*The Biology
of the Cockroach*

i do not see why men
should be so proud
insects have the more
ancient lineage
according to the scientists
insects were insects
when man was only
a burbling whatsit

archy and mehitabel by Don Marquis (by courtesy of Faber & Faber, 1958)

The Biology

of the Cockroach

D. M. Guthrie

Lecturer in Zoology, University of Aberdeen

A. R. Tindall

Lecturer in Physiology, University of Birmingham

Edward Arnold (Publishers) Ltd.

Printed in Great Britain by
William Clowes and Sons, Limited, London and Beccles

Preface

Cockroaches have long been favourite experimental material due to their large size, ease of culture and relatively generalized structure. Ever since the publication of Miall and Denny's classic monograph on *Periplaneta orientalis* in 1886, research on various aspects of cockroach biology has continued.

This book aims to review much of this work, together with some original observations. It is hoped that it will prove useful to research workers in many fields, as well as introducing the general reader to the intrinsic interest of these animals.

By far the greatest use has been made of the species listed below, so that we have found it convenient to refer to them by the abbreviations given here after the specific names. *Periplaneta americana* (L.)—*P.a.*, *Blatta orientalis* (L.)—*B.o.*, *Blattella germanica* (L.)—*Bt.g.* Where the name of the cockroach is not given it should be assumed that the research was carried out on *Periplaneta americana*. All temperatures are given in degrees Celsius.

The responsibility for the different chapters was as follows. Chapters 1, 6, 7, 8, 9, 10, 17, 18—D.M.G.; chapters 2, 3, 4, 5, 11, 12, 13, 14, 15, 16—A.R.T.

Acknowledgements

A number of specialists have drawn our attention to important papers and have given valuable advice, and we would like to thank especially Professors J. W. L. Beament, V. Kubišta and A. Glenn Richards; and Drs. D. R. Ragge and L. M. Roth. Illustrations and other original material have been provided by Professors A. R. Gilby, H. E. Hinton and J. B. Walther; and Drs. J. Box, M. A. Brooks, M. E. Cox, K. G. Davey, J. Donnellan, C. Grégoire, E. Huger, B. John, W. Judd, J. C. Lefeuvre, M. Pavan, L. M. Roth, J. Smart, D. S. Smith and J. E. Treherne, to all of whom we wish to express our indebtedness.

The following authors have kindly allowed us to reproduce figures from their published work. Professors H. Autrum, J. Boistel, A. W. A. Brown, G. M. Hughes, F. Lawson, V. Nath, J. W. S. Pringle, R. J. Pumphrey, K. D. Roeder, J. Sternburg, J. D. Smyth and V. B. Wigglesworth; and Drs. E. Anderson, P. F. Bonhag, P. C. J. Brunet, E. T. Burtt, W. T. Catton, L. E. Chadwick, P. I. Chang, A. E. Chopard, K. G. Davey, M. F. Day, M. Edwards, A. Girardie, A. Hess, G. A. Horridge, P. Howse, G. A. Kerkut, J. Lhoste, T. Narahashi, P. L. Pipa, A. Roche, P. Ruck, P. N. R. Usherwood, H. E. Vroman, R. E. Wheeler, R. B. Willey, D. M. Wilson, and J. J. Wolken.

D.M.G. would like to thank Mr. L. Panko for his assistance, especially with regard to Russian translations.

Figures 6.8, 7.7, 7.10, and 10.10 are reproduced by permission of The Rockefeller University Press, New York. The photographs for Figs. 4.2, 4.3, 4.6, 7.7, 10.10, 15.1 and 15.2 here reproduced from printed halftone copy inevitably show a loss of detail and the quality of the results is not representative of the originals.

We should also like to thank Professors G. M. Hughes and J. W. L. Beament and Drs. M. G. Guthrie and B. Singer, who have read certain chapters and given useful criticisms. In addition D.M.G. would like to record his gratitude to the typing staff of the Department of Zoology Aberdeen University for the care they have taken over the preparation of his chapters of this book, and A.R.T. would like to thank the staff of the Royal Entomological Society of London for their unfailing help on numerous occasions.

Contents

1 *Introduction*

Classification and identification

The higher classification of the 3,500 described species of cockroaches (Rehn) presents a number of difficulties. The modern classifications centre round the work of Chopard,[6] Princis,[40] Rehn[44] and McKittrick,[32] whose main interest is directed towards living forms, and Jeannel,[19] Martynov[33] and Handlirsch,[15] who have attempted to unite modern and fossil species in a classification which emphasizes the main streams in insectan evolution. Princis reviews many aspects of cockroach taxonomy. According to McKittrick, Rehn and Princis have developed separate classifications solely on the grounds of different groups of skeletal characters, and therefore he attempted to employ skeletal, myological and behavioural information on the elucidation of systematic relationships. The following outline classification is drawn largely from McKittrick, Chopard and Jeannel.

Although Karny[25] includes cockroaches, mantids and termites within a single order—Oöthecaria—and the taxonomic contiguity of termites and cockroaches is emphasized by many authors, this system is not generally accepted.

Class Insecta
　Subclass Pterygota
　　Section Polyneoptera
　　　Superorder Blattopteroidea
　　　　Order Dictyoptera
　　　　　(suborder Mantodea)
　　　　Suborder Blattodea
　　　　　Series Palaeoblattaria
　　　　　　Family　Archimylacridae
　　　　　　　　　　Mylacridae
　　　　　　　　　　Pseudomylacridae
　　　　　　　　　　Pteridomylacridae
　　　　　　　　　　Idiomylacridae
　　　　　　　　　　Neomylacridae
　　　　　　　　　　Spiloblattinidae
　　　　　Series Neoblattaria
　　　　　　Superfamily Mesoblattoidea
　　　　　　　Family　Poroblattinidae
　　　　　　　　　　Neorthroblattinidae
　　　　　　　　　　Proteremidae

Diechoblattinidae
Mesoblattinidae
Superfamily Blattoidea
    Family   Cryptocercidae
              Blattidae
Superfamily Blaberoidea
    Family   Polyphagidae
              Blatellidae
              Blaberidae

The Blaberidae are further divided by McKittrick into three groups of sub-families.

the Blaberoid complex
the Panchloroid complex
the Epilamproid complex

For details of the diagnostic features of these families, see Handlirsch for the fossil species, and McKittrick for the modern ones.[15, 32]

The Blaberoid superfamily is seen by McKittrick as embodying the most recently evolved species, and it includes the bulk of modern forms. The Blaberidae contains the newest species within the superfamily; *Blaberus* (Blaberoid complex) and *Leucophaea* (Panchloroid complex) are examples of this recent group. The Blatellids are less similar to these Blaberidae than they are to the Polyphagidae,

FIG. 1.1   *Cryptocercus punctulatus.* (From Chopard[6])

with which, according to McKittrick, they may share a distant common ancestry. The Blattidae appear in the Tertiary, and include *Periplaneta* and *Blatta*, which may thus be regarded as examples of the more archaic type of modern cockroach.[32] Using the headings of Scudder, the fossil families (Archimylacridae—Mesoblattinidae are divided into those groups confined to the Palaeozoic (Palaeoblattaria), and those found largely or exclusively in the Mesozoic and later eras (Neoblattaria). In fact, the Mesoblattoidea as here constituted contains mainly Mesozoic forms.

Recent workers (Princis, McKittrick) have been anxious to emphasize the close similarity between the wood-eating cockroach *Cryptocercus* (Fig. 1.1) and some of the less specialized Isoptera. Many structural similarities can be traced, and its gut fauna contain similar types of specialized protozoa.

The mantids mostly developed predatory specializations which make them appear superficially rather different from the cockroaches. *Lithophotina floccosa* (Cock.), according to Sharov, has a type of wing venation and other structural features suggesting a closer affinity with the Blattodea than appears in the rest of the group.[53]

The common domiciliary species and endemic British species (Fig. 1.2)

Keys to the British species of cockroach (introduced and endemic) will be found in many of the earlier monographs (there is even a very short one in Miall and Denny)[35] but, more recently, keys dealing with some of the rarer immigrants, as well as the common species, have been published by Hincks,[18] and by Ragge.[42] A brief description of the five most used types of laboratory cockroach is given below. Excellent drawings and photographs of these species will be found in Ragge,[42] in Roth and Willis,[47] and in the British Museum Economic Series.[66]

Periplaneta americana Linnaeus

Common names: Ship cockroach, Kakerlac (the name kakkerlac or kakerlak has also been applied to *B.o.*), Bombay canary, American cockroach.

Synonyms: *Stylopyga americana, Blatta americana.*

Origin: Uncertain, probably Africa or South Asia. **Distribution:** World-wide. **Description:** A large cockroach. Males 35–40 mm, females 29–37 mm in total length. Reddish-brown in colour. Wings fully developed, in the males slightly overlapping the end of the abdomen. Pronotum with indistinct pale margins. Flies weakly. Keel-like ovipositor valves in the female pronounced.

The Australian cockroach *P. australasiae* (Fab.) occurs in small numbers in Britain and has a somewhat similar appearance to *P.a.* It can be distinguished in the adult by its slightly smaller size (27–34 mm), the pale marginal ring on the pronotum being clearly marked, and by the pale yellow stripe on the humeral region of the tegmina.

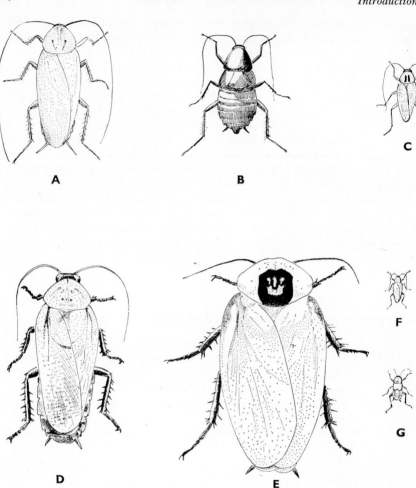

FIG. 1.2 **A.** *Periplaneta americana* (L.). **B.** *Blatta orientalis* (L.). **C.** *Blattella germanica* (L.). **D.** *Leucophaea maderae* (Fab.). **E.** *Blaberus cranifer* (Burm.). **F.** *Ectobius pallidus* (Oliv.). **G.** *E. panzeri* (Steph.). All natural size

Blatta orientalis Linnaeus

Common names: The common cockroach, blackbeetle, oriental cockroach, blackclock.

Synonyms: *Periplaneta orientalis.*
Origin: Uncertain, probably Africa or South Asia. **Distribution:** World-wide.
Description: Distinctly smaller than the foregoing species. Males 17–29 mm, females 20–27 mm. Very dark brown to black. Wings reduced. In the males, the wings do not reach the tip of the abdomen, and in the females they hardly attain the border of the second abdominal tergum.

Blattella germanica Linnaeus

Common names: shiner, steambug, steamfly, Croton bug, the German cockroach.

Synonyms: *Phyllodromia germanica, Ectobius germanicus.*
Origin: Uncertain, probably West Africa. **Distribution:** World-wide.
Description: The smallest of the laboratory cockroaches. Males 10–13 mm, females 12–15 mm. Pale yellowish-brown, with a pair of dark-brown longitudinal marks on the pronotum. Margins of the pronotum, and humeral margins of the tegmina, straw yellow. The wings are fully developed and usually extend well beyond the tip of the abdomen. A number of different colour forms are recognized, and have been genetically analysed (see below).

Leucophaea maderae Fabricius

Common names: The Madeira cockroach.
Synonyms: *Rhyparobia maderae, Panchlora maderae.*
Origin: Probably Africa, but reported from Madeira by Heevin, 1864. **Distribution:** West Indies, North and South America.
Description: A large cockroach. Males 40–44 mm, females 42–50 mm. Whitish-yellow or straw-coloured with greyish-brown speckles on the wings and thorax. Underparts and legs black or blackish-brown. Pronotum with irregular dark marks in the centre of the disc. A sluggish, heavily built cockroach in contrast to the foregoing species. Wings fully developed.

Some American laboratories also keep another rather similar species— *Nauphoeta cinerea* (Oliv.). It differs from *L. maderae*, however, in being rather smaller (24–33 mm), the dark markings are more extensive, and the wings do not cover the terminal abdominal segments.

Blaberus craniifer Burmeister

Common names: The drummer, West Indian leaf cockroach.
Origin: Probably West Africa. **Distribution:** West Indies.
Description: A very large cockroach, 55–66 mm in total length, with a rather flattened appearance due in part to the explanate margins of the pronotum and fore-wings. Upper surface dull white, with the dark abdomen showing through the wings in the centre. Central and posterior part of the pronotum with a large and clearly defined black ring, and less distinct dark markings in the humeral and costal zones of the tegmina. Legs and much of the undersurface black. The wings are fully developed. Like *Leucophaea maderae*, a heavy-bodied, sluggish insect.

In some laboratories, *Blaberus giganteus* (L.) is kept. This species is still larger (65–73 mm) than *B. craniifer*, the pronotal black patch is complete, without central light areas, and the wings are a waxy white.

Despite the apparent advantages of using such large insects as experimental material, their slow rate of development and cryptic behaviour has prevented them becoming as popular as *Blatta orientalis* and *Periplaneta americana*.

Lefeuvre points out that, in old inbred cultures of *Blaberus craniifer*, a reduction in size, accompanied by small changes in colour and form, may occur.[27]

BRITISH NATIVE SPECIES

Three species of small cockroaches belonging to the genus *Ectobius* are to be found in the southern counties of England and Wales. They are also known from other parts of Europe. In warm summer weather, they may often be found in quite large numbers in the rather dry habitats they prefer. Not a great deal is known about their life histories and feeding habits, and it is to be hoped that more attention will be focussed on them by ecologists. These species are near the extreme northern range of Dictyopteran insects (*E. panzeri*, latitude 53°N. in Britain).

General description: Small, delicate and agile cockroaches. Between 5 and 11 mm in total length in the adult stage. Grey, greyish-brown or yellowish-brown in colour, and usually no spots or distinctive markings. The species characteristics are:

Ectobius lapponicus (L.) Dusky cockroach. Total length 6–11·5 mm. Colour brown. The recess in the seventh abdominal tergum of the male with a large tubercle divided centrally. Fore-wings in the female do not cover the terminal abdominal segments.

Ectobius pallidus (Olivier). Tawny cockroach. Total length 8–9·5 mm. Colour pale yellow. The recess in the seventh abdominal tergum of the male has no tubercle. Wings fully developed.

Ectobius panzeri (Stephens). Lesser cockroach. Total length 5–8 mm. The dorsal recess in the male contains a hairy tubercle. In the female, the wings cover only the base of the abdomen. Colour brown or greyish-brown, often with a speckled appearance.

For further details, consult Lucas,[31] Burr,[3] Hincks,[18] Kevan[26] and in particular the recent publication of Ragge,[42] which gives coloured plates of the species.

Genetics and Cytology

Where large populations of *Bt.g.* are cultured, colour variants can often be observed. In *P.a.* they are much rarer, although Jefferson has recorded a white eye mutant in this species.[20] I have observed a reddish-brown colour variant of *Bt.g.* without the yellow borders to the pronotum and tegmina, or the dark brown marks on the pronotal disc.[14] Niswander,[39] and Ross and Cochran[46] describe similar variants in this species and have succeeded in isolating the factor involved through breeding experiments. Smittle and Burden, using the same kind of material, were able to show that the gene behaved as an autosomal recessive.[55]

The time taken for development from the egg to the adult may be as little as 8 weeks in this species, and this, coupled with the possibility of keeping large numbers together due to its small size, makes *Bt.g.* one of the most suitable species for breeding experiments.[66]

Gynandromorphs have been described in a few cockroaches (Chopard). Willis and Roth investigated the anatomy of a gynandromorph of *Byrsotria fumigata*. It was bilaterally divided into male and female halves, a testis being present on one side and an ovary on the other side.[64]

Morse described the chromosomal complement of *P.a.* and three other cockroach species in 1909,[37] but more recently, further information has been provided by Suomalainen,[59] and John and Lewis.[24]

In *P.a.* the diploid number is 33 in the male, and 34 in the female, there being an XO/XX sex chromosome mechanism (Fig. 1.3). The male meiotic sequence is of particular interest in that it presents a number of anomalies that help to throw light on spindle development. These are: (1) a polarized pachytene stage; (2) the absence of chiasmata; (3) absence of diplotene-diakinesis; and (4) the occurrence of a pre-metaphase stretch at the end of pachytene. John and Lewis came to the conclusion that the mechanical function normally performed by chiasmata is supplemented or replaced by matrical stickiness or terminal affinity, and that diplotene and diakinesis are suppressed by the premetaphase stretch. These

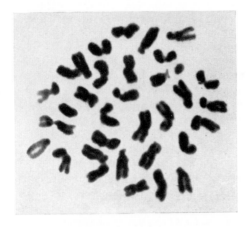

FIG. 1.3 Mitotic division in chromosomes from *Periplaneta americana*. (From John and Lewis[24])

authors also examined the chromosome structure of *P.a.* from small isolated wild populations in coal mines. Many individuals exhibited interchange heterozygosity, chromosome rings or chains being visible at meiosis. John and Lewis suggested that the establishment of interchange heterozygosity is correlated with a change from outbreeding to inbreeding.[21, 22, 28, 29]

They also found a high proportion of individuals heterozygous for independent interchanges in an inbred culture of *Blaberus discoidalis*.[23]

They conclude that genic heterozygotes and consequently interchange heterozygotes would be expected to be at a selective advantage following a change from outbreeding to inbreeding.[22]

Finally it may be pointed out that it is possible to distinguish certain cockroach species on the basis of their free amino acid patterns. Micks and Gibson obtained characteristic density curves not only for the species *P.a.*, *Bt.g.* and *P. brunnea*, but also for the males and females of those species, using paper chromatography.[36]

Palaeontology

The remains of cockroaches are a dominant feature of the insect fauna of the coal measures, and Scudder goes so far as to describe the Carboniferous as the Age of Cockroaches.[52] Cockroaches were obviously abundant and successful at this time and may be supposed already to have undergone a long period of evolution from apterygote ancestors, no survivors from this earlier period remaining to us. The environment in which this large cockroach fauna flourished is believed to have been a warm moist one, and occupied a geographical position in what is now North America, the area described as Laurentia by Suess.[58]

According to Jeannel,[19] following the system of Martynov, the cockroaches should be placed within the section or series Polyneoptera (Class Insecta, Subclass Pterygota). This group includes the majority of Hemimetabolous orders which can fold their wings at rest, and is further characterized by a jugal field with many veins, and usually possessing many Malpighian tubules (polynephridial). By definition, the Polyneoptera are more advanced than the Palaeoptera, which also appear in the Carboniferous, in which the wings are held out stiffly at the sides and lack a jugal field. The modern Palaeoptera are to be found in the Ephemeroptera and the Odonata. According to this classification, which attempts to unify the efforts of systematists of fossil as well as of modern forms, the cockroaches should be placed within the order Dictyoptera (Superorder Blattopteroidea). This order is characterized by multiarticulate cerci, no oviscope, oötheca and pentamerous tarsi. The Blattopteroidea embraces the Dictyoptera, Isoptera and a purely fossil group—the Protoblattoptera. Scudder gives a useful account of the fossil cockroaches known at that time (1886),[52] but for a fuller and slightly more recent account the reader should consult Handlirsch.[15] Not a great deal seems to have been added to the description of the fossil groups outlined by Handlirsch in 1930.

Twelve families of fossil cockroaches are recognized by Handlirsch, many of them based on few specimens, and of doubtful authenticity according to Jeannel. Of the Palaeozoic families, the most important were the Archimylacridae and the Mylacridae.

The Archimylacridae, comprising more than 350 species in 73 genera, include the most primitive forms, exhibiting resemblances to the Palaeoptera in their wing venation. They are largely Carboniferous, but small numbers appear in the Permian of North America and Russia, and even one from India, suggesting that they had spread to the dryer regions of South Asia (Jeannel).[19]

The Mylacridae include a large number of species and appeared first of all in American deposits of Middle and Upper Carboniferous age, then later in the Stephanian of France and England.

Scudder groups the Palaeozoic cockroaches in a family Palaeoblattariae, whilst the Mesozoic and modern forms constitute the Neoblattariae, although some of the Mesozoic forms are clearly intermediate in at least a few of their characteristics. These families were placed within the order Orthoptera, which Miall and Denny believed should include insects now placed in the Saltatoria, Phasmida, Isoptera, Ephemeroptera and Odonata.

Scudder distinguishes the Palaeozoic Palaeoblattariae from modern forms on three fairly minor differences: (1) The fore- and hind-wings of the Palaeozoic forms are similar as regards transparency, general disposition of veins and the development of the anal area, whilst in modern species the fore-wings are modified as leathery tegmina, and the anal area in the hind wing is notably enlarged. (2) Partial fusion of some of the veins in the fore-wings of modern cockroaches differentiates the detailed structure of the fore- and hind-wings in a manner not visible in the Palaeoblattariae. (3) The veins of the anal area run parallel to one another and to the anal furrow, terminating separately at the wing margin in Palaeozoic forms, whilst in modern forms they tend to converge or curve forwards to the anal furrow.

The Mesozoic cockroaches are seen by Scudder as generally similar to other more recent Neoblattariae, although 10 species of Palaeoblattariae were recorded from Triassic deposits.

In his enumeration of fossil cockroaches in 1886 Scudder included 177 species, 81 from the Palaeozoic, 87 from the Mesozoic and 9 from the Oligocene and Miocene. Although a considerable number of additional species have now been added to this list,[40] the general view of the fossil form as structurally very similar to the modern species, and of much the same size range, is unchanged.

The names of cockroaches

The meanings of most of the trivial or species names are usually self-explanatory, referring to a place (*maderae, floridana*), a person (*duskei, humbertiana*), or to the size (*giganteus*), structure (*emarginata*), or colour (*lutea*) of the insect. Many of the geographical attributions of origin, such as *germanica* or *orientalis*, are almost certainly incorrect.

The mainly Latinized-Greek generic names offer more interest, varying from bisyllabic words like 'Gyna' (pertaining to the female), or 'Laxta' (wide), to a great variety of rather long words, often of four or five syllables, such as the harmonius 'Nocticola' (night dweller), or the tortuous 'Hoplosphoropyga' (armoured tail?).

The most distinctive root among the scientific names for cockroaches is undoubtedly *Blatta*, with its diminutive *Blattella*. This seems to have been a Greek name for a cockroach or similar dark-haunting insect, possibly a species of Loboptera or Ectobius, or equally some kind of Coleoptera. 'Lampro' is also rather common as in *Lobolampra, Epilampra, Hololampra* and *Lamproblatta*. This refers to the smooth and shining appearance of these insects ('lampros'—shining).

Periplaneta translated freely can be taken to mean a wandering star ('peri'—about, 'planeta'—wandering star or planet) and is most likely to be intended as a description of the world-wide dispersal by ships of this cosmopolitan genus.

The origin of *Blaberus* is in 'blaberos'—harmful, referring to its fruit-eating propensities, while *Leucophaea* refers to the white and grey colour of this insect ('Leuco'—white, 'phae'—grey, dusky).

Amongst the common names applied to cockroach, only a few require explanation. The name cockroach is generally believed to derive from the Spanish word for cockroach—cucaracha, a word which seems to have been originally applied to a type of berry, noxious and inedible. It seems likely that the word was introduced into English via Central or South America, a major centre of cockroach species, rather than from Spain, although Lucas[31] notes that the Spanish word 'cuco' means bug.

The dark-coloured *Blatta orientalis* seems always to have been mistaken for a coleopteran, as witnessed by the names blackbeetle and blackclock. The two species of coleopteran involved in this confusion are almost certainly *Feronia* (Pterostichus) *madida* (Carabidae), and *Blaps muchronata* (Tenebrionidae), both frequently found in dwellings, storehouses and kitchens, and of roughly the same size and colour.

The name Croton bug applied to *Blattella germanica* is interesting in that, according to the British Museum (Nat. Hist.)[66] guide, it derives from the appearance of large numbers of this insect in the Croton aquaduct, supplying New York with water, shortly after completion. It may be noted, however, that the Greek word 'kroton' means a tick or bug.

The drummers (*Blaberus* sp.) make a light drumming sound with their wings, but the origin of the name Kakerlac (Liverpool docks), applied to *P. americana*, is obscure, although it may be East Indian.[47] Lucas[31] records it (Kakkerlak) applied to *B.o.* ("the Indian insect well known as Kakkerlak").

Geographical distribution

Princis in *Orthopterorum Catalogus*[40] gives information on the natural distribution of living species of cockroach, and additional details may be sought in the work of Roth and Willis[47] (mainly New World species), Rehn and Hebard,[43] and Chopard.[6]

As a group, the Blattodea are distributed fairly generally over the major land masses. Perhaps the richest areas in species are tropical America and West Africa. The origins of many species is undoubtedly obscured by the ease with which they have been transported on ships.

Their distribution corresponds to a preference for fairly high humidities (40–50% R.H.), and temperatures over 25°, although some species can be found to survive temperatures between -7 and 47° according to Raffy.[41] The great majority of species are found between latitudes 60°N. and 50°S., and the richest habitats are between 30°N. and 30°S. Only a few species belonging to the Corydiidae are found living under desert conditions; the thin integument and unspecialized Malpighian tubules of most cockroaches do not fit the group for desert life.

Lefeuvre has described the distribution in Central America of some species of *Blaberus* (*B. craniifer, B. discoidalis* and *B. colosseus*). *B. craniifer* is abundant on Cuba (especially in houses), where *B. discoidalis* is also found, but only the latter occurs on Haiti, Jamaica, and some of the other islands south of Cuba. This corresponds to a more northerly distribution of *B. craniifer* on the mainland of Central America, while *B. discoidalis* and *B. colosseus* are found as far south as Colombia and Venezuela[27] (see Fig. 1.4). Natural and human habitat preferences are probably involved in this pattern.

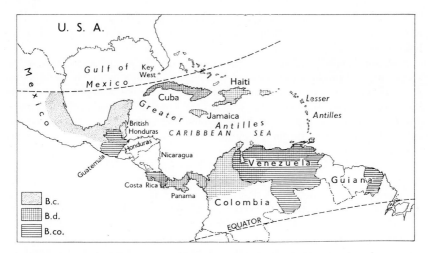

FIG. 1.4   The distribution of *Blaberus craniifer* (*B.c.*), *B. discoidalis* (*B.d.*) and
B. colosseus (*B.co.*) in Central America. (After Lefeuvre[27])

Ecology

The majority of cockroach species appear to be omnivorous and warmth-loving and this may form a basis for the commensal relationship between man and the most well-known species of cockroaches. The Carboniferous environment is believed to have been characterized by high temperatures and humidity, and unspecialized, although mainly plant, foodstuffs.[19]

Roth and Willis list 49 species recorded from houses or man-made structures in both the New and Old World.[47]

P.a. has been observed in houses, stores and meat packing plant in many countries, and has been recorded from latrines or sewers in Texas, Georgia (U.S.A.) and Iran.

B.o. and *Bt.g.* are also cosmopolitan domiciliary pests, but these two species seem to be especially noticeable where there are heating installations, as in display cases, furnace rooms and bakeries. Both species are able to hide in very small crevices. Adult German cockroaches can hide in cracks no more than 1·6 mm wide.[47]

Blaberus craniifer is a household pest in Cuba according to Deschapelles.[10] *Leucophaea maderae* has been observed in fruit stores and houses throughout the West Indies,[47] and also from Central and South America, and tropical Africa,[44] from which last geographical location it probably originated.

Cockroaches (species unstated) have been found in hospital laundry baskets, incubators for premature babies, food counters and beauty salons in department stores, and in bundles of clean towels returned from a laundry (up to 500 per bundle).[47]

Observations of cockroaches in ships and aircraft are of particular interest in view of the very wide dispersal of the most well-known species. Clearly those species which are domiciliary pests are most likely to have access to such means of transport, and will have little difficulty in obtaining entry to houses and installations on arrival.

Roth and Willis list 23 species from ships, many of them identified from a few specimens and unlikely ever to have established breeding populations on ships. *P.a., B.o.* and *Bt.g.*, on the other hand, have been recorded in large numbers from both modern steel ships as well as wooden ships of the 19th and earlier centuries. *Blattella germanica* appears to be the most successful ships' cockroach, and especially associated with the galleys, cabins and messes, while *P.a.* and *B.o.* are more often found in the holds.

Two of the earliest records of cockroaches (unidentified) from ships are provided by Moffet's observations that Drake found a captured ship to be over-run with cockroaches, and Bligh's description of a method of killing the cockroach population of the *Bounty* with boiling water. These are 17th- and 18th-century records respectively, but numerous descriptions of large cockroach populations on board ship extend to the present day. As many as 20,000 specimens have been taken from a single stateroom, and their depredations included eating and fouling the crew's food, and even eating the leather portions of boots, and the skin and nails of the persons on board.[47]

Rehn suggests that 11 of the well-known species of domiciliary pests were carried from their centre of origin to different parts of the world by ships, many of them following the slave trade route from West Africa to the Americas.

Small numbers of cockroaches, referable to perhaps as many as 20 species, have been recorded from aircraft.[47] These insects were recovered from aeroplanes landed at airports as far apart as the U.S.A., Kenya and New Zealand, and suggest that this may be a minor yet significant method of species distribution. Few details are available as to the sites within the aircraft favoured by cockroaches. *Blattella germanica* and *P.a.* are amongst the species most often reported as taking advantage of air transport.

Clearly, the habitats so far described are those made by man, and those species most similar in their requirements to man would be expected to dominate other species. Feral cockroaches were arranged in four ecological groupings by Roth and Willis. These habitat types comprised cave, desert and aquatic environments, together with a more general class described as outdoor habitats.

Chopard classifies cavernicolous cockroaches into four groups on the basis of their degree of specialization. The species that occur sporadically and accidentally in caves are described as Trogloxenes, and those that commonly and usually occur in caves but are not in any way limited to this habitat as Troglophiles (*Periplaneta cavernicola* is an example of this latter group). Two more specialized groups can be distinguished: Guanobies, feeding on deposited guano (an example is *Gyna kazungulana*); and Troglobies, specially adapted and more or less confined to caves (*Typhloblatta caeca*, eyeless but with elongated appendages, may be cited).[6]

Roth and Willis list 31 species of cavernicolous cockroach including *P.a., B.o., Bt.g.* and *B.c. P.a.* has been recorded from East Africa, India, the Malagasy Republic, in caves, and from mines (down to 2,166 ft in depth) in Great Britain,

India, South Africa and Sumatra. These authors remark that the relatively stable temperature and humidity offered by caves may be one of their attractions but, at the same time, they point out the dependence of cavernicolous cockroaches on material deposited by other cave animals as a source of food. The rôle of cockroaches as unspecialized feeders may be the major factor in this choice of habitat.[47]

Thirteen species of cockroach are listed by Roth and Willis from the burrows of various small (mainly arid habitat) mammals, nine of these species belonging to the genera *Arenivaga* and *Polyphaga*, which also appear under the heading of desert cockroaches. The cockroaches do not appear to live as commensals.

As was noted earlier in the context of general habitat preferences, many species of cockroaches require ingested water and fairly high ambient humidities. It is, thus, perhaps a little surprising to find a number of xerophilic species (Roth and Willis list 28). Some species moderate the severity of desert conditions by living in the burrows of desert rodents as mentioned above, but a few species, such as *Blattella vaga* and *Namablatta bitaeniata*, have been collected from habitats of extreme aridity. Vlasov and Miriam describe all stages of *Polyphaga indica* and *Arenivaga roseni* as 'swimming' readily in the sand and loess dust of certain habitats in the Turkmen S.S.R., a mode of locomotion that might be regarded as an adaptation for desert life.[61]

Lawson (see p.220) showed that cockroaches (*P.a.*) marooned on an experimental island would quickly learn to escape by leaping, and then swimming, and it is therefore interesting to learn that a small number of species belonging to the Epilamprinae (Chopard) favour an aquatic habitat, although the extent to which they swim varies. Roth and Willis obtained information about 10 species of aquatic cockroach.

Some species such as *Dryadoblatta scotti* lived in the water-filled leaf bases of bromeliads, a few in pools, but the majority were observed in streams. Nymphs of *Epilampra abdomen-nigrum* were observed by Cromwell to swim and dive with facility.

They could swim rapidly underwater for a minute or two and remain quiescent clinging to submerged roots for as long as 15 minutes. Many other species did not survive more than 5 min forced submersion, but if the tip of the abdomen carrying a pair of raised spiracles was allowed contact with the air the insect could breathe. Shelford, reporting on a species of *Epilampra*, described respiratory movements: 'the abdomen moves gently up and down and every 30–40 sec a bubble of air issues from the prothoracic spiracles on each side.' He was able to show that air was drawn in through the terminal abdominal spiracles, and expelled from the prothoracic spiracles.[54]

Adaptations to a partially sub-aquatic life are slight, and may include tubular extensions of the terminal abdominal spiracles (Fig. 1.5), and a hydrophobe hair pile on the underside of the thorax.[54]

By far the largest number of species whose ecological preferences have been recorded live in a variety of outdoor situations, and Roth and Willis detail some 220 species (including genera without specific identification), mostly found under rather humid conditions in the tropics and subtropics.

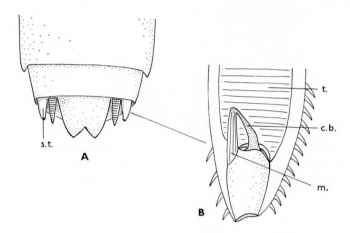

FIG. 1.5 Terminal spiracles (inspiratory) of the aquatic cockroach *Rhicnoda natatrix* (Shelford). **A**, dorsal view of the terminal segments of the abdomen: s.t.—spiracular tube. **B**, spiracular tube seen in optical section: m.—muscle attached to c.b., a cuticular bow closing the spiracle; t.—trachea. (After Shelford)

It is interesting to observe the habitat of the common domiciliary species in order to assess their independence of man-made environments.

P.a. has been recorded under decaying debris on the shore, on flowers and under timbers in a number of New World locations, as well as in sites adjacent to buildings. *B.o.* has been observed, mainly in rather small numbers, in outdoor situations in Great Britain and in the United States. Larger numbers have been observed away from houses, but it is unlikely that permanent breeding populations are present in these two countries. Feral populations may exist, however, in Southern Crimea, where they were found under dead leaves and stones in copses. *Bt.g.* appears to have the widest distribution in feral populations, having been reported from dead leaves and rubbish heaps in Algeria, Formosa, England and the U.S.A. There is some suggestion, as with the other domiciliary species, that populations invade outdoor habitats in the summer months, but many insects retreat to buildings during the winter.

A great many species of cockroach are associated with fruit, leaves, bark, roots, rotten logs or plant matter of some kind. A few depend on guano or excrement, of various types. *Parcoblatta uhleriana* and *P. virginica* have been observed to feed on aphid honeydew.

This general dependence on plants or plant products has exceptions in the small number of observations, some rather insubstantial, of cockroaches preying on other insect species. Prey species which have been reliably reported include the ant *Iridomyrmex humilis*, larvae of *Polistes* sp., a species of centipede, and unidentified termites, various hemipterans (all stages), mosquitoes and the eggs of reptiles.[47]

Cannibalism has been frequently observed in cockroaches, recently moulted nymphs and copulating and injured adults being especially susceptible. Overcrowding, shortage of food, and high temperatures may increase the tendency towards cannibalism. In most cultures it occurs only sporadically. The three commonest domiciliary species *P.a.*, *Bt.g.* and *B.o.* have been most implicated, but *Pycnoscelus surinamensis* does not resort to cannibalism even under conditions of acute food shortage (Saupe[51] and Roeser,[45] quoted by Roth and Willis).

Cockroaches have been reliably reported to attack man, to the extent of inflicting minor abrasions on the feet and hands, and small wounds on areas of more delicate skin. In certain geographical locations, this activity of cockroaches may be quite general (*P.a.* and *P. australasiae* reported by Sonan, and quoted by Roth and Willis[47]).

To summarize the foregoing ecological information, cockroaches are found living out-of-doors in a variety of situations. The larger species tend to favour tropical and subtropical locations, and most feed exclusively on plant materials. Little is known about the ecology of African and Southern Asian species. In temperate zones, a range of mostly smaller species occur, whose feeding habits may be more varied, but it is likely that while cockroaches can be described as omnivorous, they only occasionally prey on other animals.

Economic and medical importance

This topic falls under three headings (i) consumption of human foodstuffs or crops, (ii) vectors of disease or parasitic organisms of man or domestic animals, (iii) spoliation of food, and nuisance value in houses and buildings.

To what extent are cockroaches injurious insects? The short answer in the first two categories listed above is that, compared to the locust or the anopheline mosquito, cockroaches are not injurious insects. Nevertheless, there are a number of records of cockroaches causing damage to plants. Roth and Willis have collected a considerable number of observations, and should be consulted for further details.

In many instances, cockroaches (often *P.a.*) will invade greenhouses and eat the roots or blossoms of the plants. Orchids appear to be especially attractive to them. Cockroaches have also been observed to eat the bark or the fruit of trees (bananas, mangoes, papayas) growing in the open, or under cover. *Pycnoscelus surinamensis* is the species most often cited in cases of plant destruction, but other species, including *P.a.* and *B.o.*, may be involved. As an extreme example of destructiveness by *P. surinamensis*, Roth and Willis cite Roeser as giving a figure of 300,000 tobacco plants destroyed by this species, in Sumatra, in a few days. Roeser suggested that the cockroaches turned to live plant material when the organic detritus in the soil was exhausted.[45]

The importance of cockroaches as vectors of vertebrate pathogens has been discussed by Roth and Willis, and Steinhaus (consult Chapter 17). Four strains of poliomyelitis virus, 40 species of pathogenic bacteria, and 12 helminth species with primary vertebrate hosts have been traced to cockroaches, but in no case is it proved that any major rôle is played by cockroaches in human pathology. A typical example of the kind of relationship demonstrated for cockroaches and disease organisms is provided by De Coursey and Otto.[9] They investigated the dispersal of the dysentery amoeba *Entamoeba histolytica* in poorly kept dwelling-houses in Egypt, where the disease had a high incidence. Cockroaches were abundant (*P.a.* and *Bt.g.*), and lived in close association with identified persons. Examination of the cockroaches showed that *E. histolytica* was present in a small number only, so that the cockroach is unlikely to be involved as a major vector.

A few cockroaches may have a deleterious effect on domestic animals; perhaps the best-documented example is the dispersal of *Oxyspirura mansoni*, a nematode parasite of the domestic fowl, by *Pycnoscelus surinamensis*.[47] At the same time *P.a.* carries *Gongylonema neoplasticum* to the black and brown rats (*Rattus norvegicus* and *R. rattus*), an association that could be regarded as beneficial to man.[12]

In temperate zones, the domiciliary pest species are the cockroaches most at variance with human interests. *B.o.* is the species abundant in dwelling houses, *P.a.* tends to frequent kitchens and storehouses, and *Bt.g.* is associated with restaurants, bakehouses and, rather less frequently than *B.o.*, dwelling houses. There seems little doubt that some of the major objections to cockroaches are psychological ones. It is true that they may spoil food by depositing saliva and faeces on it, or leave their characteristic and often unpleasant odours (derived from the abdominal glands) on food or furniture, but very often they may simply eat food crumbs, or smears spilled on floors, and the direct damage is slight.

The indirect damage in terms of the depreciation of property values may be more considerable. The presence of cockroaches is regarded, probably correctly, as indicating badly cleaned rooms with defective walls, cracked woodwork or badly designed fittings. Cockroach invasions are taken as a sign of neglect.

To these logical reasons for dislike of cockroaches may be added more emotional effects. Many people find all insects equally repugnant, lumping them together with snakes and spiders as noxious small animals which may bite or sting. Yet cockroaches may arouse more hostility than, say, the bed bug or flea, whose positively disagreeable activities are more direct. The reasons may be connected with characteristics that help them to avoid capture, such as (i) great running speed (*P.a.*, up to 3 mph, McConnell and Richards, see p. 72), (ii) low frictional properties, resident in the smooth, wax-coated integument, and (iii) softness and flexibility of the body, due to the thin, pliable nature of the skeleton.

Also contributing to this emotional effect may be the very long fine antennae ceaselessly sweeping from side to side, and the legs covered with spines and hairs, but the texture and irregular, rapid style of movement probably contribute most to the feeling of repulsion inspired by these, on the whole, rather inoffensive insects.

Defence mechanisms

Cockroaches may escape the attentions of predatory animals by swift running (*Periplaneta*), flying (*Blatella*), diving into water and swimming underwater (*Epilampra*), burrowing (*Geoscapheus*), crawling into very narrow fissures, pulling the explanate margins of the body down against the substrate (*Blaberus*), or by protective colouration (*Panchlora*), or mimicry of a more noxious type of insect (*Prosoplecta*).

These are mostly rather unspecialized ways of escaping from predators but, in a number of species, glands secreting offensive fluids exist, and laboratory colonies of cockroaches often have a distinctive and rather acrid smell. These defensive secretions are manufactured by dorsal or ventral abdominal glands (*Eurycotis, Periplaneta*) or by tracheal glands which discharge through the spiracles (*Diploptera, Leucophaea*).[47] The best known example is provided by the ventral abdominal glands of adult *Eurycotis floridana*, whose anatomy has been described by Stay[56] and Roth *et al.*[48] They showed that an aldehyde 2-hexenal is present in the secretion which can be sprayed to a distance of several inches. The secretion effectively deters toads and frogs, and prevents lizards from eating insects they have killed. Blue jays (Cyanocitta) leave adults they have killed 5 to 10 min before eating them. The spray is a mild irritant to the human skin.[48, 49, 56]

Dorsal and ventral glands have been described in *B.o.* and *P.a.* (Liang gives details of the latter species[30]), but their functions may not be exclusively defensive according to Roth and Willis, who mention the typical gregarious behaviour as possibly linked with the activity of these glands.

In *Diploptera punctata* the tracheal glands of both nymphs and adults produce a mixture of 2-ethyl-1·4 benzoquinone; 2-methyl-1·4 benzoquinone; and parabenzoquinone. The secretion repelled a species of beetle, the ant *Pogonomyrmex badius* and a Lycosid spider, the latter only when nymphs were over a certain size[47] (see Fig. 1.6).

FIG. 1.6   Chemical defence of *Diploptera punctata*. The insect on the left has had its repugnatorial glands excised and is under persistent attack from ants. The intact insect on the right has discharged a spray of quinones (shown up by KI-starch indicator paper) and repelled the attacking ants. (By courtesy of Dr. L. M. Roth)[49]

Culture methods

The advantage of cockroaches as laboratory animals is that they survive in spite of the technical assistance available in some laboratories !

The setting up of mass cultures presents few problems, at least with *P.a.* Various designs of cages have been published,[11, 16] but any large wooden box with a glass panel to allow inspection, and a hatch with a sliding or revolving cover, will prove adequate. All joints in the woodwork should be sealed, and the sliding cover must fit tightly to prevent the escape of the first instar larvae as these can squeeze through gaps of about 1 mm. Ventilation panels can be provided, however, if a fine brass or steel wire gauze is used, and this is certainly an advantage. If a constant temperature room is not available, heat can be provided by means of an electric light bulb or bar heater located below the insects in a separate compartment. Temperatures of between 25 and 28° are suitable for most species. The floor of the cage can be covered with sawdust or wood shavings, and a number of rolls of paper or pieces of cardboard box will allow the insects suitable situations for passing 'rest' phases (see reference 16, Chapter 9). Provision of containers or niches for resting is especially desirable with *B.o.* in the author's opinion.

A very simple and effective approach to the problem of mass culture is that employed by some of the American laboratories. Moulded glass fish tanks or plastic sink units are used without a cover, the inside rim being smeared with a band of Vaseline at least 2 in. broad to prevent the escape of the insects. Reversed plastic cartons with an entrance to one side provide suitable shelters.

A dryish food is easiest to handle. Laboratory rat cake in Britain, and Purina dog chow in the U.S.A., are preferred foods. If a dry food is used, some additional water is necessary. Willis and Lewis found that *P.a.* survived twice as long on water alone, as on food without water.[47] The sawdust layer can be sprayed with water at two-day intervals, or a small jar containing a pad of cotton wool soaked in water can be arranged at a suitable height for the insects. Another alternative is to reverse a water-filled tube or jar on a Petri dish so that a narrow strip of water is exposed to the insects. The aim is to provide drinking water without allowing the insects to drown, or raising the humidity too far. Willis and Lewis kept *P.a.*, *B.o.* and *Bt.g.* successfully at 36–40% R.H. and *Leucophaea maderae* at 70%.[47]

For individual culture, perforated plastic sandwich boxes (7 in. × 4½ in.), are convenient and can be stacked in an oven, or temporarily placed in the refrigerator, to slow the insects before handling. Heal advocates separate hatching cages for gravid females which can be placed inside a rearing cage. The first instar larvae escape through the fine mesh of the hatching cage into the rearing cage and can be accurately aged.[16]

Histological methods and saline media

It may be useful to summarize briefly some of the techniques that have been successfully applied to the demonstration of cockroach structure. The student should refer to Gatenby and Beams,[13] and sections in this book on the structures concerned.

For general work, Duboscq–Brasil fixation followed by staining with Mallory's triple stain gives excellent differentiation of muscle, nerve and cuticle. Recently moulted larvae or adults, and even some parts of hardened adults can be cut in 58° m.p. paraffin wax with 1–5% Ceresin. Vacuum embedding removes air bubbles.[14] Nijenhuis and Dresden prefer a rather similar fixative, van Leeuwen's fluid (12 pt 1% picric acid in abs. alcohol, 2 pt chloroform, 2 pt 40% formol, and

1 pt acetic acid added before use) followed by 24 hr in 70% alcohol, 6 weeks in soap spirit, and final washing in 70% alcohol. Azan gave a suitable stain for the nerve trunks. Periods of fixation can be varied with the fixative, but the insect should be opened in some way, and whole insects left in the fluid for 12 to 24 hr.[38]

Cameron follows Duboscq–Brasil fixation with Peterfi's double-embedding method, leaving the insect in the methyl benzoate celloidin for several weeks before passing it into paraffin. Sections were cut either on a rotary or a sledge microtome and then stained in Weigert's haematoxylin or Van Gieson. Dehydration must be rapid. Sections of whole insects may be prepared in this way.[4] Whole insects can also be sectioned successfully in ester wax.[14]

Wigglesworth obtained sharp staining of the dictyosomes in nerve cell bodies with his ethyl gallate method,[63] and these structures often show up clearly in silver stained material.[5, 14] Willey reports obtaining little staining of brain neurosecretory material with paraldehyde fuchsin, but Guthrie obtained fairly intense staining when the stain was prepared by Gabe's method (see Fig. 6.2).[14] For nerve fibres and sense organs in sectioned material, well oxidized Hansen's trioxyhaematin gives a good sharp stain. Hess prepared sections as for the electron microscope, and then examined them with phase contrast for axon profiles.[17] Bodenstein has obtained dense staining of axons with the silver technique of Samuel,[50] but Guthrie finds that this and other silver techniques are all rather capricious with cockroach material, although much less so with larvae than with adults. Results of the Holmes method are shown in Figs. 8.8 and 8.9.[14] Methylene

TABLE 1.1

Saline media are solutions in which the tissues will survive for several hours, (Amounts are in g/l.)

Author	Tissue	NaCl	KCl	CaCl$_2$	NaHCO$_3$	Na$_2$CO$_3$	NaH$_2$PO$_4$	
Becht	Nerve, muscle	9·2	0·8	1·0	0·17	—	0·01	
Taylor	Heart	9·0	0·25	0·3	—	0·2	—	
Usherwood	Nerve, muscle	9·4	1·35	1·0	0·34	—	0·6	
Yeager and Hager	Heart	9·8	0·77	0·5	0·18	—	0·01	
Pringle	Nerves	9·0	0·2	0·2	—	—	—	Glucose 4·0
Becht, Hoyle and Usherwood	Muscle	9·32	0·77	0·5	—	—	0·01	

Roeder suggests a similar saline to Pringle's for nerve, but adds 10 ml. of phosphate buffer at pH 7·2. Usherwood's saline is oxygenated, and was used for *B. craniifer*. (For references to Becht, Usherwood, Pringle and Roeder consult the relevant chapters)

blue in the reduced form (Unna's method) often stains visceral muscle and nerve fibres brilliantly 1 to 2 hr after being injected, but Alexandrowicz leaves the insects up to 12 hr for the innervation of the heart.[1]

For the electron miscroscope, glutaraldehyde fixation followed by Palade-type osmium post-fixation often gives better results than osmium alone. Guthrie finds this satisfactory for nerve trunks. Smith finds that, to obtain good preservation of the cytoplasmic inclusions of ganglion cells, it is necessary to bisect the ganglion prior to fixation. Epon embedding, and staining the sections with 1% uranyl acetate gives good contrast. Hess[17] uses Dalton's fluid for fixation.

REFERENCES

1. ALEXANDROWICZ, J. S. (1926). The innervation of the heart of the cockroach *B.o. J. comp. Neurol.*, **41**, 291–309.
2. BEI-BIENKO, G. LA. (1950). Fauna of the U.S.S.R. Insects, Blattodea. In Russian. *Zool. Inst. Nauk. S.S.S.R. Moskva*, **40**, 1–343.
3. BURR, M. (1936). *British grasshoppers and their allies.* Janson, London.
4. CAMERON, E. (1961). *The cockroach.* Heinemann, London.
5. CHANG, P. I. (1951). The action of DDT on the Golgi bodies in insects' nervous tissue. *Ann. ent. Soc. Am.*, **44**, 311–26.
6. CHOPARD, L. (1938). La Biologie des orthoptéres. *Encycl. ent.*, A. **20**, 1–241.
7. COCHRAN, D. G. and ROSS, M. H. (1962). Inheritance of resistance to DDT in Blatella germanica. *J. econ. Ent.*, **55** (1), 88–9.
8. CROMWELL, H. H. (1946). Notes on an amphibious cockroach from the Republic of Panama. *Ent. News*, **57**, 171–2.
9. DE COURSEY, J. and OTTO, J. S. (1956). Endamoeba histolytica and certain other protozoan organisms found in cockroaches in Cairo, Egypt. *Jl. N.Y. ent. Soc.*, **64**, 157–63.
10. DESCHAPELLES, J. B. (1939). Las cucarachas. *Revta Agric., Habana*, **23**, 41–7.
11. DINNES, G. (1951). Rearing cages for cockroaches. *Sci. Tech. Ass. Bull.*, **2**, 731.
12. FIBIGER, J. A. G. and DITLEVSEN, H. (1914). Contributions to the biology and morphology of Spiroptera (Gongylonema) neoplastica n.sp. *Mindeskr. Japetus Steenstrups Føds*, **25**, 28 pp.
13. GATENBY, J. B. and BEAMS, H. W. (1950). *The microtomist's vade mecum*, 11th ed. Churchill, London.
14. GUTHRIE, D. M. Unpublished observations.
15. HANDLIRSCH, A. (1930). Blattaeformia in Kukenthals' *Handbuch der Zoologie,* Insecta I, 797–839.
16. HEAL, R. E. (1948). Rearing methods for German and American cockroaches. *J. econ. Ent.*, **41**, 329.
17. HESS, A. (1958). Experimental anatomical studies of pathways in the severed central nerve cord of the cockroach. *J. Morph.*, **103**, 479–501.
18. HINCKS, W. D. (1949). Dermaptera and Orthoptera. Handbooks for the Identification of British Insects. *R. Ent. Soc. Lond.*, **1** (5).
19. JEANNEL, R. (1965). Géonémie et insectes inférieures. *Traité de Zoologie*, ed. GRASSÉ, pp. 1–110. Masson, Paris.
20. JEFFERSON, G. T. (1958). A white-eyed mutant form of the American cockroach *P.a. Nature, Lond.*, **182**, 892.
21. JOHN, B. and LEWIS, K. R. (1957). Studies on *Periplaneta americana*. I Experimental analysis of male meiosis. *Heredity, Lond.*, **11**, 1–9.
22. JOHN, B. and LEWIS, K. R. (1958). Studies on *Periplaneta americana*. III Selection for heterozygosity. *Heredity, Lond.*, **12**, 185–97.
23. JOHN, B. and LEWIS, K. R. (1959). Selection for interchange heterozygosity in an inbred culture of *Blaberus discoidalis*. *Genetics*, **44**, 251–67.

24. JOHN, B. and LEWIS, K. R. (1960). Chromosome structure in *Periplaneta americana. Heredity, Lond.*, **15**, 47–54.
25. KARNY, H. (1921). Zur Systematik der Orthopteroiden Insekten. *Treubia*, I, pp. 1–269. G. Koleff, Weltevreden.
26. KEVAN, D. K. MᶜE. (1961). A revised summary of the distribution of British Orthopteroids. *Trans. Soc. Br. Ent.*, **14**, 187–205.
27. LEFEUVRE, J. C. (1960). A propos de *Blabera craniifer. Bull. Soc. scient. Bretagne*, **35**, 146–60.
28. LEWIS, K. R. and JOHN, B. (1957). Studies on *Periplaneta americana*. II Interchange heterozygosity in isolated populations. *Heredity*, **11**, 11–22.
29. LEWIS, K. R. and JOHN, B. (1957). Bivalent structure in *Periplaneta americana. Nature, Lond.*, **179**, 973.
30. LIANG, C. (1956). The dorsal and ventral glands of *Periplaneta americana. Ann. ent. Soc. Am.*, **49**, 548–51.
31. LUCAS, W. J. (1920). *A monograph of the British Orthoptera*. London, Royal Society.
32. MCKITTRICK, F. A. (1964). Evolutionary studies on cockroaches. *Mem. Cornell. Univ. agric. Exp. Stn*, **389**, 1–197.
33. MARTYNOV, A. B. See section in Grassé by Jeannel, *Traité de Zoologie*.
34. MARQUIS, D. (1931). *Archy & Mehitabel*. Faber and Faber, London.
35. MIALL, L. C. and DENNY, A. (1886). *The Structure and Life History of the Cockroach*, pp. 1–224. Lovell Reeve, London.
36. MICKS, D. W. and GIBSON, F. J. (1957). The characterization of insects and ticks by their free amino acid patterns. *Ann. ent. Soc. Am.* **50**, 500–5.
37. MORSE, M. (1909). The nuclear components of the sex cells of four species of cockroaches. *Arch. Zellforsch.*, **3**, 483–520.
38. NIJENHUIS, E. D. and DRESDEN, D. (1952). A micro-morphological study on the sensory supply of the mesothoracic leg of the American cockroach, *Periplaneta americana. Proc. K. ned. Akad. Wet.*, Amsterdam series C, **55**, 300–10.
39. NISWANDER, R. E. (1960). An inherited colour factor in the German roach, *Blatella germanica. Proc. Indiana Acad. Sci.*, **70**, 138.
40. PRINCIS, K. (1962–5). *Orthopterorum Catalogus*, ed. M. Beier Junk, parts, **3**, **4**, **6** and **7**.
41. RAFFY, A. (1930). Réactions des Blattes aux variations de temperature. *C.R. Soc. Biol.*, **104**, 657–8.
42. RAGGE, D. R. (1965). *Grasshoppers, Crickets and Cockroaches of the British Isles*. Warne, London.
43. REHN, J. A. G. and HEBARD, M. (1914). On the Orthoptera found on the Florida Keys and in extreme southern Florida, II. *Proc. Acad. nat. Sci. Philad.*, **66**, 373–412.
44. REHN, J. W. H. (1951). Classification of the Blattaria as indicated by their wings. *Mem. Am. ent. Soc.*, **14**, 1–134.
45. ROESER, G. (1940). Zur Kenntnis der Lebensweise der Gewachshausschabe *Pycnoscelus surinamensis. Gartenbauwissenshaft*, **15**, 184–225.
46. ROSS, M. H. and COCHRAN, D. G. (1962). A body colour mutation in the German cockroach. *Nature*, **195**, 518–19.
47. ROTH, L. M. and WILLIS, E. R. (1961). Biotic associations of cockroaches. *Smithson. misc. Collns*, **141**, 1–470.
48. ROTH, L. M., NIEGISCH, W. D. and STAHL, W. H. (1956). Occurrence of 2-hexenal in the cockroach Eurycotis floridana. *Science*, **123**, 670–1.
49. ROTH, L. M. and STAY, B. (1958). The occurrence of paraquinones in some anthropods with emphasis on the quinone secreting tracheal glands of Diploptera punctata. *J. Insect. Physiol.*, **1**, 305–18.
50. SAMUEL, E. P. (1953). Towards controllable silver staining. *Anat. Rec.*, **116**, 511–20.

22 *Introduction*

51. SAUPE, R. (1928). Zur Kenntnischer Lebensweise der Riesenschabe Blabera fusca und der Gewachshausschabe *Pycnoscelus surinamensis. Z. angew. Ent.*, **14**, 461–500.
52. SCUDDER, S. H. (1886). Palaeozoic cockroaches: a complete revision of the species of both worlds with an essay towards their classification. *Mem. Boston Soc. nat. Hist.*, **3**, 23–134. In Miall and Denny.
53. SHAROV, A. G. (1962). Redescription of *Lithophotina floccosa* (Mantodea) with some notes on Manteod wing venation. *Psyche, Camb.*, **69**, 102–6.
54. SHELFORD, R. (1907). Aquatic cockroaches. *Zoologist*, **11**, 221–6.
55. SMITTLE, B. J. and BURDEN, G. S. (1959). A Mendelian colour variant in the German cockroach. *Ann. ent. Soc. Am.*, **52**, 115–18.
56. STAY, B. (1957). The sternal scent gland of Eurycotis floridana. *Ann. ent. Soc. Am.*, **50**, 514–19.
57. STEINHAUS, E. A. (1963). *Insect Pathology*, 3 vols. Academic Press, London.
58. SUESS, E. (1965). Cited by Jeannel, in Grassé.
59. SUOMALAINEN, E. (1946). Die Chromosomenverhaltnisse in der Spermatogenese einiger Blattarien. *Ann. Acad. Sci. Fenn.*, A4, **10**, 1–60.
60. TAYLOR, A. (1935). Blood cells in the cockroach. *Ann. ent. Soc. Am.*, **28**, 135–45.
61. VLASOV, I. P. and MIRIAM, E. F. (1960). Quoted by Roth and Willis.
62. WALKER, F. (1966). *Catalogue of the Specimens of Blattariae*, in the collection of the British Museum, 1868. Johnson, London.
63. WIGGLESWORTH, V. B. (1957). The use of osmium in the fixation and staining of tissues. *Proc. R. Soc.*, B, **147**, 185–98.
64. WILLIS, E. R. and ROTH, L. M. (1959). Gynandromorphs of *Byrsotria fumigata. Ann. ent. Soc. Am.*, **52**, 420–9.
65. YEAGER, J. F. and HAGER, A. (1934). Isolated heart preparations. *Iowa St. Coll. J. Sci.*, **8**, 391–5.
66. Anonymous. *The Cockroach*. British Museum Economic Series, 14 (no date given).

2 The exoskeleton

Abbreviations used for figures in Chapter 2

A.	Abdomen, abdominal	dat.	dorsal arm of tentorium
a.	antenna	davs.	dorsal arm of vulvar sclerite
ac.	antecoxite	dg.	dorsal gonapophysis
acl.	acutolobus	di.	dikella
al.	anepisternal line	dl.	distilorus
an.	anus	dlpt.	dorsal lappet of post-tergite
ar.	arolium	dsn.	dorsal sclerite of neck
as.	anepisternum		
asap.	anepisternal apophysis	e.	eye
asl.	asperate lobe	ejd.	ejaculatory duct
at.	antetrochantin, anterior tro-chantin	epm.	epimeron
		epp.	epiproct
athl.	acantholobus	eps.	episternum
atp.	anterior tergal process	eu.	euplantula
au.	axilia		
avat.	antero-ventral arm of tentorium	FM.	foramen magnum
ax.	axillary cord	FW.	fore-wing
		f.	femur
ba.	basalare	fa.	furcal arm
bas.	basantennal sclerite	fgr.	fronto-genal ridge
bc.	basicoxale	fr.	frons
bf.	basilar cleft	fs.	furcasternum
bga.	base of galea	fsp.	fine spur
bl.	basilorus	fx.	falx
blc.	base of lacinia		
bm.	basimandibulare	g.	gena
br.	basiremigiale	ga.	galea
brm.	basal rim of left phallomere	gl.	glossa
bs.	basisternum	grl.	grumolobus
		grlbs.	basal sclerite of grumolobus
C.	costal vein	gs.	galea strut
Cu.	cubital vein		
c.	coxa	H.W.	hind-wing
ce.	cercus	hc.	head capsule
cf.	coxifer	hg.	hypogynum
cg.	colleterial glands	hgs.	sclerites of hypogynum
cgd.	duct of colleterial glands	hp.	humeral plate
chg.	cavity of hypogynum	hy.	hypopharynx
cl.	clypeus		
		ig.	inner gonapophysis
dam.	dorsal or anterior articulation of mandible	int.	internal surface
		ism.	intersegmental membrane

j.   jugum

ks.   katepisternum

L.   left hand
lavs.   lateral arm of vulvar sclerite
lc.   lacinia
li.   labium
ll.   lingualorus
lp.   labial palp
lr.   labrum
ls.   lacinia spine
lsn.   lateral sclerite of neck

M.   median vein
m.   meron
map.   maxillary appendix
mc.   cardo of maxilla
md.   mandible
mf.   median foramen
mm.   mentum
mmb.   membrane of maxilla
mp.   maxillary palp
mp_1, mp_2, mp_3 parts of medial plate of wing base
ms.   stipes of maxilla
mx.   maxilla

o.   occiput of vertex
osd.   orifice of salivary duct

pa.   pleural apodeme
paf.   perianal fold
pam.   perianal membrane
pCu.   post cubital vein
pfc.   pleurofurcal connection
pfhg.   posterior folds of hypogynum
pg.   postgena
pgl.   paraglossa
pgp.   postgenal pit
pgr.   postgenal ridge
phb.   phallobase
phg.   phallic gland
pht.   phallotreme
pl.   posttergal lappet
pla.   pleural apophysis of prothorax
plm.   pleurum, pleuron
pls.   pleural sulcus
po.   postocciput
por.   postoccipital ridge
pp.   pseudopenis
ppg.   palpiger
ppt.   paraproct
pptl.   lappet of paraproct
prm.   prementum

prt.   paratergite
ps.   preepisternum
psc.   prescutite
pscp.   prescutal process
pst.   presternum
pt.   posttrochantin
pta.   pleuro-trochantinal articulation
ptg.   protergite
ptp.   posterior tergal process
pvat.   postero-ventral arm of tentorium
pwp.   pleural wing process

R.   radial vein in Figs. 2.9 to 2.14. Right hand in other figures
Rm.   remigium
Rs.   radial sector
rc.   rectum
rfm.   rim of foramen magnum

Sc.   subcostal vein
s.   sternum
sa.   subalare
sbm.   submentum
sl.   style
slm.   scutellum
smr.   submolar
sp.   spina
sr.   spiracle
ss.   spinasternum
st.   scutum
sth.   spermatheca
stha.   aperture of spermatheca

t.   tergum
ta.   tarsus
tca.   trochantino-coxal articulation
tg.   tegula
ti.   tibia
tn.   trochantin
tr.   trochanter

u.   unguis

V.   vannal vein
Vs.   vannus
vam.   ventral or posterior articulation of mandible
vf.   valvifer
vg.   ventral gonapophysis
vlsn.   ventro-lateral sclerite of neck
vo.   vestibular organ
vsn.   ventral sclerite of neck
vu.   vulva
vus.   vulvar sclerite

The head

The strong head capsule is held in the hypognathous position. The large compound eye occupies much of the lateral wall, and the long antenna, articulating with the annular basiantennal sclerite, is placed in the antero-medial indentation of the eye (Fig. 2.2). Dorso-medial to the antennal socket is a lighter patch of cuticle covering the ocellus. From this runs dorso-medially one arm of the epicranial suture, to join the other arm in a medial suture. The epicranial sutures are very fine cracks in the sclerotization of the head capsule and are not always visible.

The anterior face of the head consists of the fused frons and clypeus. The majority of the latter is relatively unsclerotized flexible cuticle, and distal to it lies the labrum.

Dorsal to the eye is the occiput and ventral and posterior to it lies the gena which extends round dorsally to the basimandibular sclerite. This region of the gena is larger in females because their eye is smaller, and greatly reduced in males because their eye is larger. The gena is demarcated from the frons by the fronto-genal suture (Fig. 2.2).

Posteriorly, the head articulates on the lateral sclerite of the neck (Fig. 2.10) and is joined to the thorax by a large membrane. The foramen magnum is bounded laterally by the post-occipital sclerite (Fig. 2.4) with which the lateral

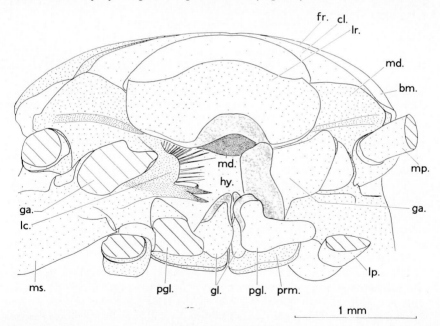

FIG. 2.1 Dissection of the head. The mouth parts. First stage: ventral view to show relationships of trophi at rest. Antennae and right paraglossa and galea removed

2+B.O.C.

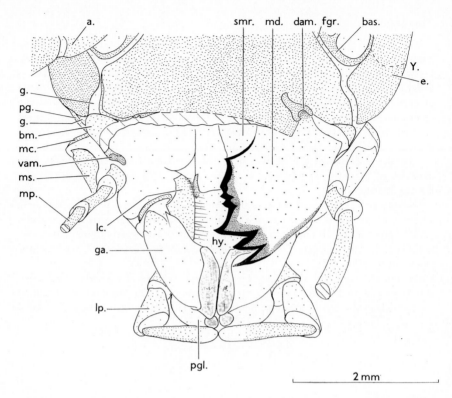

FIG. 2.2 Dissection of the head. Second stage: left antenna, right mandible, labrum and parts of clypeus and maxillary palpi also removed. Male. Y = position of the ventral edge of eye in female

sclerite of the neck, the labium and the maxilla, articulate. Lateral to the foramen magnum is the postgena separated from the gena by the postgenal ridge (Fig. 2.4). The dorsal cervical sclerite is joined to the head posteriorly (Fig. 2.11).

The antenna is long and filiform. It articulates at two points, the ventral one, the antennifer[2] being rigid and the lateral one, the surantennifer[2] being quite flexible. The basal articles are wider than long, except for the scape, while those of the apex are several times longer than wide.

The trophi or mouth-parts are the mandibles, maxillae and the hypopharynx, enclosed dorsally by the labrum and ventrally by the labium.

The mandible (Fig. 2.2) is dentate and strongly sclerotized except basally on the median edge, where there is a region of softer cuticle, the submolar.[2] The left one lies with its teeth dorsal to those of the right-hand one. Anteriorly and medially, the mandible is thinner but posteriorly and laterally it is thicker so that in posterior view it appears to be triangular with the apex near the mid-line. At the two outer basal angles, the mandible bears condyles which articulate with the head at the dorsal and ventral mandibular articulations. These are at the lateral

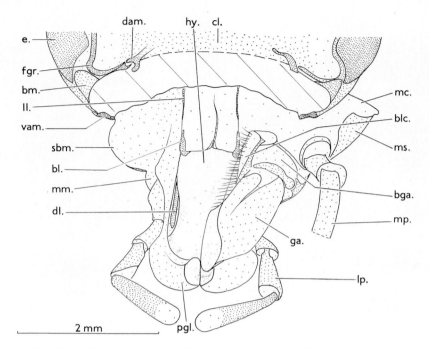

FIG. 2.3   Dissection of the head. Third stage: left mandible and right maxilla removed

edge of the clypeal region and at the ventro-posterior end of the postgena respectively (Figs. 2.2, 2.3).

The maxilla (Fig. 2.5) articulates basally with the ventral end of the post-occiput (Fig. 2.4) by means of a condyle on the basal tip of the cardo. This trophomere appears to be subdivided because it has a strong internal ridge running across it but is, in fact, a single structure without movement between the two apparent parts.

Articulating distally on the cardo is the stipes, bearing laterally a palp, though no palpifer can be discerned except for a region of articular membrane at the base of the palp. Along the medial side of the stipes is an infolding of the cuticle where a muscle is attached internally. Medial to the stipes is a wide membrane of attachment to the head.

The distal part of the maxilla consists of the outer galea and an inner lacinia (Figs. 2.1, 2.4). The galea at its tip encloses the two curved spine-like teeth of the lacinia so that when the trophi are at rest, the galeae meet distally and the laciniae are not seen externally (Fig. 2.1). On its inner surface the distal part of the galea is supported by a strut of sclerotized cuticle, the galea strut (Fig. 2.5) (the galeabacillus of Crampton[2]). The lacinia is a broad lobe with distally two inwardly curved lateral spines and a median outwardly curved projection, the maxillary appendix[2] or premaxilla.[5] Along its medial edge there is a number of

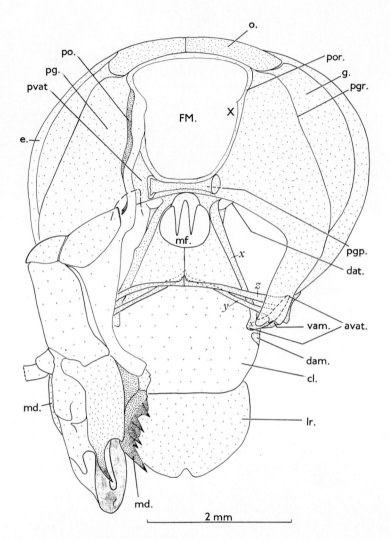

FIG. 2.4 Dissection of the head. Posterior view of head capsule and tentorium. The labrum, the right postoccipital sclerite, maxilla and mandible removed. X = point of articulation of head on lateral sclerite of neck

setae which get progressively shorter and more dense proximally. These setae are not shown except in Figs. 2.1 and 2.2.

The hypopharynx (Fig. 2.6) is a bulky median trophus occupying the space between the mandibles dorsally, the labium ventrally and maxillae laterally (Figs. 2.1, 2.2, 2.3). Largely unsclerotized, it bears several narrow sclerites, one extending alongside, the lingualorus, deep into the head, one mainly transverse,

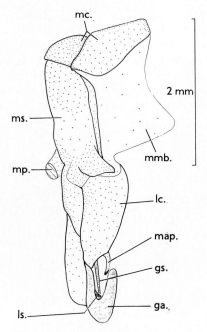

FIG. 2.5   Ventral surface of the maxilla

the basilorus, and one, the distilorus, running alongside the distal part of the structure (Fig. 2.3). In the mid-line on its ventral side is the salivary duct aperture (Fig. 2.6), and in the mid-line on the dorsal side is the mouth.

The labrum (Fig. 2.7) is a relatively simple sclerite, articulating with the head along the distal edge of the clypeus (Fig. 2.1). On its dorsal surface it is fully hardened, but the ventral surface, forming the epipharynx, is softer and un-sclerotized, although there is an arc of sclerotization with short stout setae on each side. Each arc runs anteriorly from the complex basal ring of sclerotization. The arc of one side is not necessarily identical with that on the other.

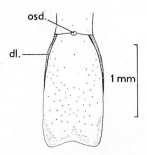

FIG. 2.6   Ventral surface of the hypopharynx

The labium (Fig. 2.8) is a composite sclerite, and consists of a basal plate, the submentum, distal to which is attached the mentum. The submentum, which is sclerotized, articulates with the head at a point adjacent to the maxillary articulation, and is indicated on the left side of Fig. 2.4 by the dotted line. The mentum is less sclerotized distally than proximally. Distal to the mentum is a slightly sclerotized region, the prementum, bearing two pairs of lobes, the glossae and paraglossae. These structures are movable on the prementum and are little

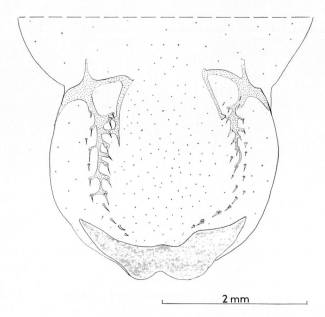

2 mm

FIG. 2.7   Ventral surface of the labrum

sclerotized, although the paraglossae are setose. Laterally the palp is inserted on to the prementum near to a small sclerite, which is claimed to be the palpiger[2] (Fig. 2.8). The inner or dorsal surface of the labium is a membrane continuous with that of the ventral surface of the hypopharynx.

The trophi fit together very neatly so that there is no space left between them at rest, and Figs. 2.1, 2.2 and 2.3 attempt to show their relationships as the trophi are removed in sequence.

There are regions on the trophi which appear to be rugose, including the tips of the glossae, paraglossae and galeae, much of the distal and dorsal surfaces of the hypopharynx, and the distal ventral surface of the labrum. The rugose appearance is due to a large number of very fine adpressed curved spines or setae, many of which lie with their tips pointing medially or posteriorly.

The tentorium (Fig. 2.4). This internal skeleton of the head capsule consists of a central mass, perforated centrally and connected to the head capsule at two main points on each side. At the antero-ventral edge of the postoccipital suture, where the rim of the foramen magnum is thickened, the tentorium is fused to it. This is the postero-ventral arm of the tentorium and is indicated externally by the posterior genal pit. This postero-ventral arm arises from the main mass of the tentorium (the eutentorium of Crampton[2]), dorsal to the medium foramen, and extends to and becomes confluent with the postgena. Ventral to the median foramen lies a larger part of the tentorium (intertentorium of Crampton[2]) and from this there arises a sheet of sclerotized cuticle stiffened by three ridges. The lateral one (x) runs to the median corner of the frontogenal ridge, just dorsal to

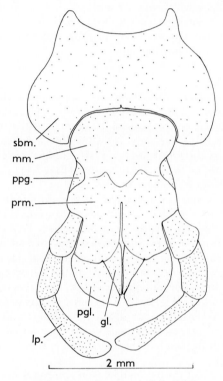

FIG. 2.8   Dorsal surface of the labium

the inner corner of the basimandibular sclerite. The two antero-ventral ones (y, z) cross to the middle and outer parts of the frontogenal ridge so that, adjacent to the postero-medial edge of the basimandibular, the frontogenal ridge is mainly formed by the ends of this massive arm of the tentorium. It is the antero-ventral arm, and is indicated externally by the pit at this position. All this part of the tentorium lies quite close to the posterior surface of the head, but there is also a very fine transparent strand, or apophysis which arises from the edge of the tentorium and runs dorsalwards to insert on to the basantennal ring immediately dorsal to the dorsal flexible antennifer articulation.

From the postero-dorsal edge of the median foramen, there is a pair of delicate transparent apophyses projecting across the foramen. These are the tendons for the oesophageal muscles.

The thorax

The thorax (Figs. 2.9 to 2.20) consists of three segments lying posterior to the head, to which it is attached by an anterior extension of the prothorax, or neck region. The skeleton of the thorax has been described in detail by Crampton[3] and in most particulars the present account agrees with his, but it is simplified by a refusal to give a separate name to every part of a sclerite. For the wing articulations too, an attempt has been made to make the terminology of the sclerites simpler and more intelligible.

THE TERGA (Fig. 2.9)

The protergum is covered by a large plate overlapping the head anteriorly, the mesothorax posteriorly, and extending laterally. This is the protergite (ptg.). It is variously darkened but, in general, the central region is lighter than the peripheral part, especially posteriorly. A median line is present which bifurcates posteriorly. Anteriorly the protergite covers the dorsal sclerite of the neck (dsn.) in the mid-line posterior to the head capsule (Fig. 2.11). This sclerite bears posteriorly an apophysis for muscle attachment.

The mesotergum is strongly sclerotized, the main sclerite being the meso-tergite. This is deeply rounded at the antero-lateral corner and has an elongated triangular region in the mid-line, the scutellum (slm.). This extends to near the anterior border and from its anterior tip there is a line extending laterally separating the narrow anterior part of the tergite from the rest. This anterior region is here called the prescutum (psc.) and consists of the antecosta and the prescutal process. The antecosta is a deep implex and bears the prescutal process running laterally towards the tegula (Fig. 2.17). This is the prealar sclerite of Crampton[3], and Snodgrass.[16] It is not a separate sclerite. Posterior to the prescutal process lies the anterior tergal process (atp.), one of the chief articulations of the fore-wing, and posterior to the notch in the lateral wall of the scutum is the posterior tergal process (ptp.).

The posterior margin of the mesotergite is in two layers, the dorsal one (dlpt.) being relatively free overlying the region of the junction between the meso- and metathorax. The articulation between the two segments occurs where the lappet of the more ventral layer (pl.) runs posteriorly to articulate with the prescutite of the mesothorax (Fig. 2.9). This region Crampton[3] calls the post-tergite and the postscutellum, but in this work the latter term is dropped because it does not seem to apply to a clearly definable part of the skeleton. The posttergite continues laterally to the jugum of the fore-wing.

The metatergum is similar to the mesotergum. The prescutum is, however, not so clearly demarcated, although it also consists of a strong antecosta with a lateral process, the prescutal process, as in the mesothorax (Fig. 2.20).

The metaposttergite (Figs. 2.9, 2.21) is also in two layers, and is very like that

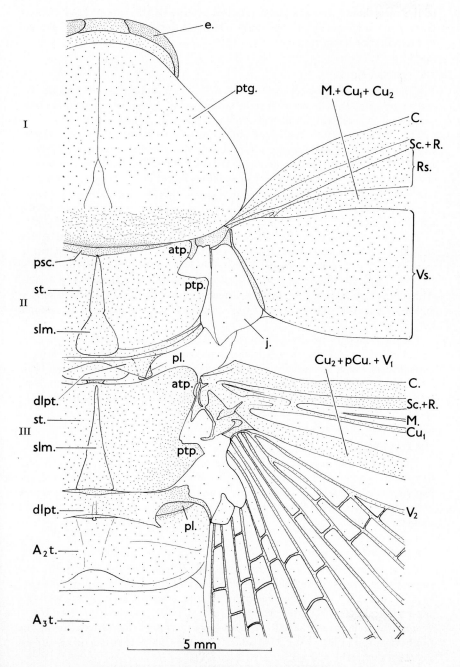

FIG. 2.9   The thorax. Dorsal sclerites. Vannal veins of fore-wing omitted

2*

of the mesothorax, but the small articular sclerite of the ventral layer is more lateral, and is connected to the lateral sclerite of the dorsal layer which extends to the posterior wing margin.

THE STERNA (Fig. 2.10)

The sterna are largely sclerotized, but their lateral limits are not obvious. For the purposes of this description only the unequivocal sternal sclerites are considered, all others being dealt with under the pleural region.

The prothoracic sternites consist of a central basisternite (bs.), posterior to which is the transverse furcasternite (fs.). Anteriorly is the ventro-lateral sclerite of the neck (vlsn.), meeting its fellow in the mid-ventral line, and, latero-dorsally, the lateral sclerite of the neck (lsn.) extending round dorsally to articulate with the dorso-lateral region of the margin of the head capsule. Anterior to the ventro-lateral sclerite there are two transverse narrow sclerites which are the ventral sclerites of the neck (vsn.). Many of the prosternites are not well sclerotized.

The mesosternites consist of the central basisternite, an anterior median spina-sternite (ss.) (sometimes not obvious externally) and a forked posterior furca-sternite (fs.). Internally the spina is more obvious, and the furcasternite can be seen to carry the furcal arm (fa.) extending laterally towards the pleurum. Although most authors put the spinasternite posterior to the furcasternite, it appears from work on the Apterygota[1] that it belongs to the position adopted here.

The metasternites are similar to those of the mesosternum but in the basisternal region a median sclerite, which is fused to the furcasternite, lies between the basisternites which lie laterally. The furcasternite is forked posteriorly and bears internally the furcal arm. Anterior to this lies the spina with a long narrow median sclerite running to the posterior edge of the furcasternite of the mesothorax. The spina is not quite so big as that of the mesothorax.

THE PLEURA

The pleurites of insects have been interpreted and named in many different ways, and no one system either commands universal support or suffices for all the many species of insects. Thus to some extent terminology is arbitrary and here the simplest system is preferred, until further comparative studies solve the many problems involved.

The propleurites

Three main pieces can be distinguished. These are the trochantin, the eupleurite and the sclerite lying anterior to the eupleurite, the preepisternite (ps., Figs. 2.10, 2.11). This latter bears an anterior point of articulation with the ventro-lateral sclerite of the neck and runs ventrally to touch basisternum I. Posteriorly it is strengthened by what may represent the antecoxite of the prothorax (ac.?, Figs. 2.10, 2.11) and it is along this posterior edge also that it articulates with the episternum (es., Fig. 2.10).

The eupleurite is deeply hollowed inwards and bears a large pleural apodeme

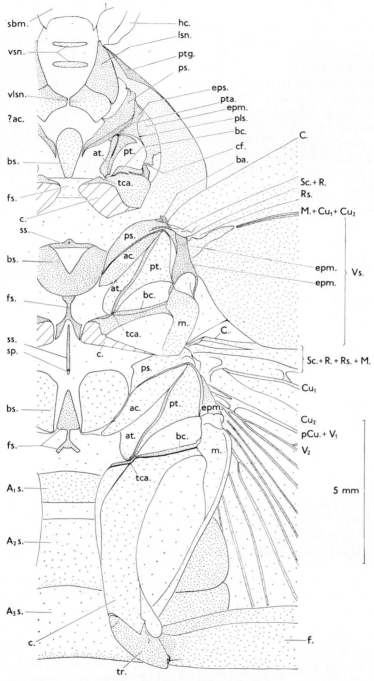

FIG. 2.10 The thorax. Ventral sclerites

(pla., Fig. 2.11) to which the sternal apophysis or furcal arm runs. This pleural groove and the corresponding internal pleural ridge divides the eupleurite into an anterior episternum and a posterior epimeron. The ventral end of the pleural groove and ridge forms the coxiferal articulation with the coxa. The epimeron (epm.) is relatively large in this segment.

Ventral to the episternum lies the trochantin which bears a ridge, appearing to divide it into two halves, the anterior and the posterior trochantins (at., pt., Figs. 2.10, 2.11). This is probably for strength since it spans the space between the pleuro-trochantinal articulation (pta., Fig. 2.10) and the trochantino-coxal articulation (tca., Figs. 2.10, 2.11).

There is often a fine transparent apophysis which runs from the base of the furcal arm to the postero-lateral wall of the segment just dorsal to the coxal rim (pla., Fig. 2.11).

The mesopleurite

The same three parts that have been noted in the prothorax are present in the two segments of the pterothorax: the eupleurite, the trochantin and the anterior sclerites running ventrally to the basisternite.

The eupleurite consists of its usual two parts: episternum and epimeron. The former is marked by a transverse line, the anepisternal line (al., Fig. 2.16), cutting off a more dorsal region, the anepisternum (as., Fig. 2.16), from a more ventral region, the katepisternum (ks., Fig. 2.16). The katepisternum continues antero-ventrally as the preepisternum (ps., Fig. 2.16) which extends anterior to the antecoxite and ends ventrally adjacent to the basisternite (Fig. 2.11). The anepisternum is rather thicker antero-dorsally and may be considered to form an apophysis which is more prominent in the metathorax (asap., Fig. 2.19). Dorsal to the anepisternum lies the basalare (20, Fig. 2.16; ba., Fig. 2.19). Posterior to the preepisternum lie the trochantins (anterior and posterior), and a longer sclerite lying adjacent to the preepisternum and running ventrally close to the basisternite. This will be called here the antecoxite (ac., Figs. 2.11, 2.16), to avoid any suggestion that theories as to its katapleural nature are more than speculation. The trochantin bears a diagonal external groove strengthening it, which extends to the trochantino-coxal articulation (tca., Fig. 2.11). The epimeron lies postero-dorsal to the pleural groove which ends in the coxiferal articulation.

The internal pleural ridge ends dorsally in a large strong process, the pleural wing process (pwp., Figs. 2.11, 2.16), and anterior to this is a less sclerotized area, the basalar cleft (bf., Fig. 2.16).

Internally, the furcasternum bears the long furcal arm which is connected by a tendinous structure to the ventral end of the pleural ridge close to the coxifer (pfc., Fig. 2.11).

The metapleurites

These are a repetition of the mesopleurites and do not need to be described further.

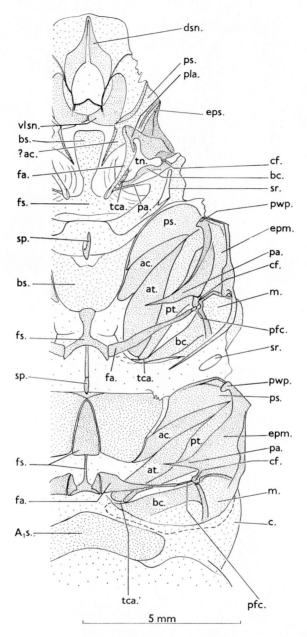

FIG. 2.11   The thorax. Internal surface of the ventral sclerites

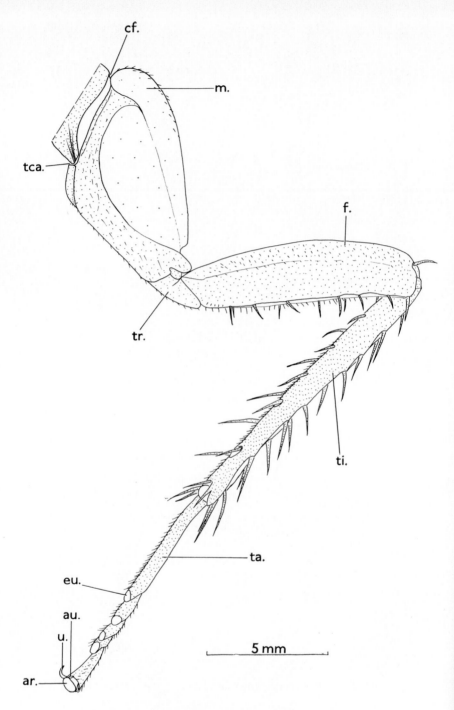

FIG. 2.12   Left metathoracic leg; posterior surface

The legs

The legs are similar in shape and structure to one another, leg 1 being the smallest and leg 3 the largest. The metathoracic leg is shown in Fig. 2.12 and further description is unnecessary.

The wings

These are shown in Figs. 2.13 and 2.14 and, again, further description is not required.

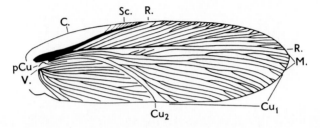

FIG. 2.13   The fore-wing. (Smart[13], relettered)

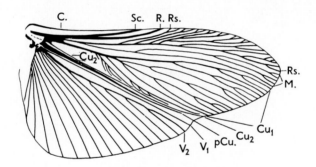

FIG. 2.14   The hind-wing. (Smart[13], relettered)

THE ARTICULAR REGION OF THE WINGS

The fore-wing (Figs. 2.15, 2.16, 2.17)

(a) *Dorsal* (Fig. 2.15). At the base of the wing there are several small sclerites which allow the movements of the wing to occur. The prescutal process (1) projects laterally close to the tegula (2), which lies medial to the base of the remigium of the wing (3). The anterior tergal process (4) is a triangular extension of the antero-lateral border of the tergite and it is with this that the anterior part of pterale I articulates (5). Posteriorly pterale I articulates with the lateral border of the tergite (6). Lateral to pterale I lies pterale II (7) and they are fused at the anterior end of the latter (8) which is also joined to the median plate (9). Laterally it is separated from the median plate by a cleft (10), posterior to which is point of fusion between pterale III and the median plate (11). Pterale III is a very irregular sclerite stretching to the posterior tergal process (12), to the basivannale (13), to the median plate (14) and to the posterior end of pterale II (15). This part is deeply inflected: only the edge is visible in dorsal view (Fig. 2.15), but in internal

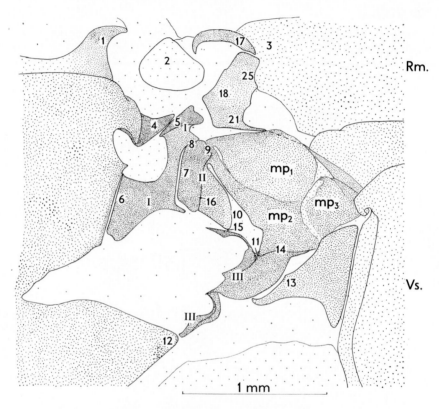

FIG. 2.15   Details of the fore-wing articular sclerites. Dorsal view

view it is seen more fully (Fig. 2.17). The median plate is subdivisible into three poorly defined areas. At the base of the remigium, there are two sclerites which are the humeral plate (17) and the basiremigiale (18).

(b) *Ventral* (Fig. 2.16). The basalare (20) lies immediately anterior to the pleural wing process and is connected to the proximal end of the basiremigiale (21). This is in turn connected to the base of the remigial region of the wing (22). Dorsal to the pleural wing process lies the ventral part of pterale II which joins the dorsal part at (16) (Fig. 2.15). Posteriorly this pterale articulates with the subalare which appears on the surface as a narrow sclerite (23) but which is more extensive internally. Dorsal to the subalare lies the ventral part of pterale III.

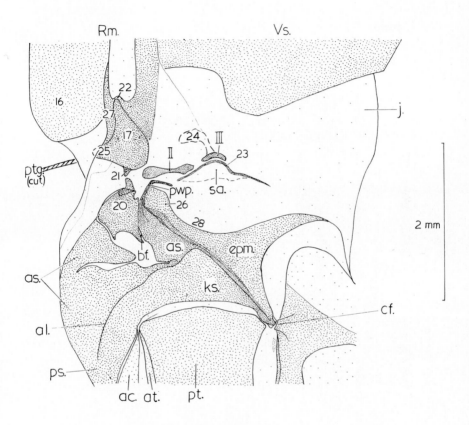

FIG. 2.16 Details of the fore-wing articular sclerites. Ventral view

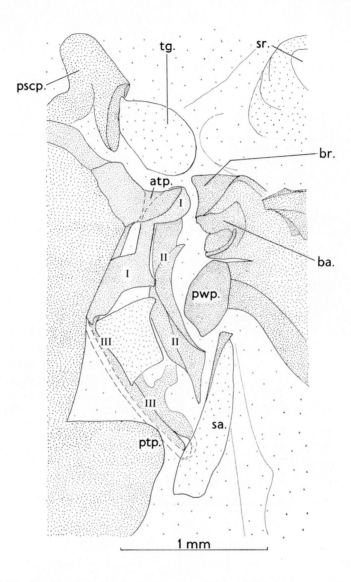

FIG. 2.17 Details of internal view of dorsal side of basal region of fore-wing. Wing flexed

The deep pit on the dorsal side at (12), where this pterale and the median plate are fused is seen on the ventral side at (24). Two struts run from the dorsal to the ventral surfaces of the basiremigiale at points (21) and (25).

The jugal membrane may be slightly sclerotized. When the fore-wing is folded at rest the ridge-lobe of the epimeron (26) lies in the groove between the humeral plate and the basiremigiale (27), while the bases of veins Sc and R lie alongside the epimeral ridge (28).

The hind-wing (Figs. 2.18, 2.19, 2.20)

(a) *Dorsal* (Fig. 2.18). The prescutal process is less well developed than in the fore-wing and there are fewer small sclerites at the base of the wing. The

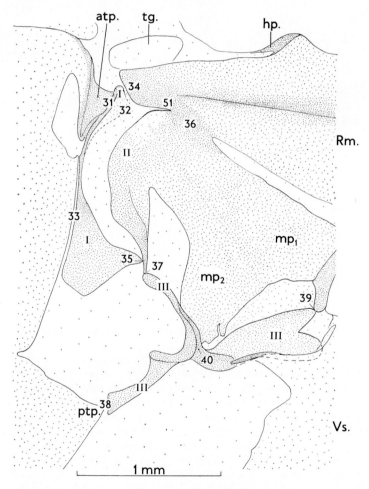

FIG. 2.18   Details of hind-wing articular sclerites. Dorsal view

The exoskeleton

anterior tergal process is fused to the anterior end of pterale I (31). This pterale
has an internal extension at the anterior end (32) and posteriorly it articulates
with the lateral edge of the tergite (33). Anteriorly it articulates with the basiremigiale (34) and posteriorly it has a triangular lateral projection which articulates with the posterior end of pterale II (35). Pterale II is a sclerite continuous
with the basiremigiale (36) and with the median plate, mp. Its posterior tip is

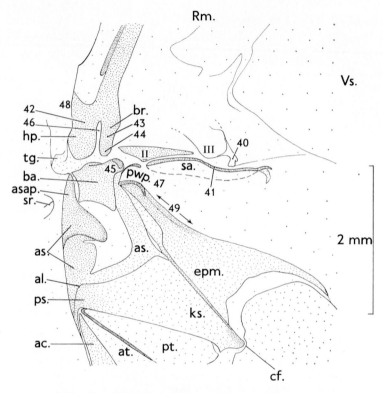

FIG. 2.19   Details of hind-wing articular sclerites. Ventral view

fused to the anterior tip of pterale III (37). The third pterale is a three-pointed
structure; the anterior part joins pterale II at (37), the posterior arm runs to the
posterior tergal process (38), and laterally, a wide arm runs out towards the basi-
vannal region of the wing. This arm is bifid at its tip and one branch is fused to a
strongly sclerotized part of the wing (39). At the centre of the three arms there is
a deep pit where all three are fused together and are fused also with the median
plate (40). The median plate is indistinctly divided into median plates 1 and 2.

(b) *Ventral* (Fig. 2.19). No part of pterale I is seen, but pterale II has a ventral
part lying immediately dorsal to the pleural wing process. The ventral part of
pterale III is seen posterolateral to pterale II and the ventral end of the pit (40)
at the centre of its three arms is shown. Ventral to pterale II and pterale III lies

the subalare (41) which is only visible on the surface as a narrow sclerite as in the fore-wing. A humeral plate (42) is present at the base of the costal region of the wing, but is only sclerotized to any extent on the ventral side. The ventral side of the basiremigium is joined to the dorsal side by a strut at (44).

When the hind wing is closed, the basalare (45) fits into the groove (46) between the basiremigiale and the humeral plate, while the basiremigiale lies

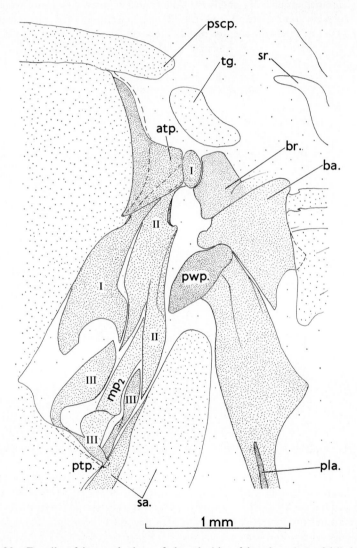

FIG. 2.20 Details of internal view of dorsal side of basal region of hind-wing. Wing flexed

between the subalare and the ridge of the epimeron (47). The edge of the wing
(48) lies dorsal to and parallel with the edge of the epimeron (49).

The abdomen

The sternite of the first abdominal segment is reduced to a small median
sclerite probably because of the great size and position of the metacoxae. The
first abdominal spiracle lies anterior to the rounded anterior angle of tergite A1,
partly beneath the lateral projecting dorsal sclerite of the metaposttergite
(Fig. 2.21). The other spiracles of the abdomen are found immediately below the

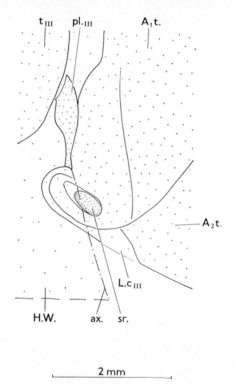

2 mm

FIG. 2.21   View of left side of first abdominal segment to show position of spiracle

antero-lateral corner of each tergite and spiracles A3 to A7 are hidden by the
postero-lateral corner of the tergite of the preceding segment. Each spiracle occurs
on a small narrow longitudinal sclerite lying between the tergite above and the
lateral edge of the sternum below. This sclerite is the pleurite (Fig. 2.22). Each
tergite, and each sternite, except the first, is crossed by a transverse line or ridge,
and bears a few short setae.

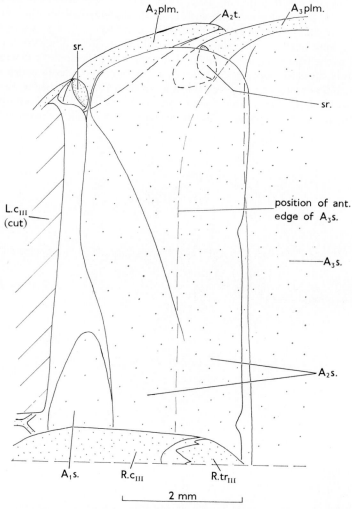

FIG. 2.22   Ventral surface of left half of first abdominal segment. Left metathoracic
leg removed

The genital appendages

FEMALE GENITAL ORGANS (Figs. 2.23 to 2.28)

The prominent features of the posterior end of the abdomen of the female *P.a.* are sternite A7 or hypogynum, the epiprocts and the cerci (Fig. 2.23). Sternum A7 bears two sclerites which are fused together at one point (Fig. 2.23) but otherwise are free to move relative to one another. The sternites of both sides lie apposed posteriorly with a fold of soft flesh between them. This fleshy fold is

continued inwards to form two folds, the posterior being larger than the anterior
(Figs. 2.24, 2.25). Dorsal to these folds of the hypogynum are the paraprocts
(Figs. 2.24, 2.27) with the anus between. The epiprocts project posteriorly, being
a partly bifid flexible projection of tergite A10 (Fig. 2.27). The cercus is found
lateral to the paraproct, with a clear articulation with the epiproct and tergite A10
anteriorly. Postero-medially there is a small curved basal sclerite which may act
as a second articulation[2] although this was not found to be the case by the writer.
The cercus is almost without setae and flat dorsally, whereas ventrally it is
rounded and with many setae. Close to the base of the cercus is the spiracle, lying

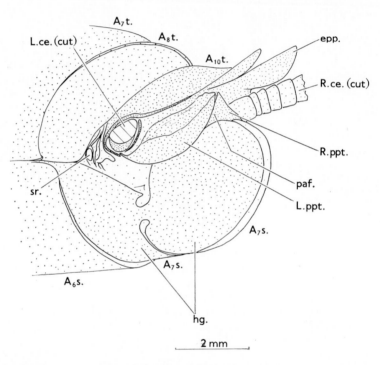

FIG. 2.23   Female genitalia. Postero-lateral view of posterior abdominal segments

just posterior to the margin of tergite A7 (Figs. 2.23, 2.28). Tergites A8 and A9
are covered by tergite A7. Sternites A8 and A9 are hidden within the genital
pouch.
    When the hypogynum is pinned back posteriorly as in Fig. 2.25, the bases of
the ovipositor appendages are visible, together with the sclerites on the dorsal
side of the hypogynum. Removal of the paraprocts, rectum and anus, and
tergite A10 leaves a membrane, whose attachment to the more ventral structures
is indicated on one side by the arrow-heads on Fig. 2.25. Within this membrane
lie various parts of the reproductive system, and when these are removed, the

internal surfaces of some of the sclerites lying round the bases of the gonapophyses or ovipositor are seen.

There are three gonapophyses: anterior or ventral, posterior or dorsal and median or inner. The inner is an outgrowth of the dorsal,[7] so that segmentally there is one gonapophysis from segment A8 (ventral) and one plus one from sternum A9 (dorsal+inner). The ventral gonapophysis is sclerotized quite extensively, and distally it lies, with the inner gonapophysis, in a hollow on the

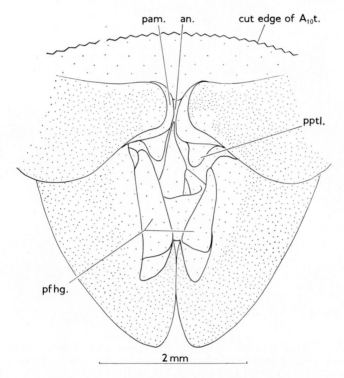

FIG. 2.24   Female genitalia. Posterior view of posterior abdominal segments. Part of tergum of the tenth abdominal segment removed

ventral side of the dorsal gonapophysis. The inner and dorsal gonapophyses are not so extensively sclerotized as the ventral one. Figure 2.26 shows the three gonapophyses at rest on the right side and spread apart on the left.

The sclerites which support the base of the ovipositor are called the valvifers, and here there are held to be two valvifers, the first supporting the ventral gonapophysis, and the second the dorsal (and inner) gonapophyses. The first valvifer (Fig. 2.26) is part of sternum A8 and the second is part of sternum A9 (Fig. 2.26). The base of the ventral gonapophysis lies laterally and its valvifer lies

on the lateral wall of the segment. It consists of a narrow vertical sclerotized bar
and a triangular piece immediately posterior to its ventral end (Fig. 2.28). Dorsal
to this triangular sclerite there is another narrow bar of sclerotized cuticle running up to terga A8 and A9. These vertical bars are the paratergites, and Gupta

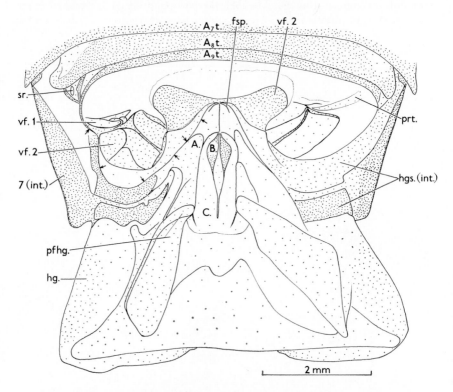

FIG. 2.25   Female genitalia. Hypogynum pinned posteriorly to show internal
structures. Tergum of the tenth abdominal segment, paraprocts and viscera dorsal
to gonapophyses removed. In this figure, the small arrows indicate, on the left side
only, the line of attachment of the membrane which extends to the paraprocts

states that they are derivatives of tergum A9 only.[7] Posterior to this at its ventral
end, there is a large sclerite which is here called the lateral part of valvifer 2. The
inner part of the second valvifer is not so obvious externally because the bases of
the dorsal gonapophyses are median. It consists of a median sclerite (Figs. 2.25,
2.26, 2.28) which bears a pair of internal apophyses (not visible in the view
drawn) and which surrounds and supports the bases of both dorsal and inner
gonapophyses.

Sternum A8 also bears three more sclerites. The lateral two (here called the
basisternite of segment A8) are attached to the postero-lateral corners of the

median sclerite (here called the presternite) of segment A8 (Fig. 2.26). The median sclerite also bears a median posterior projection, on which is the aperture of the spermathecae (Figs. 2.26, 2.27, 2.28). The cuticle lying latero-dorsal to the basisternites is ridged and rough but not heavily sclerotized.

Ventral (apparently posterior in Fig. 2.26) to basisternite A8 lie the vulva and the vulvar sclerite. The lateral arm of the latter lies vertically, external to the first valvifer (Fig. 2.28). The vulva and its sclerites lie in the intersegmental membrane between segments A7 and A8.

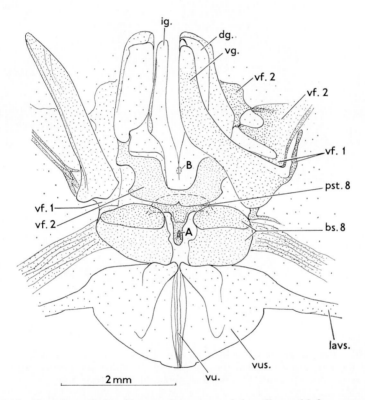

FIG. 2.26   Female genitalia. Gonapophyses turned dorsally, and left gonapophysis displaced to left. In this figure, **A** is the aperture of the spermathecae on pre-sternum 8 and **B** the aperture of the colleterial glands

The above account does not coincide with that of any other single author and the following comments should be added:

1. The gynantrium or genital chamber includes all the space around the ovipositor and between the paraprocts and hypogynum. Initially it is a simple chamber, but during ontogeny it becomes subdivided and elaborated.[7]

2. There seems to be little evidence on the development, and thus on the derivation, of the ventral sclerotized projections of tergites A8 and A9 and the sclerites at their ventral ends.

3. The opening of the colleterial glands seems to be single and rather more distal than shown by Crampton,[2] in spite of the claim by Gupta that the two glands open separately by adjacent apertures.[7]

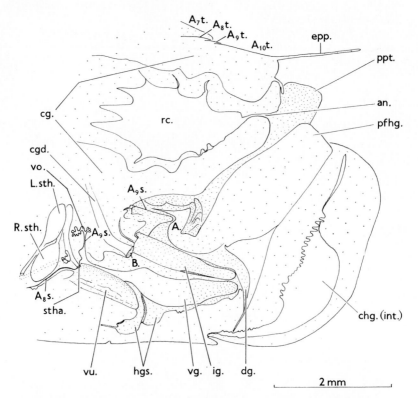

FIG. 2.27   Female genitalia. Sagittal section of posterior end of abdomen. **A** is a fold of the hypogynum, and **B** the aperture of the colleterial glands. Numbers 8 and 9 indicate the sterna of abdominal segments 8 and 9

4. The homologies of gonapophyses are a matter of dispute. The ventral and dorsal are thought to be homologous, both being coxopodites, while the inner gonapophysis is thought to be the endite of the appendage.[7, 9, 14] Denny claimed that the ventral gonapophysis was homologous to the inner gonapophysis, and that the dorsal one was the result of the division of sternum A9.[4]

5. The sclerites supporting the bases of the gonapophyses are a source of much confusion and divergence in terminology. It is for this reason that the terms used in the present account have been kept to a minimum, and they do not entirely agree with those of previous authors. The sclerotized regions which give support

to the gonapophyses have been here called valvifers. Because the gonapophyses are derived from segments A8 and A9, the valvifers are called first and second. From a functional point of view it is not profitable to try to decide which particular part of a sclerite is concerned solely with the performance of a single gonapophysis; the whole is an integrated arrangement and works as a complex unity. Most authors have, however, been concerned with the relations of the parts in comparative anatomy, with a consequent multiplication of terms.

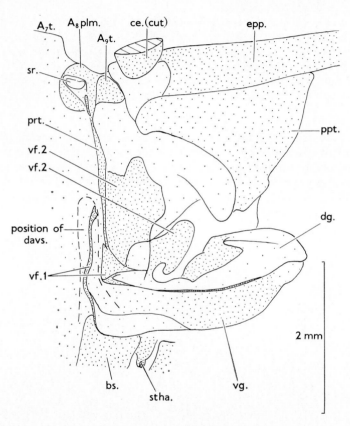

FIG. 2.28   Female genitalia. Lateral view of internal structures; the sternum of abdominal segment 8 is displaced postero-ventrally

Presternite A8 of this account is the first intervalvula of Gupta and basisternum A8 is his first basivalvula. Similarly he shows the ducts of the colleterial glands to open on his third intervalvula.[7] (This is approximately half-way between A and B on my Fig. 2.26.) The sclerite here called the second valvifer (Figs. 2.26, 2.28) is a combination of the 'second basivalvula' and the 'valvifer' of Gupta.[7] Snodgrass[15] and Marks and Lawson[8] considered the lateral part of the second valvifer to be a ventral sclerite of tergum A10, but here the work of Gupta is followed, which shows that this sclerite is derived from the lateral part of segment A9 during development.[7] This is the gonangulum of Scudder.[11, 12]

6. Crampton calls basisternite A8 'valvisclerite'; presternite A8 'medisternite'; valvifer 2 'valvijugum'; and the aperture of the colleterial glands 'valvipore'.[2]

7. Position of the vulva. The position adopted by Gupta is followed here, because he has considered the ontogeny as well as the comparative anatomy of the segments and their sclerites.[7]

The vulva and the vulvar sclerites are shown by Gupta to be formed in the intersegmental membrane between segments A7 and A8.[7] This arrangement is also accepted by Denny.[4] Gupta also maintains that the thecapore is always on segment A8.[7] On the other hand, Snodgrass,[15] Marks and Lawson,[8] and van Wyk[17] think the vulva is on sternum A8 and the basi- and presternites are sclerites on the intersegmental membrane between segments A8 and A9.

MALE GENITAL ORGANS (Figs. 2.29 to 2.34)

The posterior end of the male abdomen bears cerci and epiprocts as in the female; and, in addition, the styles found in the nymphal stages of both sexes are retained into the adult stage of the male. They are borne on the posterior edge of sternum A9, which extends deeply to the anterior within segment A8 and even segment A7 (Fig. 2.29). Terga A8 and A9 are wholly or largely hidden by tergum

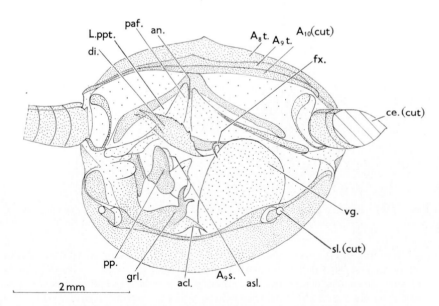

FIG. 2.29   Male genitalia. Posterior view. Epiprocts, styles and right cercus removed

A7 and the spiracle is also hidden under the postero-ventral corner of this tergum (Fig. 2.30).

The gonapophyses are carried within the cavity bounded dorsally by the paraprocts and ventrally by sternum A9. There are three gonapophyses, right, left and ventral, but the right and left are complex in structure.

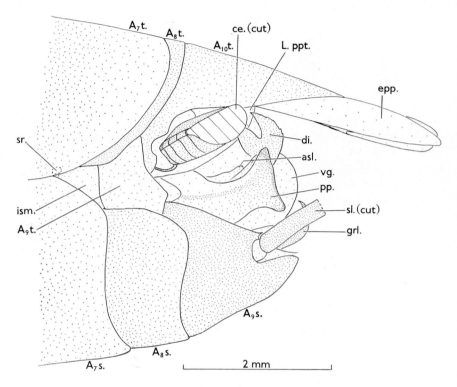

FIG. 2.30   Male genitalia. Lateral view

In posterior view (Fig. 2.29) the large smooth sclerotized surface is the ventral gonapophysis; dorsal to this but partly hidden is the right gonapophysis, and to its left lies the left one. The right gonapophysis bears a two-pronged serrated projection extending over to the left, which is shown in Fig. 2.29 with the left paraproct between the prongs. The left gonapophysis possesses a number of sharp or rounded, hard or soft lobes described below.

The ventral gonapophysis is shaped something like a boxing-glove, with the soft 'palm' dorsal and the harder 'back' ventral (Fig. 2.33). It is attached to the

56   *The exoskeleton*

body by an extensive membrane, which bears the slightly sclerotized opening of
the vas deferens. This is the phallotreme.

The right gonapophysis is seen in dorsal view in Fig. 2.31 and in ventral view
in Fig. 2.32. Neither drawing gives a complete idea of its complexity, since it
extends deeply into the posterior end of the abdomen. It is basically in three
layers, the most dorsal of which bears distally the dikella (Fig. 2.31). Proximal to
this structure, this dorsal layer is itself in two parts, one membranous, overlying

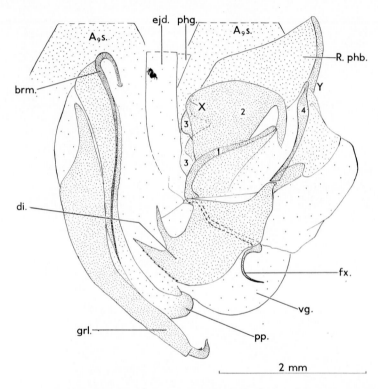

FIG. 2.31   Male genitalia. Dorsal view of internal structures. Overlying structures
removed. X and Y indicate the line on which sclerites 2 and 3 move dorso-
ventrally. The numbers 1, 2, 3 and 4 refer to the sclerites described in the text

dorsally a sclerotized region, sclerite 1, which has a projection directed to the left,
ending in the falx (Fig. 2.31).

The second, middle, layer consists of sclerite 2, which lies immediately dorsal
to sclerite 3 (Figs. 2.31, 2.32). Supporting the whole of this complex is the basal
part of the right gonapophysis, the right phallobase. This has a sclerotized medial
edge, sclerite 4 (Figs. 2.31, 2.32), which extends to support the proximal median
corner of the dikella.

Sclerites 2 and 3, or the opponentes of Crampton[2] can be separated and it is between them that the ventral gonapophyses of the female are held in copulation.[6] They articulate along a line running obliquely from the extreme median junction of sclerites 2 and 3 (X) to the base of sclerite 4 (Y) (Figs. 2.31, 2.32).

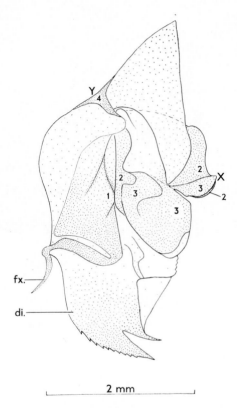

2 mm

FIG. 2.32   Male genitalia. Right phallomere, obliquely ventral view. Drawn from a specimen treated with KOH and membranes removed

The left gonapophysis has a large basal piece, extending deeply to the anterior, with a sclerotized margin. This is the base of the left phallomere or left phallobase. Distal to this there are two ventral sclerotized regions: the median one is the basal sclerite of the grumolobus (Fig. 2.34); the lateral one, the pseudopenis. This latter is also supported by the distal prolongation of the sclerotized rim of the left phallobase, on the dorsal side.

The pseudopenis ends in a prominent dark sclerotized double-headed knob (Figs. 2.30, 2.34). Lying adjacent but slightly proximal to this, are the asperate lobes, which bear a few rows of short fine setae (Figs. 2.30, 2.34), and between which the phallic gland opens. Lateral to the asperate lobes lies a short sclerotized piece bearing several short spurs, the acantholobus. Lateral again to this lies the

3 + B.O.C.

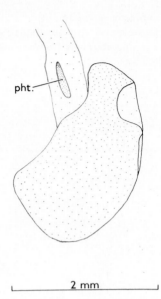

2 mm

FIG. 2.33   Male genitalia. Ventral phallomere. Ventral view

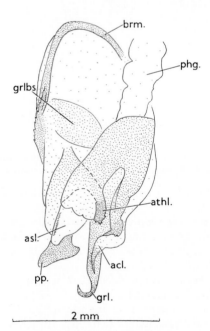

2 mm

FIG. 2.34   Male genitalia. Left phallomere. Ventral view

projection bearing the curved sharp hook, the acutolobus. Finally, dorsal to the acutolobus there is the grumolobus which ends in a double hook.

It is to be noticed that some of the above terms are new, but otherwise the terminology follows that of Crampton.[2] He calls the ventral gonapophysis the penislobus; the right phallobase the basilamina; sclerite 1 the basiserrata; sclerites 2 and 3 the opponentes; sclerite 4 the basarcus; the dikella the serrate lobe; the left phallobase the pseudopenis; and the grumolobus the titillator.

Gupta states that the phallic gland or conglobate gland opens at an aperture adjacent to the phallotreme,[6] but Qadri says it opens between the lobes of the left gonapophysis.[10] This opinion is confirmed by the writer.

REFERENCES

1. BARLET, J. and CARPENTIER, F. (1962). Le thorax des Japygides. *Bull. Annls Soc. r. ent. Belg.*, **98**, 95–123.
2. CRAMPTON, G. C. (1925). The external anatomy of the head and abdomen of the roach *Periplaneta americana. Psyche*, **32**, 195–226.
3. CRAMPTON, G. C. (1927). The thoracic sclerites and wing bases of the roach *Periplaneta americana* and the basal structures of the wings of insects. *Psyche*, **34**, 59–72.
4. DENNY, A. (1894). On the development of the 'Ovipositor' in the cockroach, *Periplaneta orientalis. Rep. Br. Ass. Advmt Sci.*, **63**, 818.
5. EIDMANN, H. (1924). Das sogenannte 'Praemaxillare' der Insekten. *Zool. Anz.*, **58**, 43–52.
6. GUPTA, P. D. (1947). On copulation and insemination in the cockroach *Periplaneta americana. Proc. natn. Inst. Sci. India*, **13**, 65–71.
7. GUPTA, P. D. (1948). On the structure, development and homology of the female reproductive organs in orthopteroid insects. *Indian J. Ent.*, **10**, 75–123.
8. MARKS, E. P. and LAWSON, F. A. (1962). A comparative study of the Dictyopteran ovipositor. *J. Morph.*, **111**, 139–71.
9. NEL, R. I. (1929). Studies on the development of the genital ducts in insects. I. Female Orthoptera and Dermaptera. *Q. Jl microsc. Sci.*, **73**, 25–85.
10. QADRI, M. A. H. (1940). On the development of the genitalia and their ducts of Orthopteroid insects. *Trans. R. ent. Soc. Lond.*, **90**, 121–75.
11. SCUDDER, G. G. E. (1957). Reinterpretation of some basal structures in the insect ovipositor. *Nature*, **180**, 340–1.
12. SCUDDER, G. G. E. (1961). The comparative morphology of the insect ovipositor. *Trans. R. ent. Soc. Lond.*, **113**, 25–40.
13. SMART, J. (1951). The wing venation of the American cockroach, *Periplaneta americana. Proc. zool. Soc. Lond.*, **121**, 501–9.
14. SNODGRASS, R. E. (1931). Morphology of the insect abdomen. I. General structure of the abdomen and its appendages. *Smithson. misc. Collns*, **85**, no. 6.
15. SNODGRASS, R. E. (1933). Morphology of the insect abdomen. II. The genital ducts and the ovipositor. *Smithson. misc. Collns*, **89**, no. 8.
16. SNODGRASS, R. E. (1935). *Principles of Insect Morphology.* McGraw-Hill, New York and London.
17. WYK, L. E. VAN (1952). The morphology and histology of the genital organs of *Leucophaea maderae. J. ent. Soc. sth. Afr.*, **15**, 3–62.

ADDITIONAL REFERENCES

18. BUGNION, E. (1920). Les parties buccales de la Blatte. *Annls Sci. nat.*, **10**, 41–108.

19. CARPENTIER, F. (1955). Pleurites thoraciques de Lèpisme et pleurites de Blatte. *Bull. Annls Soc. r. ent. Belg.*, **91**, 220–6.

20. CRAMPTON, G. C. (1923). A comparison of the terminal abdominal structures of the female of a termite (*Masotermes*) with those of the roach *Periplaneta*. *Bull. Brooklyn ent. Soc.*, **18**, 85–93.

21. CRAMPTON, G. C. (1926). Comparison of the neck and prothoracic sclerites through the orders of insects from the standpoint of phylogeny. *Trans. ent. Soc. Am.*, **52**, 199–248.

22. DASHMAN, T. (1953). The terminology of the pretarsus. *Ann. ent. Soc. Am.*, **46**, 56–62.

23. DEBOUTTEVILLE, C. D. (1952). L'homogénéité de la morphologie sternale des Blattoptèroides. *Trans. 10th. Int. Congr. Ent.*, **1**, 147–50.

24. KUPKA, E. (1946). Uber Bremsvorrichtungen an den Laufbeinen der *Blattodea*. *Öst. Zool. Z.*, **1**, 170–5.

25. LEMCHE, H. (1942). The wings of cockroaches and the phylogeny of insects. *Vidensk. Meddr dansk naturh. Foren.*, **106**, 287–318.

26. MANGAN, J. (1908). On the mouth parts of some Blattidae. *Proc. R. Ir. Acad.*, **27B**, 1–10.

27. MARTIN, J. F. (1916). Thoracic and cervical sclerites of insects. *Ann. ent. Soc. Am.*, **9**, 35–88.

28. POPHAM, E. J. (1961). The functional morphology of the mouth parts of the cockroach *Periplaneta americana*. *Entomologist*, **94**, 185–92.

29. PRESSOR, B. (1955). Structure of the integument of the maxillary palpi of the cockroach *Periplaneta americana*. *Ann. ent. Soc. Am.*, **48**, 237–406.

30. ROSS, M. (1966). Embryonic appendages of the notched sternite mutant of *Blattella germanica*. *Ant. ent. Soc. Am.*, **59**, 1160–62.

31. ROSS, M. H. (1964). Pronotal wings in *Blattella germanica* and their possible evolutionary significance. *Am. Midl. Nat.*, **71**, 161–80.

32. ROTH, L. M. and WILLIS, E. R. (1952). Tarsal structure and climbing ability of cockroaches. *J. exp. Zool.*, **119**, 483–517.

33. SNODGRASS, R. E. (1936). Morphology of the insect abdomen. III. *Smithson. misc. Collns*, **95**, no. 14.

34. SNODGRASS, R. E. (1937). The male genitalia of orthopteroid insects. *Smithson misc. Collns*, **96**, no. 5.

35. SNODGRASS, R. E. (1957). A revised interpretation of the external reproductive organs of male insects. *Smithson. misc. Collns*, **135**, no. 6.

36. TUXEN, S. L. (1956). *Taxonomists' glossary of genitalia in insects.* Munksgaard, Copenhagen.

37. VOGEL, R. (1925). Bemerkungen zum weiblichen Geschlechtsapparat der Küchenschabe. *Zool. Anz.*, **64**, 56–62.

38. WALKER, E. M. (1919). The terminal abdominal structures of orthopteroid insects. I. *Ann. ent. Soc. Am.*, **12**, 267–326.

39. WALKER, E. M. (1922). The terminal abdominal structures of orthopteroid insects. II. *Ann. ent. Soc. Am.*, **15**, 1–88.

40. YUASA, H. (1920). The anatomy of the head and mouth parts of Orthoptera and Euplexoptera. *J. Morph.*, **33**, 251–90.

3 The cuticle

In this account the following new terminology is used in an attempt to clarify a confused and unsatisfactory situation.

The initial, newly formed integument and the unaltered arthrodial membrane consist of an epicuticle outside (i), and a precuticle inside (ii) (pre-: before in time, not pro-: before in space, in front of).

(i) The epicuticle consists of a very thin outer polymer layer on the surface of a layer of 'arthrodin'. The arthrodin layer is of protein only, but may be impregnated and tanned.

Impregnated arthrodin is 'precuticulin'.

Tanned precuticulin is 'cuticulin'.

External to these layers is the 'amphion'[50] consisting of the wax or grease layer and the cement layer.

(ii) The precuticle consists of protein and chitin, which may be impregnated with lipo-protein and may or may not be tanned.

Precuticle which is impregnated but not tanned is the mesocuticle.

Precuticle which is impregnated and also tanned is the exocuticle.

The postexuvial cuticle is the endocuticle, and this grows during at least part of a stadium.

The material forming the precuticle and endocuticle is 'arthropodin'.

Impregnated but untanned arthropodin is presclerotin.

Arthropodin which is both impregnated and tanned is sclerotin.

These terms are illustrated in Fig. 3.1.

Buxton attempted to find the quantity of skeletal material in *P.a.* by removing the flesh. When he used KOH the skeleton was 11·6% of the total, but using enzymes it was 15·1 to 16·7%.[12] The area of skeleton in *Bt.g.* was found to be related to the weight by the formula $S = 12·17\, w^{0·63}$, where $S =$ surface area in mm^2 and $w =$ weight in mg. The average margin of error was 2·81%.[75] A recent investigation, using adsorbed krypton, has suggested that the surface area of a nymph of *P.a.* may be several times larger than previously estimated,[49] although the method may also include the surface area of the tracheae, so leading to an over-estimate (T).

Tauber studied the distribution of chitin in *P. fuliginosa*, expressing his results in terms of chitosan produced, a substance derived from the destructive degradation of chitin. He found a range of values from 38% in the dorsal abdominal sclerites to 18% in the hind-wing. In the crop and gizzard the figure was 19% and in the body as a whole, 30% dry wt. or 2% live wt.[77] The measurement of the percentage of chitin in cuticle by degrading it to chitosan may account for some of the discrepancy in the literature (T). In *P.a.* there is 55% of chitin in the cuticle as a whole[23] but 35% in the abdominal sclerites, in the exuvia of newly hatched nymphs and in the cuticle of freshly moulted nymphs. The wings are said to contain about 20% chitin, the exocuticle 22%, the endocuticle 60%.[13] More recently the new cuticle of the dorsal abdominal sclerites of the adults was found to contain 11·5% (females) and 10·5% (males); in the old, tanned cuticle the figures were 19% (females) and 20% (males).[19] Campbell claimed to have demonstrated the presence of chitin in *P.a.* in the peritrophic membrane, in the blastoderm membrane of the egg and throughout the exoskeleton, but not in the chorion of the egg, nor in the tracheae and air-sacs, nor in wound scabs.[13] Tsao

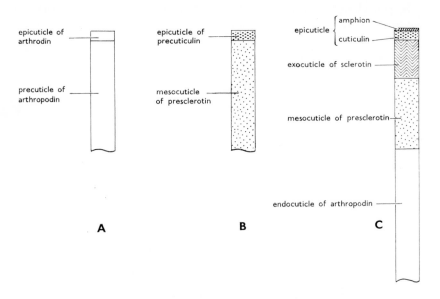

FIG. 3.1   The formation of the cuticle (diagrammatic). **A**, initial stage; **B**, intermediate stage; **C**, late stage

found in *B.o.* the chitin content of the abdominal sterna greater than that of the abdominal terga in both sexes, but the male sterna contained more than the female. It was found that although a low carbohydrate diet retarded the growth rate of *B.o.*, neither temperature nor diet affected the percentage of chitin present in the cuticle.[79] The cuticle of *P.a.* is also stated to contain 37% water, 44% proteins, 15% chitin and 4% lipoids,[64] and a considerable chitinase activity.[80]

The water content of old cuticle was 17% (females) and 24% (males) but new cuticle had 44% in both sexes. New cuticle also had more water-soluble amino acids, and proteins, in spite of the addition of the endocuticle during the growth of the cuticle. This probably reflects the addition of impregnating substances to the arthropodin during the maturation of the cuticle. This was supported by the finding that the total protein in old cuticle was greater than in new.[19] Iodine is taken up from the blood and concentrated in the cuticle,[43, 44] and may be involved in hardening of the cuticle.[78]

THE STRUCTURE OF THE CUTICLE

In *P.a.* the cuticle of the newly moulted cockroach consists of a very thin epicuticle[14] and a thicker layer, the precuticle.[64, 69] This probably primitive condition is said to be retained in the arthrodial membranes, which are about 8 μ thick in the abdominal region of male cockroaches, and consist of a simple protein,[14] although Richards and Anderson dispute this and say the arthrodial membrane is four-layered like the rest of the cuticle,[69] while Pfaff shows it as being epi-, meso- and endo-cuticle only.[64] Schatz says that some soft membranes are two-layered, but some intersegmental membranes have 'epicuticle, procuticle and endocuticle'.[72] The epicuticle and his 'procuticle' of the arthrodial membrane regions are not clearly separable, but in the regions destined to be sclerites the 'procuticle' has already at moulting become impregnated and is capable of becoming sclerotized. The 'procuticle' is pre-exuvial.[14, 18]

In older cuticle the sclerites consist of four layers, the epicuticle externally, the endocuticle internally and two intermediate layers.[14, 69, 72] The epicuticle is very thin:[15, 39] only 2–3 μ thick on the pronotal sclerite.[68, 69] The endocuticle is laminar in structure and is secreted after moulting is over, i.e. it is post-exuvial. It is soft[14] and in *B.o.* an innermost layer may be differentiated to form an inner endocuticle next to the epidermis.[72] This is the ecdysial membrane of Locke,[48] and in *P.a.* (nymphs and adults) this layer is called by Schmidt a subcuticular layer. He found it stained differently from the endocuticle, and that in the abdominal tergites of the male it was thicker than in the female. The thicker region appeared to be fibrous, the fibres being continuous with filaments penetrating the cuticle, but histochemical tests suggested it was a mucoid material, substantially protein in composition but containing carbohydrates other than glycogen. It is not chitinous but some other glycoprotein. It is suggested such material is found in other connective tissues of the cockroach body and that they may be viscous to solid gels or they may solate to liquid form. Thus they could serve to attach the cuticle to the epidermis during a stadium, and they could solate to release such attachment during the moulting period. A similar layer has been seen in the fore- and hind-gut, in the coxa and in young coxal tendon. In older tendon, it is very thin and not distinguishable, and so far it has not been possible to find it in tracheae.[73]

The two intermediate layers are structurally similar, and both are pre-exuvial, without visible laminations, are very refractory to staining, and homogeneous.[14] The outer one, the exocuticle, becomes hardened and usually darkened. The inner one is not usually darkened nor hardened. It is proposed to call the outer of these two intermediate layers the exocuticle and the inner the mesocuticle and the terminology of other authors has been changed here to fit in with this proposition (Fig. 3.1) (T). The term mesocuticle is used in an entirely anatomical sense and not in the sense first used by Schatz.[72] Thus the cuticle of the newly moulted

P.a. has two layers: epicuticle and precuticle, while the sclerites have four layers: epicuticle, exocuticle, mesocuticle and endocuticle. The exocuticle is the telo-cuticle, and the mesocuticle is the metacuticle of Dennell and Malek,[18] and the exocuticle and mesocuticle together are the inner and outer exocuticle of Pfaff. According to this author the exo- (meso-) and endocuticles have the same basic structure, i.e. long chitin micellae surrounded by a lipoprotein envelope forming fibrils which lie in lamellae. The lamellae lie at 75° to each other and between them is more protein.[47]

The pigment which may darken the exocuticle may be melanin,[69] but this is denied by Kennaugh[37] and doubted by Pennell and Tsuyuki in *P. fulginosa*.[63] The exocuticle and mesocuticle are thought to be a chitin-protein framework in layers 0·15 μ thick, alternating with wider, less dense, layers of chitin with little or no protein.[69] In adult *P.a.* 55% of the cuticle in males, and 51% in females, is pre-exuvial and the figures for the last instar nymphs are 21% to 24% respectively.[19] The pronotal sclerite of *P.a.* is 40 μ thick, the exocuticle being 10 μ thick and darker than the mesocuticle which is 28 μ thick.[69]

The abdominal sclerites are thicker anteriorly than posteriorly and the thicknesses of the different layers are shown in the following table:

	a	b	c	d
Male anterior tergite	21·0	2·5	9·0	9·5
Male posterior tergite	15·5	7·0	1·5	7·0
Female anterior tergite	35·5	9·5	8·5	17·5
Female posterior tergite	28·5	9·5	8·0	14·0

where a = total thickness, b = exocuticle, c = mesocuticle and d = endocuticle. All figures are in microns.

It may be noted that the thickness of the endocuticle relative to that of the whole cuticle remains approximately constant (male 45%, female 49%), indicating that post-exuvial cuticle is proportional to the pre-exuvial cuticle and that there is a reciprocal relationship between the thicknesses of the exocuticle and the mesocuticle.[14]

The epicuticle

This is the name given to two layers on the outside of the pre-exuvial cuticle (not the grease and cement layers), and it is without chitin.[15,40] In the new cuticle of the presumptive arthrodial membrane it consists of an inner thicker layer, and an outer very thin layer.[15,39,82]

The arthrodial membrane of the abdominal region in *P.a.* has an epicuticle about 1 μ thick; on the sclerites it is about twice as thick.[15] The inner thicker layer of the epicuticle is protein (arthrodin)[15] which is polymerized,[64] and in the sclerites it becomes tanned and hardened (cuticulin).

The outer thinner layer is said to consist of highly polymerized aliphatic compounds of various chain lengths and it is called the polymer layer. This is the first layer to be formed and is very stable, probably because it is incorporated into the arthrodin itself and is not merely on the outside of it. The outer layer is not cement layer[15] nor the lipoid layer of Richards and Anderson,[69] but it may be the same as the wax layer of Pfaff.[64]

The wax and cement layers do not remain separate but intermingle together. The cement is from the dermal glands and may be a lipoprotein, like the impregnating substance of the cuticle,[15] or a shellac-like material, at least in part.[3] The dermal glands atrophy in the adult,[39] which suggests that no further cement is formed once the animal is fully mature (T).

The wax layer on the fore-wings of *P.a.* was found to be only 0·11 μ thick,[49] but on the dorsal abdominal sclerites the newly moulted cuticle had a wax layer estimated to be 0·73 μ thick in females and 1·00 μ thick in males; in old cuticle the figures were 0·52 μ (females) and 0·41 μ (males).[19] The wax is thought to be secreted by the oenocytes via the pore-canals.[39] The grease is very mobile and is said to form spindle-shaped crystals when it is dried.[15]

The grease of *Bt.g.* has the saponification and solubility characteristics of wax.[21] According to Beament the wax of *P.a.* has a melting point of 56° and is mixed with an equal amount of 'solvent'. The molecular weight of the solvent is 120–170, and that of the wax, which is fully saturated, is 300–350.[3] The wax hydrocarbons have 27–29 carbon atoms, and the solvent hydrocarbons have 8–12 carbon atoms. They are mostly paraffins and alcohols.[3] Gilby and Cox, on the other hand, found no volatile substances to be present. They found 77% of the chloroform extracts of cast cuticle to be largely unsaturated hydrocarbons, mostly a C^{27}-diene, probably heptocose-9,18-diene. The other 23% was a mixture of 7% fatty acids, 5% esters and 9% aliphatic aldehydes. A trace of sterol was present. No alcohols were present and they suggest that the mobility of the grease is due to some of the hydrocarbons and to the free fatty acids.[25] Cockroaches in fact are stated to be killed by 5 μl. drops of C_8–C_{12} paraffins of alcohols placed on their surface.[24] The absence of alcohol is in direct conflict with the finding by Beament of cetyl alcohol, which he postulated lies with its hydroxyl groups outside until the epicuticle is tanned, when they reverse and lie inside, thus altering the surface from hydrophil to hydrofuge.[5] The existence of an alcohol monolayer is impossible without alcohol being present,[25] but some polar layer seems to function in the cuticle of *P.a.*, since the rate of penetration of a substance increases with its polarity[58] (see also below). There may be a three-dimensional network giving resistance to water evaporation,[25] a suggestion which comes close to the idea that the grease is two-layered.[58] Water in the substrate on which the grease spreads is very important. If the substrate is dry the grease spreads very slowly but if it is wet the grease spreads quickly[3] and it is postulated that the monolayer, if it is present, would be orientated in the correct way. Water in the cuticle is also important in the maintenance of stable surface properties.[35]

When the grease is left in the air it hardens and it seemed that this was due to the evaporation of the solvent,[1,25] but the grease from cuticle kept for a year had almost the same analysis as the freshly cast cuticle.[25] Thus the hardening of

3*

the grease with time probably results from chemical changes amongst the reactive compounds present.[24]

The grease is strongly reducing and is said to contain a shellac-like substance but this may be some of the cement material with which the grease is always contaminated.[3]

The pore canals

In *P.a.* these are fine tubules which run from the epidermal cells into the cuticle. They are fine, possibly helical, structures, thought to be filled with solution rather than protoplasm, and are between 0·02 and 0·002 μ in diameter in sections of dried cuticle.[69] They are present in the exocuticle, mesocuticle and endocuticle[15, 69] and are also stated to enter the epicuticle,[15] or, alternatively, not to enter it.[69] According to Pfaff, however, the pore-canals run from the boundary between the meso- and endocuticle layers up to the inner layer of the epicuticle and are thus absent from the endocuticle. He says that in mature individuals they contain a chitin filament surrounded by a protein envelope, although in the pre-moult period they convey material from the epidermal cells for the hardening and darkening of the outer part of the exocuticle.[64] The pore-canals are not always visible in the exocuticle in *B.o.*[72] They influence the flexibility and permeability of the cuticle, but their origins are uncertain.[69]

Hardening

The soft cuticle of the newly moulted cockroach is colourless, but in the sclerites both the presumptive epicuticle and exocuticle become amber in colour after tanning.[15]

In the epicuticle there is found to be a concentration of phenolic protein which has been laid down before moulting begins, changing the arthrodin to pre-cuticulin. How the protein gets there is not known but it is probably through the pore canals. Soon after moulting, or even just before, the pore canals convey to the epicuticle a steroid substance forming a lipoprotein which turns the arthrodin into precuticulin.[16, 65]

The steroid substance continues to flow from the distal ends of the pore canals and begins to diffuse inwards from the canal tips, so impregnating the arthro-podin of the exocuticular region. Meanwhile, phenolic protein begins to diffuse through the precuticle from inside outwards, meeting the steroid substance moving inwards. The protein and steroid form a lipoprotein, which changes the arthropodin to presclerotin.[16]

Cuticle impregnated with lipoprotein is greatly stabilized, giving resistance to change even before tanning takes place. The impregnated arthrodin of the epi-cuticle is precuticulin, later tanned to cuticulin;[15] the impregnated arthropodin of the mesocuticule is presclerotin, later tanned to sclerotin in the exocuticle.[51]

The steroid may undergo some degree of polymerization first[17] since it loses its yellow colour and will not stain.[51] Both steroid and phenolic protein may be produced by the oenocytes.[16, 65]

Tanning

Tanning is a process in which proteins are linked by phenolic derivatives.[18] These phenolic derivatives are quinones derived from the oxidation of a di-hydroxyphenol[17,18,37,51] but it is thought the quinone responsible is p-quinone[37] rather than o-quinone as previously suggested.[18,51]

The cuticle is capable of effecting hydroxylation of aromatic amino acids[37] so that the tyrosine-rich protein of the lipo-protein complex can be the source of the tanning quinones and, although this is denied by Malek,[51] it seems likely to occur in the early stages of tanning, when tyrosine has been found to produce dihydroxyphenols under the influence of tyrosinase. In later stages another di-hydroxyphenol diffuses into the cuticle from the blood.[17,18]

The tanning process begins in the epicuticle,[17] and it is here that there is the greatest concentration on polyphenol oxidase.[17,37] The process seems to be enzymic at first but later to lose this quality, and it spreads inwards from the epicuticle and extends through the exocuticle.[17] It does not extend to the meso-cuticle, possibly because the concentration of lipoid there is insufficient to form enough lipoprotein complex.[18]

The tanning process involves changes in a few of the amino acids of the proteins present in the cuticle. About 11 hr from the formation of the cuticle the o-tyrosine content decreases and the p-tyrosine content increases. After about 12 hr β-alanine appears and after 14 hr it increases further. Phenylalanine is found only between about $11\frac{1}{2}$ and $12\frac{1}{2}$ hr.[37] It is interesting that there was a seven-fold increase in the proline content of the cuticle mucoprotein and a decrease in the tyrosyl and phenylalanyl residues during sclerotization.[45]

No hardening nor tanning occurs in the arthrodial membrane and the epi-cuticle here is without polyphenol oxidase. Similarly the post-exuvial endo-cuticle remains unaltered, and can continue to grow during the stadium.[17] During the 20 days of cuticle synthesis in a stadium of *P.a.* nymph, the chitin content of the cuticle increased four times.[45]

In a study of the claw apophysis of *Periplaneta*, Richards and Pipa found that the proteins lay at right angles to the chitin molecules and that both lay parallel to the surface. The chitin molecules were found to be slightly bent or irregular and the proteins had side chains of various lengths all lying in the same plane as the rest of the molecule. They conclude that there is no evidence to suggest that the alteration and stabilization of the proteins is sufficient to account for the observed effect. They found the proteins of the apophysis had a refractive index of 1·554.[70]

In recent articles Locke[48] and Hackman[34] review the structure and formation of the insect cuticle, and some of the points they make are relevant to the account here of the cockroach cuticle. Locke states, for example, that all the materials of the cuticle except the cement are produced by epidermal cells, and that the poly-phenols pass outwards through the pore canals and then further through the epicuticle by 'wax canals'—structures in the epicuticle which allow the lipoids to reach the outer surface of the epicuticle. He shows that lipoids pass through the pore canals as lipid-water liquid crystals.[48]

Hackman thinks that much of the protein and chitin are covalently linked to form glycoproteins.[34] Glucose, mannose, xylose and arabinose have been isolated from the cuticle of *P.a.*, but these sugars are probably bound to the chitin chain rather than being parts of cuticular glycoproteins.[45] Hackman, however, considers that identifications and estimations of components in the cuticle are subject to large errors and that most of the ideas in connection with cuticle hardening and tanning are theories unsupported by adequate evidence. No sweeping generalizations are likely to be sound.[34] It has been shown that the cuticle is the dominant tissue in synthesis of polysaccharides[46] but, except for alanine, the amino acid content of the cuticle is equivalent to that of the blood. It is suggested that there may be an active alanine-pyruvate interconnection, which could link to high carbohydrate and alanine contents.[64] (See also Chapter 12.)

THE PERMEABILITY OF THE CUTICLE

The normal living cuticle is very impermeable to water, but an early observation was that the contact angle between the cuticles of male and female *Bt.g.* and water were different.[57] Deductions drawn from these angles, however, are unreliable, because they depend on the nature and orientation of the surface film of wax or grease,[35] and water applied to the grease-covered surface of a cockroach cuticle is immediately covered by a film of the grease.[67] Moreover, soaking in water is believed to reverse the orientation of the polar groups so that they come to the external surface of the film, and the contact angle decreases.[35]

The exuvia of the last nymph of *P.a.* was found to be 'asymmetrical', i.e. the rate of movement of water from inside outwards was less than the movement from outside inwards for equal gradients across the cuticle. The ratio of this asymmetry was 1:2·3. When the cast cuticle was washed in water a considerable asymmetry remained, although the ratio declined to 1:1·2. This was interpreted as being the result of retention of an orientated monolayer of lipoid material,[2] which is five times as impermeable as the rest of the grease.[4] When first secreted there is evidence that its polar groups are external and lipoid chains internal. Then when the precuticulin is tanned the orientation of the monolayer is reversed.[6] The asymmetry of the permeability of the cuticle to water is, however, even more remarkable because, although an asymmetry may be expected from the Hartley effect, the asymmetry actually found is the reverse of this. Beament suggests the term 'anomalous asymmetry' for it. Again hydrostatic pressure will push water through cuticle much more readily than osmosis will; and it will also push far more through inwards than outwards. The cuticle behaves as though it incorporates a valve, which may be the lipoid molecules.[6]

On boiling with chloroform, the asymmetry was lost and the rate of transpiration, i.e. rate of movement of water outwards, increased about twenty times, approaching that of a free surface of water.[2]

The formation of the lipoid monolayer depends on the presence of 'solvent' material of relatively low molecular weight in the grease,[3] and the presence of a water-containing substrate, namely the epicuticle, is probably necessary for it to take place properly.[35] One difficulty about accepting the hypothesis of the presence of a monolayer, and of its function in reducing transpiration, is that in experimental work the evaporation resistance of a monolayer on a free water surface is extremely sensitive to the presence of impurities.[41]

Above a certain critical temperature it was found that the transpiration rate of water from a cockroach was much higher than below it.[4,52,54,67,81] It is not easy to disentangle the effects of respiratory activity, changes in the grease of the amphion, and differences in the temperature of the cuticle and the ambient air (T). In dry air the rate of water loss of *B.o.* increased with temperature between 20° and 30°,[27] most of it being lost through the spiracles,[27,54] and above 30° the rate of water loss increased by three or four times, because of ventilation movements by the roach.[27] In *P.a.*, while water loss is affected by relative humidity, wind speed and temperature,[67] only temperature affects the permeability of the cuticle.[7] Above about 30° it was found that the cuticle became more permeable to water due to a change in the film of lipoid material on the cuticle.[67] A similar effect of temperature occurs at about 20° in *Bt.g.* In some experiments using dead specimens in dry air at 20°, it was found that disruption and removal of much of the grease layer caused an immediate increase in transpiration rate, followed by a partial return to normal, as the remaining grease spread back over the whole cuticle. Removing the grease fully by adsorption on aluminium dust caused an increased rate, which remained until the animal was dehydrated.[81] Clearly the grease layer of the amphion is very much involved in cuticle permeability (T), but the idea of a critical temperature at which there is a sudden change in the permeability of the cuticle has been challenged by Edney, who maintained that it is an experimental artefact. He suggested that at a constant saturation deficit the temperature transpiration curve for *P.a.* cuticle shows no abrupt change, but he did admit that there is a temperature dependence where the transpiration rate is low. This may be due to progressive melting of components of the grease or to an effect similar to the temperature-dependent coefficient of diffusion of porous membranes.[22] In both *P.a.* and *B.o.* it was found rather surprisingly that at a constant saturation deficit the rate of transpiration decreased above 50°, and it was suggested this was due to increasing desiccation or to the high relative humidity at these temperatures (73% at 55°) which allowed a hygroscopic effect to operate.[52] Indeed, cockroaches in a saturated atmosphere swell up and burst, and the rate of uptake seems to depend more on the relative humidity than on the saturation deficit.[5] When dry air was used the effects suggested a Müllerian transition phenomenon in the molecular structure of the grease, a feature only found in normal long-chain paraffins. Mead-Briggs thought that no final conclusions could be drawn and suggested that there may be two explanations for the known data, either active diffusion was at work or there was a progressive change towards greater permeability of the cuticle.[52]

In a further study of the postulated temperature change in permeability occurring at a certain critical point, Beament found that some of the earlier work was not entirely valid because it had been assumed that the temperature of the cuticle was the same as that of the air. When the temperature of the cuticle under test was measured he found that the critical temperature change was even more clearly observable, and that it occurred at about 30°. The actual temperature increased with the time which had elapsed since the last moult and Beament suggested that this was due to the loss of the more volatile substances in the grease. At temperatures less than the critical temperature, he believed that the innermost surface of the grease has a monolayer adjacent to the aqueous substrate, and that this monolayer is very resistant to water loss. The critical temperature was the moment when this innermost monomolecular layer undergoes a phase change and becomes as permeable as the rest of the grease.[4] More recently Beament has withdrawn this idea in favour of an hypothesis that the molecules of the lipoid monolayer do not stand at right angles to the surface but are positioned obliquely. As the temperature rises they become more perpendicular, so allowing more water molecules to pass through. This would account for the observation that the contact angle between a drop of water and the cuticle decreases by only 10° from 130° even at the transition temperature of 35°.[6]

One remarkable feature of the grease of cockroaches, in comparison with many other insects which have been studied, is that the grease regains its impermeability when the temperature is reduced from above the critical point. This indicates that the phase change in the lipoid monolayer is reversible,[5] or that the molecules regain the more oblique position.[6]

The cuticle even without its grease layer was still very impermeable to water,[5] and when *P.a.* was poisoned with pyrethrum applied either topically or by injection, the rate of water loss was increased five times. Water droplets were secreted on to the surface far from the site of application, and seemed to be from secretory epidermal cells. Whether it is these cells which govern the rate of water transpiration or not, it appeared that it was not the loss of water as such which always killed the animal but the rate at which this loss occurred.[36] Cockroaches also 'sweat' under deep CO_2 narcosis, but it has been suggested that this may be an effect of increased pH on the cuticular protein hydration potential. Droplets on the sclerites of cockroach are absorbed into the body more quickly than those on the arthrodial membranes, and since they are not absorbed by the cuticle of a nymph about to moult, when the outer cuticle has separated from the inner, it seems likely that the continuity of the pore canals is required for water uptake through the cuticle.[6]

The relative amounts of free and bound water within *B.o.* will not affect the transpiration rate until all the free water has been lost, and the increase in concentration of the tissue fluids is not enough to lower the rate of transpiration.[54] Nevertheless, desiccated animals tended to be hygroscopic[29] while *P.a.* can gain water from very concentrated salt solutions in contact with their surfaces,[5] and in fact leave the dry salt on the cuticle after taking up all the water. They can do this from solutions of sodium fluoride and sodium cyanide, as well as sodium chloride, without harm.[6]

WATER LOSS AND TEMPERATURE PREFERENCE

The rate of water loss in dry air at 30° is 86 mg/g/day for *P.a.*, 95 mg/g/day for *B.o.* and 159 mg/g/day for *Bt.g.* Calculating the surface areas of the three species from the formula $SA = W^{2/3}$ (where SA = surface area, and W = weight) this gives the rate of loss in mg/cm²/day as 10·5 for *P.a.*, 8·6 for *B.o.* and 7·3 for *Bt.g.*[28] The surface area figure is probably of doubtful validity, however (T). *B.o.* is reported to lose no noticeable amount of water up to 23° but above 25° the loss is obvious. Between 35° and 40° the amount lost falls off and above 40° water evaporation ceases and the animal dies.[56] The rate of water loss by *B.o.* is proportional to the saturation deficit and, at 30° in dry air, it loses 9% of its body weight per day until it dies on the fourth day.[26]

The body of *Bt.g.* contains about 67% water[11, 33] and that of *P.a.* nymphs about 65%,[55] and adults 72%, and *B.o.* can lose up to 30% of its weight by desiccation and recover afterwards.[29] In general, a cockroach tends to choose damper conditions provided the temperature is not too high and a drier atmosphere if the temperature is uncomfortably high,[31] when it is believed that evaporation is used temporarily as a cooling mechanism.[8, 56] In *B.o.*, for example, the body temperature was the same as the ambient temperature between 13° and 23°; below 13° it was higher, and in dry air above 23° it was lower. In wet air, above 23° it was higher.[56] Again in a cockroach the temperature of the genital chamber of the female in air at 45° and 90% relative humidity was the same as the air, but when the air was dried the temperature dropped to 39° in a few minutes.[53] It was found, too, that the temperature chosen by *P.a.* when it had a high water content was higher than when it was partially dehydrated,[11, 26] so that there seems to be a compromise between temperature and humidity preferences and the effect of the degree of body dehydration (T). The choice of *B.o.* is also stated to be influenced by its food and past experience.[26]

INTEGUMENTARY GLANDS

(a) Abdominal glands

Between the fifth and sixth terga of *P.a.*, infoldings of the intersegmental membranes have become glandular, the cells being specialized epidermal cells with intracellular ducts. They form the dorsal glands, and there are ventral glands between the sixth and seventh sterna. Both dorsal and ventral glands occur in both sexes, but their functions are said to be unknown.[42] Roth and Stahl suggest they may be used in a type of trophallaxis amongst groups of *B.o.* They state that a viscous secretion is produced by the cerci as well as the glands of tergites 6 and 7, and found it was 90% protein.[71] Similar glands have been described in *B.o.*[32, 38, 66, 76] and in *Bt.g.*[20, 32, 38, 74] They are found in both sexes, and even in the nymphs of *B.o.*,[32, 66] but in *Bt.g.* only the mature males have functional glands. Dusham described groups of 'dorsal pygidial glands' on the tenth tergite of *Bt.g.* females,[20] presumably similar to the cercal glands of *B.o.*[71] In *Bt.g.* they have a sexual rôle[32, 38, 74] but in *B.o.* they are probably stink glands[38, 66] and have a protective function.[32] The cercal secretion in *Blattella* is also used to cement the embryonic cuticle to the inside of the egg-case so that when hatching takes place, the escape of the first instar nymph from this membrane is facilitated.[86]

The cytoplasm of the glands cells in *B.o.* is very granular and may be vacuo-lated,[38] and the intracellular duct is said to be lined with chitin[20] opening between the bases of setae.[38] Stanislavskij stated that the single primary epidermal layer formed a double layer from which both oenocytes and skin glands develop.[76]

(b) Cervical glands (Figs. 3.2, 3.3)

Pavan has described a richly tracheated invagination of the cervical membrane of *B.o.* and *P.a.*[59,60] which secretes a colourless substance on to the surface of the body. The secretion fluoresces blue in U.V. light and was found in both sexes and

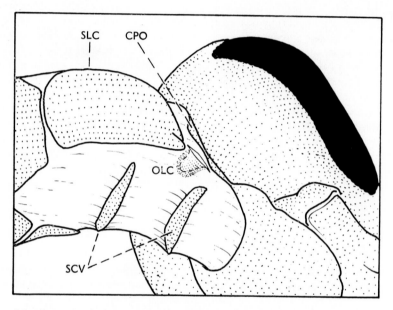

FIG. 3.2   Lateral cervical organ of *Periplaneta americana*. CPO—postoccipital condyle, OLC—lateral cervical organ, SCV—ventral sclerites of the neck, SLC—ventrolateral sclerite of the neck. (From Pavan[59])

at all stages in the life-cycle, except just after a moult, only in the Blattinae.[60] The secretion was less plentiful in the females. It is not the same material as that from the abdominal glands[61] and has been termed 'periplanetin'.[62]

Much active research continues on the ultramicroscopic structure and bio-chemistry of cuticle, and the present account can only be provisional. Much of the data on the surface area of the body, the chitin content of the cuticle, the chemical nature of the grease, the nature of the lipoprotein material, the pore canals, and aspects of water loss is suspect, and must be treated with due reserve (T).

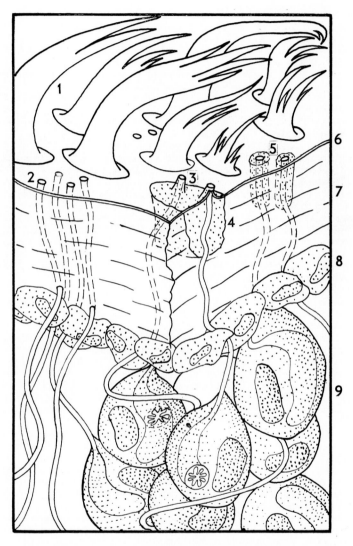

FIG. 3.3 Microscopic structure of the lateral cervical organ of *Periplaneta americana*. 1, Setae of the internal surface of the reservoir of the organ; 2 and 3, apertures of secretory ducts; 4 and 5, pigmented regions of stronger cuticle around secretory ducts; 6, epicuticle; 7, endocuticle; 8, epidermis; 9, glandular cells secreting the fluorescent material. (From Pavan[59])

REFERENCES

1. BEAMENT, J. W. L. (1951). Wax secretion in insects. *Nature*, **167**, 652–3.
2. BEAMENT, J. W. L. (1954). Water transport in insects. *Symp. Soc. exp. Biol.*, **8**, 94–117.
3. BEAMENT, J. W. L. (1955). Wax secretion in the cockroach. *J. exp. Biol.*, **32**, 514–38.
4. BEAMENT, J. W. L. (1958). The effect of temperature on the waterproofing mechanism of an insect. *J. exp. Biol.*, **35**, 495–519.
5. BEAMENT, J. W. L. (1961). The water relations of insect cuticle. *Biol. Rev.*, **36**, 281–320.
6. BEAMENT, J. W. L. (1964). The active transport and passive movement of water in insects. *Advs. Insect Physiol.*, **2**, 67–129.
7. BEAMENT, J. W. L. (1966). Personal communication.
8. BODENHEIMER, F. S. (1927). Über die Voraussage der Generationenzahl von Insekten. III. Die Bedeutung des Klimas für die landwirtschaftliche Entomologie. *Z. angew. Ent.*, **12**, 91–122.
9. BURNET, P. J. C. (1952). Periodic acid-Schiff reaction of the insect cuticle. *Science*, **116**, 126.
10. BRUNET, P. J. C. and KENT, P. W. (1955). Mechanism of sclerotin formation: the participation of a β-glucoside. *Nature*, **175**, 819–20.
11. BUXTON, P. A. (1932). Terrestrial insects and the humidity of the environment. *Biol. Rev.*, **7**, 275–320.
12. BUXTON, P. A. (1932). The proportion of skeletal tissue in insects. *Biochem. J.*, **26**, 829–32.
13. CAMPBELL, F. L. (1929). The detection and estimation of insect chitin and the irrelation of 'chitinisation' to hardness and pigmentation of the cuticula of the American cockroach, *Periplaneta americana*. *Ann. ent. Soc. Am.*, **22**, 401–26.
14. DENNALL, R. and MALEK, S. R. A. (1954). The cuticle of the cockroach, *Periplaneta americana*. I. The appearance and histological structure of the cuticle of the dorsal surface of the abdomen. *Proc. R. Soc.*, B, **143**, 126–36.
15. DENNELL, R. and MALEK, S. R. A. (1955). The cuticle of the cockroach *Periplaneta americana*. II. The epicuticle. *Proc. R. Soc.*, B, **143**, 239–57.
16. DENNELL, R. and MALEK, S. R. A. (1955). The cuticle of the cockroach *Periplaneta americana*. III. The hardening of the cuticle: impregnation preparatory to phenolic tanning. *Proc. R. Soc.*, B, **143**, 414–26.
17. DENNELL, R. and MALEK, S. R. A. (1955). The cuticle of the cockroach *Periplaneta americana*. IV. The hardening of the cuticle: phenolic tanning. *Proc. R. Soc.*, B, **143**, 427–34.
18. DENNELL, R. and MALEK, S. R. A. (1956). The cuticle of the cockroach *Periplaneta americana*. V. The chemical resistance of the impregnating material of the cuticle, and the 'self-tanning' of its protein component. *Proc. R. Soc.*, B, **144**, 545–56.
19. DENNELL, R. and MALEK, S. R. A. (1956). The cuticle of the cockroach *Periplaneta americana*. VI. The composition of the cuticle as determined by quantitative analysis. *Proc. R. Soc.*, B, **145**, 249–58.
20. DUSHAM, E. H. (1918). The dorsal pygidial glands of the female cockroach *Blattella germanica*. *Can. Ent.*, **50**, 278–80.
21. DUSHAM, E. H. (1918). The wax glands of the cockroach *Blatella germanica*. *J. Morph.*, **31**, 563–81.
22. EDNEY, E. B. (1958). A new interpretation of the relation between temperature and transpiration in Arthropods. *Proc. 10th. Int. Congr. Ent.*, **2**, 329–32.
23. FRAENKEL, G. and RUDALL, K. M. (1947). The structure of insect cuticles. *Proc. R. Soc.*, B, **134**, 111–43.

24. GILBY, A. R. (1962). Absence of natural volatile solvents in the cockroach *Periplaneta americana*. *Nature*, **195**, 729.

25. GILBY, A. R. and COX, M. E. (1963). The cuticular lipids of the cockroach *Periplaneta americana*. *J. Insect Physiol.*, **9**, 671–81.

26. GUNN, D. L. (1931). Temperature and humidity relations of the cockroach. *Nature*, **128**, 186–7.

27. GUNN, D. L. (1933). The temperature and humidity relations of the cockroach. I. Desiccation. *J. exp. Biol.*, **10**, 274–85.

28. GUNN, D. L. (1935). The temperature and humidity relations of the cockroach. III. A comparison of temperature preference, and rates of desiccation and respiration of *Periplaneta americana, Blatta orientalis* and *Blattella germanica*. *J. exp. Biol.*, **12**, 185–90.

29. GUNN, D. L. and COSWAY, C. A. (1938). The temperature and humidity relations of the cockroach. V. Humidity preference. *J. exp. Biol.*, **15**, 555–63.

30. GUNN, D. L. and COSWAY, C. A. (1942). The temperature and humidity relations of the cockroach. VI. Oxygen consumption. *J. exp. Biol.*, **19**, 124–32.

31. GUNN, D. L. and NOTLEY, F. B. (1936). The temperature and humidity relations of the cockroach. IV. Thermal death point. *J. exp. Biol.*, **13**, 28–34.

32. HAASE, E. (1889). Zur Anatomie der Blattiden. *Zool. Anz.*, **12**, 169–72.

33. HABER, V. R. (1926). The blood of insects, with special reference to that of the common household German, or croton, cockroach, *Blattella germanica*. *Bull. Brooklyn ent. Soc.*, **21**, 61–100.

34. HACKMAN, R. H. (1964). Chemistry of the insect cuticle. In: Rockstein, M. (Ed.). *Physiology of the Insecta*, vol. 3. Academic Press, London and New York.

35. HOLDGATE, M. W. (1955). The wetting of insect cuticles by water. *J. exp. Biol.*, **32**, 591–617.

36. INGRAM, R. L. (1955). Water loss from insects treated with pyrethrum. *Ann. ent. Soc. Am.*, **48**, 481–5.

37. KENNAUGH, J. H. (1958). Amino-acid metabolism, polypeptide production and the process of tanning in the cockroach, *Periplaneta americana*. *J. Insect Physiol.*, **2**, 97–107.

38. KONČEK, S. H. (1924). Zur Histologie der Rückdrüsen unserer einheimischen Blattiden. *Z. wiss. Zool.*, **122**, 311–22.

39. KRAMER, S. and WIGGLESWORTH, V. B. (1950). The outer layers of the cuticle in the cockroach, *Periplaneta americana* and the function of the oenocytes. *Q. Jl. miscrosc. Sci.*, **91**, 63–72.

40. KÜHNELT, W. (1928). Ein Beitrag zur Histochemie des Insektenskelettes. *Zool. Anz.*, **75**, 111–13.

41. LAMER, V. K. and BARNES, G. T. (1959). The effects of spreading techniques and purity of sample on the evaporation resistance of monolayers. *Proc. natn. Acad. Sci. U.S.A.*, **45**, 1274–80.

42. LIANG, C. (1956). The dorsal glands and ventral glands of *Periplaneta americana*. *Ann. ent. Soc. Am.*, **49**, 548–51.

43. LIMPEL, L. E. and CASIDA, J. E. (1957). Iodine metabolism in insects. I. In vivo metabolism of radioiodide. *J. exp. Zool.*, **135**, 19–28.

44. LIMPEL, L. E. and CASIDA, J. E. (1957). Iodine metabolism in insects. II. In vivo distribution and metabolism of iodoamino acids and related studies with *Periplaneta*. *J. exp. Zool.*, **136**, 595–613.

45. LIPKE, H., GRAINGER, M. M. and SIAKOTOS, A. N. (1965). Polysaccharide and glycoprotein formation in the cockroach. I. Identity and titer of bound monosaccharides. *J. biol. Chem.*, **240**, 594–600.

46. LIPKE, H., GRAVES, B. and LETO, S. (1965). Polysaccharide and glycoprotein formation in the cockroach. II. Incorporation of D-glucose-^{14}C into bound carbohydrate. *J. biol. Chem.*, **240**, 601–8.

47. LIPKE, H., LETO, S. and GRAVES, B. (1965). Carbohydrate–amino acid conversions during cuticle synthesis in *Periplaneta americana*. *J. Insect Physiol.*, **11**, 1225–32.

48. LOCKE, M. (1964). The structure and formation of the integument in insects. In: Rockstein, M. (Ed.) *Physiology of the Insecta*, vol. 3. Academic Press, London and New York.
49. LOCKEY, K. N. (1960). The thickness of some insect epicuticular wax layers. *J. exp. Biol.*, **37**, 316–29.
50. LOWER, H. F. (1959). The insect epicuticle and its terminology. *Ann. ent. Soc. Am.*, **52**, 381–5.
51. MALEK, S. R. A. (1952). A liproprotein precursor of sclerotin in the cockroach cuticle. *Nature*, **170**, 850–1.
52. MEAD-BRIGGS, A. R. (1956). The effects of temperature on the permeability to water of arthropod cuticles. *J. exp. Biol.*, **33**, 737–49.
53. MELLANBY, K. (1932). The influence of atmospheric humidity on the thermal death point. *J. exp. Biol.*, **9**, 222–31.
54. MELLANBY, K. (1935). The evaporation of water from insects. *Biol. Rev.*, **10**, 317–33.
55. MUNSON, S. C. and YEAGER, J. F. (1949). Blood volume and chloride normality in roaches (*Periplaneta americana*) injected with sodium chloride solutions. *Ann. ent. Soc. Am.*, **42**, 165–73.
56. NECHELES, N. (1924). Ueber Wärmeregulation bei wechselwarmen Tieren. *Pflügers Arch. ges. Physiol.*, **204**, 72–86.
57. O'KANE, W. C. and GLOVER, L. C. (1935). Studies in contact insecticides. X. Penetration of arsenic into insects. *Bull. New Hamps. agric. Exp. Stn*, **63**, 1–8.
58. OLSON, W. P. and O'BRIEN, R. D. (1963). The relation between physical properties and penetration of solutes into the cockroach cuticle. *J. Insect Physiol.*, **9**, 777–86.
59. PAVAN, M. (1954). Su un nuovo organo ghiandolare e il suo secreto in *Blatta orientalis* e *Periplaneta americana*. *Boll. Zool.*, **21**, 321–32.
60. PAVAN, M. (1954). Un nuovo organo cervicale in *Blatta orientalis* e *Periplaneta americana* produttore di secreto fluorescente alla luci di Wood. *Boll. Soc. ital. Biol. sper.*, **30**, 873–5.
61. PAVAN, M. (1954). Primi dati per la caratterizzazione del secreto dell'organo latero-cervicale di *Blatta orientalis* e *Periplaneta americana*. *Boll. Soc. ital. Biol. sper.*, **30**, 875–6.
62. PAVAN, M. (1959). Biochemical aspects of insect poisons. In LEVENBROOK, L. (ed.), Biochemistry of insects. *Proc. 4th. Int. Congr. Biochem.*, Vienna, *1958*, **12**, 15–36.
63. PENNELL, J. T. and TSUYUKI, H. (1965). An oxidase-peroxidase system in various insects. *Can. J. Zool.*, **43**, 587–8.
64. PFAFF, W. (1952). Investigation of the construction of the cuticle of insects and the mechanism of penetration by the contact insecticide E605. *Höfchenbr. Bayer PflSchutz-Nachr.*, **5**, 93–160.
65. PFLUGFELDER, O. (1958). *Entwicklunsphysiologie der Insekten*. Geest and Portig, Leipzig.
66. QADRI, M. A. H. (1938). The life-history and growth of the cockroach, *Blatta orientalis*. *Bull. ent. Res.*, **29**, 263–76.
67. RAMSAY, J. A. (1935). The evaporation of water from cockroaches. *J. exp. Biol.*, **12**, 373–83.
68. RICHARDS, A. G. (1952). Studies on arthropod cuticle. VII. Patent and masked carbohydrate in the epicuticle of insects. *Science*, **115**, 206–7.
69. RICHARDS, A. G. and ANDERSON, T. F. (1942). Electron microscope studies of insect cuticle, with a discussion of the application of electron optics to this problem. *J. Morph.*, **71**, 135–84.
70. RICHARDS, A. G. and PIPA, R. L. (1958). Studies on the molecular organization of insect cuticle. *Smithson. misc. Colln.*, **137**, 247–62.

71. ROTH, L. M. and STAHL, W. M. (1956). Tergal and cercal secretion of *Blatta orientalis*. *Science*, **123**, 798–9.
72. SCHATZ, L. (1952). The development and differentiation of arthropod procuticle: staining. *Ann. ent. Soc. Am.*, **45**, 678–86.
73. SCHMIDT, E. L. (1956). Observations on a subcuticular layer in the insect integument. *J. Morph.*, **99**, 211–32.
74. SIKORD, H. (1918). Zur Bedeutung der Rückendrüse der Männchens bei der Küchenschabe. *Z. angew. Ent.*, **4**, 374–5.
75. SIMANTON, W. A. (1933). Determination of the surface area of insects. *Ann. ent. Soc. Am.*, **26**, 247–54.
76. STANISLAVSKIJ, B. (1926). Kotázce složení hypodermy *Periplanetae orientalis*. *Spisy vydáv. přír. Fak. Karl. Univ.*, **56**, 1–15.
77. TAUBER, O. E. (1934). Distribution of chitin in an insect. *J. Morph.*, **56**, 51–8.
78. TONG, W. and CHAIKOFF, I. L. (1961). [131]Iodine utilization by the aquarium snail and the cockroach. *Biochim. biophys. Acta*, **48**, 347–51.
79. TSAO, C. H. and RICHARDS, A. G. (1952). Studies on arthropod cuticle. IX. Quantitative effects of diet, age, temperature and humidity on the cuticles of five representative species of insects. *Ann. ent. Soc. Am.*, **45**, 585–99.
80. WATERHOUSE, D. F. and MCKELLAR, J. W. (1961). The distribution of chitinase activity in the body of the American cockroach. *J. Insect Physiol.*, **6**, 185–95.
81. WIGGLESWORTH, V. B. (1945). Transpiration through the cuticle of insects. *J. exp. Biol.*, **21**, 97–114.
82. WIGGLESWORTH, V. B. (1957). The physiology of insect cuticle. *A. Rev. Ent.*, **2**, 37–54.

ADDITIONAL REFERENCES

83. BEAMENT, J. W. L. (1948). The rôle of wax layers in the waterproofing of insect cuticle and egg-shell. *Discuss. Faraday Soc.*, **3**, 177–82.
84. BEAMENT, J. W. L. (1960). Wetting properties of insect cuticle. *Nature*, **186**, 408–9.
85. BEAMENT, J. W. L. (1964). The active transport of water: evidence, models and mechanisms. *Symp. Soc. exp. Biol.*, **19**, 273–98.
86. JENKIN, P. M. and HINTON, H. E. (1966). Apolysis in arthropod moulting cycles. *Nature*, **211**, 871.
87. HINTON, H. E. (1966). Personal communication.
88. RICHARDS, A. G. and KORDA, F. H. (1948). Studies on Arthropod cuticle. II. Electron microscope studies of extracted cuticle. *Biol. Bull. mar. bio. Lab. Woods Hole*, **94**, 212–35.
89. RICHARDS, A. G. and KORDA, F. H. (1950). Studies on Arthropod cuticle. IV. An electron-microscope survey of the intima of arthropod tracheae. *Ann. ent. Soc. Am.*, **43**, 49–71.
90. WILLIS, E. R. and ROTH, L. M. (1956). Fluorescence in cockroaches. *Ann. ent. Soc. Am.*, **49**, 495–7.

4   Reproduction

Spermatogenesis

Live sperm have been found in late instars of *P.a.*, *B.o.*, *Leucophaea maderae*, and *Blaberus craniifer*,[52] and in *Leucophaea maderae* metamorphosing spermatids were seen in late sixth and seventh instars and mature sperms in late eighth and ninth instars.[51] The weights of the testes of late nymphs and adults were found to be almost the same, suggesting that they are mature towards the end of nymphal development.[49] In *B.o.* and other domestic species, the testes and rate of spermatogenesis are said to decline when the insect becomes mature and ages, whereas in the outdoor species the testes are claimed to be rapidly reduced in the adult.[61] In *B.o.* they are said to reach maximum development in the sixth instar, and after the last moult the walls of the terminal ampullae form a number of blind-ending tubes which constitute the male accessory gland. A bunch of about nine small vesicles on each side of the anterior end of the ejaculatory duct store spermatozoa and are therefore the seminal vesicles. During the week following the final moult, the follicles collapse, and the testes become almost completely reduced.[60] But Quiaoit and Lawson found that in laboratory stocks of *B.o.* the testes were still unreduced 40 days after the last moult, although there was some loss of the early stages of spermatogenesis, while in wild populations, the testes were degenerate and no sperms were present in the testes or seminal vesicles. The seminal vesicles were full of highly motile organisms which may have been bacteria. In late nymphal instars of *B.o.* most of the follicle cells of the testes were immature sperms or spermatids, with earlier stages, but some mature sperms were present. No sperms were found in the seminal vesicles which were still rudimentary.[62]

The testes in *P.a.* are said to be more or less degenerate in the adult,[81] but they are difficult to find because they are embedded in fatty tissue, each testis being a linear group of small distinct globules, lying in abdominal segments 4 and 5. They are in fact not atrophied in the adult and in a specimen 4·4 cm long the testes were about 1 cm long and contained active sperms.[63]

The details of spermatogenesis in *P.a.* have been described by Nath *et al.* (Fig. 4.1). In the spermatogonia the mitochondria are extremely delicate, granular or filamentous. The Golgi bodies arise on the mitochondria as filaments, which later become dark at their tips. The primary spermatocytes have long, thick, filamentous mitochondria and Golgi bodies which are granules, rodlets or spheroids. They are now clearly seen to be from the mitochondria, first as small granules, which become rodlets, lying against a lighter sphere. The rodlet bends to surround the spheres which, in optical section, appear as discs with a darker periphery and lighter centre. The Golgi bodies and mitochondria of the secondary spermatocytes are like those of the first spermatocytes, but in the spermatid the Golgi elements become four or five spheroids which fuse to form the acroblast at

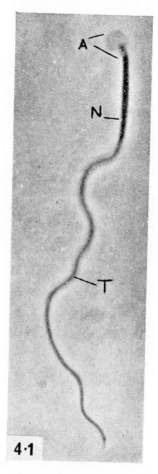

FIG. 4.1 Normal mature sperm. A—acrosome, N—nucleus, T—tail. Phase-contrast, living material. × 1600. (From Nath, Gupta and Seghal[55])

one pole of the nucleus. It is not fused to the nucleus, and later forms the pro-acrosome, which in turn becomes the acrosome. The acroblast is then lost. The mitochondria condense to form the nebenkern which shows a laminar structure, later becoming homogeneous. As the spermatid elongates the nebenkern elongates with it, and the axial filament extending from the centrosome passes through its centre. At first the elongation of the axial filament and the nebenkern is quicker than the elongation of the cell and they coil within it, but later this rights itself and the tail is formed. For a time, however, the tail has blebs of cytoplasm on it[50,55] (Fig. 4.2) similar to those described by Wassilieff in the developing sperm of *Bt.g.*[87] The sperms swim with a continuous clockwise rotation giving a straight direction of movement.[55] Many spermatids degenerate and do not become spermatozoa.[84] In the male nymphs of *Bt.g.* structures have

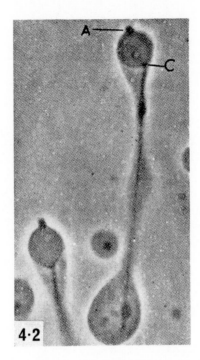

FIG. 4.2   Elongating spermatid, showing the cytoplasmic blebs being sloughed off. A—acrosome, C—centrosome. Phase-contrast, living material. × 1600. (From Nath, Gupta and Seghal[55])

been observed which have the appearance of rudimentary ovaries, and in *P.a.* some of the testicular follicles may contain ovum-like cells as well as spermatocytes.[86]

In *P.a.* the normal sperms swim with an average speed of 16 μ/sec (minimum 8·5) in saline at 15–16°, or 54 μ/sec (maximum 107) at 37–39°. The rate changes with temperature as with other body processes, but cold inactivation happens rather earlier, at 10–11°.[67] Some sperms in *P.a.* are two or three times as wide as normal sperms, which are about 85 μ long. Up to 30% of the late spermatids or sperms in the last instar nymphs are giants, but they most probably disintegrate before leaving the testes since less than 2% are found in the seminal vesicles. They may be polyploid sperms or they may be derived from multinucleate spermatids which are found in the testes of nymphs (Figs. 4.3, 4.4).[68]

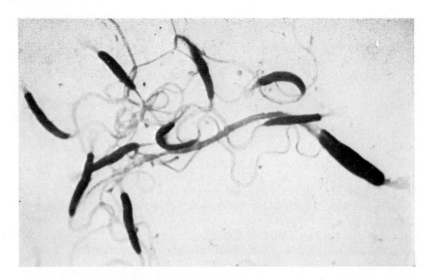

FIG. 4.3   Smear from seminal vesicle of an adult showing one giant and nine normal-sized sperm. × 1950. (From Richards[68])

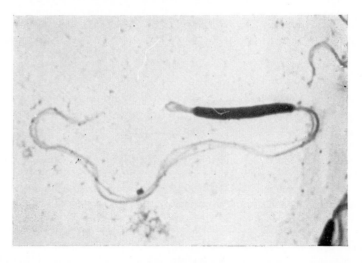

FIG. 4.4   Normal-sized sperm from adult to show duck-bill type of acrosome, and tail which in unfavourable saline solutions frays into a number of fibrils. × 3000. (From Richards[68])

The spermatophore

The spermatophore of *P.a.* is slightly larger than that of *B.o.*, which is the size of the head of a pin.[14] It forms at the end of the two ejaculatory ducts, beginning as two gelatinous masses from the utriculi majores which soon fuse to form a single mass. As this is forming, seminal fluid, with sperms, from the utriculi breviores enters and lies centrally inside it, the fluid keeping the sperms together and nourishing them. Then a second layer is added on to the outside from the epithelia of the ejaculatory ducts; this is the middle layer of the spermatophore wall. Outside this, the outside layer is said to be added by the conglobate or phallic gland when copulation takes place and the spermatophore is within the genital atrium of the female.[26] This account has not been accepted by all other workers, and Khalifa states that the spermatophores of *P.a.* and *Bt.g.* are formed during copulation, and points out that there is no ejaculatory pouch nor spermatophore mould, so that if the spermatophore is formed before copulation it is difficult to see where it is kept until mating is accomplished.[43] The formation of the outer wall is also said to be from a white secretion of the utriculi majores[60, 96] but in *Bt.g.* such a white secretion has been found to be uric acid, the amount present being inversely proportional to the frequency of mating.[71, 72] The spermatophore of *B.o.* contains a number of capsules probably derived from the secretion of the smaller and medium utriculi, each capsule containing spermatozoa.[60]

The lumen of the phallic gland is lined by epicuticle, which also extends into the ductules which penetrate inwards from the lumen through the cuticle, and into the underlying secretory cells themselves, where they become the intracellular ductules of the cells. These are lined with epicuticle only apically, while basally, that is in the deeper parts of the cells, the ductules have a reticulate lining against which microvilli abut. Golgi material, mitochondria, secretory granules and vesicles are present in the cells.[6]

Mating and copulation

The male cockroach is attracted and stimulated by the odour of the female in *P.a.*,[37, 74] having specialized sense organs[37] on the antennae for this purpose.[75] The amount of sex attractant secreted is maximum in virgin females, although the output is rather sporadic; it decreases with age and the number of oöthecae produced.[91] The males respond to objects that have been in contact with virgin females[75] and the percentage of males responding is proportional to the logarithm of the concentration of the attractant over a wide range, though they show some adaptation to the stimulus, probably through fatigue.[90] The attractant is conducive to mating in *P.a.* and vice-versa,[91] but starving *Bt.g.* will not mate.[70] The volatile substance given off by a large number of females of *P.a.* was collected from an air stream in which they were kept[95] and it was claimed that a sex attractant was present, having the structure of dimethylisopropylidenecyclopropyl propionate.[36] The existence of a sex attractant in the air stream is not doubted and it elicited great excitement in males,[34] but the chemical determination has been questioned[88] and was later withdrawn.[35] The exact structure is not yet fully elucidated, but it may be an aliphatic ester carbonyl.[88, 89]

Cockroaches which carry the oötheca for an extended period have the most pronounced periods of pheromone secretion, during which time mating is possible. The process is controlled by the secretion of the corpora allata.[5]

The courting of the females by the males in *P.a.* is in several stages and will take place in the light.[33, 91] First there are questing movements of the antennae[90] but without antennal fencing,[75] followed by questing movements of the palpi. The male then begins to search actively for the female[90] with the wings raised[75] and fluttering. When the female is contacted the posterior segments of the abdomen of the male are protruded[90] and the male pushes under the female from the front, side or rear, until connection is made by the male genital appendages. Then the male moves to be end to end with the female, in a false linear position.[75] A similar sequence also happens in *Bt.g.*, the male approaching the female from the side or front with wings raised.[23]

Copulation takes place when the adult males are 2–4 days old, and the females 4–5 days old[75] and no periodism in the frequency of copulation has been detected.[91] The process lasts 1 hr in *P.a.*[93] or 2–3 hr in *Bt.g.*,[43] and results in the deposition of the spermatophore in the female by the male. It is compressed by the sclerites of the female and attached to the spermathecal papilla, into which the sperms pass.[26] In *Bt.g.* the migration of the sperms from the spermatophore only occurs after activation by a substance produced in the spermathecal glands of the female.[43]

The process of copulation in *P.a.* has been described by Gupta, and takes place usually during the night from March to September (in Lucknow, India). The grumolobus of the male pulls down the edge of sternite 7 of the female and he inserts his genitalia until the styles press against the notches on the antero-lateral corners of sternum 7. The right phallomere lies between the dorsal gonapophyses and the ejaculatory duct aperture. The distal part of the serrate lobe of the dikella reaches to the bases of the ventral gonapophyses, while the dikella prong itself holds the base of the right ventral gonapophysis. The falx hooks round the left ventral gonapophysis. The opposed plates of sclerites 2 and 3 hold the distal ends of both left and right ventral gonapophyses.

The vulvar sclerites become tilted and the thecopore comes to face vertically downwards. The opening of the ejaculatory duct on the ventral phallomere becomes swollen and extends forwards to the entrance of the gynantrium and from it the spermatophore is expelled. It becomes attached to the spermathecal opening.

The left phallomere is arranged so that the knob of the pseudopenis is inserted into the vulva and turned transversely to the slit of the latter. The asperate lobe and the opening of the phallic gland lie close by, and the grumolobus lies ventrally in a slanting position.[27]

Oögenesis

Each ovary of *P.a.* consists of eight panoistic ovarioles and each ovariole has two sheaths. The inner one is the tunica propria consisting of the equivalent of insect connective tissue and the outer is a very unusual tissue, a network of cellular material devoid of muscle fibres and invested by tracheae and bacterio-cytes.[7,8] The diffuse cellular network is adipose tissue, rich in glycogen, and is the site of lipid and carbohydrate metabolism, and strands from it connect the ovarioles into a bundle forming the ovary.[8] A peritoneal sheath of similar struc-ture is present in *B.o.* where it probably has a nutritive function, supplying materials to the follicle cells.[3]

The tunica propria consists of a ground substance with fibrils formed by the cells of the ovariole wall. It is elastic and helps ovulation and to keep the oöcytes in place, and it may be a dialytic membrane.[8]

Each ovariole can be subdivided into six main regions or zones (Figs. 4.5, 4.6):

1. The terminal suspensory ligament which simply suspends the ovariole within the body cavity. It is syncitial but of no importance in oögenesis.

2. The germinal zone of many prefollicular cells, oögonia and young oöcytes.

3. The zone of early oöcyte growth with incomplete follicular epithelia, with the oöcytes not yet in single file.

4. The oöcytes in this zone have become large enough to lie in a single row, each in a follicle with a simple follicular epithelium.

5. In this zone the oöcytes have grown to be very large yolk-filled cells, and the oöcyte is ripe for syngamy.

6. This region is the pedicel of the ovariole which leads into the oviduct.[7]

An oöcyte begins its development as an undifferentiated cell in the germarium of zone 2. The first maturation division begins and goes as far as the diplotene stage of prophase and the cytoplasm has a low concentration of RNA. In the next region of the ovariole the follicular epithelium begins to be established,[7] with blunt processes on the follicle cells interdigitating to some extent with microvilli on the oöcytes.[2] The cytoplasm grows richer in RNA as the nucleolus of the oöcyte becomes very irregular in outline and gives off small globules, rich in RNA.[7] The nucleoli may even form emissions in zone 2 also,[2] and these growth processes continue into the anterior part of zone 4.[2,7] These nucleolar emissions migrate through the nucleoplasm to the inner surface of the nuclear membrane which is porous. They almost certainly pass from the nucleus into the cytoplasm[2] but may undergo a physico-chemical change in order to do so.[7] In the posterior part of zone 4 and in zone 5 nucleolar emissions cease, the nucleolus becoming more regular in outline and vacuolated.[2] In *B.o.* small vesicles are also reported to pass from the nucleus into the cytoplasm through which they spread or become aggregated into chains.[25]

The next major event in the maturation of the oöcyte is the provision of protein yolk bodies. This occurs in the latter part of zone 4 and zone 5 and is preceded by the slight separation of the follicular and oöcyte surfaces. The pinocytosis which the oölemma undergoes from zone 3 now becomes more obvious, taking up some dense material which probably becomes the yolk globules. The small pinosomes often fuse to form larger yolk bodies[2] and the material of which they are com-posed is probably a protein-polysaccharide complex.[1,2,7,54] Oil droplets are also found in the yolk[2] but the RNA concentration is reduced towards the end of this period.[7] No glycogen is present.[1,2,7]

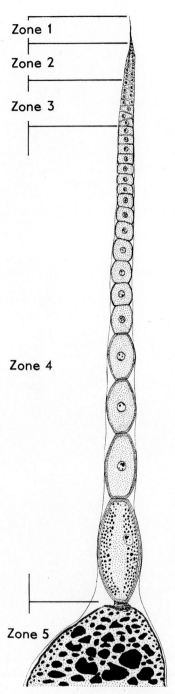

FIG. 4.5 Diagrammatic representation of ovariole in longitudinal section, showing major zones. (From Anderson[2] after Bonhag[7])

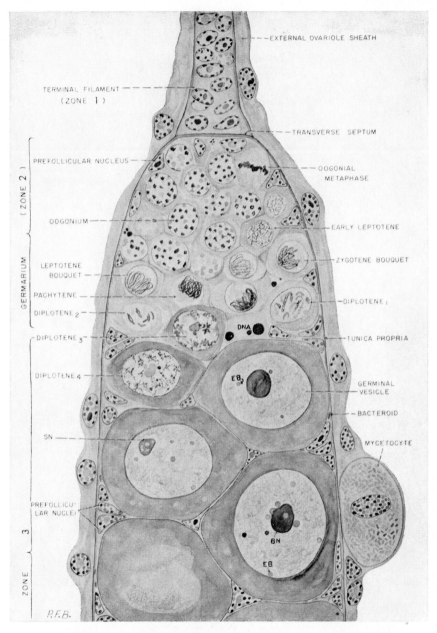

FIG. 4.6   Sagittal view of part of an ovariole to show detail of zones 1, 2 and 3. DNA—deoxyribonucleic acid, EB, BN—body emitted from nucleolus, SN—thin section of nucleolus showing vacuolate appearance. (From Bonhag[7])

The protein material forming the protein yolk is reported to be present first in the follicle cells[1,54] but this is doubted by Anderson who points out that in many insects the protein is derived from the blood.[2]

Older writers believed that in *P.a.* and *B.o.* the mitochondria[65] or the nucleolar emissions formed the protein yolk bodies[24,31,56] but recent work has shown that in *P.a.* the formation of the protein yolk is not dependent on, derived from, or associated with the nucleolar emissions[2,7] nor with any oöcyte organelles such as mitochondria or Golgi bodies.[2] Nevertheless, the high concentration of RNA in the oöplasm may be taken to indicate active protein synthesis[7] and in *B.o.* it has been suggested that the richness of the nucleolus and its emissions in RNA indicates some correlation with protein yolk synthesis.[25] This is denied by Anderson, who states that in *P.a.* it is more probably associated with maintenance of the protoplasm and that the protein of yolk is not manufactured within the oöplasm. He also points out that an organized endoplasmic reticulum was not seen in any oöcyte examined[2] but in *B.o.* both an endoplasmic reticulum and mitochondria were clearly visible.[25]

Yolk also contains lipid droplets and these were thought to be derived from the Golgi bodies[24,54,56,65] and it is unfortunate that the recent studies of oögenesis in *P.a.* have so little to say on this point,[2,7] especially as Gresson and Threadgold were unable to identify the Golgi apparatus in their electron microscope study of the oöcytes of *B.o.*[25] Only Bonhag mentions that 'agreement is not uni-

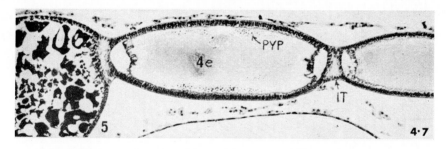

FIG. 4.7   Sagittal section of posterior end of zone 4 (4e) and part of the most anterior oöcyte of zone 5. IT—interfollicular tissue, PYP—precursor bodies of protein yolk. Magnification not stated. (From Bonhag[7])

versal'.[7] Nath *et al.* state that three kinds of lipid bodies are abundant and widely spread in the oöplasm of all oöcytes in *P.a.* Some were triglyceride surrounded by a phospholipid sheath; and some were triglyceride only. They also mention that the bacteroids between the follicular epithelium and oölemma contain free fatty acids and phospholipids and suggest that the micro-organisms may play a part in synthesizing lipids for the developing oöcyte.[54] Nath thought that only the older oöcytes, greater than 1·7 mm long, contained lipoid yolk droplets.[53]

The nuclear membrane breaks down when the yolk-filled oöcyte is mature and the first maturation division is completed. The follicular epithelium forms the chorion or egg membrane. During growth the oöcytes increase very greatly in size, and the follicle cells increase by mitosis to keep pace until zone 5, when mitoses cease and the follicle cells are stretched and flattened by the oöcyte[7] (Fig. 4.7).

Formation of the oötheca

The oötheca is formed from the secretions of the glands of the genital region in *P.a.*,[9,10,11] in *B.o.*,[58,97] in *Bt.g.* and in *Leucophaea maderae*.[83] The two major sources of material for the oöthecae are the left and right colleterial glands, the former being much larger than the latter.[10] Both are much subdivided and open by a single aperture (see page 53) on the dorsal wall of the genital chamber (T). The right gland has a main duct of cubical epithelium, lined with an intima of chitin and an external layer of circular muscles. The smaller tubes of the glands are glandular epithelium cells with small chitinogenic cells lying between their apices. The cells of the left gland are similar to those of the right gland, but the secretory cells of the smaller secretory tubules of the left gland can be subdivided into four different types (Fig. 4.8).[10] Type 1 cells are ordinary cubical cells confined to the main duct of the gland. Type 2 cells are short and contain a large endapparatus which pushes into the basal nucleus and makes its apical side concave. Cells of type 3 are tall cells with fibrillar basal cytoplasm and a narrow end apparatus; they are probably transitional cells between cells or types 2 and 4. Type 4 cells are similar to type 2 though rather longer, leaving the nucleus subspherical.[10,48]

There are in addition, groups of glandular cells in the integument, one of which forms a vestibular organ: an invagination of the dorsal wall of the vestibulum between the openings of the colleterial glands and the spermathecae. The secretion of these cells accumulates within the endocuticle, here divided into inner and outer layers with a layer of tenuous fibrillar network between. The secretion reaches the vestibule through some very wide pore canals.[9]

The oötheca of *P.a.* contains no chitin,[13] and is made of a quinone-tanned protein.[9] The left colleterial gland produces the structural protein, a β-glucoside of protocatechuic acid[42] and a polyphenol oxidase. The right colleterial gland secretes a β-glucosidase. This enzyme attacks the β-glucoside when the secretions meet and liberates protocatechuic acid. This is then oxidized to give a quinone which cross-links the protein to produce the hard resistant material of the oötheca.[11,12] Cells of types 2 and 4 secrete the protein,[9,10] cells of type 2 the oxidase,[48] which is probably a copper-protein complex and is of the laccase type.[92] The left colleterial gland has been found to secrete another substance, so far unidentified in *P.a.* and *B.o.*, and indeed in the two-day-old adult of *P.a.* almost all the secretion of the gland is this unknown material.[83] The glycogen present in the left colleterial gland is confined to the cells of type 2.[44]

Calcium oxalate crystals are frequently found in the oöthecae of blattids[30] and 15% of the weight of the oötheca of *P.a.* may be the dihydrate of calcium oxalate (equivalent to 8% of the anhydrous oxalate). In *Bt.g.* the figure was 0·03% of the dihydrate.[82] This substance is secreted by the cells of type 4.[9,10] Hackman and Goldberg found 65% calcium in the oötheca of *P.a.* of which only one third

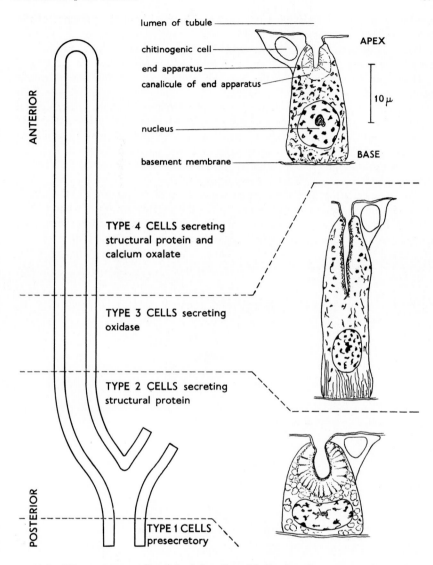

FIG. 4.8   The secretory cells of the left colleterial gland as they appear after staining with iron haematoxylin. Their approximate position in the gland is indicated. All but one branch of the gland have been omitted for clarity. (From Brunet[10])

was calcium oxalate leaving two thirds unaccounted for. They suggest that this calcium may be bound to the protein of the oötheca. In *Bt.g.* they found 0.25% calcium oxalate.[28] The lysine content of new white oöthecae $= 9.7\%$ but in old, dark oöthecae it drops to 3.6% which suggests this amino acid may be used in the

4 + B.O.C.

hardening process.[29] Darkening can occur with or without the presence of the
β-glucoside of protocatechuic acid.[16]

Both the structure of the glands and the mechanism of oöthecal production
are similar to *P.a.* in *B.o.*[58,59,97] and probably in *Leucophaea maderae* and *Bt.g.*[83]

In *P.a.* it is thought that as the eggs are being deposited and the oötheca is
being formed around them, the secretion of the vestibular organ helps to hold
the eggs together. It is of protein nature and contains diphenols. Other dermal
glands of the genital chamber secrete material which probably forms the thin
outer layer of the oötheca except for its dorsal crista[9] and this may be similar to
the waterproof layer which is reported to be found on the oöthecae of *B.o.* and
which is not the same as the cuticular grease of the rest of the insect.[76] Still other
dermal glands may secrete a lubricating material.[9]

The dorsal crista or keel of the oötheca is of a complex structure and has within
it a series of air sacs each with a fine slit to the outside air and a narrow duct
leading inwards to the dorsal part of the interior of the capsule where the
cephalic ends of the eggs are tightly packed together (Figs. 4.9, 4.10).[45]

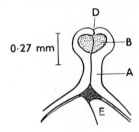

FIG. 4.9   Transverse section of keel of oötheca. A—the keel proper, B—cell within
keel, D—sutural opening to outside, E—egg. (From Lawson[45])

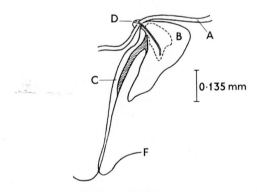

FIG. 4.10   Details of median surface of keel showing cell within. A—the keel
proper, B—cell within keel, C—tube connecting cell to interior, D—sutural
opening to outside, F—lower boundary of inner keel face with inside surface of
curved part of capsule wall. (From Lawson[45])

The oöthecae of all the cockroaches considered here all contain water and in *B.o.* this remains fairly constant in amount although during development much of the water surrounding the eggs is taken up by them. In *P.a.* this is also true, but the total water content of the oötheca falls with time in this species.[77]

The hormonal control of reproduction

Considerable effort has been devoted to studies of the hormonal and nervous control of mating, oögenesis and oviposition, especially in *Leucophaea maderae* and other cockroaches which retain the oötheca in an oöthecal chamber until the eggs are ripe.[17,18,39,70,78,99] The corpora allata are known to be necessary for egg development in *Leucophaea maderae*,[17,39,78] *P.a.*[22] and *Bt.g.*[73] but in *L. maderae* they are themselves inhibited by starvation,[39] so that oögenesis also ceases in starvation.[78] The removal of the ovaries in *L. maderae* affects the neurosecretory 'B' cells of the suboesophageal ganglia[79] and there is other evidence that neurosecretion (from the brain) is involved in the receptivity of the female for the male;[70] it has been suggested that the suboesophageal ganglion has a centre stimulating the activity of the corpora allata, and the brain one inhibiting it.[17] The corpora allata secretion is necessary for yolk deposition and to a lesser degree for the activity of the accessory glands and, when its titre is low, mating will occur.[18]

The presence of an oötheca in the brood chamber is a stimulus transmitted via the central nervous system in *Bt.g.*[73] and *L. maderae*[17,21] and removal of a oötheca stimulates the corpora allata to excite oögenesis. It was claimed that in *Bt.g.* a wax model of an oötheca was effective in inhibiting the corpora allata as a real one,[73] but later work showed that the swelling of a living one, due to the imbibition of water from the female, was necessary to prevent adaptation of the sensory or nervous systems. Otherwise, as with a dead real oötheca, it would be ejected and a new one started.[74] However, in *L. maderae* Engelmann states that the presence of an artificial oötheca interferes with the feeding of the female, so that any change in egg maturation is an indirect effect. He maintains that the inhibition of pregnancy is brought about by an agent released by the egg case or brood sac which affects neurones at various points along the central nervous system.[20]

One characteristic of the activity of corpora allata, ovaries and developing embryos is that it is cyclic[17,18,19] and when the corpora allata are transplanted, the cycles do not remain coincident.[19] It is also true that 'the neuroendocrine integration mechanism (is) of a far greater complexity than has been generally recognised heretofore'.[70]

Genetics

An early observation on the spermatocytes of *Bt.g.* was that the accessory chromosome went undivided into one of the two secondary spermatocytes in the first (reduction) division, giving an XX/XO type of sex determination.[84,87] Other cockroaches, including *P.a.* and *B.o.*, have since been found to be the same.[32,50] The diploid number for *P.a.* is 34, for *B.o.* 48 and for *Bt.g.* 34.[85]

The behaviour of the chromosomes in *P.a.* is unusual since the diplotene and diakinesis stages are absent from prophase of the reduction division in the primary spermatocyte,[40,80] or diakinesis is very brief,[15] due to the singleness of each homologue through prophase. This may be associated with premature activity of division centres, dissolution of nuclear membrane and appearance of the spindle[81] which forms at the end of the pachytene,[40] and thus there would be no time for chiasmata formation. The diplotene stage is, however, described by Bonhag in the oögenesis of *P.a.*[7] No chiasmata were found in *P.a.*[15,40,50,81,85] and it has been suggested that the mechanical functions of chiasmata are replaced by matrical stickiness and terminal affinity.[40] Alternatively, others have thought that the chiasmata are localized and usually distal, though concealed.[15,85] The occurrence of chiasmata is claimed to be supported by several lines of evidence, including (i) open-cross, ring and rod bivalent formation; (ii) multiple ring and chain associations occurring regularly in interchange heterozygotes; (iii) the bivalents may associate interstitially; (iv) the associations persist during metaphase stretch. Each of these can occur alone without chiasmata, but together they indicate its great likelihood.[47] It has been claimed recently, moreover, that chiasmata can be seen in *P.a.*, though for only a very brief part of the meiotic cycle.[64]

At premetaphase the chromosomes duplicate[80] and then undergo a pronounced elongation or stretching.[40] This phenomenon, together with complete terminalization, facilitates disjunction and this may be important in the occurrence of interchange heterozygosity found in isolated wild population of *P.a.* in two coal mines in South Wales.[41,46]

Morse reported that at the end of mitosis a body was passed out from the nucleus into the cytoplasm where it disintegrated. It was not chromatin material.[50]

About 5% of a population of *P.a.* in a coal mine were found to be white-eyed mutants, due to a recessive gene.[38] *Bt.g.* can be selectively bred for lindane resistance and is found to inherit this through the autosomal chromosomes by a muti-factorial system.[4] *Bt.g.* also has been found to exhibit red markings instead of the usual black ones, especially in late nymphal instars. Black is the dominant of a simple recessive pair.[57]

In *Byrsotria fumigata* two gynandromorph specimens have been found.[94]

The chromosomes of the primary spermatocyte prior to the bivalent orientation[47] and the chromosomes of the primary oöcyte before prometaphase have the lampbrush configuration.[7]

Ricci reports the occurrence of short-winged males in populations of *B.o.* bred for laboratory purposes, which retained this character for at least three generations.[66]

Two mutants of *P.a.*, 'pearl' and 'lavender' eye-colour, are single autosomal recessives which are inherited independently.[69]

REFERENCES

1. AGGARWAL, S. K. (1960). Histochemical studies of the carbohydrates, proteins and nucleic acids in the oögenesis of *Periplaneta americana* and *Chrotogonus trachypterus*. *Res. Bull. Panjab Univ. Sci.*, **11**, 147–53.
2. ANDERSON, E. (1964). Oocyte differentiation and vitellogenesis in the roach, *Periplaneta americana*. *J. cell. Biol.*, **20**, 131–55.

3. BACCETTI, B. (1963). Indagini ultramicroscopiche sul problema della constituzione della tuniche peritoneali ovarische e dell'esistenza negli insetti di fibre muscolari liscie. *Redia*, **48**, 1–13.

4. BARKER, J. G. (1960). Inheritance of resistance to lindane in the German cockroach, *Blattella germanica. Diss. Abstr.*, **21**, 376.

5. BARTH, R. (1965). Insect mating behavior: endocrine control of a chemical communication system. *Science*, **149**, 882–3.

6. BEAMS, H. W., ANDERSON, E. and KESSEL, R. G. (1962). Electron microscope observations on the phallic (conglobate) gland of the cockroach *Periplaneta americana. Jl R. microsc. Soc.*, **81**, 85–9.

7. BONHAG, P. F. (1959). Histological and histochemical studies on the ovary of the American cockroach *Periplaneta americana. Univ. Calif. Publs Ent.*, **16**, 81–124.

8. BONHAG, P. F. and ARNOLD, W. J. (1961). Histology, histochemistry and tracheation of the ovariole sheaths in the American cockroach, *Periplaneta americana. J. Morph.*, **108**, 107–18.

9. BRUNET, P. C. J. (1951). The formation of the ootheca by *Periplaneta americana*. I. The micro-anatomy and histology of the posterior part of the abdomen. *Q. Jl microsc. Sci.*, **92**, 113–27.

10. BRUNET, P. C. J. (1952). The formation of the ootheca by *Periplaneta americana*. II. The structure and function of the left colleterial gland. *Q. Jl microsc. Sci.*, **93**, 47–69.

11. BRUNET, P. C. J. and KENT, P. W. (1955). Observations on the mechanism of tanning reaction in *Periplaneta* and *Blatta. Proc. R. Soc.*, (B), **144**, 259–74.

12. BRUNET, P. C. J. and KENT, P. W. (1955). Mechanism of sclerotin formation: the participation of a β-glucoside. *Nature*, **175**, 819–20.

13. CAMPBELL, F. L. (1929). The detection and estimation of insect chitin, and the irrelation of 'chitinisation' to hardness and pigmentation of the cuticla of the American cockroach, *Periplaneta americana. Ann. ent. Soc. Am.*, **22**, 401–26.

14. CHOPARD, L. (1938). Biologie des Orthoptères. *Encycl. ent.*, **20**, 1–541.

15. DAGUPTA, J. (1959). Cytological observation on *Periplaneta americana. Curr. Sci.*, **28**, 461–2.

16. DUFOUR, L. (1841). Recherches anatomiques et physiologiques sur les Orthoptères, les Hyménoptères et les Neuroptères. *Mém. Acad. Sci. Inst. Fr.*, **7**, 265–647.

17. ENGELMANN, F. (1957). Die Steuerung der Ovarfunktion bei der ovoviviparen Schabe *Leucophaea maderae. J. Insect Physiol.*, **3**, 257–78.

18. ENGELMANN, F. (1960). Mechanisms controlling reproduction in two viviparous cockroaches. *Ann. N.Y. Acad. Sci.*, **89**, 516–36.

19. ENGELMANN, F. (1962). Further experiments on the regulation of the sexual cycle of females of *Leucophaea maderae. Gen. comp. Endocrinol.*, **2**, 183–92.

20. ENGELMANN, F. (1964). Inhibition of egg maturation in a pregnant viviparous cockroach. *Nature*, **202**, 724–5.

21. ENGELMANN, F. and RAU, I. (1965). A correlation between feeding and the sexual cycle in *Leucophaea maderae. J. Insect Physiol.*, **11**, 53–64.

22. GIRARDIE, A. (1962). Étude biometrique de la croissance ovarienne après ablation et implantation de corpora allata chez *Periplaneta americana. J. Insect Physiol.*, **8**, 199–214.

23. GOULD, G. E. and DEAY, H. O. (1938). Notes on the bionomics of roaches inhabiting houses. *Proc. Indiana Acad. Sci.*, **47**, 281–4.

24. GRESSON, R. A. R. (1931). Yolk formation in *Periplaneta orientalis. Q. Jl microsc. Sci.*, **74**, 257–74.

25. GRESSON, R. A. R. and THREADGOLD, L. T. (1962). Extrusion of nuclear material during oogenesis in *Blatta orientalis. Q. Jl microsc. Sci.*, **103**, 141–5.

26. GUPTA, P. D. (1946). On the structure and formation of the spermatophore in the cockroach *Periplaneta americana*. *Indian J. Ent.*, **8**, 79–84.
27. GUPTA, P. D. (1947). On copulation and insemination in the cockroach *Periplaneta americana*. *Proc. natn. Inst. Sci. India*, **13**, 65–71.
28. HACKMAN, R. H. and GOLDBERG, M. (1960). Composition of the oothecae of three Orthoptera. *J. Insect Physiol.*, **5**, 73–8.
29. HACKMAN, R. H. and GOLDBERG, M. (1963). Phenolic compounds in cockroach ootheca. *Biochim. biophys. Acta*, **71**, 738–40.
30. HALLEZ, P. (1909). Sur les cristaux de la Blatte. *C.r. hebd. Séanc. Acad. Sci., Paris*, **148**, 317–18.
31. HOGBEN, L. T. (1920). Studies on synapsis. II. Parallel conjugation and the prophase complex in *Periplaneta* with special reference to the premeiotic telophase. *Proc. R. Soc.*, (B), **91**, 305–29.
32. HUGHES-SCHRADER, S. (1950). The chromosomes of mantids in relation to taxonomy. *Chromosoma*, **4**, 1.
33. ILLINGWORTH, J. F. (1918). Notes on the mating of cockroaches. *Proc. Hawaii, ent. Soc.*, **3**, 374–5.
34. JACOBSON, M. and BEROZA, M. (1963). Chemical insect attractants. *Science*, **140**, 1367–73.
35. JACOBSON, M. and BEROZA, M. (1965). American cockroach sex attractant. *Science*, **147**, 748–9.
36. JACOBSON, M., BEROZA, M. and YAMAMOTO, R. T. (1963). Isolation and identification of the sex attractant of the American roach. *Science*, **139**, 48–9.
37. JAWLOWSKI, H. (1948). Studies on the brain of insects. *Annls Univ. Mariae Curie-Sklodowska*, (C), **3**, 1–37.
38. JEFFERSON, G. T. (1958). A white-eyed mutant form of the American cockroach *Periplaneta americana*. *Nature*, **182**, 892.
39. JOHANSSON, A. S. (1955). The relationship between corpora allata and reproductive organs in starved female *Leucophaea maderae*. *Biol. Bull. mar. biol. Lab. Woods Hole*, **108**, 40–4.
40. JOHN, B. and LEWIS, K. R. (1957). Studies on *Periplaneta americana*. I. Experimental analysis of male meiosis. *Heredity*, **11**, 1–9.
41. JOHN, B. and LEWIS, K. R. (1958). Studies on *Periplaneta americana*. III. Selection for heterozygosity. *Heredity*, **12**, 185–97.
42. KENT, P. W. and BRUNET, P. J. C. (1959). Occurrence of protocatechuic acid and its 4-0-β-D-glucoside in *Blatta* and *Periplaneta*. *Tetrahedron*, **7**, 252–6.
43. KHALIFA, A. (1950). Spermatophore production in *Blattella*. *Proc. R. ent. Soc. Lond.*, **25**, 53–61.
44. KUGLER, O. E., FRANKENSTEIN, P. W. and RAFFERTY, K. A. (1956). Histochemical localization of alkaline phosphatase, glycogen and nucleic acids in the female reproductive organs of *Periplaneta americana*. *J. Morph.*, **98**, 235–49.
45. LAWSON, F. (1951). Structural features of the oothecae of certain cockroaches. *Ann. ent. Soc. Am.*, **44**, 269–85.
46. LEWIS, K. R. and JOHN, B. (1957). Studies of *Periplaneta americana*. II. Interchange heterozygosity in isolated populations. *Heredity*, **11**, 11–22.
47. LEWIS, K. R. and JOHN, B. (1957). Bivalent structures in *Periplaneta americana*. *Nature*, **179**, 973.
48. MERCER, E. H. and BRUNET, P. C. J. (1959). The electron microscopy of the left colleterial gland of the cockroach. *J. biophys. biochem. Cytol.*, **5**, 257–62.
49. MITLIN, N. (1960). Determination of nucleic acids in the testes of three species of cockroach. *Ann. ent. Soc. Am.*, **53**, 491–4.
50. MORSE, M. (1909). The nuclear components of the sex cells of four species of cockroaches. *Arch. Zellforsch.*, **3**, 483–520.
51. MULKERN, G. B. (1957). A study of growth and molting factors in cockroaches as indicated by allatectomy, spermatogenesis and integumental transplants. *Diss. Abstr.*, **17**, 1630.

52. MULKERN, G. B. and LAWSON, F. A. (1957). Some factors affecting the male reproductive system in cockroaches. *J. Kans. ent. Soc.*, **30**, 54–7.
53. NATH, V. (1933). Microchemical tests for fats, lipoids and vacuoles with special reference to oögenesis. *Q. Jl microsc. Sci.*, **76**, 129–43.
54. NATH, V., GUPTA, B. L. and LAL, B. (1958). Histochemical and morphological studies of the lipids in oögenesis. I. *Periplaneta americana. Q. Jl microsc. Sci.*, **99**, 315–22.
55. NATH, V., GUPTA, B. L. and SEGHAL, P. (1957). Mitochondria and Golgi bodies in the spermatogenesis of *Periplaneta americana*, as studied under the phase-contrast microscope. *Res. Bull. Panjab Univ. Sci.*, **112**, 317–26.
56. NATH, V. and MOHAN, P. (1929). Studies in the origin of yolk. IV. Oögenesis of *Periplaneta americana. J. Morph.*, **48**, 253–80.
57. NISWANDER, R. E. (1961). An inherited color factor in the German roach, *Blattella germanica. Proc. Indiana Acad. Sci.*, **70**, 138.
58. PRYOR, M. G. M. (1940). On the hardening of the ootheca of *Blatta orientalis. Proc. R. Soc.*, (B), **128**, 378–93.
59. PRYOR, M. G. M., RUSSELL, P. B. and TODD, A. R. (1946). Protocatechuic acid, the substance responsible for the hardening of the cockroach ootheca. *Biochem. J.*, **40**, 627–8.
60. QADRI, M. A. H. (1938). The life-history and growth of the cockroach *Blatta orientalis. Bull. ent. Res.*, **29**, 263–76.
61. QUIAOIT, E. R. (1961). An investigation of growth, development and dimorphism in cockroaches. *Diss. Abstr.*, **22**, 950.
62. QUIAOIT, E. R. and LAWSON, F. A. (1963). Gonad degeneration in *Blatta orientalis* and other cockroach species. *J. Kans. ent. Soc.*, **36**, 56–8.
63. RAICHOUDHURY, D. P. and MITRA, H. (1941). Testes in the adult cockroach, *Periplaneta americana. Curr. Sci.*, **10**, 178–9.
64. RAJASEKARASETTY, M. R. and RAMANAMURTHY, C. V. (1963). Meiosis in the male *Periplaneta americana. Nature*, **197**, 1325–6.
65. RANADE, V. D. (1933). On the cytoplasmic inclusions in the oogenesis of *Periplaneta americana. Allahabad Univ. Stud.*, **9**, 85–121.
66. RICCI, M. (1953). Su una anomalia ereditaria osservata nei maschi di *Blatta orientalis. Boll. Soc. ent. ital.*, **83**, 109–10.
67. RICHARDS, A. G. (1963). The rate of sperm locomotion in the cockroach *Periplaneta americana* as a function of temperature. *J. Insect Physiol.*, **9**, 545–9.
68. RICHARDS, A. G. (1963). Giant sperm in the cockroach *Periplaneta americana. Ent. News*, **74**, 57–60.
69. ROSS, M. H., COCHRAN, D. G. and SMYTH, T. (1964). Eye-color mutations in the American cockroach *Periplaneta americana. Ann. ent. Soc. Am.*, **57**, 790–2.
70. ROTH, L. M. and BARTH, R. H. (1964). The control of sexual receptivity in the female cockroach. *J. Insect Physiol.*, **10**, 965–75.
71. ROTH, L. M. and DATEO, G. P. (1964). Uric acid in the reproductive system of males of the cockroach *Blattella germanica. Science*, **146**, 782–4.
72. ROTH, L. M. and DATEO, G. P. (1965). Uric acid storage and excretion by accessory sex glands of male cockroaches. *J. Insect Physiol.*, **11**, 1023–9.
73. ROTH, L. M. and STAY, B. (1959). Control of oöcyte development in cockroaches. *Science*, **130**, 271–2.
74. ROTH, L. M. and STAY, B. (1962). Oöcyte development in *Blattella germanica* and *Blattella vaga. Ann. ent. Soc. Am.*, **55**, 633–42.
75. ROTH, L. M. and WILLIS, E. R. (1950). A study of cockroach behaviour. *Am. Midl. Nat.*, **47**, 66–129.
76. ROTH, L. M. and WILLIS, E. R. (1955). Water relations of cockroach oöthecae. *J. econ. Ent.*, **48**, 33–6.
77. ROTH, L. M. and WILLIS, E. R. (1955). Water content of cockroach eggs during embryogenesis in relation to oviposition behaviour. *J. exp. Zool.*, **128**, 489–510.

78. SCHARRER, B. (1943). The influence of the corpora allata on egg development in an Orthopteran, _Leucophaea maderae. Anat. Rec._, **87**, 471.
79. SCHARRER, B. (1955). 'Castration cells' in the central nervous system of an insect, _Leucophaea maderae. Trans. N.Y. Acad. Sci._, **17**, 520–5.
80. SHARMA, G. P., PARSHAD, R. and SEHGAL, P. (1956). Meiosis without chiasmata in _Periplaneta americana. Nature_, **178**, 1004–5.
81. SHARMA, G. P., PARSHAD, R. and SEHGAL, P. (1959). Cytological analysis of the male meiosis in _Periplaneta americana. J. Genet._, **56**, 281–7.
82. STAY, B., KING, A. and ROTH, L. M. (1960). Calcium oxalate in the oöthecae of cockroaches. _Ann. ent. Soc. Am._, **53**, 79–86.
83. STAY, B. and ROTH, L. M. (1962). The colleterial glands of cockroaches. _Ann. ent. Soc. Am._, **55**, 124–30.
84. Stevens, N. M. (1905). Studies in spermatogenesis with especial reference to the 'accessory chromosome'. _Publs Carnegie Instn._, **36**, 1–32.
85. SUOMALAINEN, E. (1946). Die Chromosomenverhältnisse in der Spermatogenese einiger Blattarien. _Suomal. Tiedeakat. Toim._, (A), **sect. IV**, 1–60.
86. THIRUMALACHER, B. (1928). Ovum-like bodies in the testes of the common cockroach _Periplaneta americana._ Half-yrly _J. Mysore Univ._, **2**, 51–4.
87. WASSILIEFF, A. (1907). Die Spermatogenese von _Blatta germanica. Arch. mikrosk. Anat. EntwMech._, **70**, 1–42.
88. WHARTON, D. R. A., BLACK, E. D. AND MERRITT, C. (1963). Sex attractant of the American cockroach. _Science_, **142**, 1257–8.
89. WHARTON, D. R. A., BLACK, E. D., MERRITT, C., WHARTON, M. L., BAZINET, M. and WALSH, J. T. (1962). The isolation of the sex attractant of the American cockroach. _Science_, **137**, 1062–3.
90. WHARTON, D. R. A., MILLER, G. L. and WHARTON, M. L. (1954). The odorous attractant of the American cockroach, _Periplaneta americana._ I. Quantitative aspects of the response to the attractant. _J. gen. Physiol._, **37**, 461–9.
91. WHARTON, M. L. and WHARTON, D. R. A. (1957). Production of sex attractant substance and of oothecae by the normal and irradiated American cockroach, _Periplaneta americana. J. Insect Physiol._, **1**, 229–39.
92. WHITEHEAD, D. L., BRUNET, P. C. J. and KENT, P. W. (1960). Specificity _in vitro_ of a phenoloxidase system from _Periplaneta americana. Nature_, **185**, 610.
93. WILLIS, E. R., RISER, G. R. and ROTH, L. M. (1958). Observations on reproduction and development in cockroaches. _Ann. ent. Soc. Am._, **51**, 53–69.
94. WILLIS, E. R. and ROTH, L. M. (1959). Gynandromorphs of _Byrsotria fumigata. Ann. ent. Soc. Am._, **52**, 420–9.
95. YAMAMOTO, R. (1963). Collection of sex attractant from female American cockroaches. _J. econ. Ent._, **56**, 119–20.
96. ZABINSKI, J. (1933). Fonctionnement des différents parties des appareils copulateurs chitinés mâles et femelles de la blatte, _Periplaneta orientalis. C.r. Séanc. Soc. Biol._, **112**, 598–602.

ADDITIONAL REFERENCES

97. BORDAS, L. (1909). Recherches anatomiques, histologiques et physiologiques sur les organes appendiculaires de l'appareil reproducteur femelles des Blattes (_Periplaneta orientalis). Annls Sci. nat._, **9**, 71–121.
98. CHOLODKOWSKY, N. (1891). Die Entwicklung von _Phyllodromia germanica. Zap. imp. Akad. Nauk_, (7), **38**, no. 5.
99. CHOPARD, L. (1949). Ordre des Dictyoptères. In: Grassé, P. (ed.) _Traité de Zoologie_, **9**, 355–407.
100. ENGELMANN, F. (1957). Bau und Funktion des weiblichen Geschlechtsapparates bei der ovoviviparen Schabe _Leucophaea maderae_, und einige Beobachtungen über die Entwicklung. _Biol. Zbl._, **76**, 722–40.

101. HEYMONS, R. (1892). Die Entwicklung der weiblichen Geschlechtsorgane von *Phyllodromia germanica. Z. wiss. Zool.*, **53**, 434–536.
102. HEYMONS, R. (1895). *Die Embryonalentwicklung von Dermapteren und Orthopteren.* G. Fischer, Jena.
103. ITO, H. (1924). Contribution histologique et physiologique à l'étude des annexes des organes genitaux des Orthoptère. *Archs Anat. microsc.*, **20**, 343–460.
104. LARSEN, W. P. (1961). A study of the embryology of the cockroach *Blaberus craniifer. Diss. Abstr.*, **21**, 3565.
105. RILEY, W. A. (1904). The embryological development of the head of *Blatta. Am. Nat.*, **38**, 777–810.
106. ROSS, H. H. (1930). Notes on the digestive and reproductive systems of the German cockroach, *Blattella germanica. Trans. Ill. St. Acad. Sci.*, **22**, 206–16.
107. STÜRCHOW, B. and BODENSTEIN, W. G. (1966). Location of the sex pheromone in the American cockroach, *Periplaneta americana* (L.). *Experientia*, **22**, 851–3.
108. WHARTON, D. R. A., MILLER, G. L. and WHARTON, M. L. (1954). The odorous attractant of the American cockroach, *Periplaneta americana*. II. A bioassay method for the attractant. *J. gen. Physiol.*, **37**, 471–81.
109. WHEELER, W. (1889). The embryology of *Blatta germanica* and *Doryphora decemlineata. J. Morph.*, **3**, 291–386.
110. WIGGLESWORTH, V. B. and BEAMENT, J. W. L. (1950). The respiratory mechanisms of some insect eggs. *Q. Jl microsc. Sci.*, **91**, 429–52.
111. WILSON, F. (1965). Ploidy of some non-spherical nuclei in cockroaches calculated from photometrically measured D.N.A. content. *Ohio J. Sci.*, **65**, 212–18.

4*

5 Metamorphosis and life-cycle

The rate of growth

The growth curves of weight plotted against time in *Bt.g.* are expressed by the formula $\ln W = a + bt + c \ln t$, where W = weight; t = time and a, b and c are constants of progression. If the weight at birth is ignored, the formula can be written $\ln W = bt + c \ln t$.[63] This formula is also applicable to linear growth changes in *Bt.g.*,[64] and shows that the rate of increase tends to decrease with time.[65] In *P.a.* most linear measurements increase at each moult by 22%[13,2] and the body weight approximately doubles, but the above formula also applies to this animal.[13] The growth of nymphs of *P.a.* is similar in both sexes,[58] but in *B.o.*, although the ages and stadia are reflected in the growth of the body, the sizes of the podomeres increase in geometrical progression in the female for all the six nymphal stadia, but for only the first five of the male. The pre-imaginal instar of the male does not have such a big increase as the five previous instars, and thus the dividing line, when the rate of growth is reduced, occurs at the imaginal moult in the female, but at the penultimate moult in the male.[57] In this species linear growth at each moult is stated to increase by 24%.[56]

The rate of growth obviously depends on adequate diet (T), and it is increased in *Bt.g.* by adding excreta to its food, but it is reduced by crowding[8] and in *B.o.* the average length and weight of the adults is lower in crowded animals than in those reared singly. The crowding effect is seen even where two are reared together.[23] In *Bt.g.* growth is reduced by repeated anaesthesia with CO_2,[4,5] N_2, NO_2, cyclopropane and ethyl ether,[5] and to far-red light.[1] Mitoses in the tissues of *Bt.g.* occur during the latter half of each nymphal stadium.[3]

The mortality of the embryos in *P.a.* is 6–8%[22] and that of the nymphs is 5–10%. The mortality rate of the nymphs of *B.o.* rapidly increases with crowding. The females of *P.a.* have a decreased longevity with increased number of oötheca produced.[17]

Antennae and cerci

The antennae in newly hatched *P.a.* have 47–49 articles and the third one acts as the centre of growth, forming new ones. The number of articles increases with age so that the adult has 178 in the male and 172 in the female. In later nymphs the terminal articles are about twice as long as the basal, newly formed ones, having had longer to grow.[7] The cerci of newly hatched nymphs of *P.a.* are about 3 mm long[25] and each has 3 articles, but whereas the male has the first article two or three times as long as the second, in the female the first is the shortest article. In the adults, the male cerci have 18–19 articles, and the female 13–14.[7]

Number of eggs and oöthecae

The number of eggs in each oötheca, the number of oöthecae produced by each female and the frequency of the production of the oöthecae seem to be very variable even within one species of cockroach (T). In *P.a.* the number of eggs in each oötheca is stated to be 18–28, with 22–24 being most common,[19] or 10 arranged in 2 rows,[10] or 15 in 2 rows of 8 and 7,[22] or an average of 13·6[15] or 10–16,[42] or an average of 12 and a maximum of 18,[17] or 16[13,39] or usually fewer than 16[50] or 13 (nymphs) in an average temperature of 24·4° or 15 (nymphs) in an average temperature of 27·3°[14] or 16, one from each of the 16 ovarioles.[6] The numbers of oöthecae produced by one female *P.a.* is said to be 9·5,[42] or an average of 21·5 (10–46),[22] 58 at 24·4° or 47 at 27·3°,[14] or often 30 (one every 6–8 days)[13] or 68 maximum.[39] Both number of eggs per oötheca and numbers of oöthecae per female are affected by the diet.[50]

In *B.o.* the figures are 12–18 eggs per oötheca,[42] or 13 (nymphs) at 24·4° and 8 (nymphs) at 27·3°[14] or 6–17.[47] The number of oöthecae per female is higher at higher temperatures, but is lower in older and unmated females;[45,46] the usual number is 1–4,[42] or 1–5[40] or 5 at 24·4° or 27·3°[14] or 12 at 17–19°, 22 at 22–24° and 20 at 30°.[45,46] In *Bt.g.* the number of eggs in each oötheca is 33 (nymphs) at 24·4° or 27 (nymphs) at 27·3° or the number decreases with the number of oöthecae produced per female, averaging 37·7,[60] or 37 (18–50),[48] or about 30[36] or 40,[39] or 30 (5–45) (nymphs);[24] the average number of oöthecae produced per female is 6·6.[60] In *Leucophaea maderae* there is an average of 33·8 eggs per oötheca,[9] or 5,[39] or 7·3 (2–12)[24] or 30 (18–43) (nymphs),[9] and in *Blaberus craniifer* 34·3.[60]

Oöthecal deposition

The females of *P.a.* are reported by most observers to take some care in deposition of their oöthecae, biting out a hollow in a suitable substrate such as cardboard or wood, and sticking the oötheca down with a secretion from the mouth.[10,20,22,26,43] The oötheca is arranged with the crista dorsal,[43] then covered with debris attached by more secretion.[20,22,26,43] The secretion is clear and therefore not saliva.[43] Exposed oöthecae are eaten[20,26] and some females eat all they lay.[17] Eggs are sometimes laid by *P.a.* without an oöthecae, but they all die.[16] The oöthecae of *B.o.* were seen by Qadri to be deposited in a pit or hollow dug by the females with their mandibles and fore-legs, and then covered over,[40] but Rau found that only 38 out of 90 oöthecae were covered (with mud) by the female.[41] He describes one female scooping out a hollow, depositing an oötheca, covering it with a clear sticky secretion from her mouth and then brushing sand over the whole area.[43]

The oöthecae must be carried by the female until the young are about to emerge if they are to survive in *Bt.g.*,[48,36] and in *Blaberus craniifer*.[29] The proximal end, but not the exposed distal end, of the oötheca of *Bt.g.* is permeable to water,[51] the eggs taking water from the female.[53] Oöthecae at least 1 day old removed from the female usually develop if the humidity is adequate[52] and especially if they are in contact with physiological saline.[33] The hatching depends on the rate of water loss (which is highest at 4–6 days of age) the amount of water present and the time required to finish development. Eggs within 1 day of eclosion usually hatch even without extraneous supplies of water.[52] Even in *P.a.* a damaged oötheca rapidly loses water, and the embryos die unless the relative humidity is 90% or more and they are not less than 3 days old.[51] The dry weight of eggs decreases during development, the actual increase in weight is due to water uptake either from the female or from the water deposited with the eggs in the oötheca.[53]

Most writers say that *Bt.g.* drops the oötheca anywhere when it is ready to hatch[36] and no maternal interference occurs unless no water is available, in which case the female will eat the young.[48]

In *P.a.* copulation may be required only once,[15] and the first oötheca is laid 3–7 days after copulation,[26] or, in June, 3 days after copulation,[22] or 1 week after the imaginal moult,[10] or 1–2 weeks after,[26] or 10–17 days after, providing the temperature is not less than 21°, or 16 (6–36) days after, or 20 (8–100) days after if kept in small containers.[17] Even in warm countries it may be 6·5 months before the first oötheca is produced if the adult moult takes place in November. The minimum temperature for egg laying was found to be 18° and 37% of those laid did not develop, with a much higher proportion in spring and autumn.[22] The period between the imaginal moult and the production of the first oötheca, the pre-oviposition period, is on the average 7·8 days in *Blaberus craniifer*, 19·8 days in *Leucophaea maderae*[60] and 10½ days at 30° and 35½ days at 18° in *B.o.*[47] In *Bt.g.* the first oötheca is produced 11–12 days after becoming adult and although one copulation may be all that is necessary in this cockroach the female will copulate several times and produces in her life-time 1–2[48] or 3–4 oöthecae.[62] The removal of an oötheca from a female accelerates the production of the next.[33] In *B.o.* the rhythm of oöthecal formation is mainly due to temperature, but is also influenced by fecundity, age and other individual factors.[45] The shortest time between any two oöthecae laid by *P.a.* is 3 days in summer and 5–9 days in spring and autumn,[22] but in *Bt.g.* they appear about every 22 days.[60]

P.a. may produce oöthecae and embryos parthenogenetically, all the offspring being females.[17,21,50,54] Of 25 oöthecae produced parthenogenetically by 3 females, 9 gave nymphs[17] and 500 nymphs were obtained from 2,433 oöthecae produced by virgin females. When these became adult they laid few eggs, which did not hatch[50] but sometimes female cockroaches produced parthenogenetically can mate and lay viable eggs which grow into apparently normal insects, although their growth rate is rather below normal.[60] Oöthecae can be produced parthenogenetically by *Bt.g.*, but in this case, although the embryos develop, they do not hatch.[54]

In hatching the seam of the oötheca of *Bt.g.* splits and the young wriggle out after several hours. The volume of the embryo doubles as the young swallow air to burst open the egg case and embryonic pellicle, but later the air escapes from the gut and they return to their original size.[36] In *Blaberus craniifer* probably pressure of the female stimulates the ripe embryos to swallow air inflating themselves to open the oötheca.[29] All the nymphs press open the oötheca by inflation[10] in *P.a.* also,[15,22] taking about 5 min[10] and the young eat the egg membranes[15] before leaving the oötheca.[22] The oötheca in *Blaberus giganteus* is membranous[38] and that of *B. craniifer* is eaten by the newly hatched young.[29]

Embryonic development

The number of days required for embryonic development in *P.a.* is 40–49,[42] or 77 in the dark at 25°[19] or 40–45,[10] or 39–99[39] or about 27,[26] or 88 at 17–18° or 34 at 27–28°,[22] or 33,[12] or 57·4 at normal temperatures,[16] or 58 at 24·4° and 41 at 27·3°[14] or 53 at 17–28°, or 40 at 29°,[17] or 57 at room temperature or 30 at optimum temperature of 30°.[13] The embryonic development of *B.o.* lasts 45–56 days[42] or 62 at 24·4° or 45 at 27·3°,[14] or 41 days at 30° and 65 days at 22°;[47] of *Bt.g.* 14–15 days at 35°[48] or 21·5[36] or 24–42,[39] or 23·1 (15–30),[24] or 28 at 24·4° and 20 at 27·3°[14] or 11–13,[44] or 17·2 days; and of *Leucophaea maderae* 58 days[60] or 30 at 24–25° and 50–70% R.H.,[49] or 74 (68–84) days.[9] The embryonic development period of *P.a.* is greatly influenced by temperature, but not relative humidity,[22] and it is reduced by 2·8 days for each rise of 0·56° average temperature.[16] In *Bt.g.* the variations in the length of this incubation period are due to temperature, food and other factors.[62]

Eclosion

The oöthecae of *P.a.* average $8 \times 5 \times 3·5$ mm, with a weight of 80 mg (44–105). Ninety per cent of this weight is the weight of the eggs.[22]

The percentage hatch of the oöthecae of *Bt.g.* is 76,[60] and in *P.a.* it is 63.[22]

The nymphal period

The number of moults required to reach maturity in *P.a.* is 13[15,16] or 11 for males and 12 for females,[18] or 7[2] or 10,[10,13] or 6,[22] or 13–18,[67] or 9–13 for females and 10–13 for males,[60] or variable.[26] The figures for other species of cockroaches are:

B.o. 8–12,[67] or 7,[40,58] or 7–9 for females and 8–10 for males,[60] or 10–11;[23]

Bt.g., 6,[65] or 7,[48] or 7–11,[67] or 6 usually and 7 on poor diets with reduced growth rate throughout life[55] or 6–7 for females and 5–7 for males;[60]

Blaberus giganteus, 7;[38]

Blaberus craniifer 10;[60]

Leucophaea maderae 7–8[60] or 8.[9]

The length of each of the stadia in *P.a.* is said to be about 14 days,[10] or 33 days,[2] but most writers think the earlier stadia are shorter than later ones; i.e. 1 week for the first and 4 for the second,[26] or 1–1½ months for the first and between 1 and 11 months for the others,[22] or 4 weeks for the first and 1–6 months for the later ones,[15] or less than 3 weeks for the first and more than 30 days for the last three,[4] or 18 days for the first and 50 for the tenth.[13] Comparable data for *Bt.g.* are 8 days for the second and 7–17 days for the seventh.[48] Reasons for the wide differences reported include the effect of the winter period, or other temperature variations, individual peculiarities[22] and the presence of other individuals.[60]

The total duration of the nymphal period in *P.a.* is reported as 4–5 months with an optimum temperature of 25–30°, or as long as 14–15 months,[10] or 22 $(13\frac{1}{2}–33\frac{1}{2})$ months for females and 22 $(12\frac{1}{2}–34)$ months for males,[22] or 396 days for females and 426 days for males,[15] or 470 (285–642) days,[16] or 134–813,[39] or 520 days at 24·4° and 225 at 27·3°,[14] or 251 days for females and 276 days for males,[18] or 12 months,[44] or 143–391 days for females and 212–400 days for males.[60]

For *B.o.* the figures are 12 (10–14) months at 25°[66] or 370–419 days for females and 364–432 days for males at 24–28°,[23] or about 320 days,[42] or 533 at 24·4°, or 316 at 27·3°,[14] or 279 days at 27·5°, or 8–10 months[44] or about 270 days for females and 170 for males when reared alone or 165 days for females and 146 for males reared in groups.[60]

For *Bt.g.* the figures are 3–5 months at 25°[66] or about 54 days,[44] or 49–212,[39] or 58·2 (43–90),[24] or 135 days at 24·4° and 95 days at 27·3°,[14] or 62 (55–68) days and the females taking longer than the males,[48] or 45–53 days for females and 38–72 days for males when reared alone, or 41 days for females and 40 for males when reared in groups.[60]

For *Blaberus craniifer* the figures are 277 days for females and 257 days for males, reared alone;[60] for *B. giganteus* 174 days for females and 167 days for males,[38] and for *Leucophaea maderae* 131–63 for females and 127 days for males reared alone or 150 days for females and 121 days for males reared in groups.[60]

Isolated rearing delays the times of moulting in *Bt.g.*[37] an effect found to apply also to *P.a.*, *B. craniifer*, *L. maderae*[60] and *B.o.*,[23, 60] but crowding does not alter the number of moults in *B.o.*,[23] while the total nymphal period of *Bt.g.* is much affected by the diet of the animal but not by its sex.[27, 28]

The time of moulting in *P.a.* is delayed by the process of regenerating a part of the body, the growth rate decreasing so that often an extra moult takes place.[67] A reduced growth rate occurs in these circumstances in *Bt.g.* also[55, 61] and about 30% of them undergo an extra moult.[65] It has been found that if a leg of *Bt.g.* is amputated before a critical time in the stadium, a whole new leg is regenerated at the next moult. If the amputation occurs after this time only a blastema or papilla is formed and while the formation of a new leg delays moulting, the formation of the papilla does not.[30] With repeated amputations and regenerations as many as six extra moults may be induced but the adult is still normal,[31] and it seems that injury of muscle tissue is necessary if the moulting process is to be effected.[32] Moulting is also delayed by transferring the animal from light to darkness, and vice versa.[37]

A regenerated tarsus always has four podomeres instead of five in *Bt.g.*,[61] but in *B.o.* this effect only occurs at a minimal region of the growth profile suggesting that the gradient of growth affects morphogenesis.[57]

Life span

The life span of the adults of *P.a.* has been variously given as: 12 $(\frac{1}{2}–21)$ months for females and for males 12 $(\frac{1}{2}–19)$ months,[22] or a maximum of 6 months,[42] or a maximum of 1,502 days,[39] or for females 441 days[16] or 441 days at 24·4° and 371 at 27·3°,[14] or 181 (90–706) days if kept with males or 295 days (91–362) days if kept without males.[17] *B.o.* has a life span as an adult of 44 days for females and 40 days for males, or 41 days,[35] or 110 days at 24·4° and 100 at 27·3°,[14] or at 17–19°, 273 days for females and 217 days for males, at 22–24° 273 for females and 264 days for males, and at 30° 113 days for females. If the insects are subject to alternate temperatures of 22–24° and 30°, their life span dropped to 17–33 days.[46] For *Bt.g.* the adult life is about 2 months[48] or 232 days at 24·4° and 145 at 27·3°,[14] or 384 days.[39]

The total life span for *P.a.* from deposition to death is $16\frac{1}{2}$–25 months[42] or 35–6 months[22] and 11 months from eclosion to death. For *B.o.* it is about 12 months from eclosion to death,[42] and for *Blaberus giganteus* 612 days or more days at 29·4°.[38] (Note: the data taken from reference 60 relate to animals kept at 30°, some with occasional periods of up to 36°, and the temperatures given for reference 14 are averages, like most of the others) (T).

The moulting process

The first sign of moulting in *P.a.* is the dulling of the usually glistening black eyes. They become eventually blue in colour with an opaque overcast just before moulting.[11] The volume of the blood increases at this time[59] and the specific gravity of the blood changes two days before moulting.[34] Moulting takes 5[15] to 10 minutes,[10,16] or 20 minutes at the imaginal moult[16] and the cast skin is eaten within the next 15 minutes,[15] or seldom eaten at all,[16] or not eaten by the second and third instars.[18] The head and thorax free themselves first and hold on while the cast cuticle is pushed back over the abdomen until this also is freed;[16] if the abdomen is freed first the animal dies.[10] The newly moulted nymphs are whitish[22] or yellowish in colour[10] and darken in a few hours[22] or a few days.[10]

The first instar has a body of almost constant width, and it is not until after the first moult that the abdomen becomes the broadest part of the body.[22] The wings are manifest in the third[10,15] or fourth[15] instar and the styli of the female nymphs are lost at the penultimate moult.[10,15]

The moulting of *Bt.g.* is similar to that of *P.a.*, the new instar becoming brown in 1 or 2 hr.[36] Their mortality in the earlier moults is about 5%, but in the last moult the rate rises to almost 40%.[48]

No attempt has been made in this chapter to disguise or hide the very large variations in the accounts of different authors. It seems probable that in *P.a.* the following figures are closer to the truth than most:

Number of eggs/oötheca   about 14
Number of oöthecae/female   about 40
Time between copulation and deposition of oötheca   about 5 days
Time required for embryonic development   about 45 days
Number of moults to maturity   about 12
Duration of nymphal period   about 1 year
Duration of adult period   about 1 year

REFERENCES

1. BALL, H. J. (1958). The effect of visible spectrum irradiation on growth and development in several species of insects. *J. econ. Ent.*, **51**, 573–8.
2. BIELLMANN, G. (1960). Étude du cycle des mues chez *Periplaneta americana*. *Bull. Soc. zool. Fr.*, **84**, 340–51.
3. BROOKS, M. A. (1956). Nature and significance of intracellular bacteroids in cockroaches. *Proc. 10th. Int. Congr. Ent.*, **2**, 311–14.
4. BROOKS, M. A. (1957). Growth retarding effect of CO_2 anaesthesia on the German cockroach. *J. Insect Physiol.*, **1**, 76–84.
5. BROOKS, M. A. (1965). The effects of repeated anaesthesia on the biology of *Blattella germanica*. *Entomologia exp. appl.*, **8**, 39–48.
6. BRUNET, P. C. J. (1951). The formation of the ootheca by *Periplaneta americana*. I. The microanatomy and histology of the posterior part of the abdomen. *Q. Jl microsc. Sci.*, **92**, 113–27.
7. BUGNION, E. (1922). The growth of the antennae and cerci of the cockroach *Periplaneta americana*. *Bull. Soc. ent. Égypte*, **1921**, 56–66.
8. CHAUVIN, R. (1946). Notes sur la physiologie comparée des Orthoptères. V. L'effet de groupe et la croissance larvaire des Blattes, des Grillons et du Phanéroptère. *Bull. Soc. zool. Fr.*, **71**, 39–48.
9. ENGELMANN, F. (1957). Bau und Funktion des weiblichen Geschlechtsapparates bei der ovoviviparen Schabe *Leucophaea maderae*, und einige Beobachtungen über die Entwicklung. *Biol. Zbl.*, **76**, 722–40.
10. FISCHER, O. (1928). Die Entwicklung von *Periplaneta americana*. *Mitt. naturf. Ges. Bern.*, **1927**, V–VII.
11. FLINT, R. A. and PATTON, R. L. (1959). Relation of eye color to molting in *Periplaneta americana*. *Bull. Brooklyn ent. Soc.*, **54**, 140.
12. GIER, H. T. (1936). The morphology and behaviour of the intracellular bacteroids of roaches. *Biol. Bull. mar. biol. Lab. Woods Hole*, **71**, 433–52.
13. GIER, H. T. (1947). Growth rate in the cockroach *Periplaneta americana*. *Ann. ent. Soc. Am.*, **40**, 303–17.
14. GOULD, G. E. (1941). The effect of temperature upon development of cockroaches. *Proc. Indiana Acad. Sci.*, **50**, 242–8.
15. GOULD, G. E. and DEAY, H. O. (1938). Biology of the American cockroach, *Periplaneta americana*. *Ann. ent. Soc. Am.*, **31**, 489–98.
16. GOULD, G. E. and DEAY, H. O. (1940). The biology of six species of cockroaches which inhabit buildings. *Bull. Purdue agric. Exp. Stn*, **451**, 3–13.
17. GRIFFITHS, J. T. and TAUBER, O. E. (1942). Fecundity, longevity and parthenogenesis of the American roach, *Periplaneta americana*. *Physiol. Zöol.*, **15**, 196–209.
18. GRIFFITHS, J. T. and TAUBER, O. E. (1942). The nymphal development of the roach. *Jl N.Y. ent. Soc.*, **50**, 263–72.
19. HABER, V. R. (1919). Cockroach pests in Minnesota with special reference to the German cockroach. *Bull. Minn. agric. Exp. Stn*, no. **186**.
20. HABER, V. R. (1920). Oviposition by the cockroach, *Periplaneta americana*. *Ent. News*, **31**, 190–3.
21. HAYDAK, M. H. (1953). Influence of the protein level of the diet on the longevity of cockroaches. *Ann. ent. Soc. Am.*, **46**, 547–60.
22. KLEIN, H. Z. (1933). Zur Biologie der amerikanischen Schabe (*Periplaneta americana*). *Z. wiss. Zool.*, **144**, 102–22.
23. LANDOWSKI, J. (1938). Der Einfluss der Einzelhaltung und des gemeinschaftlichen Levens auf die Entwicklung und das Wachstum der Larven von *Periplaneta orientalis*. *Biol. Zbl.*, **58**, 512–15.
24. MORISSET, P. (1946). Comportement de la blatte germanique dans un incubateur à température constante. *Annls ACFAS*, **12**, 88–9.

25. MULKERN, G. B. (1957). A study of growth and molting factors in cockroaches as indicated by allatectomy, spermatogenesis and integumental transplants. *Diss. Abstr.*, **17**, 1630.
26. NIGAM, L. N. (1933). The life-history of a common cockroach, *Periplaneta americana. Indian J. agric. Sci.*, **3**, 530–43.
27. NOLAND, J. L., LILLEY, J. H. and BAUMANN, C. A. (1949). A laboratory method for rearing cockroaches, and its application to dietary studies on the German roach. *Ann. ent. Soc. Am.*, **42**, 63–70.
28. NOLAN, J. L., LILLY, J. H. and BAUMANN, C. A. (1949). Vitamin requirements of the cockroach, *Blattella germanica. Ann. ent. Soc. Am.*, **42**, 154–64.
29. NUTTING, W. L. (1953). Observations on the reproduction of the giant cockroach, *Blaberus craniifer. Psyche*, **60**, 6–14.
30. O'FARRELL, A. F. and STOCK, A. (1953). Regeneration and the moulting cycle in *Blattella germanica*. I. Single regeneration initiated during the first instar. *Aust. J. biol. Sci.*, **6**, 485–500.
31. O'FARRELL, A. F., STOCK, A. and MORGAN, J. (1956). Regeneration and the moulting cycle in *Blattella germanica*. IV. Single and repeated regeneration and metamorphosis. *Aust. J. biol. Sci.*, **9**, 406–22.
32. O'FARRELL, A. F., STOCK, A., RAE, C. A. and MORGAN, J. A. (1960). Regeneration and development in the cockroach, *Blattella germanica. Čas. čsl. Spol. ent.*, **57**, 317–24.
33. PARKER, B. M. and CAMPBELL, F. L. (1940). Relative susceptibility of the oötheca and adult female of the German cockroach to liquid household insecticides. *J. econ. Ent.*, **33**, 610–14.
34. PATTON, R. L. (1962). The specific gravity of insect blood and its application to physiological problems. *J. Insect Physiol.*, **8**, 537–44.
35. PEARL, R. and MINER, J. R. (1935). Experimental studies on the duration of life. XIV. The comparative mortality of certain lower organisms. *Q. Rev. Biol.*, **10**, 60–79.
36. PETTIT, L. C. (1940). A roach is born. *New Engl. Nat.*, **7**, 15–18.
37. PETTIT, L. C. (1940). The effect of isolation on growth in the cockroach, *Blattella germanica. Ent. News*, **51**, 293.
38. PIQUETT, P. G. and FALES, J. H. (1953). Life-history of *Blaberus giganteus. J. econ. Ent.*, **46**, 1089–90.
39. POPE, P. (1953). Studies of the life histories of some Queensland Blattidae. Part 1. The domestic species. *Proc. R. Soc. Qd.*, **63**, 23–59.
40. QADRI, M. A. H. (1938). The life-history and growth of the cockroach, *Blatta orientalis. Bull. ent. Res.*, **29**, 263–76.
41. RAU, P. (1924). The biology of the roach, *Blatta orientalis. Trans. Acad. Sci. St. Louis*, **25**, 57–79.
42. RAU, P. (1940). The life-history of the American cockroach, *Periplaneta americana. Ent. News*, **51**, 121–4, 151–5, 186–9, 223–7, 273–8.
43. RAU, P. (1943). How the cockroach deposits its egg-case: a study in insect behaviour. *Ann. ent. Soc. Am.*, **36**, 221–6.
44. RAU, P. (1944). Incubation of eggs of *Blattella germanica. Can. Ent.*, **76**, 212.
45. RICCI, M. (1950). Note sulla biologia di *Blatta orientalis. Riv. Parassit.*, **11**, 219–31.
46. RICCI, M. (1951). Note sulla biologia di *Blatta orientalis. Rc. Ist. sup. Sanità*, **14**, 259–70.
47. RICCI, M. (1963). Su alcuni aspetti della biologia di *Blatta orientalis. Riv. Parassit.*, **24**, 185–98.
48. ROSS, H. H. (1929). The life-history of the German cockroach. *Trans. Ill. St. Acad. Sci.*, **21**, 84–93.
49. ROTH, L. M. and STAY, B. (1959). Control of oöcyte development in cockroaches. *Science*, **130**, 271–2.

50. ROTH, L. M. and WILLIS, E. R. (1954). The reproduction of cockroaches. *Smithson. misc. Collns.*, **122**, no. 12.
51. ROTH, L. M. and WILLIS, E. R. (1955). Water relations of cockroach oöthecae. *J. econ. Ent.*, **48**, 33–6.
52. ROTH, L. M. and WILLIS, E. R. (1955). Relation of water loss to the hatching of eggs from detached oötheca of *Blattella germanica*. *J. econ. Ent.*, **48**, 57–60.
53. ROTH, L. M. and WILLIS, E. R. (1955). Water content of cockroach eggs during embryogenesis in relation to oviposition behaviour. *J. exp. Zool.*, **128**, 489–510.
54. ROTH, L. M. and WILLIS, E. R. (1956). Parthogenesis in cockroaches. *Ann. ent. Soc. Am.*, **49**, 195–204.
55. SEAMANS, L. and WOODRUFF, L. C. (1939). Some factors influencing the numbers of moults of *Blattella germanica*. *J. Kans. ent. Soc.*, **12**, 73–6.
56. SHPET, G. I. (1934). On the problem of insect growth. *Zool. Zh.*, **13**, 195–206.
57. VOY, A. (1949). Sur la croissance des pattes de la Blatte *Blatta orientalis*. *C.r. hebd. Séance. Acad. Sci.*, *Paris*, **228**, 207–8.
58. VOY, A. (1951). Étude de la croissance chez deux espèces d'Orthoptèroïdes: *Blatta orientalis, Carausius morosus* (Br) (Phasmidae). *Bull. biol. Fr. Belg.*, **85**, 237–66.
59. WHEELER, R. E. (1962). Changes in hemolymph volume during the moulting cycle of *Periplaneta americana*. *Fedn Proc. Fedn Am. Socs exp. Biol.*, **21**, 123.
60. WILLIS, E. R., RISER, G. R. and ROTH, L. M. (1958). Observations on reproduction and development in cockroaches. *Ann. ent. Soc. Am.*, **51**, 53–69.
61. WOODRUFF, L. C. (1937). Autospasy and regeneration in the roach *Blattella germanica*. *J. Kans. ent. Soc.*, **10**, 1–9.
62. WOODRUFF, L. C. (1938). Observations on roach reproduction. *J. Kans. ent. Soc.*, **11**, 94–6.
63. WOODRUFF, L. C. (1938). Normal growth rate of *Blattella germanica*. *J. exp. Zool.*, **79**, 145–65.
64. WOODRUFF, L. C. (1939). Linear growth ratios for *Blattella germanica*. *J. exp. Zool.*, **81**, 287–98.
65. WOODRUFF, L. C. and SEAMANS, L. (1939). The rate of regeneration in the German roach. *Ann. ent. Soc. Am.*, **32**, 589–98.
66. ZABINSKI, J. (1928). Élevage des Blattides soumis à une alimentation artificielle. *C.r. Séance Soc. Biol.*, **98**, 73–7.
67. ZABINSKI, J. (1936). Inconstancy of the number of moults during post-embryonic development of certain Blattidae. *Annls Mus. zool. pol.*, **11**, 237–40.

ADDITIONAL REFERENCES

68. ADAIR, E. W. (1924). Notes sur *Periplaneta americana* et *Blatta orientalis*. *Bull. Soc. ent. Égypte*, **7**, 18–38.
69. BISHOP, J. and LAWSON, F. A. (1965). Correlation of testis development with external growth in the madeira cockroach. *J. Kans. ent. Soc.*, **38**, 248–53.
70. BUGNION, E. (1917). L'accroissement des antennes et des cerques de la blatte *Blatta americana*. *C.r. Séance. Soc. Biol.*, **80**, 317–24.
71. KUNKEL, J. G. (1966). Development and the availability of food in the German cockroach, *Blattella germanica* (L.). *J. Insect. Physiol.*, **12**, 227–35.
72. POHLEY, H. J. (1959). Experimentelle Beiträge zur Lenkung des Organentwicklung, des Häutungsrhythmus und der Metamorphose bei der Schabe *Periplaneta americana*. *Arch. EntwMech. Org.*, **151**, 323–80.
73. POHLEY, H. J. (1962). Untersuchungen Über die Veränderung der Metamorphoserate durch Antennenamputation bei *Periplaneta americana*. *Arch. EntwMech. Org.*, **153**, 492–503.

74. QUIAOIT, E. R. (1961). An investigation of growth, development and dimorphism in cockroaches. *Diss. Abstr.*, **22**, 950.
75. ROSS, M. H. and COCHRAN, D. G. (1960). A simple method for sexing nymphal German cockroaches. *Ann. ent. Soc. Am.*, **53**, 550–1.
76. ROTH, L. M. and HAHN, W. (1964). Size of new-born larvae of cockroaches incubating eggs internally. *J. Insect Physiol.*, **10**, 65–72.
77. SCOTT, H. (1929). On some cases of maternal care displayed by cockroaches and their significance. *Ent. mon. Mag.*, **65**, 218–22.
78. WHARTON, D. R. A., LOLA, J. E. and WHARTON, M. L. (1967). Population density, survival, growth, and development of the American cockroach. *J. Insect Physiol.*, **13**, 699–716.
79. WILLIS, E. R. and LEWIS, N. (1957). The longevity of starved cockroaches. *J. econ. Ent.*, **50**, 438–40.

6 The endocrine system, regeneration and tissue culture

The hormonal system and regeneration

Despite their advantages of size and availability, cockroach material has proved less attractive to insect endocrinologists than species drawn from the Diptera, Hemiptera or Lepidoptera.

Indeed, some of the work that has been done has raised more problems than it has solved, and this may have persuaded researchers in need of standardized material for detailed investigations to choose insects from the groups mentioned above. Nevertheless, cockroach endocrinology offers a good deal of scope, as shown by the work of Roth and his colleagues on the causal relationships involved in oöcyte production.

In the field of tissue culture and the study of regeneration cockroaches have proved a major source of material.

The structure of the retrocerebral complex (Figs. 6.1, 8.1)

A major part of the hormone-producing system of insects consists of neuro-secretory cells within the supraoesophageal neuromeres, and paired glands with axonal connections to some of them.

Willey's important paper[85] on this topic reviews much of the previous work, and sets out a detailed description of these structures in *P.a.* and *Blaberus craniifer*. The following brief account leans heavily on this work, although Nesbitt[52] and Cazal[13] should also be consulted by the reader.

In *P.a.* three pairs of nerves arise from the brain posteriorly and run to the corpora cardiaca (see Fig. 6.1). The corpora cardiaca are elongate, rather irregularly shaped bodies, the anterior region surrounding the aorta, and the dorsal part, which contains the transverse commissures, is continued posteriorly into a process from which the aortic nerves arise. The more important nerves of the corpora cardiaca are listed in the section dealing with the topography of the nervous system. Ventrally, the corpora cardiaca are connected to a very slightly developed hypocerebral or oesophageal ganglion, and further posteriorly there is a broad connection on each side with a corpus allatum. The corpora allata are roughly oval, and joined beneath the oesophageal nerve by a transverse commissure. They possess nerves to the suboesophageal ganglion and the prothoracic gland.

The first nerve of the corpora cardiaca has been shown to arise from groups of neurosecretory cells within the pars intercerebralis (Fig. 6.2) in a variety of

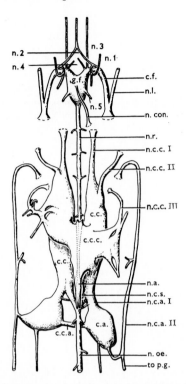

FIG. 6.1   Dorsal view of the stomodaeal nervous system of *Periplaneta americana*. Abbreviations: c.c.—corpus cardiacum, c.c.c.—corpus cardiacum commissure, c.a.—corpus allatum, c.c.a.—corpus allatum commissure, c.f.—frontal connective, g.f.—frontal ganglion, n.a.—aortic nerve, n.c.a. I and II—nerves of the corpus allatum, n.c.c. I, II and III—nerves of the corpus cardiacum, n.con.—nervus connectivus, n.c.s.—nervus cardiostomatogastricus, n.l.—labral nerve, n.oe.—oesophageal nerve, n.r.—recurrent nerve, p.g.—prothoracic gland. (From Willey[85])

insect material, and this is so in *P.a.* Willey describes three such groups (I–III) associated with the first nerve lying in the anterior region of the pars inter-cerebralis. Posteriorly two further groups of cells (IV and V) contribute fibres to the second nerve of the corpora cardiaca. Group IV includes some strikingly large cells, and one larger than the rest has an axon passing ventrally in one of the descending fibre tracts and a collateral to the central body. This cell may be neurone 19 of Bretschneider (see Chapter 8). The origin of the 10 or so fibres forming the third nerve of the corpora cardiaca is obscure. The first nerve con-tains about 40 fibres, 20 μ or so thick, as well as many smaller ones, and the second nerve contributes 7–8 fibres, 1·5–2 μ in diameter. Many branches are formed within the corpora cardiaca adjacent to the aortic lumen. According to Willey, most of the intrinsic cells of the corpora cardiaca do not stain with silver nitrate or paraldehyde fuchsin, but show an affinity for eosin and phloxin. Guthrie

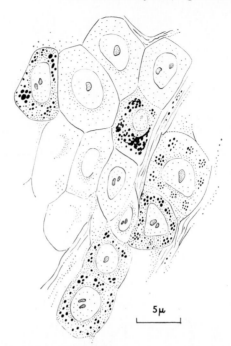

FIG. 6.2   Neurosecretory cells from the pars intercerebralis of *Periplaneta americana* (last instar larva), stained with paraldehyde fuchsin. The intracellular neuro-secretory granules exhibit various degrees of regularity in their arrangement

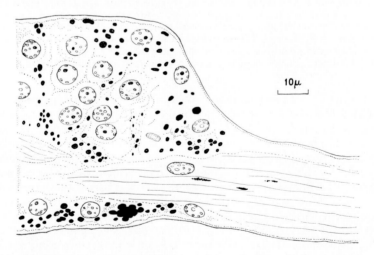

FIG. 6.3   Neurosecretory material in the corpus cardiacum (larval *P.a.*). Paralde-hyde fuchsin

obtained intense staining of neurosecretory material (Fig. 6.3), but the cells themselves did not appear stained. Willey and Chapman[86] were able to show details of ultra-structure with the electron microscope. The cytoplasm contains an abundant endoplasmic reticulum, and large secretory granules up to 6000 Å in diameter. The nucleus is large in relation to the cytoplasm. Willey discussed evidence in support of the claim that the large bulbous sacs visible at the periphery of the gland are part of the intrinsic cells.

Compared with the cells of the corpora cardiaca those of the corpora allata have restricted areas of granules, more abundant mitochondria, and they have interdigitating cell membranes. The outer connective tissue membrane of the corpus allatum is only 0·5 μ thick, while that of the corpus cardiacum is at least 2 μ.

The question of the possible presence of neurosecretory cells within the frontal ganglion is unresolved. For further details on the fine structure of retrocerebral cells consult Scharrer[74] and von Harnack's[40] work on *Leucophaea*. In addition to *P.a.*, Willey[85] examined *B.o.*, *Cryptocercus punctulatus*, *Leucophaea maderae*, *Blaberus craniifer*, *B. giganteus* and *Diploptera punctata*, and found them to differ only on small points of anatomical detail.

The structure of the prothoracic gland

Scharrer[72] first described the gland in cockroaches using *Leucophaea maderae*. In her paper she gives a number of excellent illustrations of the histology of the gland to which the reader should refer. In *Leucophaea* the gland consists of two rope-like masses of cells crossing just in front of the prothoracic ganglion. Each gland originates anteriorly near the cranial end of the first cervical sclerite and is inserted posteriorly on the contralateral coxal margin. The gland cells are arranged as a flat layer 4–12 cells wide about a central core of 6–8 muscle fibres. Intravitam methylene blue staining shows that a branch of the fourth nerve enters the organ posteriorly, and finer nerve branches comprising axons and sheath cells can be seen to ramify in the organ. While it is difficult to make this out with certainty, this author (D.G.) is of the opinion that in *P.a.* axons definitely invade the glandular layer. Scharrer observed granules of different sizes within the gland cells that stained with methylene blue and also with osmium tetroxide. She concluded that they were of a lipid nature. A tracheal trunk runs the length of the organ.

In *P.a.*, as shown by Bodenstein[8] and Chadwick,[14] the organ is similar but rather less robust. The caudal division on each side between attachments to nerve and to the coxa is seldom as pronounced as it is in *L. maderae*. Bodenstein gives a series of photographs showing stages in the degeneration of the gland following the last metamorphic moult, and Chadwick figures the organ in situ as it would be exposed for an experiment involving its removal (Fig. 6.4). According to Chadwick, Bodenstein has observed a similar organ in *B.o.*

Other cockroaches in which an essentially similar structure has been found are: *Cryptocercus punctulatus*, *Blaberus craniifer* and *Bt.g.*—by Nutting;[53] *P. australasiae*, *P. brunnea*, *P. fuliginosa*, *Blatella vaga*, *Supella supellectilium*, *Eurycotis floridana, Nauphoeta cinerea, Pycnoscelus surinamensis, Neostylopyga rhombifolia* and *Diploptera dytiscoides*—by Chadwick.[14]

Chadwick points out that many of these species are less suitable for extirpation experiments than *P.a.*, due to the fact that there tend to be more supernumerary branches in their glands, and these cannot be removed with certainty.

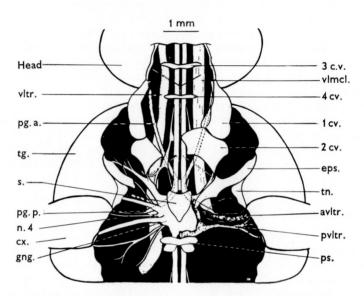

FIG. 6.4   Ventral view of the prothoracic gland and surrounding structures. Dashed lines indicate the position of cuts to be made if attempting to remove the gland. Abbreviations: avltr.—principal anterior ventral leg trachea, 1c.v. . . . 4c.v.—first . . . fourth cervical selerite, cx.—coxa, eps.—episternum, gng.—prothoracic ganglion, n.4—fourth prothoracic segmental nerve with small branch innervating the prothoracic gland, pg.a.—anterior limb of prothoracic gland, pg.p.—posterior limb of prothoracic gland, ps.—poststernum, pvltr.—principal posterior ventral leg trachea, s.—sternum, tg.—tergum, tn.—trochantin, vlmcl.—ventral longitudinal muscle, vltr.—ventral longitudinal tracheal trunk. (From Chadwick[14])

The cervical glands

The ventral glands of insects, which are the major source of the moulting hormone, have been observed to arise in the region of the labium. In many of the less specialized Hemimetabolous orders these glands form compact structures in the ventral part of the head, and while there is not a great deal of experimental evidence as to their function, the phasing of mitotic activity and timing of degeneration suggest that they possess a similar function to the ventral glands of the prothorax. In the much more investigated species belonging to the higher Hemimetabola and the Holometabola, the ventral glands have moved posteriorly into the thorax.[83]

According to Rae and O'Farrell,[60] some of the Dictyoptera occupy an intermediate position between these two conditions, in that both cephalic (near cervical region) and thoracic glands are present in the larvae.

Following the work of Bodenstein[5] and Chadwick,[14] who showed that removal of the prothoracic glands did not prevent moulting in cockroaches, Rae[59] discovered glandular tissue of a similar type arranged in the form of a pair of ovoid bodies near the edge of the foramen magnum. Rae found these cervical glands in *P.a.* and *Bt.g.*, and his microphotographs show that each gland consists of an inner zone of small cells with large nuclei, and an outer zone of large cells with a glandular appearance. In the centre of the organ is a cavity lined with cuticle, from which fine ducts pass into the inner cell layer. The organ is richly tracheated. That this organ in the cockroach has an endocrine function has yet to be convincingly demonstrated.

THE PHYSIOLOGY OF THE ENDOCRINE ORGANS

1. The brain-prothoracic gland system

Scharrer showed that the prothoracic gland degenerated shortly after metamorphosis in *Leucophaea maderae*, and had a clearly glandular appearance.[72] Bodenstein followed this up by showing that in *P.a.* the metamorphic moult was dependent on a diffusible factor in the blood which caused implanted limbs to moult synchronously with the host. Active prothoracic glands implanted into an adult caused the host insect to moult again forming a giant adult, and where a limb had been regenerating in the operated insect this could be exteriorized at the additional moult. It was found that inclusion of fragments of corpus cardiacum augmented the effect of the prothoracic glands, presumably by supplying small quantities of brain hormone. Two pairs of nymphal prothoracic glands are required for the production of a post-adult moult.

Towards the end of each instar the neurosecretory cells of the pars intercerebralis in *P.a.* can easily be seen after staining with paraldehyde fuchsin, and the secretion can easily be traced to the descending axons, and eventually appears in large quantities in the peripheral layers of the corpora cardiaca (examine Fig. 6.3).[35]

However, there is one striking anomaly. As shown by Bodenstein,[5] Nutting[53] and Chadwick,[14] removal of the nymphal prothoracic glands does not prevent the operated insect moulting or the regeneration of damaged structures. Chadwick discusses the possible significance of these findings in his second paper and comes to the conclusion that another source of ecdysone must be present in the cockroach, so far undiscovered.

The prothoracic gland normally degenerates a few days after metamorphosis in *L. maderae* and *P.a.*, according to Scharrer[73] and Bodenstein[5] respectively.

Considerable quantities of ecdysone can be extracted from the excrement of a number of species, mainly from the larvae. Hoffmeister, Rufer and Ammon showed that the number of Calliphora units per 1 mg of methanol extract was 5,000 in *P.a.* as compared with 20,000 in the larvae of *Locusta migratoria* or 200 in Bombyx larvae.[44]

According to Fraenkel and Hsiao, the tanning of the adult cuticle which occurs a short while after the metamorphic moult is probably due to the secretion into the blood of a hormone, to which they gave the name bursicon. They were able to demonstrate it in *P.a.*, as well as in blowflies, and compared the concentration of hormone in different organs of *P.a.* Appreciable quantities were found in all parts of the central nervous system, none in the prothoracic gland and the largest amounts in the corpora cardiaca. It appears to be quite distinct from ecdysone. The pars intercerebralis cells (median cells) with axons in the corpora cardiaca are suggested by the authors as the main source of the hormone, although its wide distribution is enigmatic. In the cockroach the hormone is present in both adults and larvae, rather than just for a brief period round about emergence, as in the blowfly. The authors are cautious as to the actual rôle of roach tanning factor on the roach cuticle as tests were made using blowflies as the assay subjects. Evidence is produced that suggests that the hormone is a protein.[29]

Earlier, Bodenstein and Sprague had produced evidence to suggest that the development of the proteinaceous secretion of the left colleterial gland was controlled by corpus allatum hormone—neotenin—[9] but Fraenkel and Hsiao contend that no juvenile hormone is found in the adult roach.[29] Bodenstein and Sprague did demonstrate convincingly that the differentiation of the colleterial gland is dependent on prothoracic gland hormone. Anlagen transplanted into adults will not develop further unless prothoracic glands are implanted.[9]

Bodenstein was able to show by parabiotic experiments that prothoracic gland hormone had a positive effect on leg regeneration in *P.a.*,[7] and Marks and Reinecke showed a similar effect in tissue culture experiments, prothoracic ganglion being as effective as brain fragments in stimulating prothoracic gland activity.[49]

2. The corpora allata

The early work of Scharrer on *Leucophaea maderae* demonstrated that the secretion of the corpora allata determined juvenile characteristics in the larva and was responsible for oöcyte development and the secretions of secondary sexual organs in the adult.[72, 76]

Bodenstein and Sprague used the high sensitivity of the colleterial gland to neotenin to detect small quantities of the hormone. They transplanted glands and classified them eventually on a scale of 4 (0–3), 3 indicating tubules very full of secretion. Insects which had been allatectomized still showed traces of secretion; this is interesting in view of the possibility of alternative hormone sources. The interaction of ecdysone and neotenin is well shown by the responses of this organ; a high enough allatum titer reducing organ differentiation to a minimum in the presence of ecdysone.[9]

Lüscher and Engelmann have tried to investigate in more detail the changes in the corpora allata which must be associated with its declining output of neotenin, thus allowing the final moult to be a metamorphic one. They used estimates of total glandular volume and the density of nuclei to determine whether the fall in activity was simply a case of negative allometry or involved active inhibition.

Nuclear and volume measurements were combined to give a value known as the activity volume (difference between the volume of the gland, and the minimal volume of a gland with the same number of nuclei). This appears to be a measure of cytoplasmic volume.[47,48] Scharrer and von Harnack had shown earlier that the histology of the corpora allata in *L. maderae* varied with its secretory activity.[77]

The activity volume decreases during early larval life, but increases rapidly during the third instar, and drops to zero during the last instar. This suggests active inhibition and the authors found that if the corpus allatum nerves were sectioned the activity volume was maintained, and supernumerary larval moults occurred.

Killing of a number of the pericardial cells, shown by Engelmann and Lüscher in an earlier paper[27] to be implicated in corpus allatum function, had a similar effect to section of the corpus allatum nerve in maintaining the activity volume. Nevertheless, the idea put forward in the earlier paper that the pericardial cells produce a factor inhibiting corpus allatum activity and thus favouring metamorphosis was not borne out in detail by the later experiments.

That a secretion of the corpora allata had a gonadotrophic effect was first demonstrated by Scharrer in *L. maderae*,[78] and later found to be true of a variety of other species (see Fig. 6.5). The effect is reliable enough to have been

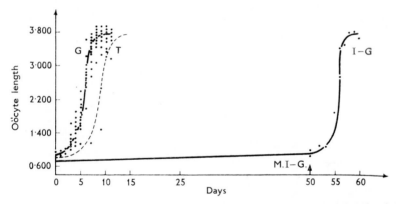

FIG. 6.5   Delay in oöcyte growth due to a supernumerary moult. Growth of the oöcyte (in mm) after the final moult (tenth) is slightly precocious in insects with implanted corpora allata (G), as compared with controls (T). But where a supernumerary instar (eleventh) has resulted from the implantations (I–G), oöcyte growth has been delayed till after final moult (arrow). M.I-G—metamorphosis of giant imagos. (From Girardie[32])

made the basis for an assay method by Bowers, Thompson and Uebel, who showed that a number of epoxy analogues of farnesol had much greater gonadotrophic effects than farnesol itself. The identification of farnesol with neotenin has been prevented by the relative ineffectiveness of the hormone mimic. 10,11-Epoxy farnesenic acid methyl ester was found to be 1,000 times as effective as farnesol, and effective concentrations are near those for crystalline silkworm ecdysone.[11] Oöcyte development is under the control of the corpora allata, and the oöcyte growth can be measured by the increase in weight, or by measurements of oöcyte length (Girardie).[32] While the substances involved in oöcyte development undoubtedly consist largely of protein, so far only the mobilization of fats has been demonstrated. Bodenstein and Sprague[9] noted that there were increased deposits of fat in the fat bodies of allatectomized roaches, and Gilbert (cited by Wigglesworth) has shown that the juvenile hormone induces synthesis of ovarian lipids in the fat body.[30] This topic was investigated in more detail by Vroman, Kaplanis and Robbins, who followed rate of appearance of ^{14}C in the lipid fractions after injection as acetate. Following allatectomy they found 66% more total lipid than in controls. The major lipid group in normal insects was triglyceride, and the proportion of triglyceride increased with allatectomy, but the turnover of triglycerides and phospholipids decreased following operation most notably in the former group. These results suggest the effects of reduced utilization, as ovarian lipid has been shown to be 70% triglyceride (Fig. 6.6).[81]

The effects of food, mating and carrying oöthecae have been investigated by authors using several species; in the viviparous cockroach *Diploptera punctata* (Roth and Stay),[66] *Nauphoeta cinerea* and *Pycnoscelus surinamensis* (Roth),[61,62,63] *Leucophaea maderae* (Roth;[62] Engelmann and Rau[28]) and *Byrsotria fumigata*

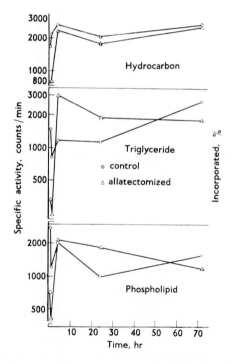

FIG. 6.6   The effect of allatectomy on the turnover of different lipid fractions in *P.a.* (females). (From Vroman, Kaplanis and Robbins[81])

(Barth[2]). In *L. maderae* a centre in the brain affects the receptivity of the females to males. Under conditions of starvation it is inactive in *L. maderae*, but starvation has no effect on the receptivity of *N. cinerea*, although the oöcytes may not develop. In *N. cinerea* spermatophoral stimulation at mating makes the insects unreceptive and augments oöcyte development. Development of the oötheca causes stretching of the uterus wall, and this is followed by reduction of oöcyte development. This inhibitory effect of uterine stretch receptors is not effective before the first ovulation (*N. cinerea* and *P. surinamensis*).

Diploptera punctata differs from the above species in that mating stimuli are the only factor required for the activation of the corpora allata and the development of the oöcytes.

The rôle of the corpora allata in mating behaviour was investigated in more detail in *N. cinerea* by Roth. He found that mating involved the female feeding on the tergal gland of a displaying male, and this was initiated by the activity of the corpora allata. Mating results in loss of receptivity by suppressing feeding behaviour. Transection of the nerve cord just before or after mating may result in excessive sexual behaviour, suggesting that pathways in the nerve cord may exist capable of damping down the humoral effects.[61]

At one time Roth seemed uncertain whether a pheromone was involved in mating in *N. cinerea*,[61] but more recently he has shown this to be so.[67] In addition, the male may stimulate the female by song (see sound production, p. 249).

In *B.g.* Roth showed that a chemical attractant picked up by contact chemo-receptors was released by the female, and in *B. fumigata* Barth presented good evidence for sex pheromones. A volatile sex pheromone is produced by the females, controlled by the corpora allata. Its production is prevented by alla-tectomy. Successful matings could be shown to depend on an adequate supply of the pheromone. The question of the possible rôle of the corpora allata in various aspects of male reproduction was also investigated by Barth, and no effect of allatectomy could be demonstrated.[1]

A further possible effect of corpus allatum secretion is provided by the work of Sägesser who showed that juvenile hormone may maintain the high larval level of oxygen consumption.[68] Wigglesworth, however, argues that this effect of allatectomy may well be an indirect one, and does not necessarily support the idea of a metabolic hormone.[83]

3. Secretions of the corpora cardiaca

In the cockroach the corpora cardiaca are sufficiently separate from the corpora allata to make their removal without parts of the latter organ a practical proposition.

Corpora cardiaca extracts applied to the central nervous system markedly increased activity in peripheral nerves and connectives according to Milburn, Weiant and Roeder.[51] They suggested that the substance might act by suppressing the activity of inhibitory fibres originating at the suboesophageal level. The extracts may be preserved by quick freezing, and their potency lasts longer if they are heated to between 90 and 100° for 5 min, although prolonged heating decreases potency. The substance does not affect sensory-interneurone synapses.

A variety of biologically active substances were tested for comparison with extract of corpus cardiacum but none had a similar effect. These substances were: DDT, DDT-toxin ethyl alcohol, picrotoxin, pilocarpine, DFP, *d*-tubocurarine, eserine, 5-hydroxytryptamine, 5-hydroxytryptophane, lysergic acid diethylamide, γ-aminobutyric acid, catechol, adrenaline, noradrenaline, dopamine, reserpine, strychnine and tetanus toxin. The last two substances have the effect of blocking the action of corpus cardiacum extract.

That the corpus cardiacum secretes substances affecting the contractility of visceral muscle was first shown by the work of Cameron. Cameron showed that these substances affected the musculature of the gut, the malpighian tubules and the heart.[12]

Recent work by Davey has helped to demonstrate the nature and mode of action of the factors involved. He showed that the heart tissues contained a substance necessary for the heart-accelerating effect of corpus cardiacum extract which appeared to be exhausted by prolonged exposure to the hormone. Excised heart preparations responded by 20% increase in rate of beat which declined to normal after three hours, but addition of fresh extract had little effect. Exposure of the heart to Trypan blue, Carmine or Indian ink clogged the pericardial cells, and greatly decreased the effect of the extract. Davey suggests that the corpus cardiacum factor causes the pericardial cells to release the cardio-accelerator.[16]

Cockroaches fed a 10% glucose solution show an immediate increase in heart-beat rate of 13–21%, and this is not affected by allatectomy or sectioning the nerve cord. Pericardial blockage, or removal of the corpus cardiacum on the other hand, prevents this effect. By waxing and burning techniques the nervous pathway involved was shown to consist of labral receptor fibres, passing to the brain in the labral nerve with connections to the frontal ganglion and by the recurrent nerve to the corpora cardiaca.[17]

The nature of the substances involved was investigated by Davey who showed that the secretion of the corpus cardiacum was probably a peptide, while the substance produced by the pericardial cells was an *o*-dihydroxy-indolalkylamine. Since it was believed that the latter substance was elaborated from an inert precursor, stages in secretion were looked for among pericardial cells exposed to corpus cardiacum extract. Under these conditions the cells become markedly larger, and the nuclei send out branches to the peripheral cytoplasm. Secretory droplets appear near the nuclei and then more gradually in the cytoplasm. At a later stage small residual droplets may be seen near the cell membrane. During their secretory cycle the pericardial cells can be shown to contain argentaffin granules, a significant similarity to vertebrate cells of similar function. The decline in effectiveness of corpora cardiaca extract on the heart cells coincides with decreased histological evidence of secretion in pericardial cells following long exposure.[18] This suggests the depletion of some, perhaps nuclear, precursor. This cardiac accelerator can be released by enforced activity, when it appears in effective quantities in the blood.[20] Hodgson and Geldiay demonstrated the depletion of NSM from the corpus cardiacum following enforced activity or electrical stimulation, and correlated this with the decreasing effectiveness of corpora cardiaca extracts to inhibit central nervous activity.[43]

By the use of amino acid decarboxylase inhibitors such as semicarbazide hydrochloride and isonicotinic acid hydrazide, Davey showed that the normal response of the heart to corpora cardiaca extract could be reduced, thus supporting the idea that a decarboxylase was involved in the formation of the pericardial amine.[21]

An adrenergic substance from the corpus cardiacum has been demonstrated by Barton-Browne *et al.*, following electrical stimulation,[3] and this appears to be a separate substance to the cardiac accelerator investigated by Davey.

A similar relationship to that existing between the corpus cardiacum and the pericardial cells may involve the endocrine glands and secretory cells in the hind-gut. Davey was able to demonstrate increased regularity, tonus, amplitude and frequency in the spontaneous contractions of suspended hind-gut preparations, following treatment with corpora cardiaca extracts (see Fig. 6.7).[19] Bromolysergic acid diethylamide inhibits this effect, and this points to the involvement of a tryptamine derivative such as an indolalkylamine.[19]

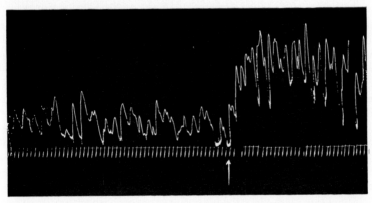

FIG. 6.7 The effect of corpus cardiacum extract on rhythmic spontaneous contractions of the hind-gut. There is increase in tonus, frequency and amplitude. The time marker is at 10 sec. (From Davey[19])

Other neurosecretory cells

Wall and Ralph have shown that neurosecretory cells in *B.a.* may produce an anti-diuretic hormone under conditions of dehydration or injection of 4 N NaCl. Cells in the pars intercerebralis and in the thoracic ganglion can be seen to contain neurosecretory granules when the insects have been subjected to this treatment. Later work showed that recta from *P.a.* could be studied in vitro. Extracts from the corpora allata, metathoracic and some abdominal ganglia from hydrated insects increased water reabsorption by the recta of hydrated animals, and a similar effect was produced by extracts of brain and prothoracic ganglia from dehydrated animals.[82] One of the most striking examples of neurosecretory action has been provided by the work of Harker,[36, 38] Harker and Brown.[39] She showed that a cockroach with a well-developed diurnal rhythm of activity, if joined parabiotically to an arhythmic cockroach (*P.a.*), induced its own rhythm in its partner. Arhythmic insects were produced by exposure to continuous light or dark. Transplantation of suboesophogeal ganglia from a rhythmic to an arhythmic insect had a similar effect, a rhythm being induced in the host that lasted for three days or so. It was shown that by painting over the eyes and ocelli, photic stimuli especially via the ocelli provided the input necessary for the initial timing of secretion. Cooling the suboesophageal ganglion in situ (Harker and Brown) delayed the activity cycle, but histological evidence of secretion so readily demonstrated in other neurosecretory cycles could not be found.[39]

REGENERATION, WOUND HEALING AND TISSUE CULTURE

Many of the earlier papers on regeneration in insects described experiments on Phasmids, or Mantids (Suster, Friedrich), but for studies on limb-bud formation the semi-transparent limbs of cockroaches offer considerable advantages, and operations on the nervous system can draw on an extensive background of knowledge. The regeneration of appendages, the peripheral and central nervous system, the gut and the tracheal system have been studied.

Bodenstein[7] gives a clear picture of the events that lead to the formation of a new limb in larvae of *P.a.* When the leg is removed distal to the trochantero-femoral articulation, a new limb can be reconstituted after the next moult if the period of regrowth is sufficiently long. The progress of the limb primordium can be seen through the wall of the coxa. Up to 5 days after amputation little change is visible, but after 7 days a small bud can be seen at the distal extremity of the coxa, and some of the coxal muscles undergo regression. At 14 days a tubular primordium doubled on itself, and about one-third to one-quarter the length of the coxa is evident, and this gradually increases to half the coxal length at 28 days (stage 7). Thirty-two days after amputation the new limb may occupy much of the coxal cavity, and extend to three-quarters or more of the coxal length.

When moulting takes place the limb is exteriorized through the trochanter.

In the adult there is no sign of limb regrowth up to 4 months after amputation, and there is little doubt that the absence of growth hormone is responsible, as shown by the tissue culture experiments of Marks and Reinecke.[49]

The origin of the limb-bud cells was shown to be in part from de-differentiated muscle cells, as removal of coxal muscle reduced the size of the regenerated limb according to Bodenstein.

That adult insects can regenerate a limb if blood hormone levels are altered to promote growth and moulting was shown by Bodenstein in parabiosis experiments, and by the implantation of prothoracic glands. The effects on growth and moulting are separable in that more glands have to be implanted to produce moulting than to initiate the early stages of regeneration.[7]

No evidence was found for the presence of a factor produced by the wound surface accelerating regeneration, or for a specific nerve supply being necessary for limb regeneration, as postulated for some other animals (Needham).

O'Farrell and Stock[54,55,56,57] investigated the question of the length of the pre-moult growth period necessary for regeneration in more detail, and found that a control situation existed between the endocrine system and the regenerate in *Bt.g.* An all-or-nothing growth response follows tarsal removal. Before the critical period removal results in a 4- or 5-segmented tarsus, after this only a minute papilla is exteriorized at the following moult. Intermediates total less than 1%. This suggests an effect of hormone level on the regenerate. However, amputation over a certain time range before the critical period could delay the moult, indicating a feed-back effect from limb to glands.

Removal of the cercus, on the other hand, does not result in all-or-nothing regeneration and intermediate-sized regenerates occur. No effect on the moulting cycle was observed.[57]

O'Farrell and Stock also believed they could distinguish different limb regions in the primordium sufficiently well to see that regeneration proceeded proximo-distally following amputations before the critical period, and in the reverse polarity if made after the critical period.

The formation of muscles within the limb primordia was investigated with cytochemical techniques by Cowden and Bodenstein, but the findings were not compared with muscle formation during normal development and must be accounted of general rather than specific interest (see Chapter 10). The elementary myotubes were believed to fuse to form syncytial fibres, rather than to acquire additional nuclei by amitoses. An interesting point to be compared with Cohen and Jacklet's findings[15] on nerve cells was that at an early stage the myotube nuclei were surrounded by a cytoplasmic zone of high RNA content, suggesting localized protein synthesis.

Little attention was paid to the regenerative capacity of the insect nervous system before Bodenstein observed the effect of sectioning peripheral nerves and central connectives in *P.a.* Both adults and larvae exhibited considerable powers of regeneration, new fibres or fibre branches sprouting from the severed ends of connectives and nerves, and invading other parts of the nervous system and muscles in the course of 4–6 weeks. Histological studies showed that haemocytes gathered between the stumps and formed a physical bridge which the new fibres traversed after 11–57 days. The formation of this blood cell aggregate may, he suggested, govern the rapidity with which the union of the stumps occurs. The course of axon regeneration is reflected in the excitability of the coxal muscles as shown by electrical stimulation, and external recording techniques. Very little difference was detected between adults and larvae. Up to 5 days after nerve section the coxal muscles remained inexcitable, and this inexcitability lasted to 56 days in adults, 67 days in larvae. In this second positive phase the muscle potentials again appeared and muscular contractions followed stimulation.

When a ganglion was removed altogether fine axon processes grew out from the connectives, some of them into the denervated limb, but very atypical connections were established.

A thoracic ganglion transplanted into the coxa of another insect survived and appeared to make functional contacts with the muscles, which remained excitable after the host nerves had been cut.[8]

Guthrie examined the relative growth capability of larval and adult nerves and found that adults formed functional connections with comparatively distant muscles such as the tibial depressor[34] much less readily than larvae after, section of n.5.

Crushed nerves (n.5) regenerated more rapidly (2–4 weeks), than cut nerves (3–6 weeks), and similar differences were observed by Case[12] on the spiracular nerves (crushes 9–15 days, cut nerves 16–32 days).

A very few adult larval parabioses appeared to demonstrate increased adult regenerative growth after section.[34]

Electron micrographs of stump junctions appeared to show much reduced glial cell investment (Fig. 6.8), and this often corresponded to a region in which the maximum conduction velocities fell from 6 m/sec to 3 m/sec or less. In the stump before union lysosomes are often abundant, and small bundles of collagen fibres occur, presumably before incorporation into the neural lamella[35] (Fig. 6.9).

Attempts were made to incorporate ganglia into the course of a severed fifth nerve. This was successful using either abdominal or thoracic ganglia, but only thoracic ganglia made functional connections with local musculature (Fig. 6.10). While recording from these implanted ganglia was hampered by the growth of overlying tissues there was no doubt that local facilitating pathways could be formed through them[33].

Reinnervated muscles often gave greater isometric tensions to maximal motor nerve stimulation than were observed in the normal unoperated muscles. This may be due to an extension of the limited slow fibre innervation, in terms of whole muscle fibres, or an extension of fast fibre innervation, in terms of additional endplates on fibres already innervated.

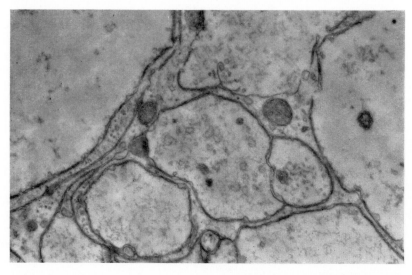

FIG. 6.8   Region of the stump junction in a mended nerve 6 weeks after severance, characterized by the very simple condition of the interaxonal sheath material. Contrast with Fig. 8.13. × 16,000

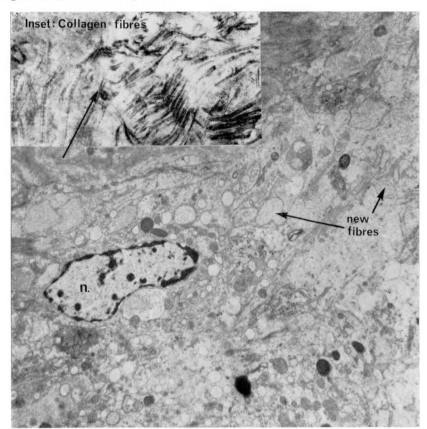

FIG. 6.9   Reconstruction zone in a regenerating nerve stump (n.5) 3 weeks after
severance. Areas of new collagen and nerve fibres can be seen. × 9,200

Wigglesworth observed that section of a major nerve caused changes in the
ganglionic cell bodies with axons in the nerve. The dictyosomes and associated
tubular structures undergo changes in density when stained by the ethyl gallate
technique.[84] Cohen and Jacklet were able to demonstrate increases in perinuclear
RNA in cell bodies whose axons had been sectioned,[15] and together with
Wigglesworth's observations furnish valuable tools for tracing the position of
motor cell bodies whose end organs are known.

Guthrie observed that the dictyosomes of cell bodies in transplanted ganglia
were stained in a striking manner by silver nitrate.[35]

Before regeneration occurs in nerves and connectives, parts of axons no longer
in contact with cell bodies undergo degeneration. Hess has described the
degeneration in the larger fibres of the central nervous system. The process
occurs quite rapidly, the axon having totally collapsed after 8 days and little
further change occurring up to 30 days after the axons are cut. Initial changes
in the axons were observed after 4 days, the axoplasm becoming regionally
localized as the axon membrane lost its regular contour.[42]

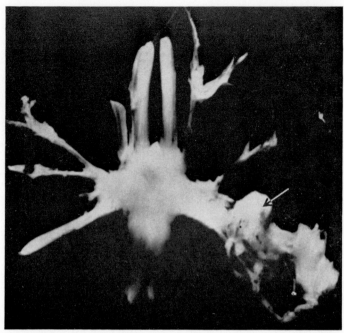

FIG. 6.10   Implanted ganglion ↓ incorporated into a gap in the fifth mesothoracic nerve. Many of these implanted ganglia could be shown to be independently functional after 12 weeks. × 20

In both connectives (Hess[42]) and peripheral nerves (Guthrie[34]), degenerated axons become surrounded by an unusually large number of glial folds, so that they appear as dense rings under the light microscope (Fig. 6.11). In peripheral nerves 2–6 extra glial folds could be seen in electron microscope preparations (Guthrie).

The problem of limb/segment specificity in insects has been investigated by earlier authors using Phasmids or Diptera as their material, and the ablation technique; transplantation of limbs has been less often attempted. The proportional effect of host tissue and graft in determining the limb has been investigated by Urvoy in *Blaberus craniifer*. He finds that three kinds of implantation site can be characterized: (i) neutral areas which do not impose their own pattern on the graft, but will react positively to the presumptive fate of the graft; (ii) negative areas, which have no morphogenetic identity of their own and are unable to react to a specific graft; (iii) positive areas, with a strongly developed organ specificity capable of dominating the identity of the graft. These areas, termed also by Urvoy 'territoires de régéneration', are readily activated to the formation of a new limb by the implant.[80]

Other peripheral organs can also be transplanted into new sites. The compound eyes can be transplanted in this way together with parts of the optic lobe, and will survive for some time, although no growth seems to occur.[10,87] Day showed that while the regeneration of tracheae occurred rapidly in larvae, this capability was almost entirely lost in the adults of *P.a.* After six weeks detracheated areas still lacked tracheae. Since cuticular growth as a whole is at a standstill in the adult this is not perhaps surprising.[22]

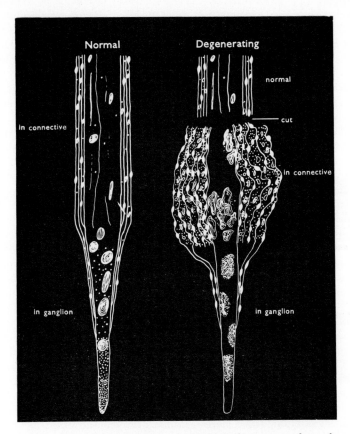

FIG. 6.11   The effect on sheath and axon material of severance from the neurone cell body of the nerve fibre. (From Hess[41])

Day also investigated the regeneration response of the mid-gut to localized wounds in *P.a.* Within hours of the operation blood cells began to accumulate at the wound site. This blood cell aggregate would not take up injected Chinese white particles as free blood cells would. During the first 3 days the epithelium undergoes little change. The gut muscles contract locally and haemocytes bridge the gap in the gut wall. All necrotic tissue and cellular debris is encapsulated by haemocytes at the end of 3 days, and epithelial regeneration now commences. Phosphate granules normally present in mid-gut cells disappear in the wound area about this time, and may not reappear for 8 weeks or more. The wound attains its maximum size after 3 or 4 days, and begins to decrease in size after 3 weeks. The wound tissue behaves in some respects like a neoplasm, but if transplanted it soon becomes encapsulated and does not spread.[22]

All the experiments on isolated organs so far described, have depended on in vivo operational procedures. Marks and Reinecke have managed to obtain cell growth in leg tissue explants cultivated in vitro. Regenerating limbs were removed from larvae of *Leucophaea maderae*. In early experiments the time of removal had a definite relationship to the growth capabilities of the explant, and this was believed to be due to the effect of different stages in the endocrine cycles of the donor insect.

In later experiments prothoracic ganglia or brains, and prothoracic glands were placed near the limb primordia, and this often had a positive effect on the development of cell buds and vesicles, provided that the primordium had experienced at least 7–9 days in vivo growth. Primordia which had experienced even longer periods of in vivo growth (10–20 days) would produce a high ratio of vesicles to cells without endocrine tissues being added to the culture. Not only was there a critical period at the 7–10-day level in the responsiveness of leg primordia, but prothoracic glands aged more than 10 days in vivo tended to suppress vesicle formation, and were often associated with cell degeneration, although this latter effect could be antagonized by the addition of the brain and corpus allatum.

In a number of instances axonic outgrowths were observed from the fifth root of the mesothoracic ganglia in vitro, and these appear similar to outgrowths from this structure in vivo.[8,34] Fibre growth was greatest in explants with 7–9 days in vivo growth, and a prothoracic ganglion and gland placed with them in the culture.[49]

Recently Larsen has been able to maintain heart fragments from the embryos of *B. craniifer* for periods up to 260 days in tissue culture. Sterile precautions were taken at all stages of the removal of heart tissue from the gravid female insect. The medium used was TC 199 fortified with 2% bactopeptone, and micro-organisms were inhibited with streptomycin and mycoban. Cultures were maintained at 25°. Heart fragments continued to beat for several weeks with synchrony between the chambers, and asynchronously up to 260 days. Earle balanced salt solution, and Scherer maintenance medium were almost as satisfactory. Fat body cells attached to the heart were used up after a time. Malpighian tubes, hind-gut muscles and cibarial muscles pulsated for 30, 67 and 68 days respectively in TC 199. There was no evidence of growth in any of these tissues.[44]

Although cell division and proliferation have not occurred in these cultures, this field of study offers great possibilities for the elucidation of growth requirements.

Tumours

Scharrer[69,72] showed that severance of the recurrent nerve in *Leucophaea maderae* causes the development of tumours in the fore-gut, anterior mid-gut and salivary glands which are innervated by this nerve. The level at which the nerve is cut does not matter. Of the operated animals 70–80% developed tumours. Males survive less well than females, but the incidence between the sexes is about the same. That a sexual factor is involved is indicated by the fact that castrates of both sexes survive better than males, but not so well as females. Examination of the fat content,[73] of the tumour-bearing insects showed that the males had an abnormally low fat content, while females had a normal level. Castrated females often had a rather higher content than normal females. Histology: In the anterior mid-gut a thickening is first seen in the ventricular region and then occurs in the intestinal region, the epithelial and muscular layers being replaced by a double layer of cells (less differentiated). Melanization occurs later and may be due to cell injury. Cell enlargement is responsible for much of the increase in size, and mitoses are rare. Necrosis occurs at a later stage. The epithelial cells appear to be involved in the primary effect. Fore-gut tumours are rare and look like sarcomas; salivary reservoir tumours look epithelial. These tumours are invasive and may penetrate the body wall.

Tumours may be induced in *P.a.* by imposing extra secretory cycles.[37] Harker had shown that neurosecretory cells in the suboesophageal ganglion controlled the two-hour diurnal rhythm via light receptors. When ganglia from an insect in which dark/light periods have been reversed are implanted into normally rhythmic roaches, and implants are given on four successive days, tumours may appear in the mid-gut and occasionally in the fore-gut.[37]

If a synchronous ganglion implant or synchronous injection of ganglion extract coincides with the secretory activity of the host no tumour results, and implanted tumours can be prevented from size increase by synchronous ganglion implants. The site of implantation has little to do with position of tumour. The tumours usually metastasize, and are transplantable.

In the mid-gut tumour growth can also result from the implantation of out-of-phase ganglia.[37]

REFERENCES

1. BARTH, R. H. (1964). Cockroach mating behaviour; neuroendocrine control of a chemical communication system. *12th Int. Cong. Ent.* London.
2. BARTH, R. H. (1962). The endocrine control of mating behaviour in *Byrsotria fumigata. Gen. Comp. Endocr.*, **2**, 53–69.
3. BARTON-BROWNE, L., DODSON, L. F., HODGSON, E. S. and KIRALY, J. K. (1961). Adrenergic properties of the cockroach corpus cardiacum. *Gen. comp. Endocr.*, **1**, 232–6.
4. BODENSTEIN, D. (1953). Studies on the hormonal mechanisms in growth and metamorphosis of the cockroach *P. americana*. I. Transplantation of integumental structures and experimental parabiosis. *J. exp. Zool.*, **123**, 189–232.
5. BODENSTEIN, D. (1953). Studies on the hormonal mechanisms in growth and metamorphosis of the cockroach *P. americana*. II. The function of the prothoracic gland and the corpus cardiacum. *J. exp. Zool.*, **123**, 413–33.
6. BODENSTEIN, D. (1953). *The role of hormones in moulting and metamorphosis in Insect Physiology*. Ed. Roeder, John Wiley, New York.
7. BODENSTEIN, D. (1955). Contributions to the problem of regeneration in insects. *J. exp. Zool.*, **129**, 209–24.

8. BODENSTEIN, D. (1957). Studies on nerve regeneration in *P. americana. J. exp. Zool.*, **136**, 89–116.
9. BODENSTEIN, D. and SPRAGUE, E. (1959). The developmental capacities of the Accessory Sex glands in *P.a. J. exp. Zool.*, **142**, 177–202.
10. BODENSTEIN, D. Personal communication.
11. BOWERS, S., THOMPSON, M. J. and UEBEL, E. C. (1965). Juvenile and gonadotrophic hormone activity of 10,11-epoxy farnesenic acid methyl ester. *Life Sciences*, **4**, 2323–31.
12. CAMERON, M. L. (1953). The secretion of an orthodiphenol in the corpus cardiacum of the insect. *Nature*, **172**, 349–50.
12a. CASE, J. F. (1957). The median nerves and cockroach spiracular function. *J. Insect Physiol.*, **1**, 85–94.
13. CAZAL, P. (1948). Les glandes endocrines rétrocerebrales des insectes. *Bull. Biol. Fr. Belg.* supplement **32**, 1–227.
14. CHADWICK, L. E. (1956). Removal of prothoracic glands from the nymphal cockroach. *J. exp. Zool.*, **131**, 291–306.
15. COHEN, M. J. and JACKLET, J. W. (1965). Neurons of Insects: RNA changes during injury and regeneration, *Science*, **148**, 1237–9.
16. DAVEY, K. G. (1961). The mode of action of the heart accelerating factor from the corpus cardiacum of the insects. *Gen. comp. Endocr.*, **1**, 24–9.
17. DAVEY, K. G. (1962). The release by feeding of a pharmacologically active factor from the corpus cardiacum of *P.a. J. Insect Physiol.*, **8**, 205–8.
18. DAVEY, K. G. (1962). The changes in the pericardial cells of *P.a.* induced by exposure to homogenates of the corpus cardiacum. *Q. Jl microsc. Sci.*, **103**, 349–58.
19. DAVEY, K. G. (1962). The mode of action of the corpus cardiacum on the hind gut in *P.a. J. exp. Biol.*, **39**, 319–24.
20. DAVEY, K. G. (1963). The release by enforced activity of the cardiac accelerator from the corpus cardiacum of *P.a. J. Insect Physiol.*, **9**, 375–82.
21. DAVEY, K. G. (1963). The possible involvement of an amino acid decarboxylase in the stimulation of the pericardial cells of *P.a.* by the corpus cardiacum. *J. exp. Biol.*, **40**, 343–50.
22. DAY, M. F. (1952). Wound healing in the gut of the cockroach. *Aust. J. scient. Res.*, **B5**, 282–9.
23. ENGELMANN, F. (1957). Die Steuering der Ovarfunktion bei der ovoviviparen Schabe *Leucophaea maderae. J. Insect Physiol.*, **1**, 257–78.
24. ENGELMANN, F. (1960). Mechanism controlling reproduction in two viviparous cockroaches. *Ann. N.Y. Acad. Sci.*, **89**, 516–39.
25. ENGELMANN, F. (1962). Further experiments on the regulation of the sexual cycle in females of *Leucophaea maderae. Gen. comp. Endocr.*, **2**, 183–92.
26. ENGELMANN, F. (1964). Pheromones and mating behaviour. *12th Int. Cong. Ent.* London.
27. ENGELMANN, F. and LÜSCHER, M. (1956). Die hemmende Wirkung des Gehirus auf die Corpora allata bei *Leucophaea maderae* (Orthoptera). *Verh. dt. zool., Ges. Hamburgh.*, 215–20.
28. ENGELMANN, F. and RAU, I. (1965). A correlation between feeding and the sexual cycle in *Leucophaea maderae. J. Insect Physiol.*, **11**, 53–64.
29. FRAENKEL, G. and HSIAO, C. (1965). Bursicon, a hormone which mediates tanning of the cuticle in the adult fly and other insects. *J. Insect Physiol.*, **11**, 513–56.
30. GILBERT, L. I. (1965). (The juvenile hormone and ovarian lipids) cited in WIGGLESWORTH, V. B. The Juvenile Hormone. *Nature, Lond.*, **208**, 522–4.
31. GIRARDIE, A. Étude du développement normal et experimental chez *P.a.* Thése de Science, Universite de Strasbourg.
32. GIRARDIE, A. (1962). Etude biometrique de la croissance ovarienne après ablation et implantation de corpora allata chez *P.a. J. Insect Physiol.*, **8**, 199–204.

33. GUTHRIE, D. M. (1966). Physiological competition between host and donor ganglia in an insect. *Nature, Lond.*, **210** (5033), 312–13.
34. GUTHRIE, D. M. (1962). Regenerative growth in insect nerve axons., *J. Insect Physiol.*, **8**, 79–92.
35. GUTHRIE, D. M. Unpublished observations.
36. HARKER, J. (1956). Factors controlling the diurnal rhythm of activity of *P.a. J. exp. Biol.*, **33**, 224–34.
37. HARKER, J. (1958). Experimental production of midgut tumours in *P.a. J. exp. Biol.*, **35**, 251–9.
38. HARKER, J. E. (1960). The effect of perturbations in the environmental cycle of the diurnal rhythm of activity of *Periplaneta americana* L. *J. exp. Biol.*, **37**, 154–63.
39. HARKER, J. E. and BROWN, R. H. J. (1960). The effect of cooling on neurosecretory cells. *Nature, Lond.*, **185**, 392.
40. HARNACK, M. VON (1958). The effect of starvation on the endocrine control of the ovary by the corpus allatum in the insect *Leucophaea maderae*. *Anat. Rec.*, **130**, 446.
41. HESS, A. (1958). Experimental anatomical studies of pathways in the severed central nerve cord., *J. Morph.*, **103**, 479–502.
42. HESS, A. (1960). The fine structure of degenerating nerve fibres, their sheaths and their terminations in the central nerve cord of the cockroach, *P.a. J. Biophys. Biochem., Cytol.*, **7**, 339–44.
43. HODGSON, E. S. and GELDIAY, S. (1959). Experimentally induced release of neurosecretory materials from roach corpora cardiaca. *Biol. Bull.*, **117**, 275–83.
44. HOFFMEISTER, H., RUFER, C. and AMMON, H. (1965). Annscheidung von Ecdyson bei Insekten. *Z. Naturf.*, **20** (2), 130–3.
45. KHAN, T. R. and FRASER, A. (1962). Neurosecretion in the embryo and later stages of the cockroach (*P.a.*). *Mem. Soc. Endocr.*, **12**, 349–69.
46. LARSEN, W. (1963). The maintenance of embryonic cockroach heart fragments in vitro. *Life Sciences*, **8**, 606–10.
47. LÜSCHER, M. and ENGELMANN, F. (1955). Uber die Stenrerung der Corpora allata Funktion bei der Schabe *Leucophaea maderae*. *Revue suisse zool.*, **62**, 649–57.
48. LÜSCHER, M. and ENGELMANN, F. (1960). Histologische and experimentelle untersuchungen uber die Auslsing der metamorphose bei *Leucophaea maderae* (Orthoptera). *J. Insect Physiol.*, **5** (3/4), 240–58.
49. MARKS, E. P. and REINECKE, J. P. (1965). Regenerating tissues from the cockroach *Leucophaea maderae*: effects of endocrine glands in vitro. *Gen. comp. Endocr.*, **5**, 241–7.
50. MILBURN, N. S. and ROEDER, K. D. (1962). Control of efferent activity in the cockroach terminal abdominal ganglion by extracts of corpora cardiaca. *Gen. comp. Endocr.*, **2**, 70–6.
51. MILBURN, N., WEIANT, E. A. and ROEDER, K. D. (1960). The release of efferent nerve activity in the roach *P.a.*, by extracts of the corpus cardiacum. *Biol. Bull.*, **118**, 111–19.
52. NESBITT, H. H. J. (1941). A comparative morphological study of the nervous system of Orthoptera. *Ann. ent. Soc. Am.*, **34**, 51–81.
53. NUTTING, W. L. (1955). Extirpation of roach prothoracic glands. *Science*, **122**, 30–1.
54. O'FARRELL, A. F. and STOCK, A. (1953). Regeneration and the moulting cycle in *Blattella germanica* L. I. Single regeneration initiated during the first instar. *Aust. J. biol. Sci.*, **6**, 485–500.
55. O'FARRELL, A. F. and STOCK, A. (1954). Regeneration and the moulting cycle in *Blatella germanica* L. III. Successive regeneration of both mesothoracic legs. *Aust. J. biol. Sci.*, **7**, 525–36.

56. O'FARRELL, A. F., STOCK, A. and MORGAN, J. A. (1956). Regeneration and the moulting cycle in *Blattella germanica* L. IV. Single and repeated regeneration of both mesothoracic legs. *Aust. J. biol. Sci.*, **9**, 406–22.
57. O'FARRELL, A. F. and STOCK, A. (1958). Some aspects of regeneration in cockroaches. *Proc. 10th Int. Cong. Ent.*, vol. **2**, 1956.
58. OZBAS, S. and HODGSON, E. S. (1958). Action of insect neurosecretion upon central nervous system in vitro and upon behaviour. *Proc. natn. Acad. Sci.*, **44**, 825–30.
59. RAE, C. A. (1955). Possible new elements in the endocrine complex of cockroaches. *Aust. J. Sci.*, **18**, 33–4.
60. RAE, C. A. and O'FARRELL, A. F. (1959). The retrocerebral complex and ventral glands of the primitive orthopteroid *Grylloblatta campodeiformis*, with a note on the homology of the muscle core of the 'prothoracic gland' in Dictyoptera. *Proc. R. Ent. Soc. Lond.*, A, **34**, 76–82.
61. ROTH, L. M. (1962). Hypersexual activity induced in females of the cockroach *Nauphoeta cinerea*. *Science*, **138**, 1267–9.
62. ROTH, L. M. (1964). Control of reproduction in female cockroaches with special reference to *Nauphoeta cinerea*. I. First pre-oviposition period. *J. Insect Physiol.*, **10**, 915–45.
63. ROTH, L. M. (1964). Control of Reproduction in female cockroaches with special reference to *Nauphoeta cinerea*. II. Gestation and post-parturition. *Psyche, Camb.*, **71**, 198–244.
64. ROTH, L. M. and STAY, B. (1962). A comparative study of oöcyte development in false ovoviviparous cockroaches. *Psyche*, **69**, 165–208.
65. ROTH, L. M. and STAY, B. (1962). Oöcyte development in *Blattella germanica* and *B. vaga*. *Ann. ent. Soc. Am.*, **55**, 633–42.
66. ROTH, L. M. and STAY, B. (1961). Oöcyte development in *Diploptera punctata*. *J. Insect Physiol.*, **7**, 186–202.
67. ROTH, L. M. and DATEO, G. P. (1966). A sex pheromone produced by males of *Nauphoeta cinerea*. *J. Insect Physiol.* **12**, 255–65.
68. SÄGESSER, H. (1960). Uber die wirkung der Corpora allata auf den sauerstoffverbrauch bei der schabe *Leucophaea maderae*. *J. Insect Physiol.*, **5**, 264–85.
69. SCHARRER, B. (1945). Tumours and nerve section in cockroach. *Proc. Soc. exp. Biol. Med.*, **60**, 184–9.
70. SCHARRER, B. (1946). Effect of corpus allatum removal in *Leucophaea maderae*. *Endocrinology*, **38**, 35–45.
71. SCHARRER, B. (1948). The prothoracic glands of *Leucophaea maderae*. *Biol. Bull. mar. biol. Lab. Woods Hole*, **95**, 186–98.
72. SCHARRER, B. (1948). Malignant characteristics of experimentally induced tumours in the insect *Leucophaea maderae*. *Anat. Rec.*, **100**, 774–5.
73. SCHARRER, B. (1949). Tumour mortality and sex in *Leucophaea maderae*. *Anat. Rec.*, **105**, 624–36.
74. SCHARRER, B. (1952). Neurosecretion XI. The effects of nerve section on the intercerebralis–cardiacum–allatum system of the insect *Leucophaea maderae*. *Biol. Bull. mar. biol. Lab. Woods Hole*, **102**, 261–72.
75. SCHARRER, B. (1961). Functional analysis of the corpus allatum of the insect *Leucophaea maderae*, with the electron microscope. *Biol. Bull. mar. biol. Lab. Woods Hole*, **121**, 370–81.
76. SCHARRER, B. (1961). Histophysiological studies on the corpus allatum of *Leucophaea maderae* III. The effects of castration. *Biol. Bull. mar. biol. Lab. Woods Hole*, **121**, 193–208.
77. SCHARRER, B. and HARNACK, M. VON (1958). Histophysiological studies on the corpus allatum of *Leucophaea maderae* I. Normal life cycle in male and female adults. *Biol. Bull. mar. biol. Lab. Woods Hole*, **115**, 508–20.

78. SCHARRER, B. and HARNACK, M. VON (1961). Histophysiological studies of the corpus allatum III. The effects of castration. *Biol. Bull. mar. biol. Lab. Woods Hole*, **121**, 193–208.

79. STOCK, A. and O'FARRELL, A. F. (1954). Regeneration and the moulting cycle in *Blattella germanica* L. II. Simultaneous regeneration of both metathoracic legs. *Anat. J. Biol. Sci.*, **7**, 302–7.

80. URVOY, J. (1964). Sur la transplantation d'appendices chez la blatte *Blaberus craniifer*. *XIIth Int. Congr. Ent.*, **2**, 156.

81. VROMAN, H. E., KAPLANIS, J. N. and ROBBINS, W. E. (1965). Effect of allatectomy on lipid biosynthesis and turnover in the female american cockroach, *P.a. J. Insect Physiol.*, **11**, 897–904.

82. WALL, BETTY, J. and RALPH, C. L. (1962). Responses of specific neurosecretory cells of the cockroach *Blaberus giganteus* to dehydration. *Biol. Bull.*, **122** (3), 431–8.

83. WIGGLESWORTH, V. B. (1965). The Juvenile Hormone. *Nature, Lond.*, **208**, 522–4.

84. WIGGLESWORTH, V. B. (1960). Axon structure and the Dictyosomes (golgi bodies) in the neurones of the cockroach, *P.a. Q. Jl microsc. Sci.*, **101**, 381–8.

85. WILLEY, R. B. (1961). The morphology of the stomodaeal nervous system in *P.a. J. Morph.*, **108**, 219–47.

86. WILLEY, R. B. and CHAPMAN, G. B. (1960). The ultrastructure of certain components of the corpora cardiaca in orthopteroid insects. *J. Ultrastruct. Res.*, **4**, 1–14.

87. WOLBARSHT, J. B. Personal communication.

ADDENDUM

Osinchak has recently studied the localization of phosphatases in the pro-thoracic gland of *Leucophaea maderae*. Prominent sites of acid phosphatase activity include large membrane bound disc bodies or lysosomes, and certain cisternae of the Golgi apparatus. Thyamine phosphatase activity was traced to certain elements of the Golgi apparatus, endoplasmic reticulum and in lysosome-like dense bodies. The regression of the prothoracic glands has been shown by Scharrer to occur within a few days of the final moult in *Blaberus* and *Leucophaea*. Resorption is the result of physiological autolysis and is aided by the action of phagocytic haemocytes. These changes could be followed with the electron microscope.

The understanding of the mode of action of the tanning hormone—bursicon—has been considerably extended by the work of Mills and his colleagues. Mills and Nielsen were able to prepare the hormone in purified form. They found that it was stable up to 55° but inactivated by repeated freezing and thawing. High salt concentrations and extremes of pH inhibited the tanning process. Copper and magnesium had an acceleratory effect, while other ions inhibit darkening. Maximum tanning occurred between 35° and 45°, but bursicon activity was destroyed by short-chain alcohols. A good agreement between the molecular weight found by gel filtration and by chromatography was obtained. The former gave a value between 30 and 50,000, and the latter gave 40,000.

Mills had shown in a previous paper that the isolated ganglion could secrete bursicon, but Fraenkel and Hsiao found that severance of the central nervous system eliminated the tanning response. Mills confirmed this observation and

132   *The endocrine system, regeneration and tissue culture*

also noted that disruption of the stomatogastric nervous system did not affect
tanning. By means of an ingenious in vitro preparation in which the nerve cord
could be stimulated electrically while the attached terminal ganglion dipped into
a chamber containing a piece of untanned cuticle, he was able to produce tanning
via the central nervous system. The strength and duration of the stimulus was
not proportional to the intensity of the reaction.

The observation of Harker that the histology of neurosecretory cells in the
suboesophageal does not change with the different stages in the circadian rhythm
has been confirmed recently by Brady. He could distinguish six pairs of PAF
stained cells in this region. At the height of locomotor activity he observed slight
changes in the nuclei of one of the pairs of cells.

ADDITIONAL REFERENCES

BRADY, J. (1967). Histological observations on circadian changes in the neurosecretory cells of the cockroach suboesophageal ganglion. *J. Insect Physiol.*,
13, 201–3.

MILLS, R. R., MATHUR, R. B. and GUERRA, A. A. (1965). Studies on the hormonal
control of tanning. Release of an activation factor from the terminal
abdominal ganglion. *J. insect Physiol.*, **11**, 1047–53.

MILLS, R. R., MATHUR, R. B. and GUERRA, A. A. (1965). Hormonal control of tanning
in the cockroach. Assay for the hormone and the effect of wound healing.
J. Insect Physiol., **11**, 1268–75.

MILLS, R. R., MATHUR, R. B. and GUERRA, A. A. (1966). Hormonal control of tanning
in the cockroach. Hormone stability and postecdysial changes in hormone
titre. *J. Insect Physiol.*, **12**, 275–80.

MILLS, R. R. and NIELSEN, DONOVAN, J. (1967). Hormonal control of tanning in the
cockroach. Some properties of the purified hormone. *J. Insect Physiol.*, **13**,
272–81.

MILLS, R. R. and NIELSEN, DONOVAN, J. (1967). Control of cuticular tanning in the
cockroach. Bursicon release by nervous stimulation. *J. Insect Physiol.*, **13**,
815–30.

OSINCHAK, J. (1966). Ultrastructural localization of some phosphatases in the prothoracic gland of the insect *Leucophaea maderae. Z. Zellforsch.*, **72/2**, 236–
48.

SCHARRER, B. (1966). An ultrastructural study of the regressing prothoracic glands
of Blattarian insects. *Z. Zellforsch.*, **69**, 1–21.

7   *Sense organs*

INTRODUCTION

The cryptic habit of the laboratory species of cockroach is undoubtedly associated with the rather slight development of some sense organs, such as the eyes, and the refined sensitivity of others, notably the vibration receptive subgenual organs. Attention has been focused on the physiology of trichoid mechanoreceptors in the cockroach since the earliest days of zoological neurophysiology,[5] and much of our understanding of these sense organs in insects has been derived from a study of cockroach material. Certain sense organs on the other hand have been largely neglected, for example the long antennae with their numerous chemoreceptor hairs.

MECHANORECEPTORS

(a) Cuticular hairs

Tactile bristles, large spines and auditory hairs can be distinguished. In addition some of the bristles form well-defined groups or hair plates at the leg joints, and have a proprioceptive function.

(i) TACTILE BRISTLES

Sihler figures a bristle type of sense organ from the cockroach cercus. A single eccentrically placed sense cell supplies a process to the base of the hair.[50]

Barnes observed that bursts of electrical activity could be recorded in the leg nerves of the cockroach, when the limb was moved, and that the frequency of discharge was proportional to the extent and rapidity of the movement. He believed that a 'tension receptor' in the muscle might be involved in the sensory response but histological studies failed to reveal a sense organ of this type.

He concluded that a slow adapting muscle receptor of the kind found in Crustacea did not occur in the insect limb. Pringle suggests that the sensory responses observed by Barnes were mainly from campaniform sensilla. It should be noted that critical analysis of the responses was not possible as Barnes relied on a loudspeaker for the display of signals.[2]

Pumphrey in a short communication refers to the response of the fine body hairs to maintained deflection as a rapidly adapting one and notes their similarity to vertebrate tactile receptors, but few details are given.[38]

Lefeuvre has described a rather unusual type of trichoid sensillum from the larvae of *Blaberus craniifer*.[26]

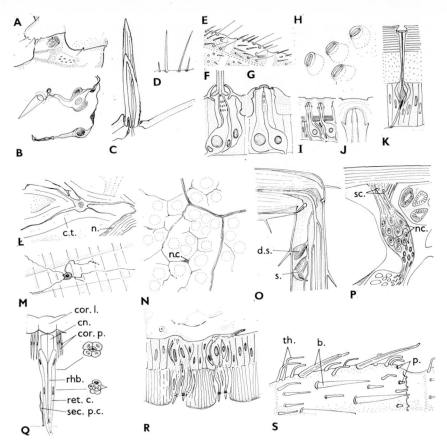

FIG. 7.1 Various types of sense organ. **A**, sensory structures on the trochanter and coxa; tactile bristles, a hair plate and a group of campaniform organs. **B**, hair sense organs from the abdominal terga. **C**, tibial spine (with eccentric neurone). The fine threads running up inside it appear to be connective tissue lamellae. **D**, different sizes of hair organ from the legs. **E**, upper and lower surfaces of the cercus showing bristles, fine auditory hairs and campaniform organs. **F**, vertical section through an auditory hair organ (after Hsü [24]). **G**, vertical section through a campaniform organ from the cercus (after Hsü [24]). **H**, surface view of a group of campaniform organs from the trochanter. **I**, vertical section through campaniform organs from trochanter. **J**, similar to **I**, but showing detail of neurone insertion on the cuticle. **K**, vertical section through plate organ of unknown function from the trochanter. **L**, stretch receptor from the abdominal tergum. n.—nerve, c.t.—connective tissue. **M**, stretch receptor lying between gut epithelium and circular muscle in the crop. **N**, free nerve endings ramifying between hypodermal cells. Abdominal sterna. n.c.—neurilemma cell. **O**, tibial chordotonal organs. d.s.—distal subgenual organ, s.—subgenual organ. **P**, vertical section through femoral chordotonal organ. N.c.—neurone cell bodies, sc.—scolops. **Q**, vertical section through ommatidium of compound eye. cor.l.—corneal lens, cn.—cone, cor.p.—corneal pigment cell, rhb.—rhabdome, ret.c.—retinular cell, sec.p.c.—secondary pigment cell. To the right are shown transverse sections at the levels indicated. (After Hesse) **R**, sense organs from the tarsal pads. These are most likely to be chemoreceptors, or temperature receptors. **S**, sensory hairs on the antenna. b.—bristles, th.—thin-walled hairs (probably hygroreceptors) and p.—pegs

(ii) LARGE SPINES

On the femora and tibiae of *Periplaneta americana,* and some other forms, hollow socketed spines are found (see Fig. 7.1C).

Nijenhuis and Dresden figure a single sense cell at the base of each spine with a distal process passing up into a small perforation in the expanded proximal end of the spine. In some specimens they observed what appeared to be a fine nerve branch passing into the lumen of the spine.[30]

Pumphrey showed that the tibial spines adapted slowly to prolonged stimulation as compared with finer hairs. The magnitude of the response varied according to the direction of the applied force, being largest when the spine was deflected proximally or against the cuticular stop on that side. This is the direction the spine is moved in when the leg makes its propulsive stroke against the ground. The initial frequency of nerve impulses depends on the speed of deflection of the spine, but falls after one second from the start of stimulation to a level roughly proportional to the magnitude of deflection in any given direction. The response may take 10 sec to fall to near the original level (Fig. 7.2). Pumphrey

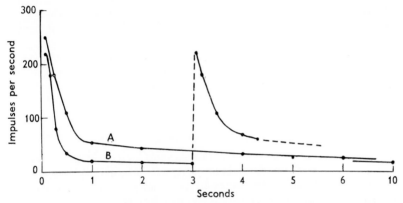

FIG. 7.2   The response of a tibial spine to maintained deflection. In *B* a small initial deflection was suddenly increased after 3 sec. (From Pumphrey and Rawdon-Smith[38])

points out that this response shows a greater similarity to that of a proprioceptor, than of a touch receptor, and might be important in such reflexes as those involved in cleaning behaviour.[38] *

Pringle and Wilson employed the response of the large spine sensillum to study the response of a sense organ to a harmonic stimulus. The severed leg was fixed to a support, and the spine driven against its cuticular stop by the action of an oscillating steel spring. The highest frequency of nerve impulses recorded in the leg nerve preceded maximum tension at moderate or low stimulus amplitudes, but became more exactly synchronized at high amplitudes. This effect was non-

* Very recently Chapman has shown that campaniform organs may occur on the spines.

linear, and more nearly proportional to the logarithm of the stimulus intensity. It was believed to be a corollary of the adaptation of the response to a transient stimulus.

If stimulation frequencies are gradually raised the response begins to adapt out between 0·6 and 1·0 c/s. The response to a transient stimulus produced a peak discharge rate of 350 impulses/second, dropping to 150 in a half-second, and then to 50. A comparison with control theory was possible.[36]

(iii) HAIR PLATES

At certain points on the integument, most frequently where there is a cuticular overlap, small groups of hairs are aggregated to form hair plates (Fig. 7.1A). Pringle investigated the receptor properties of three hair plates on the borders of the coxa of a walking leg.[35] Earlier workers such as Lowne had described hair plates in other insects and Barnes had recorded increased activity in the leg nerves of the cockroach during forced movements.

Because of their location these hair plates will only be stimulated in certain positions of the limb segments. The numbers of hairs in each hair plate ranged from 11 to 81 as follows: inner coxal hair plate 69–81, outer coxal hair plate 11–39, trochanteral hair plate 42–54. These numbers are for the legs of all three thoracic segments and do not show the segmental differences that were observed.

The responses of single hairs of the inner coxal hair plate were elicited by mechanical stimulation with a needle, and were found to be rather variable. Adaptation was fairly slow, proceeding rapidly in the first second, but taking as much as 12 sec to return to normal levels. The hairs were responsive to very small displacements, not visible under a magnification of $\times 100$.[35]

(iv) AUDITORY HAIRS (Trichobothria, Fadenhaare of Sihler[50])

The cercal sense organs of a number of insect species including *B.o.* and *P.a.* were described by Sihler.[50] In addition, a figure showing the distribution of domed sensilla in *Blattella* (*Phyllodromia*) *germanica* is given. Three kinds of sensory structures were found on cockroach cerci: long fine hairs (thread hairs— Fadenhaare of Sihler), short bristles (bristle hairs—Borstenhaare, Sinnes- börstchen of Sihler) and a domed type of receptor—probably a campaniform organ—(Sinnesküppeln, Sihler); the latter were much more abundant on the basal and terminal parts of the cercus than in between (Fig. 7.1E and G).

There seems little doubt that the Fadenhaare are the auditory receptors of Pumphrey and Rawdon-Smith[37, 39] and therefore they will be referred to by the latter name.

The auditory sensilla are shown by Sihler[50] to have a rather complex socket in the form of a double collar. The dendrite from a single large sense cell passes up inside a cuticular sleeve to be inserted more or less symmetrically on the base of the hair. Transverse sections through the dendrite show a thick neurilemma surrounding the cell process. The boundary between the two elements appears as a dark ring. There are traces of an axial structure within the cell process in longitudinal sections. The single large formative cell at the base of the hair is described as a trichogen cell; a tormogen cell is not figured. Hsü's figure of the auditory hair socket from the cercus of *P.a.* appears less complex than that of Sihler, while the upper region of the dendrite is shown to be more elaborate. Three tiers of rods or folds (four tiers as seen laterally) can be seen within the expanded end of the dendrite (Fig. 7.1F).[24]

The function of these sense organs is discussed by Sihler, who points out that Schaxel had suggested an auditory function for similar hairs in spiders and Sihler gives examples of crickets' sensitivity to footfalls. He also suggests their function as touch receptors in the narrow galleries of field crickets.[50]

Pumphrey and Rawdon-Smith published five papers in the years 1936–7 on the physiology of these receptors, two of these using *P.a.* and three using a species of *Gryllus*.[37,39,40,41,42] Although on behavioural grounds it might be expected that the sensitivity of the cricket preparation was higher or more complex than the cockroach one, no striking difference seems to have appeared, and therefore this work will be described as a whole.

Pumphrey and Rawdon-Smith found that the cercal hairs of *Gryllus domesticus* and *P.a.* responded to gross air movements and to sounds of low frequency. The upper limit of effective auditory stimulus was between 3 and 4 kc/s. They noted that the response to sound is in many ways similar to that of the mammalian cochlear nerve. At the lowest end of the frequency range the response is synchronous with the stimulus, but at higher stimulus frequencies the response is no longer synchronous, the stimulus response ratio dropping to 2:1. Equilibration, another characteristic of the cochlear nerve, was observed (Fig. 7.3). Response amplitude dropped off with continuous auditory stimulation due to lengthening of refractory periods, but could be shown to recover smoothly by stimulating at

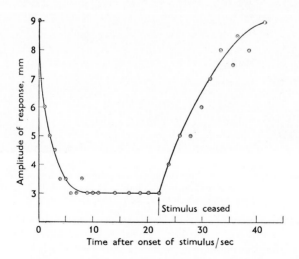

FIG. 7.3 Response of the auditory hair organ. A graph of a recording from the afferent fibres in the cercal nerve, demonstrating equilibration (see text). The stimulus intensity is constant and the stimulus frequency 300 c/s. (From Pumphrey and Rawdon-Smith[40])

intervals with brief periods of sound.[37] In another communication the range of synchronous response is given as 50–400 c/s, of partial synchrony 400–800 c/s, and of some kind of completely asynchronous response to 3,000 c/s. The argument for supposing alternation to occur is examined. A synchronous response at 800 c/s would indicate a latency of 1·25 msec, which would be unlikely in an unmedullated invertebrate fibre; therefore it is likely that alternation similar to that described by Davis in the mammal, occurs. This is supported by the occasional observation of frequency doubling (say, a response of 800 c/s to 400 c/s stimulus) at low frequencies, and the fact that a reduction of intensity of 20 db causes the response to 800 c/s to drop to 400 c/s.[40] In the same year Pumphrey and Rawdon-Smith were able to demonstrate alternation ratios of 1:3 and 1:4 as responses to a single frequency at different intensities; some fibres responding to every third

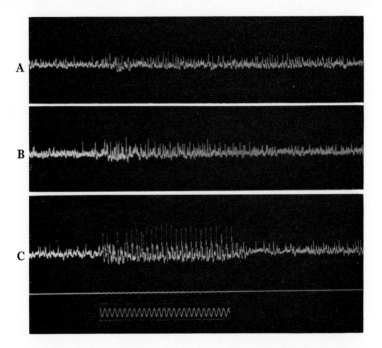

FIG. 7.4   Response of auditory hair organs (*Henschoutedenia epilamproides*). Records from the cercal nerve at a stimulus frequency of 50 c/s, but at different sound intensities. **A**, 60 db; **B**, 75 db; **C**, 100 db

or fourth stimulus wave. That the effect was less marked than in the vertebrate was regarded as due to the smaller number of slower fibres. This experiment demonstrated the large measure of functional parity existing between the complex mammalian preparation and the much simpler insectan one.[39]

Comparing the frequency sensitivity of human ear, locust tympanum, locust body hair and cricket cercus Pumphrey and Rawdon-Smith show that the outstanding ability of the cercal hair is to discriminate sound below 100 c/s. The unspecialized body hair of the locust has its most sensitive range between 800 and 1,200 c/s.[41]

Pumphrey and Rawdon-Smith extended their studies to the auditory synapses in the central nervous system.[42] This is described in Chapter 5.

Few other cockroach species have been investigated, but Guthrie obtained some information on the auditory responses of the large East African species *Henschoutedenia epilamproides* Shel.

Responses in the cercal afferents followed stimulation by very light air currents, but pure tones were ineffective in producing a response over 500 c/s, even when the intensity was raised to 100 db. Greatest synchrony and sensitivity was found at 50 c/s (intensity 60 db) (Fig. 7.4).[19]

(b) **Campaniform stress receptors** (Figs. 7.1G–J and 7.5)

Campaniform organs of a considerable variety of form have been described by the earlier morphologists (Snodgrass[51]). In the more specialized types the cuticular area is oval rather than circular and a thickened ridge lies along the long axis of the organ as seen in plain view (Fig. 7.1H). This type of receptor is found on many of the limb segments and has been investigated by Pringle[33,34] (and other papers on reflexes) in *P.a.* and to a lesser extent *B.o.* Chapman has shown that campaniform organs may occur on the spines of the leg.

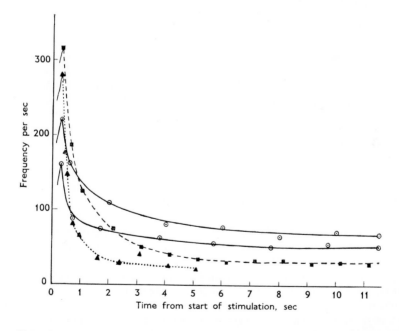

FIG. 7.5   Campaniform organ responses—adaptation curves—from the maxillary palps. Sense organs between segments 1 and 2—▲; between 3 and 4—◯; between 4 and 5—■ (this curve may be anomalous). (From Pringle[33])

Pringle found that recordings from the cut end of the maxillary nerve showed a constant discharge, which largely disappeared when the lacinia and galea were cut away, and responses from the palp could then be observed. Manipulation of the different segments resulted in clear-cut discharges resembling single fibre responses. Adaptation was slow and incomplete although there was a 20% frequency drop in the first half-second of stimulus (Fig. 7.5). Differential sensitivities of the palpar segments was apparent. Responses of joint 1–2 between segments 1 and 2 were characterized by large impulses, high threshold and rapid adaptation. On the other hand, impulses from joint 3–4 were of small amplitude; there was greater sensitivity and slower and less complete adaptation. It was found that normal muscular movements did not initiate regular responses, but restraints or forced movements did. The most effective stimulus was direct pressure on the cuticle. Lateral forced movements were more effective than those made in the plane of the limb.

Microscopic examination of the palps showed that the segments bore small groups of campaniform organs, each of 1–5 units. On the labial palp they only occurred on joint 2–3. Internally each group of campaniform organs appeared to be innervated by a single nerve fibre, thus bearing out the physiological findings. The author discusses the theoretical implication of common fibre innervation, which would appear to result in the most active sensillum determining the impulse rate in the fibre.[33]

In the walking leg Pringle showed that there were larger numbers of campaniform organs and he described 9 groups altogether. The trochanter is especially well endowed, having 5 groups of between 7 and 20 units in the mesothoracic leg.

These campaniform organs were shown to be functionally similar to those of the palps in responding to cuticular stresses. In each group the long axes of the cuticular caps were aligned parallel and this suggests sensitivity to one axis of compression, and helps to explain innervation by only one nerve fibre. The accuracy of alignment was not as great in some groups as others. The different sensilla of a group may extend the range of the fibre quantitatively but not qualitatively.

A theory of selective response to distortion was elaborated on the basis of a model, each unit responding to a compression component of shear which raised the sclerotized ridge when acting along the greatest diameter of the cuticular dome, but had no effect when acting transversely.[34]

The campaniform organs are placed so as to respond maximally when the animal is in the standing position. This study provides a detailed basis for the sense of contact pressure postulated by earlier workers on insects such as Fraenkel, Hoffmann and Holst.

The Sinnesküppeln of the cercus may also be campaniform organs and were figured in some detail by Sihler.[50] A domed cuticular cap is innervated by a single dendrite at the apex of which a single rod appears. These organs are most abundant on the terminal and basal segments of the cercus. In *P.a.* a fine channel is to be seen in the centre of the cap, but is absent in *B.o.* The structure of the (*P.a.*) Sinnesküppeln of the cercus is also figured by Hsü. The cuticular structures agree with Sihler's description, but the upper part of the dendrite is shown to be more complex with two tiers of rods visible from the side (Fig. 7.1G),[24] and the perforation is not visible.

A few workers have used the reliability of campaniform organ response to study the effects of certain drugs. Milburn has shown that the drug 5 hydroxy-tryptamine produces prolonged excitatory activity.[29]

Chordotonal organs

The chordotonal organs consist of groups of rather complex sensilla arranged in a fan-like or parallel array (Fig. 7.1O). Each sensillum is composed of several cells, and typically possesses an apical system of dense rods—the scolops (Fig. 7.1P).

Scolopophorous sensilla or scolopidia have been described in the walking legs of *P.a.* by Nijenhuis and Dresden,[30] and in *B.o.* and *Blattella* (*Phyllodromia*) *germanica* by Friedrich,[11] and Debaisieux.[9]

In *Periplaneta* there appear to be at least 9 such organs in the leg (one of them is partly divided) and their sensory axons contribute to nerves 3 and 5. Most of them are inserted on unspecialized cuticle, although according to Nijenhuis and Dresden the proximal coxal organ is surrounded by muscle and inserted on an apodeme. Attention has been mainly focussed on the tibial organs and their function as vibration receptors.

Nijenhuis and Dresden make a distinction between chordotonal organs *sensu strictu* which have their cuticular insertions near joints and the subgenual organs which have their insertions away from the joints. Classified on this basis there are four coxal (n.3), and one femoral (n.5) chordotonal organs; two tibial subgenual organs (n.5); tibial and tarso-pretarsal chordotonal organs of Debaisieux (n.5).

Nijenhuis and Dresden publish microphotographs of the femoral group and of the tibial organs in which the large cell bodies of the femoral scolopidia are clearly seen.[30] Friedrich illustrates quite well the appearance of the subgenual organ of the tibia and distinguishes between the transverse subgenual organ (s.s.) and an oblique distal organ (distal subgenual organ of Nijenhuis and Dresden). He is also able to arrange the tibial organs of Orthopteroid insects in a series of increasing complexity, from the single transverse organ of Dermaptera to the Gryllid with subgenual, intermediate (Zwischenorgane) and enlarged distal organ (Crista acoustica). In this series the cockroaches are seen to possess a structurally simple arrangement. Friedrich gives some details of the terminal scolops.[11]

Debaisieux gives the number of scolopidial groups in each organ as follows: (i) Femoral—1 dispersed and 1 condensed, (ii) subgenual—1 subgenual, and 1 distal subgenual, (iii) tibial (distal)—1 or 2, (iv) Tarso-pretarsal—probably 3.[9]

Autrum and Schneider,[1] and Howse[22, 23] have investigated electrical activity in the leg nerves resulting from the repetitive application of small displacements to the legs. It is presumed that the organ stimulated is the tibial subgenual organ (Fig. 7.1O), but the evidence for precise localization of the response is equivocal.

Autrum and Schneider examined a number of different species, and their results expressed as a displacement/frequency plot indicate for most species an increase in sensitivity with frequency increase. In the more sensitive species the response declines above 1,500 c/s. *Periplaneta americana* appears to be more sensitive than other species at all frequencies, with the exception of *Liogryllus* at about 8,000 c/s. Over the range 800–2,000 c/s *Periplaneta* is very much more sensitive than other species (less than 10^{-2} mμ displacement provides a stimulus at about 1,500 c/s) (Fig. 7.6). Behaviourally it could be noted that those insects with subgenual organs responded more obviously to substrate vibrations than insects without them.[1]

Howse[22] in a preliminary communication noted the fact that the legs of *P.a.* responded to continuous stimulation at, say, 1,000 c/s by a brief response with a latency of 10–20 msec. Adaptation was rapid occupying $\frac{1}{2}$ sec or less. If the stimulus was given in bursts at 30/sec, however, a synchronous non-adapting response occurred. Howse examined the suggestion by Autrum and Schneider[1] that stimulation of the scolopidia occurred as a result of vortices in the blood, but a theory of direct stimulation seemed adequate.[22] In a fuller treatment of his results Howse[23] gives further details. In the cockroach he obtained non-adapting responses to pulsed vibration up to 50/sec, while in the termite such a response failed about 3/sec. Comparing the displacement/frequency curve obtained from his cockroach material with that of Autrum and Schneider,[1] that of Howse shows a slightly reduced sensitivity at most frequencies. The shape of the curves is roughly similar except for an extra peak of greater sensitivity at about 3,000 c/s in the more recent work. This still makes the sensitivity of the termite preparation one-hundredth down on the cockroach.

Recordings were made both from the leg and from the ventral nerve cord of the cockroach giving a range of latencies of 12·5–14·5 msec, and 15–18 msec respectively. Natural damping will curtail the magnitude of transient vibration, and this natural damping might be expected to be greater in the closely organized fan-shaped cockroach organ than in the more loosely disposed one of the termite. Indeed, Howse showed that the 'time constant' (as defined by Haskell—the time taken to return to a state of rest) is 7 msec in the roach and 30 msec in the termite. Evidence is also brought forward to support the view that the differences in the mechanical responsiveness of scolopale and accessory cells may lead to stimulating forces being developed at their junctions.[23]

Becht has investigated the effect on the excitability of a coxo-trochanteral group of Scolopidia in *P.a.* of DDT and lindane. Three organs were found in this area, the largest innervated by six thick fibres, the two smaller ones by six thin fibres. The correspondence with Nijenhuis and Dresden's map of sensilla is not clear. Stimulation by tension produces a phasic response of large value impulses (250 μv), and a sustained response of smaller value impulses (250 μv). The tonic discharge drops from a level of 240/sec to near 100/sec in 15 sec, and then may remain at this level for at least 3 min. DDT poisoning results in stimulation evoking a high-frequency response (350/sec) involving both types of fibre, followed an hour or so later by a great reduction in responsiveness. Lindane, on the other hand, has no effect on the normal response.[3]

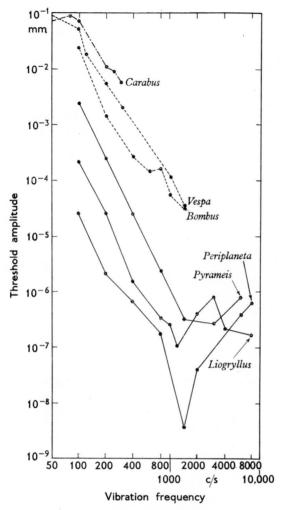

FIG. 7.6   The vibration thresholds of various insect species, as measured by the electrical activity of the leg nerves. (From Autrum and Schneider[1])

Stretch receptors

Although Orlov had figured stretch receptors in the gut muscle of beetle larvae in 1924, non-cuticular sense organs were little investigated in insects until the work of Slifer, Finlayson, Lowenstein and Osborne, from 1956 onwards. Some of the earlier work on sense organs and reflexes was influenced by the supposed absence of non-cuticular proprioceptors.

Finlayson and Lowenstein[10] describe abdominal stretch receptors in 9 insect orders, including adult specimens of *P.a.* In the cockroach a pair of receptors occur in the dorsal region of abdominal segments 2–7. Each consists of a single multipolar cell embedded in a strand of connective tissue. It lies dorsal to the fourth and fifth muscle bands counting from the mid-line, and its axon joins the main tergal nerve (Fig. 7.1L). This paper includes details of the connective tissue strands which are complex.

The functional characteristics of this type of receptor were demonstrated in a moth (*Antheraea*) and a dragonfly (*Aeschna*), but it is unlikely to be markedly dissimilar in the cockroach. In *Antheraea* there was a resting discharge of 20 impulses/sec that rose to two or three times this frequency on the connective tissue strand being stretched; both the initial and subsequent frequency depending on the amount of extension. It was suggested that this receptor behaved like the static receptor of Crustacea. The authors, furthermore, were able to arrange the different types of stretch receptor in a series progressing from superficial elements associated only with connective tissue, to those lying more deeply and associated also with muscle. The cockroach organs could be seen to be of the less advanced type.[10]

In a later paper Osborne and Finlayson included further structural details of the cockroach stretch receptor (*P.a.* and *Blaberus craniifer*) together with information about seven other orders.

In both *P.a.* and *Blaberus* a vertical receptor is also present, lying very close to the longitudinal receptor described previously. In *P.a.* they are joined together by a connective tissue strand, but this is not the case in *Blaberus*. A dendrite running back close to the axon could be seen in some *Blaberus* receptors, and both receptors could be identified in segments 1–7. The lower part of the vertical connective tissue strip is attached to a muscle band or to a motor nerve.

In this paper the authors elaborate the thesis that the receptor may have been derived from a migrated cuticular receptor, the most primitive orders of the series being represented by the Ephemeroptera and the Plecoptera, in which the sense cell lies very superficially.[31]

Osborne examined the longitudinal stretch receptor of *Blaberus craniifer* with the electron microscope. Schwann cells invest the axon, cell bodies and dendrites, but the terminal regions of the dendrites are naked, and embedded in the connective tissue matrix. He suggests that the connective tissue may be derived from the basement membrane of peripheral nerves.

The sensory terminations are simple and resemble those of vertebrate muscle spindles.[32]

While it was difficult to demonstrate, Osborne suggests that the connective tissue matrix may be sufficiently elastic normally to prevent the anomalous responses due to overstretch demonstrated by Finlayson and Lowenstein.

Beside these abdominal stretch receptors this author (D.M.G.) has observed similar sense cells in the inner muscular layers of the crop, and Davey has identified an element of this type from the hind-gut.[8] A large multipolar receptor is also to be found lying against the dorsal femoro-tibial articulation in *P.a.* (see Addendum).

LIGHT AND TEMPERATURE RECEPTION

The structure of the lateral eyes

Miall and Denny give quite a detailed description of the cockroach eye in their monograph.[28]

The eye is observed by them to be roughly oval and in its longest axis to have 67 facets. A figure taken from Grenacher demonstrates the structure of an ommatidium, showing lens, crystalline, cone, rhabdome and retinal elements. In the middle and lower region of the ommatidium there appear to be 4 retinular cells with rhabdomes at their inner borders separated by a small axial canal. Hesse extended and confirmed these observations. In *P.a.* the eye is of the eucone apposition type, with a distinct and well-developed cone, and rhabdomeres extending up, and to the sides of the cone (Fig. 7.1Q). The retinular cells are only semi-stratified in contrast to apterygotes where the cells are stratified into a distal and proximal group, or as in some of the higher orders where there is one set (unstratified). Cross-sections at the distal end show 4 retinular cells and 4 rhabdomes; further proximally there are 7 retinular cells and 4 or 5 rhabdomeres.[21]

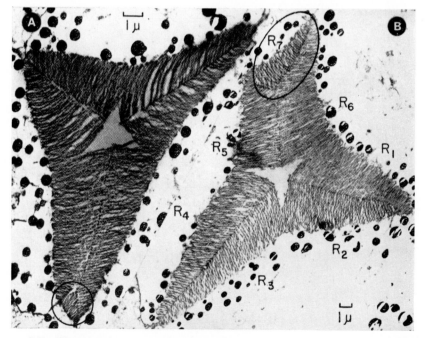

FIG. 7.7 Electronmicrograph of rhabdomeres and retinular cells. **A** is proximal to **B**. (From Wolken and Gupta[57]). These authors interpret the number of rhabdomeres present as shown in **B**, but Hesse and Goldsmith describe 4 rhabdomeres at this level

Wolken and Gupta examined the cockroach rhabdome with the electron microscope. Their transverse sections show a structure in the form of a three-pointed star with an axial cavity, and one eccentric rhabdome lying near the tip of one of the arms of the star. They could identify seven rhabdomeres (Fig. 7.7), and note that the cockroach has the large rhabdom characteristic of 'slow' eyes; it has five times the volume of the *Drosophila* rhabdom. The retinular cells also conform to the 'slow' pattern in that the entire inner margin of the cells form the wedge-shaped rhabdomeres.

The rhabdomeres contain a visual pigment complex containing retinene, and its concentration per rhabdomere was 1×10^8 molecules. This was within the normal photoreceptor range and would just cover the surface area of a rhabdomere as a monolayer.[57]

Physiology of the compound eye

Burtt and Catton[5,6] have studied the electrical changes in the ommatidia and optic lobe of *P.a.* following illumination. The cockroach experiments were subsidiary to work on *Locusta* and other species.

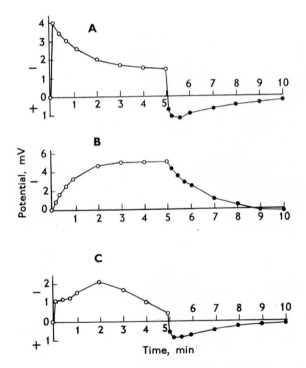

FIG. 7.8   Potential changes accompanying light-adaptation ($\bigcirc$) and dark adaptation ($\bullet$) in the retinula cell zones of A, *Phormia*, B, *Aeschna* (larva) and C, *Periplaneta* (adult). (From Burtt and Catton[6])

A characteristic profile of potential exists along the axis of the eye and optic lobe, in both light and dark adapted states. In the cockroach (*P.a.*) the potential profile was similar to that of *Locusta* with three negative peaks. The first peak at a depth of 850 μ could be localized anatomically in the first synaptic layer of the optic lobe. The profile of *Schistocerca* was less like the *Locusta* type, than that of *Periplaneta*, and those of dragonflies and Diptera exhibited a clear-cut deviation from this form, although changes in potential accompanying light or dark adaptation revealed similarities to *Aeschna* (Fig. 7.8).

Transient responses also occurred, at 'on' and 'off' points with light flash stimulation, but this type of response was of small magnitude in *P.a.* as compared with other insects. In the retinula cells no transient response occurred in *Periplaneta* or *Aeschna*, although it occurred in locusts and flies.

The spectral sensitivity of the cockroach eye has been explored by Walther and Dodt,[52] and Walther.[53,54,55]

It is not entirely clear to what extent the ocellus was used in the earlier work but *Calliphora* and *Periplaneta* eyes were shown to be similar in responding with a greater electrical effect to U.V. and green light than to other parts of the spectrum. At the red end, however, there was a large peak in the *Calliphora* eye absent in *Periplaneta*. A similar spectral sensitivity curve was demonstrated in the roach ocellus, and it was shown that the sensitivity to U.V light varied according to the state of light or dark adaptation quite independently of the response to other wavelengths.[52]

Later work showed that the dorsal and ventral areas of the eye differed in their spectral sensitivity and confirmed the importance of the state of adaptation of the eye in determining sensitivity (Fig. 7.9).[53]

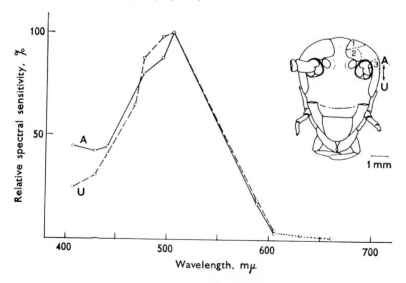

FIG. 7.9   Relative spectral sensitivity of upper (*A*) and lower (*U*) parts of the eye during dark adaptation. .... = whole eye. (From Walther[53])

In the ventral parts of the eye there is only a single sensitivity peak with a maximum at 507 mμ. This is unaltered by the state of adaptation. The dorsal areas on the other hand show a peak in the U.V. as well as this one, when they are dark-adapted. Adaptation with selected monochromatic light significantly alters the sensitivity of dorsal areas, and significant changes in the wave form of the electrical response to different light wavelengths occur in dorsal ommatidia.

It is suggested that there are two different types of receptors or receptor systems appearing most distinct under conditions of red and blue-violet light adaptation.[53,54,55]

Comparisons between the roach eye (*P.a.*) and those of diurnal species is of interest. Ruck showed that in the former the flicker fusion perception range extended to 45–60 c/s, while in day-flying insects such as *Apis*, *Pachydiplax* and *Phormia* it occurred up to 190–350 c/s. This confirmed Autrum's general theory of 'fast' and 'slow' eyes, but Ruck found himself in disagreement over Autrum's correlation of 'fast' eye type with typical electroretinogram, low photic sensitivity and extremely rapid rate of adaptation. He found that the bee and roach electroretinogram were of similar form.[48]

The ocelli

In Miall and Denny's monograph[28] The ocelli are described as 'white fenestrae, which . . . may represent two simple eyes which have lost their dioptric apparatus'. This is a reasonable statement of the main anatomical feature of these eyes, but in many of the later popular treatises, the two pale areas between the antennal bases are described as organs of unknown function (Marshall and Hurst,[27] Bullough[4]). In superficial appearance they differ from the ocelli of many other insects in their not forming an ocellar triangle, their pale colour due to lack of masking pigment, and their large slightly concave lenses. Ruck refers to them as the dorsal ocelli, following Snodgrass[51] and earlier workers, who thus distinguished them from the ventral ocelli of some larvae; in the case of Blattodea, however, this gives a somewhat erroneous idea of their position.

Due largely to the work of Ruck,[46,47,48,49] a considerable amount of information is forthcoming as to the structure and function of these organs, to which the reader should refer for details. The ocelli of *P.a.* and *Blaberus craniifer* were examined.

Below the flattened corneal lens the sense cells are arranged in groups of three to five to form retinulae, scattered at different depths. A rhabdom formed of the inner margin of retinula cells is visible, the retinular axons passing down in groups to a synaptic layer at the base of the ocellus. Within the synaptic layer large fibres from the ocellar nerve can be seen. There are about 25 fibres, 4 of which are especially thick (6–10 μ). Between the synaptic and sensory zones lies a layer of whitish material composed of small spheres, some of which are radially striated like urate spheres.

Fine stainless-steel macroelectrodes were used to record at different depths within the ocellus, the indifferent lead being taken from the antenna. The ocellar response was investigated as a function of log. intensity and the state of light or dark adaptation. A slow wave response with small on–off spikes was obtained in both states of adaptation increasing with stimulus intensity. The increase in response with intensity was regular in the dark-adapted state, but fell off rather sharply in the light-adapted eye above -3.0, and was at all times less than in the dark-adapted state (Fig. 7.10).

The author suggests that there is evidence for negative and positive components in the retinogram. The positive 'off' spike increases in a regular stepwise manner over a certain intensity range, and it seems likely that this is due to the recruitment of ocellar fibres. The 'on' response has a positive and a negative component. Thus there are three components—a positive and a negative slow wave which sum algebraically in various ways; and 'off' spikes. Severing the ocellar nerve abolishes the 'off' spikes and these might be expected to originate from ocellar nerve fibres, but they could not be recorded directly from the intact ocellar nerve.

Ruck discusses his results in comparison with recordings made from locust material by Hoyle and Parry and underlines the importance of the position of both leads. Ruck also examined the responses of the ocellus of *Melanoplus*, and although generally similar to the roach, differences of detail are evident.

Both cockroach and *Melanoplus* ocelli were highly sensitive, responding to between 10^{-4} and 10^{-5} ft candles in the case of the *Periplaneta* 'off' spike (Fig. 7.10).[46]

The effect on response of light and dark adaptation was investigated in more detail by Ruck. Exposure to rather bright light (12,000 ft candles) reduces the sensitivity of the ocellus by a factor of about 30,000. Increase in responsiveness during dark adaptation was slow, after one minute it was only two to three times that of the fully light-adapted state.[47]

In a study on the eyes and ocelli of a number of insect species Ruck found that the greatest sensitivity was found in the dragonfly ocellus, but it did not dark adapt more rapidly than the roach ocellus even though other characteristics differed (such as flicker fusion frequency perception), as it might have been expected to on the grounds of Autrum's classification.

Ruck is of the general opinion that electroretinogram, photic sensitivity, adaptation rate and fusion frequency perception are probably unrelated properties of the eye, and that flicker frequency resolution depends on the retinula cells, rather than on post-synaptic events as suggested by Autrum.[48]

Walther and Dodt figure a bimodal curve for the spectral sensitivity of the ocellus very similar to that of the compound eye, the height of the U.V. peak being dependent on the state of light or dark adaptation.[52]

Goldsmith and Ruck studied the spectral sensitivity of the roach ocellus (*Periplaneta americana* and *Blaberus craniifer*). The relative number of quanta needed to produce a constant size electrical response in the ocellus were measured at various wavelengths between 302 mμ and 523 mμ. The wave form of the dark-adapted ocellar response depended on the intensity but not the wavelength of stimulating light. They suggested that a single type of receptor was present with a maximum sensitivity of about 500 mμ, but they do not seem to have observed the peak at the U.V. end of the spectrum observed by Walther and Dodt,

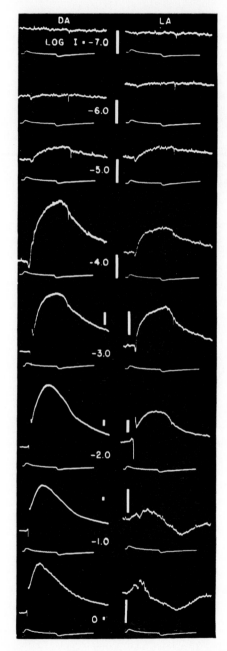

FIG. 7.10   Ocellar responses to illumination for $\frac{1}{8}$ sec in dark (DA), and light (LA) adaptation. All calibration strips equal 1 mV. The upper trace is the response from the receptor cell layer, the lower trace the stimulus duration. (From Ruck[46])

although they point out that the bee has receptors corresponding to sensitivity peaks at 490 mμ and 335–340 mμ. The spectral absorption of the ocella cornea in *Blaberus* was not significant between 350 and 700 mμ.

Goldsmith and Ruck note the complete absence of pigment and the white reflecting layer of the ocellus.[14]

The work of Harker suggests that at least one of the important functions of the ocelli may be in relation to the regulation of activity via diurnal light fluctuation and the hormonal system. She showed that insects (*P.a.*) would still respond to changes in light intensity when the eyes were painted over, but that this response disappeared when the ocelli were covered (consult Chapter 6).[20]

Dermal light sense

Graber[15] suggested that a dermal light sense unconnected with the major photoreceptors might be present in the cockroach.

That the peripheral nervous system might be directly responsive to light stimuli is a suggestion that gains some indirect support from the transparent nature of much of the cuticle, and from the complexity of the dermal innervation. Fine nerve branches can be seen in methylene blue preparation ramifying between the epidermal cells and apparently unconnected to any well-defined cuticular sensilla (Fig. 7.1N).

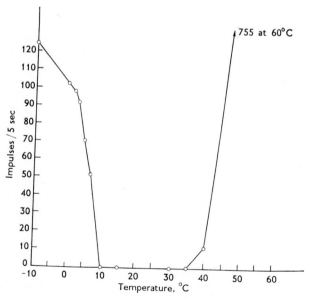

FIG. 7.11   Response of tarsal receptors to changes in temperature. Impulses per second in tibial n.5 at the temperature shown, after acclimatization at 22°. (From Kerkut and Taylor[25])

Temperature reception

It must be clear that changes in temperature will eventually affect directly the rate of heartbeat and many other functions, and it might be argued that directional responses based on localized receptors are not logically to be expected in most non-parasitic species.

Temperature preferences have been studied in *P.a.* by Gunn[16,17] and by Gunn and Cosway,[18] in the later papers in relation to humidity.

The preferred temperature range of *B.o.* is 20–29°, while the upper limit extended to 33° in *P.a.* and *Blaberus giganteus*. The lower limits of temperature preference were less well defined than the upper ones, presumably due to heat injury levels.[17] Desiccation lowered the preferred range in *B.o.*[16]

Kerkut and Taylor provided evidence for the existence of temperature receptive areas in the tarsus of *P.a.* These gave well-defined responses over three ranges of temperature (Fig. 7.11). Recordings were made from the tibia as near the nerve as possible, and the receptive areas were located in the pad between the claws in the first–fourth tarsal segments.

Over the range 0–28° ascending temperatures produced momentary increases in activity, intervals of 5° being distinguished. Cooling over the range 13–0° has the effect of producing a gradual increase in activity, discrimination being at the level of 1°. Above 30° prolonged electrical activity occurs.

The number of receptor types involved is obscure.[25]

CHEMORECEPTION

The antennae

In *P.a.* the antennae in the adult are normally one to one-and-a-half times the length of the body and composed of many annuli. If the tip of the antenna is examined it is often found to be broken at its extremity, the annuli separating rather readily.

In *P.a.* the antennae are clothed with many hairs, although in *Blaberus craniifer* there are few. The antennal hairs of *P.a.* can be grouped in two categories: thick-walled bristles, and thin-walled hairs (Fig. 7.1S). The tapered bristles are similar in shape, but vary in size and have fluted surfaces. The inner channel is clearly visible and runs to the tip which is slightly recurved. The bristles have straight shafts and are socketed. The largest of the thin-walled hairs are often sickle-shaped and more abundant at the joints and towards the extremity of the antennae than at the base or between joints. The distal part of these hairs often tapers little and the tip is bluntly rounded. Smaller and less-curved hairs of a similar type are present, the smallest appearing as short conical pegs (Fig. 7.1S).

A similar range of hair types has been described by Roth and Willis in *Bt.g.* The bristles were described by them as sensilla chaetica, the long thin-walled hairs as sensilla trichodea, and the thin-walled pegs as sensilla basiconica. Males and females of this species differ in the abundance of thin-walled sensilla on the proximal annuli. In the males segment 3 is without them, but they are found on annuli 4 to 13 or more. In the female, however, they are absent from annuli 3 to 8.[43]

Glaser performed a number of simple experiments with *P.a.* and noted that in the presence of food, rapid oscillation of the antennae occurred. Using Roquefort cheese as an odour source, he noted that roach without antennae were much retarded in their ability to locate food. This effect was slightly increased by removing the palps also, but from the way in which the palps were used it was suggested that the antenna bore distance chemoreceptors, the palps contact chemoreceptors.[13]

Male individuals of *P.a.* respond to extracts of a substance produced by the female by a stereotyped behaviour involving posture, antennal movements, wing fluttering and protrusion of the abdomen. Wharton, Miller and Wharton investigated the response of males to different dilutions of the attractant. The responses are only well developed when the male roaches are in groups. The percentage response is proportional to the log of the concentration throughout a wide range. A rather slow form of adaptation appeared in repetitive tests.[56]

Roys examined the receptivity of antennal receptors in *P.a.* to various odour stimuli, using a method of d.c. amplification to obtain summed records of small responses. Changes in tip to base potentials were obtained from the excised antenna.[44]

From this small amount of work it would appear that cockroaches have a well-developed sense of smell, but the attractions for researchers of other insect orders, especially of the Diptera, have so far outweighed the advantages of cockroach material.

Contact chemoreception, gustatory responses

As pointed out by Frings,[12] these probably lie on the tips of the maxillary and labial palpi, and on the inner surface of the mouth-parts, and the wall of the mouth and pharynx. The palps are densely covered with the bristle type of hair described on the antenna. The apex of the last segment has an especially close pile of sensilla; some very short peg-like structures are visible between the bases of the larger hairs. It seems also likely that chemoreceptors lie in other regions of the gut, and may be involved in the muscular and secretory cycles of the gut. Davey and Treherne identified groups of bipolar sense cells in the wall of the pharynx, with peg-like tips projecting into the pharyngeal lumen (Fig. 7.12). They believe this sense organ may be an osmo-receptor involved in the mechanism of crop emptying.[7]

Frings used the drinking response of cockroaches mounted on glass rods to determine the acceptability of various substances. Sucrose solutions were acceptable down to a threshold of 0·026 M, so a 0·1 M sucrose solution was used as a base to which other solutions were added. Rejection thresholds for 4 acids, 5 hydroxides and 28 salts were determined.

Many electrolytes, especially acids at 'below rejection' concentrations, were preferred to sugar water, suggesting that rejection thresholds were not true sensory thresholds.

Acid and hydroxide thresholds were much lower than those for neutral salts.

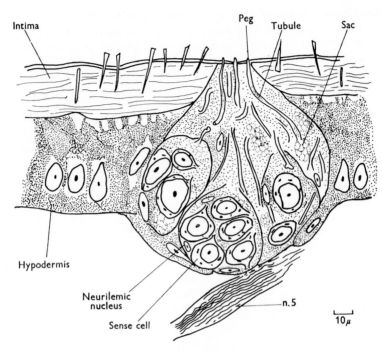

FIG. 7.12   Receptor from the wall of the pharynx, possibly an osmoreceptor.
(From Davey and Treherne[7])

H_3O^+ and OH^- ions had a general stimulatory effect, but the H_3O^+ ion concentration at rejection threshold was 8–13 times lower with CH_3COOH^- than for HCl, H_2SO_4 or HNO_3. Similarly the OH^- ion concentration for NH_4^+OH was 12 times down at the rejection threshold, than for NaOH, KOH, LiOH and $Ca(OH)_2$.

The order of stimulative efficiency of the cations as reciprocals of the threshold normalities in ascending order was Li^+, Na^+, Mg^+, NH_4^+, H_3O^+; and for anions $-PO_4^-$, CH_3COOH^-, SO_4^- and Cl^-, Br^-, I^-, No_3^-, OH^-.

The order for the cations reflected their ionic mobilities and that for the anions is empirical, but may be related to their penetration into cells.

In this research the cockroach was used as an example from the Insecta and no comparison with other insect species was attempted.[12]

Roys has shown that even quite unspecialized parts of the nervous system would respond to solutions containing NaCl, HCl, sucrose and quinine.

A successive lowering of the threshold of response to NaCl, was obtained from the tarsus, from the tarsus slit open, from the nerve cord, and from the desheathed nerve cord. An unspecialized responsiveness to the other substances was also shown.[45]

Hygroreceptors, humidity responses

Hygroreceptors were tentatively identified by Roth and Willis in *B.g.* They found that the reaction of the insect to a choice between 0% and 100% relative humidity declined as successive annuli were removed from the antennae. As has been already mentioned in connection with antennal structure, the male has thin-walled hair sensilla on annuli 4 to 8, while the female does not (Fig. 7.1S). This sexual difference is paralleled by the reaction of insects with partly amputated antennae, to humidity differences. A greater number of segments have to be left intact in the female than in the male for a standard level of reaction to humidity to be scored. This suggests that the thin-walled receptors play a significant part in humidity responses.[43]

Gunn[17] showed that desiccated cockroaches (*B.o.*) that had lost 70% of their initial weight showed a preference for a much lower temperature range, than had been previously the case. The range shifted from 20–29° to 12–23°. The choice of air of lower evaporating power may be mediated by some direct effect of blood concentration on the nervous system. When cockroaches were placed in a humidity gradient at a given temperature (Gunn and Cosway[18]) they became distributed at random, but as the temperature was raised they mostly became rather hygropositive.

The responses of cockroaches to different humidities does not seem as clear cut as in some other insect species.

REFERENCES

1. AUTRUM, H. and SCHNEIDER, W. (1948). Vergleichende Untersuchungen über den Erschütterungsinn der Insekten. *Z. vergl. Physiol.*, **31** (1), 77–88.
2. BARNES, T. C. (1931). The kinesthetic sense of insects. *Ann. ent. Soc. Am.*, **24**, 824–6.
3. BECHT, G. (1958). The influence of DDT and lindane on chordotonal organs in the cockroach. *Nature, Lond.*, **181**, 777–9.
4. BULLOUGH, W. S. (1954). *Practical Invertebrate Anatomy*. MacMillan, London.
5. BURTT, E. T. and CATTON, W. T. (1964a). The potential profile of the insect compound eye and optic lobe. *J. Insect. Physiol.*, **10**, 689–710.
6. BURTT, E. T. and CATTON, W. T. (1964b). Potential changes in the eye and optic lobe of certain insects during light and dark adaptation. *J. Insect Physiol.*, **10**, 865–86.
6b. CHAPMAN, K. M. (1965). Campaniform organs on tactile spines. *J. exp. Biol.*, **42**, 191–203.
7. DAVEY, K. G. and TREHERNE, J. E. (1963). Studies on crop function in the cockroach. II. The nervous control of crop-emptying. *J. exp. Biol.*, **40**, 775–80.
8. DAVEY, K. G. (1962). The mode of action of the corpus cardiacum on the hindgut in *Periplaneta americana*. *J. exp. Biol.*, **39**, 319–24.
9. DEBAISIEUX, P. (1938). Organes scolopidianx des pattes des insectes. *Cellule*, **47**, 79–202.
10. FINLAYSON, L. H. and LOWENSTEIN, O. (1958). The structure and function of abdominal stretch receptors in insects. *Proc. R. Soc.*, B, **148**, 433–49.
11. FRIEDRICH, H. (1929). Vergleichende Untersuchungen über der tibialen Scolopalorgane einiger Orthoptera. *Z. wiss. Zool.*, **134**, 84–148.
12. FRINGS, H. (1946). Taste thresholds, sucrose and electrolytes in cockroach. *J. exp. Zool.*, **102**, 23–50.
13. GLASER, R. W. (1927). Antennal sense of smell in *Periplaneta*. *Psyche, Camb.*, **34**, 209–15.

14. GOLDSMITH, T. H. and RUCK, P. (1958). The special sensitivities of the dorsal ocelli of cockroaches and honeybees. *J. gen. Physiol.*, **41**, 1171–85.
15. GRABER, V. (1883). Dermal light sense in Blattella. *Sber. Akad. Wiss. Wien*, **87**, 201–36.
16. GUNN, D. L. (1934). Temperature preference in the cockroach. *Z. vergl. Physiol.*, **20**, 617–25.
17. GUNN, D. L. (1935). Temperature preference and rates of desiccation in the cockroach. *J. exp. Biol.*, **12**, 185–90.
18. GUNN, D. L. and COSWAY, C. A. (1938). Temperature and humidity responses in *Blatta orientalis*. *J. exp. Biol.*, **15**, 555–63.
19. GUTHRIE, D. M. (1966). Sound production and reception in *Henschoutedenia epilamproides*. *J. exp. Biol.* **45**, 321–8.
20. HARKER, J. (1956). Factors controlling the diurnal rhythm of activity of *P.a.* The Ocellar contribution to behaviour. *J. exp. Biol.*, **33**, 224–34.
21. HESSE, R. (1901). Untersuchungen über die Organe der Lichtempfindung bei niederen Thieren. VII—von den Arthropoden Augen. *Z. wiss. Zool.*, **70**, 347–473.
22. HOWSE, P. E. (1962). The perception of vibration by the subgenual organ in *Zootermopsis angusticollis* Emerson and *Periplaneta americana* L. *Experientia*, **18**, 457–9.
23. HOWSE, P. E. (1964). An investigation into the mode of action of the subgennal organ in the termite *Zootermopsis angusticollis* Emerson, and in the cockroach, *Periplaneta americana* L. *J. Insect Physiol.*, **10**, 409–24.
24. HSÜ, F. (1938). Étude cytologique et comparée sur les sensilla des insectes. *Cellule*, **47**, 1–60.
25. KERKUT, G. A. and TAYLOR, B. J. R. (1957). A temperature receptor in the tarsus of the cockroach *P.a.* *J. exp. Biol.*, **34**, 486–93.
26. LEFEUVRE, J.-C. (1961). Les sensilla trichodea de *Blabera craniifer*. *Bull. Soc. Sci. Bretagne*, **36**, 67–80.
27. MARSHALL, A. M. and HURST, C. H. (1892). *A Junior Course of Practical Zoology*. Smith and Elder, London.
28. MIALL, L. C. and DENNY, A. (1886). *The Cockroach*. Lovell Reeve, London.
29. MILBURN, N. (1960). Pharmacology of campaniform organs of roach trochanter (private communication).
30. NIJENHUIS, E. D. and DRESDEN, D. (1952). A micro-morphological study on the sensory supply of the mesothoracic leg of the American cockroach *Periplaneta americana*. *Proc. K. Ned. Akad. Wet*, Series C., **55**, 3, 300–10.
31. OSBORNE, M. P. and FINLAYSON, L. H. (1962). The structure and topography of stretch receptors in representatives of seven orders of insects. *Q. Jl microsc. Sci.*, **103**, 227–42.
32. OSBORNE, M. P. (1963). An electron microscope study of an abdominal stretch receptor of the cockroach. *J. Insect Physiol.*, **9**, 237–45.
33. PRINGLE, J. W. S. (1938). Proprioception in insects. I. A new type of mechano-receptor from the palps of the cockroach. *J. exp. Biol.*, **15**, 101–13.
34. PRINGLE, J. W. S. (1938). Proprioception in insects II. The action of the campaniform sensilla on the legs. *J. exp. Biol.*, **15**, 114–31.
35. PRINGLE, J. W. S. (1938). Proprioception in insects III. The function of the hair plates. *J. exp. Biol.*, **15**, 467–73.
36. PRINGLE, J. W. S. and WILSON, V. J. (1952). The response of a sense organ to a harmonic stimulus. *J. exp. Biol.*, **29**, 220–34.
37. PUMPHREY, R. J. and RAWDON-SMITH, A. F. (1936). Synchronized action potentials in the cercal nerve of the cockroach in response to auditory stimuli. *Proc. physiol. Soc., Camb.* in *J. Physiol., Lond.*
38. PUMPHREY, R. J. (1936). Slow adaptation of a tactile receptor in the leg of the common cockroach. *J. Physiol.*, **87**, 6P–7P.

39. PUMPHREY, R. J. and RAWDON-SMITH, A. F. (1936). 1 to 3, and 1 to 4 alternation in the cercal nerve of the cricket. *Proc. Physiol.*, **87**, 57–9.

40. PUMPHREY, R. J. and RAWDON-SMITH, A. F. (1936). Response of auditory receptors including anal cerci of cockroach. *Proc. R. Soc.* B, **121**, 18–27.

41. PUMPHREY, R. J. and RAWDON-SMITH, A. F. (1936). Sensitivity of insects to sound. *Nature, Lond.*, **137**, 990.

42. PUMPHREY, R. J. and RAWDON-SMITH, A. F. (1937). Synaptic transmission of nervous impulses through the last abdominal ganglion of the cockroach. *Proc. R. Soc.*, B, **122**, 106–18.

43. ROTH, L. M. and WILLIS, E. R. (1952). Possible hygroreceptors in *Aedes aegypti* (L.) and *Blattella germanica* L. *J. Phys.*, **91**, 1–14.

44. ROYS, C. C. (1954). Olfactory nerve potentials a direct measure of chemo-reception in insects. *Ann. N. Y. Acad. Sci.*, **58**, 250–5.

45. ROYS, C. C. (1956). A comparison between the thresholds of taste receptors and of non-gustatory nerve tissue to taste stimuli (in *P.a.*). *Anat. Rec.*, 125, 555.

46. RUCK, P. (1957). The electrical responses of dorsal ocelli in cockroaches and grasshoppers. *J. Insect Physiol.*, **1**, 109–23.

47. RUCK, P. (1958). Dark adaptation of the ocellus in *P.a.*: A study of the electrical response to illumination. *J. Insect Physiol.*, **2**, 189–98.

48. RUCK, P. (1958). A comparison of the electrical responses of compound eyes and dorsal ocelli in 4 insect species. *J. Insect Physiol.*, **2**, 261–74.

49. RUCK, P. (1961). Electrophysiology of the insect dorsal ocellus. 1 Origin of the components in the electroretinogram. *J. gen. Physiol.* **44**, 605–27.

50. SIHLER, H. (1924). Die Sinnesorgane an den Cerci der Insekten. **45**, 519–80.

51. SNODGRASS, R. E. (1935). *Principles of Insect Morphology*. McGraw-Hill, New York and Maidenhead.

52. WALTHER, J. B. and DODT, E. (1957). Electrophysiologische Untersuchungen über die Ultraviolettempfindlichkeit von Insektenaugen. *Experientia*, **13**, 333.

53. WALTHER, J. B. (1958). Untersuchungen am Belichtungspotentiel des Kom-plexauges von *Periplaneta* mit farbigen Reien und Selektive Adaptation. *Biol. Zbl.*, **77**, 63–104.

54. WALTHER, J. B. (1958). Changes in spectral sensitivity and form of retinal action potential of the cockroach eye by selective adaptation. *J. Insect Physiol.*, **2**, 142–51.

55. WALTHER, J. B. and DODT, E. (1959). Die Spektralsensitivität von Insekten—Komplex augen im Ultraviolett bis 290 mμ. *Z. Naturf.*, **14b**, 273–8.

56. WHARTON, D. R. A., MILLER, G. L. and WHARTON, M. L. (1954). The odorous attractant of the American cockroach *Periplaneta americana*. *J. gen. Physiol.*, **37**, 461–9.

57. WOLKEN, J. J. and GUPTA, P. D. (1961). Photoreceptor structures IV. The retinal cells of the cockroach. *J. biophys. biochem. Cytol.*, **9**, 720–3.

ADDENDUM

Sense organs

Florentine claims to have identified areas of sound receptive hairs in the lateral abdominal folds of *P.a.* These hairs respond to 1 msec clicks at 79 to 90 db. Guthrie has noticed a similar responsiveness to apparatus switch noises in the cercal hair response of *Henschoutedenia*.

Florentine also noted that substratum vibrations were stimuli for the ab-dominal hairs. To what extent these hairs are more specialized for sound re-ception than general body hairs is not clear.

A most interesting association of receptors has recently been discovered by

Moulins. A large multipolar receptor lies with many of its processes on a transverse connective tissue lamella in the hypopharynx of *Blaberus*. Other processes run on to the cuticle. The axon joins the hypopharyngeal branch of the labral nerve. At either end of the lamella lie small ganglia on the course of the hypopharyngeal branches of the mandibular nerves. Each ganglion contains three cells each with a pair of peripheral processes extending into the connective tissue band. Moulins believes that the tension in this lamella is influenced by the volume of the cibarium.

Roth and Barth have followed up an earlier line of work by Roth, on the sense organs involved in mating. The copulatory behaviour in a number of cockroach species is described, together with the results of amputating sense organ bearing structures. As had been indicated previously chemoreceptors play a key rôle.

ADDITIONAL REFERENCES

FLORENTINE, GERARD J. (1967). An abdominal receptor of the American cockroach *Periplaneta americana* and its response to airborne sound. *J. Insect Physiol.*, **13**, 215–18.

GUTHRIE, D. M. (1967). Multipolar stretch receptors and the insect leg reflex. *J. Insect Physiol.* **13**, 1637–1644.

MOULINS, M. (1966). Presence d'un recepteur de tension dans l'hypopharynx de *Blabera craniifer* Burm. *C.R. Acad. Sci. Paris*, **262**, 2476–9.

MOULINS, M. (1967). Les cellules sensorielle de l'organe hypopharyngien de *Blabera craniifer*. *C. R. Acad. Sc. Paris*, **265**, 44–47.

ROTH, L. M. and BARTH, R. H. (1967). The sense organs employed by cockroaches in mating behaviour. *Behaviour*, **28**, 58–95.

8   *The nervous system*

THE TOPOGRAPHY OF THE NERVOUS SYSTEM
NERVES OF THE HEAD
Where appropriate, muscle numbers are given in brackets, after the nerve.

The supra-oesophageal ganglion (Fig. 8.1A)

(a) PROTOCEREBRUM

This is divided clearly into right and left lobes. *The dorsal integumentary nerve (n.1)* (nt. Willey) arises near the boundary between the proto- and deutocerebrum, but the internal root runs into the neuropile at the tritocerebral level.[104] As in the locust, it probably collects axons from trichoid mechanoreceptors and thermoreceptors on the vertex and frons.

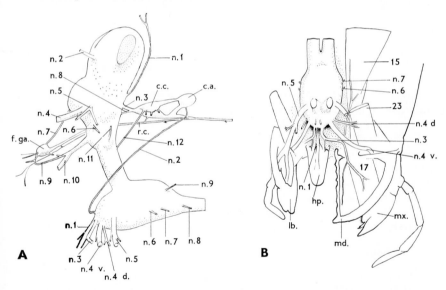

FIG. 8.1   The nervous system of the head. **A,** The supra- and sub-oesophageal ganglia, lateral view. Nerves numbered in order. c.a.—corpus allatum, c.c.—corpus cardiacum, f.ga.—frontal ganglion, r.c.—recurrent nerve. (After Willey[104]). **B,** Suboseophageal ganglion seen from above (dorso-anterior dissection). n.4 d., n.4 v.—dorsal and ventral roots of nerve 4, lb.—right half of the labium, md.—mandible, mx.—maxilla, hp.—hypopharynx. Muscles 15, 17 and 23 are shown

Ocellar nerve (n.2). The large shallow ocelli receive broad nerves from the proto-cerebrum. According to Ruck, the ocelli probably receive the centrifugal axons of interneurones.[86]

Dorsal cardiac nerve (n.3) (ncc.II Willey).[104] This nerve runs postero-ventrally to the corpus cardiacum.

Optic lobes. The outer chiasma may correspond to a distinct nerve, but the elaboration of this region obscures homology with other head nerves.

(b) DEUTOCEREBRUM

Antennal nerve (n.4). This is a thick nerve passing antero-laterally into the antennal lumen, where it receives fibres from the many sense organs, and inner-vates the intrinsic muscles (1 and 2). Eggers describes the type of Johnston's organ found in the antenna of orthopteroid insects.[25]

Dorsal deutocerebral nerve (n.5). Arises laterally and dorsally and innervates the three large extrinsic dorsal muscles (3–5).

Ventral deutocerebral nerve (n.6). A small nerve to the ventral extrinsic antennal muscle (6), and to the positional sense hair organs at the base of the antennal socket.

Median frontal connective (n.7) (n.conn. Willey).[104] A median nerve running anteriorly to the frontal ganglion.

Main cardiac nerve (n.8) (ncc.1 Willey). A broad short nerve connecting the deutocerebrum to the corpus cardiacum posteriorly.

(c) TRITOCEREBRUM

Lateral frontal connective (n.9) (l.f.conn., Willey). Runs forward on either side to join the frontal ganglion. The labral levators (12 and 13) are innervated via this root according to Willey.[104]

Labral nerve (n.10). A large, predominantly sensory trunk arising anteriorly with n.9, it innervates the sensory areas of the clypeus and labrum. There appears to be no labral ganglion.

Lateral integumentary nerve (n.11) (n.t. Willey). A small nerve innervating sensory structures on the genal areas of the head.

Ventral cardiac nerve (n.12) (n.cc.III Willey). A small nerve running dorsally from the boundary between tritocerebrum and circumoesophageal connectives, to the corpus cardiacum.

The circumoesophageal connectives are short and broad. A large and a small transverse commissure join the two connectives beneath the oesophagus.

Sub-oesophageal ganglion (Fig. 8.1B)

The neuromeres of this ganglion cannot be easily distinguished externally, so the nerves will not be segregated on this basis. The ganglion is often best dissected from the anterior aspect. Passing from the anterior to the posterior region the nerves are:

Hypopharyngeal nerve (n.1). This fine nerve originates near the mid-line, and innervates some hypopharyngeal muscles (19, 21 and 22). A ventral ramus runs down into the hypopharynx.

Corpus allatum nerve (n.2) (n.c.a.II Willey).[104] A fine nerve arising slightly dorsal to n.1 and running postero-dorsally to the corpus allatum. A side branch may run to the prothoracic gland.

Mandibular nerve (n.3). This stout nerve gives off a few fine branches to the cibarial wall and hypopharynx before turning laterally into the mandible. Within the mandible, it divides into a dorsal ramus to muscles 15 and 16, and a ventral ramus to the triturating wall of the mandible and the internal adductor (17).

Maxillary nerve (n.4). This nerve has two roots.

(i) Dorsal trunk. This smaller nerve innervates the majority of the muscles at the base of the maxilla (23–28).

(ii) Ventral trunk. This divides into a palpal ramus with three sensory branches to the three basal palp segments, and ramus divided again into a branch to the galea and another to the lacinia. Muscles 29–38 are largely innervated by trunk (ii). Hypopharyngeal muscle 20 appears to receive fibres from this nerve.

Labial nerve (n.5). Arising as a single root, but soon giving off small side branches to the muscles at the base of the labrum (39–41). It then divides into two rami, one to the palp, the other to the ligula.

Cervical nerves (n.6, 7 and 8). Lying behind the labial nerve root are a pair of small nerves which appear to innervate cervical muscles inserted on the tentorium, n.6 running to muscle 54 and n.7 to 55. Still further posteriorly is a small nerve trunk (n.8) running posteriorly to innervate muscles 52 and 53 (prothoracic nerves innervate part of these muscles).

Prothoracic gland nerve (n.9). A fine dorso-posterior nerve (p.g.n. Willey) running posteriorly to the prothoracic gland.

THE THORACIC NERVOUS SYSTEM

Each thoracic ganglion possesses eight nerve roots according to the classification of Pipa, Cook and Richards, if the interganglionic connectives are included under the heading of nerves. The descriptions of Dresden and Nijenhuis[22,60,61] and the previous authors[66] have been slightly reduced in detail for the purposes of this work, and additional information should be sought with the authors quoted. A fuller description of the spiracular nerve trunks is placed in a section near the end of this chapter. Nerves are numbered and lettered anterior to posterior. Nerve 1 is the anterior connective. 3Ar1b is nerve 3A, ramus 1, branch b.

Prothoracic ganglion

Nerve 2. Branches are as follows: 2Ar1 (muscles 55 and 84); 2Ar2 fuses with the interganglionic connective. 2B fuses with 2Br1e from the mesothorax, and one of the resulting nerves (O) joins part of CA innervating muscle 56. Other nerves from the first fusion innervate muscles 54, 63, 64 and muscles inserted on the fore-gut. A small branch joins n.1. Nerve 2C supplies muscles 59–62 and accepts sensory axons from the protergum. A chiasmic nerve arises from the antero-dorsal region of the ganglion, and its end organs were tentatively identified as muscle 64, a cervical hair plate and sensory areas near the trochantin.

6*

Nerve 3. 3Ar1a supplies the sense organs of the first cervical plate, and 3Ar1b that of the second. Nerve 3Ar1c supplies muscles 57 and 58. Nerve 3Ar1a (rather variable) accepts sensory axons from the episternum. 3Ar3 innervates muscles 71 to 73, and muscles 65, 69, 70 and 74 receive fibres from nerve 3Ar2. A number of sensory branches arise at this level; 3Br1a supplies antero-medial tergal areas, 3Br1b the antero-lateral tergum and a small adjacent sclerite, 3Br2 the medial protergum, and 3Br3 the antero-lateral tergum and epimeron. 3br1 is a sensory nerve to the second trochantin, and 3br2 supplies a coxo-trochantinal chordotonal organ. 3br3 innervates the first trochantin, and a coxal hair plate near the pleuron. The outer coxal hair plate is innervated by 3br4, and 3br5 is a sensory nerve to the proximal coxal chordotonal organ, other branches (3br5b) passing to the setae of the anterior coxal wall.

Nerve 4. A purely motor nerve. 4r1b supplies the small muscle 82b while 4r2 innervates muscle 83. 4r3 supplies motor fibres to tergal (a and b) and pleural (c and d) parts of the large trochanteral depressor 85.

Nerve 5. 5r1a innervates other parts of muscle 85 (e, f, g and h). Nerve 5r2 is a sensory ramus supplying setae on the meron. Muscles 86 and 87 are innervated by 5r1b. A more detailed description of the end organs of this important nerve will be given in the section on the mesothoracic nerves.

Nerve 6. 6A supplies various tergomeral (76–79), and tergo-coxal muscles (80 and 81). 6Br1 sends axons to muscle 98, while 6Br2 innervates the episternal muscle (97). 6Br2b supplies muscle 82, and the sensory branch 6Br3 accepts axons from setae on the meron. An important motor branch 6Br4 runs to muscles 88 (a and b), and 89.

Nerve 7. This small sensory nerve arises on the ventral surface of the ganglion and supplies setae in the sternal region.

Nerve 8. This is a spiracular nerve and will be dealt with in a separate section.

Mesothoracic ganglion (Figs. 8.2, 8.3)

Nerve 2. Trunk 2A divides into 2Ar1a supplying muscles 99 and 102; 2Ar1b innervating muscles 100 and 101; and 2Ar2 which fuses with the interganglionic connective. Nerve 2Br1a supplies the transverse ventral muscle 103, and the very delicate 2Br1b fuses with n.8. According to Pipa, Cook and Richards, nerve 2Br1b can be mistaken for a trachea. 2Br1c innervates a fine muscular strand identified by the above authors, and described by them as muscle Z (114B). It also innervates muscle 96. Nerve 2Br1d innervates the setae above the first spiracle, but part of the nerve may be fused with another ramus (n.8).

Nerve 2Br2b is an important nerve branch supplying the numerous sense organs of the wing surface (see Flight, p. 252). It divides into rami traversing the main wing veins. In the metathorax the wing nerve has a similar origin.

In the wingless cockroach *Loboptera decipiens* lateral thoracic lobes similar to those characteristic of larvae are visible, but although the innervation of these lobes is much reduced as compared with the pattern of nerves in the wing; costal, subcostal, radial, cubital, first anal and anal nerves can still be made out arising from 2Br2b.[69]

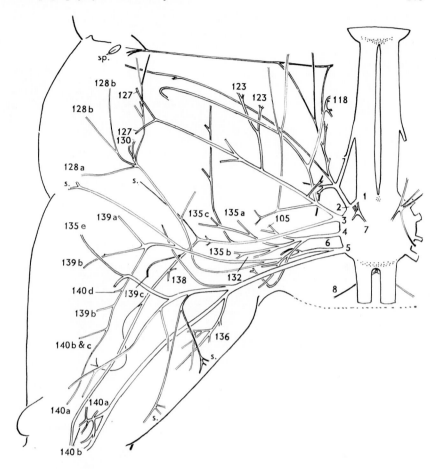

FIG. 8.2 The nervous system of the mesothorax, ventral view. Numbers 1 to 8—
nerves, numbers 105 to 140—muscles, s.—sensory terminal, sp.—spiracle. (Based
largely on Dresden and Nijenhuis[61], with material from Pipa, Cook and Richards[66]
and other sources)

Nerve 3. This nerve divides very near its ganglionic origin into large anterior
and posterior trunks.

3A. This branch innervates coxal adductors 118, 119, 120, 122, 123 and 124,
and the promotors 126, and 127. Trunk muscles 114–16, and 121, also receive
motor fibres from this source. Nerve 3Ar1b runs to the pleural arm and fuses
with 6Ar4 to innervate muscles 114–16 so it is not certain that all these muscles
receive axons from n.3A. A small anterior trunk (3Ar1a) runs to a sensory area
on the medial border of the episternum.

3B. This is an important sensory nerve. Four branches, however, supply

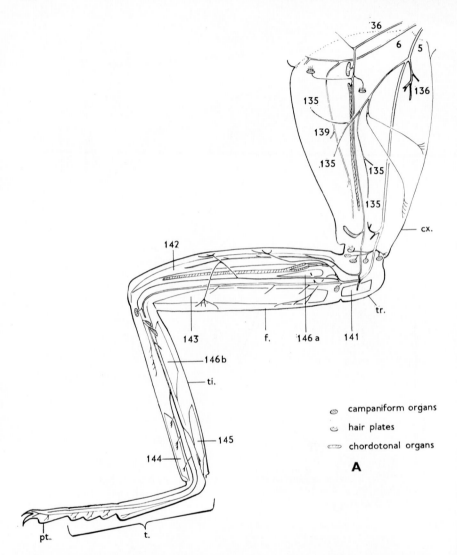

FIG. 8.3**A**   The innervation of the mesothoracic leg, ventral view. Proximal part
after Nijenhuis and Dresden. Numbers 3 to 6—nerves, numbers 135 to 146—
muscles. Types of sense organ as shown. cx.—coxa, f.—femur, pt.—pretarsus,
t.—tarsus, ti.—tibia, tr.—trochanter

muscles: 3Br6 to muscle 138, r7 to 139c, 410 joins a branch of n.5 which runs to
muscle 141, and r11 innervates muscle 142. The sense organs supplied all lie
proximal of the coxo-trochanteral joint. Nerve 3Br1 innervates a sensory area of
the skin ('singular' sensillae of Nijenhuis and Dresden[60]) on the trochantin, as

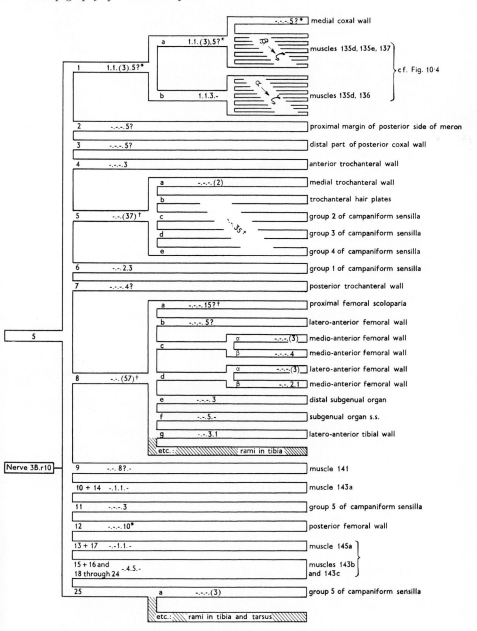

Fig. 8.3 **B**

does 3Br3b; and 3Br5b and 3Br8b innervate separate areas in the distal part of the coxa. Four chordotonal organs send fibres to this nerve: the coxotrochantinal to 3Br2, proximal coxal to 3Br5, and posterior and anterior distal coxal organs to 3Br8c. Inner and outer coxal hair plates are supplied by 3Br3 and to 3Br4 respectively, but n.3 seems to have no campaniform organ axons.

Nerve 4. This small motor nerve supplies muscles 135a, b and c, 105 and 132.

Nerve 5. The fifth nerves of the pterothorax are the largest peripheral nerves. They innervate a few muscles, and most of the sense organs of the leg. See Fig. 8.3 **A** and **B**. Within the coxa, this nerve innervates 135d, 135e, 136 and 137, whilst more distally it innervates all the muscles below the trochanter, except muscle 142, 141 is shared with 3Br10.

The campaniform organs, important in postural reflexes, are largely innervated by n.5. Using Pringle's notation the campaniform group and corresponding nerve branch are as follows: 1–5r6, 2–5r5c, 3–5r5d, 4–5r5e, 5–5r11, 6–5r25a.[70] Group 6 are tibial, so any more distal groups must also be innervated by unspecified branches of the fifth nerve. The scolopidial organs not innervated by the third nerve pass axons into the fifth nerve; the femoral chordotonal organ into nerve 5r8a; the subgenual organ into 5r8f; and the distal subgenual to branch 5r8f. Nijenhuis and Dresden were able to distinguish a number of cuticular sensory areas innervated by branches of n.5 ('singular' sensory areas) in different limb segments. The nerve branches corresponding to the areas of each segment were as follows: coxa—5r1a; meron—5r2; trochanter—5r4, and 5r7; apodemes of muscles 135–7—5r5a; femur—5r8b–d and 5r12; tibia—5r8g–i.

Numerous spines and setae are innervated by branches of n.5 but space only allows mention of a specialized trichoid organ, the trochanteral hair plate supplied by 5r5b (Figs. 8.3 **A** and 8.3 **B**).

Nerve 6. This nerve has an important motor function as well as sensory rami.

6A. Muscles 128, 129, 130 and 131 are innervated by this nerve. As previously mentioned 6A is connected to muscles 114–16 through a plexus formed by 6Ar4 and 3Ar1b so the precise motor supply is obscure.

6B. Two closely adjacent cuticular sensory areas are innervated by n.6 in the proximal part of the coxa (6Br3a and b). This area is described as the meron by Nijenhuis and Dresden. Anterior of the coxa this nerve innervates muscles 117, 133 and 134, and within the coxa, muscles 139a, 139b and 140.

Nerve 7. Innervates the setae of the basisternum.

Nerve 8. A spiracular nerve.

Metathoracic nerves

To a considerable degree, the nerves of this segment duplicate topographically those of the more anterior pterothoracic segment. Only the major differences will be noted.

Nerve 2. A branch from 2Ar1 supplies 151 and 189. 2Ar1b sends motor fibres to muscle 148, and according to Pipa, Cook and Richards may innervate muscles 100, 125, 151, 189 and 152.[67] Nerve 2Ar2a supplies 101, 104 and 106, and 2Br1c innervates muscle 125 instead of muscle 114B (muscle 2). 2Br2a supplies some of the structures in mesothorax (tegula, spiracular sclerite) innervated by 2Br1d. Nerve 2C runs to muscles 153–6.

Nerve 3. Branch 3Ar2a could not be found in the metathorax, and a homologue of muscle 121 was also absent. Nerve 3Ar3 innervates the tergal muscles of the trochantin 161–3, 150A and 150B. The coxal levator 180 is innervated by branches of nerve 3B (3Br6 and 3Br7).

Nerve 4. Muscle 173 (the probable mesothoracic homologue of muscle 105) is supplied by 4r1a, and 4r3 supplies muscles 177A and C.

Nerve 5. This has a very similar distribution to n.5 in the mesothoracic segment. It innervates 177D and E, 178, 179, 182A, and has many sensory branches throughout the limb.

Nerve 6. Follows much the same distribution as in the mesothorax. Anterior branches innervate muscles 157–9, 169, 174–6 and 6Br3 collects sensory fibres from the meron. 6Br4 innervates muscles 181a, b and c.

Nerve 7. This ventral nerve supplies basisternal sense organs as in the mesothorax.

Nerve 8. Spiracular nerve (muscles 201 and 202 of the first abdominal segment).

THE ABDOMINAL NERVOUS SYSTEM

Six free abdominal ganglia occur, 5 simple and 1 composite. Segment 1 is innervated by nerves arising from the metathoracic ganglion, while segments 2 to 6 are each associated with separate segmental ganglia. The more anterior are closer together than the more posterior ones so that as their segments are of roughly the same size the ganglia often do not appear to lie in the segments of the innervate. Ganglia 1–4 lie in the segment anterior to the one they innervate, and ganglion 5 lies on the border of segments 5 and 6. The sixth ganglion lies rather further dorsally than the others due to the ventral position of reproductive structures, and it lies largely within the eighth segment, innervating segments 7, 8, 9 and 10. Ganglia 1–5 appear about the same size, but the sixth ganglion is at least twice this size.

Nerves to the first abdominal segment. (Arising from the metathoracic ganglion)

Nerve 2. 2Ar2a supplies muscles 151, 152 and 189, while muscles 192 and 193 are innervated by the branch 2Ar1b. 2Br1d is a sensory nerve to the spiracular setae. The tergosternal muscle 190 is supplied with motor fibres from nerve 2Br1c. Muscles 194–200 are innervated by this nerve.

Nerve ABn2. This nerve innervates a small muscle extending between the first and second abdominal sternite. There are many cuticular branches.

THE GENERALIZED NERVOUS SYSTEM OF AN ABDOMINAL SEGMENT. (Segment 4) (Fig. 8.4)

The arrangement of nerves and muscles in segments 2, 3, 4, 5 and 6 is very similar and it is only necessary to describe the basic pattern. For the sake of

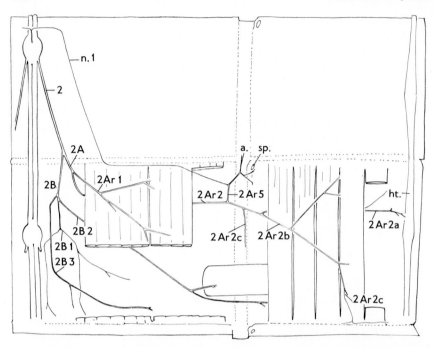

FIG. 8.4   The nervous system of an abdominal segment, dorsal view. The tergum
is shown pinned outwards to display the heart (ht.). According to Schmitt, nerve a.
joins the nervous system of the anterior segment. sp.—spiracle

muscle numbers segment 4 can be taken as a typical segment. A single major
nerve trunk, n.2 passes postero-ventrally from the ganglion. Schmitt illustrates a
slightly different pattern of nerves and should be consulted.[88]

Nerve 2. 2Ar1 supplies muscles 246 and 247, and 2Ar2 runs to the pleural
region where a branch 2Ar2S passes forward to fuse with the spiracular nerve.
2Ar2a runs dorsal to the main tergal muscles supplying cuticular sense organs
and finally running to the heart. 2Ar2b divides into an anterior and a posterior
ramus and these innervate muscles 235–9, while nerve 2Ar2c innervates sense
organs in the lateral tergal areas. The medial sternal areas receive branches of the
sensory nerve 2B1, while the more lateral areas of the sternum are innervated by
2B3. 2B3 also innervates the oblique muscle 246. Most of the other segmental
muscles appear to receive motor axons from nerve 2B2a, that is to say muscles
240–245. A small branch 2B2b that runs back towards the mid-line appears to
end on muscle 246.

The sixth ganglion. (Fig. 8.5)

The nerves will be enumerated as they would be if they proceeded from a
ganglion composed of a single neuromere. The description is based on the male
ganglion. Some variability is encountered, especially with the posterior nerves.

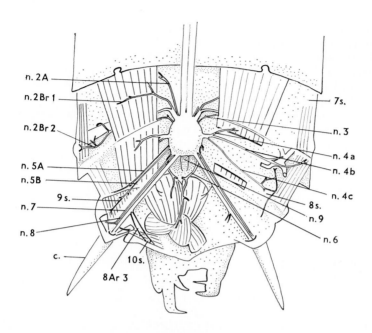

FIG. 8.5 The sixth abdominal ganglion and its nerves, dorsal view. 7 to 10s.—seventh to tenth segments, n.2 to n.9—nerves, c.—cercus. The specimen shown is a male

Nerve 2. This nerve arises not far behind the anterior end of the ganglion. 2A runs anteriorly to innervate sensory areas of the anterior and median sternal region, while the larger trunk divides into 2Br1 to the sternal muscles 295–296. 2Br2 runs laterally to the heart and the dorsal muscles 283–287.

Nerve 3. A slender nerve arising near the root of n.2, it passes along the posterior edge of the seventh sternum to innervate the smaller segmental muscles (288–294).

Nerve 4. A stout nerve originating near the middle of the ganglion. 4A runs a short course to the longitudinal sternal muscles 312–315, while nerve 4B passes beneath these muscles to the region of the spiracle, beyond which nerve branches can be traced to the dorsal muscles 299–303. Branch 4c is a rather thinner nerve and passes across the posterior areas of the sternum branching at the spiracular level. Most of these branches appear to be sensory. One branch at least joins a fine lateral nerve running up to the spiracle and probably innervating its muscles.

Nerve 5. This nerve consists of two rami often arising so close to the ganglion that they appear to be two separate nerves. Trunk 5A appears to run to the sensory areas in the ninth segment, while nerve 5B can be traced to the small dorsal muscles 318–322.

Nerve 6. This nerve, the phallic nerve, often appears to originate from the seventh nerve, but usually a closer examination will reveal a separate root ventral to this nerve. Curving posteriorly towards the mid-line it gives off a conspicuous median branch 6B to the more anterior phallic muscles (338–340), and then proceeds posteriorly branching repeatedly. It appears to innervate most of the phallic muscles.

Nerve 7. This nerve is closely associated with the eighth nerve, and in some, especially female specimens, they appear to have a common root. Both are essentially nerves of the tenth segment. It runs parallel and just anterior to the eighth nerve without major branches until it attains the base of the cercus where it divides into branches to the cercal muscles and to the sensory areas of the tenth tergum.

Nerve 8 (the cercal nerve). Although in some specimens there appear to be motor branches, this is predominantly a sensory nerve, and the thickest nerve arising from the sixth ganglion. It passes postero-laterally and slightly dorsally into the cercus. About half-way along its course, a small nerve 8B is given off to the rectum, and further posteriorly other fine branches (8Ar2, 8Ar3) pass to the rectal dilator muscles (329–332).

Other nerves. In the female a small nerve may be seen arising from the sixth ganglion and running to the gonoducts; whether this nerve (n.9) occurs in the male is uncertain.

THE TOPOGRAPHY OF FIBRE GROUPS WITHIN THE BRAIN

The arrangement of fibre tracts within the brain of *P.a.* has been studied by non-specific staining methods. Most of the tracts and glomeruli that can be recognized in the brains of other insects can be recognized in *P.a.* Thus the central body, protocerebral bridge, α- and β-lobes of the corpora pedunculata, optic peduncle as well as other less striking parts of the brain can be distinguished.

Fig. 8.6 is based on sections stained in Mallory's triple stain and interpreted by means of the work of Bretschneider,[9, 10] and illustrates the position of some of the more easily recognizable structures. Details of structure and function derived from the study of other insect groups have been added in this section, but only where these features have been shown to be true for insect brains in general.

THE PARS INTERCEREBRALIS

Anteriorly, cells in this region are associated with the ocellar tracts; laterally, there are contributions to the protocerebral bridge. A number of strikingly large cells can be shown to be neurosecretory and compose part of the first corpora cardiaca nerve on each side. The fine structure of neurones within the pars intercerebralis of *Blaberus craniifer* has been studied by Willey and Chapman (Chapter 6).

THE PROTOCEREBRAL BRIDGE

Lying immediately posterior to the pars intercerebralis, this region has connections with ocellar or optic tracts in insects, but its major source of fibres is found in the protocerebral lobes.

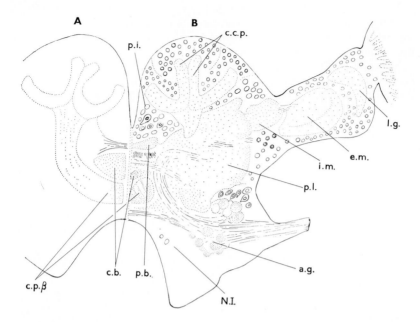

FIG. 8.6 Transverse sections through the 'brain'. **B** illustrates a more anterior level than is shown in **A**. a.g.—antennal glomeruli, c.b.—central body, c.c.p.—calyces of the corpora pedunculata, c.p.β—β lobe of the corpora pedunculata, i.m.—inner medulla, e.m.—external medulla, l.g.—lamina ganglionaris, N.l.—Nebenlappen, p.b.—protocerebral bridge, p.i.—pars intercerebralis, p.l.—protocerebral lobe

THE OPTIC BODY OR TUBERCLE

A small glomerulus with connections with the anterior optic tract in a number of insects, it lies near the base of the optic lobes.

THE NEBENLAPPEN OR ACCESSORY LOBES

They lie ventrally to the main protocerebral lobes, and may be confused with other structures in this region. There is a transverse commissure linking the lobes of either side and connections with the corpora pedunculata.

THE CORPORA PEDUNCULATA

These are large, striking, and closely textured glomeruli often with a conspicuous dorsal double calyx (as in *B.o.*). From the main dorso-ventral corpus, α- and β-lobes are differentiated, the latter usually the more ventral. Very distinctive connections can be demonstrated with antennal centres, and fibres may also be demonstrated from the optic lobes. The work of Maynard[46] has thrown some light on the functional connections of these glomeruli in the cockroach (see behavioural physiology, p. 192).

As can be seen from a casual inspection of sections of the brain of *P.a.* (Fig. 8.6) the corpora pedunculata are of remarkably large size compared with the rest of the brain. In some insects large interneurones with collaterals in the corpora pedunculata send axons to the ventral ganglia, but these have not been described in cockroaches. The work of Goustard and others (see Behaviour, p. 219) suggests that antennal function has a dynamic rôle in modifiable behaviour, and it may be that this is linked with the activity of the corpora pedunculata.

The possible function of these structures has long attracted interest. One suggestion that has been advanced is that they perform a sensory mixing process involved in orientation.

THE CENTRAL BODY

This is an ovoid mass of fine terminals lying near the centre of the proto-cerebrum. Its connections are perhaps the most diverse of major brain regions, indeed some fibres can be traced to almost all parts of the brain, as well as to the ventral ganglia. Fibres from the optic and antennal lobes to the central body have been demonstrated in a number of different insects.

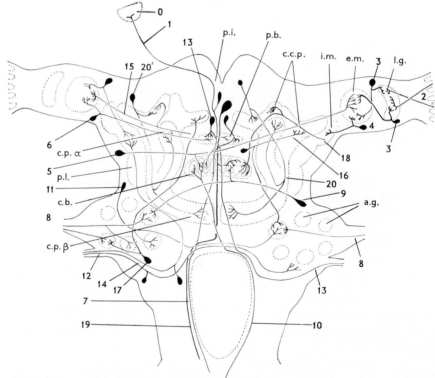

FIG. 8.7   Diagram of neurone types in the 'brain'. See text for further details. Abbreviations as in Fig. 8.6. α and β lobes of the corpora pedunculata are shown. (From Bretschneider[9])

Little is known about changes in brain structure during growth and development, but Panov found that the brain of larvae *Bt.g.* exhibits few differences compared with the brain of adults, even to small details of structure in the corpora pedunculata. This is not so in the higher insects.[62]

Detailed neurone patterns

The brief résumé of prominent brain regions given above holds good for the cockroaches *B.o.* and *P.a.* Some more detailed information has been obtained using the impregnation methods of Golgi and Apathy.[9, 30]

Figure 8.7 is taken directly from Bretschneider[9] except for neurone 1, which has been shown in the form illustrated by Bullock and Horridge.[11] This conforms to the now generally accepted origin of ocellar cell bodies. In addition, there are large elements with collaterals in the protocerebral lobes which pass down to the ventral centres, and what appear to be ascending fibres from the ventral nerve cord with arborizations in the corpora pedunculata β-lobes. These two neurone types are added to 20 and 20[1] (slightly different forms of the same neurone) as 21 and 22. Table 8.1 sets out the connections of these neurones, the convention that the short process is the collateral and the longer one the axon, being employed throughout.

TABLE 8.1

No. of neurone	Cell body	Collateral	Axon
1	Protocerebrum	Central body and Protocerebral bridge	Ocellus
2	Optic lobe	—	Optic glomerulus
3	Optic lobe	Optic glomerulus	Optic glomerulus
4	Optic lobe	Optic glomerulus	Protocerebral lobe
5	Protocerebrum	Central body	Optic glomerulus
6	Protocerebrum	Optic glomerulus	Protocerebral bridge
7	Pars intercerebralis	Protocerebral bridge	Ventral nerve cord
8	Antenna		Antennal glomerulus
9	Protocerebrum	Central body	Antennal glomerulus
10	Ventral nerve cord		Central body
11	Antennal lobe	Antennal glomerulus	Antennal glomerulus (contralateral)
12	Antennal lobe		Antennal glomerulus (contralateral)
13	Pars intercerebralis	Protocerebral bridge	Antennal muscles
14	Antennal lobe		Protocerebral lobe
15		C. pedunculata calyx	Optic glomerulus
16	Protocerebral lobe	C. pedunculata calyx	Antennal glomerulus
17	Antennal lobe	Antennal glomerulus	C. pedunculata calyx
18		C. pedunculata calyx	Central body

8.1—*continued*

No. of neurone	Cell body	Collateral	Axon
19	Pars intercerebralis	Central body	Ventral nerve cord
20	C. pedunculata globuli	C. pedunculata calyx	C. pedunculata (1) α lobe (2) β lobe
20[1]	C. pedunculata globuli	C. pedunculata calyx	C. pedunculata (1) α lobe (2) β lobe
21	Protocerebral lobes	(2) Protocerebral lobes	Ventral nerve cord
22	Ventral nerve cord		C. pedunculata β-lobe

Fibre pathways in the ventral nerve cord

No effective work on the complete arrangement of neurones in the ventral nerve cord has yet been accomplished, but the distribution of the larger axons is fairly easily determined by the application of unspecific staining methods. As far as more specific total staining methods are concerned, there is little doubt that many of the silver-on-the-slide techniques that can be applied successfully to other Hemimetabola (methods of Holmes, Palmgren, Bodian, Samuels, see Chapter 1) do not give results which are of a comparable excellence when applied to the cockroach nerve cord, although occasionally good results can be achieved, especially with larvae. Pipa, Cook and Richards[67] applied the Bodian protargol method to the study of the ventral ganglia but, as can be seen from their figures, the axoplasm and axon membrane were usually much less well stained than the sheath material. Bodenstein obtained some excellent results of high clarity with the method of Samuels. Guthrie has found that the Holmes method following glutaraldehyde fixation often gives good results (Figs. 8.8, 8.9), but the method cannot be depended on with adult material.[29]

Hess obtained good pictures of axons in transverse section by imbedding in methacrylate, cutting thin sections as for the electron microscope and then examining them by phase contrast.[31] In this laboratory (Guthrie) we have obtained only poor results with the partial metal impregnation procedures such as the Golgi technique.

The giant fibre system of the ventral nerve cord was investigated by Pumphrey and Rawdon-Smith;[74] Roeder, Kennedy and Samson;[83] Roeder;[79] Hess;[31] and Pipa, Cook and Richards.[67] Some of the physiological data suggests morphological correlates. Transverse sections of the abdominal nerve cord in the interganglionic regions reveal the presence of many fibres, the great majority of which, as shown by Roeder, are below 15 μ in diameter. Of the larger ones, a conspicuous tier of 3 axons lies slightly below the centre of the section, and above this there are 3 slightly smaller axons in an L-shaped configuration. The maximum diameter of the ventral fibres is placed at 45 μ by Pipa, Cook and Richards, and 50 μ by Roeder using permanently mounted sections, and by Hess at 60 μ (about 60 μ) using electron microscope techniques of preparation. The point is of interest in relation to conduction velocity measurements. Both

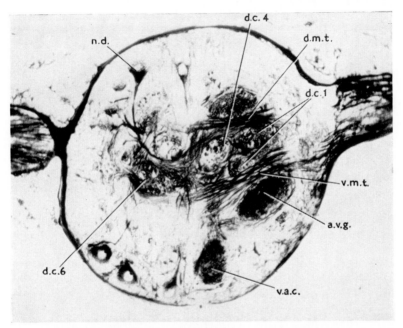

FIG. 8.8 Longitudinal vertical section through a mesothoracic ganglion close to the mid-line. Anterior is to the right. Abbreviations for this, and following figures, are: a.v.g.—anterior ventral glomerulus, d.c.1 to 6—dorsal commissures 1 to 6, d.i.t.—dorsal intermediate longitudinal tract, d.m.t.—dorsal median longitudinal tract, l.d.t.—lateral dorsal longitudinal tract, m.d.t.—median dorsal tract, n.d.—neurone of d.m.t., p.v.c.—posterior ventral commissure, v.a.c.—ventral association centre, v.c.l. 1 and 2—ventral commissural loops 1 and 2, v.i.t.—ventral intermediate tract, v.l.t.—ventro-lateral longitudinal tract, v.m.t.—ventral median longitudinal tract, v.t.—ventral tract, s.m.c.—supramedian commissure. (Holmes method)

Roeder, and Pipa, Cook and Richards note that the giant fibres narrow where they pass through abdominal ganglia. Roeder also described anterio-posterior tapering of the larger fibres. Guthrie attempted to obtain diameter measurements of the larger axons by examining just-thawed sections of nerve cord obtained by the freezing technique. Seventy-four measurements were made at different levels in the nerve cord, the largest axon averaging out at 30·8 μ; this includes ganglionic diameters. The narrowing of the fibres in the ganglion can be seen to entail a loss of diameter of about 25%. The largest axon tapers from a maximum of 53 μ near the first ganglion to a maximum of about 30 μ near the sixth. Pipa *et al.* suggest that the abdominal giants continue anteriorly through the thoracic ganglion,[67] but the physiological observations of Roeder,[79] and the degeneration experiments of Hess suggest that they terminate at the metathoracic level.[31] Gahery and Boistel, however, found that the prolonged repetitive discharge produced in sub-giant fibres by treating the sixth abdominal ganglion with 3-hydroxytyramine could be detected at the mesothoracic ganglion level. These fibres which provide two distinct voltage values (0·2 and 1·0 mV) are not giants, and may be the smaller fibres of Hess.[27] The question of the position of the giant fibre cell bodies

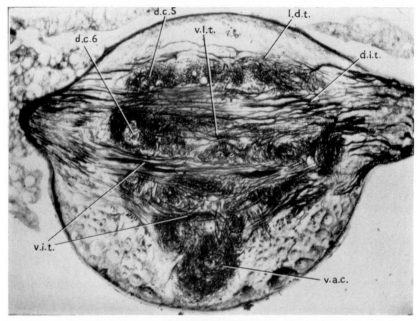

FIG. 8.9   Longitudinal vertical section through a mesothoracic ganglion lateral to the one illustrated in Fig. 8.8. See Fig. 8.8 for abbreviations

remains somewhat obscure. Cuts made in the nerve cord between the first and second, and the fourth and fifth abdominal ganglia were followed by proximal degeneration, but little or no distal degeneration (Hess). The dorsal trio of fibres, with two adjacent smaller fibres, and the most median of the ventral group degenerated, an observation consistent with the view that the cell bodies of these fibres occupied the terminal ganglion. The difficulty of observing single large cells in a state of chromatolysis may, it is suggested, be due to the origin of each of these fibres from a number of small cell bodies. The origin of the two outer axons (numbers 1 and 2 of Hess) of the ventral group may be from cell bodies in different abdominal ganglia, since they are unaffected by cuts at either level.[31]

Hughes, using orthodox recording together with a specialized pulse-sorting device, obtained information supporting the idea that the abdominal giants consist of two essentially separate groups. These might correspond to the two categories demonstrated by Hess (see Behavioural physiology, p. 192).

The abdominal ganglia of unspecialized segments have a much simpler internal structure than can be seen in the ganglia of the thorax. Methylene blue preparations suggest that there are a few large motor axons which enter the abdominal ganglion and pass directly forward to the ganglion in front (Fig. 8.29, A cells). At least three are visible. Finer fibres end anteriorly (B cells), or posteriorly (C cells) in the neuropile of their ganglion of entry. Within the connectives, intersegmental fibres, A cells and fibres with transverse rami can be made out.

Hughes and Wilson showed that motor axons originating from cell bodies in the abdominal ganglion of one segment can be shown electrophysiologically, to descend to a more posterior segmental level before emerging in a nerve.[38]

The fibrous anatomy of the thoracic ganglia was first examined by Miall and Denny, who include in their famous monograph figures demonstrating at least 8 of the major tracts.[49] More recently Pipa, Cook and Richards describe the number and orientation of 8 tracts, together with notes on the range of fibre diameters characteristic of each tract.[67] This author (Guthrie) also examined the structure of the mesothoracic ganglion in order to determine the position of n.5. motor neurone collaterals (Fig. 8.11). Rowe has investigated the fibre tracts of the thoracic ganglia, but his results were not available at the time of compilation of this chapter.[85]

Pipa, Cook and Richards describe 8 longitudinal tracts, arranged at 4 levels within the ganglion, and 10 tracts which in whole or in part lie in the transverse plane. In addition, a zone of fine terminals termed the ventral association centre could be observed in the ventral neuropile. Using this description to identify tracts within the mesothoracic ganglion, it was found (Guthrie) that the imprecise location of many of the labels in the photographic illustrations provided

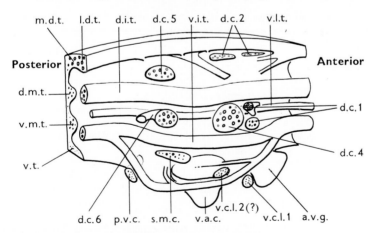

FIG. 8.10   Diagram indicating the position of the major tracts in the right half of a mesothoracic ganglion, viewed laterally. For abbreviations see Fig. 8.8. (Labelling follows Pipa, Cook and Richards[67])

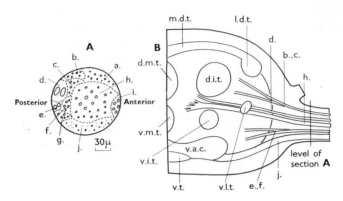

FIG. 8.11   Diagram to illustrate position within the ganglionic nerve root of different axon groups in mesothoracic n.5. **A**, The section is at right angles to the nerve root. **B**, Half of a transverse section through the ganglion. Fibre groups a. to j. For other abbreviations see Fig. 8.8

by these authors made the process difficult, but all save dorsal commissure 3 and ventral commissural loop 2 could be found.[67] Another ventral glomerulus was observed[29] (Figs. 8.8, 8.10).

A list of the tracts identified by Pipa, Cook and Richards, together with the diameters of component fibres and comments, is given below. This should be compared with Fig. 8.10, which is based in part on a diagram of longitudinal tracts published by the above authors.

TABLE 8.2

Fibre tracts and glomeruli in the thoracic ganglia of *P.a.* (see Fig. 8.10)

Tract	Orientation	Fibres
Median dorsal	Longitudinal	10 or more fibres 20–25 μ
Lateral dorsal	Longitudinal	4 fibres 15–30 μ
Dorsal median	Longitudinal	Mostly less than 10 μ
Dorsal intermediate	Longitudinal	Many large fibres
Ventral median	Longitudinal	Most are 5–10μ
Ventral intermediate	Longitudinal	4 fibres 14–25 μ, rest 10 μ
Ventral lateral	Longitudinal	2, 14–15 μ, but most 8–12 μ
Ventral	Longitudinal	Majority 10 μ
Dorsal commissure I	Transverse	Mostly intraganglionic fibres less than 10 μ
Dorsal commissure II	Transverse, part vertical	Mostly intraganglionic fibres less than 10 μ
Dorsal commissure III	Transverse	Mostly intraganglionic fibres less than 10 μ

8.2—*continued*

Tract	Orientation	Fibres
Dorsal commissure IV	Transverse	Mostly intraganglionic fibres less than 10 μ
Dorsal commissure V	Transverse, part vertical	Mostly intraganglionic fibres less than 10 μ
Supramedian commissure	Transverse	Mostly intraganglionic fibres less than 10 μ
Posterior ventral commissure	Transverse	Mostly intraganglionic fibres less than 10 μ
Ventral commissural loop I	Curves round v.a.c. centre anteriorly	Mostly intraganglionic fibres less than 10 μ
Ventral commissural loop II	Curves beneath the v.a.c.	Mostly intraganglionic fibres less than 10 μ
Ventral association centre		Mostly intraganglionic fibres less than 10 μ
Anterio-ventral glomerulus	Lies anterior and dorsal to the v.a.c.	Mostly intraganglionic fibres less than 10 μ

THE FINE STRUCTURE OF THE PERIPHERAL AND CENTRAL NERVOUS SYSTEM

Wigglesworth classified the elements to be found in a more complex part of the cockroach nervous system, such as a ganglion, as follows, proceeding from the periphery inwards: (i) A fibrous neural lamella, (ii) a layer of cells—the perineurium, (iii) outer glial cells associated with a sinus system, and (iv) inner glial cells of the neuropile (see Fig. 8.12). The neurone cell bodies lie in the outer glial cell zone, the neuropile being composed of axons and other neurone processes partially or entirely surrounded by folds of glial membrane. The glial nuclei tend to be scarcer in the central regions of the neuropile than they are peripherally. This nomenclature seems to be generally accepted now for the different cell layers, although Hess in one of his early papers seems to have named the neural lamella and perilemma (perineurium) in the reverse positions.

These elements will be described below in more detail.

The term neural lamella now tends to be used to describe the outer sheath of nerves and ganglia which, with the light microscope, appears as more or less homogeneous material,[3, 66, 87] although Hess in his outer perilemmal sheath shows flattened nuclei. Richards and Schneider applied x-ray diffraction methods to the study of the constituents of the neural lamella and came to the conclusion that small (10–20%) amounts of collagen were present, probably as small fibres in a non-fibrous matrix.[77] The presence of collagen was confirmed histochemically by Ashurst, who demonstrated a collagenous protein in the sheath. A neutral polysaccharide, perhaps associated with plasticity, was also present.

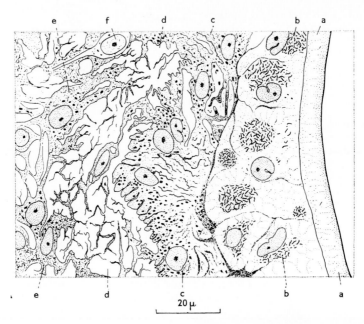

FIG. 8.12   Horizontal section through a ganglion to demonstrate the cell layers. a, neural lamella; b, perineurium cells; c, outer glial cells; d, glial sinus system; e, inner glial cells; f, small neurone. (From Wigglesworth[102])

Hess then showed that, under the higher resolutions of the electron microscope, the constituent fibres of the neural lamella could be clearly seen to have the periodic banding already demonstrated in vertebrate collagen. The fibres are imbedded in an amorphous matrix, and appear to be orientated along many axes.

The detailed form of the fibres has been further investigated in *P.a.* by Treherne and Smith.[97] The outer region of the sheath (*c.* 3 μ) appears structureless and below there is a narrow region of fine filaments, each *c.* 50 Å across. Below this is the main zone of collagen-like fibres. These vary in diameter, and the banding can be characterized as consisting of a series of macroperiods each *c.* 560 Å long, and consisting of a single dense subperiod line and five apparently double sub-period lines. This pattern of banding is generally similar to that of other insects, but differs from that of rat-tail collagen in the omission of an extra double sub-period line.

The neural lamella is permeable to silver nitrate,[98] a variety of dyes,[102] and ^{24}Na, ^{42}K, and ^{14}C labelled inulin molecules.[91]

Below the neural lamella is a layer of cells described by Scharrer as the perineurium, and figured by Wigglesworth as a layer of variable thickness often characterized by deeply indented nuclei and clumps of filamentous mitochondria. Large quantities of glycogen can be demonstrated within the perineurial cells by histochemical techniques[3, 102] and probably correspond to the deeply staining granules *c.* 300–350 Å in diameter observed by Treherne and Smith in electron-micrographs, similar to granules seen in glycogen-rich fat body. Besides these dense granules, the perineurial cells have large populations of mitochondria closely packed together, and profiles of smooth-membraned vesicles and cisternae. The synchronous depletion of glycogen in the fat body and peri-neurium of starved roaches points to a trophic function for these cells (Wiggles-worth), but the connection with the formation of the overlying neural lamella remains obscure.

Lipids may be localized in the perineurial cells. Ashurst demonstrates lipo-chondria perhaps of a phospholipid or cerebroside nature in these cells,[3] and some of Treherne and Smith's figures show lacunae after lipid solvent treat-ment,[97] but Wigglesworth rarely observed triglycerides in the perineurium.[102]

Wigglesworth described an ill-defined zone of outer glial cells in the region of the neurone cell bodies often associated with extracellular spaces.[102] This is figured in electronmicrographs by Treherne and Smith, who believe that it may play an important rôle in the ionic balance between the haemolymph and the central nervous system. The tracheoles pass through this glial lacunar system and cavities of the system surround their terminations on the inner glial complex. The mesaxonal channels may be continuous with the glial lacunar system. There are also very fine channels *c.* 100–200 Å, permeating all parts of the neuropile.[97]

Due to the small dimensions involved, relatively little detail can be resolved in the axon membrane or the cell inclusions bounded by it with the light micro-scope. In successful preparations made by one of the silver techniques, the axon membrane and the axoplasm do appear distinct against a nearly colourless back-ground of interstitial sheath cell material. But examination of the 'axon mem-brane' with the higher powers of the light microscope suggest that fine particles of reduced silver adhere to it producing a thickened image of the membrane. In preparations made by the osmium-ethyl gallate method, Wigglesworth could observe some axoplasmic inclusions, such as mitochondria.[103]

Hess examined sections taken through the metathoracic leg of *P.a.*, which contained large nerve trunks (probably parts of n.5), with the electron micro-scope. He observed the axon membrane bounding a granular axoplasm containing small numbers of objects tentatively identified as mitochondria. Each of the larger axons was surrounded by folds of membrane described by analogy with vertebrates as Schwann cells. The nerve fibre is described as resting in the cyto-plasm of the Schwann cell. The dense zones associated with these sheath mem-branes are suggested as being of a lipid nature, presumably due to their reaction with osmium.

Treherne and Smith demonstrate clearly the structure of an axon in a non-synaptic region of a ganglion; fine neurofilaments or neurotubules are arranged longitudinally, mitochondria are well characterized and small vesicular profiles occur.[97]

The glial processes, that wrap the larger axons individually and the smaller axons in small groups, are more distinct in Smith's electronmicrographs[97] than in the much earlier figures of Hess[33] and Edwards.[23] Smith is in agreement with Hess's view of the glial processes as ribbon-like extensions from a more peripherally situated cell body and he uses the term mesaxon (also used by Edwards to describe the channel between adjacent double membrane folds). The glial cell membrane can be seen to be separated from the axon membrane by an extracellular gap of about 100 Å, and is thus not within the sheath cell cytoplasm as suggested by Hess. Smith sees the sheath associated with one of the larger axons as similar in many ways to the myelin turns of a Schwann cell formed by

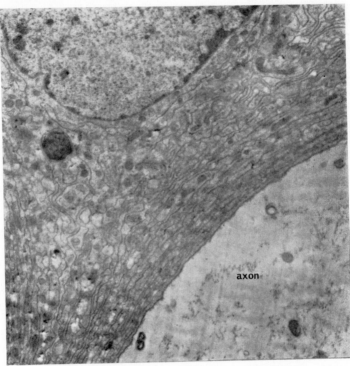

FIG. 8.13   Electronmicrograph of glial cell membranes surrounding an axon in a growing nerve. The nucleus can be seen at the top of the figure. × 10,000

mesaxonal invagination, and the term Schwann cell is employed. This would seem not entirely appropriate in view of the irregularity of the insect glial processes (Fig. 8.13), and the exact characterization of vertebrate Schwann cell structure by Finean and his colleagues.

Dense accretions were observed by Hess enclosed within the glial membranes and were described as lipid droplets. Smith shows them to lie within the fairly regular dilations of the mesaxon, and thus to be essentially extracellular. No detail can be seen in them, and larger masses of visually similar material can be seen within the glial lacunar system. Smith and Treherne suggest the PAS-positive material of Wigglesworth,[102] or the acid mucopolysaccharide of Ashurst,[2] as possible biochemical identities of this material.

In some of their light microscope photographs Pipa, Cook and Richards show a fine basketwork of protargol-stained threads surrounding axons.[67] Whether these are glial-cell processes or a meshwork of amorphous matter of the kind mentioned above is not clear. At one point, Edwards appears to refer to this mesaxonal material as chitinous bars, although no sharp profile is visible. Inclusions of a considerable variety of form are found within the perineurial and glial cell processes, and were recognized as proteinaceous and distinct from

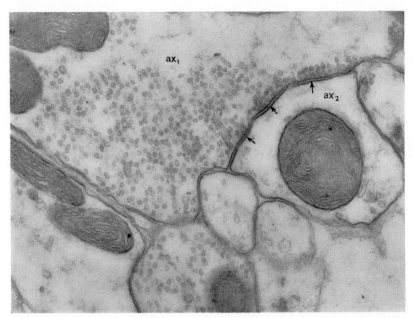

FIG. 8.14   Synaptic contact between two axons, ax_1 and ax_2 (electronmicrograph). Synaptic vesicles can be seen clustered in ax_1 and at the dense zones of the two axon surfaces, indicated by arrows. × 31,500. (From Treherne and Smith[97])

glycogen by Scharrer in light microscope preparations. More recently, Pipa has described a number of different types. Usually a limiting membrane is present, but the central region may be homogeneous, full of small vesicles, or partly occluded by myelin figures. Guthrie has observed gliosomes especially abundant in regenerating nerves. They may be compared to the acid-phosphatase, mito-chondria-associated lysosomes of vertebrates.

In the synaptic regions of the ganglia, axonal profiles with various types of inclusions are visible. Hess lists three main size categories of inclusion: (i) 300–500 Å, granules, (ii) 100–1,500 Å, vesicles, (iii) 1,200–2,500 Å, droplets. He also shows mushroom-shaped synapses with granular inclusions poking into larger fibres, but many other vesicle-laden axon profiles, as pointed out by Smith, are not necessarily synapses.[32] In this part of the ganglion Hess showed that there was little sheath material.[32, 34] The granules were recognized by Smith and Treherne, but only a single category of larger inclusions of this type, between

800 and 1,100 Å in overall diameter. The former category have a lightly staining content, the latter a limiting membrane and dense centre. The former type are described as synaptic vesicles and adjacent axon profiles with many vesicles on one side and few on the other, appear to represent pre- and post-synaptic elements (Fig. 8.14). It is tentatively suggested that the larger inclusions are neurosecretory.[97]

The distribution peak diameters for large numbers of these two vesicle types are given as 450 Å and 100 Å respectively, and homogeneous populations of the first type have a concentration of 4,000 μ. Both types may occur together.[97]

The structure of neurone cell bodies within the ventral ganglia

With the standard silver techniques, the cell bodies of neurones show up clearly as large subspherical cells with distinctive nucleoli and a differentiated cytoplasm. As pointed out by Hess, Wigglesworth, and Pipa, some of the cells appear much darker than others, possibly due to a larger population of sub-cellular components or, as suggested by Pipa, to homogeneously distributed RNA.

Sections of thoracic ganglia cut very thin and stained by his ethyl gallate method were found by Wigglesworth to show more detail than could be easily seen by other methods. Mitochondria could be seen and the cell membrane was observed to have numerous infoldings extending into the cytoplasm. Also visible were the dictyosomes often associated with tubules that may have been part of the neurofibrillar system. The identity of the dictyosomes, especially with regard to the Golgi bodies of vertebrate cells, has long interested histologists and it has been suggested that the dictyosomes represent the Golgi apparatus without any of the RNA material found in the reticular complex of the vertebrate cell.

Wigglesworth's figures show the dictyosomes as lying around the course of tubules and with a darker outer cortex. The walls of these canals become noticeably darker in regenerating neurones. The dictyosome body thus appears mushroom-shaped or annular according to the plane of section.[103]

Preparations made by the Holmes method often show the dictyosomes very clearly, when, in most cases, a basket-like form is evident, the ribs bearing granules of some stainable substance. No canals can be seen, but all other inclusions are poorly stained.[29]

The distribution of RNA has been investigated by Cohen and Jacklet, using specific staining methods, and it was found by these authors that the cytoplasm gave a generally positive reaction. In regenerating neurones, however, the reaction was noticeably more intense in the vicinity of the nuclear membrane, and this observation furnishes a useful tool for the identification of specific cell bodies with peripheral axons.[16]

Smith uncovered much additional detail in the structure of the neurone cell body by cutting thin sections for examination with the electron microscopes. Difficulties of fixation are discussed by him. The invaginations of the cell membrane could be seen clearly and parts of the sheath cell membrane were visible within the cell membrane folds. Within the cytoplasm could be seen mito-

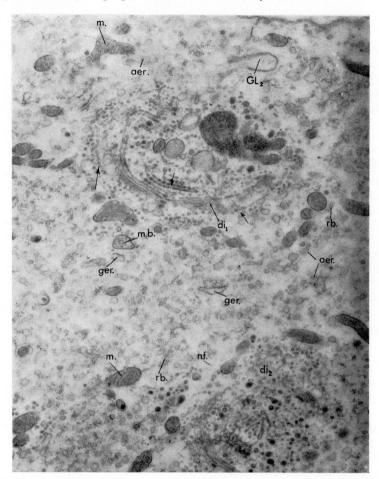

FIG. 8.15   Cytoplasmic inclusions from a ganglionic neurone (electronmicrograph). GL—glial invaginations, aer.—agranular endoplasmic reticulum, ger.—granular endoplasmic reticulum, di.—dictyosome profile, m.—mitochondrion, m.b.—multivesicular bodies, nf.—neurofilaments, rb.—ribosomes. Arrows indicate parts of the dictyosome. × 20,000. (From Treherne and Smith[97])

chondria with parallel cisternal membranes, fine neurofibrils, free ribosome clusters, granular vesicles, rough-surfaced vesicles with attached ribosomes, sub-spherical multi-vesiculate bodies, and dictyosomes (Fig. 8.15). It seems that ribosomal RNA may be either attached to a membrane system as in many vertebrate cells or be present as unattached groups.

The dictyosomes were examined in some detail and many anatomical features were convincingly demonstrated,[97] although a general similarity can be seen to the early work of Gatenby and Beams on the grasshopper dictyosome using the electron microscope.

7+B.O.C.

The dense outer layer seen with the light microscope is represented by a number of hemispherical membrane shells with regular perforations, arranged one over the other so that meridional sections reveal three or four of these curved double-walled structures divided into smaller cisternae by the perforations. At the equatorial margin of these double membranes, smaller vesicles appear to be split off. Partially enclosed by the membranes are a number of large osmiophilic vesicles, some nearly spherical with an outer region differentiated, others with a less regular profile, and the outer region not defined. These large vesicles are interesting as they appear to be fairly specific to cockroaches.[97]

The canals observed by Wigglesworth are not visible in the electronmicrographs, while the striking vesicles observed by Smith near the centre of the dictyosome do not appear readily demonstrable under the light microscope.[103]

Pipa has adopted a more histochemical approach to the study of neurone cell body inclusions.[63,64,65] The outer region of the dictyosome (externa) was markedly sudanophilic as compared with the interior, and tests for RNA were negative. Two other types of inclusions could also be identified; both appeared yellow in fresh cells and were PAS positive and sudanophilic. Pipa suggests that these reactions were due to the presence of glycolipid. These inclusions were either numerous, closely grouped, with a sharply defined profile, and about 1 μ across—beta granules, or they were scattered and ranged in size from 5–10 μ in delta granules. These two categories could be recognized under the electron microscope.[65]

THE MEMBRANE PHYSIOLOGY OF THE COCKROACH AXON

Most of the detailed information that has been established refers to the giant fibres of the ventral nerve cord of *P.a.*, the structure and distribution of which has been described above, and comparatively little is known at the membrane level about other axon types. Some details of motor axon properties are to be found in the section dealing with the neuromuscular apparatus. The animal can be assumed to be *P.a.* unless otherwise stated.

The magnitude of the resting and the action potential. These were determined by Boistel and Coraboeuf in the giant fibres of *P.a.* as 78 mV and 85 mV respectively.[6] In a later communication, Boistel decided that some degree of attenuation would have been imposed on the action potential by the resistance of the electrodes and estimated the true values as 70 mV and 100–110 mV respectively.[8] These figures coincide quite well with the measurements made by Yamasaki and Narahashi of 64·5 mV and 92·2 mV, the value of the action potential being adjusted by calculation.[56] Later work by these authors produced slightly different values of 70·3 mV and 94·5 mV, closer to Boistel's later figures. The sodium concentration of the saline was in this case raised to 214 mM, a level comparable to that used by Boistel. Another yet more recent series of measurements made by Narahashi and Yamasaki[57] yielded the following values, probably the most reliable so far made. Resting potential: $77 \pm 0·7$ mV (24 observations). Action potential: $99 \pm 1·4$ mV (19 observations). These values are within the range described for other animals (Fig. 8.16).

It should be possible to describe these membrane potentials in terms of the concentrations of potassium and sodium ions on either side of the membrane, as established by workers on the squid axon. This was done for the cockroach giant axon by Narahashi using the estimations of Tobias for the haemolymph serum and the sheathed nerve cord, and taking into account the specific permeability of the membrane to Na, K and Cl; potassium and sodium equilibrium potentials can be calculated. The values thus obtained were 97·7 mV for the potassium

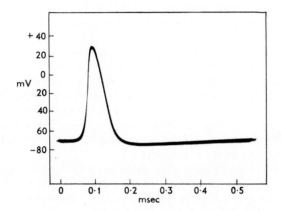

FIG. 8.16   Record of an action potential from a giant axon in the ventral nerve cord.
(From Narahashi[56])

equilibrium potential, and the sodium equilibrium potential (to be compared with positive overshoot) was 24·0 mV.[56] The major discrepancy is thus between the observed and calculated values for the resting potential, assuming that this will be near the potassium equilibrium potential. This discrepancy of about 20 mV is probably associated with a well-marked positive after-potential, according to Narahashi. The amount of the after-potential can be altered by negative or positive adjustment of the resting potential.

The voltage-current relationships of cockroach axons are similar to those of other types of nerves studied, where current intensity is plotted against the steady-state magnitude of the electrotonic potential (Narahashi).[56] When the two microelectrodes are inserted less than 50 μ apart, and catelectrotonic and anelectrotonic potentials are recorded simultaneously, a slight hump appears at the beginning of the catelectrotonic trace at about $11·8 \times 10·9$ A and an action potential at $4·42 \times 10-8$ A (Narahashi),[106] but a lower value for critical depolarization current was obtained in later experiments: $3·4 \times 10-8$ A (Narahashi).[55] The value for the critical depolarization itself obtained in the later experiments was 25 mV at 30·2°, both mean values.

The electrical membrane constants obtained by Narahashi and his colleagues are given below.[106] These entail assumptions as to the axoplasmic resistance and the axon diameter.

Effective membrane resistance	283 kΩ
Specific membrane resistance	800 Ω cm^2
Specific membrane capacity	6·3 μF cm^{-2}
Membrane time constant	4·2 msec
Membrane length constant	0·86 mm

All these values, except that for membrane capacity, are close to measurements made on other invertebrate axons (Narahashi), the figure for capacity being five or six times that for squid, crab and lobster axon.[56]

Conduction-velocity measurements have been made by a number of workers and it must be assumed that these apply to the largest axons, as most of them were made on intact nerve cords or nerves, or by intracellular techniques without precise knowledge of the identity of the axon penetrated.

Pumphrey and Rawdon-Smith,[74] Roeder,[79] and Roeder, Kennedy and Samson,[83] obtained values for the maximum conduction velocity in the ventral abdominal nerve cord of 5–12 metres per second, but undoubtedly some of these measurements were too high, as Boistel and Coraboeuf,[6] and Boistel[8] found a range of 6·6–7·2 m/sec using intracellular methods on the giant axons. The giant axons are believed to be 40–50 μ across.

The fine fibres of the sensory cercal nerve have also been examined from this point of view and Pumphrey and Rawdon-Smith,[74] Roeder, Kennedy and Samson,[83] and Roeder[79, 81] agree that the range of highest conduction velocities to be expected is 1·5–2·0 m/sec.

Guthrie has made some measurements on the mesothoracic crural nerve which contains some large motor axons. The maximum conduction velocity was found to vary considerably and this was believed to be due to the fact that these fibres taper considerably. Maximum values were between 6·25 and 8·3 m/sec. Axon diameters from frozen sections were 52 μ–37 μ (largest fibres). These values are fairly near what could be expected on the basis of measurements made on other insect axons, and conform fairly well to a velocity/diameter relationship of 0·15–0·25 m/sec/μ diameter, the large cockroach axons, however, being at the lower end of this range, i.e. they are slow for their size.[29]

The relative refractory period of cockroach (*P.a.*) nerve cord is 13 msec, and the absolute refractory period is 2 msec (Boistel),[8] these are close to figures for other insect axons.[56]

The effect of altering the external concentration of potassium and sodium ions on membrane potential is of interest. Yamasaki and Narahashi found that the resting potential was reduced by high external potassium, but low potassium had little effect. When the drop in resting potential was plotted against the logarithm of external potassium concentration, it could be seen that there was a linear relationship above 20 mM, and for a tenfold increase in potassium, the potential fell by 42 mV, instead of the calculated 59 mV, implying the involvement of other ions in the development of the resting potential (Fig. 8.17).[106, 107] This helps to explain the discrepancy between the calculated potassium equilibrium potential and the observed resting potential mentioned earlier.

Reduced external sodium concentration has the effect of lowering the size of

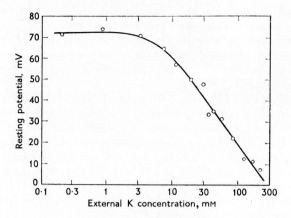

FIG. 8.17   Abdominal giant axon: the effect of changes in external potassium concentration on the magnitude of the resting potential. (From Narahashi[56])

the action potential, but has little effect on the resting potential (Fig. 8.18). The dependence of the action potential on the Na gradient has been noted in axons and muscle fibres of a number of different animals since the classical work of Hodgkin and Katz. This dependence is underlined by the observation by

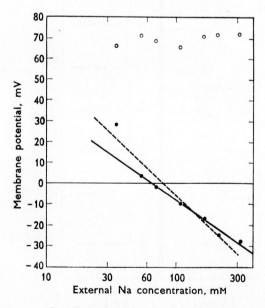

FIG. 8.18   Giant axon: the effect of varying external sodium concentrations on the magnitude of the resting potential (○) and active membrane potential (●). ––––––––––, calculated values. (From Yamasaki and Narahashi[56])

Narahashi and Yamasaki that the rising phase of the action potential is reduced more rapidly than the falling phase in Na-deficient media.[107]

The magnitude of the ionic current during the action potential was calculated from the membrane electrical constants, and the inward ionic current when the rate of rise is greatest was 6·9 mA cm^{-2}; this is three to ten times higher than the other examples quoted.[56,107]

As in the other excitable tissues, low external calcium drastically reduces the electrical responsiveness of the membrane, decreasing both the resting and action potential. In high Ca, the resting potential is slightly increased, and in high and low Ca the rising phase of the action potential is slowed. There is evidence that the effect of some insecticides is linked to the rôle of Ca in excitation as shown by Gordon and Welsh,[28] and Welsh and Gordon.[101] Repetitive responses are not observed in the cockroach axon in low Ca media,[57] as have been observed in other animals, although low Ca accelerates the effect of DDT in eliciting a train of impulses in response to a single shock.[28]

It has been shown in other animals that, to some extent, barium can substitute for sodium as a physiological medium for conduction, and the effect of external barium was investigated by Narahashi. Complete substitution produced immediate inexcitability in the axons, but a solution containing 100 mM Na and

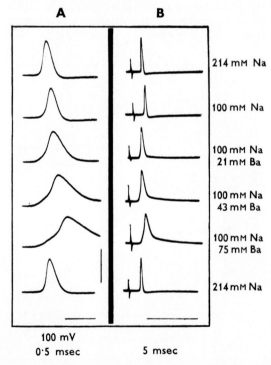

FIG. 8.19   Giant axon: the effect of differing concentrations of barium on the shape of the action potential at, **A**, fast and, **B**, sweep speeds. (From Narahashi[56])

21–75 mM Ba allowed the formation of near-normal action potentials. In the higher concentrations of Ba, the rate of rise was slowed and the after-potentials appeared much modified (Fig. 8.19). The change in the rate of rise was seen by Narahashi as a depression of sodium conductance associated with increase in membrane resistance.[55] Lithium, on the other hand, could be used as a complete substitute for Na.[56]

A feature of the impulse as recorded oscillographically in the cockroach giant axon is that the spike potential is followed by a brief positive rise and then a slower negative fall in the trace. These after-potentials are more clearly defined at low sweep speeds, and they are affected by a variety of changes in the external medium.[57,58,59] An increase in temperature increases the size of the negative after-potential without having much effect on the positive potential (Fig. 8.20).[56]

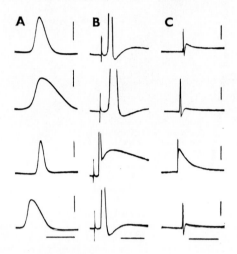

FIG. 8.20   The effect of temperature on the shape of the action potential. Temperatures, from top to bottom, 20°, 11°, 32°, 20°. Differences in gain and sweep speed as follows: **A**, 50 mV, 1 msec; **B**, 5 mV, 5 msec; **C**, 5 mv, 50 msec. (From Narahashi[56])

The resting potential is also increased by a rise in temperature. Polarization of the membrane by applied current affects both after-potentials in a symmetrical manner. Depolarization increased the positive phase and decreased the negative phase, hyper-polarization increases the negative phase and decreases the positive phase.[106] This suggests that the effect of temperature on after-potentials is in part a reflection of the temperature sensitivity of the resting potential. The positive phase is interpreted by Narahashi as being due to a temporary rise in potassium conductance during the falling phase, producing the brief period of high membrane potential observed. The negative after-potential is seen as the result of potassium ion retention in the vicinity of the axon membrane.[56]

High calcium markedly increases the negative after-potential, as does the presence of barium ions.

THE CONSTITUTION OF THE HAEMOLYMPH AND ITS EFFECT ON CONDUCTION

The Na/K ratio varies much in different insect species, and also according to diet. In *P.a.*, the Na/K ratio is fairly high, but in media containing high potassium or very low sodium, conduction is only affected after some time, however the blocking of conduction is rapid if the nerve cord is desheathed[96] (Fig. 8.21). The

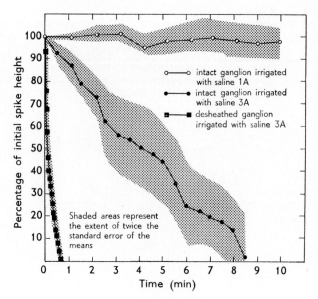

FIG. 8.21   The rate of loss of conduction through the fourth abdominal ganglion when irrigated with normal saline (○), and with high potassium saline when intact (●), and when desheathed (■). Shaded areas represent the extent of twice the standard error of the mean. (From Treherne[97])

sheath is also effective in restraining the action of acetylcholine.[98] In the case of ion permeability, this is not due to passive impermeability but rather to a dynamic steady-state, as demonstrated by Treherne.[95]

The behavioural physiology of the nervous system

Under this heading may be grouped all those observations which are focused at the neuronal level, usually involving the activity of several cells, but which do not depend on a detailed examination of membrane properties by the use of intracellular electrodes. This kind of information may be considered to extend from descriptive synaptic physiology to the statistical analysis of mass activity. Observations on small numbers of fibres will be described first of all.

One of the earliest workers in the field of locomotor reflexes was Rijlant, who recorded changes in motor impulse frequency associated with both passive and active leg movements, suggesting a division between fast and tonic motor activity. However, the precise definition of sensori-motor arcs involved in leg movements awaited the investigations of Pringle.

Pumphrey and Rawdon-Smith (see Chapter 7, p. 137) were able to describe the properties of cercal sensory–giant fibre synapses by the use of external recording methods, and their work may be regarded as the starting-point of analytical insect electrophysiology. Recording points were on the cercal nerve and abdominal connectives of *P.a.*, thus obtaining indirect information about transmission through the sixth or last abdominal ganglion. In response to acoustical or electrical stimulation of the cercal elements, a rapid and a delayed response were recorded in the connectives, and this was interpreted as an indication that some sensory fibres synapsed in the ganglion, while others ascended directly to higher levels.[74] Roeder, Kennedy and Samson, however, in some later work found no evidence either physiological or morphological for the existence of straight-through fibres of the kind envisaged by these early workers.[83]

It was also shown by Pumphrey and Rawdon-Smith that some of the cercal fibres were so arranged with regard to the ascending interneurones that impulses crossed over to the contralateral side in the sixth ganglion, and this was confirmed by Roeder.[79] It is worth noting that either ascending fibre collaterals or contra-lateral arborizations of cercal fibres could route the impulses as observed.[74]

At frequencies of electrical stimulation between 25 c/s and 400 c/s a 1:1 stimulus to response ratio occurred, but the synapses showed fatigue (adaptation), the response soon declining to near zero. The response could be brought back by raising the stimulus intensity which appears to recruit more fibres. Increasing the stimulus frequency also raised the response level, as did adding another type of stimulus, but, in the latter case, the effect was momentary. Thus the refractoriness of the post-synaptic membrane was overcome by activating more presynaptic fibres, i.e. by spatial summation; increase of response at higher frequency probably indicates temporal summation rather than enhancement of frequency-sensitive fibres.[74]

In the non-adapted state, the interneurone threshold may be set so low that deflection of a single trichoid sensillum will cause discharge, and Roeder argues that this wide variation in threshold suggests that this must be intrinsically adjusted.[80]

The unadapted preparation may show a train of secondary spikes in response to a single stimulus, and Roeder, Kennedy and Samson showed that the anti-cholinesterase DFP (di-isopropylfluorophosphonate) produced a similar condition of high synaptic facilitation, alternating with synaptic block. DFP does not affect spontaneous activity. What is perhaps not entirely clear is the extent to which parallel ascending fibre synapses, perhaps of a quick-adapting, high threshold type, could be responsible for the appearance of delayed discharge under conditions of minimal input and artificially raised ACH.[83] Hughes has shown that two groups of responding abdominal giants can be detected in this preparation, and has pointed out that a much more complex system may exist than has been so far described physiologically.[37]

Roeder, Kennedy and Samson,[83] and Roeder[79,81] estimated the delay at the cercal sensory-giant fibre synapse. In chronological order of publication values

7*

were: 0·7–2·0 msec (interval between direct and transynaptic spikes), 0·7–1·2 msec and 1·1–1·5 msec. The range given in each case takes into account the shortening of the delay with increased stimulus strength and probably corresponds to increase in quanta of transmitter per unit time at the giant synapse with afferent fibre recruitment. Callec and Boistel have obtained more detailed information on transmission in the synaptic zones of the sixth abdominal ganglion by recording with glass capillary electrodes during stimulation of the cercal nerve in excised preparations (Fig. 8.22). The observed potentials could

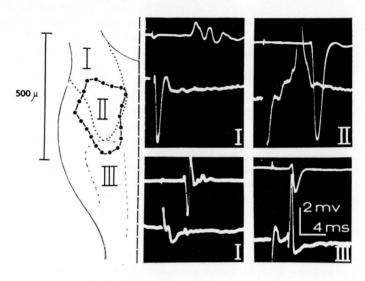

FIG. 8.22   Potentials from the synaptic zone of the cercal nerve, following electrical stimulation of the cercal nerve. To the left is shown the areas of the sixth ganglion from which the records were obtained: I includes the root of the cercal nerve, II the synaptic area and III the root of the connective. In the records the upper trace was taken from the connectives between the first and third abdominal ganglion, the lower one from the areas illustrated. The vertical scale does not apply to the upper trace. (From Callec and Boistel[12])

be referred to the region of the cercal nerve root (I), the synaptic zone anterior to it (II), or an area at the base of the connective (III). Region I yielded an early potential of 1·2 msec duration, and often of small amplitude. Region II was characterized by a potential lasting 10 msec, with a delay of 2 msec, the rising phase often appearing as a spike imposed on a slow potential. This slow potential may be the excitatory post-synaptic potential. In Region III a large spike without a slow phase and slightly in advance of the giant fibre response was observed. It seems that these potentials were leaked rather than true trans-membrane potentials.[12]

Following this important work, Bernard, Gahery and Boistel showed that a greater number of cercal afferents were required for a criterion giant fibre response at low temperatures than at high (11–26°), and slow and fast temperature changes produced different effects on peripheral and central neurones.[5] Gahery and Boistel demonstrated that GABA (γ-amino-butyric acid) inhibited the excitatory synapses while leaving the responsiveness of ascending giant fibres unaffected.[27]

This work on temperature effects on synapses extends earlier research by Kerkut and Taylor who found that ventral ganglia showed a transient increase in spontaneous electrical activity when subjected to a drop in temperature (25–15°), while the result was reversed when the temperature was raised. Transients occupied about five seconds.[42]

The response to cercal stimulation of ascending abdominal fibres can be sorted by magnitude, according to Roeder, large spikes of 10–1·5 mV being distinguishable from small spikes in the range of 100–300 μV. Conduction times, and fibre thresholds, taken together with the characteristic voltages obtained by external recording, allowed Roeder to build up a picture of the larger ascending fibres which accorded well with morphological studies he also made.

Three large and three smaller giant fibres ascended to the metathoracic ganglion on each side and at least four of these synapses with cercal afferents. Two small elements on each side receive contralateral cercal afferents. Within the metathoracic ganglion, synapses between the ascending fibres and motor neurones occur. These ascending fibre-motor synapses are highly unstable, much more so than the synapses of the sixth ganglion, and the synaptic delay may be more than 4·0 msec. One of the reasons for the variability of this synapse is the inhibitory effect of descending fibre synapses, which may block motor conduction. Furthermore, Roeder points out that the range of synaptic delays may mask the existence of more than one synapse at this locus.

The three large abdominal giants are in synaptic relationship with two large and one smaller giant fibre in the connective to the mesothoracic ganglion, and these synapse again with one large and one smaller giant fibre extending into the prothoracic ganglion. From this point, a small fibre may continue longitudinal transmission into the head ganglia. There is thus a scaling down of number and speed of pathways towards the anterior end of the nerve cord.[79]

Recently published work by Hughes suggests that the large spontaneous spikes that can be easily observed in the ventral nerve cord are independent of the large ascending spikes resulting from stimulation of the cercal hairs, and may be due to activity in descending giant fibres[37] (Fig. 8.23).

There seems little doubt that, as in other invertebrates with non-medullated nerve fibres, the giant fibres provide a rapid conduction pathway for avoidance or escape reactions. Roeder has measured the total time involved in this startle response, the shortest times in the unadapted cockroach being as follows: cercal cell response, about 0·5 msec; conduction time in cercal fibres, 1·5 msec; synaptic delay in the sixth abdominal ganglion, 1·1 msec; giant fibre conduction, 2·8 msec; synaptic delay in metathoracic ganglion, 4·0 msec; conduction time in motor fibres, 1·5 msec. As shown earlier by Pringle, only the fast motor fibres are primarily involved in the cercal response; neuromuscular delay and muscle potential, 4·0 msec; development of contraction, 4·0 msec; total time, 19·4 msec; the range of behaviourally measured response times was 28–90 msec.

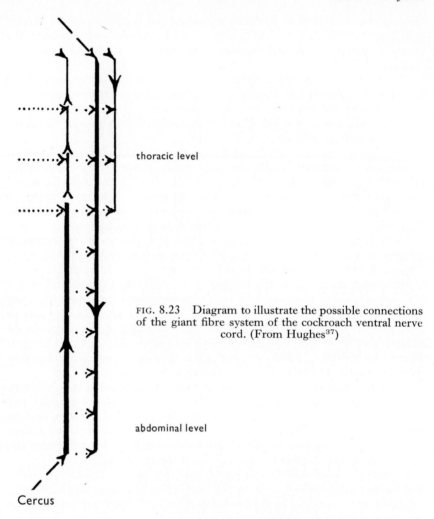

thoracic level

FIG. 8.23   Diagram to illustrate the possible connections of the giant fibre system of the cockroach ventral nerve cord. (From Hughes[37])

abdominal level

Cercus

The variability of the behavioural response may be due to the instability of the thoracic synapses and slowness of mechanical events.[81]

Recently, Hughes has investigated changes in the cercal nerve-giant fibre response to repetitive air current stimulation. If air puffs are repeated at half-minute intervals in isolated abdomen preparations the larger spikes (above a standard voltage) fall off in numbers rather sharply, but if a substantial rest period is allowed (50 min) initial response levels are largely recovered (Fig. 8.24). Hughes concluded that the processes underlying the waning of the response were localized at the level of the sixth abdominal ganglion and he viewed this pheno-menon of adaptation at the afferent interneurone synapse as being involved in the habituation of the response of the whole animal to repeated puffs of air.[37]

The basis of our present understanding of segmental reflexes was laid down by Pringle in a study published shortly after his descriptions of the sense organs and the dual motor innervation of the cockroach leg (see Sense organs, p. 139, and Neuromuscular physiology, p. 242). The tibial extensor and the coxal group of trochanteral extensors are used as examples of a levator and a depressor respectively, the basic approach being a Sherringtonian one. External recordings

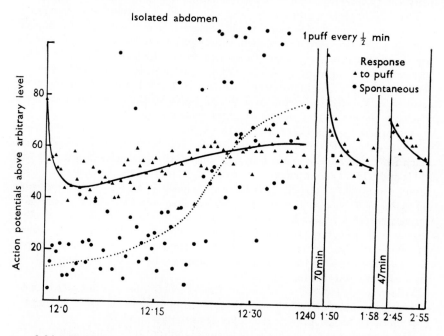

FIG. 8.24   *Periplaneta*: waning of the response of giant fibres in the ventral nerve cord to stimulation of the cercal hairs by standard air puffs. The count of spikes above a constant voltage is plotted (▲) for successive puffs given at half-minute intervals. The spontaneous activity of the preparation was also counted between the puffs (●) and the mean level is indicated by the dotted line. (From Hughes[37])

were made by inserting fine wire electrodes at either end of the muscle, tonic and phasic responses being obtained.

Under no-stimulus conditions, a regular discharge occurred in the trochanteral depressor, an abrupt increase in frequency following levation of the leg. When allowed to return to its previous position, the tonic discharge rate drops to its original level.

Pringle found that the tonic fibre frequency was unaffected by limb position—which would have been the case if hair plates had been stimulated—neither did artificially stretching the muscles affect it—as would have occurred if the chordotonal organs had been involved. Direct pressure on the campaniform sense organs confirmed the deduction that they supplied the afferent component in this reflex. The application and release of maintained pressure produces remarkably sudden changes in frequency, sometimes made more striking by a brief silent period following the initial change.

Electrical stimulation of the fifth nerve root resulted in silent periods in the tonic discharge to the tibial levator, while the removal of pressure levating the trochanter caused increases in frequency. Frequency increases were often marked by a rebound burst of pulses sometimes including fast axon spikes.

The results clearly support the idea of mutual inhibition between pairs of tonic motor neurones, each pair corresponding to a levator and depressor muscle.

Pringle also demonstrated bilateral intrasegmental reflexes, depression of the leg of one side producing slight decrease, levation slight increase, in tonic fibre discharge to the depressor muscles of the opposite side. However, intersegmental reflexes although sought for were not found. Lateral pressure on the body resulted in lowered tonic discharge to depressors of the same side, and raised discharge to contralateral depressors, thus resisting this pressure.[72]

Wilson has recently introduced on-line computing techniques into the study of input–output relationships in leg reflexes (Fig. 8.25). Recording leads were taken from electrodes implanted in the tibial extensor muscles of different legs (142a and b in the mesothorax), one leg being stimulated mechanically by a lever driven sinusoidally at 2–20 c/s. Ipsilateral responses followed input frequences up to 20 c/s or more without shift of phase. The contralateral leg gave weaker responses with a phase change of 180° compared to stimulus phase, and other segments showed very weak and variable responses only detectable by storing successive sweeps. Nevertheless, these intersegmental responses are of interest in view of failures by earlier workers to demonstrate them (note, however, the early observations by Hughes[36]).

Wilson concluded that input-output phasing contains information on which co-ordination can be based at all normal speeds of limb movement, and he suggests that muscular factors provide the upper limit to this speed.[105]

The control of efferent fibre activity by inhibitory fibres descending from the brain has been demonstrated for thoracic motor neurones by Pringle, and in the case of efferent axons of the sixth abdominal ganglion by Roeder *et al.* It may be that Roeder's early work in inhibitory pathways in the insect C.N.S., based on work on *Mantis*, can be applied with caution to the cockroach.[82, 84]

Janda states the effect of decapitation on *B.o.* is to make it walk more slowly, and with less assurance, although it walks more efficiently than *Bt.g.* after the same treatment. Cuts isolating the thoracic ganglia from the rest of the nerve cord made the clawing or scratching reflex (Wischreflex) appear much clearer in these segments.[39]

Pringle showed that decapitation produced hyperactivity of all slow fibres to leg muscles, but especially to depressors, a condition similar to decerebrate rigidity in mammals often occurring. Lack of coordination was observed in the levator responses, and the preparation was usually very responsive to air currents. However, isolation of the ganglion involved, by cutting anterior and posterior connectives, resulted in a return to more or less normal reflexes, suggesting the presence of local augmentor elements.[72] Roeder *et al.* found that transection of

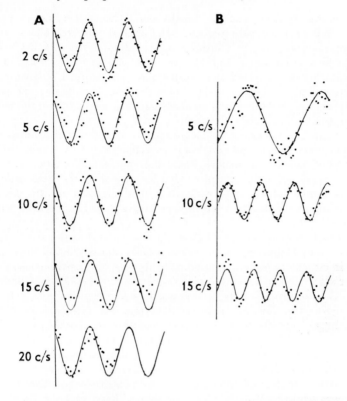

FIG. 8.25   Efferent fibre responses resulting from sinusoidal mechanical stimulation of the leg plotted over stimulus cycles. **A**, cross-correlogram for ipselateral response. Deviations were not systematic with change of frequency. **B**, cross-correlogram for contralateral responses. The phase is inverted compared to **A**.
(From Wilson[105])

the abdominal nerve cord in front of the sixth ganglion, or removal of the head ganglia resulted in large increases in efferent activity. Removal of the supra-oesophageal centres alone produced a slight increase in small spike activity in some preparations, leading to the conclusion that the suboesophageal ganglion was the head centre mainly responsible for the observed inhibition. One peculiarity was that heightened activity following cord transection might not appear for as much as 15 min, and this Roeder suggests may be due to the slow action of a chemical mediator; if perhaps the descending inhibitory pathways consist of hierarchical series rather than single fibres, a similar slow run down might occur following cord transection. Pathways involved are certainly complex, and Roeder showed that ganglion bisection, and unilateral transection of the cord, both produced heightened efferent activity. These results were interpreted as evidence of the decussation of descending inhibitory fibres, and the presence of transverse intra-ganglionic inhibitory elements.

The increase in efferent activity usually took the form of regular volleys rather than the raising of a steady frequency, the frequency of the volleys varying in different fibres of a nerve.[84] The descending inhibitory system cannot be blocked by KCl or anelectrotonus, but Milburn *et al.* found that extracts of corpus cardiacum had a similar effect to cord transection. Corpus cardiacum extract application produced heightened activity in thoracic efferents also, and again this is interpreted as blocking of inhibition as there is no evidence that this substance has any action on excitatory synapses.[50]

The isolated nerve cord of the cockroach, in common with the central nervous system of other insects and vertebrates as demonstrated by Adrian, exhibits a high level of spontaneous activity. Roeder has touched on certain aspects of this activity—mainly in so far as it provides a useful tool for the observation of the effects of various substances on conduction. The functional identity of the units involved and the significance of their repetitive activity remains to a great extent obscure.[80]

The effect on limb position of direct current applied to thoracic ganglia has been shown by Hughes to vary with the polarity and position of the electrodes. Thus, if current is passed longitudinally through the metathoracic ganglion, anterior negativity causes leg flexion, posterior negativity causes extension. When current is passed transversely, flexion occurs at the negative pole, extension at the positive pole. Hughes suggested that this was evidence for differently orientated and current-sensitive neurones, and illustrates possible configurations. So far it has not been possible to extend these observations.[36]

The possibility of finding a preparation containing relatively few neurones that would exhibit some form of learning has until recently received little attention from invertebrate neurophysiologists. Using an experimental layout that avoids nonspecific artefacts, Horridge has now shown that a cockroach limb and its associated nervous system minus the head centres can be trained to maintain a posture that avoids reception of an electric shock. Headless cockroaches (presumed to be *P.a.*) are mounted in pairs so that a circuit is completed through a prothoracic leg of each insect when the leg of one of each pair of insects (P animals) falls below a certain level and makes contact with a saline bath (Fig. 8.26A). Shocks are delivered at 1/sec, the second (R) animal receiving shocks to the tarsus irrespective of the leg position. After 30–45 min of training, the animals were removed, and, following a wait of 10 min, remounted in an experimental set-up that delivers shocks independently to both of them only when the individual prothoracic leg falls to the critical level. It is now seen that the P animals receive significantly less shocks than the R animals (during the first 2 min this is at the 0·1 level of a rank order test). The use of pairs helps to allow for inherent variability in the material (which, it is pointed out, is quite high), and differences in testing procedure. It might be thought that the changes observed must be localized within the prothoracic segment, but if a metathoracic leg is left intact in each, not used in the preliminary test, and then used for the retest, its error curve in the P animal is significantly better than in the R animal. Thus the changes involved cannot be confined to one segment.[35]

More recently, Luco and Aranda have shown that plastic changes in central

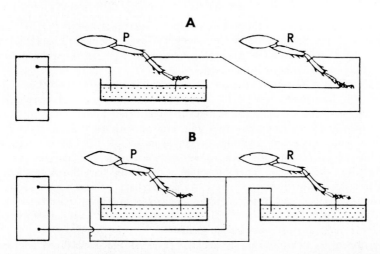

FIG. 8.26   Experimental layout for learning trials on headless insects. The circuit is completed through the legs and saline baths. See text. (From Horridge[35])

nervous system function in *B.o.* may involve changes in facilitation and synaptic delay that can be directly demonstrated. These authors had previously shown that in a small number (10%) of normal cockroaches, stimulation of the anterior connectives of the metathoracic ganglion with a single shock could elicit a single post-synaptic spike. A monosynaptic pathway was believed to be involved and the single all-or-none response termed the servile response. These authors found that if the forelimbs of a cockroach are amputated after 3 or 4 days, it learns to stand and walk with the remaining legs, and functions such as cleaning of the antennae are transferred to one of the mesothoracic limbs. When the nerve cord is removed and examined in vitro by electrophysiological methods 90% of preparations exhibit the servile response and the synaptic delay has shortened from 4·42 msec to 1·86 msec (mean values). To what extent the observed facilitation and shortened synaptic delay are independent changes is not clear. Details of technique and reasoning are not made fully explicit in this paper.[43]

Finally it may be pointed out that very little information based on localized recording is available on the activity of the many hundreds of neurones in the head ganglion, although Maynard has provided a picture of the probable fibre pathways between the deutocerebrum and the corpora pedunculata. He observed a large monophasic potential (up to 30 mV) in the calyx of the c.p. consequent on antennal nerve stimulation, and a smaller biphasic response in the α- and β-lobes. Maynard suggests that his observations support the idea of a functional pathway from the antennal glomeruli to the calyx, then to peduncle, α-lobe and finally to the antennal lobe.[47] The symptoms of chlordane poisoning are interesting from the point of view of corpora pedunculata function (see Chapter 18).

THE SPIRACULAR NERVOUS SYSTEM. (Fig. 8.27)

The median nerves and their branches have been described in *P.a.* by Case,[13] Pipa *et al.*[66] and Schmitt.[88] The spiracular nervous system is remarkable onto-genetically in that the main ganglionic root arises from an unpaired group of nerve cells in the embryo (Johannsen and Butt).[40]

In *P.a.* Pipa *et al.* refer to the thoracic ganglionic root as nerve 8 (Case—n.6). As in other insects this root divides soon after leaving the dorsal surface of the ganglion into right and left rami, which run transversely to the spiracles. Nerve 8 of the prothoracic ganglion has three anastomoses with nerve 2Br1 of the meso-thoracic ganglion before reaching the single muscle of the first spiracle. Fine branches of 2Br1d (mesothoracic) innervate the cuticle and hair sense organs surrounding the spiracle. The spiracular nerve of the mesothorax has a rather similar relationship to the ganglion of the segment behind it, but only two anastomoses occur, and in the metathorax there is only one, again between n.8 and 2Br1. Case,[13] and Matsuda[46] (*Bt.g.*) indicate a generally similar arrangement but show fewer anastomoses and other details.

According to Schmitt the spiracular nerves of the generalized abdominal segment run laterally from a root near the anterior margin of each abdominal ganglion, and Case shows the median nerve dichotomy at this point, but indicates an additional root running forwards from near the division to the surface of the right anterior connective just posterior to the preceding ganglion. He also claims that a ganglion of small size is present on the dorsal part of each transverse nerve. Schmitt shows this nerve running out to the pleural fold where it divides into an anterior ramus to n.2B of the preceding segment, from which comes the branch to the spiracular muscles, and a posterior ramus joining n.2A of its own segment.[88] The anterior branch is often rather obscure, and Case does not figure it.[13] The terminal branch to the spiracular muscles appears to come off directly rather than from the main trunk of 2B.

The spiracle of the eighth segment is within the area innervated by the sixth abdominal ganglion, and according to Case arises from a T-shaped junction, without a root from the connective, near the anterior edge of the ganglion. A further eighth nerve root from the posterior region of the ganglion fuses with the base of the cercal nerve, but in *Leucophaea maderae* Engelmann shows this posterior root fusing with n.2A of the eighth segment (dorsal nerve) which gives rise terminally to a branch to the spiracle.[26]

Methylene blue preparations clearly demonstrate a pair of thick axons in the ganglionic root of the abdominal spiracular nerves bifurcating into right and left branches at the T-junction. Other fine fibres can be seen. The ganglion described by Case appears to contain at least two small neurones with processes in a fine connection to one of the segmental nerves (Fig. 8.27).[29] In the thoracic ganglia fibres from the eighth nerve root could be seen to descend to a more posterior level in the connectives (Fig. 8.27).

The function of these nerves had been demonstrated by Case in *P.a.* and *B.c.*[13] Section of the nerves does not abolish opening of the spiracle in response to a high external concentration of CO_2, but it does abolish rhythmic valvular con-

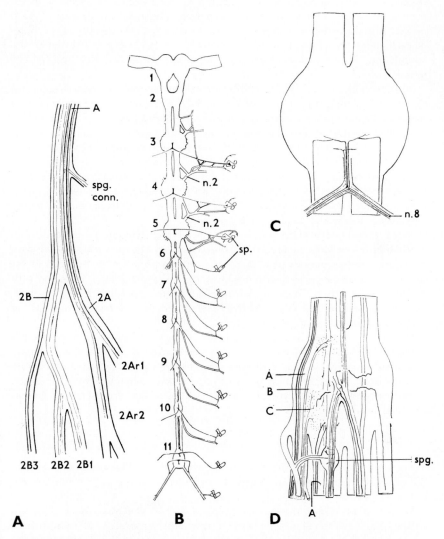

FIG. 8.27 Nervous system of the spiracles, and parts of the abdominal nervous system. **A**, fibres of different diameters within the main abdominal nerve trunk; spg. conn.—connective of spiracular ganglion. **B**, the spiracular nervous system. Ganglia numbered as a single series; sp.—spiracle. (Information from various sources, including Case, Schmitt, and Pipa, Cook and Richards) **C**, branches of median nerve fibres in the mesothoracic ganglion. **D**, details of fibre arrangement in an abdominal ganglion; spg.—spiracular ganglion. Three groups of fibres can be distinguished in the main nerve trunk (n.2). **A**, **C** and **D** from methylene blue preparations

tractions. These contractions are synchronous with bursts of impulses in the transverse nerves, and they can be elicited by electrical stimulation of these nerves. Impulses are grouped in such a way as to suggest the activity of two fibres in each nerve. No afferent impulses could be demonstrated in the nerve, but stimulation of mechanoreceptors near the spiracle produced electrical activity in n.2.

That axon branches from one cell innervate spiracle muscles on both sides was shown by crushing the eighth nerve root, then when one transverse nerve was stimulated electrically the spiracular muscles on both sides contracted. Furthermore, the impulses in the transverse nerves of both sides were synchronous. The pathway involved in closure of the spiracle in response to mechanical stimulation was shown to be from the hair organs through the second nerve, forwards in the connectives to the ganglion in front, and then out to the spiracular muscle through the median root. This agrees with morphological findings.[13] Finally, Case concluded that the centre controlling the timing of spiracular and ventilatory movements was in the metathoracic ganglia.[14, 15]

More recently Myers and Fisk have examined the timing of neural control of ventilation in the large cockroach *Byrsotria fumigata*. Section of the nerve cord at various levels suggested that there was a respiratory centre localized in the abdominal nerve cord, normally inhibited by descending fibres from the suboesophageal ganglion. These in turn received augmentor fibres from the brain. CO_2 had a well-defined effect on the isolated abdomen, 6 contractions/min at 11% CO_2 rising to about 30 per min at 27% CO_2.[52]

Myers and Retzlaff extended these observations neuro-physiologically and produced convincing evidence that the pacemaker is in the first separate abdominal ganglion, which continues to produce accurately timed discharges when isolated. Three different types of impulse were obtained from the lateral nerves, suggesting three types of axon. The maximum conduction velocities observed were about 2 m/sec.[53]

THE INNERVATION AND NEURAL CONTROL OF GUT MUSCLE

Not a great deal of information exists on this topic. The admirable work of Willey,[104] however, describes clearly the topography of the gut nervous system in *P.a.* (Fig. 8.28).

According to Willey the frontal ganglion lies on the pharynx, and nerves arising from it run to the median labral retractors (12), the lateral labral retractors (13) and the pharyngeal dilators (7, 8, 9 and 10, posterior ramus). In this study, however, a fine lateral nerve linked to the frontal ganglion appeared to innervate the median and lateral labral retractors (12 and 13). A recurrent nerve connects the frontal ganglion with the retrocerebral complex. Beneath the corpus cardiacum the recurrent nerve is slightly expanded into a hypocerebral ganglion. Fibres from this region pass to the corpora cardiaca, the intrinsic pharyngeal muscles, and, according to Nesbitt, the aorta. Posteriorly the nerve tract continues as the oesophageal nerve along the dorsal surface of the crop giving off lateral nerves to the salivary glands. About halfway between brain and proventriculus the

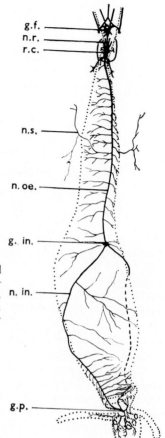

g.f.
n.r.
r.c.

n.s.

n. oe.

g.. in.

n. in.

g.p.

FIG. 8.28 Stomodaeal nervous system, dorsal view. Abbreviations: g.f.—frontal ganglion, g.in.—ingluvial ganglion, g.p.—proventricular ganglion, n.in.—ingluvial nerve, n.oe.—oesophageal nerve, n.r.—recurrent nerve, n.s.—salivary nerve, r.c.—retrocerebral complex. (From Willey)

oesophageal nerve bifurcates, giving rise to two ingluvial nerves, one passing to the ventral surface of the crop while the other continues on the dorsal surface. At the point of dichotomy there is a flat triangular ganglion—the ingluvial ganglion. Willey describes this as a small ganglion, but it can normally be seen clearly in dissections. The dorsal ingluvial nerve runs posteriorly to a point at which a number of especially large branches are given off to the crop musculature (shown as a single ramus in figure 1 of Willey's paper).[104] Here there is another ganglion, not mentioned in Willey's account, with at least 20 nerve cell bodies. This structure (Fig. 8.29) will be termed the second ingluvial ganglion. In methylene blue preparations some of the ganglion cells can be made out in considerable detail. The pyriform cell bodies give rise to two or more short processes. One interesting feature are fine processes running to other cell bodies through the cell body layer, rather than through the neuropile.[29]

The dorsal ingluvial nerve continues posteriorly to a terminal proventricular

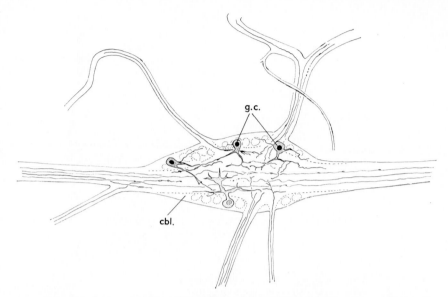

FIG. 8.29   The second ingluvial ganglion of the crop. A number of ganglion cells (g.c.) can be seen, and the cell body layer (cbl.) is visible; 20–25 cells appear to be present. Methylene blue

ganglion just in front of the proventriculus. Nerves from this ganglion pass over the proventriculus and some run along the gastric caeca.

The rectum receives nerve fibres from two branches of the eighth (cercal) nerve in *P.a.*, and a similar arrangement has been described in *Leucophaea*. Davey demonstrated nerve cells in the upper colon with arrows running to the rectal nerves in *P.a.*[17] The innervation of the mid-gut is obscure, but according to Day and Waterhouse this region of the gut has few nerve fibres in many species of insects.[21]

Sense organs in the pharynx consisting of nests of receptor cells with peg-like tips have been observed by Davey and Treherne, and multipolar sense cells similar in appearance to stretch receptors occur in the crop, and hind-gut.[19]

Davey and Treherne have made a study of the mechanism of crop emptying. Treherne found that the rate of crop emptying and the frequency with which the proventricular valve was opened was related to the osmotic pressure of the fore-gut contents. Cutting various stomodaeal nerves showed that the fifth nerve of the frontal ganglion was involved, and this received axons from the pharyngeal sense organs, suggested as possible osmoreceptors by these authors. Cutting nerves at any level on the ingluvial-recurrent nerve pathway reduced crop emptying. The pressure of the crop contents is related to the operation of the valve.[18,19,20]

Davey showed that corpus cardiacum extract stimulated argentaffin cells in the upper colon to produce an indolalkylamine that acts on the muscles of this region through local neurones.[17]

THE INNERVATION OF THE HEART,
AND THE CONTROL OF HEARTBEAT

In many insects the blood is propelled through the complex cavities of the haemocoele by the muscles of the heart and ventral diaphragm. In the cockroach (*P.a.*) the ventral diaphragm is only slightly developed (Richards is of the opinion that it is absent in *B.o.* and *P.a.*,[76] but a fine system of muscle fibres has been described in *Leucophaea*,[26] and a somewhat similar structure can be demonstrated in *P.a.*[29]). The abdominal spiracular nerve passes across the ventral diaphragm in *P.a.* but nerve branches could not be seen.

Four possible sources of nerve terminals on the heart have been described. (1) The retrocerebral complex (corpora cardiaca). (2) Transverse branches of the dorsal segmental nerve (in the abdomen 2A). (3) Intrinsic cardiac neurones. (4) Oblique branches of the dorsal segmental nerve, or branches of other nerves from the segmental ganglia.[1,41]

In fact, a lateral nerve can be distinguished running along the side of the dorsal vessel and this contains separate ganglion cells, but appears to arise anteriorly in the retrocerebral complex. Willey describes the origin of the aortic nerves from posterior extensions of the corpora cardiaca in *P.a.*, but did not trace them to the segmental level described by Alexandrowicz in *B.o.* Near the transverse commissure of the corpora cardiaca two groups of nerve fibres run forward into the wall of the aorta, and from the anterior region of the commissure a further ten groups of fibres run forward to form a plexus in the wall of the aorta. Willey suggests that fibres from this plexus may innervate the antennal pulsatile organs.[104]

The dorsal nerve (2A) of an abdominal ganglion can be fairly easily traced to the wall of the heart, and according to Schmitt it then divides into an anterior and posterior ramus running parallel to the main axis of the heart in *P.a.*[88] In the same insect McIndoo shows a segmental ramus running to the aorta from n.2 (possible 2C) in the meso- and metathorax, and an unidentified nerve in the prothorax,[45] but these were not described by Pipa and Cook.[66]

Alexandrowicz shows fibres from the dorsal nerve (2A and 2a) in *B.o.* joining the lateral nerve. Recurrent branches of these fibres run to the alary muscles.[1]

Lying on either side of the heart, but separated from it by an interval of several microns, are the lateral cardiac nerves. In *P.a.* they contain up to 32, mostly bipolar, neurones according to McIndoo,[44,45] and in *B.o.* Alexandrowicz counted as many as 40[1] (see also Metcalf, Winton and Fukoto[48]). The segmental vessels contain tripolar neurones (*P.a.*). Short processes run from the cardiac neurones to the myocardium and alary muscles. McIndoo found that when teased apart 10 or 12 fibres could be seen in the lateral nerve, but his drawings of sections indicate many more to be present.[45] Edwards and Challice were able to identify parts of these ganglion cells in electronmicrographs, as well as axons.[24]

The fourth source of nerve terminals is described in the work of Alexandrowicz, who postulated the existence of a purely sensory innervation entering the heart from its dorsal side.[1] This originates from the fine integumentary branch of 2Ar2a (integ. Schmitt).

McIndoo was of the opinion that, compared with other insects he had studied, the cockroach heart was well innervated.[45]

The physiology of the nerve elements of the cockroach has been investigated hardly at all by direct means.

Decapitation of *P.a.* and thus removal of effects from the corpora cardiaca fibres produces a very gradual decline in frequency (Orser and Brown) and an immediate reduction in the amplitude of heart beats, according to Jones.[41] A variety of cardio-accelerator substances have been extracted from the corpora cardiaca, but for the most part it is likely that their effects are direct ones on the heart muscle.

The response to acetylcholine of heart muscle has by certain authorities (Prosser) been regarded as a criterion by which neurogenic and myogenic hearts can be distinguished. Thus myogenic molluscan hearts tend to be depressed by Ach, while the hearts of *Limulus* and many crustaceans with pacemaker neurones are accelerated.[73] The heart of *P.a.* is accelerated by Ach down to concentrations of 5×10^{-8},[54] an effect potentiated by pyrethrum, paraoxon and eserine. Nicotine has a depressive effect on heartbeat,[54] a result believed to follow when nerve-cell bodies rather than simply axon terminals are affected.[110]

The temperature characteristic for insect heartbeat rates is also believed to have some correlation with the presence or absence of local neurones (for a discussion, see Jones). The aneural hearts of mosquitoes provide values below 9,000, while *P.a.* and *B.o.* have values between 12,000 and 14,000.[41] Finally, Steiner showed that electrical stimulation of the nerve cord in the neck region following decapitation produced acceleration.[89] These considerations would favour the idea of local pacemaker neurones, segmental accelerator fibres, and perhaps a separate aortic control system localized anteriorly, but more direct evidence is required.

THE NUTRITION OF THE CENTRAL NERVOUS SYSTEM

Treherne studied the fate of carbohydrates within the central nervous system of *P.a.* using ^{14}C; detecting radioactivity by means of a scintillation counter, and identifying substances chromatographically. He found that ^{14}C labelled glucose was largely converted to trehalose. The rate of entry of these sugars into the central nervous system was studied by estimation of the amount of ^{14}C in the abdominal nerve cord, and found to be equivalent to 1·09 mM glucose/litre of nerve-cord water/minute. The rate of entry into different parts of the nerve cord was closely similar. Only about 7% of ^{14}C entered as glucose, but the rate of entry was 2·5 times that of the larger trehalose molecules. More than half the absorbed ^{14}C was incorporated as glutamic acid and glutamine, while smaller amounts of glycogen, trehalose, glucose, aspartic acid and occasional traces of alanine were found. Where the nerve cord had been isolated and exposed to ^{14}C in vitro, substantial amounts of alanine could be demonstrated, and the formation of the other amino acids was reduced. Treherne felt that the prompt appearance of ^{14}C, supplied as trehalose and glucose, in aspartic and glutamic acids in vivo, and in alanine in vitro, suggests the presence of the Krebs tricarboxylic acid cycle enzymes in the nervous system.[90]

More recently Ray has provided information on the free amino acids. Chromatograms of nerve cord extracts yielded arginine, *glutamine*, *γ-amino-n-butyric acid*, alanine, aspartate, glutamate, serine, glycine, taurine and *proline*. Those in italic type above are all linked with glutamate, and derived from the Krebs cycle intermediate α-oxoglutarate. Aspartate is derived from oxaloacetate, and alanine is derived from pyruvate.

Iodacetate was shown by Yamasaki and Narahashi to inhibit glycolysis in cockroach nerve. Iodacetate duplicates the depletion of proline caused by DDT, and this suggests that the nerve failure observed at the final stage of DDT prostration is due to this. Ray suggests that proline acts as a temporary metabolic reserve in cases of hyperactivity, or when the usual glycolytic pathway is blocked. Alanine can arise as a result of proline oxidation, or as the endproduct of carbohydrate metabolism when pyruvate metabolism is blocked.

REFERENCES

1. ALEXANDROWICZ, J. S. (1926). The innervation of the heart of the cockroach, *B.o. J. comp. Neurol.*, **41**, 291–309.
2. ASHURST, D. E. (1961). An acid mucopolysaccharide in cockroach ganglia. *Nature, Lond.*, **191**, 1224–5.
3. ASHURST, D. E. (1961). A histochemical study of the connective tissue sheath of the nervous system of *P.a. Q. Jl microsc. Sci.*, **102**, 455–61.
4. ASHURST, D. E. and PATEL, N. (1963). Hyaluronic acid in the cockroach nervous system. *Ann. ent. Soc. Am.*, **56**, no. 2.
5. BERNARD, J., GAHERY, Y. and BOISTEL, J. The effects of temperature changes applied to the cercal nerves and to the sixth abdominal ganglion of the cockroach (*Blaberus craniifer* Burm). *The Physiology of the Insect Central Nervous System*, ed. ROCKSTEIN, pp. 67–72. Academic Press, New York and London.
6. BOISTEL, J. and CORABOEUF, E. (1954). Potentiel de membrane et potentiel d'action de nerf d'insecte récuellis à l'aide de microelectrode intracellulaire. *C.r. hebd. Séanc. Acad. Sci., Paris*, **238**, 2116–18.
7. BOISTEL, J. and CORABOEUF, E. (1955). Quelques aspects de la microphysio logique nerveuse chez les insectes. *Colloques int. Cent. natn. Rech. scient.*, **67**, 57–72.
8. BOISTEL, J. (1960). *Caracteristiques fonctionelles des fibres nerveuses et des récepteurs tactiles et olfactifs des insectes.* Librairie Arnette, Paris, 1–147.
9. BRETSCHNEIDER, F. (1913). Der Central Korper und die pilzformigen Korper im Gehirn der Insekten, *Zoo. Anz.*, **41**, 560–9.
10. BRETSCHNEIDER, F. (1914). Uber die gehirne der Kuchenschabe und des Mehlkafers. *Jena. Z. Naturw*, **52**, 269–362.
11. BULLOCK, T. H. and HORRIDGE, A. G. (1965). *Structure and Function of the Nervous System of Invertebrates.* Freeman, London.
12. CALLEC, J. J. and BOISTEL, J. (1965). Analysis with microelectrodes of the synaptic transmission at the level of the sixth abdominal ganglion of a cockroach, *P.a.* In *The Physiology of the Insect Central Nervous System*, ed. ROCKSTEIN, pp. 59–65. Academic Press, New York and London.
13. CASE, J. F. (1957). The median nerves and cockroach spiracular function. *J. Insect Physiol.*, **1**, 85–94.
14. CASE, J. F. (1961). Organisation of the cockroach respiratory center. *Biol. Bull.*, **121**, 385.

15. CASE, J. F. (1961). Effects of acids on an isolated insect respiratory center. *Biol. Bull.*, **121**, 385.

16. COHEN, M. J. and JACKLET, J. W. (1965). Neurons of Insects: RNA changes during injury and regeneration. *Science*, **148**, 1237–9.

17. DAVEY, K. G. (1962). The mode of action of the corpus cardiacum on the hind gut. *J. exp. Biol.*, **39**, 319–24.

18. DAVEY, K. G. and TREHERNE, J. E. (1963). Studies on crop function in the cockroach (*P.a.*). I. The mechanism of crop emptying. *J. exp. Biol.*, **40**, 763–73.

19. DAVEY, K. G. and TREHERNE, J. E. (1963). Studies on crop function in the cockroach (*P.a.*). II. The nervous control of crop emptying. *J. exp. Biol.*, **40**, 775–80.

20. DAVEY, K. G. and TREHERNE, J. E. (1964). Studies on crop function in the cockroach (*P.a.*). III. Pressure changes during feeding and crop emptying. *J. exp. Biol.*, 513–24.

21. DAY, M. F. and WATERHOUSE, D. F. (1953). Chapter 10. The structure of the alimentary system. In *Insect Physiology*, ed. ROEDER, K. D. John Wiley, London.

22. DRESDEN, D. and NIJENHUIS, E. D. (1958). Fibre analysis of the nerves of the second thoracic leg in *P. americana*. *Verh. K. Akad. Wet.*, **61**, 213–23.

23. EDWARDS, G. A. (1959). The fine structure of a multi-terminal innervation of an insect muscle. *J. biophys. biochem Cytol.*, **5**, 241–4.

24. EDWARDS, G. A. and CHALLICE. The ultrastructure of the heart of the cockroach *B.g. Ann. ent. soc. Am.*, **53**, 369–83.

25. EGGERS, F. (1923). Ergebnisse von Untersuchungen an Johnstonchen organe der Insekten. *Zool. Aug.*, **57**, 224–40.

26. ENGELMANN, F. (1963). Die Innervation der Genital und Postgenitalsegmente bei Weibchen der Schabe *Leucophaea maderae*. *Zool. Jb. Anat.*, **81**, 1–16.

27. GAHERY, Y. and BOISTEL, J. Study of some pharmacological substances which modify the electrical activity of the 6th abdominal ganglion of the cockroach *P.a.* In *The Physiology of the Central Nervous System*, ed. ROCKSTEIN, pp. 73–8. Academic Press, New York and London.

28. GORDON, H. T. and WELSH, J. H. (1948). The rôle of ions in axon surface reactions to toxic organic compounds. *J. cell. comp. Physiol.*, **31**, 395–419.

29. GUTHRIE, D. M. Unpublished observations.

30. HANSTROM, B. (1928). *Vergleichende Anatomie des Nervensystems der Wirbellosen Tiere*. Berlin.

31. HESS, A. (1958). Experimental anatomical studies of pathways in the severed central nerve cord of the cockroach. *J. Morph.*, **103**, 479–501.

32. HESS, A. (1958). The fine structure of nerve cells, and fibres, neuroglia, and sheaths of the ganglionic chain in the cockroach (*P. americana*). *J. biophys. biochem. Cytol.*, **4**, 731–42.

33. HESS, A. (1958). The fine structure and morphological organisation of the peripheral nerve fibres and trunks of the cockroach (*P. americana*). *Q. Jl microsc. Sci.*, **99**, 333–40.

34. HESS, A. (1960). The fine structure of degenerating nerve fibres, their sheaths and their termination in the central nerve cord of the cockroach (*P. americana*). *J. biophys. biochem. Cytol.*, **7** (i).

35. HORRIDGE, G. A. (1962). Learning leg position by the ventral nerve cord in headless insects. *Proc. R. Soc. B.*, **157**, 33–52.

36. HUGHES, G. M. (1952). Differential effects of direct current on insect ganglia. *J. exp. Biol.*, **23**, 387–402.

37. HUGHES, G. M. (1965). Neuronal pathways in the insect central nervous system. In *The Physiology of the Insect Central Nervous System*, ed. ROCKSTEIN. Academic Press, New York and London.

38. HUGHES, G. M. and WILSON, V. J. (1965) (unpublished). Cited in Hughes[37].

39. JANDA, O. (1939). Nervous control of walking following decapitation in insects (in Czech). German summary, *Sb. ent. Odd. nár. Mus. Praze*, **17**, 50–68.
40. JOHANNSEN, O. A. and BUTT, F. H. (1941). *Embryology of Insects and Myriapods*. McGraw-Hill, New York and Maidenhead.
41. JONES, J. C. (1964). The circulatory system of insects. In *The Physiology of the Insecta*, vol. **3**, pp. 1–94 (Chapter 1), ed. ROCKSTEIN. Academic Press, New York and London.
42. KERKUT, G. A. and TAYLOR, B. J. R. (1956). The effect of temperature on spontaneous activity of slug, cockroach and crayfish ganglia. *Nature, Lond.*, **178**, 426.
43. LUCO, J. V. and ARANDA, L. C. An electrical correlate to the process of learning. Experiments in *Blatta orientalis*. *Nature Lond.*, **201**, no. 4926, 1330–1.
44. MACINDOO, N. E. (1939). The lateral blood vessels of the cockroach heart. *J. Morph.*, **65**, 323.
45. MCINDOO, N. E. (1945). The innervation of the insect heart. *J. comp. Neurol.*, **83**, 141.
46. MATSUDA, R. (1956). The comparative morphology of 2 species of insects. *Microentomology*, **21** (1), 1–65.
47. MAYNARD, D. (1956). Electrical activity in the cockroach cerebrum. *Nature, Lond.*, **177**, 529–30.
48. METCALF, R. L., WINTON, M. Y. and FUKOTO, T. R. (1964). *J. Insect Physiol.*, **10**, 353.
49. MIALL, L. C. and DENNY, A. (1886). *The Cockroach*. Lovell Reeve, London.
50. MILBURN, N., WEIANT, E. A. and ROEDER, K. D. (1960). The release of efferent nerve activity in the cockroach *Periplaneta americana* by extracts of the corpus cardiacum. *Biol. Bull.*, **118**, 111–19.
51. MULIYIL, A. (1935). The effect of ultracentrifuging on the ganglion cells of certain orthoptera. *Z. Zellforsch. mikrosk. Anat.*, **23** (4), 627–56.
52. MYERS, T. B. and FISK, F. W. (1962). Breathing movements of the Cuban burrowing cockroach. *Ohio J. Sci.*, **62**, 253–8.
53. MYERS, T. and RETZLAFF, E. (1963). Localization and action of the respiratory centre of the cuban burrowing cockroach. *J. Insect Physiol.*, **9**, 607–14.
54. NAIDU, M. B. (1955). Physiological action of drugs and insecticides on insects. *Bull. ent. Res.*, **46**, 205–20.
55. NARAHASHI, T. (1961). Effect of barium ions on membrane potentials of cockroach giant axons. *J. Physiol.*, **156**, 389–414.
56. NARAHASHI, T. (1963). The properties of insect axons. *Recent Advances in Insect Physiology*, **1**.
57. NARAHASHI, T. and YAMASAKI, T. (1960). Mechanism of the after-potential production in the giant axons of the cockroach. *J. Physiol.*, **151**, 75–88.
58. NARAHASHI, T. and YAMASAKI, T. (1960). Mechanism of increase in negative after-potential by dicophanum (DDT) in the giant axons of the cockroach. *J. Physiol.*, **152**, 122–40.
59. NARAHASHI, T. and YAMASAKI, T. (1960). Behaviour of membrane potential in the cockroach giant axons poisoned by DDT. *J. cell. comp. Physiol.*, **55**, 131–42.
60. NIJENHUIS, E. D. and DRESDEN, D. (1952). A micro-morphological study on the sensory supply of the mesothoracic leg of the American cockroach *Periplaneta americana*. *Proc. K. ned. Akad. Wet.*, Series C, **55**, 3, 300–10.
61. NIJENHUIS, E. D. and DRESDEN, D. (1956). On the topographical anatomy of the nervous system of the mesothoracic leg of the American cockroach, *P.a. Proc. K. ned. Akad. Wet.*, Series C, **58**, 121–36.
62. PANOV, A. (1957). Development of the insect brain (in Russian). *Ent. Obozr.*, **36**, 271–4.
63. PIPA, R. L. (1961). Histochemistry of cockroach nervous system. *J. comp. Neurol.*, **116**, 15–26.

64. PIPA, R. L. (1961). Studies on the hexapod nervous system IV. *Biol. Bull.*, **121** (3), 521–34.
65. PIPA, R. L. (1962). A cytochemical study of neurosecretory and other neuroplasmic inclusions in *P.a. General and Comparative Endocrinology*, **2** (1), 44–52.
66. PIPA, R. L. and COOK, E. F. (1959). Studies on the hexapod nervous system I. The peripheral distribution of the thoracic nerves of the adult cockroach, *P.a. Ann. ent. Soc. Am.*, **52**, 695–710.
67. PIPA, R. L., COOK, E. F. and RICHARDS, A. G. (1959). Studies on the hexapod nervous system II. The histology of the thoracic ganglion of the adult cockroach, *P.a. J. comp. Neurol.*, **113**, 401–33.
68. PIPA, R. L., RUDOLPH, L., RICHARD, S., NISHIOKA and HOWARD, A. BERN. (1962). Studies on the hexapod nervous system. V. *The Ultrastructure of Cockroach Gliosomes*, **6** (2), 164–70.
69. POISSON, R. A. and LEFEUVRE, J. C. (1962). A propos de l'innervation alaire de Loboptera decipiens (Blattidae). *Bull. biol. Fr. Belg.*, **96**, 169–75.
70. PRINGLE, J. W. S. (1938). Proprioception in insects II. The action of the campaniform sensilla on the legs. *J. exp. Biol.*, **15**, 114–31.
71. PRINGLE, J. W. S. (1939). The motor mechanism of the insect leg. *J. exp. Biol.*, **16**, 220–31.
72. PRINGLE, J. W. S. (1940). The reflex action of the insect leg. *J. exp. Biol.*, **17**, 8–17.
73. PROSSER, C. L. (1952). *Comparative Animal Physiology*. Saunders, London.
74. PUMPHREY, R. J. and RAWDON-SMITH, A. F. (1937). Synaptic transmission of nervous impulses through the last abdominal ganglion of the cockroach. *Proc. R. Soc.*, B., **122**, 106–18.
75. RAY, J. W. (1965). The free amino acid pool of the cockroach (*P.a.*) central nervous system. In *The Physiology of the Insect Central Nervous System*, ed. ROCKSTEIN. Academic Press, New York and London.
76. RICHARDS, A. G. (1963). The ventral diaphragm of insects. *J. Morph.*, **113**, 17–48.
77. RICHARDS, A. G. and SCHNEIDER, S. (1958). Uber den Komplexen Bau der Membranen des Bindegewebes von Insekten. *Z. Naturf.*, **13** (10), 680–7.
78. ROEDER, K. D. (1937). Tonus and activity in Mantids. *J. exp. Zool.*, **76**, 353–74.
79. ROEDER, K. D. (1948). Organization of the ascending giant fibre system in the cockroach (*Periplaneta americana* L.). *J. exp. Zool.*, **108**, 243–62.
80. ROEDER, K. D. (1953). Electric activity in nerves and ganglia. In *Insect Physiology*. John Wiley, New York and London.
81. ROEDER, K. D. (1959). A physiological approach to the relationship between prey and predator. *Smithson. misc. Collns.*, **137**, 287–306.
82. ROEDER, K. D. and WEIANT, E. A. (1950). Neuromuscular events in cockroach. *J. exp. Biol.*, **27**, 1–13.
83. ROEDER, K. D., KENNEDY, N. K. and SAMSON, E. A. (1947). Synaptic conduction to the giant fibres of the cockroach and the action of anticholinesterases. *J. Neurophysiol.*, **10**, 1–10.
84. ROEDER, K. D., TOZIAN, L. and WEIANT, E. (1960). Endogenous nerve activity and behaviour in the mantis and cockroach. *J. Insect Physiol.*, **4**, 45–62.
85. ROWE, E. (1965). Neurons in the thoracic ganglia (personal communication).
86. RUCK, P. (1957). The electrical responses of dorsal ocelli in cockroaches and grasshoppers. *J. Insect Physiol.*, **1**, 109–23.
87. SCHARRER, B. (1939). The differentiation between neuroglia and connective sheath in the cockroach (*P. americana*). *J. comp. Neurol.*, **70**, 77–88.
88. SCHMITT, J. B. (1954). The nervous system of the pregenital abdominal segments of some Orthoptera. *Ann. ent. Soc. Am.*, **47**, 677–82.
89. STEINER, G. (1932). Die Automatie und die zentrale Beeinflussung des Herzens von *P.a. Z. vergl. Physiol.*, **16**, 290–304.

90. TREHERNE, J. E. (1960). The nutrition of the central nervous system of the cockroach *P. americana* L. The exchange and metabolism of sugars. *J. exp. Biol.*, **37**, 513–33.

91. TREHERNE, J. E. (1961). Sodium and potassium fluxes in the abdominal nerve cord of the cockroach, *P. americana* L. *J. exp. Biol.*, **38**, 315–22.

92. TREHERNE, J. E. (1961). Exchanges of sodium ions in the central nervous system of an insect (*P. americana*). *Nature, Lond.*, **191**, 1223–4.

93. TREHERNE, J. E. (1961). The movements of sodium ions in the isolated abdominal nerve cord of the cockroach, *P. americana*. *J. exp. Biol.*, **38**, 629–36.

94. TREHERNE, J. E. (1961). The efflux of sodium ions from the last abdominal ganglion of the cockroach (*P. americana*). *J. exp. Biol.*, **38**, 729–36.

95. TREHERNE, J. E. (1961). The kinetics of sodium transfer in the central nervous system of the cockroach, *P. americana* L. *J. exp. Biol.*, **38**, 737–46.

96. TREHERNE, J. E. (1962). Some effects of the distribution of water and inorganic ions in the central nervous system of an insect (*P. americana* L.). *Nature, Lond.*, **193**, 750–2.

97. TREHERNE, J. E. and SMITH, D. S. (1963). Functional aspects of the organization of the insect nervous system. Chapter in *Recent Advances in Insect Physiology*, **1**, 401–97.

98. TWAROG, B. M. and ROEDER, K. D. (1956). Properties of the connective sheath of the cockroach abdominal nerve cord. *Biol. Bull. mar. biol. Lab., Woods Hole*, **111**, 278–86.

99. TWAROG, B. M. and ROEDER, K. D. (1957). Pharmacological observations on the desheathed last abdominal ganglion of the cockroach. *Ann. ent. Soc. Amer.*, **50**, 231–7.

100. WEIANT, E. A. (1953). Endplates in *Periplaneta*. In the chapter by ROEDER, K. D. in *Insect Physiology*, p. 451.

101. WELSH, J. H. and GORDON, H. T. (1947). The mode of action of certain insecticides on the arthropod nerve axon. *J. cell. comp. Physiol.*, **30**, 147–71.

102. WIGGLESWORTH, V. B. (1960). The nutrition of the central nervous system in the cockroach *P. americana* L. The rôle of the perineurium and glial cells in the mobilization of reserves. *J. exp. Biol.*, **37**, 500–12.

103. WIGGLESWORTH, V. B. (1961). Axon structure and the dictyosomes (Golgi bodies) in the neurones of the cockroach, *P. americana*. *Q. Jl microsc. Sci.*, **101** (4), 381–8.

104. WILLEY, R. B. (1961). The morphology of the stomodaeal nervous system in *Periplaneta americana* and other Blattaria. *J. morph.*, **108**, 219–61.

105. WILSON, D. M. (1965). Proprioceptive leg reflexes in cockroaches. *J. exp. Biol.*, **43**, 397–409.

106. YAMASAKI, T. and NARAHASHI, T. (1958). Effects of potassium and sodium ions on the resting potentials of the giant axon of the cockroach. *Nature, Lond.*, **182**, 1805.

107. YAMASAKI, T. and NARAHASHI, T. (1959). The effects of potassium and sodium ions on the resting and action potentials of the cockroach giant axon. *J. Insect Physiol.*, **3**, 146–58.

108. YAMASAKI, T. and NARAHASHI, T. (1959). Electrical properties of the cockroach giant axon. *J. Insect Physiol.*, **3**, 230–42.

109. YAMASAKI, T. and NARAHASHI, T. (1960). Synaptic transmission in the last abdominal ganglion of the cockroach. *J. Insect Physiol.*, **4**, 1–13.

110. YEAGER, J. F. and GAHAN, J. B. (1937). Effects of the alkaloid nicotine on the rhythmicity of the isolated heart preparation from *Periplaneta americana* and *Prodenia eridania*. *J. Agric. Res.*, **55**, 1–9.

ADDENDUM

Nervous system

Shankland has recently described the nerves of the pregenital abdominal segments in *P.a.* This paper came to hand too late to be embodied in the relevant section of the book, but it should be consulted by anyone working in this area. The externally visible ganglia are labelled 2 to 7, a practice avoided here. The variations in the longitudinal junctions between the nerves of adjacent segments is described, and details of all the major nerve terminations are given. Especially useful are the figures of nerves in the abdominal folds. A discrepancy between this account and that given earlier in the present work is over the innervation of the heart, where only a single branch from the nerve to the large longitudinal tergal muscles is shown.

The permeability of the abdominal nerve cord in *P.a.* to aliphatic alcohols has been studied by Eldefrawi and O'Brien. The rates of efflux and influx of ^{14}C and ^3H labelled alcohols was measured. Fifty minutes of exposure resulted in higher internal than external concentrations in all compounds except methanol. Influx rates of alcohols were lower than those of their analogous fatty acids, the differences being attributed to the absence of metabolism of the alcohols in the nerve cord.

ADDITIONAL REFERENCES

COHEN, M. J. and JACKLET, J. W. (1967). The functional organization of motor neurones in an insect ganglion. *Phil. Trans.*, **B.252**, 561–72.

ELDEFRAWI, M. E. and O'BRIEN, R. D. (1967). Permeability of the abdominal nerve cord of the American cockroach to aliphatic alcohols. *J. Insect Physiol.*, **13**, 691–8.

MAYNARD, D. M. (1967). The organization of central ganglia. In *Invertebrate Nervous Systems*, ed. WIERSMA, C. University of Chicago Press.

SHANKLAND, D. L. (1965). Nerves and muscles of the pregenital abdominal segments of the American cockroach *Periplaneta americana*. *J. Morph.*, **117**, 353–86.

WOGWIAK, A., ALVAREZ, R., WILSON, E. and GARA AUSTT, E. (1967). Cercal potentials in *P.a. Acta. physiol. Lat. Amer.*, **17**, 102.

9   *Behaviour*

Although a certain number of field observations on cockroach behaviour have been made, they are not easily related to one another. The material in this chapter is therefore restricted to externally observed reflexes, and the analysis of modifiable behaviour under well-defined conditions.

The study of reflex behaviour in the intact animal has to a large extent been superseded by more analytical work on the specific nerves and muscles involved, but Hoffman performed the useful function of describing easily observable reflexes in female *B.o.* The righting reflexes in this species occur if a specimen is placed on its back on a smooth surface, and, in most instances, involve body torsion towards one side, searching movements of the legs on that side, and the extension of the hind-leg of the opposite side against the substrate to form a strut (Stemmbein). The turn may be made to either side, and has a bearing on the question of whether cockroaches are right- or left-handed. In a sample of 35 individuals run through 20 times each, right- and left-hand turns were about equal, but some individuals were markedly biased towards one side (17:3 left to right in one example). Less often the insect may right itself by turning a forward somersault, both hind-legs being used equally to turn the body over. Wille[22] describes this righting movement as the one usually employed in *Blattella germanica*, rather than unilateral torsion. In *B.o.*, the insect would still turn itself on a particular hind-leg, even if that leg was incomplete or had been partially amputated. If a current of air is directed against a roach when it is lying on its back, a peculiar extension of limbs and trunk occurs (Ausbreitungsreaktion), which, as pointed out by Hoffmann,[11] probably has something in common with the falling reflex described by Diakonoff[3] and others. By shielding various parts of the body, it can be seen that it is a reflex rather than a local reaction, and that the suspension of movement that occurs is the primary effect of the mechanical stimulus of the air current, the spreading and extension being an effect of loss of contact with the substrate.

Hoffmann and Turner[21] have both described the cleaning reflexes in *B.o.* in considerable detail, and Turner concluded that the way in which the limbs transferred matter to the mouth was similar to the way in which a cat cleaned itself. The spines on the hind-legs are used to clean dirt from the auditory hairs of the anal cerci.

Hoffmann noted[11] that as in phasmids seizure of a limb is often followed by autotomy at the trochanteral–femoral boundary, but this author finds that only a proportion of cockroaches (*P.a.*) appear to be able to do this, although the mechanical situation is important.

Turner,[20] and Lawson[14] describe leaping in *B.o.* and *P.a.* respectively, in association with maze running. In *P.a.* this is not necessarily associated with an attempt to fly, but usually takes place when the roach is standing on a raised edge of some kind. Both Lawson and Turner were impressed by the behaviour of the roach prior to leaping, which suggested appraisal of the spatial characteristics of the environment.

The most coherent body of work on cockroach behaviour deals with learning and retention, and provides a valuable background for physiological work of the kind recently initiated by Horridge.

Although some work of Grabers touches on this problem, the observations of Szymanski[19] performed 25 years later used a training procedure which has been employed by many later workers. The cockroach (*B.o.*) was placed in an illuminated run containing a dark box. The photonegative tendency of the insect would result in an attempt to enter the dark box, but an electrified wire on the threshold of the dark box caused the insect to turn back. The number of successive trials required for a correct response varied widely, from 16 to 118 (mean 51). Retention was poor, lasting less than an hour in most instances and was not related to the number of shocks received. Retraining had to be given before the correct response was established, but it remained unstable on later tests. Turner suggests that this trained avoidance of the dark is not a reversal of photonegativity but a reaction connected specifically with the disagreeable properties of this particular dark box.

Turner,[20, 21] who repeated Szymanski's experiments in much the same form, was able to distinguish Szymanski's three categories of behaviour in training: (1) rapid progress, slow fatigue, (2) rapid progress, rapid fatigue and (3) slow progress and slow fatigue. Turner was also able to resolve more detail in the material (*B.o.*). Male roaches learned more quickly than females, and larvae learned more quickly than adults, but the great differences between individuals might mask this,[20] and Eldering[4] noted no differences in learning ability with age or sex.

Moulting did not affect retention, but retentiveness was markedly impaired in sickness or just prior to death.[20]

The rôle of the antennae in a learning situation was considered by Turner, and was regarded as important by Turner,[20] Chauvin,[1] Hullo[12] and Eldering,[4] but from their tactile rather than their olfactory function. Turner wiped down his copper maze with alcohol, and Eldering replaced the paper partitions in her maze, but these precautions made no significant difference to the error curves obtained. When Turner amputated the antennae of his roach, their ability to learn was drastically reduced, as was their general level of activity, and Goustard[6] believed that antennal function had an effect on the general level of excitation.

Turner's second series of experiments[21] employed a maze of copper strip with four blind alleys, one of which had three additional culs-de-sac. The goal was a tilted pathway running down to a cage of the type to which the insect was accustomed. The whole maze was arranged above a water surface and initially many of the roaches jumped into the water, the first stage of training involving the suppression of this behaviour. When roaches were tested for their ability to take the correct path to the cage, errors fell off steeply to near zero in 20 trials, and number of minutes to reach the cage decreased from 40 to 4.

In this training situation, unlike the simpler darkness-shock test, adults tended to do better than larvae. The larvae moved about rapidly and with less co-ordination than the adults, and thus committed more errors. The adults appeared to display more caution. No specific punishment was given and this may be the reason why Turner was able to achieve complete training in a day, while Eldering using shocks in training had to reduce the number of successive tests to between 5 and 10 due to the inhibiting effect of repeated shocks. Turner found a lapse of 12 hr in training sufficient to produce a rise in errors.

Eldering[4] employed mazes of a simpler type, one of her first experiments being concerned with conditioning *P.a.* to turn either to the right or the left to avoid an electric shock. Over a period of 7 days, errors were reduced to the 10% level in the majority, but great individual variation was observed. Made to choose a light rather than a dark box most roaches took 9 days to reach 10% errors, but as in the training to right or left preference, errors were not reduced smoothly.[4]

The form of some of these learning curves is interesting in that it exhibits a backsliding tendency also observed in ants, but not in higher animals such as rats (see Schneirla[18]). It can also be seen in Turner's results, and those of Gates and Allee.[5] Often Eldering's roaches might reduce errors to 20% in 3 days, then they would fluctuate between 20 and 40% for 2 days, and this would be followed either by a smooth reduction of errors to 10% in the final 2–3 days, or in a minority by a rise to 40% or more. This suggests the interpolation of a phase of instability in the course of training, which then gives way to a more steady response in most insects, as might occur if the supply of some substrate had been temporarily reduced.

The problem of retention was investigated by Eldering[4] using animals habituated to turning left. These gave 100% errors at the commencement of training for right turning, but they reached the 10% level of errors in 9 days (7 days in untrained roaches). They were given 9 days of rest, and then retested when they gave 60% errors (mean) at the first test, but none on succeeding tests, or on 3 successive days of testing 1 month later. Although retention was poor at the first retest, subsequent trials seem to indicate a much greater capability of retention than would appear from Szymanski and Turner's experiments, where initial training occupied a much shorter period.

It might be expected that the photonegative response itself which forms part of the experiments of many workers, was capable of modification, and this was shown to be so by Eldering. Measured in seconds, the mean time taken for a batch of roaches to enter a dark box in an illuminated background fell from 160 to under 20 in 29 trials. Any change in the intensity or type of illumination (day-light or artificial) temporarily elevated the escape time. It is perhaps surprising that raising the intensity of illumination does not increase the strength of the photonegative response, at least insofar as it is reflected in the escape time.

Turner[21] observed the importance of the tactile properties of the maze even of the raised type, and this factor was accentuated in the walled mazes used by Eldering.[4] The pathway taken through a maze having a left- and a right-hand

8+B.O.C.

turning was always very close to the walls, only occasional excursions into the centre of each corridor being made. Cockroaches learnt to run these mazes as rapidly as they learnt other types of problems, although running times rose temporarily if the maze was rotated 90° relative to the light source, suggesting at least some dependence on visual cues. If an extra turning was introduced, and the shape of the maze altered so that the insect had to go further to the right or left in passing from one compartment to another in the maze, the test proved too severe for the animals to learn successfully. Electric shock treatment improved times only slightly.

Recent workers have tended to concentrate more on the conditions that retard or accelerate learning or retention. Hunter[13] has studied the effect of low temperatures (3–6°C) on *Bt.g.* when conditioned in the electrified dark box test. The trials were run in two series separated by a rest period, the second or relearning tests constituting a trial of retention. With a 1 hr rest period at normal temperature the 10% errors level was reached in the learning tests with 7·10 mean number of shocks, and at relearning after 1·6 shocks. Two hours in the cold before learning increased shocks at learning to 10·05, but a similar period of cold between learning and relearning had no effect and it might be thought that retention is not affected by cold. If, however, 4 hr of cold are given at the rest period together with 1 hr at normal temperatures, retention is adversely affected and this effect persisted when the period at normal temperature following cold was increased to 4 hr.

Most of these experiments were conducted with single insects, and the effect of other roaches in the test area could not be gauged. Gates and Allee,[5] using a simple maze with three lanes, one of which ended in a dark box containing food, showed that roaches run in pairs performed much less well than single ones (average times 7·19 against 4·076 min). Groups of three showed a slower decrease again in the time taken to reach the goal. These authors found no evidence of retention from day to day, and the numbers of errors appear to have remained above the 10% level even in insects tested singly. These are much poorer results than were obtained by other workers.

Observations on mammals suggest that sleep and activity may effect learning and retention and Minami and Dallenbach[16] investigated these factors in the American cockroach *P.a.* in a detailed manner. The dark-avoidance test was used as in Hunter's experiments, and the roaches were subjected to three types of treatment at an interval in training: forced locomotion in a motor-driven treadmill at 135 in./minute, slow perambulation in circular arena offering poor contact (rest), and being allowed to remain passively within a paper-filled dark box (inactivity). Relearning after learning resulted in few shocks being required to attain the 10% error level, as found by other workers, but forced locomotion before relearning was followed by high scores and the general behaviour of such insects was irritable and overactive. If the forced locomotion is given and then a 2hr rest period allows recovery before relearning, scores are near normal, suggesting that forced activity prevents relearning rather than destroys retention.

Inactivity was a state believed by these authors to be similar to sleep, and it was found that relearning scores were much lower if a period of inactivity preceded relearning rather than simply a period of rest. If a period of inactivity preceded learning it had little effect on scores, suggesting that it affected retention rather than learning. Like Eldering[4] and Hunter,[13] Minami and Dallenbach[16] did not find any difference between male and female learning capabilities as had been found by Turner, but they did find evidence of retention for as long as 2 days, and this concurred with other workers, excepting Gates and Allee.[5]

The French researchers Chauvin,[1] Hullo[12] and Goustard[6] have turned their attention more to the overall balance of different sensory factors involved in learning and their relation to the general level of excitation shown by the training animal, rather than to single elements in learning behaviour.

Chauvin trained his insects (*Bt.g.*) to a more complex maze (nine blind alleys) than had been employed by other workers. The goal was a dark box. These mazes were composed of separable T-pieces that could be arranged in a variety of configurations. Chauvin found, rather surprisingly perhaps, that the difficulty of a maze did not depend largely on the number of blind turnings, but on the total configuration of the maze. In general, the mazes with fewest turnings were the most difficult, although the mean errors could be related to the number of cul-de-sacs by the expression $y \times ax^2 + bx^3$, where x equalled the number of blind turnings. Chauvin found, using the learning-relearning method, that errors were reduced in a fairly regular way as shown by other authors, but he finds raising the intensity of background illumination reduces errors, and this seems at variance with Eldering's results. He believed that the sensory data used are mainly tactile, especially antennal, and postural; the latter presumably involving the campaniform proprioceptors of the legs. Optic and olfactory senses are of secondary importance. Hunger, sexual attraction and temperature (upper range) have little effect on learning. Hullo[12] performed a similar series of experiments with the same species of cockroach and type of maze construction, and on the whole comes to generally very similar conclusions, except in so far as he believes that the antennae are even more important than suggested by Chauvin. He found that waxing the antennae in one position was sufficient to inhibit learning almost completely. Like Eldering,[4] Hullo[12] found that changing the position of the light source considerably modified the pattern of errors, but he nevertheless believes photic responses in learning are secondary. He also noticed a tendency in his subjects to make turns in the contrary direction of the previous turn, and the T-maze construction tended to favour this error.

Goustard[6] performed a large number of experiments, many of them designed to define more clearly the rôle of different senses, but photic stimulation was the main object of study. Much earlier work is surveyed in his 1958 paper. Although cockroaches (*Bt.g.*) are photonegative, light has an excitatory effect proportional to the relative intensity of different parts of the background. A point of interest related to this photonegativity is that as the light intensity of a source is raised, movement towards the light is inhibited much more than movement away is accelerated, but it can be observed that inhibition decreases markedly with trials. Both ocelli, eyes and a general photic sensitivity possibly localized in the nerve cord, were involved in responses to light. Ocelli and eyes were much more sensitive to blue and yellow light than of other wavelengths, a statement that does not accord with the results of physiologists (see Chapter 7) who found sensitivity peaks in the green and U.V. for compound eyes, and for green only in ocelli, although different species were used.

Goustard believed that the threshold for a behavioural response to white light was much lower for the general light sense, than for eyes or ocelli, but again this seems unlikely in view of the extremely high sensitivity of ocelli demonstrated by Ruck.[17] According to Goustard,[6] the effect of light stimulation in learning can be seen as changes in speed of movement, general excitation and thirdly, orientation to a light source. General excitation is increased considerably by responses mediated through the general light sense, much less by stimulation of eyes or ocelli. Speed and orientation to a light source is increased by optic, decreased by ocellar stimulation. These receptors control a level of response that is affected by removal of any one of them; thus removal of the ocelli increases orientation by means of the eyes.

Some of Goustard's experiments appear to demonstrate latent learning, in that insects placed in a maze with a transparent shelter rather than a dark one, learnt much more rapidly when a dark shelter was placed in the maze than those which had been trained to a dark shelter from the beginning. Furthermore, he believes that an anticipatory element is present in exploratory behaviour rather than it being based simply on trial and error. Chauvin, in summing up his results, concludes that learning in the white rat is guided by 'general methods' transferable to different problems, whilst in the cockroach the response varies with the type of question asked.

However, Lawson[14] believes that the type of question posed by the maze experiment, while it produces steep learning curves in ants which live in underground galleries, is not suited to displaying the potentialities for modifiable behaviour of an animal living a different kind of life such as the cockroach. He examined the behaviour of *P.a.* when placed on a wooden island standing in water, and noted the time taken to escape, a feat often achieved by leaping, and then swimming. Most adults escaped within ten minutes, but fewer nymphs escaped, the percentage falling with the size of the nymph. The production of watery or gaseous faeces was common in the training situation, and the larger insects which did not escape spent a good deal of time in grooming and cleaning activities. Adults tested a second time escaped more rapidly, but an insufficient number of successive trials were given for it to be clear whether cockroaches performed better in this type of test, than in the maze test.

That cockroaches exhibit marked rhythmicity in their general level of activity was recognized by many of the earlier workers, but Szymanski[19] appears to have been the first to record this accurately by means of an aktograph. He found that *B.o.* spend the day and most of the night at rest, becoming active mainly between 7.0 and 10.30 p.m. and for a few minutes at 6.0 a.m. Although the main phase of activity coincides with darkness, cockroaches were indifferent to a half-dark half-light cage in this active phase, as they were to other stimuli. Gunn[7] kept cockroaches (*B.o.*) in an aktograph for most of their adult life, and took pains to maintain a uniform humidity and temperature. Total activity per day varied from 6 to 1,300 journeys (average 150), and in 155 days one cockroach made 22,000 journeys ($5\frac{1}{2}$ km). About 2 weeks before death, there were often a few days of great activity. In alternating light and dark periods (12-hr intervals) the total activity remained the same, but it tended to be concentrated in the dark period. High activity occurs during the first hour of darkness and has reached a low level some time before the light comes on again. If the insects are placed once more in a continuous light or darkness, the rhythm persists for some days. Under the conditions of alternating light and dark, if the onset of darkness is advanced by four hours each day, the beginning of activity is also advanced but by a much shorter period of time. Gunn did not observe the early morning burst of activity described by Szymanski and concludes that the cockroach is essentially mono-phasic in its activity rhythms.

All these observations were made on confined insects, but Mellanby[15] was able to verify these observations on a wild population. He noted also that darkening the room by day in which the animals lived, only caused activity if it had been illuminated the previous night.

The physiological factors controlling the diurnal rhythm were investigated by Harker,[8, 9] who found that a rhythmic cockroach (*P.a.*) grafted on to an arhythmic cockroach caused the latter to develop patterned activity. This suggested the involvement of the endocrine system. It was also shown that the eyes and ocelli helped to determine rhythmicity, an observation made earlier by Cloudesley-Thompson.[2] The site of secretory activity was localized in the suboesophageal ganglion, a ganglion from a rhythmic cockroach effecting the appearance of a rhythm in an arhythmic headless cockroach—when implanted into the latter.

More recently, Hocking[10] has shown that one cockroach can affect the diurnal rhythms of another roach in an adjacent cage. He found that a male cockroach (*Bt.g.*) exposed to normal daylight and darkness, retained its diurnal rhythm of activity only if the adjacent cage held a male, and in the case of a female if the neighbouring insect was a male. All other combinations: a single female; a single male; two females, and the male of a male/female pair tend to lose their avoidance of daylight excursions, and the diurnal rhythm disappeared. A point of interest was that, in the normal rhythm, the activity of the females during darkness was usually much higher than that of males. Hocking suggests that a substance secreted by the tergal gland of the male, perhaps controlled by the suboesophageal ganglion, may be the controlling agent in the retention of diurnal rhythm.

REFERENCES

1. CHAUVIN, R. (1947). Études sur le comportement de *Blatella germanica* dans divers types de labyrinth. *Bull. biol. Fr. Belg.*, **81**, 92–128.
2. CLOUDESLEY-THOMPSON, J. L. (1953). Studies in diurnal rhythms III. Photo-periodism in the cockroach (*P.a.*). *Ann. Mag. Nat. Hist.*, **12** (6), 705.
3. DIAKONOFF, A. (1936). Nervous factors in the control of flight in the cockroach. *Archs néerl. Physiol.*, **21**, 104–29.
4. ELDERING, F. J. (1919). Sur les habitudes acquises chéz les insects. Troisiéme Reunion Ann. d. Physiol. *Archs. néerl. Physiol.*, **129**, 469–90.
5. GATES, M. F. and ALEE, W. C. (1933). Conditioning in the roach. *J. comp. Psychol.*, **13**, 331–58.

6. GOUSTARD, M. (1958). Reaction phototropique et régulation du comportement chez l'imago male de *Blattella germanica*. *Bull. Biol. Fr. Belg.* Supplement **45**, 1–112.

7. GUNN, D. L. (1940). The daily rhythm of activity of *B.o. J. exp. Biol.*, **17**, 267–77.

8. HARKER, J. E. (1954). Diurnal rhythms in *Periplaneta americana*. *Nature, Lond.*, **173**, 689.

9. HARKER, J. E. (1960). Internal factors controlling the suboesophageal ganglion neurosecretory cycle in *P.a.* L. *J. exp. Biol.*, **37**, 164–70.

10. HOCKING, B. (1958). On the activity of *Blattella germanica*. *Proc. Xth Congr. Ent.*, **2**, 201–4, 1956.

11. HOFFMANN, R. (1933). Zur analyse des reflexgeschehens bei *Blatta orientalis* L. *Z. vergl. Physiol.*, **18**, 740–95.

12. HULLO, A. (1948). Role des tendences motrices et des donnees sensorielles dans l'apprentissage du labryinthe par les Blattes (*B. germanica*). *Behaviour*, **1**, 297–310.

13. HUNTER, W. S. (1932). The effect of inactivity produced by cold on learning in the cockroach, *Blattella germanica*. *J. genet. Psychol.*, **41**, 253–66.

14. LAWSON, J. W. H. (1965). The behaviour of *P.a.* in a critical situation and the variation with age. *Behaviour*, **24**, 210–28.

15. MELLANBY, K. (1940). Daily rhythm in *Blatta. J. exp. Biol.*, **17**, 278–85.

16. MINAMI, H. and DALLENBACH, K. M. (1949). Activity and learning in the cockroach. *Am. J. Psychol.*, **59**, 1–58.

17. RUCK, P. (1958). Dark adaptation of the roach ocellus. *J. Insect Physiol.*, **2**, 189–98.

18. SCHNEIRLA, T. C. (1953). Basic problems in the nature of insect behaviour. *Insect Physiology*, pp. 656–84, ed. ROEDER, K. D. John Wiley, New York and London.

19. SZYMANSKI, J. S. (1912). Modification of innate behaviour in the roach. *J. Anim. Behav.*, **2**, 81–90.

20. TURNER, C. H. (1912). An experimental investigation of an apparent reversal of the responses to light of a roach (*B.o.*). *Biol. Bull.*, **23**, 371–86.

21. TURNER, C. H. (1913). The behaviour of the common roach (*B.o.*) on an open maze. *Biol. Bull.*, **25**, 325–32.

22. WILLE, J. (1920). *Biologie und Bekämpfung der Deutschen Schabe. Monogrn. angew. Ent.* **5**. Berlin.

10 *Musculature and locomotion*

Abbreviations used for figures in Chapter 10

---

a.	anterior	ob.	oblique
ab.	abductor	p.	pleuron
ad.	adductor	p.a.	pleural arm
ax.	axillary sclerite	ph.	phragma
al.	abdominal	pl.	proximal
a.n.w.p.	anterior notal wing process	po.	posterior
c.	cervical	pr.	protractor
cx.	coxa or coxal	prm.	promotor
d.	dorsal	pro.	prothoracic
dep.	depressor	re.	retractor
dil.	dilator	rem.	remotor
dl.	distal	ro.	rotator
e.s.	episternum	s.	sternum
ex.	extrinsic	sa.	subalar plate
h.	horizontal	s.a.	sternal arm
i.	inner	sr.	small or smaller
in.	intrinsic	sp.	spina
ins.	insertion	st.	segment
l.	lateral	t.	tergum
ll.	longitudinal	t.-s.	tergo-sternal
lev.	levator	tent.	tentorium
lr.	larger or large	tn.	trochantin
m.	muscle	tr.	trochanter
me.	median	u.p.	unguitractor plate
mr.	meron	v.	ventral
o.	outer	vl.	vertical

The muscles of an insect can be classified so as to fall into several groups, but the most clear-cut division is between skeletal muscles and visceral muscles. Even here muscles which do not fit easily into either of these categories can be found, for example some of the oesophageal muscles originating from the cuticle of the head.

Intrinsic heart muscles and alary muscles, and the intrinsic musculature of the gut are placed at the end of the chapter under the heading of visceral muscles.

THE TOPOGRAPHY OF THE SKELETAL MUSCULATURE (*P.a.*)

The musculature of the three major tagmata has attracted unequal attention from insect anatomists. The thoracic musculature has been thoroughly and accurately described by Carbonell, and subsidiary studies by Maki (on *Bt.g.*), and by Chadwick (on *P.a.* and other species), provide additional detail, while Dresden and Nijenhuis have added some information on intrinsic leg muscles. Snodgrass in his papers on insect mouth-parts uses the cockroach as an example of unspecialized structure, and a good deal of information about the head musculature is included here and in his book. Carbonell mentions that the head contains 51 muscle pairs, but without giving the source of this observation. Mangan, Pringle and earlier workers, who have studied the mouth-parts, contribute descriptions of their intrinsic muscles. Some attention has been paid to the muscles of the genital segments by Gupta and McKittrick and they have been mainly relied on in these accounts to supplement original work. Comparatively little research has been done on the muscles of generalized abdominal segments, apart from the work of Ford on *Blaberus* and *Parcoblatta*.

As the space available is limited a detailed description of the 370 or so pairs of muscles is not possible. A system of abbreviated enumeration has thus been adopted for the thoracic muscles, the number series employed being based on the one introduced by Carbonell.

Each muscle has been given a number, but where in the head or the legs the numbers left by Carbonell are too few, small letters have been added as follows:

Small letters after muscle numbers indicate branches or divisions of this muscle. Large letters indicate additional muscles added from other sources. After the muscle number and description the insertion (Ins.) and origin (O) are given.

Head (Fig. 10.1)	No.	Ins.	O	No.	Ins.	O
Antenna in.	1 d.lev.	2nd st.	1st st.	2 v.dep.	2nd st.	1st st.
ex.	3 d.me.lev.	1st st.	tent.	4 d.l.lev.	1st st.	tent.
	5 v.dep. pulsatile	1st st.	tent.	6 v.me.dep.	1st st.	tent.
Antennal pulsatile organ	7 h.muscle	p.organs	frons	8 d.dil.	pharynx	d.frons
Pharynx	9 l.dil.	pharynx	l.v.frons	10 v.dil.	pharynx	v.clypeus
Clypeus	11 cibarial dil.	cibarium	clypeus			
Labrum	12 me.lev.	me.labrum	frons	13 l.lev.	l.labrum	frons
	14 i.dep.	Across labral cavity				
Mandible	15(3)d.m. ad.,i.	mandible	vertex	16 d.l.ab. (red)	mandible	gena
	17 i.ad.	mandible	tent.	18 hypo-pharynx	l.mandible	
Hypo-pharynx	19 d.re. salivarium	duct	hypo-pharynx	20 re.	1 hypo-pharynx	occiput
	21 pr., l.	hypo-pharynx	labium	22 v.re.v.	1 hypo-pharynx	labium
Maxilla ex.	23 re.	d.maxilla	tent.	24 ad. cardo l.me.	cardo.	tent.
	25 ad. cardo 2	cardo	tent.	26 ad. cardo 3	l.cardo	tent.

Head	No.	Ins.	O	No.	Ins.	O
	27 h.ad.	stipes	joins contra-lateral m.	28 l.ad.	stipes	tent.
in.	29 ro.lacinia, base	lacinia	stipes	30 re.galea	tip galea	stipes
	31 re.galea	tip galea	stipes	32 re.galea	tip galea	stipes
palp. ex.	33 lev. (lr.),d.	1st st.	stipes	34 dep. (sr.)v.	1st st.	stipes
in.	35 lev. 2nd st.	2nd st.	1st st.	36 lev. 3rd st.	3rd st.	2nd st.
	37 dep. 4th st.	4th st.	3rd st.	38 dep. 5th st.	5th st.	4th st.
Labium	39 m.re.	ligula	post-mentum	40 re.	a.post-mentum	tent.
	41 l.re.	l.ligula	l.post-mentum			
	42 re. glossa	glossa	ligula base	43 re.para-glossa	paraglossa	pre-mentum
Labial/ ex. Labium	44 lr.lev.	1st st.	post-mentum	45 h.dep.	1st st.	base ligula
palp	46 ro.	1st st.	post-mentum	(sometimes appears to have 2 rami)		
in.	47 lev. 2nd st.	2nd st.	1st st.	48 dep. 3rd st.	3rd st.	2nd st.
	49 lev. 3rd st.	3rd st.	2nd st.			
Oesophagus	50 p.dil.	oesophagus	vertex	51 v.dil.	oesophagus	tent.

NOTES ON HEAD MUSCLES

The interpretation of some of the muscles as to whether they comprise separate muscles, or merely separate bundles of muscle fibres within a muscle is often doubtful. Muscle 16 is notable for its reddish colour.

Prothorax and neck. (Figs. 10.1 and 10.2)

Cervical	52 d.l.re., head, d.c.sclerite			53 d.re., head, t.l.		
	54 d.tent.re., tent., c.			55 A v.tent.re., tent., s.a.l.		
	55B pro.gland, 1st c.sclerite, l. 1st cx.					

Dorsal thoracic	60 lr.t.re.	1st ph.	t.	61 st.t.re.	1st ph.	t.
	62 ph.re.	1st ph.	1st ph.	63 d.c.m.	1st c. sclerite	t.
	64 spiral c.m.	1st c. sclerite	t.	65 p.m.(1st)	p.a.	t.

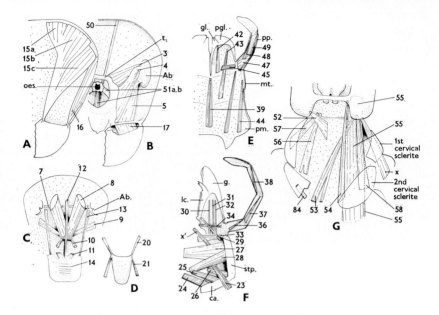

FIG. 10.1   The muscles of the head and neck. **A**, frontal view of the extrinsic mandibular muscles. **B**, posterior view of the head showing seven anterio head muscles. Ab.—antennal base, oes.—oesophagus, t.—tentorium. **C**, head muscles revealed by moving the frons, clypeus and labrum. **D**, the hypopharynx and its muscles. **E**, muscles of the labium, dorsal view. gl.—glossa, mt.—mentum, pp.—palp, pgl.—paraglossa, pm.—postmentum. **F**, muscles of the maxilla, dorsal view. ca.—cardo, g.—galea, lc.—lacinia, stp.—stipes, x′—a muscle observed in a few specimens. **G**, diagrammatic representation of the neck muscles, dorsal view. x—undetermined muscle

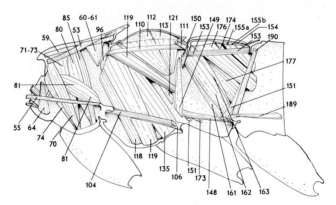

FIG. 10.2   Lateral view of the thoracic musculature of the right side viewed from the mid-line

	No.	Ins.	O	No.	Ins.	O
	66 po.p.m. (2nd)	p.a.	t.	67 p.m. (3rd)	p.a.	a.t.
	68 a.p.m. (4th)	p.a.	a.t.	69 vl.c.m.	c.	a.t.
	70 tn.m. (1st)	po.tn.	po.t.	71 tn.m. (2nd)	po.tn.	po.t.
	72 tn.m. (3rd)	me.tn.	me.t.	73 tn.m. (4th)	a.tn.	a.t.
	74 cx.prm.	cx.	a.t.	75 cx.prm.	cx.	a.s.
	76 mr.m. (1st)	mr.	po.t.	77 o.mr.m. (2nd)	mr.	po.t.
	78 mr.m. (3rd)	mr.	po.t.	79 lr.mr.m. (4th)	mr.	po.t.
	80 cx.re.	cx.	me.t.	81 lr.cx.re.	cx.	a.t.
Ventral thoracic	82 s.ad.	cx.	s.a.	82B sr.s.ad.	cx.rim	(MXl)
				(See Pipa, Cook and Richards[50])		
	84 s.c.m. (2nd)	c.s.	s.a.	83 cx.re.m.	cx.	s.a.
Trochanteral apodeme	85(8) main trochanteral depressor.			2 originate t. 2 on p.		4 from cx.wall
	86 po.dep.	tr.	po.cx.	87 a.dep.	tr.	a.cox.
	88(2) lr.lev.tr.	tr.	a.&po.cx.	89 sr.lev.tr.	tr.	po.cx.

Muscle numbers 90–95 were left by Carbonell for the prothoracic leg muscles originating in the trochanter or further distally. Dresden and Nijenhuis gave a detailed enumeration of the muscles of the mesothoracic leg which appears similar to that for the pro- and metathoracic legs at least as far as the non-coxal segments are concerned.[17] Their modifications of Carbonell's coxal (extrinsic and intrinsic) muscle list[6] are given under the heading of the mesothorax.

Intrinsic leg muscles of the 3 thoracic segments (non-coxal)

Femur	90, 141, 183	femoral ab., femur, tr.
Tibia	91, 142, 184	(a) lr. tibial lev., tibia d. femur (b) sr. tibial lev., tibia, d. femur.
	92, 143, 185	(a) tr. tibial dep., tibia, tr.
		(b) lr. tibial dep., tibia, v. femur.
		(c) sr. tibial dep., tibia, v. femur.
Tarsus	93, 144, 186	tarsal lev., tarsus, tibia. 94, 145, 187 dep.
		tarsal m., tarsus, tibia.
Pretarsus	95, 146, 188	pretarsal m., u.p., (a) femur. (b) tibial origin

	No.	Ins.	O	No.	Ins.	O
Posterior	96 ph.m.	s.a.	1st ph.	97 2nd p.m.	cx.	ep.2
Ventral	98 sp.cx.m.	cx.	1st sp.	99 3rd sp.m.	1st sp.	s.a.1
thoracic	100 s.a.m.	s.a.1	s.a.2	101 4th sp.m.	2nd sp.	s.a.1
muscles	102 1st ep.m.	ep.1	s.a.1	103 po.ep.m.	ep.2	1st sp.
	104 po.sp.m.	1st sp.	s.a.2	105 mr.m.	1st sp.	meral ridge
	106 2nd sp.m.	1st sp.	s.a.2			

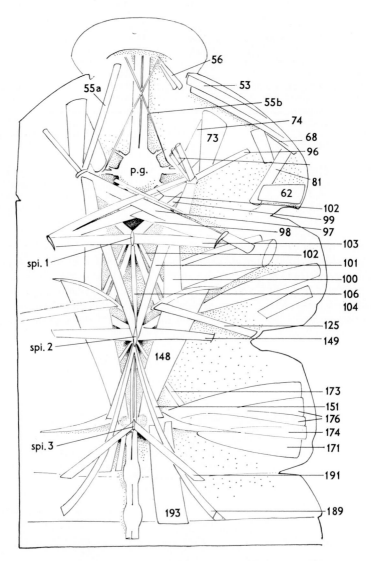

FIG. 10.3   Ventral musculature of the thorax exposed by cutting through the terga in the mid-line and pinning them out laterally. p.g.—prothoracic ganglion, spi. 1 to 3—spina 1 to 3

2nd **Thoracic**

	No.	Ins.	O	No.	Ins.	O
Spiracular	107 Occlusor m.					
Dorsal muscles	108 (1st) ph.m.	a.c.s.	me. 2nd ph.	109 (2nd) ph.m.	a.e.s.	l. 2nd ph.
	110 d.11.m.	1st ph.	2nd ph.	111 sr.ph.m.	po.t.	m. 2nd ph.
	112 m.ph.m.	po.t.	l. 2nd ph.	113 lr.ph.m.	m.t.	l. 2nd ph.
	114A lr.t.p.m.	l.t.	p.ridge	114B (muscle z^{50})	l.me.t.	v.l. thorax
	115 p.ax.m.	3rd ax.	p.ridge	116 sr.t.p.m.	a.n.w.p.	p.ridge
	117 v.p.m.	p.a.	s.a.			

Muscles 118–140 were studied by Dresden and Nijenhuis[17] and the enumeration they imposed on Carbonell's system[6] is used below (105 is also mentioned).

	No.	Ins.	O	No.	Ins.	O
Ventral muscles	118 l.tn.m.	t.n.	a.t.	119 me.tn.m.	tn.	a.me.t.
	120 sr.tn.m.	tn.	a.me.t.			
	121 vl.ph.m.	s.	l.ph.	112 (1st) c.s.m.	tn.	a.c.s.
	123 v.c.s.m.	tn.	a.e.s.	124 l.c.s.m.	l.tn.	a.c.s.
	125 (4th) c.s.m.	s.a.	l. 2nd ph.			
Coxal (cx.)	126 s.prm.cx.	a.cx.		127 s.p.prm.cx.	ex.p.	c.x.
	128(a) sa.m.	within cx.	sa.	(b) sa.m.	cx. margin	sa.
	129 sr.t.rem.	po.cx.	t.	130 t.rem.	po.cx.	t.
	131 lr.t.rem.	po.cx.	a.me.t.	132A s.rem.	po.cx.	sa.
	132B sr.s.ad.	cx.rim	sa.MX2^{50}	133 s.cx.m.	a.cx.	sa.
	134 sp.m.cx.	v.cx.	2nd sp.			
Coxal (mainly in)	135 (a) tr. dep.	tr.apodeme	a.l.t.	(b) origin: s.a.		
	(c) origin from basalar plate			(d) m.cx. wall	(e) edge cx.	
	130 po.tr.dep.	tr.apodeme	po.cx.	137 a.tr.dep.	tr.apodeme	me.cx. wall
	138 a.lev.tr.	tr.apodeme	a.cx.	139 (a) lr.tr. lev.	tr.	po.cx. wall
	(b) lr.tr.lev.	tr.	a.cx.rim	(c) lr.tr.lev.	tr.	a.cx. wall
	140 (a) po.cx. lev.	tr.	po.cx. wall	(b) po.cx.lev.	tr.	po.cx. wall
	(c) po.cx.lev.	tr.	po.cx. wall	(d) ob.ramus	tr.	po.cx. wall

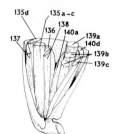

FIG. 10.4 The coxa (2) split open from the ventral side to display the muscles. Muscle 135 has its origin inside the thorax.

141–146 muscles intrinsic to limb segments distal to the coxa.

	No.	Ins.	O	No.	Ins.	O

3rd **Thoracic**

	No.	Ins.	O	No.	Ins.	O
Spiracular	147 occlusor					
Anterior	148 v.11.m.	sa.2	sa.3	149 h.v.m.	e.s.3	2nd sp.
Ventral muscles	150A ph.e.s.m.	ph.2	c.s.3	150B ph.m. (PEP[50])	ph.2	c.s.3
	151 ob.s.m.	2nd sp.	sa.3	152 11.s.m.	2nd sp.	sa.3 (v)
Dorsal muscles	153 d.11.m.	al.t.l.	ph.2	154 m.d.ob.m.	me.al.t.l.	t.
	155 (2) lr.d. ob.m.	a.al.t.l.	me.t.	156 l.d.ob.m.	l.al.t.l.	t.
	157 lr.t.p.m.	p.ridge	l.t.	158 p.ax.m.	3rd ax.	p.ridge
	159 sr.t.p.m.	a.n.w.p.	p.a.	160 p.s.m.	p.a.	sa.
Coxal (cx.)	161 lr.tn.m.	tn.	a.t.	162 me.tn.m.	tn.	a.me.t.
	163 sr.tn.m.	tn.	a.me.t.	164 1st e.s.m.	tn.	a.e.s.
	165 v.e.s.m.	tn.	a.e.s.	166 e.s.m.	1 tn.	a.e.s.
	167 e.s.prm.	c.edge	po.l.e.s.	168 e.s.prm.	cx.edge	po.l.e.s.
	169 sa.m.	sa.	mr.	170 cx.ro.(sr.)	mr.	sa.
	171 cx.ro.(lr.)	mr.	p.s.a.	172A s.rem.	po.cx.	p.s.a.
	172B sr.s.ad. (MX3 see [50])	cx.rim.	sa.	173 sp.m.	a.cx.	2nd sp.
	170 po.cx.rem.	po.cx.	a.t.	175 a.cx.rem.	po.cx.	a.t.
	176 lr.me.cx. rem.	po.cx.	a.t.			
Coxal (in)	177 very similar to 135 in the mesothorax					
	178 similar to 136			179 a.tr.dep.	tr.apodeme a.cx.	
	180 similar to 138			181 as 139, but (c) origin a.cx.rim		
	182 similar to 140, but (c) and (d) originate from po.cx.rim					
Leg muscles	183–188 are distributed among the other intrinsic leg muscles, as 90–95.					

The following muscles run between the metathorax and abdominal segments 1 and 2. They are for the most part specialized muscles which do not fit into the series of generalized abdominal muscles.

No.	Ins.	O	No.	Ins.	O
189 sp.m.	al.s.2	2nd sp.	190 t.s.m.	al.t.1.	sa.
191 ob.v.m.	a.al.s.1	sa.	192 v.11.v.m.	a.al.s.l.	v.s.a.
193 d.11.v.m.	a.al.s.2, originates on both sides of 190.				

Chadwick has described and compared the ventral thoracic muscles of *P.a.*, *B.o.*, *Bt.g.*, *Blaberus craniifer*, *Leucophaea maderae* and 14 other species of cockroaches.[10] Differences between the species were on the whole quite minor. Chadwick makes a number of small alterations to Carbonell's description and the student should consult this work.

Abdominal muscles (Fig. 10.5)

The musculature of segments 2–6 in the female, and 2–7 in the male conforms fairly closely to a standard pattern of 16 muscle pairs including those of the spiracles. Segment 1 in both sexes, and segment 8 in the male still exhibit a musculature of a generally similar topography to that of the most generalized segments, while segments 7–10 in the female, and 9–10 in the male, are highly

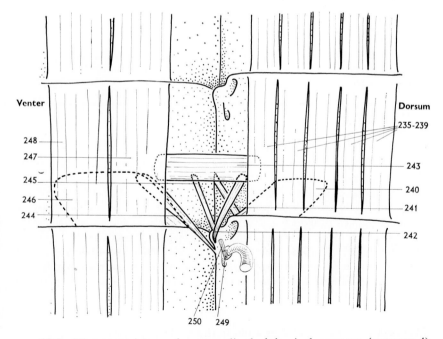

FIG. 10.5   The musculature of a generalized abdominal segment (segment 4). Dorsal view of a pinned-out preparation. sp.—spiracle

modified in association with the genitalia. The latter will be dealt with separately under muscles of the genital segments.

SEGMENT 1. Longitudinal intersegmental

          194–198 d.11. muscles   199–200 v.11. muscles

In the male only one muscle, 199, appears to be present. In the first segment, these muscles are orientated obliquely, associated with the membranous sternum. Spiracle occlusor 201, spiracle dilator 202.

GENERALIZED SEGMENTS (2–6, ♀; 2–7, ♂) 2–7 shown here as in the male

	Seg-ment 2	3	4	5	6	7
Muscle d.11.m.(5)	203–207	219–223	235–239	251–255	267–271	283–287
d.ob.m.	208	224	240	256	272	288
i.t.m.	209	225	241	257	273	289
o.t.m.	210	226	242	258	274	290
vl.t.-s.m.	211	227	243	259	275	291
st.ob.-s.m.	212	228	244	260	276	292
1r.ob.t.-s.m.	213	229	245	261	277	293
v.ob.m.	214	230	246	262	278	294
v.11.m. (2)	215–216	231–232	247–248	263–274	279–280	295–296
Spiracle occlusor	217	233	249	265	281	297
Spiracle dilator	218	234	250	266	282	298

Dorsal and ventral longitudinal muscles could be regarded as single muscles with 5 and 2 parts respectively, but their innervation suggests them to be separate functional units.

Ford has described the abdominal musculature of *Blaberus atropos* and *Parcoblatta pennsylvanica*,[21] but these descriptions differ in a number of respects from the pattern observed in *P.a. P. pennsylvanica* was most similar to *P.a.* Taking the muscle series of segment 4 as an example, Ford identified 235–239, 240, 243, 245 and 247–248. A muscle similar to 241, but tergosternal in position is shown by her, and a smaller one parallel to this one which I cannot identify. Also shown is a small muscle running from the anterior region of the tergum to near the spiracle. A number of fine connective tissue strands lie in this region.

Musculature of genital segments in the male

Muscles not directly attached to the phallic lobes.

SEGMENT 8

d.11.m.(5) 299–303, small dorsal muscles 304–306 (numbered as in generalized segment).

vl.t.-s.m. 307, small ventral muscles 308–311.

v.l.m.(3) 312–315.

Some of the smaller segmental muscles could not be positively identified in this segment, but the ventral longitudinal muscles have an extra part inserted on the rounded ninth sternum—315.

Spiracular occlusor 316.
Spiracular dilator 317.

SEGMENT 9

d.11.m.(5) 318–322 very short muscles.

v.o.m. There appears to be few ventral muscles in this segment, but a triangular muscle runs to the tenth segment: 323.

SEGMENT 10

d.11.m. (5) 324–328. These muscles are considerably larger than those of the preceding segment.

Rectal dilators (4) 329–332. Each muscle consists of 4 or 5 radiating muscle fibres. In some specimens 329 (ventral) appears to originate on the eighth segment.

Cercal muscles (3). i.d.rem. 333; o.d.prm. 334; v.ob.m. 335. These muscles produce a mainly horizontal movement of the cercus through about 35°, moving it clear of the wings. Occasionally the cercus is rapidly vibrated; presumably a cleaning movement.

PHALLIC MUSCLES (see Fig. 10.6 for positions)

Ventral area of left phallic lobe (grumolobus, etc., left phallobase). ex. 335, origin 9s.: in. 337.

Dorsal area of left phallic lobe (pseudopenis, asperate lobe). ex. all originating near border 8–9s. 338, 339, 340. in. 341–344.

Ventral or median phallic lobe (ventral gonapophysis). ex. 345 (origin as 327–9), 346–348 originate anterior margin s.10. in. 349 and 350.

Right phallic lobe (dibella, falx, right phallobase). ex. 351 origin from median lobe. 352–3 hind margin of s.9. in. 355–357.

Musculature of the genital segments in the female

SEGMENT 7

d.11.m. (5) 283–287 (288–290) small dorsal muscles (as in male).

vl.t.-s.m. 291 (292–294) small ventral muscles (as in male).

d.o.m. 288 large well-developed muscle.

The ventral longitudinal muscles appear to be specialized to form 4 retractors of the eighth sternum numbered from the mid-line 295a, 295b, 295c and 296. 295a, b and c have a common area of origin.

Spiracular muscles 297 and 298.

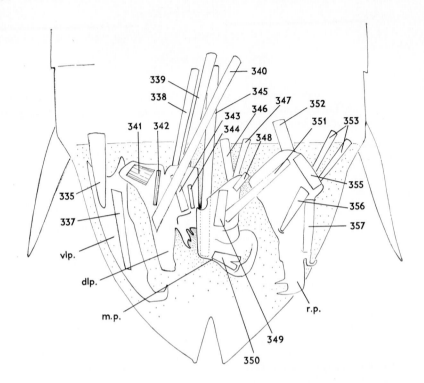

FIG. 10.6 Dorsal view of the musculature of the phallic lobes (rather diagrammatic). dlp.—dorsal left phallic lobe, m.p.—median phallic lobe, r.p.—right phallic lobe, vlp.—ventral left phallic lobe. The segments are numbered

SEGMENT 8

d.11.m. (5) 299–303 (shorter than 283–287).

vl.t.s.m. (27). Two rather oblique retractors of the ninth segment occupy the position that would normally be occupied by this muscle. 306a—anterior muscle, 306b—posterior muscle. 306a appears homologous with (304–305, small dorsal muscles, 308–311 small ventral muscles), 312–315 are left for derivatives of the v.11 muscles, but they were not positively identified.

Spiracular muscles 315–317.

SEGMENT 9

d.11.m. (3) 318–322. Very short muscles, indistinctly separated.

v.o.m. a small triangular muscle may be homologous with 323 in the male.

SEGMENT 10

d.11.m. 324–328.

Rectal dilators 329–332.

Cercal muscles (as in the male) 333–335.

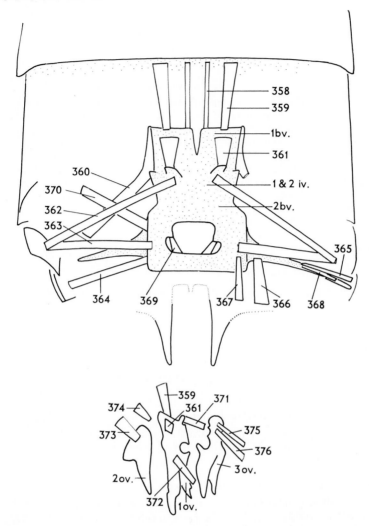

FIG. 10.7   Dorsal view of the muscles of the ovipositor system in the female (diagrammatic). 1 and 2bv.—first and second basivalvulae, 1 and 2iv.—first and second intervalvulae, 1 to 3ov.—first to third ovipositor valves

Muscles of the female genitalia (Fig. 10.7)

Gupta[25] has enumerated these muscles, and where these could be positively equated with muscles observed by us they are placed in brackets.

Six sclerites can be clearly distinguished: first and second valvifers, and 3 pairs of ovipositor valves projecting posteriorly. Since it is difficult to homologize these muscles with those of the phallic lobes with any degree of certainty, a separate number series following 336–337 is employed.

2ND VALVIFER (1st basivalvula of Gupta)

Ex. 358 (1) m.re. Arises from 7s. 359 (3) l.re. origin 7s. larger than 358.
   360 (2) 1. pr. origin 8s. Broad insertion.
In. 361 (5) re. first valvifer. Inserted on a process of the second valvifer.

1ST VALVIFER (intervalvula and 2nd basivalvula of Gupta)

Ex. 361 (above). 362 (4) pr. second valvifer. Arises on the eighth tergum.
Ex. 363 (9) t.pr. arises 8t. 364 (10) v.t.pr. arises on 9t. 365 (6) a.l.pr. arises on the
8t. inserted on the basal part of the lateral arm. 366 (8) po.pr. arises posteriorly on
borders of ninth and tenth segment, inserted on base of lateral arm (further medial
than shown by Gupta[25]). 367 (11) me.po.pr. This looks like an intrinsic muscle in
Gupta's figure, but is shown here as lying medial to 368 (inserted on base).
In. 368 (7) po.l.pr. Runs from inner to outer part of first valvifer lateral arm.
369 (12) Occlusor muscle. Very small muscle at the side of the main internal opening of the valvifer.
   Other muscles. Muscle 13 of Gupta was not positively identified, but a large
retractor 370 appears to arise on the eighth sternum and is inserted on the anterior
angle of the first valvifer.

MUSCLES OF THE OVIPOSITOR VALVES

   The inner margins of some of these valves are confused with areas mentioned
above, so that muscle 361 (5) is in fact inserted on the inner end of the first
ovipositor valve.

(dorsal gonapophysis) *first ovipositor valve*

   Beside muscles 359 (3), and 361 (5), there appears to be two other muscles, one
attached basally—362, the other inserted between the two lobes of the valve: 363.
Both are extrinsic.

(Inner gonapophysis) *second ovipositor valve*

   One large dorsal muscle runs down from the ninth segment to this sclerite:
364, and a smaller muscle 365 is inserted on the membrane between ovipositor
valves 1 and 2.

(Ventral gonapophysis) *third ovipositor valve*

   Two small protractor muscles lie close together on the base of this valve: 366
(anterior), 367 (posterior). They originate in the ninth segment.
   McKittrick figures the musculature of the female genitalia excellently in a
number of species including *Bt.g.*[42] It is not easy to compare the pattern shown
in *Bt.g.* with that of *P.a.*

Light microscope histology

   The muscles in *Bt.g.* whether flight muscles or normal trunk muscles are of the
radial-lamellar type, the fibrils forming radiating lamellae as seen in transverse
section. In a few thin fibres there may be an outer radial-lamellar part surrounding an inner core of evenly distributed sarcostyles. The muscle nuclei are more or
less randomly distributed. The Z-membrane can be seen clearly in the fresh fibre

as well as after fixation and staining, but the M-membrane is not clear. In *Oniscosoma granicollis*, *Platyzosteria analis*, *Panesthia australis* and *Periplaneta americana* the fibres are of similar form although in the last two species they are of larger size.[65]

In the coxal muscles of the cockroach *P.a.* the Z-membrane or telophragma usually shows very clearly after staining with Hansen's Trioxyhaematin or Heidenhain's Iron Haematoxylin, and the peripheral position of many of the

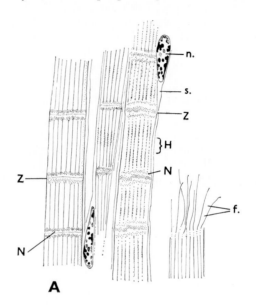

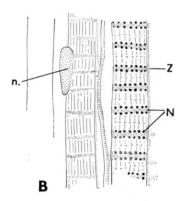

FIG. 10.8   Histology of muscle fibres. **A**, from the coxa (Heidenhains Iron Haemotoxylin). **B**, from the crop. Meth. Blue. The nuclei (n.), sarcolemma (s.), fibrils (f.), accessory disc (N), Z-membrane and *H*-discs, can be seen

large nuclei is well demonstrated (Fig. 10.8). The dark disc (A- or Q-band) is well defined, although in the relaxed fibre it may be narrow and lightly stained. The fibrils themselves are convincingly demonstrated by treatment with the iron stains and appear often to be continuous through many sarcomeres (Fig. 10.8).[26]

When the fibres are stained by means of a silver nitrate technique such as the Holmes method for the nervous system, the transverse structures appear more distinct and the fibrils less well marked. The Z-membrane is differentiated and sometimes has a slightly beaded appearance. The A- and I-bands often show great contrast in density. In many fibres granules may be seen at the edge of the A-band, corresponding in all probability to the accessory discs of the classical micro-scopists. It is tempting to see in these argyrophilic regions the transverse component of the sarcoplasmic reticulum described by electron microscopists.[26]

The development of muscles involved in flight

In *Bt.g.* the muscle fibres of the pterothorax are not much specialized as compared with the normal leg muscles. Apart from the small wing adjustor muscles there is only one muscle—a tergosternal muscle which is an exclusive wing muscle. The other muscles are either trunk muscles in the larva whose attachments change during development, or muscles that combine the rôle of leg and wing muscle.

One of the tergo-coxal muscles may be taken as an example of a muscle of the latter type and this functions during the larval period. In the first instar it consists of about 60 fibres, 35 of them of the thin type already described. At this stage the thin fibres occupy a disproprotionately large part of the muscle, but as development proceeds the thicker fibres increase in size and outstrip the growth of the thin fibres. The lamellate arrangement of the sarcostyles now appears, and the nuclei which had been largely confined to the axial core migrate peripherally. In the half-grown larva, fibre cleavage now begins, greatly increasing the size of the muscle.

In the tergo-sternal muscle, which has a purely alary function, development occurs from a very small rudiment. In the early larva this is a delicate strand 5 μ across, with a sarcolemma and fibrils with cross-striations. Nuclei are few but it can be seen that the rudiment is a single muscle fibre. At a later stage splitting occurs to produce the 12 fibres of the adult muscle.

In *P.a.* fibre cleavage is more active. The tergo-coxal muscle similar to that described in *Bt.g.* has about 500 fibres of radial lamellar type with an accessory bundle of thin fibres in the adult. Nuclei migrate peripherally as in *Bt.g.* One very interesting point is that in frozen sections of cleaving fibres the sarcolemma is very distinct and from the way it can be seen transecting the plane of adjacent lamellae an impression is gained of the sarcolemma taking an active rôle in fibre cleavage.[65]

Electron microscope histology

In the abdominal muscles of *Bt.g.*[18] the fibres have the same general charac-teristics as the thoracic muscle of *P.a.*[61,62] The Z-membrane, A- and I-bands are distinct, but under the electron microscope the M-line can be seen to be absent, although the H-band appears as a low density striation. The mitochondria or sarcosomes are arranged regularly opposite the I-bands near the telophragma, in the abdominal muscles of *Bt.g.* and are 0·5–1·5 μ in length. In *Periplaneta* coxal muscles, however, the sarcosomes are larger (5 μ in length) and are randomly distributed. The distribution and size of sarcosomes differs much according to species and type of muscle.

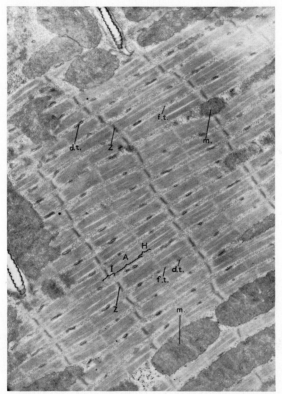

FIG. 10.9   An electronmicrograph of the fine structure of muscle fibres. A—A-disc, d.t.—dense tubular component, f.t.—fine tubules, H—H-band, I—I-disc, m—mitochondria, Z—Z-membrane. (From Smith[62])

One of the most complex parts of the fibre concerns the endoplasmic[18, 20] or sarcoplasmic reticulum,[62] a tubular complex visible between the fibrils (f.t. above).

In *Bt.g.* aggregation of tubules could be seen at the level of the Z-membrane, and junctional structures known as triads at the boundary between A- and I-bands. Definite connections between the plasmamembrane and the tubular system could be demonstrated, at such points the plasma membrane being infolded to form a deep groove or funnel.[18]

In the coxal muscles of *P.a.* the picture is generally similar, but a dense tubular component transverse to the axis of the fibrils can be seen as distinct from the close packed fine tubules arranged in sheets running out between the fibrils (Fig. 10.9). This dense component can be seen in sections cut parallel to the fibre lamellae to be a regionally dilated tubule system with regularly formed junctions.

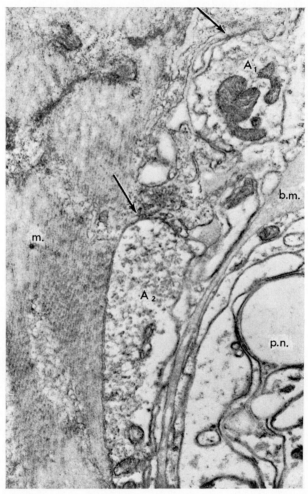

FIG. 10.10   Fine structure of neuromuscular junction (abdominal muscle of *Bt.g.*). m.—muscle, A_1 and A_2—small and large axons containing synaptic vesicles and in close contact with the muscle, b.m.—bounding membrane, p.n.—peripheral nerve, arrows—endoplasmic reticulum. (Electronmicrograph from Edwards[18])

This dual system of tubules may be regarded as comparable to that demonstrated in vertebrate muscle fibres, and may be involved in the coupling of the excitable membrane to the contracting fibril.

The sarcolemma of the light microscopist can be separated into two membranes, the cell membrane and the basement membrane of the muscle fibre.[62]

Pattern of innervation

As shown by the preparations of the early insect histologists, insect muscle fibres each receive several nerve terminals. A good way of demonstrating this for class purposes is to inject a dilute solution of reduced methylene (Unna's method of preparation [67]) into the abdomen of living *P.a.*, removing some of the abdominal muscles after approximately one hour.

Preparations made by the use of intravitam methylene blue also demonstrate that in many of the motor nerves at least two axons, often of different diameters, are distributed side by side over parts of the musculature, some of the muscle fibres receiving endings which include more than one axon, that is to say the muscle fibres receive a polyneuronal innervation. Furthermore, each muscle fibre has more than one terminal on it so that the innervation can also be described as multiterminal.

In the abdominal muscles of *Bt.g.* the endings are approximately 30 μ apart,[18] and in leg muscles of *P.a.* 40 μ apart.[72]

Edwards has demonstrated the fine structure of neuromuscular junctions in the abdominal muscles of *Bt.g.* (Fig. 10.10). In this region the nerve terminal could be seen to contain a single large axon (up to 8 μ in diameter), and three to seven other axons 0·5–1·5 μ thick. The axons were ensheathed by a common lemnoblast. On the muscle side the lemnoblast fuses with the sarcolemma of the muscle fibre, and mesaxons may be observed round the axons at certain points formed by the invagination of the plasmamembrane of the lemnoblast.[18]

One odd point here is that Edwards interprets the dense zones between the folds of axon sheath as chitinous bars. These have been interpreted by other authors (see Chapter 8), as of a lipid or at any rate non-chitinous nature.

As many as four neuromuscular junctions could be seen in a single plane of section. Synapsing axons contained mitochondria and many vesicles 50 Å in diameter, the interspace between the plasmamembrane of the muscle and of the axon being often as little as 15 Å. The muscle cytoplasm in the synaptic region contains granules, vesicles and tubules of the endoplasmic reticulum, but few mitochondria,[18] in this last particular differing from wasp or cicada muscle.[20]

THE PHYSIOLOGY OF THE NEUROMUSCULAR APPARATUS

Pringle[52] demonstrated that the legs of the cockroach *P.a.* contained two types of motor axon associated with slow or fast kinds of muscular contraction. The fast system responded to low frequency shocks with single twitches and with tetanic contractions following stimuli above about 30 per sec. The slow system on the other hand did not respond to low-frequency excitation, but repetitive shocks produced a slowly augmenting contraction that continued up to at least 100 c/s. By means of the local application of nicotine to the thoracic ganglion it was possible to determine the numbers and types of fibre in different muscles, as neurones were first excited, then paralyzed. His brief table of motor components is given below.

Pringle,[52] and Wilson,[75] also showed that externally recorded potentials presumably near nerve terminals in the muscle allowed the recognition of larger fast potentials, and smaller slow potentials.

TABLE 10.1

(compare with Table 10.2)

Nerve	Fast fibres	Slow fibres	Muscle
3a	2 or more	2 or more	Depressors and remotors of the coxal (120, 122, 123, 124)
3b	2		Trochanteral flexor (138, 139c)
3b		1	Femoral reductor (141)
3b	1	1	Tibial extensor (142)
4		1	Coxal rotator (105)
4	1	1	Pleural extensor of trochanter (135)
5	1	1	Trochanteral extensor (136, 137)
5	2 or more	2 or more	Tibial flexor (143) tarsal depressor (146) and meta tarsal (144)
6	2	2	Trochanteral flexor (139a, b, 140)

It was observed that where a muscle was supplied by more than one fibre, that axonal territories did not overlap.

Behaviourally the slow system was seen as responsible for postural contraction and slow walking movements, and the fast system as involved in quick running movements.

That only a percentage of all the muscle fibres composing a muscle received both slow and fast axons was demonstrated in other insects by intracellular recording methods, and then also in *P.a.* by Smyth and Hoyle.[63] In the tibial extensor of the hind-leg it can be seen that a wedge-shaped zone near the trochanteral end of the muscle is innervated by both axons, the rest of the muscle receiving only fast axons.[63] This localization of a slow zone does not occur in some of the coxal muscles, however, where dually innervated fibres are randomly distributed according to Becht.[2]

Following the work of Dresden and Nijenhuis on the anatomy of the cockroach leg Dresden,[16] Becht and Dresden,[3] and Becht[2] investigated the type of mechanical responses characteristic of the coxal muscles using isotonic recording methods.

Three types of response were elicited following electrical stimulation of the motor axons. Fast muscles gave a large twitch response, fatigued rapidly and twitch/tetanus force ratio was higher. Slow muscles gave only a small response to a single maximal stimulus, were slow to fatigue and the twitch/tetanus ratio was low. However, some muscles did not separate easily into either of these categories, having characteristics of both, and it was supposed that in these muscles fast and slow functions may be restricted to separate groups of muscle fibres.

The numbers given to the muscles followed Dresden and Nijenhuis (in outline derived from Carbonell's series). Examples of fast muscles quoted by Becht and Dresden are 136 and 137, of slow muscles 135b, and of 'mixed' muscles 138 and 139c. All from mesothoracic coxae.[3]

The possible rôle of synaptic transmission in determining these differences was investigated by Becht *et al.*, using intracellular recording techniques. No evidence of large differences in the electrical properties of the junctions or muscle membrane appeared and variations in the contractile or coupling mechanisms are involved.

Usherwood[69] reinvestigated the nature of these differences in the neuromuscular physiology of mesothoracic coxal muscles, using intracellular microelectrodes and isometric tension recording. The errors inherent in the isotonic recording methods used by Becht and Dresden are discussed by this author, but it may be pointed out that some difficulties do arise in isometric recording, albeit of a less fundamental nature, due to the difficulty of adjusting accurately the resting length of the muscle.

The information derived from this study is summarized in Table 10.2 and Figs. 10.11 and 10.12.

Usherwood's conclusion was that the mechanical responses of the various coxal muscles of the cockroach to motor nerve stimulation are basically similar to each other when differences in the innervation pattern are taken into account, the number and type of axon present varying.

The occurrence of an inhibitory axon has now been established in locusts, and while it has not so far been demonstrated in the cockroach, it seems likely that this third axon type may be of general occurrence. In locusts marked reduction of the mechanical effect produced by slow fibre stimulation was demonstrated when the inhibitory fibre was also stimulated. The action of the inhibitory fibre is associated with muscle membrane hyperpolarization, increased chloride conductance, and can be mimicked by γ-amino-butyric acid.

Miniature end-plate potentials believed to be due to the spontaneous release of occasional quanta of transmitter substance have been shown to occur by Usherwood in *Blaberus giganteus*. Their magnitude is usually about 0·25 mV and they may occur several times a second.[70]

The effect of specific ions and of drugs on neuromuscular transmission has not been studied intensively in cockroach muscles. Hoyle showed that a high concentration of magnesium ions and a low concentration of calcium ions both lowered the height of intracellularly recorded potentials observed in the extensor tibial muscles of *P.a.* Following excess magnesium a delay in the appearance of the reduced postsynaptic potention can also be seen.[29] Usherwood found that the alkaloid ryanodine (empirical formula—$C_{25}H_{35}O_9N$) converts the normal graded response to all-or-none responses in many fibres. The excitability of the fibre is

TABLE 10.2

Summary of electrical and mechanical recordings obtained from the mesothoracic coxal muscles of *Periplaneta americana*

In column 2 figures in brackets represent the number of motor axons innervating the muscles; histological data from Dresden and Nijenhuis (1958). In columns 5, 6 and 7 figures in brackets represent number of measurements made.

Muscle	Innervation (established by electrical recordings)	Mechanical responses to graded stimulation	Peak tension developed following a single maximal stimulus (g)	Rise time of twitch ±S.E. of mean (msec)	Decay time of twitch ±S.E. of mean (msec)	Half-decay time of twitch ±S.E. of mean (msec)	Estimated cross-sectional area of muscle (cm²)	Approximate isometric twitch tension (g cm^{-2})	Becht and Dresden's classification
136 and 137	1 'fast' axon (1)	1 'fast' contraction	4–7.5	13.5±1.0 (23)	30.2±2.5 (14)	10.3±1.2 (14)	8.2×10^{-3}	850	'Fast' muscle
135a and c	4 'fast' axons (4)	4 'fast' contractions	2–5	10.6±0.1 (7)	33.7±1.9 (6)	10.01±0.6 (6)	7.2×10^{-3}	700	'Fast' muscle
135d and e	2 'fast' axons (4) 2 'slow' axons	2 'fast' contractions 2 'slow' contractions	0.5–2	12.1±1.4 (19)	41.9±3.2 (11)	12.9±0.5 (10)	—	—	'Mixed' muscle
135b	2 'fast' axons (4) 1 'slow' axon	2 'fast' contractions 1 'slow' contraction	0.1–0.75	13.3±0.6 (24)	71±4.7 (11)	15.1±1.1 (10)	8.4×10^{-4}	850	'Slow' muscle
138 and 139c	3 'fast' axons (7) 1 'slow' axon	3 'fast' contractions 1 'slow' contraction	1–2	11.4±0.7 (8)	29.5±0.9 (8)	9.2±1.0 (11)	3.6×10^{-3}	550	'Mixed' muscle
139a and b and 140	5 'fast' axons (7)	5 'fast' contractions	2–5	11.7±0.6 (13)	30.1±0.5 (10)	9.7±1.0 (7)	6.6×10^{-3}	800	'Mixed' muscle

increased and repetitive spikes appear. These changes in excitability are believed to be due to diminished potassium conductance.[68]

Denervation has a variety of effects dependent in some degree on the type of

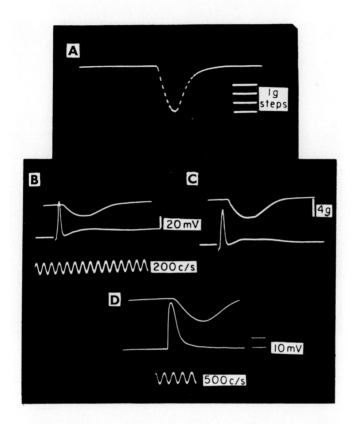

FIG. 10.11   Mechanical and electrical responses from muscle group 136 and 137. **A,** mechanical response to maximal indirect stimulation. Record modulated at 500 c/s. **B–D,** simultaneous records of the electrical (intracellular) and mechanical response from three preparations. Time and tension calibration the same for **B** and **C.** The electrical response is the lower trace, and the mechanical response is the upper trace. (From Usherwood[69])

muscle involved, but spontaneous shifts in the membrane potential of the muscle fibres so affected have been recorded in a number of different insects. In the spiracular muscle of *Blaberus* and *P.a.*, Case found that denervation produced fasciculation or brief incomplete contractions of some muscle fibres in a muscle.[8] Bodenstein also observed this in the coxal muscles of *P.a.* which after a period of five or six days lost their ability to respond to direct electrical stimulation. Spontaneous activity has also been observed in the denervated femoral muscles of *P.a.*[5]

The way in which the controlled contraction of separate motor units is used to build up complex limb movements has been recently the subject of investigation by Hoyle. While the classical picture of reciprocal inhibition in opposing

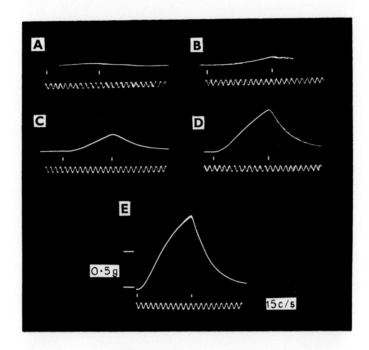

FIG. 10.12   Mechanical response of muscle group 135d and e to stimulation of the slow axon at the following frequencies. **A**, 10 c/s; **B**, 25 c/s; **C**, 35 c/s; **D**, 80 c/s; **E**, 125 c/s. (From Usherwood[69])

muscles undoubtedly holds for certain movements the simultaneous contraction of antagonists (cocontraction) may be observed in a significant number of instances in *P.a.* It is suggested that the contraction of a muscle may act as an additional restoring force in limb movements and supplement the effects of gravity and cuticular elasticity.[30]

TERRESTRIAL LOCOMOTION

(i) Speed of running

Many species of cockroaches can run swiftly and this may be associated with their often rather weak powers of flight. McConnell and Richards[39] give details of the running speeds of *P.a.*, the average adult speed (males and females) being 74 cm/sec at 25°. The highest individual speed recorded at the more elevated temperature of 35° was 130 cm/sec (2·9 miles/hr), but this temperature is at the upper side of the optimum temperature range and may not reflect a normal capability. Males appeared to run rather faster than females (66 against 57 cm/sec, at 22°). Wille has examined the running speed of the much smaller *Bt.g.* and obtained speeds of 2·7, 18·2 and 29·3 cm/sec for the first instar nymph, adult female and adult male respectively.[73] It seems probable that if these and other insect running speeds were expressed as body lengths per sec more comparable values for different species would be obtained; values near 1 cm/sec/mm could be expected. The dependence of speed on temperature up to about 28° was demonstrated by McConnell and Richards, rate and temperature increasing smoothly up to this level ($Q_{10} = 1·8$).

The nature of the surface also effects running speed in that smooth surfaces produce, as would be expected, lower speeds for adults. The larvae, however, with their adhesive pulvilli can run effectively on glass.

While the running speeds of few insects are known, cockroaches have the highest speeds recorded.

(ii) **The sequence and mechanics of walking movements**

The walking movements of *B.o.* have been analysed by Hughes[31, 32, 33] (Fig. 10.13), who was able to show that the alternate tripod mode of locomotion proposed by Müller and others was an over-simplification of the actual sequence of movements. More recently this work has been embodied in a review with additional observations.[33]

The walking leg of the cockroach functions both as a strut and as a lever, serving both to support and move the body. These are to some extent antagonistic functions and a delicate balance exists with reference to each limb, altering according to limb-position. The fore-limb tends to resist forward movement, the hind-limbs revolving it towards the vertical position where it becomes a lever.

The coxal articulations of the mid- and hind-limbs allow limited arcs of movement at a fixed angle to the body, but the fore-coxae due to the arrangement of the trochantin have two axes of movement which also allows a wide arc of movement to the limb. The hind- and mid-legs can be regarded largely as rigid extensions of the coxae.

It is probable that the retractors commence their activity while the limb is moving forward and before it touches the ground, so that their contraction will help to stop the forward movement of the limb; a phase absorbing much energy in non-rotary motion. If a similar action occurs with reference to the protractor on the backswing, then a considerable overlap in the contraction cycles of opposing muscles may be supposed to occur, thus breaking down the distinction between agonists and antagonists. Support for this comes from observations on other insects.

The hind-limbs are the longest and undergo the greatest effective change in length during walking. The whole limb is orientated very near the horizontal plane in the cockroach so that there is very little vertical strut component involved in its mechanics and the abdomen is frequently dragged on the ground. This may be associated with life in narrow crevices and fissures.

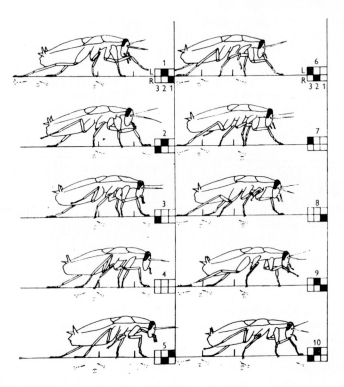

FIG. 10.13   Normal walking as shown by successive frames of cine film (30 frames/ sec) (*Bt.g.*). The black squares on the right of each drawing indicate which legs are off the ground, and the scores made on smoked paper are also shown. (From Hughes[31])

In the theory of alternation of triangles of support proposed by earlier workers it was necessary that only three legs touched the ground at a time. Ciné film records showed that four or five limbs might be applied to the substrate at any one instant, the gait being flexible and varied. Usually, however, the order in which the legs are lifted is as follows: R1, L2, R3, L1, R2, L3. The first three legs and the second three make up two triangles and these are protracted soon after one another. At high speeds the intervals between leg movements may be very short. When the cockroach is exposed to very low temperatures a striking and unusual rhythm may occur as follows: R3, R2, R1, L3, L2, L1. This has been observed in other insects.

In normal progression no fore- or middle-leg is lifted until the leg behind has taken up its supporting position, and each leg alternates with the contralateral limb of the same segment. These axioms, especially the first one, can be applied to other insects.

As might be expected, the ratio between protraction and retraction time alters with the speed of the whole animal. In *Periplaneta* it was shown that the ratio ose from 0·07 at low speeds to 1·0 at high speeds (2·0–9·8 cm/sec), whilst the ange in *Blatta* was 0·31 to 0·8 at 3·2 and 17·5 cm/sec. Such changes[31, 33] are orrelated with differences in the sequence of leg movements.

The sequence of limb movements in *Blatta* does not remain a normal one vhen the animal is suspended, as occurs in some other insects.

More recently Wilson has reviewed work on insect walking, and added some of is own observations on *B.o.*[75]

SOUND PRODUCTION

It is perhaps surprising that cockroaches—which together with crickets provide is with an outstanding example of a simple auditory sensillum, the cercal hair organ—appear to depend very little on environmental sounds, and recorded nstances of sound production are rare.[60]

Quite recently, however, a number of new observations have been made which onsiderably extend the information available on this topic.

Two main methods of sound production occur. Expulsion of air from the tracheal system (species of *Gromphadorhina*), and stridulation produced by the rubbing together of cuticular files on the posterior edge of the pronotum and the costal region of the tegmina (a variety of different genera and species).

Roth and Willis describe a hissing sound made by females of *Gromphadorhina laevigata* when they are with recently hatched larvae, and a shadow passes over them. This sound is produced by the expulsion of air from the second abdominal spiracles. A similar phenomenon has been observed in *G. coquereliana* by Chopard.[11]

Vosseler described thoracic stridulatory organs in *Leucophaea* (originally identified as *Rhyparobia*) and observed that they consisted of fine raised striae approximately 5 µ apart. The insect emits a high-pitched sound when alarmed.[71]

Hartmann working in Roth's laboratory has identified a similar type of stridulatory structure in a number of other species. These were: *Jagrehnia gestroiana*, *Oxyhalsa buprestoides*, *Henschoutedenia flexivittata*, *Panchlora nivea* and *Nauphoeta cinerea*.[28]

About the same time Guthrie found an apparatus in *Henschoutedenia epilamproides* of a similar form,[27] and Howse started an examination of stridulation n the related *Blaberus discoidalis*.

At the time of writing the most comprehensive information is available for two species *N. cinerea* and *H. epilamproides*.

Hartmann observed that the males of *N. cinerea* stridulated when they were courting non-receptive females. A pheromone termed seducin by Roth and Dateo is normally produced by the male and this tends to bring the female into a receptive state. However, if mating is unsuccessful the male stridulates to the female from a distance of about 2 cm. Each phrase begins with 2–6 complex pulse trains each with a duration of 500–750 msec. These are then followed by a series of disyllabic chirps, each of 40–80 msec duration. Phrases last 7–10 sec. Each pulse train appears to be produced by posterior, anterior and side to side displacement of the pronotum over the costal veins, and the chirps are produced by rapid

9+B.O.C.

minute movements of the pronotum, first in a posterior and then in anterior direction only. This is the only recorded instance of stridulation during courtship in a cockroach.[28]

In *H. epilamproides* an alarm call consisting of brief repeated chirps follows handling or occasionally a movement near the insect. The structure of the sound is complex (Fig. 10.14), the basic 'carrier' frequency 4·5–5 kc/s being amplitude modulated at 1–2·5 kc/s to produce chirp subunits. Each chirp lasts about $\frac{1}{10}$ sec. The sound intensity at a range of 1 cm is about 70 db (reference $0 = 0 \cdot 0002$ dyn/cm^2).

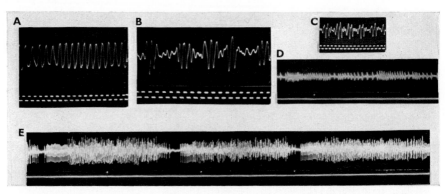

FIG. 10.14   Sounds made by *Henschoutedenia epilamproides* displayed at different sweep speeds. Time marker **A**–**C** 5 kc/s, **D** 50 c/s, **E** 20 c/s

Recordings were made from the auditory nerve (cercal, eighth) to determine whether the sound can be heard by the insect, using artificial tones and pre-recorded sound from the cockroach. Very little response was obtained to frequencies above 500 c/s (up to 100 db). Over the range 500–20 c/s the response curve conformed generally to that described for cercal hair organs by Pumphrey and Rawdon-Smith. Much of the stridulatory movement was produced by a muscle (62), the pterothoracic homologues of which are flight muscles. It was suggested that the call might frighten predators because of its resemblance to the sound components in mammal cries. Small voles (*Clethrionomys glareolus*) were frightened by the sound, and the low-frequency components of rat noise were shown to resemble *Henschoutedenia* sound.[27]

FLIGHT

Cockroaches are among the least specialized fliers, and many species are characterized by reduction of the wing apparatus in one or both sexes. Where the wings are fully developed, flight is often weak and orientation poor, in contrast to the ease with which they run, climb, burrow or swim.

The fibres of the indirect muscles of flight differ little from leg muscles in *Bt.g.* according to Tiegs. The fibres (12–20 μ), and the fibrils (0·5 μ) are of small diameter[65] compared to those of specialized flight muscle—Dipteran fibres 120–1,800 μ, fibrils 1·6–3·5 μ (Pringle).[54] In *Bt.g.* the fibres are of a tubular type, rather than fibrillar. Tiegs also found that tracheation was superficial, and the flight muscle was developed by fibre proliferation rather than by the incorporation of myoblasts into a pre-existing rudiment.

Perez-Gonzalez and Edwards were able to show that the oxygen consumption and succinic dehydrogenase activity of leg and wing muscle in *P.a.* differed hardly at all. The substrate used for energy requirements during flight may be fat rather than carbohydrate (Diptera), but it is probable that oxidative breakdown products must be made available, since fatty acids cannot be metabolized directly.[49] Barron and Tahmisian showed that flight muscle extracts of *P.a.* could not utilize butyric acid, but acetate formed a suitable substrate, probably involving the citric acid cycle.[1] The finding is supported by McShan, Kramer and Schlegel who found low fatty acid oxidase activity in the thoracic muscles of *Leucophaea maderae*.[43] Undoubtedly glycolysis is also important in providing energy for flight, but the end-product is pyruvic or phosphopyruvic acid rather than lactic acid according to Barron and Tahmisian.[1]

Insects can be divided into two groups as far as the neural control of the indirect flight muscles is concerned. The more specialized fliers with high wing-beat frequencies are dependent on the mechanical attributes of the skeleton and its effect on properties of the muscle fibrils; a low-frequency neural input serving merely to maintain excitability. In less specialized fliers, such as cockroaches, the indirect flight muscles are driven by motor axons similar to the fast axons of leg muscles, there being a 1:1 ratio between nerve impulse and muscular contraction (Roeder).[58] The wing muscles are not easily excitable by direct electrical stimulation, as was found in other insects, but Roeder observed that the tergal remotor was an exception.[58]

Roeder illustrated a preparation from *P.a.* in which electrical and mechanical events in the wing muscles can be clearly seen during contractions at 28 c/s (Fig. 10.15). The electrical response can be observed to slightly precede the onset of contraction.[58] The route followed by motor axons to the longitudinal indirect flight muscles had been shown to lie partly through the interganglionic connectives,[54] and Chadwick supported this idea in *P.a.* by showing that section of

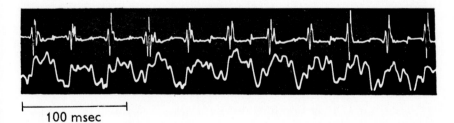

100 msec

FIG. 10.15 Electrical responses (upper trace) and mechanical movements (lower trace) of the thoracic muscles from a cockroach in flight. (From Roeder[58])

the connectives between meso- and metathoracic ganglion abolished hind-wing movements, and between pro- and mesothoracic ganglion eliminated flight movements generally.[9]

The degree of resting tension is an important factor in determining activity in asynchronous flight muscle, but not nearly so important in an insect such as the cockroach. Roeder concluded that the tension in the cockroach thorax was insufficient to produce resonance, and therefore the nerve impulse was a determining factor.[58]

Chordotonal and campaniform sensilla on the wing surface undoubtedly provide important information to the central nervous system about mechanical stresses arising in the wings during flight. Pringle has compared the data provided by Zacwilichowski and others on the distribution of these sense organs in different species[54]. In *Bt.g.* Zacwilichowski found only 16 campaniform organs, and 14 chordotonal organs on each fore-wing, and 6 chordotonal organs on each hind-wing (maximum numbers). This total of 36 sense organs can be compared with 43 in *Chorthippus* (Saltatoria) and 1,295 in *Apis* (Hymenoptera), although many species have more than 100.[78]

The wing-beat frequency is a function of the ambient temperature in *P.a.* Over the range 17–40° the wing-beat frequency rises from 24 to 41 beats/sec. Between 17 and 30° the rate of increase averages 56 c/min/deg, but above 30° it drops to 38 c/min/deg. The corresponding Q_{10} values for these ranges are 1·35 and 1·15, and these are lower than the Q_{10} values for other activities such as heartbeat frequency and running speed. The rates of increase in wingbeat were not greatly different from those observed in high-frequency asynchronous fliers such as *Drosophila*. Cold-acclimated cockroaches could still flutter their wings at 7°.[57] Wing-beat frequency is also affected by the load and air resistance of the wings, as in other insects. The frequency rises from 28 c/s to 33 c/s when the wings are cut short close to the body.[58]

Flight can be initiated in cockroaches by withdrawal of pressure or contact from the tarsi, as in many other insects (Pringle), and light pinching of the abdomen may be effective in maintaining flight in a suspended insect.[54] Laboratory cockroach species do not fly readily, even in the most conducive circumstances, but some laboratory cultures of *P.a.* show much greater willingness to fly than others, and Zimmerman (quoted in Roth and Willis) describes *P.a.* flying about street lamps at night, on the gulf coast of Texas.[79] In Lawson's behavioural experiments, which involved the escape of adult *P.a.* from wooden rafts on water, jumping and then swimming was preferred to flight as a method of escape.[38] On the other hand, many feral cockroach species fly very readily at night if air temperatures are high enough, and *Panchlora nivea*, a rather delicately built species, is a good example. Princis and Kevan record it flying to light in Trinidad.[51]

To sum up, it is not surprising that cockroaches, which have changed little since the Carboniferous, offer a good example of an unspecialized flight apparatus, as compared with the large Holometabolous orders originating with flowering plants in the Mesozoic, and this accords with a cryptic habit in many species.

VISCERAL MUSCLE

Some aspects of the physiology of gut and heart muscle have been dealt with in the sections on incretory organs, and on the nervous system, and morphological details may be found in these sections, and in the chapters devoted to the gut and circulatory system. The purpose of this brief section is to draw the attention of the reader to details omitted under these other headings. The reviews by Davey on visceral muscle physiology,[15] and by Jones on heart structure and function,[34] contain much recent information.

The muscles of the gut

Extrinsic dilator muscles increase the diameter of the cibarium, pharynx and oesophagus (8–11, 50 and 51), and the rectum is dilated by eight radiating groups of muscles in the abdomen (329–332). In all these muscle groups the muscle fibres are arranged apart from one another, so as to have the appearance of separate, very small muscles.

The muscular coat of the gut consists of a well-developed layer of circular muscle, and adjacent fibres branch and anastomose. Lying inside this layer are small widely spaced groups of longitudinal fibres accommodated within the folds of the epithelium. The fibres of the muscular coat have a conspicuous striation (Fig. 10.8 **B**). The development of the inner muscular layer varies considerably in different regions of the gut. In the mid-gut the longitudinal muscle bands are rather weakly developed, but they are complex and powerful over the proventriculus. The crop is characterized by narrow longitudinal muscles in its posterior region, but these become much more powerful as the crop merges into the oesophagus, and the colon and rectum have both layers well developed. The innervation has been described in Chapter 8.

When freshly exposed all regions of the gut may exhibit slight peristaltic movements, which usually die away quite soon. Pinching small areas of the crop musculature causes a local contraction spreading slowly from the point of stimulation in a manner reminiscent of coelenterate column musculature.[26] Davey found that the hind-gut if excised and suspended under light tension in a saline bath, would after an initial delay, pulsate rhythmically and give a useful kymograph record.[13]

The factors involved in crop emptying have been extensively investigated by Treherne and Davey. Meals of high osmotic pressure are emptied into the mid-gut more slowly than those of low osmotic pressure. When the rate of flow through the proventricular valve is compared with the rate of flow through an idealized orifice, taking into account viscosity, the drop in pressure, frequency and duration of opening, and the dimensions of the orifice, it can be seen that some additional factors are involved.

High-viscosity meals, for instance, are emptied more rapidly than would be expected. Davey suggests, taking into account work on locusts, that information from mechanoreceptors and osmoreceptors in the pharyngeal region may be the basis on which retrocerebral ganglion cells regulate crop emptying.[14]

Cameron[7] and Davey[13] investigated the effect of corpora cardiaca extracts on rhythmic contractions in isolated preparations of the hind-gut. Both workers found that these extracts had a stimulating effect, producing increases in amplitude.

Acetylcholine at low concentrations (10^{-8} M) stimulates the activity of gut muscle in *P.a.* according to Kooistra, and this effect is potentiated by eserine.[35] Indolalkylamines also augment the contractions of the gut[13] (see Chapter 6).

The muscles of the heart and ventral diaphragm

Like the gut the heart possesses extrinsic dilator muscles, as well as intrinsic muscle fibres causing constriction.

The dilator muscles consist of fan-shaped groups of fine muscle fibres. Although these alary muscles are best developed in the abdominal segments, according to McIndoo[40, 41] they are found at boundaries between segments from the first to second thoracic, to the eighth to ninth abdominal, in *P.a.* (11 pairs). The alary muscles are arranged so that their fibres converge on a point near which the dorsal diaphragm meets the lateral wall of the tergum. Ford[21] describes the alary muscles together with the rest of the abdominal musculature, but their association with the cuticle is indirect, and they do not form part of any other series. The fibres run from the dorsal diaphragm to the sides of the heart.

The heart itself is very largely formed of a thin circular layer of delicate striated muscle fibres with strikingly large nuclei. This layer is the myocardium. In the abdomen there are segmental vessels, but these contain little or no muscle tissue.[40]

In the prothoracic and cervical region a short aorta can be seen and this passes forward into the head, and between the tritocerebral lobes of the brain expanding anteriorly into a large blood sac associated with the antennal pulsatile organs. The form of this system is complex, but the pulsatile vesicles are muscular sacs medial to the bases of the antennae and dilated by a comparatively large horizontal muscle. In frontal dissection this muscle has the appearance of a modified antennal muscle, and therefore it has been described together with the other skeletal muscles (muscle 7). For details of the anatomy of the antennal and cephalic pulsatile system, consult Pavlova.[48]

The remains of a very reduced ventral diaphragm comprising both a connective tissue lamella and a system of muscles is visible in *P.a.* It can be found overlying the nerve cord in the abdomen, but it does not extend very far laterally. The muscles comprise three or four bundles of longitudinal fibres on either side of the nerve cord, with a few transverse fibres. Rhythmic movements are absent, but small alterations in tension appear to control the depth of the blood space beneath. Nerve fibres seem to enter the diaphragmal musculature from the spiracular nerve root, but this was not determined with certainty.[26]

Some information on the fine structure of heart muscle has been provided by Edwards and Challice in *Bt.g.* Intercalated discs are present between the muscle cells of the myocardium as in vertebrate heart muscle. The plasmamembrane of the fibres is often deeply indented in association with the endoplasmic reticulum. Intracellular or interaxonal vesicles of several types could be seen, perhaps corresponding to transmitter or neurosecretory material. The ergastoplasm and mitochondria of the fibres are complex; the mitochondria are numerous and appear to be located between the myofilaments.[19]

The nervous control of heartbeat has been discussed elsewhere, but it is likely that cockroach heart contractions are largely myogenic.

The effect of differing ratios of ions on the heart beat has been examined by Ludwig, Tracey and Burns in *P.a.*, and there is other work bearing on this topic. Ludwig *et al.*, found that a wide range of ion ratios could be tolerated for some time, but the heart would beat with great regularity for 24 hr or more in a solution made up thus: (g/l.)—NaCl—11·0, KCl—1·4, $CaCl_2$—1·1. Na/K ratios between 3 and 30 are tolerated, but K/Ca ratios must be between 0·9 and 3·5. Thus the heart is much more sensitive to variations in the balance between K and Ca ions, than between Na and K.[37]

Acetylcholine accelerates the heart beat in *P.a.* and *B.o.*, and this occurs even at low concentrations ($2 \times 10^{-9}\%$). Naidu believes that this has a direct effect on the myocardium in *P.a.*,[47] while Metcalf Winton and Fukoto suggest that it is due to effects on the cardiac neurones of the lateral nerve.[46] Eserine potentiates, and atropine abolishes the effect of Ach.[34]

Nicotine arrests the heart of *P.a.* when applied in fairly high concentrations ($10^{-2}\%$), but lower concentrations (less than $2·5 \times 10-4\%$) tend to have an acceleratory effect. Adrenalin produces a temporary increase in the rate of beat, and the heart may then slow and stop altogether.[34]

Systole, diastole and diastasis (slow relaxation) phases can be distinguished in the cardiac cycle of *P.a.*[76] Electrical stimulation of the heart during the contraction cycles will produce extra systoles according to Yeager, and at a sufficiently high frequency a gradual summation and then smooth tetanus is produced. The alary muscles on the other hand although innervated are electrically inexcitable.[76] Information from other insect species (see Jones) suggest that the alary muscles of *P.a.* may be of the type which undergo only very slight shortening, perhaps as a direct response to tension exerted by the myocardium, and provide a source of controlled elasticity rather than contractual tension. Jones notes that the isolated heart never maintains the same rate as it does in the intact animal.[34]

Ralph obtained six factors from the corpora cardiaca–allata system which accelerated the heart, and five factors from the central nervous system which decelerated heart action. Another accelerator occurred in all neural structures.[56] Gersch *et al.*,[22, 23] and Unger[66] have isolated and characterized physiologically and chromatographically two substances (C and D) which are found in a number of nervous and endocrine structures. Both substances accelerate the heart of *B.o.*, but substance D may reduce heartbeat rate at high concentrations.

REFERENCES

1. BARRON, E. S. G. and TAHMISIAN, T. N. (1948). The metabolism of cockroach muscle. *J. cell. comp. Physiol.*
2. BECHT, G. (1959). Studies on insect muscles. *Bijdr. Dierk.*, **29**, 1–40.
3. BECHT, G. and DRESDEN, D. (1956). Physiology of the locomotory muscles in the cockroach. *Nature, Lond.*, **177**, 836–7.

4. BECHT, G., HOYLE, G. and USHERWOOD, P. N. R. (1960). Neuromuscular transmission in the coxal muscles of the cockroach. *J. Insect Physiol.*, **4**, 191–201.

5. BODENSTEIN, D. (1957). Studies on nerve regeneration in *Periplaneta americana*. *J. exp. Zool.*, **136**, 89–116.

6. CARBONELL, C. S. (1947). The thoracic muscles of the cockroach *P. americana* L. *Smithson misc. Collns.*, **107**, 1–23.

7. CAMERON, M. L. (1953). Secretion of an orthodiphenol in the corpus cardiacum of insects. *Nature, Lond.*, **172**, 349, 350.

8. CASE, J. F. (1957). The median nerves and cockroach spiracular function. *J. Insect Physiol.*, **1**, 85–94.

9. CHADWICK, L. E. (1953). The flight muscles and their control. In *Insect Physiology*, ed. ROEDER, K. D. John Wiley, New York.

10. CHADWICK, L. E. (1957). The ventral intersegmental muscles of cockroaches. *Smithson. misc. Collns.*, **131**, 1–30.

11. CHOPARD, L. (1950). Sur l'anatomie et le developpement d'une blatte vivipare. *8th Int. Congr., Stockholm*, 218–22.

12. COWDEN, R. R. and BODENSTEIN, D. (1961). A cytochemical investigation of striated muscle differentiation in regenerating limbs of the roach, *P.a. Embryologia*, **6**, 36–50.

13. DAVEY, K. G. (1962). The mode of action of the corpus cardiacum on the hindgut in *P.a. J. exp. Biol.*, **39**, 319–24.

14. DAVEY, K. G. and TREHERNE, J. E. (1964). Studies on crop function in the cockroach *P.a.* III. Pressure changes during feeding and crop emptying. *J. exp. Biol.*, **41**, 513–24.

15. DAVEY, K. G. (1964). The control of visceral muscles in insects. In *Advances in Insect Physiology*, **2**, 219–42.

16. DRESDEN, D. (1956). A technique for recording muscle contractions in an insect on a kymograph. *Nature, Lond.*, **177**, 835–6.

17. DRESDEN, D. and NIJENHUIS, E. D. (1952). On the anatomy and mechanism of motion of the mesothoracic leg of *P. americana*. *Verh. K. ned. Akad. Wet.*, (C), **56**, 39–47.

18. EDWARDS, G. A. (1959). Fine structure of a multi-terminal innervation of an insect muscle. *J. biophys. biochem. Cytol.*, **5**, 241–7.

19. EDWARDS, G. A. and CHALLICE, C. E. (1960). The ultrastructure of the heart of the cockroach. *Ann. ent. Soc. Am.*, **53**, 369–83.

20. EDWARDS, G. A., RUSKA, H. and DE HARVEN, E. (1958). *J. biophys. biochem. Cytol.*, **4**, 251–60.

21. FORD, NORMA (1923). A comparative study of the abdominal musculature of Orthopteroid insects. *Trans. R. Can. Inst.*, **14**, 207–319.

22. GERSCH, M., FISCHER, F., UNGER, H. and KOCH, H. (1960). Die Isolierung hormonaler factoren aus dem nervensystem der Kuchenschabe (*P.a.*). *Z. Naturf.*, **15**, 319–22.

23. GERSCH, M., FISCHER, F., UNGER, H. and KABITZA, W. (1961). Vorkommen von Serotonin in nervensystem von *Periplaneta americana*. *Z. Naturf.*, **16**, 361–51.

24. GRIFFITHS, J. T. and TAUBER, O. E. (1943). Effects of pH and of various concentrations of sodium, potassium and calcium chloride on muscular activity of the isolated crop of *P.a. J. gen. Physiol.*, **26**, 541–58.

25. GUPTA, P. D. (1948). On the structure development and homology of the female reproductive organs in orthopteroid insects. *Indian J. Ent.*, **10**, 75–123.

26. GUTHRIE, D. M. Unpublished observations.

27. GUTHRIE, D. M. Sound production and sound reception in a cockroach. *J. exp. Biol.*, **45**, 321–8.

28. HARTMANN, H. B. (1966). Stridulation by a cockroach during courtship behaviour. (In press. Communicated to me by Dr. L. M. Roth in whose laboratory this work was done.)

29. HOYLE, G. (1955). The effect of some common cations on neuromuscular transmission in insects. *J. Physiol.*, **127**, 90–103.
29b. HOYLE, G. (1965). The neural control of skeletal muscle. In *The Physiology of the Insecta*, ed. ROCKSTEIN. Academic Press, New York.
30. HOYLE, G. (1957). The nervous control of insect muscles. In *Recent Advances in Invertebrate Physiology*. U. Oregon Publications.
31. HUGHES, G. M. (1952). The coordination of insect movements. I. The walking movements of insects. *J. exp. Biol.*, **29**, 267–84.
32. HUGHES, G. M. (1957). The coordination of insects' movements. III. The effects of limb amputation and the cutting of commissures in the cockroach (*Blatta orientalis*). *J. exp. Biol.*, **34**, 306–33.
33. HUGHES, G. M. (1965). Locomotion: Terrestrial. In *The Physiology of the Insecta*, pp. 227–53, ed. ROCKSTEIN, Academic Press, New York and London.
34. JONES, J. C. (1965). The circulatory system of insects. *The Physiology of the Insecta*, ed. ROCKSTEIN, Academic Press, New York and London, 1–94.
35. KOOISTRA, G. (1950). Contribution to the knowledge of the action of acetylcholine in the intestine of *Periplaneta americana*. *Physiologia comp. Oecol.*, **2**, 75–80.
36. KOZHANCHIKOV, I. W. (1965). Cited in Jones.
37. LUDWIG, D., TRACEY, K. M. and BURNS, M. (1957). Ratio of ions required to maintain the heart beat of the American cockroach *Periplaneta americana*. *Ann. ent. Soc. Am.*, **50**, 244–52.
38. LAWSON, J. W. H. (see Chapter 9).
39. MCCONNELL, E. and RICHARDS, A. G. (1955). How fast can a cockroach run? *Bull. Brooklyn ent. Soc.*, **50**, 36–43.
40. MCINDOO, N. E. (1945). The innervation of the insect heart. *J. comp. Neurol.*, **83**, 141–55.
41. MCINDOO, N. E. (1939). The heart and lateral blood vessels of the cockroach. *J. morph.*, **65**, 323–47.
42. MCKITTRICK, F. A. (1964). Evolutionary studies of cockroaches. *Mem. Cornell Univ. agric. Exp. Stn*, **389**, 1–197.
43. MCSHAN, W. H., KRAMER, S. and SCHLEGEL, V. (1954). Oxidative enzymes in the thoracic muscles of *Leucophaea maderae*. *Biol. Bull.*, **106**, 341.
44. MAKI, T. (1938). Studies on the thoracic musculature of insects. *Man. Fac. Sci. Agr. Tainhoku. Imp. Univ.*, **24**, 1–343.
45. MANGAN, J. (1938). Cited by PRINGLE, J. W. S. *J. exp. Biol.*, **15**, 114–31.
46. METCALF, R. L., WINTON, N. Y. and FUKOTO, T. R. (1964). The effects of cholinergic substances upon the isolated heart of *Periplaneta americana*. *J. Insect Physiol.*, **10**, 353–61.
47. NAIDU, M. (1955). Physiological action of drugs and insecticides on insects. *Bull. ent. Res.*, **46**, 205–20.
48. PAVLOVA, M. (1895). Uber ampullenartige Blutzirkulationsorgane im Kopf verschiedener Orthopteren. *Zool. Anz.*, **18**, 7–13.
49. PEREZ-GONZALES, M. D. and EDWARDS, G. A. (1954). Metabolic differences among several specialized insect muscles. *Bolm. Fac. Filos. Cienc. Univ. S. Paulo*, **19**, 373–81.
50. PIPA, R. L., COOK, E. F. and RICHARDS, A. G. (1959). Studies on the hexapod nervous system. I. The peripheral distribution of the thoracic nerves of the adult cockroach, *P.a. Ann. ent. Soc. Am.*, **52**, 695–710.
51. PRINCIS, K. and KEVAN, D. K. MCE. (1955). Cockroaches from Trinidad, B.W.I., with a few records from other parts of the Caribbean. *Opusc. Ent.*, **20**, 149–69.
52. PRINGLE, J. W. S. (1939). The motor mechanism of the insect leg. *J. exp. Biol.*, **16**, 220–31.
53. PRINGLE, J. W. S. (1940). The reflex mechanism of the insect leg. *J. exp. Biol.*, **17**, 8–17.

9*

54. PRINGLE, J. W. S. (1957). *Insect Flight.* University Press, Cambridge.

55. PROSSER, C. L. *et al.* (1952). *Comparative Physiology.* Saunders, New York.

56. RALPH, C. L. (1962). Heart accelerators and decelerators in the nervous systems of *P.a. J. Insect Physiol.*, **8** (7/8), 431–9.

57. RICHARDS, A. G. (1963). The effect of temperature on wing-beat frequency in the male of the cockroach, *P.a. Ent. News*, **74**, 4, 91–4.

58. ROEDER, K. D. (1951). Orthopteran flight. *Biol. Bull.*, **100**, 95–106.

59. ROTH, L. M. and DATEO, G. P. (1966). A pheromone in *Nauphoeta cinerea. J. Insect Physiol.*, **12**, 255–62.

60. ROTH, L. M. and WILLIS, E. R. (1960). Biotic associations of cockroaches. *Smithson misc. Collns.*, **141**, 1–470.

61. SMITH, D. S. (1961). The structure of insect fibrillar flight muscle. *J. biophys. biochem. Cytol.*, **10** suppl., 123–58.

62. SMITH, D. S. (1962). Cytological studies of some insect muscles. *Revue can. Biol.*, **21**, 279–301.

63. SMYTH, T. and HOYLE, G. (1965). Cited in ROCKSTEIN (ed.), The neural control of skeletal muscle. *The Physiology of Insecta*, ed. ROCKSTEIN. Academic Press, New York.

64. SNODGRASS, R. E. (1935). *Principles of Insect Morphology.* Mcgraw-Hill, New York and Maidenhead.

65. TIEGS, O. W. (1955). Flight muscles of insects. *Phil. Trans. R. Soc. B.*, **238**, 221–52.

66. UNGER, H. (1957). Untersuchungen zur neurohormonalen Beeinflussung der herztätigkeit bei Schaben. *Biol. Zbl.*, **76**, 204–25.

67. UNNA, P. G. (1946). Method for preparing leuco-methylene blue. In *Notes on Microscopical Techniques for Zoologists.* PANTIN, C. F. A. University Press, Cambridge.

68. USHERWOOD, P. N. R. (1962). The action of the alkaloid ryanodine on insect skeletal muscle. *J. comp. Biochem. Physiol.*, **6**, 181–99.

69. USHERWOOD, P. N. R. (1962). The nature of 'slow' and 'fast' contractions in the coxal muscles of the cockroach. *J. Insect Physiol.*, **7**, 31–52.

70. USHERWOOD, P. N. R. (1963). Spontaneous miniature potentials from insect muscle fibres. *J. Physiol.*, **169**, 149–60.

71. VOSSELER, J. (1907). Beobachtungen uber Ouest-afrikanischen Insekten. *Ent. Z.*, **5**, 527–32.

72. WEIANT, E. (1965). Cited in HOYLE; The neural control of skeletal muscle. In *The Physiology of the Insecta.* ed. ROCKSTEIN. Academic Press, New York and London.

73. WILLE, J. (1920). Biologie und Bekampfung der Deutschen Schabe, *B.g. Monogrn angew. Ent., Z. augern Ent.*, **1** (7), 1–140.

74. WILSON, D. M. (1966). Insect walking. *A. Rev. Ent.*, **11**, 103–22.

75. WILSON, V. J. (1954). Slow and fast responses in cockroach leg muscle. *J. exp. Biol.*, **31**, 280–90.

76. YEAGER, J. F. (1939). Stimulation of the isolated heart in the cockroach. *J. agric. Res.*, **59**, 59–121.

77. YEAGER, J. F. and HAGER, A. (1934). The cockroach heart. *Iowa St. Coll. J. Sci.*, **8**, 391–5.

78. ZACWILICHOWSKI, J. (1934). Über die Innervierung und die Sinnesorgane der Flügel von *Bt.g. Bull. int. Acad. Sci. Lett. Cracovie*, B., **2**, 89–104.

79. ZIMMERMAN, E. C. (1961). Cited in ROTH and WILLIS. See above.

ADDENDUM

Muscles

Shankland has recently described the muscles of the pregenital abdominal segments in *P.a.* This paper came too late to hand to be used as the basis for the relevant section of this book, but the description of the musculature seems to agree fairly closely with the one given here. Shankland's enumeration runs from 1 onwards, rather than trying to continue the thoracic series. This paper should be consulted by anyone working in this area.

Research on the fine structure and physiology of the muscles of other animals has suggested that invertebrate muscles, including those of insects, may contain slow and fast muscle fibres in addition to the terminations of 'slow' and 'fast' motor axons. The unguitractor muscle of the locust is probably a muscle of this kind, according to Usherwood, and it is likely that similar muscles occur in the cockroach, thus contradicting the basic theory of muscle uniformity elaborated earlier.

Guthrie has recently published some information on the pattern of re-innervation of the tibial depressor (muscle 143) which appears to receive 5 'fast' axons, 2 'slow' axons and an inhibitory axon. Unpublished work by Pearson and Bergman promises to throw much more light on the peripheral inhibitory axon of the cockroach. They have shown that it is a common inhibitor, as in Crustacea, and is capable of completely reducing slow contractions. As many as 80% of the fibres receive inhibitory and slow axons in muscle 182C and D.

The role of glutamic acid as the major transmitter at the excitatory nerve-muscle synapse in locusts is strongly supported by recent work by Usherwood, and was suggested earlier by Kerkut, Shapira and Walker using the cockroach leg muscle preparation.

ADDITIONAL REFERENCES

GUTHRIE, D. M. (1967). The regeneration of Motor axons in an Insect. *J. Insect Physiol.*, **13**, 1593–1611.

KERKUT, G. A., SHAPIRA, A. and WALKER, R. J. (1965). The effect of acetylcholine, glutamic acid and GABA on the contractions of the perfused cockroach leg. *Comp. biochem. Physiol.*, **16**, 37–48.

KERKUT, G. A. and WALKER, R. J. (1966). The effects of L. glutamate, acetylcholine and GABA on the miniature end plate potentials and contractures of the coxal muscles of the cockroach, *P.a. Comp. Biochem. Physiol.*, **17**, 435–54.

PEARSON, K. G. and BERGMAN, S. J. (Personal communication.)

ROTH, L. M. and HARTMAN, H. B. (1967). Sound production and its evolutionary significance in Blatteria. *Ann. ent. Soc. Amer.*, **60**, 740–52.

SHANKLAND, D. L. (1965). Nerves and muscles of the pregenital abdominal segments of the American cockroach *Periplaneta americana. J. Morph.*, **117**, 353–70.

USHERWOOD, P. N. R. (1967). Personal communication.

11 *The alimentary canal and nutrition*

The anatomy of the gut

The alimentary canal in cockroaches begins at the mouth, includes the pharynx, and ends at the anus with a sphincter muscle. Two salivary glands open into the pharynx and the mid-gut has eight digestive diverticula or hepatic caeca attached to its anterior end. The hind-gut consists of the ileum, colon and rectum, the last possessing 'glands'. The gizzard may be called the proventriculus and the mid-gut the ventriculus (T).

In *P.a.* the total length of the gut is 6·7 cm,[98] and the pharynx joins to the oesophagus in the posterior or dorsal part of the head. It has many external dilator muscles and its internal surface is smooth. The junction with the oesophagus is thick and muscular[9] and a sphincter is present which can close the lumen at this point.[19]

The oesophagus is normally closed by its internal folds[98] and extends as far back as the posterior part of the prothorax, where it leads into the crop, and internally it is irregularly grooved and ridged.[9] Its wall is a layer of cuboidal cells, between which lie muscle cell processes and tracheal cells, and within is a chitinous intima with small projections, on the tips of which are fine bristles. Externally there is a layer of circular muscle.[98]

Dorsal to the oesophagus lies the fused part of the salivary glands and alongside it lie the rest of the glands and the two reservoirs, which extend back as far as the mesothorax. The reservoirs have an intima similar to that of the trachea,[9] and there are two kinds of cells present in the secretory acini of the gland (Figs. 11.1, 11.2). The first is usually filled with secretory granules and the endoplasmic reticulum is prominent in electronmicrographs during the formation of secretion. The second, or parietal, cell is less common and has an intracellular duct lined with many microvilli. Few secretory granules are found in these cells, but mitochondria, multivesicular bodies and coarse endoplasmic reticulum are noticeable. The intercellular ducts are lined with chitin, but the plasma membrane adjacent to them has many small infoldings into the cell associated with large numbers of mitochondria. These ducts may be more than simply conduits.[60, 61]

The crop is large and is used for storing food.[9] It has a wall of four layers: a chitinous intima, an epithelium and circular and longitudinal muscle layers.[98] The intima of the stomodeum and gizzard in *B.o.* is stated to arise not as a secreted chitinous layer, but as a peculiar transformation, called 'cuticularization' of the apical parts of the epithelial cells.[1]

The gizzard is conical and 3·5 mm long. It can be divided into two halves,

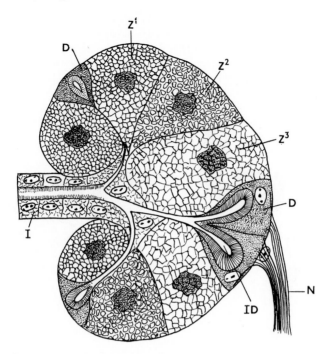

FIG. 11.1   Semi-diagrammatic section of acinus of salivary gland of *Periplaneta*.
I—intercalated duct, Z^1–Z^3—zymogenic cells in phases of secretion, D—ductule-
containing cell, ID—intra-cellular ductule, N—nerve. (From Day[24])

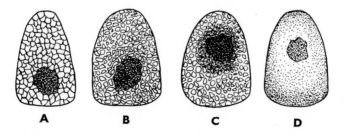

FIG. 11.2   **A–D** = phases in secretion of zymogenic cells. **A**, regenerating or non-
secreting phase. Note acidophilic, finely vacuolate cytoplasm. **B**, early secreting
phase. Cytoplasm granular and intensely basophilic. **C**, late secreting phase. Baso-
philia partly replaced by acidophilic cytoplasm. **D**, excreting phase. Cytoplasm
completely acidophilic. (Redrawn, from Day[24])

anterior and posterior. The anterior part bears internally six large sclerotized teeth which project into the lumen and are shaped so that at rest their tips fit together. Two pairs of teeth are mirror images of each other; those of the third pair are not.[59] Sanford stated that there are smaller teeth with short spines lying between the six large ones,[98] but Judd maintains that there are only three finely setose parallel folds in the channels between them.[59] The fit of the teeth is so close that they prevent the movement of food from the crop. They are held closed by circular muscle. The teeth are opened by the action of opposed longitudinal muscles (Fig. 11.3).[19]

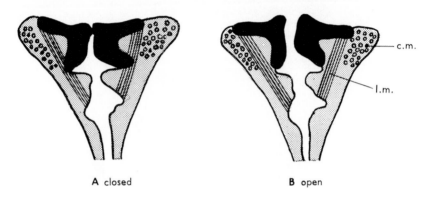

A closed   B open

FIG. 11.3 Diagrammatic representation of the proventricular valve in the open and closed positions. c.m.—circular muscle; l.m.—longitudinal muscle. (From Davey and Treherne[19])

External to the chitinous layer is a layer of columnar epithelial cells, and these are surrounded by connective tissue with many fine tracheae. Outside these there is a thick layer of circular muscle.[98]

In the posterior half of the gizzard there are pulvilli or 'cushions' covered with setae arranged as an anterior group and as a posterior group, with smaller ones between them (Fig. 11·4).[59] The anterior cushions carry larger 'spines' which are inserted into sockets.[98] Posteriorly the gizzard projects as a narrow tube 2–3 mm long into the mid-gut. This may be a valvular mechanism,[8] but it is also used in the regurgitation of mid-gut enzymic fluid into the crop for digestion there. It may also be used to close the fore-gut when air is swallowed by the nymph to inflate itself during moulting. It is not likely to be concerned in forming the peritrophic membrane since it is too far from the mid-gut wall.[25]

The diameter of each digestive diverticulum or caecum is about one third that of the mid-gut and the lengths of the caeca vary with the amount of food eaten. The outer layer of the mid-gut is a loose network of muscle fibres and the luminal border of the epithelial cells bears very fine filaments projecting into the lumen. Older cells are replaced by newer ones developing from the epithelium, which is folded forming the crypts of Frenzel between small villi-like structures. These are not for secretion but for the efficient regeneration of the epithelial cells. A

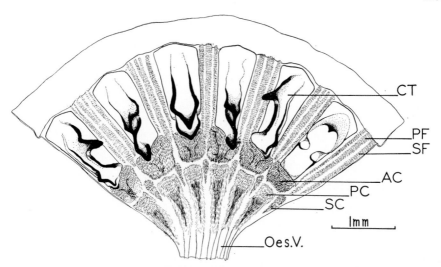

FIG. 11.4 Sclerotized intima of proventriculus of *Periplaneta americana*. Teeth (CT) numbered from left to right, 1, 2, 3, 4, 5, 6. AC—anterior cushion, Oes. V.— oesophageal valve, PC—posterior cushion, PF—primary fold, SC—secondary cushion, SF—secondary fold. (From Judd[59])

membrane lining the wall of the mid-gut is said to be shed at intervals. The caeca have a similar histological structure to the mid-gut.

Posterior to the mid-gut is a very short ileum, or small intestine, with a narrow lumen, thin epithelium, and a chitinous intima bearing short spines. Externally there is a coat of irregular muscle fibres.

The ileum leads into the colon, with an epithelium of long narrow cells in more or less regular folds, over which lies the chitinous layer. This is not setose.

The rectum has a thin muscle layer, and its glands are groups of very long cells bulging into the lumen. A distinct chitinous intima is present.[98]

THE PERITROPHIC MEMBRANE

At the junction of the gizzard and the mid-gut, the peritrophic membrane is formed by a ring of specialized endodermal epithelial cells. It is produced continuously and ends in the anterior part of the hind-gut, where it is torn up by the internal spines. There is considerable disagreement at present as to its detailed structure and mode of action. Some colloidal substances can pass through it and others cannot, and in general this is related to particle size. Nevertheless, some substances which can diffuse easily in gelatine do not pass through the peritrophic membrane and vice versa, and in carnivorous and omnivorous insects larger particles pass through the peritrophic membrane than in herviborous kinds.[80] It is not disputed that it is permeable to some extent, but the problem is to clarify just what are the properties of this permeability.[57] It may be that the epithelial cells also play a major rôle in selective permeability.[80] In *B.o.* it is said to be encrusted with calcium salts or carbohydrates which are responsible for its permeability characteristics.

The nature of the peritrophic membrane is not known but its structure has been described from phase-contrast and electron microscopy. It seems to be of several layers, orientated at random in *B.o.* Each layer is a network of thicker fibrils embedded in a thinner layer of amorphous ground substance. These areas of thinner ground substance between the fibrils, of about 0·08 μ diameter, are supposed to be the sites of diffusion.[57] The fibrils are about 100 Å in diameter.[122]

In a recent investigation Lee found that the peritrophic membrane of *P.a.* was produced in several layers, the main layer being produced by the most anterior cells of the mid-gut epithelium. Other layers are formed by cells of the mid-gut epithelium more posteriorly, and cells at the bases of the caeca secrete more material which is incorporated into the membrane. There is evidence of chitin synthesis in the formation of the peritrophic membrane, from an acid mucopolysaccharide produced as granules in the cells forming the peritrophic membrane.[69]

Electronmicrographs of saliva deposited on the screen of the instrument show, in about 25% of the attempts, a structure very like that of the peritrophic membrane. The fibril pattern is probably of chitin and usually shows up as three systems of parallel strands at 60° to each other, giving a regular hexagonal array. The ground substance is probably protein. The regular array suggests the deposition of the layers by similarly regular secretory cells. Sometimes the arrays are irregular,[79] but it should be remembered that the electron beam tends to break down such a delicate membrane.[57] The membrane found in the saliva is said to be peritrophic membrane and to have come from the mid-gut by regurgitation.[79]

The movement of the gut

Peristalsis and antiperistalsis occur in the crop of *P.a.* and there are also contractions confined to the posterior one-third of the crop.[44] The crop activity is greater in the male than in the female.[44,45] The activity of the crop does not require the central nervous system to be intact, in contrast to the gizzard, although both are innervated by the visceral nervous system.[20,44] The tonus, amplitude, frequency and co-ordination of the contractions of the hind-gut of *P.a.* are affected by the secretion by the anterior part of the colon of indolalkylamine acting via the peripheral nerves, the secretion being provoked by a factor released by the corpora cardiaca,[18] although peristalsis of the fore-gut is inhibited.[12]

Contraction of the muscles of the fore-gut of *P.a.* causes elongation and the application of iodoacetic acid makes the fore-gut lengthen by such contraction.[82]

The factors affecting the emptying of the crop and the activity of the gizzard are complex and have been shown to depend on the osmotic pressure of the ingested fluid, the frequency of opening of the valve of the gizzard teeth, the duration of each opening of the valve, changes in the size of the opening, and differences in pressure between the crop and the mid-gut[19,20,21,118] but do not depend much on the viscosity of the ingested material.[19] The nervous system is concerned in the activity of both crop and gizzard, and sensory receptors in the pharynx are thought to be osmoreceptors monitoring the concentration of the food intake.[20]

The emptying of the crop after a feed occurs in an exponential manner, as does the frequency of opening of the valve; but there is no simple correlation between the two.[19] Other factors are involved such as pressure changes. It is found that there is a positive pressure in the crop and negative pressure in the mid-gut, i.e. a hydrostatic gradient from crop to mid-gut. The value of this pressure difference also declines exponentially with time after feeding. At the same time it can be deduced that there must be a corresponding increase in either the duration of the opening of the gizzard valve or its diameter or both. The precise details of this are not yet known.[21] The true volume of the crop does not vary very much with filling and emptying because the unoccupied volume is filled by a variable amount of air.[19,21] The time taken for the crop to lose half an ingested meal ranges from 2 hr for distilled water to 13 hr for 2 M glucose solution,[19] or even longer in some cases.[98]

A similar relation was found between the rate of crop emptying and the absorption of tripalmitin in *P.a.*, suggesting that it is the rate of leaving the crop which limits the absorption of fat rather than the rate of its uptake in the mid-gut.[119]

Secretory mechanisms

The digestive diverticula and the mid-gut are the chief secretory and absorptive regions of the gut, and in *P.a.* they are said to contain both secretory and absorptive cells[103] in separate groups.[98] However, old cells are said to contain both food and secretory granules.[110] In *B.o.* the secretory cells are said to be mainly in the anterior part of the mid-gut and in the diverticula, while the absorptive cells are chiefly in the posterior part of the mid-gut. The secretory cells degenerate after a time and the younger cells which replace them are thought to be absorptive at first.[43] Old cells are also found to degenerate and to be squeezed out by new ones developing in their place in *P.a.*[98,112] Secretory cells of the mid-gut and caeca of *B.o.* have many microvilli at their luminal border. They have mitochondria with irregular cristae. Absorptive cells occur in groups amongst the secretory cells, and are in general like them. Their mitochondria may contain a clear vacuole-like space inside them, and may be typical of the degenerating cells. Each of the replacement cells has an irregular large nucleus and many mitochondria.[117]

It is not certain by what means the secretion passes from the cells to the gut lumen, but it is reported that secretory granules pass out of the cells of the mid-gut epithelium by merocrine action after one month's starvation,[110] and the secretion is said to be released as small sacs from the epithelial cells in *P.a.*[98] and in *B.o.* Indeed, in *B.o.* Gresson states a cell may discharge a vesicle containing secretory granules more than once before it degenerates and that such a vesicle may be seen free in the lumen of the gut.[43] On the other hand, most workers think that in *P.a.* the secretion diffuses out, without any apical extrusions or globuli being formed,[111] and that many apparent extrusions are the result of poor fixation of the material.[112] Day and Powning, working mainly with *Bt.g.*, present a picture of the activity of the mid-gut epithelium in which the epithelial cells grow from nidi or centres each of several immature cells. As the cells age they move laterally away from their nidus, gradually degenerate and are eventually pushed out into the lumen of the gut in the form of globules of cytoplasm. The epithelial cells begin to secrete and absorb as soon as they are mature and reach the luminal surface of the epithelium (Fig. 11.5).[25]

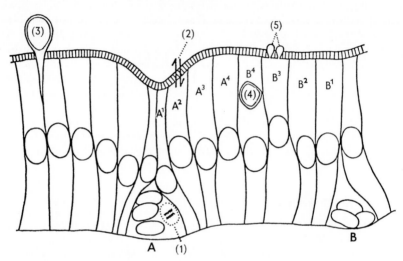

FIG. 11.5   Diagram of epithelium of *Blattella* midgut showing the sequence of changes occurring from the origin of the cells in the nidi A and B, to degeneration (3). A^1–A^4 and B^1–B^4 represent cells of increasing age, which have originated from regenerative nidus A and regenerative nidus B, respectively; (1), a mitotic figure; (2) indicates that secretion of digestive enzymes and absorption occur in the same epithelial cell; (3), the final stage in cell degeneration showing extrusion of nucleus and adherent cytoplasm; (4), a cytoplasmic granule in an old cell; (5), cytoplasmic globules in process of being expelled through the striated border. (From Day and Powning[25])

    The groups of long cells found in the epithelium of the mid-gut and caeca of *P.a.* are older cells, and mixed up with them are younger cells growing at their bases. Sometimes the younger cells squeeze the base of the older cell and displace the nucleus apically, but no nuclear extrusion is seen.[111]

    The mitochondria of the mature epithelial cells of the mid-gut of *P.a.* are filamentous and rod-shaped, but those of degenerating cells are granular.[103] In *B.o.* the mitochondria are filamentous and granular in both secretory and absorptive cells of the mid-gut and caeca, but the Golgi apparatus is close to the nucleus in the secretory cells, and nearer to the lumen in the absorptive cells.[43] There are no glands in the wall of the fore-gut of *B.o.* and no secretion of enzymes.[26]

DIGESTION

The movement of food through the gut

Experiments with banana paste mixed with carmine particles showed that after fasting for 2 days the food eaten by *P.a.* reached the caeca of the mid-gut within half an hour, the end of the mid-gut in 2 hr, the end of the colon in 8 hr and the end of the rectum in 20 hr. These are average times with a range of 9 to 33 hr, but the food was in the rectum for more than half its total time in the gut. The food used was soft and required no grinding but nevertheless the speed of its movement through the crop was surprising,[106, 107] especially as the crop is said to be capable of storing a large meal for up to 2 months and to be able to store more than enough for 2 months' supply.[98] No differences were found in the times taken by the food to pass through the gut in males, females or nymphs,[107] but the rate of its passage was slowed down by the presence in the crop, of food eaten previously.[106] The gizzard sphincter may retain the food in the fore-gut and withhold it from the mid-gut for several days.[98] In *B.o.* digestion is said to take up to 4 days,[101] and in *Bt.g.* after a 2-day fast starch reached the mid-gut within 10 min and the rectum in 5 hr.[25] Cysts of *Giardia* sp. reached the colon of *P.a.* in 2–3 hr,[136] and food is said to take 6 to 48 hr to pass from the crop to the mid-gut.[74]

Some experiments studying the passage of glucose through the gut of *P.a.* have shown that the rate at which it passes from the crop depends upon its osmotic pressure, the greater the concentration the slower its release into the mid-gut. The reason for this seems to be to keep down the concentration of glucose in the mid-gut, and the rate of emptying is probably the limiting factor in glucose absorption.[118] A similar situation is true for fat also, since the rate of absorption of fatty acids and fats is dependent on the rate at which they are allowed to leave the crop.[119, 120]

Conditions within the gut—pH and redox potential

Much of the acidity found in the crop of *Bt.g.* and *P.a.* is the result of the action of the yeasts and bacteria present there, on sugars, especially glucose, in the food. Thus the pH is to some extent dependent on the diet, but in *Bt.g.* the average pH is 5·2;[128, 131] after feeding on carbohydrates it is 4·8,[128] after glucose 4·6, after starch 5·5[131] and after protein 6·2.[128, 131] The pH of the mid-gut is more constant in *Bt.g.*, perhaps due to rapid absorption of sugar in this region, and averages 6·2, but after feeding on starch it is 6·3 and after protein 6·4. The pH of the saliva of this cockroach is 6·9.[128] In *P.a.* the pH of the colon determined by indicators averages 7·3 (females) and 7·4 (males). With glass electrodes the pH averages 7·7 in both males and females.

The redox potential decreases from fore-gut to hind-gut in *Bt.g.*, but in the rectum it increases again. The higher values and less reducing conditions in the crop and rectum are presumably due to the richer tracheation of these regions of this insect.[25] In *P.a.* too there is a gradient from the crop to the colon. Using indicators the average values were $+150$ mV in the crop to -120 mV in the colon; using Pt-Ir electrodes the values for the colon averaged -170 mV, but the range found was from -84 to -241 mV.[121]

Digestion of carbohydrates

The saliva contains amylase[26,101] and invertase but no lactase in *B.o.*,[26] amylase and invertase in *Bt.g.*,[25,129] cellulase[126,127] and amylase but not invertase in *P.a.*[24,25,129] and in *Leucophaea maderae* it acted on cellulose,[127] starch, α-glucosides, cellobiose and lactose.[28] The salivary amylase of *B.o.* degraded starch to achroodextrins.[26]

In the mid-gut and caeca, amylase is reported from *B.o.*,[26,116] *Bt.g.* and *P.a.*;[129] maltase from *B.o.*,[26] *Bt.g.* and *P.a.*;[129] invertase from *B.o.*,[26,116] *Bt.g.* and *P.a.*;[129] glycosidase from *B.o.*;[26] lactase from *Bt.g.* and *P.a.*;[129] and β-glucosidase from *P.a.*, reported to hydrolyse cellobiose and salicin,[83] which is probably not of importance in the metabolism of the animal.[27] No lactase was found in *B.o.*[26,116] nor cellulase in either *B.o.*[26] or *Blaberus craniifer*.[3] However, recent investigation has demonstrated significant amounts of cellulase in the saliva and intestine of many cockroaches including *P.a.*, *B.o.*, *Blaberus craniifer* and *Leucophaea maderae*, but not *Bt.g.*[126] The enzyme detected in the gut is derived from the intestinal microorganisms.[127]

Maltase, invertase, amylase and many other enzymes have been found in the crop of different cockroaches, but they are derived from the saliva or from the mid-gut by regurgitation.[101,116,129,130] An unidentified substance in wheat bran is said to encourage the production of enzymes by the caeca and mid-gut and their regurgitation into the crop.[101] Maltase, invertase and lipase have been found in the cells of the fore-gut of *P.a.* and they may be in the process of being secreted or absorbed.[116]

The optimum pH for the amylase of *Bt.g.* is 5·9, for the invertase and maltase 5·0–6·2, and for the lactase 5·0–6·4. Thus the enzymes digesting carbohydrates work at the pH usually found in the crop.[129] These figures are largely confirmed by Day and Powning, who found in *Bt.g.* that the optimum pH for the amylase and the invertase was about 6.[25] Most fructose in the diet of *P.a.* is converted to glucose in the mid-gut before it is absorbed, and as it is never found in the caeca it is thought this conversion takes place very rapidly.[91]

Digestion of fats

Lipase is found in the crop, mid-gut and caeca of *B.o.*[26,116] and in *P.a.*[29,98,119] and in the epithelial cells of the mid-gut and hind-gut of *Bt.g.* but not in the crop epithelium.[25] The lipase found in the crop is there by regurgitation[29,119,130] and in *B.o.* it is inhibited by NaF and $MgCl_2$. The optimum pH of the lipase in *Bt.g.* is 8 and therefore it cannot be very active in the crop.[130,131] In *P.a.* a large percentage of triolein and tripalmitin fed to the cockroaches remained un-hydrolyzed and the fatty acids produced may be responsible for the slowing down of the enzyme action.[29,119] Nevertheless, after a few hours tripalmitin reached the mid-gut and was absorbed, but it is not certain whether or not it was rapidly hydrolyzed by the lipase which is secreted by the mid-gut and caeca.[119]

The rate of lipolysis is higher in well-fed than in starved animals.[29] After partial hydrolysis the crop content of fat and fatty acids are allowed to pass gradually into the mid-gut.[119]

Digestion of proteins

Pepsin has not been found in cockroaches,[116,130] but erepsin and trypsin are said to occur in the mid-gut, caeca and hind-gut of *B.o.*,[116] as well as a proteinase in the saliva,[26] which may be produced by the zymogen cells of the salivary glands.[61] The protease of the mid-gut of *Bt.g.* and *P.a.* is very similar to mammalian trypsin. It has the same optical density[93] and a similar activity (μ value $= 15{,}000$–$16{,}000$),[70] but it is not inhibited by ovomucoid as mammalian trypsin is[93] and its pH range is wider, extending on the acid side.[93,130] Its optimum pH with gelatine is 8·4 at 37°, and it is not affected by enterokinase.[93] In the mid-gut there are di- and tripeptidases with a pH optimum of 8·5.[130] In *B.o.* the proteinase found has the same activity and pH optimum as mammalian trypsin, but no activator has been discovered. It is strongest in the crop, but it is regurgitated to the crop from the mid-gut and caeca. Dipeptidases are also present, the activity increasing the more posterior is the region of gut studied. This suggests an enzyme chain for protein digestion, especially as an amino-peptidase, and a carboxypeptidase have been detected also.[101] The optimum pH for the proteinase of *P.a.* and *Bt.g.* is about 8, and in *P.a.* much proteinase activity occurs in the crop when it is full, but when it is empty the activity decreases to about one tenth of the maximum. Proteinase occurs in the mid-gut and caeca of *P.a.*, and in *Bt.g.* its activity is the same in both sexes.[25] The proteinase of *P.a.* is an endopeptidase;[120] no collagenase is found in *Periplaneta*.[122]

Digestion of other foods

The gut of *Blaberus craniifer* contains amylase, α- and β-glucosidases, α-fructofuranosidase and α- and β-galactosidases.[3] The β-glucosidase found in the caeca of this roach is probably an enzyme with an active sulphydryl group and it is said to attack all β-glucosides.[32] In *P.a.* the gut contains a β-glucosidase and a different β-N-acetylglucosaminidase.[94] The latter is probably the 'chitinase' reported from the gut and saliva of *P.a.*[96,123,124] which has an optimum pH of 5·4 to 6·0.[123] The mid-gut and caeca have the highest activity of the gut and liberate 70 μg N-acetylglucosamine per ml. of digestive juice, while the saliva liberates 870 μg N-acetylglucosamine per ml. The activity of the gut is not due to the micro-organisms present.[124] In *P.a.* hyaluronidase is present[114,115] which may be involved in the permeability of the peritrophic membrane or the gut wall[114] or in the digestion of hyaluronic acid in the diet.[115]

The saliva also contains mucoid substances,[23,24] which may be an enzyme precursor, and the cytoplasm of the zymogen cells of the glands passes through a secretory cycle, being first very basophilic, but later acidophilic. The secretion passes into ductules which may contribute substances to the saliva.[24]

Mucoid substances are not found in the mid-gut of cockroaches but they are abundant in the striated border of its epithelial cells.[23]

An alkaline phosphatase is known to occur in the fore-gut and hind-gut of *Bt.g.*,[22, 25] with an optimum pH of 5·0, being strongly concentrated in the circular muscles at the anterior end of the mid-gut. Its functional significance is not clear, but it is in this region of the wall of the mid-gut that a concentration of glycogen also occurs, in amounts which remain more or less constant even in starvation or with different kinds of diet. The glycogen is found with a characteristic distribution in the cells lying just apical of the nuclei and in the striated border.[25]

It seems probable that in *Bt.g.* sterol esters are hydrolyzed in the gut[84] and enzymes for sterol esterification are most concentrated in the mid-gut and caeca.[13] Unfortunately, the presence of the micro-organisms of the gut complicates the study of sterol metabolism,[40] but the hydrolyzed esters are believed to reform after absorption.[84, 85] Several esterases have been found in the gut.[15]

No enzyme inhibitors are known to occur in the gut or Malpighian tubules of *B.o.*, yet the digestive enzymes entering the hind-gut disappear,[101, 116] but by what means is not known.[101]

The activities and quantities of the enzymes in the gut are affected by the food eaten by the cockroach[25, 101] and the process of digestion itself also affects them. Digestion greatly increases the concentrations of proteinase and amylase in *B.o.*, and to a lesser extent the lipase, but not the other enzymes. Feeding with white bread reduced the general level of proteinase and amylase but addition of peptone caused both to increase, although no increase in peptidases was found. No adaptation of the enzymes to a diet of white bread and wheat bran was found even after 8 weeks, and the animal is not able to alter its digestive juices to be most suitable for all the foods eaten. This is true of *Bt.g.* also, and during starvation of this cockroach the titre of enzymes decreased. As in *B.o.*, too,[101] the activity of an enzyme tended to be reduced in *Bt.g.* when its diet contained a large proportion of the substrate of that enzyme. Feeding after a period of starvation caused an increase in some of the enzymes in *Bt.g.*[25]

Absorption

Most of the products of digestion are absorbed in the mid-gut and caeca,[116] while water and salts are absorbed by the hind-gut and particularly by the rectal glands.[116, 120] Gresson thought that the anterior part of the mid-gut of *B.o.* was mainly secretory and the posterior part mainly absorptive[43] but Day and Powning considered that different substances were absorbed in different regions of the gut of an insect and the same substance was absorbed in different regions of the gut in different species. The mid-gut epithelial cells are short-lived, but when they are mature enough to reach the lumen of the gut, they begin to secrete and absorb without visible changes taking place.[25]

In *P.a.* almost all the glucose is absorbed from the caeca.[91, 118, 120] If the concentration of glucose in the gut in *P.a.* is high, the amount in the haemolymph rises, as does the amount of trehalose. The production of trehalose may reduce back diffusion into the gut. Fructose is absorbed in this roach more slowly than glucose.[120]

The absorption of fat is not so clearly understood as the absorption of carbohydrates. The crop in *P.a.* is said to digest fats, the maximum rate being about two days after feeding on the fat, and to absorb and store the fat droplets in the epithelial cells. The tracheal end cells are also said to absorb fatty substances from the crop.[98] In *Leucophaea maderae* the cells of the fore-gut, mid-gut and caeca contain much fat, and the fore-gut is said to be important in fat absorption. The hind-gut cells contain little fat.[100] In *P.a.* the absorption of triolein occurred from the crop to some extent and was enhanced by the presence of a small proportion of long chain fatty acids. They reduced the viscosity of the fat and hastened its appearance in the cells of the crop epithelium.[29] The absorption of tripalmitin, however, occurred only from the anterior part of the mid-gut and the caeca [119] and the fat droplets in the crop epithelium of this roach cannot be translocated.[120] It is remarkable that fat droplets can occur in the blood, and the epithelia of the crop and mid-gut of *B.o.* even when no fat is present in the diet [102] and 6·2% of the dry weight of whole body of *P.a.* is fat.[11] The glycerol fraction of digested fat is almost certainly not absorbed by the crop in *P.a.*[118,120]

It is not known whether proteins have to be wholly degraded to amino acids before absorption can take place.[25]

In *Bt.g.* and *P.a.*, ascorbic acid is absorbed in the mid-gut and caeca, and ferric iron absorption occurs only in one region of the hind-gut.[25]

Transaminases occur in the rectum of *P.a.*[16]

Water is absorbed from the hind-gut and rectum of *Bt.g.*,[132] and from the mid-gut also in *P.a.*[36]

NUTRITION AND NUTRITIONAL REQUIREMENTS

There are several important conditions to be fulfilled before any results from nutrition experiments can be accepted and utilized (T). The first of these is that the physical features of the food and its surroundings—its texture, position, the light intensity etc.—are suitable [4] and that it is attractive to the experimental animal; extracts of natural food enhance this.[71] The second is that sampling techniques and numbers are adequate, especially where different numbers of males and females are used in experiments whose results are to be compared.[52] The diet used to discover essential nutrients must be minimal and therefore it must be suboptimal, and it cannot be assumed that the nutrients are not interconvertible.[42] The presence of the oötheca in the brood sac of *Leucophaea maderae* suppresses feeding, but when the eggs are being produced, the female eats more than usual.[30]

The cockroach *Bt.g.* is three times as efficient as a pig in converting food into flesh, but even so it eats three times as much food as its increase in weight.[76] During starvation it utilizes many of the non-nitrogenous constituents of its body, but the metabolism of proteins is very limited.[90] On a synthetic diet, *Bt.g.* and *B.o.* can be stopped from growing but on returning to the normal diet they begin to grow again, the rate being the same as it was just before the beginning of the standstill period. This may happen even after a period as long as the entire nymphal period, and ends in normal maturity.[138,139,140,141]

It is important to use the term 'essential nutrients' to mean substances required for indefinite growth and reproduction. In practice, growth through two or three generations suffices as a basis for this test, but some substances, not themselves essential nutrients, may be necessary for the maximum nutrient utilization if not maximum growth rate. In fact the balance of the nutrients in the diet must be satisfactory. Again, the synthesis of nutrients by the animal depends on the supply of its precursor, but since the conversion metabolism may not be 100% efficient, even more of the precursor may be needed than expected. Some amino acids are utilized for their side chains or become non-essential amino acids or nucleic acids or amino sugars. If the rate of their utilization equals the rate of their endogenous synthesis, then there is no need for that amino acid in the diet. If the former is more than twice the latter, then the substance is usually considered to be an essential nutrient. An embryo therefore with a high rate of growth and metabolism could have a very different requirement for essential nutrients from other stages in the life cycle.[42]

The nutrients of a diet may be divided into three main classes: (i) the precursors which are useless until converted, such as betaine, a precursor of choline; (ii) substances which are directly useful but which are not easily converted into other substances, e.g. lysine; (iii) substances which may be utilized directly but which also can be easily converted. An example is glutamic acid. This third class includes (a) substances such as glucose which can be converted to many compounds and (b) those like phenylalanine which are converted to only a relatively few other compounds. It should be noted here that radioactive tracer studies have revealed many processes in metabolism which are of little importance in nutrition work so that the term convertible here is used only in the nutritional sense.[42]

Suitable diets

It is not easy to give the natural diet of cockroaches but *B.o.* is reported to be caught best in traps baited with cinnamon bun![95]

Zabinski claimed to have maintained *Bt.g.* throughout its entire life cycle on a synthetic diet, even with glycine as the only source of nitrogen,[138,139,141] but Chauvin found that a diet of farinaceous matter with added yeast was insufficient to maintain the fertility of *Bt.g.* through two or three generations and fresh salad was necessary to complete the diet. The missing constituents supplied by the salad were said to be sterols.[13] A diet of equal parts of skimmed milk and whole wheat gave good growth and reproduction of this cockroach, but reproduction was prevented by linseed oil meal and growth stopped on a diet of cooked starch 22 parts, cellulose 2, lard 10, sugar 10, mineral salt mixture 6 and casein 40. Growth was satisfactory when 5 parts each of cod-liver oil and dried yeast were added to this diet.[75] Similarly, dried milk alone is not enough for growth, but with ground wheat[76,78] or meat products, it is sufficient.[78] A diet of purified casein, starch, mineral salts and yeast is also stated to be all right for the growth of *Bt.g.*[10] Casein is claimed to be a complete and balanced protein[67] but if it is replaced by its known amino acids, poorer growth occurs. Addition of cystine, not present in casein, gives better growth. Sterilization of a chemically defined diet adequate for the normal growth of aseptically reared *Bt.g.* altered it in some way, possibly by killing bacteria present or by a partial breakdown of some of the constituents, and it no longer was sufficient for their normal growth.[54]

In *B.o.* dietary glycosides can be replaced by glucosides, although then the growth is slower and food consumption is reduced. Moulting and reproduction are normal and it is supposed that the chitin is derived from the glycogenic amino acids. In fact proteins can replace both glycosides and glucosides for this animal.[67]

Lack of one essential nutrient can depress the efficacy of the others present, so that the excess amounts of these have to be destroyed by the animal—a process which may lead to reduced growth. Thus a proper balance of nutrients in a diet is as important as the presence or absence of a particular nutrient.[42]

Requirements for specific substances

PROTEINS AND AMINO ACIDS

P.a. is sensitive to its dietary supplies of amino acids and therefore to different qualities of protein.[91] *Bt.g.* showed good growth with casein[75, 87] and fibrin,[87] moderate growth with gelatine,[75] steamed egg albumen, lactalbumen and wheat gluten[87] and poor growth with zein,[75, 87] enzymically hydrolyzed or oxidized casein, gelatine and haemoglobin.[87] *B.o.* is said to have large reserves of proteins[137] and in *P.a.* the accumulations of protein waste material in the fat body may be used if the diet is deficient in protein.[39] *Bt.g.*, however, has a reduced growth rate if its dietary supply of nitrogen is reduced and its nymphal period is longer.[138, 140, 141] It is stated to utilize gelatine just as well as albumen,[139, 141] but requires carbohydrates to make use of the albumen if this is its only source of nitrogen.[138, 140]

Lafon stated that the optimum intake of protein by *B.o.* is 15–45% of its diet, and that the animal will select a diet within this range if given an adequate choice.[67] In *B.o.*, *P.a.* and *Bt.g.*, the protein level in the diet and the longevity of the animal are inversely related. If the optimum intake of protein is assumed to be the level which gives the quickest development and lowest mortality then the optimum level of dietary protein in the adults is 11–24% for *Bt.g.*, 22–24% for *B.o.* and in the nymphs, 22–24% for *Bt.g.* and *B.o.*, and 49–79% for *P.a.* The level for the adults of *P.a.* is said to be of a wider range.[49]

Haydak stated that if the diet contains too great a proportion of protein, the growth of *Bt.g.* stops but that of *P.a.* and *B.o.* does not, or is only slightly affected;[49] but Gier found that *P.a.* can only live until the fat of the fat body had been metabolized.[39] The whole life span is shortened, however, because the longevity of the adults is reduced, and white deposits accumulate in the fat body, head and legs. This material may be reabsorbed if the roach is fed on a diet containing dextrin and little protein and the longevity is increased. Dried egg yolk in the diet causes the duration of the nymphal period to be reduced in *Bt.g.*, but not in *P.a.* or *B.o.*[49]

The output of endogenous nitrogen in *B.o.* adult is 84 mg/kg live weight/day and with a diet of 2·5% protein, nitrogen metabolism is at equilibrium. Using casein the protein minimum requirement is only one-third greater than the endogenous nitrogen output.[67]

Attempts to elucidate the amino acids essential to *Bt.g.* have led to some conflicting results, but it seems that both sexes require leucine in the diet equally, but otherwise they have varying needs.[51] However, Gordon states that lysine and histidine are necessary, the animal having no reserves of these. Arginine or threonine or tryptophan deficiency only shows up in the adult, and the nymphs appear to have considerable reserves of these amino acids, so that they can grow at 80% of the normal rate even without supplies of arginine. He also considers the data for leucine, isoleucine and valine to be inconclusive. An absence of all three allows growth of the first generation, but viable eggs are not produced.[42] Hilchey's work suggests that glutamic acid is toxic to both males and females[51] but Gordon says that 80% of the dietary nitrogen may be glutamic acid, and he treats it as a class (iii) substance, i.e. it can be converted to many other substances.[42]

Sulphate or organic sulphur compounds are suitable sources of this element in *Bt.g.* for the production of cystine and methionine[42, 53] and if it is reared on oxidized casein which is deficient in tyrosine and methionine, normal amounts of both amino acids are nevertheless found in their tissues.[87]

House found that valine, tryptophane, histidine and probably arginine are essential for normal growth and that cystine seems to be necessary for development.[55]

CARBOHYDRATES

The carbohydrates most useful for *Bt.g.* are glucose, sorbitol, glycerol, maltose, sucrose and melibiose; moderately useful are mannose, mannitol, fructose, galactose, lactose, melezitose, raffinose and α-methyl-D-glucoside. L-sorbose, dulcitol, D-xylose, mesoinositol, turanose and L-rhamnose are more or less useless.[42]

FATS

Little is reported on requirements of fats. In starvation the reserve fat of *Bt.g.* may be utilized and if the diet contains glycerol or fatty acids but not both, the missing part is said to be supplied and the complete fat formed.[46]

MINERAL SALTS

Magnesium and iron are essential for *Bt.g.*, and zinc, copper and manganese probably are. Any need for calcium is undetectable.[42]

Accessory growth factors

Inositol is required by *P.a.* for the first 14 weeks of its development and probably much longer, even for all the nymphal period[34] and a diet lacking this substance produced a marked reduction in growth and survival, and more or less no maturation. The critical amount required is 100 mg/kg diet.[33] In the newly emerged nymphs the figure is 40 to 80 mg/kg of diet, but they probably retain some from the embryonic stage.[35] Inositol is not required by *Bt.g.*[88] but this is only true of the first generation, if it is true at all. Cholesterol is required by *Bt.g.*[42]

Choline is essential for *Bt.g.*[88] and the optimum supply is 2–4 mg/g of diet.[86] Signs of avitaminosis in this insect include lack of mobility and lack of a sheen to the cuticle.[141] Zabinski found addition of vitamin B, yeast or bran did not improve the growth of the animal[138,140] but the vitamin B complex in yeast has proved to be necessary,[76,78] although an individual may live as long as 5 months with a reduced supply of vitamin B complex.[76] The ether extract of yeast contains a non-saponifiable growth factor,[78] which seems to be different from the thiamin and flavin in the yeast.[76] Later work has shown that pantothenic acid and nicotinic acid are essential and pyridoxine, thiamine and riboflavin are desirable. Biotin, vitamin K and *p*-aminobenzoic acid are not essential,[88] although Gordon states that biotin, folic acid and cyanobalamine are necessary for reproduction and growth beyond the first generation.[42] The addition of folic acid slightly reduced the growth rate, while the bodies of roaches contain more riboflavin than they receive in the diet, indicating that this substance is synthesized by them or their micro-organisms.[88] Linoleic acid is necessary for *Bt.g.*, too, although this may not become apparent until after the first generation,[42] but it does not require vitamins A and D[75,76] nor carotene. Its fat is without vitamin A.[10]

B.o. is stated to contain reserves of vitamins[137] and it does not require vitamin E.[66]

Vitamins are necessary for *P.a.*,[104] but it is difficult to get a clear-cut vitamin deficiency in this insect. Antivitamins have been used to show a requirement for the corresponding vitamin. *P.a.* requires for optimum growth niacin and pantothenic acid, but anti-metabolites against *p*-aminobenzoic acid, riboflavin, pyridoxine and vitamin K indicate that these substances are not essential dietary requirements. When the diet contained the antimetabolite against thiamine but no thiamine itself, the result was no growth and high mortality. This suggests that the animal or its micro-organisms are synthesizing the vitamin so that its absence from a normal diet produces no symptoms of avitaminosis. The antimetabolite against folic acid led to a reduced growth rate and a moderate mortality rate.[105]

An interesting observation by Goetsch was that feeding blattids with torutilin or vitamin T (=torulin?=thiamine), in the absence of enough protein, led to accelerated moulting, but if torutilin and enough protein were present during a critical phase the nymphs become deformed and, like the soldiers of termites, with excessively large heads.[41]

At a relative humidity of 36%, *P.a.* females lived for 42 days with no food or water, for 40 days with dry food and no water, and 90 days with water but no food; for males the figures are 28, 27 and 44 days respectively.[133]

There are differences of opinion about the exact internal anatomy of the gizzard, and about the physiology, formation and fate of the peritrophic membrane. The report claiming fragments of regurgitated peritrophic membrane in the saliva is so odd that confirmation would be desirable. Crop function has been elucidated by thorough careful work but details of the secretory activity of the intestinal epithelial cells remain undecided, in spite of much painstaking study.

The accounts of the pH and redox potentials seem to be acceptable in view of the many variables which affect their measurement, but the same can hardly be said about the accounts of food absorption. It seems likely that fat, fatty acids and glycerol are all absorbed by the mid-gut and its caeca, and not by the crop.

The study of the diet has led to many sharply differing statements and has emphasized the need for great caution before conclusions are drawn. It is necessary to accept as a criterion a diet adequate only for survival, or one sufficient for some growth, or one which allows indefinite reproduction to occur, before any attempt is made to define what the minimal diet is. Accounts which claim to define a single diet for all three must be suspect or spurious (T).

Organisms found in the gut of cockroaches

The following organisms have been reported to occur in the gut of cockroaches and Table 11.1 supplements those given in Chapter 17. Reference numbers are given here in italic figures.

TABLE 11.1

	P.a.	B.o.	Bt.g.	Remarks
PROTOZOA				
Balantidium blattarum	37			
B. ovatum	38			
B. praenucleatum		65		7·6% of individuals affected.
Bodo sp.	134	134		
Coccidioides periplanetae (spores)		2		Epithelial cells of mid-gut and caeca.
Coelosporidium periplanetae		108		100% infection of the Malpighian tubules. Forms sphores. Trophozoites amoeboid.
Embadomones blattae		143		
Endamoeba blattae	56	56, 62 73, 74 99		In the colon. Nuclear division seen.[62]
Endolimax blattae	73	72, 99		
Entamoeba dofleini		31		
E. hertwigi		31		
E. histolytica	97			In the gut.
E. thompsoni	56, 73	56, 72 73, 99		

11.1—*continued*

	P.a.	B.o.	Bt.g.	Remarks
Giardia sp., cysts	*136*			
Gregarina blattarum	*81, 92*	*99*	*92*	
Hartmanella blattae = *Glaseria blattae*		*58*		
Hexamita periplanetae = *Octomitus periplanetae*		*6, 99*		
Isotricha caulleryi	*125*			
Leptomonas periplanetae		*68*		
Lophomonas blattarum	*48, 56*	*56, 63, 99*		32% infected and commensal.[63] Not common.[48]
L. striata	*56, 74*	*56, 64, 99*		29% infected in *B.o.*; 2 out of 30 in *P.a.*[64] 100% infected in *P.a.*, and seen to form double cysts and then divide transversely. Occurs in the colon.[74]
Monocercomonas orthopterorum = *Trichomonas orthopterorum*		*89, 56, 99*		
Monocercomonoides orthopterorum	*56*	*6, 56*		
Nyctotherus ovalis	*56, 74, 48, 92*	*56, 99, 74*	*56, 92*	100% infection; in hind-gut, together with cysts.[74]
Oikomonas sp.		*134*		
Plistophora kudoi (spores)		*109*		Ovoid spores, $32 \times 1\cdot75$ μ. 75% infection; in epithelia of mid-gut and caeca.
Polymastix melolontha	*121*			
Retortomonas blattae		*56*		
Tetratrichomastix blattidarum	*135*	*135*	*135*	In the rectum.
Trimitus blattae		*56*		
NEMATODA				
Ancylostoma duodenale	*97, 92*		*92*	May encyst in fat body or muscle.[97]
Ascaris lumbricoides	*97*			May encyst in fat body or muscle.
Gongylonema neoplasticum	*97, 47*	*47*	*47*	
G. orientale	*47*			
G. pulchrum		*47*		
G. scutatum		*47*		

11.1—*continued*

	P.a.	*B.o.*	*Bt.g.*	Remarks
Hammerschmidtiella diesingi	17, 48, 92, 14	92	92	In rectum.[92] Common, especially in nymphs and adult females. Least heavy infections in nymphs. Occur in hind-gut near to Malpighian tubules.[17]
Leidynema appendiculata	48, 17, 92	92		In large intestine.[92] Uncommon, with distribution as previous example.[17]
Protospira columbiana		47		
Protrellina künckeli	92			In rectum.
Spiura gastrophila	97			May encyst in fat body or muscle.[97]
Telastoma bulhoesi	48, 92			Common.[48] In large intestine.[92]
T. riveroi	92			In large intestine.[92]
Trichuris trichura	97			May encyst in fat body or muscle.
ACANTHOCEPHALA				
Moniliformis moniliformis	47	47		
PLATYHELMINTHES				
Hymenolepis sp.	97			May encyst in fat body or muscle.
FUNGI				
Aspergillus niger	97			
Blastocystis hominis		99		
BACTERIA				
Aerobacter cloacae			113	In immature oöthecae and gut.
Aerobacter sp.	7			
Achromobacter hyalinum = *Acinetobacter hyalinum*	48			In faeces.
Alcaligenes fecalis	7			In hind-gut.
Bacillus albolactis	48			In faeces.
B. subtilis	97			In hind-gut.
Clostridium sp.	97			In hind-gut.
Eberthella oedematiens = *Salmonella oedematiens*	7			

11.1—*continued*

	P.a.	B.o.	Bt.g.	Remarks
Escherichia coli			113	
Escherichia sp.	7			
Micrococcus parvulus = *Veillonella parvula*	48			In faeces.
Mycobacterium laticola = *M. smegmatis*	97			In the hind-gut.
M. leprae	97			In the hind-gut.
M. phlei	97			In the hind-gut.
M. piscium = *M. marinum?*	97			In the hind-gut.
Mycobacterium sp.	97			In the hind-gut.
Nocardia sp.	97			In the hind-gut.
Parcolobactrum sp.	7			In the hind-gut.
Proteus mirabilis	7			In the hind-gut. At a maximum in June, declining to an absence of infection by November.
P. morganii	7			
P. rettgeri	7			
P. vulgaris	7			
Pseudomonas aeruginosa	7, 97			In the hind-gut.
Salmonella anatis	97			
S. bovis-morbificans	77			Very uncommon.
S. bredeney	7			In the hind-gut.
S. oranienberg	7			In the hind-gut.
S. schottmuelleri	7			In the hind-gut.
S. typhimurium	5			On the body surface and in the gut of *P.a.*
S. typhi	97			
Streptococcus faecalis			113	In the mid-gut.
Treponema parvum		99		
T. stylopygae = *Spirochaeta stylopygae*		99		
Vibrio comma	97			

Bacillus subtilis, *B. albolactis* and *Achromobacter* are normally strict aerobes, and therefore are not likely to be found in the gut of cockroach. They are perhaps contaminants or misidentified organisms (T).

Henry considers that the intestinal organisms do not always exert a beneficial effect on the cockroach and considers them to be of little importance in *Bt.g.*[50] but Hilchey *et al.* state that they are important in the synthesis of cystine and methionine by this roach[53] and in *P.a.* and *Leucophaea maderae* they produce the cellulase present in the mid-gut and caeca.[127]

The optimum growth of the organisms in the hind-gut of *B.o.* occurred when the pH was 7·5–8, and *Endamoeba* thrived best on spores of fungi, but the ciliates thrived best on starch. A diet of bread encouraged a large increase in the numbers of organisms present, but meat produced acidity which, like starvation or heat, reduced the numbers.[99] *Polymastix melolontha* was only found in *P.a.* gut where there was a large amount of yeast present.[121]

REFERENCES

1. ALVARADO, S. and LEQUEROS, C. (1957). La estructura de la cuticula de los insectos. I. El epitelio estomodeal de los blatidos. *Boln R. Soc. esp. Hist. nat.*, **55**, 159–84.
2. AVRECH, V. V. (1931). Zur Frage der Parasiten der Botschabe. *Arch. Protistenk.*, **74**, 236–48.
3. BANK, W. M. (1963). Carbohydrate digestion in the cockroach. *Science*, **141**, 1191–2.
4. BECK, S. D. (1956). The European corn borer, *Pyrausta nubilalis* Hubn., and its principal host plant. *Ann. ent. Soc. Am.*, **49**, 582–8.
5. BECK, O. and COFFEE, W. B. (1943). Observations on *Salmonella typhimurium*. *J. Bact.*, **45**, 200.
6. BĚLAŘ, K. (1916). Protozoenstudien. II. *Arch. Protistenk.*, **36**, 241–302.
7. BITTER, R. and WILLIAMS, O. B. (1949). Enteric organisms from the American cockroach. *J. infect. Dis.*, **85**, 87–90.
8. BORDAS, L. (1897). Classification des orthoptères d'après les charactères tirés de l'appareil digestif. *C.r. hebd. Séanc. Acad. Sci., Paris*, **124**, 821–3.
9. BORDAS, L. (1898). L'appareil digestif des Orthoptères. *Annls Sci. nat.*, **5**, 1–208.
10. BOWERS, R. E. and MCCAY, C. M. (1940). Insect life without vitamin A. *Science*, **92**, 291.
11. BUXTON, P. A. (1932). The proportion of skeletal tissue in insects. *Biochem. J.*, **26**, 829–32.
12. CAMERON, M. (1953). Secretion of an Orthodiphenol in the corpus cardiacum of the insect. *Nature*, **172**, 349–50.
13. CHAUVIN, R. (1949). Les sterols dans le régime alimentaire de certains Orthoptères. *C.r. hebd. Séanc. Acad. Sci., Paris*, **229**, 902–3.
14. CHITWOOD, B. G. (1932). Synopsis of nematodes parasitic in insects of the family Blattidae. *Z. ParasitKde.*, **5**, 14–50.
15. COOK, B. J. and FORGASH, A. J. (1965). The identification and distribution of the carboxylic esterases in the American cockroach, *Periplaneta americana*. *J. Insect Physiol.*, **11**, 237–50.
16. CRAIG, R. (1960). The physiology of excretion in the insect. *A. Rev. Ent.*, **5**, 53–68.
17. DABROVOLNY, C. and ACKERT, J. (1934). Life-history of *Leidynema appendiculata* (Leidy) a nematode of cockroaches. *Parasitology*, **26**, 468–80.
18. DAVEY, K. G. (1962). The mode of action of the corpus cardiacum on the hind gut of *Periplaneta americana*. *J. exp. Biol.*, **39**, 319–24.
19. DAVEY, K. G. and TREHERNE, J. E. (1963). Studies on crop function in the cockroach *Periplaneta americana*. I. The mechanism of crop-emptying. *J. exp. Biol.*, **40**, 763–73.
20. DAVEY, K. G. and TREHERNE, J. E. (1963). Studies in crop function in the cockroach *Periplaneta americana*. II. The nervous control of crop emptying. *J. exp. Biol.*, **40**, 775–80.
21. DAVEY, K. G. and TREHERNE, J. E. (1964). Studies on crop function in the cockroach, *Periplaneta americana*. III. Pressure changes during feeding and crop-emptying. *J. exp. Biol.*, **41**, 513–24.
22. DAY, M. F. (1949). The distribution of alkaline phosphatase in insects. *Aust. J. scient. Res.* (B), **2**, 31–41.

23. DAY, M. F. (1949). The occurrence of mucoid substances in insects. *Aust. J. scient. Res.* (B), **2**, 421–7.

24. DAY, M. F. (1951). The mechanism of secretion by the salivary gland of the cockroach, *Periplaneta americana. Aust. J. scient. Res.* (B), **4**, 136–43.

25. DAY, M. F. and POWNING, R. F. (1949). A study of processes of digestion in certain insects. *Aust. J. scient. Res.* (B), **2**, 175–215.

26. DIRKS, E. (1922). Liefern die Malpighischen Gefässe Verdauungssekrete? *Arch. Naturgesch.*, **88**, 161–200.

27. DUTTON, G. J. (1962). The mechanism of o-aminophenyl glucoside formation in *Periplaneta americana. Comp. Biochem. Physiol.*, **7**, 39–46.

28. EHRHARDT, P. and VOSS, G. (1962). Beitrag zum Wirkungsspektrum kohlen-hydratspaltender Fermente und ihre Verteilung im Verdauungstrakt der Schaben *Blaberus discoidalis* (Sv.) und *Leucophaea maderae. J. Insect Physiol.*, **8**, 165–74.

29. EISNER, T. (1955). The digestion and absorption of fats in the fore-gut of the cockroach *Periplaneta americana. J. exp. Zool.*, **130**, 159–82.

30. ENGELMANN, F. and RAU, I. (1965). A correlation between feeding and the sexual cycle in *Leucophaea maderae. J. Insect Physiol.*, **11**, 53–64.

31. EPSTEIN, H. W. (1941). *Parasitic Amoebae.* State Med. Publ. Moscow–Lenin-grad. (Not seen—from HOYTE, H. M. D., 1961.)

32. FISHER, F. M. (1964). The properties and specificity of a β-glucosidase from *Blaberus craniifer. Biol. Bull. mar. biol. Lab. Woods Hole*, **126**, 220–34.

33. FORGASH, A. J. (1958). The effect of inositol on growth, survival and maturation in *Periplaneta americana. Ann. ent. Soc. Am.*, **51**, 406–9.

34. FORGASH, A. J. (1962). Inositol requirement of *Periplaneta americana* during development. *Ann. ent. Soc. Am.*, **55**, 703–6.

35. FORGASH, A. J. and MOORE, R. F. (1960). Dietary inositol requirement of *Peri-planeta americana. Ann. ent. Soc. Am.*, **53**, 91–4.

36. GERSCH, M. (1942). Fluoresgensmikroskopische Untersuchungen über die Ausscheidung von Farbstoffen bei *Periplaneta*. I. Beitrag zur Exkretion bei Insekten. *Z. vergl. Physiol.*, **29**, 473–505.

37. GHOSH, E. (1922). On a new ciliate, *Balantidium blattarum* sp. nov., an in-testinal parasite in the common cockroach (*Blatta americana*). *Parasitology*, **14**, 15–16.

38. GHOSH, E. (1922). On a new ciliate, *Balantidium ovatum* sp. nov. an intestinal parasite in the common cockroach (*Blatta americana*). *Parasitology*, **14**, 371.

39. GIER, H. T. (1947). Growth rate in the cockroach, *Periplaneta americana. Ann. ent. Soc. Am.*, **40**, 303–17.

40. GILBY, A. R. (1965). Lipids and their metabolism in insects. *A. Rev. Ent.*, **10**, 141–60.

41. GOETSCH, W. (1947). Der Einfluss von Vit. T auf Gestalt und auf Gewohn-heiten von Insekten. *Öst. Zool. Z.*, **1**, 193–274.

42. GORDON, H. T. (1959). Minimal nutritional requirements of the German roach, *Blattella germanica. Ann. N.Y. Acad. Sci.*, **77**, 290–351.

43. GRESSON, R. A. R. (1935). The cytology of the mid gut and hepatic caeca of *Periplaneta orientalis. Q. Jl microsc. Sci.*, **77**, 317–34.

44. GRIFFITHS, J. T. and TAUBER, O. E. (1940). Motility of the excised fore-gut of *Periplaneta americana* in various salt solutions. *Iowa St. Coll. J. Sci.*, **14**, 393–403.

45. GRIFFITHS, J. T. and TAUBER, O. E. (1943). The effects of pH and of various concentrations of sodium, potassium and calcium chloride on muscular activity of the isolated crop of *Periplaneta americana. J. gen. Physiol.*, **26**, 541–58.

46. HABER, V. R. (1926). The blood of insects, with special reference to that of the common household German or Croton cockroach, *Blattella germanica. Bull. Brooklyn ent. Soc.*, **21**, 61–100.

47. HALL, M. C. (1929). Arthropods as intermediate hosts of helminths. *Smithson. misc. Collns.*, **81**, no. 15.
48. HATCHER, E. (1939). The consortes of certain North Carolina blattids. *J. Elisha Mitchell Scient. Soc.*, **55**, 329–34.
49. HAYDAK, M. H. (1953). Influence of the protein level of the diet on the longevity of cockroaches. *Ann. ent. Soc. Am.*, **46**, 547–60.
50. HENRY, S. M. (1962). The significance of micro-organisms in the nutrition of insects. *Trans. N.Y. Acad. Sci.*, **24**, 676–83.
51. HILCHEY, J. D. (1953). Studies on the qualitative requirements of *Blattella germanica* for amino acids under aseptic conditions. *Contr. Boyce Thomson Inst.*, **17**, 203–19.
52. HILCHEY, J. D. and PATTON, R. L. (1952). Effects of irregular sex ratios on growth response data from nutritional assays upon *Blattella germanica*. *Contr. Boyce Thomson Inst.*, **16**, 455–9.
53. HILCHEY, J. D., BLOCK, R. J., MILLER, L. P. and WEED, R. M. (1955). The sulfur metabolism of insects. I. The utilization of sulfate for the formation of cystine and methionine by the German cockroach *Blattella germanica*. *Contr. Boyce Thomson Inst.*, **18**, 109–23.
54. HOUSE, H. L. (1949). Nutritional studies with *Blattella germanica* reared under aseptic conditions. II. A chemically defined diet. *Can. Ent.*, **81**, 105–12.
55. HOUSE, H. L. (1949). Nutritional studies with *Blattella germanica* reared under aseptic conditions. III. Five essential amino acids. *Can. Ent.*, **81**, 133–9.
56. HOYTE, H. M. D. (1961). The protozoa occurring in the hind-gut of cockroaches I. *Parasitology*, **51**, 415–36.
57. HUBER, W. R. (1950). Recherches sur la structure submicroscopique de la membrane péretrophique de l'intestine moyen chez quelques insectes. *Archs Anat. Histol. Embryol.*, **33**, 1–19.
58. IVANIĆ, M. (1937). Körperbau, Ernährung und Vermehrung einer in Enddarme der Küchenschabe lebenden *Hartmanella*-Art. *Arch. Protistenk.*, **88**, 339–52. (Not seen.)
59. JUDD, W. W. (1948). A comparative study of the proventriculus of Orthopteroid insects. *Can. J. Res.* (D), **26**, 93–161.
60. KESSEL, R. G. and BEAMS, H. W. (1962). The fine structure of the salivary glands and associated ducts in *Periplaneta americana*. *Anat. Rec.*, **142**, 313.
61. KESSEL, R. G. and BEAMS, H. W. (1963). Electron microscope observations on the salivary gland of the cockroach *Periplaneta americana*. *Z. Zellforsch. mikrosk. Anat.*, **59**, 857–77.
62. KUDO, R. (1926). Observations on *Endamoeba blattae*. *Am. J. Hyg.*, **6**, 139–52.
63. KUDO, R. (1926). Observations on *Lophomonas blattarum*, a flagellate inhabiting the colon of the cockroach, *Blatta orientalis*. *Arch. Protistenk.*, **53**, 191–214.
64. KUDO, R. (1926). A cytological study of *Lophomonas striata* Bütschli. *Arch. Protistenk.*, **55**, 504–15.
65. KUDO, R. R. and MEGLITSCH, P. A. (1938). On *Balatidium praenucleatum* n.sp. inhabiting the colon of *Blatta orientalis*. *Arch. Protistenk.*, **91**, 111–24.
66. KUDRJASCHOW, B. A. and PETROWSKAJA, O. A. (1937). Vitamin E und Lebensfähigkeit der Keimzellen von Insekten (Versuche an *Periplaneta orientalis*). *Bull. Biol. Méd. exp. URSS*, **4**, 490–2.
67. LAFON, M. (1951). Essais sur l'alimentation d'un insecte: *Blatta orientalis*. I. Données quantitatives sur la nutrition azotée. *Physiologia comp. Oecol.*, **2**, 224–40.
68. LAVERAN, A. and FRANCHINI, G. (1920). Contribution à l'étude des Flagellés des Culicides, des Muscides, des Phlebotomes et de la *Blatte Orientale*. *Bull. Soc. Path. exot.*, **13**, 138–47.
69. LEE, R. F. (1965). Personal communication.
70. LIN, S. and RICHARDS, A. G. (1956). A comparison of two digestive enzymes in the house-fly and American cockroach. *Ann. ent. Soc. Am.*, **49**, 239–41.

71. LIPKE, H. (1957). Nutritional considerations for rearing insects. *Proc. N. cent. Brch Am. Ass. econ. Ent.*, **12**, 90–1.
72. LUCAS, C. L. T. (1927). The intestinal amoebae of the cockroach. *J. Parasit.*, **13**, 220.
73. LUCAS, C. L. T. (1927). Two new species of amoebae found in cockroach: with notes on the cysts of *Nyctotherus ovalis* Leidy. *Parasitology*, **19**, 223–35.
74. LUCAS, C. L. T. (1928). A study of excystation in *Nyctotherus ovalis*. *J. Parasit.*, **14**, 161–76.
75. MCCAY, C. M. (1933). An insect test for vitamin B factions. *J. biol. Chem.*, **100**, lxvii–lxviii.
76. MCCAY, C. M. (1938). The nutritional requirements of *Blattella germanica*. *Physiol. Zool.*, **11**, 89–103.
77. MACKERRAS, M. J. and MACKERRAS, I. M. (1948). Salmonella infections in Australian cockroaches. *Aust. J. Sci.*, **10**, 115.
78. MELAMPY, R. M. and MAYNARD, L. A. (1937). Nutritional studies with cockroach *Blattella germanica*. *Physiol. Zool.*, **10**, 36–44.
79. MERCER, E. H. and DAY, M. F. (1952). The fine structure of the peritrophic membranes of certain insects. *Biol. Bull. mar. biol. Lab. Woods Hole*, **103**, 384–94.
80. MONTALENTI, G. (1930). L'origine e la funzione della membrana peritrofica dell'intestino degli Insetti. *Boll. Ist. Zool. Univ. Roma*, **8**, 36–64.
81. NARAIN, N. (1960). Gregarine parasites from the intestine of *Periplaneta americana*, *Gryllodes melanocephalus*, Serv. and *G. sigillatus* Walk. *Proc. natn. Acad. Sci. India*, **30**, 31–6.
82. NATALIZI, G., BETTINI, S., and BOCCACCI, M. (1957). Osservazioni sulle differenze di comportamento dell'intestino anteriore di blatta (*Periplaneta americana*) e di ditisco (*Cybister lateralimarginalis*) in seguito all'azione di sostanze contraturanti, e descrizione di una nuova tecnica di registrazione. *Rc. Ist. sup. Sanità*, **20**, 410–31.
83. NEWCOMER, W. S. (1954). The occurrence of β-glucosidase in digestive juice of the cockroach *Periplaneta americana*. *J. cell. comp. Physiol.*, **43**, 79–86.
84. NOLAND, J. L. (1954). Sterol metabolism in insects. I. Utilization of cholesterol derivatives by the cockroach *Blattella germanica*. *Archs Biochem. Biophys.*, **48**, 370–9.
85. NOLAND, J. L. (1954). Sterol metabolism in insects. II. Inhibition of cholesterol utilization by structural analogs. *Archs Biochem. Biophys.*, **52**, 323–30.
86. NOLAND, J. L. and BAUMANN, C. A. (1949). Requirement of the German cockroach for choline and related compounds. *Proc. Soc. exp. Biol. Med.*, **70**, 198–201.
87. NOLAND, J. L. and BAUMANN, C. A. (1951). Protein requirement of the cockroach *Blattella germanica*. *Ann. ent. Soc. Am.*, **44**, 184–8.
88. NOLAND, J. L., LILLY, J. H. and BAUMANN, C. A. (1949). Vitamin requirements of the cockroach *Blattella germanica*. *Ann. ent. Soc. Am.*, **42**, 154–64.
89. PARISI, B. (1910). Su alcuni flagellati endoparassiti. *Arch. Protistenk.*, **19**, 232–8. (Not seen.)
90. PILEWICZÓWNA, M. O. (1926). Przemianie azotowey u owadów. *Pr. Inst. M. Nenck.*, **3**, 1–25.
91. PILLAI, M. K. K. and SAXENA, K. N. (1959). Fate of fructose in the alimentary canal of the cockroach. *Physiol. Zool.*, **32**, 293–8.
92. PORTER, A. (1930). Cockroaches as vectors of hookworms in gold mines of the Witwatersrand. *J. med. Ass. S. Afr.*, **4**, 18–20.
93. POWNING, R. F., DAY, M. F. and IRZYKIEWICZ, H. (1951). Studies on the digestion of wool by insects. II. The properties of some insect proteinases. *Aust. J. scient. Res.* (B), **4**, 49–63.

94. POWNING, R. F. and IRZYKIEWICZ, H. (1962). β-glucosidase in the cockroach (*Periplaneta americana*) and in the puffball (*Lycoperdon perlatum*). *Comp. Biochem. Biophys.*, **7**, 103–15.

95. RAU, P. (1945). Food preferences of the cockroach *Blatta orientalis*. *Ent. News*, **56**, 276–8.

96. RAZET, P. (1953). Recherches sur la localisation des enzymes uricolytiques chez les Insectes. *C.r. hebd. Séanc. Acad. Sci.*, **236**, 1304–6.

97. ROTH, L. M. and WILLIS, E. R. (1957). The medical and veterinary importance of cockroaches. *Smithson. misc. Collns.*, **134**, no. 10.

98. SANFORD, E. W. (1918). Experiments on the physiology of digestion in the Blattidae. *J. exp. Zool.*, **25**, 355–411.

99. SASSUCHIN, D. N. (1930). Lebensbedingungen, Cytologie, und Entwicklung von *Endamoeba blattae* Büt. (Leidy). *Arch. Protistenk.*, **70**, 681–6.

100. SCHARRER, B. (1947). Fat absorption in the fore-gut of *Leucophaea maderae*. *Anat. Rec.*, **99**, 638.

101. SCLOTTKE, E. (1937). Untersuchungen über die Verdauungsfermente von Insekten. III. Die Abhängigkeit des Fermentgehaltes von der Art der Nahrung. Versuche an *Periplaneta orientalis*. *Z. vergl. Physiol.*, **24**, 463–92.

102. SCHLÜTER, C. (1912). Beiträge zur Physiologie und Morphologie des Verdauungsapparates des Insekten. *Z. allg. Physiol.*, **13**, 155–200.

103. SHAY, D. E. (1946). Observations on the cellular enclosures of the mid-gut epithelium of *Periplaneta americana*. *Ann. ent. Soc. Am.*, **39**, 165–9.

104. SIEBURTH, J. F., BONSALL, M. G. and MCLAREN, B. A. (1951). A simplified biological assay method using the cockroach *Periplaneta americana* for protein utilization. *Ann. ent. Soc. Am.*, **44**, 463–8.

105. SIEBURTH, J. F. and MCLAREN, B. A. (1953). Growth studies with the cockroach *Periplaneta americana*, fed with vitamin-deficient diets substituted with corresponding anti-vitamins. *Ann. ent. Soc. Am.*, **46**, 43–8.

106. SNIPES, B. T. (1938). Passage time of various types of normal and poisoned foods through the alimentary tract of the cockroach *Periplaneta americana*. *Iowa St. Coll. J. Sci.*, **13**, 93–4.

107. SNIPES, B. T. and TAUBER, O. E. (1937). Time required for food passage through the alimentary tract of the cockroach *Periplaneta americana*. *Ann. ent. Soc. Am.*, **30**, 277–84.

108. SPRAGUE, V. (1940). Observations on *Coelosporidium periplanetae* with special reference to the development of the spore. *Trans. Am. microsc. Soc.*, **59**, 460–74.

109. SPRAGUE, V. and RAMSEY, J. (1942). Further observations on *Plistophora kudoi*, a microsporidian of the cockroach. *J. Parasit.*, **28**, 399–405.

110. SRIVASTAVA, R. P. (1955). On the secretory and absorptive activity of the mid-gut of *Periplaneta americana*. *Curr. Sci.*, **24**, 57–8.

111. SRIVASTAVA, R. P. (1962). On the manner of the discharge of secretion from the epithelial cells in mid-gut and hepatic caeca of certain insects. *Proc. natn. Acad. Sci. India*, **32**, 33–6.

112. SRIVASTAVA, R. P. (1962). On the nature of the cell extrusions from the epithelium in mid-gut and hepatic caeca of certain insects. *Proc. natn. Acad. Sci.*, **32**, 65–71.

113. STEINHAUS, E. A. (1941). A study of the bacteria associated with thirty species of insects. *J. Bact.*, **42**, 757–90.

114. STEVENS, T. M. (1956). A preliminary study of hyaluronidase in several species of non-venomous insects. *Ann. ent. Soc. Am.*, **49**, 617–20.

115. SUTHERLAND, D. J. (1960). Hyaluronidase and its function in the American cockroach *Periplaneta americana*. *Diss. Abstr.*, **21**, 1234.

116. SWINGLE, H. S. (1925). Digestive enzymes of an insect. *Ohio J. Sci.*, **25**, 209–18.

117. THREADGOLD, L. T. and GRESSON, R. A. R. (1962). Electron microscopy of the epithelial cells of the mid-gut and hepatic caeca of *Blatta orientalis*. *Proc. R. Soc. Edinb.*, **68**, 162–70.

118. TREHERNE, J. E. (1957). Glucose absorption in the cockroach. *J. exp. Biol.*, **34**, 478–85.

119. TREHERNE, J. E. (1958). The digestion and absorption of tripalmitin in the cockroach *Periplaneta americana*. *J. exp. Biol.*, **35**, 862–70.

120. TREHERNE, J. E. (1962). The physiology of absorption from the alimentary canal in insects. *Viewpoints in Biol.*, **1**, 201–41.

121. WARHURST, D. (1964). Growth and survival, *in vitro* and *in vivo* of *Endolimax blattae*, an entozoic amoeba of cockroaches. Thesis, University of Leicester.

122. WATERHOUSE, D. F. (1957). Digestion in insects. *A. Rev. Ent.*, **2**, 1–18.

123. WATERHOUSE, D. F., HACKMAN, R. H. and MCKELLAR, J. W. (1961). An investigation of chitinase activity and termite extracts. *J. Insect Physiol.*, **6**, 96–112.

124. WATERHOUSE, D. F. and MCKELLAR, J. W. (1961). The distribution of chitinase activity in the body of the American cockroach. *J. Insect Physiol.*, **6**, 185–95.

125. WEILL, R. (1929). Notes protistologiques indochinoises (première série). *Archs Zool. exp. gén.*, **69**, 12–37.

126. WHARTON, D. R. A. and WHARTON, M. L. (1965). The cellulase content of various species of cockroach. *J. Insect Physiol.*, **11**, 1401–5.

127. WHARTON, D. R. A., WHARTON, M. L. and LOLA, J. E. (1965). Cellulase in the cockroach, with special reference to *Periplaneta americana*. *J. Insect Physiol.*, **11**, 947–59.

128. WIGGLESWORTH, V. B. (1927). Digestion in the cockroach. I. The hydrogen ion concentration in the alimentary canal. *Biochem. J.*, **21**, 791–6.

129. WIGGLESWORTH, V. B. (1927). Digestion in the cockroach. II. The digestion of carbohydrates. *Biochem. J.*, **21**, 797–811.

130. WIGGLESWORTH, V. B. (1928). Digestion in the cockroach. III. The digestion of proteins and fats. *Biochem. J.*, **22**, 150–61.

131. WIGGLESWORTH, V. B. (1930). Some notes on the physiology of insects related to human disease. *Trans. R. Soc. trop. Med. Hyg.*, **23**, 553–70.

132. WIGGLESWORTH, V. B. (1932). On the function of the so-called 'rectal glands' in insects. *Q. Jl microsc. Sci.*, **75**, 131–50.

133. WILLIS, E. R. and LEWIS, N. (1957). The longevity of starved cockroaches. *J. econ. Ent.*, **50**, 438–40.

134. YAKINOFF, W. L. and MILLER, G. A. (1922). Ueber die Darmprotozooen von *Periplaneta orientalis*. *Arkh. russk. protist. Obshch.*, **1**, 131–3.

135. YOUNG, M. D. (1935). Description, incidence and cultivation of *Tetratrichomastix blattidarum* n. sp. from the cockroach. *J. Parasit.*, **21**, 309–10.

136. YOUNG, M. D. (1937). Cockroaches as carriers of *Giardia* cysts. *J. Parasit.*, **23**, 102–3.

137. ZABINSKI, J. (1926). Observations sur l'élevage des Cafards nourris avec des aliments artificiels. *C.r. Séanc. Soc. Biol.*, **94**, 545–8.

138. ZABINSKI, J. (1928). Badania nad wzrostem karalucha (*Periplaneta orientalis*) i prusaka (*Blattella germanica*) na pozywkach sztucznych i niepelnowartosciowych. *Acta Biol. exp.*, *Vars.*, **2**, 123–63.

139. ZABINSKI, J. (1928). Élevage des Blattides soumis à une alimentation artificielle. *C.r. Séanc. Soc. Biol.*, **98**, 73–7.

140. ZABINSKI, J. (1928). Nouvelles recherches sur l'élevage des Blattides soumis à une alimentation artificielle. *C.r. Séanc. Soc. Biol.*, **98**, 78–80.

141. ZABINSKI, J. (1929). Growth of blackbeetles and of cockroaches on artificial and on incomplete diets. Part I. *J. exp. Biol.*, **6**, 360–86.

ADDITIONAL REFERENCES

142. ABBOTT, R. L. (1926). Contributions to the physiology of digestion of the Australian cockroach, *Periplaneta australasiae. J. exp. Zool.*, **44**, 219–53.
143. BISHOP, A. (1931). A description of *Embadomonas* n. sp. from *Blatta orientalis, Rana temporaria, Bufo vulgaris, Salamandra maculosa* with a note upon the 'cyst' of *Trichomonas batrachorum. Parasitology*, **23**, 286–300.
144. EIDMANN, H. (1924). Untersuchungen über die Morphologie und Physiologie des Kaumagens von *Periplaneta orientalis. Z. wiss. Zool.*, **122**, 281–309.
145. HOPKINS, T. L. (1961). Functions of the Madeira cockroach (*Leucophaea maderae*) alimentary tract in the absorption, metabolism and excretion of 'Ronnel'. *J. econ. Ent.*, **54**, 224–30.
146. NOLAND, J. L., LILLY, H. H. and BAUMANN, C. A. (1949). A laboratory method for rearing cockroaches, and its application to dietary studies on the German roach. *Ann. ent. Soc. Am.*, **42**, 63–70.
147. PETRUNKEWITSCH, A. (1900). Die Verdauungsorgane von *Periplaneta orientalis* and *Blatta germanica. Zool. Jb.*, **13**, 171–90.
148. RAMME, W. (1913). Die Bedeutung des Proventriculus bei Coleopteren und Orthopteren. *Zool. Jb.*, **35**, 419–56.
149. ROTH, L. M. and WILLIS, E. R. (1960). The biotic associations of cockroaches. *Smithson. misc. Collns.*, **141**, 1–470.
150. TONG, W. and CHAIKOFF, I. L. (1961). [131]Iodine utilization by the aquarium snail and the cockroach. *Biochim. biophys. Acta*, **48**, 347–51.
151. WALL, B. J. (1967). Evidence for antidiuretic control of rectal water absorption in the cockroach, *Periplaneta americana* L. *J. Insect Physiol.*, **13**, 565–78.
152. YEAGER, J. F. (1931). Observations on crop and gizzard movements in the cockroach *Periplaneta fulginosa. Ann. ent. Soc. Am.*, **24**, 739–45.
153. YOUNG, P. L. (1961). Studies on the transmission of helminth ova by cockroaches. *Diss. Abstr.*, **22**, 1760.

12 *Metabolism*

CARBOHYDRATES

These substances are the most commonly used for respiration and the production of cellular energy. The many steps catalyzed by different enzymes in this process may differ slightly in different tissues but in basic pattern the process is similar in all living organisms. The detailed steps are to be found in various textbooks of biochemistry[41] and are not included here.

The main outlines of carbohydrate katabolism are:

(i) The phosphorylation of glucose derived from oligo- or polysaccharides in which one or two molecules of ATP become ADP, and the splitting of the phosphorylated hexose into glyceraldehyde-3-phosphate and dihydroxyacetone phosphate. The former is oxidized with the help of NAD to 1,3-diphosphoglycerate which becomes, after several steps, pyruvate. The dihydroxyacetone phosphate can become glyceraldehyde phosphate, but it may also be reduced to glycerol-1-phosphate.

(ii) The reoxidation of the NADH to NAD. This can happen in three ways. The pyruvate derived from the glyceraldehyde phosphate may be reduced to lactate as it reoxidizes the NADH. Or the NADH can pass directly, but with difficulty and slowly, into the mitochondria where other hydrogen acceptors will oxidize it. The NAD can then return to the cytoplasm for more hydrogen. Or, thirdly, the reduction of the dihydroxyacetone phosphate, mentioned above in (i), is at the expense of the NADH. The resulting glycerol phosphate diffuses quickly into the mitochondria and is reoxidized, returns to the cytoplasm as dihydroxyacetone phosphate and reoxidizes more NADH.

The small size of the molecule of glycerol phosphate gives it a great advantage over NADH in transferring hydrogen to the mitochondria, because it moves so much faster and penetrates the mitochondrial membrane so easily.

(iii) The pyruvate passes into the mitochondria where it enters the tricarboxylic acid cycle (TCAC). It is further oxidized to carbon dioxide and hydrogen.

(iv) The hydrogen is passed to the terminal oxidation chain and becomes water.

The main result of the release of energy which occurs at various points in this complex series of events, is that the phosphagen arginine phosphate is synthesized, and acts as the energy store of the cell.

Some workers have maintained that in resting tissues and in muscles which are not working as fast as flight muscles, these processes are all likely to occur, but that in active flight muscle the ability of glycerophosphate to function as a hydrogen carrier from NADH to the mitochondria is utilized to a very great degree, so much so that it allows the very great energy release of flight muscle to take place without any oxygen debt being incurred.

The great value of using glycerophosphate as the 'hydrogen carrier' from

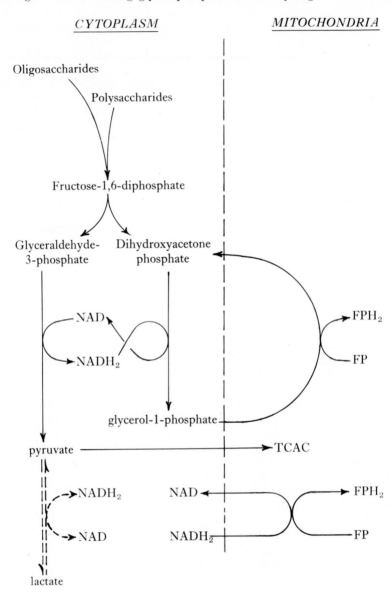

CYTOPLASM   *MITOCHONDRIA*

NADH to the mitochondria is that it acts quickly, and it obviates the need for pyruvate to become lactate. Since there is little lactic dehydrogenase in, for example, flight muscle, this is probably essential for the working of the muscle. It should be noted that it remains vital for the pyruvate to pass into the TCAC, since this is the source of much of the energy by means of which energy-rich phosphate bonds are formed. It is also important that in non-flight muscles and other tissues lactate can be formed from pyruvate during glycolysis if the oxygen supply is temporarily inadequate. The lactate in mammals passes to the liver for metabolism, but in the absence of this organ in insects it is to be assumed that it becomes pyruvate, which then becomes glycogen or carbon dioxide and water, in all the tissues.

It should be emphasized that it has proved extremely difficult to isolate mito-chondria without damage, so that study of their insoluble enzymes has not proved very satisfactory. Undoubtedly much remains to be understood, and some of the above suggestions are likely to be greatly elaborated or proved wrong in the future (T).

Glycolysis

All the work on glycolysis has been done using muscle tissue and the results clearly show that in their physiology muscles fall into two kinds: the 'red' in-direct flight muscles, i.e. most of the muscles of the pterothorax, and others which are 'white'. The coxal muscles are the most widely used example of the latter,[54,55,56, 90] although some of them are classed as red by some authors.[11,14] Both types of muscle use glycogen as the main substrate of their carbohydrate metabolism,[24,25,53,46,55,56,90] although the amount found can vary widely. In the coxal muscles of the male *P.a.* the amount is 5·8 times that of the female.[10] The glycogen content of the flight muscle in male *P.a.* is $1,360 \pm 280$ mg glucose equivalents per 100 g muscle and after flight to exhaustion this goes down to 490 ± 290. After two hours rest it has reached 880 ± 130. At the same time the glycogen content of the rest of the body (mainly the abdomen) decreases from $1,580 \pm 275$ before flight to $1,000 \pm 270$ immediately after flight, but it continues to fall as the flight muscle reserves are rebuilt, to 830 ± 200 after two hours. Much of this glycogen is thought to come from the fat body. The trehalose content of the blood also falls during flight from 880 ± 80 mg glucose equivalents per cent to 380 ± 80.[90]

The chief products of anaerobic glycolysis are glycerophosphate, pyruvic acid and lactic acid[10,23,24,47,51,53,54,90,103,104] but the amounts formed differ in the two kinds of muscles and are the subject of dispute. The flight muscles are found to produce little lactate,[53,54,55,56] while the amount produced by the coxal muscles is less than expected[104] and less than the total acidity produced.[10] It has been suggested that acids produced other than lactic include phosphopyruvic and that this can enter the TCAC without becoming pyruvate first.[94] Glycero-phosphate produced from glycogen accounts for an equivalent of half of the glycogen metabolized,[53,56] and it is thought that at the triose phosphate level half becomes glycerophosphate and half goes on to pyruvate. This in turn becomes acetate and also lactate and possibly malate.[53,54]

10*

The amount of lactate formed by the metathoracic muscles of *P.a.* in 40 min of anaerobiosis was equivalent to only 3·3% of the glycogen consumed.[54] In both coxal and thoracic muscle glycerophosphate dehydrogenase is stated to be high and lactic acid dehydrogenase to be low.[23] Since the rate of glycogen metabolism and the activity of triose phosphate dehydrogenase is increased by 100 times in flight, the formation of lactate would lead to an impossible oxygen debt.[54] Thus it is concluded that the dihydroxyacetone–glycerophosphate pair is the major route by which NADH is reoxidized,[23,24] and it has been shown that by inhibiting the formation of glycerophosphate, the production of carbon dioxide decreases, and lactate accumulates; i.e. under abnormal conditions pyruvate will reoxidize NADH and become lactate.[24] However, it has been suggested that malate and oxaloacetate may act as a hydrogen transfer pair, reoxidizing NADH between cytoplasm and mitochondria,[41] and the enzyme malic acid dehydrogenase has been demonstrated in the fat body of *Bt.g.*[118] and in nymphs of *P.a.*[39]

The enzyme phosphohexoseisomerase catalysing the reaction glucose-6-phosphate $\rightleftharpoons$ fructose-6-phosphate has been identified in the cockroach.[94]

Control mechanisms

The greater the work output of the cell the faster its metabolism and vice versa, and muscles such as flight muscle, which at times have a very high metabolic output, tend to have a high basal metabolic rate. This probably helps them to recover quickly since it is the resting metabolism which provides the energy for the recovery processes.[55] The mechanisms controlling this adaptation to demand are not fully understood but several suggestions have been put forward. Sacktor[12] suggested accumulation of metabolites, or changes in the divalent ions could be involved, while Bücher, Klingenberg and Zebe[19] thought the ratio of ATP/ADP to be very important.

More recently Cochran, working with isolated mitochondria from the thoracic muscles of cockroach, confirms that the rate of oxidation of several of the intermediate compounds in the TCAC corresponds with the ATP/ADP ratio. He also discovered an inhibitory effect on glycerophosphate by the accumulation of the products of oxidation in the mitochondria. When the ratio of reactants to product, i.e. glycerophosphate to dihydroxyacetone phosphate, is approximately 3, the rate of oxidation of glycerophosphate is very low. He suggests that the situation is as follows. It is assumed that the muscle at rest has:

(i) a high concentration of NAD in the sarcoplasm relative to the concentration of NADH;
(ii) a high ATP/ADP ratio;
(iii) access to oxygen sufficient for all needs.

When the muscle becomes active the ATP is used and forms ADP, which causes pyruvate to be oxidized via the TCAC to provide energy to synthesize more ATP. The Embden–Meyerhof pathway of glycolysis then begins to replace the pyruvate so that the concentrations of dihydroxyacetone phosphate and NADH begin to increase. This upsets the equilibrium between dihydroxyacetone phosphate and glycerophosphate, so beginning the dihydroxyacetone phosphate/

glycerophosphate cycle for reoxidizing the NADH. When activity ceases these processes continue only until the glycerophosphate/dihydroxyacetone phosphate ratio is again 3, i.e. until it reaches the resting level.[30]

The work has been criticized by Lewis, Fowler and Greenfield, who found that the oxygen taken up by the mitochondria of the thoracic muscles of *P.a.* was only that required to oxidize the L-isomer of α-glycerophosphate to dihydroxy-acetone phosphate. This is because the α-glycerophosphate oxidase is specific to the L-form, so that theories of respiration control based on experiments in which the substrate used is the DL-mixture cannot be valid.[65]

Kubišta and his co-workers emphasize the rôle of the balance between in-organic phosphate, adenosine phosphates and phosphagens in at any rate limiting carbohydrate metabolism. The amount of inorganic phosphate is thought to have a regulatory or limiting rôle in anaerobiosis of muscle (especially as far as the reactions in the mitochondria are concerned) but this is not true in aerobiosis and its mechanisms are not yet understood. (But see also Hofmanova *et al.*[129] where it is concluded that the main role for the regulation of the intensity of respiration in resting insect muscle should be ascribed to phosphate acceptors which react with the respiratory chain through ADP.)

They have shown that in anaerobiosis the concentration of inorganic phosphate in the metathoracic muscles remains constant, while that of glycerophosphate increases and arginine phosphate and ATP decrease. When oxygen is then admitted to the preparation, the inorganic phosphate level immediately drops and the arginine phosphate level quickly increases. The ATP is not resynthesized so quickly since the available ADP is at a low level. The glycerophosphate con-centration begins to decrease and after 100 minutes the levels of glycerophosphate, inorganic phosphate and arginine phosphate are all approaching their initial level. The ATP still remains low although the ATP/ADP ratio regains its usual value, because of depletion of the ADP. It is thought some of the ADP is changed to AMP and inosine phosphate, which is itself also probably dephosphoryl-ated.[54,57,60,61,63,85,90]

There are wide variations in the ratios of ATP/ADP and phosphagen/ inorganic phosphate at different times and under different conditions in muscle and it is thought there are two kinds of ATP present; one is 'turnover' ATP, in equilibrium with the phosphagen and used in the contraction processes; the other is 'store' ATP which is not in equilibrium with phosphagen and is not used in contraction. The amount of the latter is thought to be about twice the former. It may be also that these two types of ATP are not only functionally different but are spatially separated in some way in the cell, e.g. in the plasma and in the mito-chondria.[61,85] This concept of the compartmentalization of the reactants has, however, been questioned since it does not account for all observations, and Kubišta concludes that a satisfactory explanation is still required.[61]

TCAC

This cycle of reactions is well known. It begins with pyruvate which is decarboxylated and combined with coenzyme A. The acetyl-*S*-CoA so produced combines with 4C oxaloacetate to form citrate. This undergoes a series of reactions in which two carbon atoms are removed (together with hydrogen atoms) so that oxaloacetate is re-created to start the cycle with more pyruvate residues again.

Various vitamins and enzymes including pantothenic acid, thiamin, nicotinamide, NAD and NADP are involved in these reactions, which result in the release of energy. This is used to synthesize ATP and phosphagen (T).

In cockroaches, very little information is available on the TCAC itself, but from studies on ^{14}C-labelled glucose uptake and the resulting carbon dioxide output it seems some of the carbonyl and methyl carbon atoms may pass into polysaccharides or amino acids.[103]

The terminal oxidation pathway

This consists of a series of cytochromes which transfer in series one electron from each hydrogen atom, the resulting H^+ ions passing into solution as H_3O+. At the end of the chain of cytochromes the electrons take up a H^+ ion and unite with oxygen to become water.

There are three cytochromes typically involved in insects (four in some); they are lettered b, c and a. Cytochrome b takes electrons from reduced flavo-proteins, so splitting off the hydrogen and in effect oxidizing them. The electrons transfer to cytochrome c, and then to cytochrome a. This cytochrome is some-times called cytochrome oxidase, and promotes the formation of water. In some cases reduction of certain substances may be effected by cytochromes without the intervention of flavo-proteins.[41]

In *P.a.*, the succinoxidase system, in which succinate is oxidized via flavo-proteins and the cytochromes and water is produced, is similar to that found in the horse.[43] Succinic oxidation in *P.a.* may occur by direct reduction of cyto-chrome c, which is then reoxidized by cytochrome a. The succinic oxidase is stated to be bound to coenzyme A, and the amount of coenzyme A found, in *P.a.*, in the whole coxa is 11·4 units/g fresh material; in the 'white' muscle, 6·1 units/g and in the 'red' muscles 28·0 units/g.[14] The thoracic red muscles have greater amounts of succinic oxidase activity[11] and cytochrome oxidase than the white muscles, the activity of the latter being proportional to the basal metabolic rate and to $W^{2/3}$ (W=weight). All these differences are correlated with the much greater activity of the red flight muscles which also have higher concentrations of glycogen,[62] more active respiratory enzymes and a greater consumption of oxygen.[58]

Different tissues of *P.a.* have different degrees of succinic oxidase and cyto-chrome a activity. The muscles showed strong succinate oxidation and, in decreasing order, the activity of the other tissues tested were, hind-gut, fat body, mid-gut, Malpighian tubules and central nervous system. The ratio of cyto-chrome activity to succinate oxidase was 16:1 for central nervous system, decreasing to 4:1 for some other tissues.[97] Harvey and Beck cautiously conclude that there is no evidence that any of the components of the typical mammalian succinoxidase system are absent, nor any evidence that non-mammalian components are present in leg muscles of *P.a.*

The cytochrome a activity changes with age[43] and in *P.a.* the level in the coxal muscles of males rises to double the nymphal level within 3 days of the last moult and at 11 days has almost reached the triple level characteristic of the old adults. In females the activity does not exceed the nymphal level by more than one-third and there is little further increase after the fourth day of adult life. The colour of the muscles of the males deepened progressively with this increase in cytochrome oxidase content.[16,17]

There are interesting differences between the coxal muscles of male and female *P.a.* The oxygen uptake of these muscles at 38° in the male was 13·6 µl O_2/mg dry wt/hr, i.e. at the same rate as in pigeon breast muscle, and in the female 6·2; while addition of succinate increased the oxygen uptake by 155% in the male and 108% in the female. Addition of acetate, on the other hand, increased the oxygen uptake of the male by 34% and of the female by 100%. The concentration of NAD, of cytochrome c, of diphosphothiamine, and of total ion are all higher in the male than in the female.[10] The succinic oxidase activity is two or three times more active in the leg muscles of the male cockroach than in those of the female.[10,43,97]

In general, lactic acid is not a prominent metabolite of carbohydrate katabolism but there is a high concentration of lactic dehydrogenase in the mid-gut and nerve cord of *P.a.*, suggesting that lactic acid is formed here in the (anaerobic) breakdown of glucose.[24] Kubišta has studied the carbohydrate metabolism of the metathoracic muscles of *P.a.* under conditions of carbon monoxide and cyanide poisoning. He found that a CO/O_2 mixture caused an increased gas consumption, possibly because the CO itself was being oxidized.[52] Cyanide caused increased oxygen consumption, with a decrease in glycogen, phosphagen and ATP, suggesting that its effect is to uncouple the mechanism of oxidative phosphorylation; the usual inhibitory effect of cyanide on cytochrome oxidase is not seen, possibly because the enzyme is far from being fully saturated.[52,63] The production of lactic acid increases to three times that when the tissue is in nitrogen.[51] Obviously the normal metabolism is not anaerobic, but the muscles show great ability to recover from a period of anaerobiosis, resynthesizing glycogen and phosphagen.[54,58] Cleary, however, found no sign of glycogen resynthesis from glucose after a period of anaerobiosis.[29]

The activity of cytochrome c oxidase was investigated by Sacktor and Bodenstein. They found that the enzyme was more active in the central nervous system and fore-gut of the female than in the male, but in the muscles of the coxa the opposite was true. In decreasing order the activities in various tissues were: muscles of male, heart, muscles of female, brain of female, mid-gut, fore-gut of female, hind-gut, nerve cord of female, Malpighian tubules, fore-gut of male, brain of male, fat body of male, nerve cord of male, fat body of female, testes and accessory gland of male. They point out that in general this order corresponds with the tracheation and respiration of the structures, and that the hind-gut has a high metabolic activity because its resorption function needs a considerable amount of energy.[96]

The pentose pathway

Some glucose is not katabolized as described above but enters the pentose sugar cycle. The details of this cycle are given in Gilmour[41] but in outline it forms the important pentoses of nucleotides and nucleic acids, with the production of glyceraldehyde-3-phosphate as a by-product. This enters the Embden–Meyerhof pathway of glycolysis.

Glucose injected into *P.a.* is largely metabolized via the usual Embden–Meyerhof pathway,[103] especially in the female,[25] but between 4% and 9% uses a pathway of the phosphogluconate decarboxylation type by which it enters the pentose cycle.[103] Chefurka thinks these figures may be too low.[25] The enzyme phosphogluconate dehydrogenase is found in the fat body of *Bt.g.*[118] and *P.a.* nymphs, and in the latter the maximum activity, ten times that of the minimum, occurs 4 to 8 days after a moult. Significant differences are found between the sexes and the instars used, showing the care required in comparing data.[39]

GENERAL METABOLISM OF CARBOHYDRATES

Glycogen is one of the main carbohydrate reserves, although its structure in insects is not known.[23, 25] It may occur in several forms[25] or in two, free and bound.[55, 59] Glycogen is the main source of trehalose in the blood and injection of extract of the corpora cardiaca causes the trehalose concentration of the blood to increase, and the body glycogen to decrease in amount.[15, 105, 106] The maximum trehalose concentration in the blood is reached after 5 hr and the level returns to normal after 48 hr;[106] the glycogen content of the fat body decreased by 55% in *Blaberus craniifer* after a similar treatment. However, injection of water into *B. craniifer* causes the blood trehalose level to rise[15] so that the obvious conclusions may be a little uncertain. The trehalose contents of the muscles and gut are not affected by the extract of the corpora cardiaca, but a substance present, which is probably polypeptide,[32] may increase the activity of the phosphorylase in the fat body which is necessary for glucose or glycogen to be katabolized.[9] This is in parallel with the vertebrates in which intracellular glycolysis requires the activation of inert phosphorylase b to active phosphorylase a.

The trehalose content of the thoracic muscles of *P.a.* decreases in flight,[25] and in *Leucophaea maderae* trehalose has been shown to be present in the mitochondria of the thoracic muscles. This enzyme has an optimum pH of 6 and it can synthesize trehalose from glucose. It is present in the epithelium and contents of each of the fore- and mid-gut but not in the hind-gut.[119] *Blaberus discoidalis* has trehalose activity in the membrane fraction of centrifuged muscle not identical with soluble trehalose.[117]

In the fat body of *P.a.* increased activity of the phosphorylase is accompanied by a decrease in the glycogen,[106] suggesting that the synthesis and breakdown of this substance are by different routes.[25] In fact, glycogen synthesis probably follows the usual pattern,[41] since it has been shown that in the fat body of *P.a.* the enzymes uridine diphosphate glucose pyrophosphatase and uridine diphosphate glucose glycogen-transglucosylase are present and the activity of the latter is stimulated by glucose-1-phosphate but not by glucose-6-phosphate. This indicates the synthesis is by glucosyl transfer from uridine diphosphate glucose.[111] The ability to form glycosides by transference of glucose from uridine diphosphate glucose is used in *P.a.* to detoxify various potentially dangerous substances, especially phenols, forming β-glucosides. The homogenized fat body, for example, can form *o*-aminophenyl-β-D-glucoside from *o*-aminophenol under the influence of uridine diphosphate glucose glucosyltransferase.[38] Protocatechuic acid, an aromatic derivative of tyrosine, may be synthesized from glucose, although it is not certain whether it is the bacteroids of *P.a.* which are responsible.[18]

Nervous tissue is also unusual because the perineurium cells contain considerable glycogen, and lesser amounts also occur in the glial membranes, neuropile and nerves.[116] Glucose becomes glutamine and glutamic acid after absorption into the central nervous system, together with smaller amounts of glycogen, trehalose and aspartic acid, demonstrating a link between carbohydrate and amino acid metabolism.[108]

Carbonic anhydrase activity was found in vitro in preparations of head, fat body and gut of *P.a.* The enzyme was soluble in water, heat labile and sensitive to cyanide, but not to several insecticides.[4] Its function and importance in these tissues have not been investigated (T).

The metabolism of adenine nucleotide has not been extensively studied in insects but various organs in *P.a.* have been tested for ATP dephosphorylating activity.[10, 98] The highest activity found was in the muscles and then in decreasing order in fat body, Malpighian tubules, nerve cord, brain, hind-gut, fore-gut and mid-gut. The activity was enhanced by the presence of magnesium ions and less so by calcium ions. The activity of the muscles and hind-gut of the female was greater than that of the male, which is perhaps surprising when it is recalled that the cytochrome oxidase activity of the muscle of the male was greater than that of the female.[96] It is interesting that fluoride did not inhibit this activity in muscle, as happens in house-fly muscle, suggesting the processes are not identical in these two animals.[98]

Three pyrophosphatases were discovered in the mitochondria of cockroach thoracic muscles with different pH optima and different Michaelis constants. All required magnesium ions for maximum activity.[79]

Phosphatases have been found in the mid-gut and Malpighian tubules of *B.o.* The optimum pH for the enzyme in the mid-gut was 8·6 to 9·0 and it was not activated by Mg^{2+}.[37] In *P.a.* adenosine triphosphatase was activated by Mg^{2+}, and Ca^{2+} to a lesser degree,[98] but the activity in the female was less affected by Ca^{2+} than that in the male.[77] The breakdown of ATP in the thoracic muscles was found to be more rapid in the female than in the male, but in the Malpighian tubules the reverse is true.[98]

Day found that the phosphatase was an alkaline phosphatase and that it was present in the 'storage tissue' (yolk, fat body?), nervous tissue and reproductive tissue in the embryo, but in the adult it was mostly in the fore- and mid-gut and the nervous tissue.

Inorganic phosphate (as $NaH_2{}^{32}PO_4$) taken up by *Bt.g.* was found to be most concentrated in the epithelial cells of the mid-gut, the gonads and gonoducts; a lesser concentration occurred in the muscles, nerve ganglia and Malpighian tubules, and least in the fat body.[66]

Hydrocarbons

These compounds have various functions in insects, such as acting as attractants, repellants, pheromones and some hormones, e.g. juvenile hormone. Some of the hydrocarbons of the cuticular waxes have an antibiotic action against bacterial and fungal attack.[41]

Little definite is known about these compounds in cockroaches but an analysis of the blood and the whole body of *P.a.* showed that the three main constituents were n-pentacosane (11%), 3-methylpentacosane (20%) and 6,9-pentacosadiene (65%)[1, 8] or 9,18-heptacosadiene.[41] The male had a concentration of 0·35% of hydrocarbons in its blood, and the female had 0·68%.[8] Acree *et al.* confirm that the total concentration of the three main hydrocarbons is much higher in the females than in the males at 24 days of adult age, but at 13 days of age they found the sexes were similar. This may be due to differences in blood volume, but they also found differences with age, the concentration of the pentacosene increasing almost three times between 2 and 92 days of age, probably due to metabolic activities. The concentrations of the other compounds remained fairly constant.[1] *P.a.* is stated to be able to synthesize labelled acetate, after injection, into a number of saponifiable and unsaponifiable substances. Of the latter 59–68% were hydrocarbons, forming a complex mixture of branched chain, saturated or unsaturated compounds. No squalene was found.[70]

Phospholipids

Some of these compounds and their derivatives are of importance in insects, and in *P.a.* seven different kinds are reported, as well as a cerebroside from sphingomyelin.[102]

Pterins and carotenoids

Little is known about these compounds in spite of their general biological importance (T).

FAT METABOLISM

There is a great dearth of information about fat metabolism in most living organisms, and especially in insects. Few have worked out the details of its biochemistry, and it is usually assumed that the scheme in insects is similar to that believed to occur in other animals (T).

It is thought that fatty acid chains are synthesized in the cytoplasm 2-carbon units at a time from acetyl CoA, which unites with malonyl CoA to give a 4-carbon compound. One molecule of CO_2 and CoA are liberated in this reaction. This 4-carbon compound takes up a second 2-carbon unit from another molecule of malonyl CoA, which has been formed from acetyl CoA by carboxylation, with biotin as the catalyst. This process continues until fatty acids of usually 16 to 18 carbon atoms have been formed. Subsequently the ketone groups are reduced to methylene groups by $NADPH_2$.

The molecules seem to be closely bound to the enzyme(s) until fully made, since no intermediates have been detected, and it seems likely that each fatty acid will have its own enzyme.

Most animals can synthesize fatty acids with no more than one double bond, but some insects contain fatty acids with several double bonds, i.e. they are polyunsaturated compounds. These have perhaps been synthesized by the micro-organisms in the insect or taken in with the diet.

The fatty acids may be (left) free or more usually they are combined with glycerol. This process involves the reaction of the acyl compounds with α-glycerophosphate to form a diacylphosphatidic acid, which then becomes a triglyceride.

It might be expected that fat would form carbohydrates in such conditions as diapause, pupation or embryological development but so far no evidence of the required glyoxylate cycle has been found.[41]

The katabolism of fat begins with the hydrolysis of the triglyceride by lipase, an enzyme found in insect tissues as well as in the gut. The glycerate is metabolized via pyruvate, while the fatty acid is degraded by a reversal of the anabolic processes[81] or as in higher animals by the process of β-oxidation. This takes place in the mitochondria and begins with the combination of the fatty acid and CoA. Each 2-carbon unit is removed in a cycle which is repeated until the whole of the fatty acid chain has become 2-carbon units. The cycle involves four main steps: firstly, dehydrogenation to give a double bond between the α- and β-carbon atoms. Secondly, hydration to form a β-hydroxy compound which, thirdly, is dehydrogenated to form a β-keto derivative. Finally, this reacts with another molecule of CoA in such a way that an acetyl CoA unit is freed, and the remaining fatty acid chain is also combined with CoA. The acetyl CoA then enters the tricarboxylic acid cycle as in carbohydrate metabolism.[41]

It has been suggested that the fat is katabolized not in the muscles, but in other tissues, especially the fat body, and that the acetate formed is carried to the site of its further metabolism.[94] On the other hand, in flight muscles the sarcosomes may be the site of the fatty acid breakdown.[114]

In cockroaches almost nothing is known about the biochemical details. Most accounts refer to the quantity of fat or its degree of saturation, but in one study using ^{14}C-acetate, it was found that the amount found in the fatty acids synthesized by *P.a.* was much more than the amount which was incorporated into unsaponifiable substances (mostly hydrocarbons). This was more especially true of the male in which the saponifiable fraction was 14–17 times the unsaponifiable fraction, while the unsaponifiable fraction was about the same in the two sexes. Most of the fatty acids were 16- to 18-carbon compounds, but 17 different kinds were found.[70]

The fat body of the fourth instar nymph of *P.a.* contained several enzymes, including fatty acid activator enzymes for acetate, butyrate, laurate and palmitate with an intensity similar to that of rat mammary tissue. It also contained lipase and showed a strong anaerobic glycolysis activity.[81]

The degree of saturation of fatty acids or fats is indicated by the iodine number; the higher the number the more unsaturated is the compound. The value found for *P.a.* is 60–72,[80] for *B.o.* 68·8[107] and for *Bt.g.* 55–57[73] or 69–74.[78] In *P.a.* the fat in both sexes has the same iodine value and it is found that the iodine value changes from 60 at 17° to 72 at 32°.[80] There is a greater rate of maturation at the higher temperature, however, which may affect the results. The fat is also stated to become more unsaturated as *Bt.g.* is starved.[78]

The amount of fat present in the female cockroach is much greater than in the male, partly because of the yolk of the eggs, but it is highest in the nymphs of *Bt.g.* Various estimates have been made of the percentage of fat in the bodies of roaches:

TABLE 12.1

	% wet weight	% dry weight
P.a. male[101]	7·1	25·55
P.a. female[101]	9·5	28·63
Bt.g. male[78]	1·70	—
Bt.g. female[78]	4·78	—
Bt.g. nymphs[78]	5·72	—
Bt.g.[73]	5·24–6·1	15·6–17·1
B.o.[107]	4·3	—

There are many factors which affect the fat content both in quantity and quality, including stadium, sex, phase, starvation, systematic position, temperature and diet, of which the last two are most important.[80] Fat is probably used in starvation,[21,78] although the fat body was not reduced in *B.o.*[89] Protein is changed to fat when the diet contains little fat,[78] and fat, as well as carbohydrate, has been found to give rise to protein in *P.a.* by Schweet.[100,101] He also found that diets containing between 1% and 30% fat did not alter the fat content of the body, while in *Bt.g.* the iodine number of the body fat is only half that of the dietary fat.[73] The corpora allata control the synthesis and metabolism of phospholipid and the triglyceride portion of fats, but do not influence that of the hydrocarbon fraction.[113]

STEROLS

Insects possess little or no power to synthesize their sterol requirements, but some of the micro-organisms they harbour can do so, although some cholesterol is always an essential dietary constituent as far as is known at present. Some insects can utilize β-sitosterol and ergosterol either directly or after small changes to the side-branch of the molecule.

Sterols are concerned, with proteins and lipids, in the formation of cell membranes. Some hormones, such as ecdysone, are also thought to be steroids.[41]

In cockroaches, most information relates to *P.a.* and *Bt.g.* The distribution of sterols amongst the tissues of the body, including the haemolymph, is wide in *P.a.*[20,48] Interchange occurs between the tissue and blood sterols[48] but the rate of movement of cholesterol in and out of the tissues is slow, compared with that of mammals.[112] The distribution of free sterols, sterol esters and polar steroids found in the different tissues is not uniform, the blood containing the least concentration of esterified sterols and the fat body the most, which may indicate their importance. More than 80% of the intake is retained for at least 20 days. Little polar sterol was found.[48] On the other hand, the free sterol and sterol esters are said to slowly equilibriate,[112] which would not facilitate storage.

Not less than 40% of the body cholesterol was exchangeable with the dietary cholesterol[112] but injected labelled cholesterol remained largely unchanged as free sterol,[110] although some was esterified. *P.a.* shows great efficiency in its utilization of dietary cholesterol, being able to survive with only 0·1% cholesterol in the diet; it is also stated to be able to incorporate labelled acetate into sterol,[20] but only 5–8% of labelled acetate injected into *P.a.* was recovered as substances which precipitate digitonin, indicating little incorporation of the acetate.[70] Agarwal and Casida state that the natural sterol of *P.a.* nymphs is not cholesterol, and that they convert dietary cholesterol to their major natural sterol.[2]

Noland has made a detailed study of sterol metabolism in *Bt.g.* He found this animal could reach maturity with a dietary intake of cholesterol of 0·025%, although the optimum level was 0·05%.[82,83] Of the dietary cholesterol 90% is retained.[93] Noland found ergosterol was about half as effective in the diet as cholesterol and β-sitosterol to be about 60% as effective.[82,83] The latter compound can be the only source of sterol for *Bt.g.* Of tritiated β-sitosterol taken in with the diet, 93% is found to remain as free sterol, while 97% of it is a Δ^5-fraction; four-fifths of this fraction is cholesterol. Thus the majority of the β-sitosterol is changed to cholesterol, and *Bt.g.* can remove the 24-ethyl group from the sitosterol side chain.[92] The work of Noland has been criticized by Gordon, who claimed that *Bt.g.* uses plant sterols and dihydrocholesterol instead of cholesterol, but is unable to use ergosterol and 7-dehydrocholesterol.[42] On the other hand, this roach is said to be able to convert ergosterol to 22-dehydrocholesterol which is then incorporated directly into further metabolites without being changed to cholesterol first.[26,27]

The micro-organisms of the gut can synthesize ergosterol from sodium acetate in *Bt.g.*, so that this cockroach could apparently mature on a diet containing acetate, but even aseptic roaches can form some cholesterol. This is not sufficient without further supplies, although 0·1% cholestenol with not less than 0·004% cholesterol gives satisfactory growth and development.[27] Noland found cholesterol chloride antagonistic to the uptake of cholesterol from the diet by the adult,[82] but Robbins *et al.* state that the inhibiting effect in the nymph is much less than expected.[93]

Cholestanol is converted to cholestenol slowly and irreversibly,[71] probably in the gut caeca, and may be able to substitute for cholesterol in *Bt.g.*[28] Chauvin found both cholesterol and ergosterol were necessary for maturation in *Bt.g.* and that additional yeast in the diet was insufficient to supply them.[22]

AMINO ACIDS

The amino acids found in the blood of *P.a.* are: Ala, Arg, CyS, Glu, Gly, Ile, Leu, Met, Pro, Ser, Tyr, Val and Glu (NH$_2$).[91] The amino acids found in the body of *P.a.*, excluding the head, are: Ala, Arg, Asp, CySH in the form of cysteic acid, Glu, Gly, His, Ile, Leu, Met, Pro, Thr, Tyr and Glu (NH$_2$).[86]

Transamination and deamination

In most living organisms these two processes are interlinked. The first involves the transfer of amino groups from amino acids to some α-oxo-acid, the most active of which is α-oxoglutaric acid, which becomes glutamic acid. Other substances used as acceptors of the amino group are oxaloacetic acid, which becomes aspartic acid, and pyruvic acid, which becomes alanine. These reactions are reversible so that given the corresponding keto acid, interchange can occur with, for example, glutamate, and another amino acid is synthesized. In this way the synthesis of some of the non-essential amino acids can be accounted for.

A suggested scheme illustrating these reactions is given by Auclair:[7]

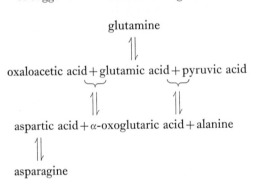

Deamination is a process which requires consideration of the L-series and D-series of amino acids separately. Nearly all known deaminases are D-amino acid oxidases, in spite of the fact that most amino acids in living organisms are L-amino acids (T). The only L-amino acid oxidase reported is a weak enzyme in the fat body of *P.a.* which acts on L-leucine,[6] but L-glutamine dehydrogenase deaminates L-glutamine. The deamination process produces ammonia and the corresponding keto acid. Glutamate deamination is reversible so glutamate can be synthesized from α-oxoglutarate, and ammonia. Moreover, if this glutamate deamination is linked to transamination this could account for the deamination of L-amino acids in a two-step process:

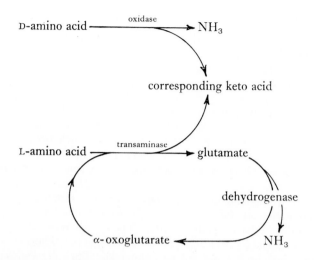

A most important process is the storage of amino groups in the form of amines, of which glutamine is the most important in animals. This process is reversible and is catalysed by the widely distributed enzyme glutaminase. Asparagine is another amine often used (T).

In cockroaches, the typical glutamate/α-oxoglutarate transaminase has been found in the fat body and Malpighian tubules of *P.a.* by McAllen[72] and in the leg muscles the reaction

$$\text{glutamate} + \text{pyruvate} \rightleftharpoons \alpha\text{-oxoglutarate} + \text{alanine}$$

occurs at rates which, if extrapolated from 25° to 38°, would be similar to those of rat.[10] The synthesis of several amino acids is known to occur in the fat body of *Bt.g.*, in part as a result of the symbiotes therein. These are considered further in Chapters 11 and 13 (T).

D-amino oxidases have been shown to be present in the fat body and Malpighian tubules of *P.a.*,[6,12] and to be absent in other tissues; it is not yet certain whether the enzyme in the fat body is the result of the activity of the bacteroids.[6,36]

Glycine, formate and the metabolism of single carbon units

Glycine and formate will react reversibly to form serine. This reaction occurs in the fat body of *P.a.*[15,20] In reverse this reaction yields formate which can be used to incorporate a single carbon unit into various reactions, in particular that of purine synthesis. The carbon of the formate becomes the β-carbon of the serine.[99] The serine formed in the fat body of *P.a.* gradually decreases, and the possibilities of its further metabolism are wide. It may be incorporated into proteins, or become pyruvate, or lose carbon dioxide by oxidation of the β-carbon,[76] and there is evidence that the metabolism of serine is linked with that of cystine and β-alanine.[7]

Transmethylation

By means of folic acid derivatives, formate can normally be utilized to provide methyl groups for methylation of such substances as homocysteine which becomes methionine (T). McEnroe and Forgash found this did not happen in the fat body of *P.a.*, though it can occur in other animals.[76] Thus the usual pathway for the source of methyl groups may not be available and an external source of methyl groups is required. Both choline and methionine are the usual sources of methyl groups in most insects although a few, such as *Bt.g.*, have bacteroids in the fat body which can synthesize methionine, provided enough choline is available.[40] Similarly, so long as some choline is available, ethanolamine or dimethylethanolamine can also be utilized by this roach, and betaine could quantitatively replace choline.[84]

A common compound in insect blood is proline, which can be utilized by oxidation to glutamate, followed by the transamination of this with pyruvic acid to form alanine and α-oxoglutaric acid.[41] The reverse reaction, of glutamate to proline, was studied by McEnroe and Forgash, who found labelled formate was incorporated into proline but not into glutamate. They suggest that either the glutamate was not involved or it was used too quickly for any activity to be detected.[76] Using radioactive glucose, it has been found that the glutamic acid–proline relation indicates that they may share a common precursor.[68]

Studies by Treherne of *P.a.* show that, in the central nervous system at least, there is an interchange of carbohydrate and amino acid metabolism,[108] and Schweet is reported as showing proteins can be synthesized from both carbohydrates and fats in *P.a.*[100] There is no doubt of the importance of transamination as a process in which carbohydrates are used to form non-essential amino acids and in *P.a.* the bacteroids were found to form the essential amino acids valine, tyrosine, phenylalanine, histidine, threonine of the cuticle and fat body, but leucines were not formed.[68]

Metabolism of tyrosine

This amino acid is of importance, for several of its derivatives play important rôles in the metabolism of cockroaches, e.g. production of melanin, tanning of the exoskeleton, the formation of certain defensive secretions and in nerve physiology. Tyrosine is normally acquired by hydroxylation of phenylalanine, which is an essential dietary amino acid, except in *Bt.g.*, in which the bacteroids can synthesize threonine, phenylalanine and tyrosine from glucose.[40, 41] In *P.a.* also, tyrosine was produced by the bacteroids of the fat body and it seems likely that the phenylalanine–tyrosine relation may derive from their having a common precursor.[68] It has been suggested that shikimic acid plays this rôle.[33]

Metabolism of sulphur

Aposymbiotic *P.a.* and *Bt.g.* do not incorporate ^{35}S-labelled inorganic sulphur compounds, but those with their bacteroids can form methionine, cysteine, glutathione and methionine sulphoxide. Strangely, however, the labelled sulphur appears in the Malpighian tubules and gut and does not show in the fat body of *Bt.g.* It is therefore suggested that the fat body produces an essential enzyme, or intermediate compound, without which the synthesis of the sulphur-containing amino acids cannot occur.[44] Inorganic sulphate is also stated to be incorporated by *Bt.g.* into cystine and methionine[45,67] by different pathways, and that the micro-organisms of the gut probably play a part in this since the rate of sulphate uptake was much less in aseptic roaches.[45] This cockroach can also satisfy its needs for sulphur from homocysteine, methionine sulphoxide, cysteic acid, taurine and β-hydroxyethanesulphonic acid.[42]

The work of Bloch and Henry on *Bt.g.* has greatly extended the understanding of these processes. They administered labelled methionine, cystine and their oxidation products, to xenic and aposymbiotic cockroaches. They found cysteine and cystine were quickly converted to glutathione, taurine and sulphate, in both states of the cockroaches, but only the xenic state gave methionine from cysteine. Cysteic acid gave taurine and some sulphate in both states of cockroach, most of the taurine being excreted. The sulphate may form cystine. On the other hand, the sulphur of labelled sodium sulphate was hardly found in taurine. Methionine and methionine sulphoxide are interconvertible in both xenic and aposymbiotic cockroaches.

The authors propose that methionine and cystine are linked to sulphate by two pathways. The more usual one is:
Methionine sulphoxide —— methionine —— homocysteine —— cystathionine —— cysteine —— cysteinesulphinic acid —— β-sulphinyl pyruvic acid —— sulphite —— sulphate.
The alternate route is:
Methionine —— homocysteine —— cystathionine —— cysteine —— cysteine-sulphinic acid —— 2-aminoethane sulphinic acid taurine —— ? —— sulphate.[13]

Purine metabolism

The pathways of purine metabolism in insects are only partly known so that their similarity to those found in vertebrates is partly supposition. The first step is a union of glycine with an amide of ribose phosphate, and this has been found to occur in vitro in the fat body,[74] followed by the addition of a formate 1-carbon radical, a step which occurs in the fat body in vivo.[75,76] The formate is transferred to the purine molecule by tetrahydrofolic acid.[50] Next, amine groups from glutamine and aspartate and another formate radical are added to form hypoxanthine ribose phosphate. This is hydrolysed and loses the phosphate group to become hypoxanthine ribonucleoside, which is then reduced to hypoxanthine. The last step was shown by Cochran and Bruno to occur in the mitochondria of the thoracic muscles of *P.a.*[31]

The hypoxanthine is then oxidized to xanthine and then to uric acid by xanthine oxidase. The enzyme xanthine oxidase has been demonstrated in cockroaches by several workers.[5,35,69,87]

Hypoxanthine may also be derived from other purines such as adenine and

guanine and/or their corresponding ribonucleotides.[31,35] The uric acid so produced may be, in its turn, broken down through a series of compounds to CO_2
and NH_3 as shown below:

$$\text{uric acid} \xrightarrow{\text{uricase}} \text{allantoin}$$

$$\text{allantoin} \xrightarrow{\text{allantoinase}} \text{allantoic acid}$$

$$\text{allantoic acid} \xrightarrow{\text{allantoicase}} \text{urea}$$

$$\text{urea} \xrightarrow{\text{urease}} CO_2 + NH_3$$

In cockroaches this degradation series is of little importance, although uricase
has been found in the fat body of *P.a.*[34,88] and *Leucophaea maderae.*[69]

A more detailed account of the contributions of various workers, which tend
to confirm that the above outline of uric acid metabolism also occurs in cockroaches, follows.

The fat body of *P.a.* has been found to synthesize uric acid in vitro from
glycine and a source of ammonia[74] and a transformylase occurs, involving tetrahydrofolic acid, which incorporates carbon atoms 2 and 8 into the purine from
formate.[50,74,75,76] It is true, however, that the ratios of formate incorporated
into the two possible positions was not the same in vivo and in vitro, so there may
be further factors involved as yet unknown.[36]

Xanthine oxidase is reported from the fat body of *P.a.*[74] and the fat body of
L. maderae[69] or the bacteroids therein.[87] It is found in the Malpighian tubules
and the gut of *P.a.*,[35] but it was not found in *Bt.g.* nor *B.o.*[109]

Uricase was reported from the fat body of *P.a.* by Cordero,[34] from the gut and
the Malpighian tubules of *P.a.*,[35] and from the fat body of *L. maderae*,[69] and/or
the bacteroids of the fat body.[87,88] On the other hand, it is stated to be absent
from *P.a.* completely[115] or at least from the fat body,[74] and it was not present
either in *B.o.* or *Bt.g.*[109]

Guanase was found in the gut, Malpighian tubules and leg muscles of *P.a.*[35]
and in the fat body of *P.a.* by Anderson[3] as well as in the fat body of *L. maderae*[69]
and its bacteroids.[87]

Adenase is known from the fat body of *P.a.*[3, from 5] and adenosine deaminase
in the gut and Malpighian tubules of *P.a.* oxidize adenosine to hypoxanthine
ribonucleoside.[35] Adenosine deaminases have been found in the mitochondria of
the thoracic muscles of *P.a.*[31]

Certainly the fat body has a central rôle in the synthesis of purines.[74,76]

A great deal of research is devoted to the metabolism of the cockroach, and it
has not been possible to include work published after 1965. There is no doubt
that care is needed in using the results so far published because there are real
differences between species, ages, stages in development, and even between sexes
and the different types of muscles of the same animal. It is not safe to assume any
result is true of anything except that to which it refers (T).

REFERENCES

1. ACREE, F., TURNER, R. B., SMITTLE, B. J. and BURDEN, G. S. (1965). Hydrocarbons in haemolymph of cockroaches of different ages. *J. Insect Physiol.*, **11**, 905–10.
2. AGARWAL, H. C. and CASIDA, J. E. (1960). Nature of house fly sterols. *Biochem. biophys. Res. Commun.*, **3**, 508–12.
3. ANDERSON, A. D. (1953). Thesis, Cornell University. From: LISA, J. D. and LUDWIG, D. (1959), and ANDERSON, A. D. and PATTON, R. L. (1955).
4. ANDERSON, A. D. and MARCH, R. B. (1956). Inhibitors of carbonic anhydrase in the American cockroach *Periplaneta americana. Can. J. Zool.*, **34**, 68–74.
5. ANDERSON, A. D. and PATTON, R. L. (1955). *In vitro* studies of uric acid synthesis in insects. *J. exp. Zool.*, **128**, 443–52.
6. AUCLAIR, J. L. (1959). Amino acid oxidase activity in the fat body and Malpighian tubes of some insects. *J. Insect Physiol.*, **3**, 57–62.
7. AUCLAIR, J. L. (1959). The influence of dietary amino acids on the blood amino acids of the German cockroach, *Blattella germanica. J. Insect Physiol.*, **3**, 127–31.
8. BAKER, G. L., VROMAN, H. E. and PADMORE, J. (1963). Hydrocarbons of the American cockroach. *Biochem. biophys. Res. Commun.*, **13**, 360–5.
9. BANK, W. M. (1963). Carbohydrate digestion in the cockroach. *Science*, **141**, 1191–2.
10. BARRON, E. S. G. and TAHMISIAN, T. H. (1948). The metabolism of cockroach muscle. *J. cell. comp. Physiol.*, **32**, 57–76.
11. BETTINI, S. and BOCCACCI, M. (1954). Localizzazione e distribuzione della succinodeidrogenasi nel muscolo di insetti. *Rc. Ist. sup. Sanità*, **17**, 188–91.
12. BLASCHKO, H., COLHOUN, E. H. and FRONTALI, N. (1961). Occurrence of amine oxidase in an insect, *Periplaneta americana. J. Physiol.*, **156**, 28P.
13. BLOCK, R. J. and HENRY, S. M. (1961). Metabolism of the sulphur amino acids and of sulphate in *Blattella germanica. Nature*, **191**, 392–3.
14. BOCCACCI, M. and BETTINI, S. (1956). Coenzyme A content in American cockroach, *Periplaneta americana* and housefly *Musca domestica. Experientia*, **12**, 432–3.
15. BOWERS, W. S. (1963). The relationship between hormonal activity and sugar metabolism in *Protoparce sexta* and *Blaberus craniifer. Diss. Abstr.*, **23**, 2575.
16. BROOKS, M. A. (1957). Succinoxidase in the American cockroach. *Ann. ent. Soc. Am.*, **50**, 122–5.
17. BROWN, B. E. and BROWN, A. W. A. (1956). The effects of insecticidal poisoning on the level of cytochrome oxidase in the American cockroach. *J. econ. Ent.*, **49**, 675–9.
18. BRUNET, P. J. C. (1963). Synthesis of an aromatic ring in insects. *Nature*, **199**, 492–3.
19. BÜCHER, T., KLINGENBERG, M. and ZEBE, E. Discussion of DR. SACKTOR's paper. In LEVENBROOK, L. (1959).
20. CASIDA, J. E., BECK, S. D. and COLE, M. J. (1957). Sterol metabolism in the American cockroach. *J. biol. Chem.*, **224**, 365–71.
21. CERVENKOVA, E. (1960). Metabolismus svaba *Periplaneta americana* za hladoveni. *Věst. čsl. Spol. zool.*, **24**, 183–93.
22. CHAUVIN, R. (1949). Les sterols dans le régime alimentaire de certains Orthoptères. *C.r. hebd. Séanc. Acad. Sci., Paris*, **229**, 902–3.
23. CHEFURKA, W. (1958). On the importance of α-glycerophosphate dehydrogenase in glycolysing insect muscle. *Biochim. biophys. Acta*, **28**, 660–1.
24. CHEFURKA, W. (1959). Glucose metabolism in insects. In LEVENBROOK, L. (1959).
25. CHEFURKA, W. (1965). Some comparative aspects of the metabolism of carbohydrates in insects. *A. Rev. Ent.*, **10**, 345–82.

26. CLARK, A. J. and BLOCK, K. (1959). Conversion of ergosterol to 22-dehydro-cholesterol in *Blattella germanica*. *J. biol. Chem.*, **234**, 2589–94.
27. CLAYTON, R. B. (1960). The rôle of intestinal symbionts in the sterol metabolism of *Blattella germanica*. *J. biol. Chem.*, **235**, 3421–5.
28. CLAYTON, R. B. and EDWARDS, A. M. (1963). Conversion of 5α-cholestan-3β-ol to Δ⁷-5α-cholesten-3β-ol in cockroaches. *J. biol. Chem.*, **238**, 1966–72.
29. CLEARY, M. B. (1948). The anaerobic glycogen consumption and the question of post-anaerobic glycogen resynthesis in some invertebrates. *Biol. Stud. Cath. Univ. Am.*, **7**, 1–18.
30. COCHRAN, D. G. (1963). Respiratory control in cockroach-muscle mitochondria. *Biochim. biophys. Acta*, **78**, 393–403.
31. COCHRAN, D. G. and BRUNO, C. F. (1963). A partial pathway for the synthesis of uric acid in the American cockroach. *Proc. 16th. Int. Congr. Zool.*, **2**, 92.
32. COLHOUN, E. H. (1963). The physiological significance of acetylcholine in insects and observations on other pharmacologically active substances. *Advs. Insect Physiol.*, **1**, 1–46.
33. COOK, T. W. and HENRY, S. M. (1963). Symbiotic bacteria and aromatic amino acid metabolism in cockroaches. *Amer. chem. Soc. Abstr. Mtgs.*, **145**, 24C.
34. CORDERO, S. M. (1958). Purification and activity of purine enzymes in various tissues of American cockroach, *Periplaneta americana*. Thesis, Fordham University. From: PIERRE, L., 1964.
35. CORDERO, S. M. and LUDWIG, D. (1963). Purification and activities of purine enzymes from various tissues of the American cockroach, *Periplaneta americana*. *Jl N.Y. ent. Soc.*, **71**, 66–73.
36. CRAIG, R. (1960). The physiology of excretion in the insect. *A. Rev. Ent.*, **5**, 53–68.
37. DRILHON, A. (1943). Sur la présence et l'activité des phosphatases chez les insectes. *C.r. Séanc. Soc. Biol.*, **137**, 390–1.
38. DUTTON, G. J. (1962). The mechanism of o-aminophenyl glucoside formation in *Periplaneta americana*. *Comp. Biochem. Physiol.*, **7**, 39–46.
39. GARY, N. E., BERGER, R. S. and TUONG, R. G. (1959). Biology and dehydrogenase activities of the fat body of late instar American cockroach. *Ann. ent. Soc. Am.*, **52**, 570–3.
40. GILMOUR, D. (1961). *Biochemistry of insects*. Academic Press N.Y.
41. GILMOUR, D. (1965). *The metabolism of insects*. Oliver and Boyd, Edinburgh and London.
42. GORDON, H. T. (1959). Minimal nutritional requirements of the German roach, *Blattella germanica*. *Ann. N.Y. Acad. Sci.*, **77**, 290–351.
43. HARVEY, G. T. and BECK, S. D. (1953). Muscle succinoxidase in the American cockroach. *J. biol. Chem.*, **201**, 765–73.
44. HENRY, S. M. and BLOCK, R. J. (1960). The sulfur metabolism of insects. IV. The conversion of inorganic sulfate to organic sulfur compounds in cockroaches. The rôle of intracellular symbionts. *Contr. Boyce Thomson Inst.*, **20**, 317–29.
45. HILCHEY, J. D., BLOCK, R. J., MILLER, L. P. and WEED, R. M. (1955). The sulfur metabolism of insects. I. The utilization of sulfate for the formation of cystine and methionine by the German cockroach, *Blattella germanica*. *Contr. Boyce Thomson Inst.*, **18**, 109–23.
46. HOFMANOVÁ, O., ČERKASAVOVÁ, A., FOUSTKA, M. and KUBIŠTA, V. (1966). Metabolism of the thoracic musculature of *Periplaneta americana* during flight. *Acta Univ. Carol.*, **1966**, 183–89.
47. HUMPHREY, G. F. (1949). Invertebrate glycolysis. (1949). *J. cell. comp. Physiol.*, **34**, 323–5.
48. ISHII, S., KAPLANIS, J. N. and ROBBINS, W. E. (1963). Distribution and fate of 4-¹⁴C-cholesterol in the adult male American cockroach. *Ann. ent. Soc. Am.*, **56**, 115–19.

49. KILBY, B. A. (1963). The biochemistry of the insect fat body. *Advs. Insect Physiol.*, **1**, 111–74.
50. KISLINK, R. L. and SAKAMI, W. (1955). A study of the mechanism of serine biosynthesis. *J. biol. Chem.*, **214**, 47–57.
51. KUBIŠTA, V. (1957). The influence of carbon monoxide and cyanide on the resting metabolism of insect muscle. *Věst. čsl. Spol. zool.*, **21**, 126–34.
52. KUBIŠTA, V. (1957). Accumulation of a stable phosphorus compound in glycolysing insect muscle. *Nature*, **180**, 549.
53. KUBIŠTA, V. (1958). Anaerobe Glykolyse in den Insektenmuskeln. *Biochem. Z.*, **330**, 315–23.
54. KUBIŠTA, V. (1959). Stoffwechsel der isolierten Insektenmuskulatur. *Sber. Ges. Beförd. ges. Naturw. Marburg*, **81**, 17–31.
55. KUBIŠTA, V. (1961). Adaptation of energy metabolism. *Proc. 5th. Nat. Congr. Czechoslov. Physiol. Soc.*, **V**, 251–6.
56. KUBIŠTA, V. (1963). Adaptation of muscle energy metabolism. In GUTMANN, E. and HNÍK, P. (Eds.). *The effect of use and disuse on neuromuscular functions.* Liblice, 1962. Prague, 1963.
57. KUBIŠTA, V. (1963). Changes in the system of energy-rich phosphorus compounds in insect thoracic muscles and their relation to the carbohydrate metabolism. *Acta Univ. Carol.*, **1963**, 283–300.
58. KUBIŠTA, V. (1966). Preparations of isolated insect musculature. *Acta Univ. Carol.*, **1966**, 197–208.
59. KUBIŠTA, V. and BARTOS, Z. (1960). Free and fixed glycogen in insect muscle. *Physiologia bohemoslov.*, **9**, 235–9.
60. KUBIŠTA, V. and FOUSTKA, M. (1962). Inorganic phosphate and the rate of glycolysis in insect muscle. *Nature*, **195**, 702.
61. KUBIŠTA, V. and FOUSTKA, M. (1963). Anaerobic and postanaerobic changes of soluble phosphorus compounds in insect muscle. *Physiologia bohemoslov.*, **12**, 183–90.
62. KUBIŠTA, V., NOVOTNÝ, I. and CERKASOV, J. (1958). Metabolismus glykogenu ve hmyzim svalu. *Acta Univ. Carol.*, **1958**, 145–151. [From: KUBIŠTA, 1963; ref. 57.]
63. KUBIŠTA, V. and URBANKOVA, J. (1962). Evidence for the uncoupling action of cyanide. *Biochim. biophys. Acta*, **62**, 175–6.
64. LEVENBROOK, L. (ed.) (1959). The biochemistry of insects. *Proc. 4th. Int. Congr. Biochem.*, Symp. 12.
65. LEWIS, S. E., FOWLER, K. S. and GREENFIELD, C. (1963). α-glycerophosphate oxidation. Report of Pest Infestation Laboratory, Slough.
66. LINDSAY, E. and CRAIG, R. (1942). The distribution of radio-phosphorus in the wax moth, mealworm, cockroach and firebrat. *Ann. ent. Soc. Am.*, **35**, 50–6.
67. LIPKE, H. and FRAENKEL, G. (1956). Insect nutrition. *A. Rev. Ent.*, **1**, 17–44.
68. LIPKE, H., LETO, S. and GRAVES, B. (1965). Carbohydrate-amino acid conversions during cuticle synthesis in *Periplaneta americana*. *J. Insect Physiol.*, **11**, 1225–32.
69. LISA, J. D. and LUDWIG, D. (1959). Uricase, guanase and xanthine oxidase from the fat body of the cockroach *Leucophaea maderae*. *Ann. ent. Soc. Am.*, **52**, 548–51.
70. LOULOUDES, S. J., KAPLANIS, J. N., ROBBINS, W. E. and MONROE, R. E. (1961). Lipogenesis from C^{14}-acetate by the American cockroach. *Ann. ent. Soc. Am.*, **54**, 99–103.
71. LOULOUDES, S. J., THOMPSON, M. J., MONROE, R. E. and ROBBINS, W. E. (1962). Conversion of cholestanol to Δ^7-cholestenol by the German cockroach. *Biochem. biophys. Res. Commun.*, **8**, 104–6.
72. MCALLEN, J. W. (1958). Thesis, University of Western Ontario, Canada. From: BHEEMESWAR, B. Some aspects of amino acid metabolism in insects. In: LEVENBROOK, L., 1959.

73. MCCAY, C. M. (1938). The nutritional requirements of *Blattella germanica*. *Physiol. Zool.*, **11**, 89–103.
74. MCENROE, W. D. (1957). Uric acid metabolism in American cockroach. *Diss. Abstr.*, **17**, 2338.
75. MCENROE, W. D. and FORGASH, A. J. (1957). The *in vivo* incorporation of ^{14}C-formate in ureide groups of uric acid by *Periplaneta americana*. *Ann. ent. Soc. Am.*, **50**, 429–31.
76. MCENROE, W. D. and FORGASH, A. J. (1958). Formate metabolism in the American cockroach, *Periplaneta americana*. *Ann. ent. Soc. Am.*, **51**, 126–9.
77. MCSHAN, W. H., KRAMER, S. and OLSON, N. F. (1955). Adenosine triphosphatase activity of American cockroach and woodroach thoracic muscles. *Biol. Bull. mar. biol. Lab. Woods Hole*, **108**, 45–53.
78. MELAMPY, R. M. and MAYNARD, L. A. (1937). Nutrition studies with cockroach, *Blattella germanica*. *Physiol. Zool.*, **10**, 36–44.
79. MILLS, R. R. and COCHRANE, D. G. (1965). Isolation and properties of inorganic pyrophosphatases from cockroach thoracic muscle mitochondria. *J. Insect Physiol.*, **11**, 1463–74.
80. MUNSON, S. C. (1953). Some effects of storage at different temperatures on the lipids of the American roach and on the resistance of this insect to heat. *J. econ. Ent.*, **46**, 657–66.
81. NELSON, W. L. (1958). Fat metabolism with reference to insects. *Proc. 10th. Int. Congr. Ent.*, **2**, 359–64.
82. NOLAND, J. L. (1954). Sterol metabolism in insects. I. Utilization of cholesterol derivatives by the cockroach *Blattella germanica*. *Archs Biochem. Biophys.*, **48**, 370–9.
83. NOLAND, J. L. (1954). Sterol metabolism in insects. II. Inhibition of cholesterol utilization by structural analogs. *Archs Biochem. Biophys.*, **52**, 323–30.
84. NOLAND, J. L. and BAUMANN, C. A. (1949). Requirement of the German cockroach for choline and related compounds. *Proc. Soc. exp. Biol. Med.*, **70**, 198–201.
85. NOVOTNY, I., KUBIŠTA, V. and FOUSTKA, M. (1963). The effect of 2,4-dinitro-phenol on the level of acid-soluble phosphorus compounds in insect muscles in aerobic and anaerobic conditions. *Physiologia bohemoslov.*, **12**, 191–5.
86. PANT, R. and AGARWAL, H. C. (1963). Free amino acids of some insect tissue homogenates. *Curr. Sci.*, **32**, 20–1.
87. PIERRE, L. L. (1961). Functions of the symbionts in the fat body of the tropical cockroach *Leucopheae maderae*. *Diss. Abstr.*, **22**, 983.
88. PIERRE, L. L. (1964). Uricase activity of isolated symbiotes and the aposymbiotic fat body of a cockroach. *Nature*, **201**, 54–5.
89. PILEWICZÓWNA, M. O. (1926). Przemianie azotowey u owadów. *Pr. Inst. M. Nenck.*, **3**, 1–25.
90. POLACEK, I. and KUBIŠTA, V. (1960). Metabolism of the cockroach *Periplaneta americana* during flight. *Physiologia bohemoslov.*, **9**, 228–34.
91. PRATT, J. J. (1950). A qualitative analysis of the free amino acids in insect blood. *Ann. ent. Soc. Am.*, **43**, 573–80.
92. ROBBINS, W. E., DUTKY, R. C., MONROE, R. E. and KAPLANIS, J. N. (1962). The metabolism of H^3-β-sitosterol by the German cockroach. *Ann. ent. Soc. Am.*, **55**, 102–4.
93. ROBBINS, W. E., KAPLANIS, J. N., MONROE, R. E. and TABOR, L. A. (1961). Utilization of dietary cholesterol by German cockroaches. *Ann. ent. Soc. Am.*, **54**, 165–8.
94. SACKTOR, B. (1955). Cell structure and the metabolism of insect flight muscle. *J. biophys. biochem. Cytol.*, **1**, 29–46.
95. SACKTOR, B. (1959). Biochemical basis of flight muscle activity. In LEVEN-BROOK, L. (1959).

96. SACKTOR, B. and BODENSTEIN, D. (1952). Cytochrome *c* oxidase activity of various tissues of the American cockroach *Periplaneta americana*. *J. cell comp. Physiol.*, **40**, 157–61.
97. SACKTOR, B. and THOMAS, G. M. (1955). Succino-cytochrome *c* reductase activity of tissues of the American cockroach *Periplaneta americana*. *J. cell. comp. Physiol.*, **45**, 241–6.
98. SACKTOR, B., THOMAS, G. M., MOSER, J. C. and BLOCK, D. I. (1953). Dephosphorylation of adenosine triphosphate by tissues of the American cockroach *Periplaneta americana*. *Biol. Bull. mar. biol. Lab. Woods Hole*, **105**, 166–73.
99. SAKAMI, W. (1948). The conversion of formate and glycine to serine and glycogen in the intact rat. *J. biol. Chem.*, **176**, 995–6.
100. SCHWEET, R. S. Thesis, Iowa St. University, 1941. From SCOGGIN, J. K. and TAUBER, O. E. (1950).
101. SCOGGIN, J. K. and TAUBER, O. E. (1950). Survey of literature on insect lipids. *Iowa St. Coll. J. Sci.*, **25**, 99–124.
102. SIAKOTOS, A. N. and ZOLLER, H. S. (1960). Phospholipids of the American cockroach. *Fedn Proc. Fedn Am. Socs exp. Biol.*, **19**, 232.
103. SILVA, G. M., DOYLE, W. P. and WANG, C. H. (1958). Glucose catabolism in the American cockroach. *Nature*, **182**, 102–4.
104. SLATER, W. K. (1927). The aerobic and anaerobic metabolism of the common cockroach *Periplaneta orientalis*. *Biochem. J.*, **21**, 198–203.
105. STEELE, J. E. (1961). Occurrence of hyperglycaemic factor in the corpus cardiacum in an insect. *Nature*, **192**, 680–1.
106. STEELE, J. E. (1963). The site of action of insect hyperglycaemic hormone. *Gen. comp. Endocrinol.*, **3**, 46–52.
107. TIMON-DAVID, J. (1930). Recherches sur les matières grasses des insectes. *Annls Fac. Sci. Marseille*, **4**, 29–207.
108. TREHERNE, J. E. (1960). The nutrition of the central nervous system in the cockroach *Periplaneta americana*. The exchange and metabolism of sugars. *J. exp. Biol.*, **37**, 513–33.
109. TRUSZKOWSKI, R. and CHAJKINOWNA, S. (1935). Nitrogen metabolism of certain invertebrates. *Biochem. J.*, **29**, 2361–5.
110. VANDENHEUVEL, W. J. A., ROBBINS, W. E., KAPLANIS, J. N., LOULOUDES, S. J. and HORNING, E. C. (1962). The major sterol from cholesterol-fed American cockroaches. *Ann. ent. Soc. Am.*, **55**, 723.
111. VARDANIS, A. (1963). Glycogen synthesis in the insect fat body. *Biochim. biophys. Acta*, **73**, 565–73.
112. VROMAN, H. E., KAPLANIS, J. N. and ROBBINS, W. E. (1964). Cholesterol turnover in the American cockroach *Periplaneta americana*. *J. Lipid Res.*, **5**, 418–21.
113. VROMAN, H. E., KAPLANIS, J. N. and ROBBINS, W. E. (1965). Effect of allatectomy on lipid biosynthesis and turnover in the female American cockroach, *Periplaneta americana*. *J. Insect Physiol.*, **11**, 897–904.
114. WEIS-FOGH, T. Power in flapping flight. In RAMSEY, J. A. and WIGGLESWORTH, V. B. (eds.) (1961). *The Cell and the Organisms*. The University Press, Cambridge.
115. WHARTON, D. R. A. and WHARTON, M. L. (1961). Effects of radiation on nitrogen and phosphorus excretion by the cockroach *Periplaneta americana*. *Radiat. Res.*, **14**, 432–43.
116. WIGGLESWORTH, V. B. (1960). The nutrition of the central nervous system in the cockroach *Periplaneta americana*. *J. exp. Biol.*, **37**, 500–12.
117. WYATT, G. R., GUSSIN, A. E. and GILBY, A. R. (1965). The activation of insect muscle trehalose. *Fedn Proc. Fedn Am. Socs exp. Biol.*, **24**, 220.
118. YOUNG, R. G. (1958). Dehydrogenase systems of fat body of susceptible and chlordane-resistant *Blattella germanica*. *J. econ. Ent.*, **51**, 867–9.
119. ZEBE, E. C. and MCSHAN, W. H. (1959). Trehalase in the thoracic muscles of the woodroach, *Leucophaea maderae*. *J. cell comp. Physiol.*, **53**, 21–9.

ADDITIONAL REFERENCES

120. BABERS, F. and PRATT, J. J. (1951). A comparison of the cholinesterase in the heads of the house-fly, the cockroach and the honey bee. *Physiol. Zool.*, **24**, 127–31.
121. COOK, B. J. and FORGASH, A. J. (1965). The identification and distribution of the carboxylic esterases in the American cockroach *Periplaneta americana*. *J. Insect Physiol.*, **11**, 237–50.
122. BHAKTAN, N. M. G. (1965). Certain biochemical properties of insect muscle lipase. *J. Anim. Morph. Physiol.*, **11**, 285–93.
123. DAY, M. F. (1949). The distribution of alkaline phosphatase in insects. *Aust. J. scient. Res.* (B), **2**, 31–41.
124. HENRY, S. M. and BLOCK, R. J. (1961). The sulfur metabolism of insects. VI. Metabolism of the sulfur amino acids and related compounds in the German cockroach *Blattella germanica*. *Contr. Boyce Thomson Inst.*, **21**, 129–44.
125. HOFMANOVÁ, O., MANOWSKA, J., PELOUCH, V. and KUBIŠTA, V. (1967). Free and bound adenosine diphosphate in insect muscle and its relation to adenosine triphosphate. *Physiologia bohemoslov*, **16**, 97–103.
126. KINSELLA, J. E. (1966). Sterol metabolism during embryogenesis of *Periplaneta americana* (L). *J. Insect Physiol.*, **12**, 435–8.
127. KINSELLA, J. E. (1966). Metabolic patterns of the fatty acids of *Periplaneta americana* (L) during its embryonic development. *Can. J. Biochem., Physiol.* **44**, 247–58.
128. KINSELLA, J. E. (1966). Phospholipid patterns of *Periplaneta americana* during embryogenesis. *Comp. Biochem. Physiol.*, **17**, 635–40.
129. KINSELLA, J. E. and SMITH, T. (1966). Lipid metabolism of *Periplaneta americana* L. during embryogenesis. *Comp. Biochem. Physiol.*, **17**, 237–44.
130. LIPKE, H., GRAVES, B. and LETO, S. (1965). Polysaccharide and glycoprotein formation in the cockroach. II. Incorporation of D-glucose-^{14}C into bound carbohydrate. *J. biol. Chem.*, **240**, 601–8.
131. MANSINGH, A. (1966). Metabolism of labeled glutamic acid in adult German cockroaches. *J. econ. Ent.*, **59**, 234–5.
132. MCENROE, W. (1966). In vivo preferential oxidation of ureide carbon no. 2 of uric acid by *Periplaneta americana*. *Ann. ent. Soc. Am.*, **59**, 1011.
133. MILLS, R. R. and COCHRAN, D. G. (1965). Isolation and properties of inorganic pyrophosphatases from cockroach thoracic muscle mitochondria. *J. Insect Physiol.*, **11**, 1463–74.
134. MILLS, R. R. and COCHRAN, D. G. (1967). Adenosinetriphosphatases from thoracic muscle mitochondria of the American cockroach. *Comp. Biochem. Physiol.*, **20**, 919–23.
135. MUTCHMOR, J. A. and RICHARDS, A. G. (1961). Low temperature tolerance of insects in relation to the influence of temperature on muscle apyrase activity. *J. Insect Physiol.*, **7**, 141–58.
136. PEARSE, A. G. E. and SCARPELLI, D. G. (1958). Cytochemical localization of succinic dehydrogenase in mitochondria from *Periplaneta americana*. *Nature*, **181**, 702–3.
137. ROSEDALE, J. L. and MORRIS, J. P. (1930). Amino acids of tissue. IV. The diamino acid content of muscular tissue of different classes of animals. *Biochem. J.*, **24**, 1294–6.

13 The fat body and its bacteroids

The identity of the bacteroid

There has been much dispute about the identity of the organisms in the bacteriocytes or mycetocytes. Gier claimed that all those from different cockroaches were generically the same,[37] but Richards and Brooks consider that there is no real information on which to base the specificity of the bacteroids.[81] They have been variously identified as diphtheroids,[35,56] called *Corynebacterium* in *P.a.*,[39] and *C. blattellae* in *Bt.g.*[40] In *Leucophaea maderae* they are claimed to be *Aerobacter* of the Enterobacteriaceae;[76] in *P.a.*, Rickettsiae,[35,37] or unclassified bacteria most closely resembling *Vibrio*;[28] in *B.o. Blattabacterium cuenoti*[50] or *Rhizobium uricophilum*[55] and in cockroaches *Bacillus cuenoti*.[62]

Various writers have stated that the symbiotic bacteroids of the fat body are cell inclusions,[42,80] or, more particularly, chondriosomes[86] or mitochondria. Those of *Bt.g.* react positively to both bacterial and mitochondrial stains, but unlike mitochondria the organisms are not attacked by bile salts.[12] In *P.a.* they are said to differ from mitochondria in staining reactions, morphology and occurrence.[35] X-ray and serological tests on the organisms of *Bt.g.* are said to show they are organisms intermediate between bacteria and yeasts and are best called bacteroids,[72,73,74] an opinion shared by Silva,[88,89] but others also claim that there is no doubt of their bacterial nature.[52,62]

The bacteroids are Gram-positive in *Bt.g.*,[12,22,42,72,90] in *B.o.*,[22] and in *P.a.*[39,45] and in cockroaches in general,[66,67,68,69] or with only a few Gram-negative in *P.a.*[92] or with all Gram-negative.[28] However, the test to determine the Gram reaction is of doubtful reliability[12] and indeed in *B.o.* the bacteroids may be Gram-positive at first, later Gram-negative, and later still Gram-positive again.[31] The change from Gram-positive to Gram-negative may be brought about by antibiotics in this species.[32]

The bacteroids are immotile in *B.o.*, *Bt.g.*[22] and *P.a.*,[35,39] except that they may move by lysis in *B.o.* and *Bt.g.*[22] and Mercier claimed that they are motile.[66,67,68,69]

They show constrictions and/or transverse walls or partitions in *Bt.g.*,[38,72,90] in *B.o.*[32,38,50,52] and in *P.a.*[45,48] which may lead to equal or unequal budding or fission.[39] There are granules present in the bacteroids of *Bt.g.*,[22,90] in *P.a.*[23,90] and in *B.o.*[22,32,50,52] or in those of all species of cockroach.[62,66,67,68,69] Often they occur in pairs (as in *P.a.*[90]) and are the points from which the transverse walls begin their growth.[23] In some cases no granules could be seen in the bacteroids of *Bt.g.* or *P.a.*, but these are thought to be immature.[90] According to

Lwoff the fission of the bacteroids shows affinities with the Schizosaccharo-mycetes.[62]

In *B.o.* they appear to have no nucleus nor nucleolus,[70] but they do have a clear zone[50, 82] around a granule which it has been suggested may be a nucleus.[50] In *P.a.*, a nuclear zone has been described which is without membranes and resembles the corresponding structure of the blue-green algae,[23] but two or three clear zones have been described,[45] and these may be equivalent to the vacuoles that may occur in those of *Bt.g.*[22, 72] and *B.o.*[22]

Spore formation is said by Mercier[66, 67, 68, 69] to occur in all cockroaches, and this is confirmed in *B.o.*[70] On the other hand, only a minority of the bacteroids does so in *B.o.* according to Wolf.[92] Lwoff found spores to be formed in *Bt.g.*,[62] but no spore formation was found in *B.o.*[50, 55] nor in *P.a.*[39]

The bacteroids are said to show transverse banding, clear transparent bands alternating with more opaque ones in *Bt.g.*;[22, 90] for *B.o.* a similar appearance is both claimed[22, 52] and denied.[82] The cytoplasm is homogeneous, granular and without vacuoles in *B.o.*[70]

The bacteroids have no capsule in *Bt.g.*[45] and *P.a.*[39]

They are stated to have lengths in *B.o.* of 2·5–3·5 μ[22] or 1·5–2·0 μ[55] or 6–8 μ[3] or 3 μ[22] and either 3·4 μ (average) or, after treatment with antibiotics which probably allows a resistant bacteroid to multiply, 7·8 μ (average).[32] In *Bt.g.* they are said to have lengths of about 6–8 μ[3, 38] or 3 μ[22] and in *P.a.* about 6–8 μ[38] or 2·5–3·5 μ[1] or 1·5–6·5 μ, average 3·5 μ.[35] Their widths in *B.o.* are 0·5 μ[55] or 1·0 μ[32] and in *P.a.* 0·9–1·0 μ,[35] or 0·5–1·5 μ.[1]

The bacteroids are not acid-fast.[22, 39, 42, 45, 66, 67, 68, 69]

The bacteroids have been thought to contain ribonuclease in *B.o.* which is active in cell multiplication,[70] and in *Bt.g.* deoxyribonucleic acid, ribonucleic acid, and polysaccharides have been detected.[12] The nucleoids of the bacteroids of *B.o.* may be DNA.[32] This substance is also stated to be present in those of *Bt.g.*, although it is not typical since it is resistant to deoxyribonuclease unless it has previously been attacked by pepsin.[83] The bacteroids of *P.a.* also react positively to the Feulgen test, and in this case the reaction can be abolished by deoxyribo-nuclease.[1] Even if no positive reaction occurs, in the Feulgen test, DNA may still be present, however.[91]

The culture of the bacteroids in vitro

Whether the bacteroids from cockroach fat body have been cultivated or not has been a vexed and controversial question for many years. It is important to know the nature of the medium used for cultivation of the organism, the source of the bacteroids, and all other conditions of the experiments before any con-clusions can be drawn. In addition, reinfection of aposymbiotic individuals by the organism cultured to form normal bacteriocytes is necessary to demonstrate real identity (T).

The bacteroids of *P.a.* were thought to have been cultured in 14% of the attempts made by Glaser, who also claimed that subculturing the organism enhances its survival and suggested it had become adapted to the medium. He found three morphologically distinct types in this cockroach, but usually only one type was found in any one host animal.[39] The same applies in general to *Bt.g.*,[40] while three types of organism have been isolated also from *Cryptocercus punctulatus*.[51] The bacteroids of *P.a.* have also been said to grow slowly on a yeast-dextrose agar[56] and in lactose broth,[33] but other writers state that no bacteroids could be cultivated from *P.a.*[37,44,49] They may survive in vitro in fat body or other normal host tissue cultures.[36] Similarly the bacteroids of *Bt.g.* could not be cultured in artificial media[45,46,49,90] nor those of *B.o.*,[49,52,54] although in one case they were reported to appear after about 16 days.[90] The bacteroids of *Leucophaea maderae* were cultured on lactose agar.[76]

Bode says that if a large enough inoculum is used some organisms can be cultured in meat broth, but he also points out that one cannot be sure they are the bacteroids of the fat body.[5] Others have also had reservations about the nature of the organisms cultured and Javelly found that they had different staining reactions from the bacteroids of the fat body, the egg and the embryo.[54] Moreover, the identification of bacteria in culture remains very difficult and, so far, reinfection of cockroaches has not been established.[81] Grafts of normal *Bt.g.* fat body into specimens of *Bt.g.* from which the fat body had been removed, were not destroyed, although the recipients all died within three days; but all grafts from other species of cockroach were immediately destroyed.[45]

Fragments of fat body and ovary can be kept alive on agar plates and in one experiment a fragment of ovary survived for 39 days and in seven other experiments fragments of fat body were kept for 14 to 39 days. All were infected with the bacteroids and in four of the experiments with fat tissue, the bacteroids were reported to have multiplied although the host tissue died. As the bacteriocytes degenerated the cell membranes broke down and the bacteroids migrated to neighbouring cells until all the tissue was infected.[45,46] Keller was able to culture the micro-organisms from *B.o.* on agar with fresh ground fat body and on agar containing 0.2% of uric acid. The organisms took about 10 days to grow at an optimum temperature of $24°$, and were cocco-bacilli and cocci. The identity of the organisms cultured was checked by serological tests and Keller states that, although the results can only be almost certain, it is most probable that they were identical with the bacteroids of the fat body.[55]

Since the bacteroids are known to be transmitted to the next generation through the eggs, several workers have cultured the contents of the oöthecae (T). Mercier claimed that the oöthecae were sterile apart from the bacteroids, which he found developed a filiform shape in broth culture. He thought they were like *Bacillus mesentericus* or *B. subtilis*.[66,67,68,69] Gropengiesser found in some of the oöthecae of *Bt.g.* a bacillus which could be *B. cuenoti*; in others a fungus was present with oval cells $3.5–4 \mu \times 1.8–2 \mu$, having vacuoles, oil-droplets, but showing no gas, alcohol or acid formation, nor spore formation, and forming freed daughter cells. In other oöthecae both organisms were present, and in still others, neither. In a few cases a Sarcina was present, with cells of about 1.6μ diameter, which were Gram-positive, but had no flagella. It was not thought these organisms could be extraneous infections, but also it was not thought that the bacillus was from the fat body of the embryo, especially as the bacteroids of the fat bodies of

11 + B.O.C.

different cockroaches were considered to be different. The fungus, however, was believed to be the symbiotic organism, of the fat body, but it utilized very little nitrogen from the culture medium, although in vivo there could be greater rate of uptake. Both bacillus and fungus showed proteolytic activity and were without antagonism in mixed culture.[42] But *B. cuenoti* is always a contaminant according to Hertig.[49] A fungal form is reported by Brooks in the fat body of *Bt.g.*[12]

Donellan claims to have cultured the organisms aerobically on a medium at pH 7·2 containing 0·15% sodium urate, 0·5% potassium dihydrogen phosphate, 0·03% Lam-lemco and 0·04% magnesium sulphate, with or without 0·1% ammonium sulphate; and on a similar medium in which 0·2% allantoin replaced the urate. The organism was not a classified bacterium but was Gram-negative and resembles the *Vibrio* genus.[28]

The bacteriocytes

The cells containing the bacteroids are called bacteriocytes or mycetocytes. In *Bt.g.* they are variously reported as being in paired groups in the fat body of abdominal segments 2 to 6 (10 in all),[12] in an axial row mixed with fat cells,[42] in 4 rows,[29, from 45] in 3 to 4 rows,[22] in several rows,[3] or scattered.[45] These cells are without urates or fat.[3, 42, 45] In *B.o.* they lie in a single longitudinal axial row.[3, 42]

Even in aposymbiotic cockroaches the bacteriocytes are retained, albeit without contents.[18] The number of bacteroids in *P.a.* approximately doubles in each instar until the imaginal moult when the number remains roughly constant until a decline occurs in old age.[36] In *B.o.* the nymphs have few bacteroids[93] and in the adult, where there are many more, the female has more than the male, and the fat body contains more than the eggs.[92] It is also said that after death of the host the bacteroids form a central structure which could be interpreted as a spore or resistant stage.[62]

The bacteriocytes are large cells,[81] with large nuclei and 'fibrous' cytoplasm even in aposymbiotic animals[18] and contain much glycogen.[8] In *P.a.* the nuclei are also very large relative to the cell volume and each bacteriocyte of *Bt.g.* has 1 or 2 nuclei.[45] In *B.o.* the bacteriocytes have more mitochondria, lying irregularly near the nucleus, than the usual fat body cell.[57, 70] Both typical fat body cells and bacteriocytes contain reserve materials, but no Golgi apparatus, and the bacteroids lie in the superficial indentations of the nucleus. One of the remarkable features of the mitochondria of the bacteriocytes of *B.o.* is that they have oblique christae,[70] while those of the fat body of *P.a.* have christae which are thought to be in the form of a single continuous spiral.[75] In aposymbiotic *Bt.g.* the empty bacteriocytes never divide and there are therefore only 10 clusters present. It seems probable that they must undergo division at an early stage in their development if they are to divide at all, because those without bacteroids increase to about 200 times the normal volume when the host is reinfected with bacteroids. They do not divide to accommodate the increasing population of bacteroids.[18]

The nuclei of the bacteriocytes in *Bt.g.* are said to divide amitotically in *Bt.g.*[45, 58] and *P.a.*,[22] or mitotically in *Bt.g.*[18] and *P.a.*[2] The nuclear division occurs in the latter half of a stadium in *Bt.g.*[81] and in *P.a.* it is so late in the stadium that the new cuticle has already been formed.[2] For a short time the bacteriocytes of *B.o.* are binucleate until cell division occurs[31] and this may account for the observation that those of *P.a.* may contain 1 or 2 nuclei.[45] In *Bt.g.* the bacteriocytes, urate cells and plain fat body cells all divide at the same time.[18, 22]

The nuclei of the bacteriocytes are polyploid,[2, 81] being in *P.a.* 4-, 8-, or 16-ploid, even in the late embryo. Calculating from the nuclear volume fully mature bacteriocytes become 256- or 512-ploid. The normal fat body cells are 2- or 3-ploid and urate cells are 2-ploid. No endomitoses were seen.[2]

The removal of the bacteroids from cockroaches is usually accomplished by adding antibiotic drugs to the food,[16] or by injecting them into the animal. The bacteroids of some species of cockroaches are susceptible, however, to other treatments, and the bacteroids of *P.a.* can be greatly reduced in numbers by starvation or poor diet.[36] It is said that *Bt.g.* can be made aposymbiotic only by antibiotics,[45, 81] but Brooks found that diets deficient in manganese made *Bt.g.* grow poorly and produce progeny without bacteroids.[13] The action of manganese in assisting the ovarian transmission of bacteroids is synergized by zinc and antagonized by calcium.[14, 15] Other aposymbiotic *Bt.g.* were produced by feeding them on a diet containing particular ratios of calcium and zinc or other salts, but all died even on a fortified diet of dog-biscuit and yeast.[13] Whatever method is used to remove the bacteroids the results are the same and cannot be attributed to the antibiotics used.[12] Feeding *B.o.* with antibiotics appeared to remove the original population of bacteroids, but it allowed a new organism to grow, of about twice the size of the bacteroids. It was perhaps another organism rather than another strain of the normal bacteroids; the new organism was hardly able to infect the eggs so that the next generation were found to possess deformed infected bacteriocytes.[31, 32] In the same roach, *B.o.*, the bacteroids found in animals treated to remove them look like 'pathological forms' and if the progeny of these animals survived they had defective bacteriocytes although some bacteroids might be present.[31] In the fat body of the *B.o.* there were some bodies present which were neither bacteroids nor mitochondria;[70] they could be the microsporidian, *Plistophora* sp., reported to occur in the fat body of *B.o.* where they cause abnormal mitoses as in some tumours.[69] A microsporidian was also found in the fat body of *P.a.* by Porter.[79] Bacteriocytes in aposymbiotic *Bt.g.* may or may not shrink and disappear.[87]

Nature and functions of the bacteroids

Buchner[20] thought the bacteroids of *P.a.* are symbiotes (quoted by Glaser) but Glaser himself thought they are exparasites which have adapted themselves to their special rôle.[38] In *Bt.g.* they seem to be symbiotes[45] and in *B.o.* there is said to be a complete equilibrium between the bacteroids and the bacteriocytes.[70] It is not, however, easy to prove in what ways the bacteroids benefit the host, and even less easy to show how the host benefits the bacteroids. The data produced by different workers have been very varied (T).

Nymphs of *Bt.g.* made aposymbiotic grow poorly, die easily[12, 16, 19, 45] and take two or three times as long to mature [17,41] as normal nymphs, while the fat body becomes distended with accumulation of urates in both *Bt.g.* and *B.o.*[12,32] Aposymbiotic *B.o.* and *P.a.* are also 40% smaller than normal, showing poor growth, with poor reproductive capacity in the adult stage,[81] while aposymbiotic *Bt.g.* has a shortened life span[87] and lays fewer and less viable eggs.[16] Adult *B.o.*,[31,32,81] adult *P.a.*[81] and nymphs of *Bt.g.*[12] are lighter in colour than normal roaches, but in *B.o.* they may later regain the normal colour. This lightening of the colour is not due to any dietary change but probably from the loss of one of the steps in the formation of tyrosine so that melanin production is reduced.[31] Reduction in development of both male and female gonads is reported to occur in aposymbiotic *Bt.g.*,[17] and reproductive capacity is reduced in the adults.[12] Ovarian atrophy in *Bt.g.*[45] and other cockroaches[41] has been reported, while in *B.o.* either the ovaries remain very immature[31] or degenerative changes occur in oögenesis.[32] The changes in *B.o.* begin at a definite time after the removal of the bacteroids, and lead to the rejection of the oöcytes as foreign bodies. These effects on oögenesis, moreover, can be produced by feeding the nymphs with penicillin for the first 4 months of life, and are then not manifest until 7 or 8 months later. Injection of fat body brei into aposymbiotic females did not allow the development of viable nymphs, although oöthecae were produced,[32] and a similar result was found with the supernatant fluid from centrifuged fat body suspension.[31] This suggests that some soluble factor necessary for oögenesis is secreted by the bacteroids. Brooks and Richards found no evidence for an hormonal effect, however, in experiments with *Bt.g.*, in which aposymbiotic females could accept implants of normal fat body tissue which sometimes led to more normal functioning although the bacteroids did not infect the ovaries.[19] It is interesting to find that in *Bt.g.* mature ovaries grew during a period of 35 to 50 days following a period when aureomycin had been used to suppress the bacteroids.[87] In male cockroaches, it is claimed there is little or no effect on the gonad[31,41] but the first few oöthecae formed by normal females mated with aposymbiotic males were infertile.[16] Keller points out that some cockroaches are known in which only the female harbours bacteroids, and there certainly seems to be some symbiosis between the bacteroids and the female.[41]

The metabolic activity of the fat body

The fat body is the centre of much metabolic activity in cockroaches, and in *P.a.* it has been shown to oxidize NADH, sugar phosphates, isocitrate, succinate, oxoglutarate and hydroxybutyrate[97] and it contains several esterases.[25] It contains in *Bt.g.* NAD, NADP, glucose-6-phosphate, 6-phosphogluconate dehydrogenase and malic dehydrogenase.[96] The last two are found in the fat body of *P.a.* and vary in amount with the time after moulting, the maximum occurring 4 to 8 days after moulting, being 10 times the minimum.[34] Glycogen varies also during a stadium: the fat body content of this substance increases 60 times during the 20-day period of maximum cuticle synthesis,[59] and shows the importance of using nymphs of known age for valid comparisons. There were also significant differences between the sexes and the different instars.[34]

The adenosine nucleotide content of the fat body of *Leucophaea maderae* has been found to vary during the reproductive cycle, the ATP apparently being destroyed and later resynthesized. Changes occur in the ATP content of the fat body during the phase when water is being passed into the eggs, but this may be an artefact if the water content of the fat body decreases during this time. It is thought there may be a hormone secreted by the corpora allata which uncouples the process of oxidative phosphorylation.[61]

In the nymphs of *Bt.g.* the bacteroids seem to be concerned in uric acid metabolism, since urates accumulate so readily in aposymbiotic animals.[19] In *B.o.* the abdomen of an aposymbiotic female becomes distended and stretched by this accumulation of urates.[31] Moreover, transplants of normal fat body are accepted by the aposymbiotic nymphs of *Bt.g.*, after which some of the urate accumulations go, but the older the recipient, the less successful are the transplants.[19]

Uricase has been detected in the fat body of *P.a.*[26, from 78] and in *L. maderae*.[60] In aposymbiotic *L. maderae* the nymphs contained little of this enzyme but the adults contained so much that they ought not to require the uricase activity of the bacteroids.[78] Recently, Donnellan has isolated an organism from the fat body of *P.a.*, which degrades uric acid to glyoxylate and urea via allantoin and allantoic acid. Urease present breaks down the urea, and the glyoxylate is synthesized to malate via tartronic semialdehyde, glycerate and pyruvate.[27]

Removal of the corpora cardiaca causes deposition of urates in the fat body, and an increase in the fat of the adipose cells of this organ.[6]

The fat body of *P.a.* fixes ammonia injected into the haemocoel and its uric acid content varies with the amount of protein in the diet. When the diet contains 25% protein, the fat body uric acid equalled 12.7 ± 3.9 mg; with a protein-free diet, the amount present was 1.2 ± 0.3 mg, after 30 days. With a 60% protein diet, the uric acid content rose to 39 ± 3.6 mg. The decrease in uric acid when the diet contained no protein could not be accounted for by the excretory loss. Thus the bacteroids had probably metabolized it.[64] The same thing is probably true for *Bt.g.*[45] Injected glycine or urea did not increase fat body uric acid in *P.a.*[64]

The fat body does not form vitamin E[55] nor does it appear to have any humoral function,[19] but it does have, in *P.a.*, amine oxidase,[4] high catalase activity,[71] and may act as a store for sterols which are found as esters in high concentration.[53] Vitamin C is synthesized by the bacteroids in *Bt.g.*,[95] in *Leucophaea maderae*[76] and in *P.a.*,[33] in spite of the fact that the vitamin appears to be unnecessary for the normal health of the animals.[33,77,95] *P.a.* can synthesize ascorbic acid from mannose,[77,85] glucose, fructose, galactose, xylose and sucrose.[85] It is possible that the bacteroids are synthesizing it for their own use or as a by-product of some other reaction (T).

Bacteroids have been thought to synthesize cholesterol[24] and other vitamins or proteins, for example, in *Bt.g.*,[45,84,94] but much of the evidence is derived from experiments in which the absence of various substances in aposymbiotic cockroaches was taken to indicate the production of the missing compound by bacteroids. In *B.o.* they are said to produce the vitamin B needed by the roach,[81] but *L. maderae* requires dietary vitamin B.[77] This divergence is emphasized by the report that there is a factor in yeast which is not a B vitamin (factor 'X') supposedly formed by the fat body bacteroids of *Bt.g.*, which is necessary for the host's satisfactory growth, fertility and cuticle darkening.[12] McCay[63] also remarks on a substance in yeast necessary to the roach, which he says is not vitamin B_1 nor flavin. In this cockroach 9 amino acids are essential for the normal animal; if it is deprived of its bacteroids, it requires more than 19 amino acids, as well as the factor 'X' of yeast;[12] this presumably gives an indication of the synthetic value of the bacteroids. One noticeable result of reduced tyrosine production in aposymbiotic roaches is their lighter colour, due to the consequent inability to synthesize melanin and tanning phenols. Aposymbiotic *Bt.g.* were able to synthesize from glucose: alanine, glutamic acid, aspartic acid, glycine, proline and possibly serine,[47] but not leucine, tyrosine, valine, phenylalanine, threonine, isoleucine, arginine and lysine.[47, 48] Cultures of bacteroids from *P.a.* were able to synthesize pantothenic and folic acids.[33] The total amino acid counts of normal and aposymbiotic *B.o.* are the same.

The bacteroids of *B.o.* may be involved in lipid metabolism.[31]

Attempts have been made to compensate for the loss of the bacteroids by an artificial, enriched diet, but yeasts and mildews are reported to be necessary for *P.a.* On the other hand, unbalanced diets are not compensated for by the bacteroids.[5] Aposymbiotic *P.a.* kept without vitamins of the B group died, but those which received only folic and pantothenic acids lived, though with less colour.[33] Yeast added to a complete diet of *B.o.* causes accelerated growth which distorts the wing structure, but a diet without yeast or vitamins usually results in the death of the aposymbiotic cockroach, and there seems to be a connection with, if not a full dependence on, the bacteroids in normal animals.[31] In this roach, however, it is reported that a full diet with yeast is not able to reverse the degenerative changes in oögenesis due to removal of the bacteroids.[32]

The interrelations of bacteroids and roach remain obscure. Brooks reports experiments in which the progeny of *Bt.g.* which had been subjected to abnormal salt ratios in the diet were unable to survive even on a fortified diet, although they contained abundant bacteriocytes and bacteroids. This could be due to disturbance of a delicate balance between host and bacteroids, or to a competition between the two organisms for essential nutrients or vital factors.[13] Could it also be due to the toxic effects of the unusual amounts of different salts in the diet (T)? It is of interest to find that Bode found the bacteroids of *P.a.* were affected by the absence of the normal gut micro-organisms,[5] whereas in *Bt.g.* Wollman noted that the number of bacteroids present was unaffected by such conditions.[94]

The surface of the bacteroids of *B.o.* is provided with many microtubules which may have an absorptive function.[70]

The bacteroids and ovarian transmission

The bacteriocytes in *Bt.g.* migrate from the fat body to lie close to the ovaries[14, 22] and between the ovarioles.[45] The bacteroids infect the ovaries and in due course the older oöcytes; they do not affect the younger oöcytes.[22, 42, 45] This is also true of *P.a.*[38]

A similar migration of some of the bacteriocytes occurs to the testes in males of *Bt.g.*[12, 22] and *P.a.*, but no infection of them has been seen.[2] The timing of the infection and the site on the egg where it occurs are specific to the host concerned[30] as are the number of bacteroids present, the structure of the ovary and the details of the embryonic development.[35]

The details of the transference of the bacteroids from the bacteriocytes of the adult to the embryonic bacteriocytes of the developing fat body of the embryo, are not wholly agreed,[8] although some recent work with the electron microscope clearly supersedes some older investigations (T).

In *P.a.* the bacteroids penetrate the ovarian sheath between the follicle cells but do not enter them,[7, 22] accumulating between the oöcytes and the follicle cells, until the mass of bacteroids is two or three deep. As the oöcyte grows it presses against the follicle cells and squeezes the bacteroids towards both ends so that the accumulations are much more fully at the poles of the developing egg.[7, 21, 35, 38] The bacteroids pass into the oöcyte but exactly how is not clear. The eggs have microvilli which surround the bacteroids and these may be a means of drawing them actively into the egg.[23] According to Anderson, however, the evidence for any bacteroids being intracellular is at least dubious if not false. Moreover, the bacteroids are so numerous that, although at first they lie tangentially, later they lie palisade fashion and this causes indentations in the oölemma[1], which may be the reason for the appearance of the microvilli.[22]

On the other hand it is stated that the polar regions of the oöcyte pucker and fold, so forming invaginations which are crowded with bacteroids from the polar accumulations. These form a yolk-free zone about 15 μ thick and 150 μ diameter just beneath the surface.[22] Another account states that the cleavage nuclei in the yolk mass migrate to the periphery of the oöcyte, where some of them pick up bacteroids and retreat with them back into the yolk. There they congregate and form a transitory mycetome, or collection of bacteriocytes. In later development some pass posteriorly through the yolk and through the incomplete margins of the gut epithelium and so into the developing body cavity. From here they make their way into the lateral lobes of the fat body.[35] The migration from the yolk takes place when the germ band grows round it.[38]

In *Bt.g.* the process of infecting the oöcytes is very similar. The eggs are infected when they reach a size of about 0·13 mm long[42] and again no bacteroids have been seen in the follicle cells.[9] At first the multiplication of the bacteroids is equal to the growth of the egg so that they cover all the surface of the egg. Later the egg grows too big and they come to lie in two polar masses.[11, 42]

The critical stage in the life cycle is at the entry of the bacteroids into the eggs.[12] As indicated above, the details of this process are not known, and Borghese states that either it occurs very quickly or it is obscured by the staining of the follicle cells.[11] The bacteroids come to lie immediately beneath the oölemma in the peripheral oöplasm which is without yolk.[9, 11] Here they multiply[9, 42] and begin to move into the yolk to form a central collection[11, 42] either without any special connection with the yolk nuclei[9, 10] or by means of the vitellophag nuclei.[12] They later pass from the yolk, between the endoderm cells, while the embryo is still in the ventral lamina stage, and so into the bacteriocytes formed previously in the developing fat body.[9, 12, 45, 58] These are the non-vesicular cells of the developing fat body, and during their migration, they are said to pass into the epineural sinus where they begin to multiply.[11] Only the visceral abdominal lobes of the fat body are infected at first,[9] but later the bacteriocytes increase in number and spread throughout the fat body.[12]

The processes of oöcyte infection in *B.o.* are probably essentially similar. The young oöcytes were found to be surrounded by a layer of bacteroids, which migrated into the peripheral oöplasm from the follicle cells[43] or at least bacteroids were seen in the follicle cells as well as in the peritoneal tunic cells.[68] They lay within a layer of a much folded membrane, forming a honeycomb-like layer which was seen to have connections to the bacteroids, and which could arise from them. In older oöcytes the bacteroids were congregated at each pole.[43]

The bacteroids are probably symbiotic organisms. They are almost certainly immotile, and may multiply by the formation of transverse partitions. They probably do not form spores, and their dimensions cannot be stated without further work to confirm one of the numerous statements already made. Whether the organism has been cultured in vitro is a question whose answer must also remain in abeyance at present, although it is very likely that Keller and Donnellan have successfully accomplished this. The interrelation between the bacteroids and the organisms in the gut merits investigation and much remains to be learnt about both the bacteriocytes and the bacteroids.

There is no doubt that the term 'fat body' is an unfortunate one for an organ in which so much metabolic chemistry goes on, especially as it is so intimately concerned with the metabolism of nitrogenous compounds.

Accounts of the transference of the bacteroids into the developing eggs leave much to be desired, but improvement will have to wait until an adequate account of the embryology of *P.a.* is given (T).

REFERENCES

1. ANDERSON, E. (1964). Oocyte differentiation and vitellogenesis in the roach *Periplaneta americana. J. cell. Biol.*, **20**, 131–55.
2. BAUDISCH, K. (1956). Zytologische Beobachtungen an den Mycetocyten von *Periplaneta americana. Naturwissenschaften*, **43**, 358.
3. BLOCHMANN, F. (1887). Uber das regelmässige Vorkommen von bakterien-ähnlichen Gebilden in den Geweben und Eiern verschiedener Insekten. *Z. Biol.*, **24**, 1–15.
4. BLASCHKO, H., COLHOUN, E. H. and FRONTALI, N. (1961). Occurrence of amine oxidase in an insect, *Periplaneta americana. J. Physiol.*, **156**, 28P.
5. BODE, H. (1936). Untersuchungen über die Symbiose von tieren mit Pilzen und Bakterien. V. Die Bakteriensymbiose bei Blattiden und das Verhalten von Blattiden bei aseptischer Aufzucht. *Arch. Mikrobiol.*, **7**, 391–403.
6. BODENSTEIN, D. (1953). Studies on the humoral mechanisms in growth and metamorphosis of the cockroach, *Periplaneta americana*. III. Humoral effects on metabolism. *J. exp. Zool.*, **124**, 105–15.
7. BONHAG, P. F. (1959). Histological and histochemical studies on the ovary of the American cockroach, *Periplaneta americana. Univ. Calif. Publs Ent.*, **16**, 81–124.

8. BONHAG, P. F. and ARNOLD, W. J. (1961). Histology, histochemistry and tracheation of the ovariole sheaths in the American cockroach, *Periplaneta americana*. *J. Morph.*, **108**, 107–18.
9. BORGHESE, E. (1946). Richerche sul batterio simbionte della *Blattella germanica*. *Boll. Soc. ital. Biol. sper.*, **22**, 106–7.
10. BORGHESE, E. (1948). Il ciclo del batterio simbionte di *Blattella germanica*. *Mycopath. Mycol. appl.*, **4**, 85–102.
11. BORGHESE, E. (1948). Osservazioni sul batterio simbionte della *Blattella germanica*. *Monitore zool. ital.*, **56**, 252–3.
12. BROOKS, M. A. (1956). Nature and significance of intracellular bacteroids in cockroaches. *Proc. 10th. Int. Congr. Ent.*, **2**, 311–14.
13. BROOKS, M. A. (1957). Investigation of possible antagonism between host and symbiote. *Anat. Rec.*, **128**, 527–8.
14. BROOKS, M. A. (1960). Some dietary factors that affect ovarial transmission of symbiotes. *Proc. helminth. Soc. Wash.*, **27**, 212–20.
15. BROOKS, M. A. (1962). The relationship between intracellular symbiotes and host metabolism. *Symp. genet.*, **9**, 456–63.
16. BROOKS, M. A. and RICHARDS, A. G. (1954). The necessity for intracellular bacteroids (symbiotes) in growth and reproduction of cockroaches (Blattariae). *Anat. Rec.*, **120**, 742.
17. BROOKS, M. A. and RICHARDS, A. G. (1955). Intracellular symbiosis in cockroaches. I. Production of aposymbiotic cockroaches. *Biol. Bull. mar. biol. Lab. Woods Hole*, **109**, 22–39.
18. BROOKS, M. A. and RICHARDS, A. G. (1955). Intracellular symbiosis in cockroaches. II. Mitotic division of mycetocytes. *Science*, **122**, 242.
19. BROOKS, M. A. and RICHARDS, A. G. (1956). Intracellular symbiosis in cockroaches. III. Reinfection of aposymbiotic cockroaches with symbiotes. *J. exp. Zool.*, **132**, 447–65.
20. BUCHNER, P. (1912). Studien an intrazellularen Symbionten. I. Die intracellularen Symbionten der Hemipteren. *Arch. Protistenk.*, **26**, 1–116.
21. BUCHNER, P. (1921). *Tier und Pflanzen in intrazellular Symbiose*. Gebrüder Borntraeger, Berlin.
22. BUCHNER, P. (1953). *Endosymbiose der Tiere mit pflanzlichen Mikroorganismen*. Verlag Birkhauser, Basel und Stuttgart.
23. BUSH, G. L. and CHAPMAN, G. B. (1961). Electron microscopy of symbiotic bacteria in developing oocytes of the American cockroach *Periplaneta americana*. *J. Bact.*, **81**, 267–76.
24. CLAYTON, R. B. (1960). The rôle of intestinal symbionts in the sterol metabolism of *Blattella germanica*. *J. biol. Chem.*, **235**, 3421–5.
25. COLHOUN, E. H. (1963). Synthesis of 5-hydroxytryptamine in the American cockroach. *Experientia*, **19**, 9–10.
26. CORDERO, S. M. (1958). Dissertation, Fordham Univ.
27. DONNELLAN, J. F. (1965). Personal communication.
28. DONNELLAN, J. F. (1965). Personal communication.
29. FRÄNKEL. No reference, 1918. From HALLER, G. DE. (1955).
30. FRAENKEL, H. (1921). Die Symbionten der Blattiden im Fettgewebe und Ei, insbesondere von *Periplaneta orientalis*. *Z. wiss. Zool.*, **119**, 53–66.
31. FRANK, W. (1955). Einwirkung verschiedener Antibiotica auf die Symbionten der Küchenschabe *Blatta orientalis* und die dadurch bedingten Veränderungen am Wirtstier. *Zool. Anz.*, **18** (suppl.), 381–8.
32. FRANK, W. (1956). Entfernung der intrazellulären Symbionten der Küchenschabe *Periplaneta orientalis* durch Einwirkung verschiedener Antibiotica, unter besonderer Berücksichtigung der Veränderungen am Wirtstier und an den Bakterien. *Z. Morph. Ökol. Tiere*, **44**, 329–66.
33. GALLAHER, M. R. (1963). Vitamin synthesis by the symbionts in the fat body of the cockroach *Periplaneta americana*. *Diss. Abstr.*, **23**, 3449–50.

11*

34. GARY, N. E., BERGER, R. S. and TUONG, R. G. (1959). Biology and dehydrogenase activities of the fat body of late instar American cockroach *Periplaneta americana*. *Ann. ent. Soc. Am.*, **52**, 570–3.
35. GIER, H. T. (1936). The morphology and behaviour of the intracellular bacteroids of roaches. *Biol. Bull. mar. biol. Lab. Woods Hole*, **71**, 433–52.
36. GIER, H. T. (1937). Growth of the intracellular symbionts of the cockroach *Periplaneta americana*. *Anat. Rec.*, **70**, 69.
37. GIER, H. T. (1947). Intracellular bacteroids in the cockroach, *Periplaneta americana*. *J. Bact.*, **53**, 173–89.
38. GLASER, R. W. (1920). Biological studies on intracellular bacteroids. *Biol. Bull. mar. biol. Lab. Woods Hole*, **39**, 133–45.
39. GLASER, R. W. (1930). On the isolation, cultivation and classification of the so-called intracellular 'symbiont', or 'rickettsia' of *Periplaneta americana*. *J. exp. Med.*, **51**, 59–82.
40. GLASER, R. W. (1930). Cultivation and classification of 'bacteroids', 'symbionts' or 'Rickettsiae' of *Blattella germanica*. *J. exp. Med.*, **51**, 903–7.
41. GLASER, R. W. (1946). The intracellular bacteroids of the cockroach in relation to symbiosis. *J. Parasit.*, **32**, 483–9.
42. GROPENGIESSER, C. (1925). Untersuchungen über die Symbiose der Blattiden mit niederen pflanzlichen Organismen. *Zentbl. Bakt. ParasitKde.*, **64**, 495–511.
43. GRESSON, R. A. R. and THREADGOLD, L. T. (1960). An electron microscope study of bacteria in the oocytes and follicle cells of *Blatta orientalis*. *Q. Jl microsc. Sci.*, **101**, 295–7.
44. GUBLER, H. V. (1948). Versuche zur Züchtung intrazellulären Insektensymbionten. *Schweiz. Z. allg. Path. Bakt.*, **11**, 489–93.
45. HALLER, G. DE (1955). La symbiose bactérienne intracellulaire chez la Blatte *Blattella germanica*. *Archs Sci. Genéve*, **8**, 229–304.
46. HALLER, G. DE (1955). L'isolement du symbiote intracellulaire de la Blatte. *Revue suisse Zool.*, **62** (Suppl.), 164–70.
47. HENRY, S. M. (1962). The significance of microorganisms in the nutrition of insects. *Trans. N.Y. Acad. Sci.*, **24**, 676–83.
48. HENRY, S. M. and BLOCK, R. J. (1962). Amino acid synthesis, a ruminent-like effect of the intracellular symbionts of the German cockroach. *Fedn Proc. Fedn Am. Socs exp. Biol.*, **21**, 9.
49. HERTIG, M. (1921). Attempts to cultivate the bacteroids of the Blattidae. *Biol. Bull. mar. biol. Lab. Woods Hole*, **41**, 181–7.
50. HOLLANDE, A. C. and FAVRE, R. (1931). La structure cytologique de *Blattabacterium cuénoti* (Mercier) n.g. symbiote du tissue adipeux des Blattides. *C.r. Séanc. Soc. Biol.*, **107**, 752–4.
51. HOOVER, S. (1945). Studies on the bacteroids of *Cryptocercus punctulatus*. *J. Morph.*, **76**, 213–25.
52. HAVASSE, R. (1936). Protistologica 24. *Bacillus cuenoti* Mercier, bacteroide de *Periplaneta orientalis* à la morphologie d'une bactérie. *Archs Zool. exp. gén.*, **70**, 93–6.
53. ISHII, S., KAPLANIS, J. N. and ROBBINS, W. E. (1963). Distribution and fate of 4-C^{14}-cholesterol in the adult male American cockroach. *Ann. ent. Soc. Am.*, **56**, 115–19.
54. JAVELLY, E. (1914). Les corps bactéroides de la blatte (*Periplaneta orientalis*) n'ont pas encore été cultivées. *C.r. Séanc. Soc. Biol.*, **77**, 413–14.
55. KELLER, H. (1950). Die Kultur der intrazellularen Symbioten von *Periplaneta orientalis*. *Z. Naturf.*, **5B**, 269–73.
56. KETCHEL, M. M. and WILLIAMS, C. M. (1953). Isolation of the intracellular symbiont of the roach. *Anat. Rec.*, **117**, 650.
57. KOCH, A. (1930). Über das Vorkommen von Mitochondrien in Mycetocyten. *Z. Morph. Ökol. Tiere*, **19**, 259–90.

58. KOCH, A. (1949). Die Bakteriensymbiose der Küchenschaben. *Mikrokomos*, **38**, 121–6.

59. LIPKE, H., GRAINGER, M. M. and SIAKOTOS, A. N. (1965). Polysaccharide and glycoprotein formation in the cockroach. I. Identity and titer of bound monosaccharides. *J. biol. Chem.*, **240**, 594–600.

60. LISA, J. D. and LUDWIG, D. (1959). Uricase, guanase and zanthine oxidase from the fat body of the cockroach *Leucophaea maderae*. *Ann. ent. Soc. Am.*, **52**, 548–51.

61. LÜSCHER, M. and WYSS-HUBER, M. (1964). Die Adenosin-Nukleotide im Fettkörper des adulten Weibchens von *Leucophaea maderae* im Laufe des Sexualzyklus. *Revue suisse Zool.*, **71**, 183–94.

62. LWOFF, A. (1923). Nature et position systématique du bacteroides des Blattes. *C.r. Séanc. Soc. Biol.*, **89**, 945–6.

63. MCCAY, C. M. (1938). The nutritional requirements of *Blattella germanica*. *Physiol. Zööl.*, **11**, 89–103.

64. MCENROE, W. D. (1957). Uric acid metabolism in the American cockroach. *Diss. Abstr.*, **17**, 2338.

65. MERCER, E. H. and BRUNET, P. C. J. (1959). The electron microscopy of the left colleterial gland of the cockroach. *J. biophys. biochem. Cytol.*, **5**, 257–62.

66. MERCIER, L. (1906). Les corps bactéroides de la Blatte (*Periplaneta orientalis*): *Bacillus Cuénoti* n. sp. *C.r. Séanc. Soc. Biol.*, **61**, 682–4.

67. MERCIER, L. (1907). Recherches sur les bactéroides des Blattides. *Arch. Protistenk.*, **9**, 346–58.

68. MERCIER, L. (1907). Cellules à *Bacillus Cuenoti* dans la paroi des gaines ovariques de la Blatte. *C.r. Séanc. Soc. Biol.*, **62**, 758–9.

69. MERCIER, L. (1908). Néoplasie du tissue adipeux chez les Blattes (*Periplaneta orientalis*) parasitées par une Microsporidie. *Arch. Protistenk.*, **11**, 372–81.

70. MEYER, G. F. and FRANK, W. (1957). Electronmikroskopische Studien zur intracellulären Symbiose verschiedener Insekten. I. *Z. Zellforsch. mikrosk. Anat.*, **47**, 29–42.

71. NELSON, W. L. (1958). Fat metabolism with reference to insects. *Proc. 10th. Int. Congr. Ent.*, **2**, 359–64.

72. NEUKOMM, A. (1927). Sur la structure des bactéroides des Blattes. *C.r. Séanc. Soc. Biol.*, **96**, 306–8.

73. NEUKOMM, A. (1927). Action des rayons ultra-violets sur les bactéroides des Blattes (*Blattella germanica*). *C.r. Séanc. Soc. Biol.*, **96**, 1155–6.

74. NEUKOMM, A. (1932). La réaction de la fixation du complément appliquée à l'étude des bactéroides des Blattes (*Blattella germanica*). *C.r. Séanc. Soc. Biol.*, **111**, 928–9.

75. PEARSE, A. G. E. and SCARPELLI, D. G. (1958). Cytochemical localization of succinic dehydrogenase in mitochondria from *Periplaneta americana*. *Nature*, **181**, 702–3.

76. PIERRE, L. L. (1961). Functions of the symbionts in the fat body of the tropical cockroach *Leucophaea maderae*. *Diss. Abstr.*, **22**, 983.

77. PIERRE, L. L. (1962). Synthesis of ascorbic acid by the normal fat body of the cockroach *Leucophaea maderae* and by its symbionts. *Nature*, **193**, 904–5.

78. PIERRE, L. (1964). Uricase activity of isolated symbionts and the aposymbiotic fat body of a cockroach. *Nature*, **201**, 54–5.

79. PORTER, A. (1930). Cockroaches as vectors of hookworms in gold mines of the Witwatersrand. *J. med. Ass. S. Afr.*, **4**, 18–20.

80. PRÉNANT, A. (1904). *Traité d'histologie*, vol. 1. Schleicher (Masson), Paris.

81. RICHARDS, A. G. and BROOKS, M. A. (1958). Internal symbiosis in insects. *A. Rev. Ent.*, **3**, 37–56.

82. RIES, E. (1932). Experimentelle Symbiosestudien. I. Mycetomtransplantationen. *Z. Morph. Ökol. Tiere*, **25**, 184–234.

324 The fat body and its bacteroids

83. RITZI, M. T. M. (1954). Desoxyribose nucleic acid in the symbiotic micro-organisms of the cockroach. *Science*, **120**, 35–6.
84. ROTH, L. M. and WILLIS, E. R. (1957). The medical and veterinary importance of cockroaches. *Smithson. misc. Collns.*, **134**, no. 10.
85. ROUSELL, P. G. (1956). Effects of various factors on the synthesis of ascorbic acid by the American cockroach. *Trans. N.Y. Acad. Sci.*, **19**, 17–18.
86. SCHNEIDER, K. C. (1902). *Lehrbuch der vergleichenden Histologie der Tiere.* G. Fischer, Jena.
87. SELMAIR, E. (1962). Beiträgezur Wirkung wachstumsförderner Stoffe auf die Entwicklung der Blattiden (*Blattella germanica*). *Z. ParasitKde.*, **21**, 321–62.
88. SIVA, J. P. (1954). La naturaleza de los simbiotes intracellulares de *Blattella germanica*. *Microbiologia esp.*, **7**, 51–60.
89. SILVA, J. P. (1954). Cultivo 'in vitro' de simbiotes intracellulares de insectos. *Microbiologia esp.*, **7**, 187–254.
90. TACCHINI, I. (1946). Ricerca sui batteri simbionti intracellulari delle Blatte. *Boll. Soc. ital. Biol. sper.*, **22**, 113–14.
91. TRAGER, W. (1952). Mitochondria or microorganisms? *Science*, **116**, 332.
92. WOLF, J. (1924). Contribution à la morphologie des bactéroides dans les Blattes (*Periplaneta orientalis*). *C.r. Séanc. Soc. Biol.*, **91**, 1180–2.
93. WOLF, J. (1924). Contribution à la localisation des bactéroides dans le corp adipeux des Blattes (*Periplaneta orientalis*). *C.r. Séanc. Soc. Biol.*, **91**, 1182–3.
94. WOLLMAN, E. (1926). Observation sur une lignée aseptiques des Blattes (*Blattella germanica*). *C.r. Séanc. Soc. Biol.*, **95**, 164–6.
95. WOLLMAN, E., GIROUD, A. and RATSIMAMANGA, R. (1937). Synthèse de la vitamine C chez un insecte orthoptère (*Blattella germanica*) en élevage aseptique. *C.r. Séanc. Soc. Biol.*, **124**, 434–5.
96. YOUNG, R. G. (1958). Dehydrogenase systems of fat body of susceptible and chlordane-resistant *Blattella germanica*. *J. econ. Ent.*, **51**, 867–9.
97. YOUNG, R. (1959). Oxidative mechanisms of the insect fat body. *Ann. ent. Soc. Am.*, **52**, 567–70.

ADDITIONAL REFERENCES

98. BROOKS, M. A. and RICHARDS, K. (1966). On the in vitro culture of intracellular symbiotes of cockroaches. *J. invert. Pathol.*, **8**, 150–7.
99. BRUES, C. T. and DUNN, R. C. (1945). The effect of penicillin and certain sulfa drugs on the intracellular bacteroids of the cockroach. *Science*, **101**, 336–7.
100. COOK, B. J. and EDDINGTON, L. C. (1967). The release of triglycerides and free fatty acids from the fat body of the cockroach *Periplaneta americana*. *J. Insect Physiol.*, **13**, 1361–72.
101. DUBOWSKY, N. and PIERRE, L. L. (1966). Malic enzyme activity in the fat bodies of the cockroach *Leucophaea maderae*. *Ann. ent. Soc. Am.*, **59**, 1012–21.
102. LUDWIG, D. and GALLAGHER, M. R. (1966). Vitamin synthesis by the symbiotes in the fat body of the cockroach *Periplaneta americana* (L). *Jl N.Y. ent. Soc.*, **74**, 134–9.
103. MALKE, H. and SCHWARTZ, W. (1966). Untersuchungen über die Symbiose von Tieren mit Pilzen und Bakterien. *Arch. Mikrobiol.*, **53**, 17–32.
104. MILBURN, N. S. (1966). Fine structure of the pleomorphic bacteroids in the mycetocytes and ovaries of several genera of cockroaches. *J. Insect Physiol.*, **12**, 1245–54.
105. NELSON, D. R., TERRANOVA, A. C. and SUKKESTEAD, D. R. (1967). Fatty acid composition of the glyceride and free fatty acid fractions of the fat body and hemolymph of the cockroach *Periplaneta americana* (L). *Comp. Biochem. Physiol.*, **20**, 907–12.

106. PIERRE, L. L. (1965). Guanase activity of the symbiotes and fat bodies of the cockroach *Leucophaea maderae. Nature,* **208,** 666–7.
107. RAMAZZOTTO, L. J. and LUDWIG, D. (1967). Differences in composition of the fat body of normal and aposymbiotic cockroaches. *Ann. ent. Soc. Am.,* **60,** 227–30.
108. WALKER, P. A. (1965). The structure of the fat body in normal and starved cockroaches as seen with the electron microscope. *J. Insect Physiol.,* **11,** 1625–31.

14 Excretion

The morphology and position of the Malpighian tubules

Henson studied the tubules in *B.o.* He found they occur at the junction of the mid-gut and the hind-gut in 6 groups, of which only 4 arise in the embryo. The other 2 groups develop in the nymphal stage and all 6 groups then form numerous secondary tubules until a large number is present.[21] In *P.a.* there are 6 bundles of about 12[7] or 15 to 20 tubules in the adult insect.[5] Henson maintains that they are mesenteric (endodermal) derivatives or outgrowths, and this is supported by the absence of an inner cuticle or intima.[33]

Lison found 3 kinds of tubules in *B.o.*, and suggests that they are stages in the development from a single type,[28] while Srivastava and Gupta claim there are 2 different kinds of tubule in *P.a.*, one of which stains much darker than the other with silver nitrate.[43]

Histology

Coriphosphin is a vital stain for the nuclei of the epithelial cells of the tubules.[19]

Dirks found no carbohydrate enzymes,[16] but Bank found β-fructofuranosidase, α- and β-glucosidases, and α- and β-galactosidases.[3] The cells appear to have no Golgi bodies, but this may be because they are of a different and unrecognized kind. Granules seen with the light microscope do not correspond to those found by the electron microscope.[33]

Functioning

There has been much controversy over the functioning of these organs. Surprisingly large quantities of vitamins are found in the tubules of *P.a.*[23, 32] In µg per gram of fresh tissue the approximate amounts found by Metcalfe were: thiamin 40, riboflavin 900, nicotinic acid 300, pantothenic acid 80 and ascorbic acid 750. He also found that thiamin and pantothenic acid injected into a cockroach promoted the release of the riboflavin of the tubules into the blood, and he therefore suggested that the vitamins must be bound in some way to the tissue to prevent them interacting within the tubules. The riboflavin is in two forms:[8, 32] free in the lumen apically, and as small particles in the cytoplasm of the cells of the basal parts of the tubules; it occurs in both forms in the middle region of the tubule. When the cockroach is reared on a riboflavin-free diet, the free form is first taken into the body, then the particulate form disappears, presumably having been converted into free riboflavin and absorbed.[32]

Studies by fluorescent microscopy show that the particulate form in *P.a.* may be a phosphorylated form of riboflavin[32] or, in *B.o.*, riboflavin conjugated with a protein.[8] Phosphate granules have been detected in the tubule cells of *Bt.g.*[14] In *P.a.* some of the tubules contain no riboflavin, some have the free form and some have the particulate form.[31] Several other fluorescent substances are known to occur in the tubules of *B.o.*[8] Kubistova confirms the presence of great concentrations of riboflavin, which he says occur in the free form but with only traces of riboflavin phosphate present. The amounts he found in the two sexes were equal at the beginning of imaginal life, but the concentration in the female decreased from then on.[23]

Meyer describes in *Blatta* the movement of substances through the micropits of the basal membrane into the cells of the tubule from the haemocoel, a process in which mitochondria probably play a part. Particles observed by the electron microscope may be in the form of cell inclusions which are 'emptied' into the lumen, or they may grow within the cytoplasm and pass through the 'brush border' into the lumen.[33] Lison described the excretion of acidic and basic dyes by the tubules of *B.o.* Basic dyes are excreted into the lumen of the distal part of the tubule, and then taken up and held as granules by the arthrocytes or storage cells of the middle part of the tubule. Acidic dyes are not reabsorbed and Lison claims that the apical membrane of the cell is permeable to acidic dyes from cell to lumen, but not in the reverse direction. Some granules are found in the cytoplasm of the cells of the middle region of the tubule stained by acidic dyes, but Lison states these are existing granules, stained by the dye on its way through from blood to lumen, whereas the particles found when basic dyes are used are (new) particles of the dye itself.[26,27,28] Indigo-carmine has been used to show the elimination of this substance by the tubules in *P.a.*[36] and in *B.o.*,[34] and that the process may be primarily a secretory system energized by an oxidative enzyme.[36] Excretion of this dye was optimum at 35°[36] and it was found by Sawaya to be eliminated rapidly into the lumen of the tubule.[41] Wall and Ralph studied the antidiuretic activity of extracts of the C.N.S. and corpora cardiaca using this dye,[44] although it was also claimed that only 3·5% of the total 60 μg N_2 excreted per day per male cockroach, starved for 20 to 72 hours, was uric acid.[46]

The use of tubules for excretion of nitrogenous substances has not yet been convincingly shown in the roach, and Srivastava and Gupta think they do not take an active part in nitrogen excretion and are probably mainly osmoregulatory.[43] This opinion is shared by Dirks, although she suggests the fluid from the tubules affects the pH and redox potential of the hind-gut.[16] The redox potential of the tubules of *P.a.* lies between $-0·125$ V and $-0·289$ V.[32] On the other hand, labelled uric acid is recovered from the tubules as well as the fat body after being injected into the animal.[29] Radioactively labelled iodine as the free amino acid monoiodohistidine, and labelled diiodotyrosine and thyroxine were excreted by the Malpighian tubules and the hind-gut.[24,25]

The elimination of nitrogen from the body is, certainly, necessary and uric acid is the main excretory product of *P.a.*,[35] and Wall and Ralph consider that there is an antidiuretic hormone produced by the brain and stored in the corpora allata, which reduces the activity of the Malpighian tubules in animals with hyperosmotic blood.[45] According to Srivastava and Gupta uric acid and urates diffuse from the blood into the ileum and colon, the excess water subsequently being reabsorbed by the rectum.[43] Some of the uric acid found in the fat body may act as a nitrogen store,[37,43] although Ludwig[12] disagrees with this view. There was a decrease in the uric acid deposits in the fat body when the diet was low in protein in *Bt.g.*[20] and in *P.a.*, in which the decrease could not be wholly accounted for by the amount excreted. This strongly suggests that some must have been metabolized in a time of nitrogen deficiency.[29] The amount of uric acid in the fat body increased when the bacteriods were killed[6,18] which tends to support the idea that these organisms play an important part in nitrogen metabolism (T). It is also increased in *Bt.g.* when it was fed with a high-protein diet, so much so that the abdomen was distended. White deposits of urates or uric acid were found in the head and legs as well as the fat body.[20] Large deposits of uric acid have recently been noticed in the utriculi majores of the males of *Bt.g.* This uric acid is stored until copulation, when it is poured over the spermatophore and may help to protect this. No such uricose glands, however, are present in *P.a.*, *B.o.* and *Leucophaea maderae*.[39,40]

The studies of Gersch[19] using solutions of sodium fluorescein injected into the haemocoel of *Periplaneta* are of interest. With solutions of 1 part per million (1 ppm), the dye was very quickly absorbed by the mid-gut and eliminated through the hind-gut. With solutions of 10 ppm to 100 ppm the tubules as well as the mid-gut helped to eliminate it; and when the concentration used was 1000 ppm the dye penetrated into the fat body and central nervous system, not being removed fast enough to prevent its distribution in the body. Gersch also points out that only part of the tubules are used in eliminating the fluorescein dye,[19] while Lison has described differentiation along the length of the tubule, mentioned above. The distal region may be concerned with excretion, as well as the production of a sulphonated colloidal substance,[28] the middle region for storage and the proximal or basal region with other functions. The tubules certainly act as vitamin stores, and it seems possible that the tubules are used to excrete only such substances as occur in concentrations greater than the gut can handle. If this is so, it explains why uric acid has not been found to imitate the behaviour of the large doses of dyes in the experimental work, since it is very unlikely to reach high concentrations in the blood, and would be removed by the gut in normal circumstances (T). In addition, Cordero and Ludwig report a large concentration of uricase in the tubules in *P.a.*, so that the absence of uric acid, so often reported, may be an indication of the activity of this enzyme.[11] On the other hand, the uricolytic enzymes in *Blaberus fusca* are found in the fat body and not in the Malpighian tubules.[38]

Support for the belief that the hind-gut in *Bt.g.* has an excretory function comes from the observation that dyes incorporated into food never get into the blood, but if they are injected into the haemocoel they are soon found in the hind-gut.[15]

The tubules of *B.o.* show rhythmical waving movements with a rate of about 5 per min at 20°. No peristalsis was seen by Koller,[22] but Yeager and Hager suggest there are 10 such contractions per minute.[47] This is probably to bring them into contact with a greater volume of blood and is nothing to do with the movements of fluid from the lumen of the tubules into the gut, which continues when the tubule is not moving. No movements are observed at temperatures much less than 20° and the optimum temperature for maximum activity is approximately $35° \pm 3°$.[22] A secretion of the utriculi majores of *P.a.* increases the rate of movement of the tubules in concentrations of 10^{-8} to 10^{-9} M. This substance was reported by Davey to be a dihydroxyindolealkylamine[13] but this was doubted by Colhoun.[10] The movement of the tubules is also affected by a secretion of the corpora cardiaca which may be an *o*-diphenol[9] or again indolealkylamine.[13]

The tubules of *P.a.* contain amino acid oxidases[4] which actively form keto acids on incubation with, for example, methionine,[2] and also transaminases (Judson and Craig, unpublished, from Craig[12]). They contain β-fructofuranosidase, α- and β-glucosidases and α- and β-galactosidases.[3] In *Bt.g.* they contain amylase, maltase, saccharase and trehalase activity,[17] and in *B.o.* peptidases, especially dipeptidase and a little amylase.[42]

REFERENCES

1. ANDERSON, A. D. (1953). Uric acid synthesis in insects. Thesis, Cornell University.
2. AUCLAIR, J. L. (1959). Amino acid oxidase activity in the fat body and Malpighian tubes of some insects. *J. Insect Physiol.*, **3**, 57–62.
3. BANK, W. M. (1963). Carbohydrate digestion in the cockroach. *Science*, **141**, 1191–2.
4. BLASCHKO, H., COLHOUN, E. H. and FRONTALI, N. (1961). Occurrence of amine oxidase in an insect, *Periplaneta americana*. *J. Physiol.*, **156**, 28P.
5. BORDAS, L. (1898). L'appareil digestif des Orthoptères. *Annls Sci. nat.*, **5**, 1–208.
6. BROOKS, M. A. and RICHARDS, A. G. (1956). Intracellular symbiosis in cockroaches. III. Reinfection of aposymbiotic cockroaches with symbiotes. *J. exp. Zool.*, **132**, 447–65.
7. BUCK, J. B. and KEISTER, M. L. (1950). In BROWN, F. (ed.). *Selected invertebrate types*. Wiley, New York and London.
8. BUSNEL, R. G. and DRILHON, A. (1942). Recherches sur la répartition de la riboflavin (vitamin B₂) et de quelques autres substances fluorescentes chez les insectes. *Archs Zool. exp. gén.*, **82**, 321–56.
9. CAMERON, M. (1953). Secretion of an Orthodiphenol in the corpus cardiacum of the insect. *Nature*, **172**, 349–50.
10. COLHOUN, E. H. (1963). Synthesis of 5-hydroxytryptamine in the American cockroach. *Experientia*, **19**, 9–10.
11. CORDERO, S. M. and LUDWIG, D. (1963). Purification and activities of purine enzymes from various tissues of the American cockroach, *Periplaneta americana. Jl N.Y. ent. Soc.*, **71**, 66–73.
12. CRAIG, R. (1960). The physiology of excretion in the insect. *A. Rev. Ent.*, **5**, 53–68.
13. DAVEY, K. G. (1960). A pharmacologically active agent in the reproductive system of insects. *Can. J. Zool.*, **38**, 39–45.
14. DAY, M. F. (1949). The distribution of alkaline phosphatase in insects. *Aust. J. scient. Res.* (B), **2**, 31–41.
15. DAY, M. F. and POWNING, R. F. (1949). A study of the processes of digestion in certain insects. *Aust. J. scient. Res.* (B), **2**, 175–215.
16. DIRKS, E. (1922). Liefern die Malpighischen Gefässe Verdauungssekrete? *Arch. Naturgesch.*, **88**, 161–200.

17. EHRHARDT, P. and VOSS, G. (1962). Beitrag zum Wirkungsspektrum kohlen-hydratspaltender Ferments und ihre Verteilung im Verdauungstrakt der Schaben *Blaberus discoidalis* (Sv.) und *Leucophaea maderae. J. Insect Physiol.*, 8, 165–74.
18. FRANK, W. (1956). Entfernung der intrazellulären Symbioten der Küchenschabe (*Periplaneta orientalis*) durch Einwirkung verschiedener Antibiotica, unter besonderer Berücksichtigung der Veränderungen am Wirtstier und an den Bakterien. *Z. Morph. Ökol. Tiere*, 44, 329–66.
19. GERSCH, M. (1942). Fluoreszensmikroskopische Untersuchungen über die Ausscheidung von Farbstoffen bei *Periplaneta*. I. Beitrag zur Exkretion bei Insekten. *Z. vergl. Physiol.*, 29, 473–505.
20. HAYDAK, M. H. (1953). Influence of the protein level of the diet on the longevity of cockroaches. *Ann. ent. Soc. Am.*, 46, 547–60.
21. HENSON, H. (1944). The development of the Malpighian tubules of *Blatta orientalis*. *Proc. R. ent. Soc. Lond.*, 19, 73–91.
22. KOLLER, G. (1948). Rhythmische Bewegung und hormonale Steurung bei den Malpighischen Gefässe der Insekten. *Biol. Zbl.*, 67, 201–11.
23. KUBISTOVA, J. (1957). Riboflavin bei *Periplaneta americana*. *Věst. čsl. Spol. zool.*, 21, 135–8.
24. LIMPEL, L. E. and CASIDA, J. E. (1957). Iodine metabolism in insects. I. In vivo metabolism of radioiodide. *J. exp. Zool.*, 135, 19–28.
25. LIMPEL, L. E. and CASIDA, J. E. (1957). Iodine metabolism in insects. II. In vivo distribution and metabolism of iodoamino acids and related studies with *Periplaneta*. *J. exp. Zool.*, 136, 595–613.
26. LISON, L. (1936). Études histophysiologiques sur le tube de Malpighi des insects. I. L'elimination des colourants acides chez les Orthoptères. *Archs Biol.*, 48, 321–60.
27. LISON, L. (1936). Études histophysiologiques sur le tube de Malpighi des insectes. II. Phénomènes d'athrocytose dans le tube de Malpighi chez les Orthoptères. *Archs Biol.*, 48, 489–512.
28. LISON, L. (1938). Études histophysiologiques sur les tubes des Malpighi des insectes. III. L'elimination des colorants basiques chez les Orthoptères. *Z. Zellforsch. mikrosk. Anat.*, 28, 179–209.
29. MCENROE, W. D. (1957). Uric acid metabolism in the American cockroach, *Periplaneta americana*. *Diss. Abstr.*, 17, 2338.
30. MCENROE, W. D. and FORGASH, A. J. (1958). Formate metabolism in the American cockroach, *Periplaneta americana*. *Ann. ent. Soc. Am.*, 51, 126–9.
31. METCALFE, R. L. (1943). The storage and interaction of water-soluble vitamins in the Malpighian system of *Periplaneta americana*. *Archs Biochem.*, 2, 55–62.
32. METCALFE, R. and PATTON, R. (1942). A study of riboflavin metabolism in the American roach by fluorescence microscopy. *J. cell. comp. Physiol.*, 19, 373–6.
33. MEYER, G. F. (1957). Elektronmikroskopische untersuchungen an den Malpighi Gefässen verschiedener Insekten. *Z. Zellforsch. mikrosk. Anat.*, 47, 18–28.
34. MOSELEY, H. N. (1871). On the circulation in the wings of *Blatta orientalis* and other insects, and on a new method of injecting the vessels of insects. *Q. Jl microsc. Sci.*, 11, 389–95.
35. NATION, J. L. and PATTON, R. L. (1961). A study of nitrogen excretion in insects. *J. Insect Physiol.*, 6, 299–308.
36. PATTON, R. L., GARDNER, J. and ANDERSON, A. D. (1959). The excretory efficiency of the American cockroach, *Periplaneta americana*. *J. Insect Physiol.*, 3, 256–61.
37. PIERRE, L. (1964). Uricase activity of isolated symbiotes and the aposymbiotic fat body of a cockroach. *Nature*, 201, 54–5.

38. RAZET, P. (1953). Recherches sur la localisation des enzymes uricolytiques chez les insectes. *C.r. hebd. Séance. Acad. Sci.*, *Paris*, **236**, 1304–6.
39. ROTH, L. M. and DATEO, G. P. (1964). Uric acid in the reproductive system of males of the cockroach, *Blattella germanica*. *Science*, **146**, 782–4.
40. ROTH, L. M. and DATEO, G. P. (1965). Uric acid storage and excretion by accessory sex glands of male cockroaches. *J. Insect Physiol.*, **11**, 1023–9.
41. SAWAYA, P. (1940). Sôbre a histophysiologia dos orgãos excretores de alguns insectos. I. Orthoptera. *Revta Ent. Rio de J.*, **11**, 232–52.
42. SCHLOTTKE, E. (1937). Untersuchungen über die Verdauungsfermente von Insekten. III. Die Abhängigkeit des Fermentgehaltes von der Art der Nahrung. Versuche an *Periplaneta orientalis*. *Z. vergl. Physiol.*, **24**, 463–92.
43. SRIVASTAVA, P. N. and GUPTA, P. D. (1961). Excretion of uric acid in *Periplaneta americana*. *J. Insect Physiol.*, **6**, 163–7.
44. WALL, B. J. and RALPH, C. L. (1962). Factors from the nervous system of the cockroach that influence excretion rates of the Malpighian tubules. *Am. Zoologist*, **2**, 455–6.
45. WALL, B. J. and RALPH, C. L. (1964). Evidence for hormonal regulation of Malpighian tubule excretion in the insect, *Periplaneta americana*. *Gen. comp. Endocrinol.*, **4**, 452–6.
46. WHARTON, D. R. A. and WHARTON, M. L. (1961). Effects of radiation on nitrogen and phosphorus excretion by the cockroach, *Periplaneta americana*. *Radiat. Res.*, **14**, 432–43.
47. YEAGER, J. F. and HAGER, A. (1934). On the rates of contraction of the isolated heart and Malpighian tube of the insect *Periplaneta orientalis*. *Iowa St. Coll. J. Sci.*, **8**, 391–5.

15 Circulation

The specific gravity of the blood of the nymphs of *P.a.* is 1·029 in both sexes and it rises to its maximum two days before ecdysis.[63,64] The blood of adult males and females of *B.o.* has a specific gravity of $1·0150 \pm 0·0113$ and that of the nymphs is $1·0182 \pm 0·0108$.[112] The pH of the blood of nymphal and adult *P.a.* lies between 7·5 and 8·0.[34] The freezing point depression of the blood of *B.o.* is 0·76°.[73]

About one-third of the water content, or one-fifth of the body weight, of *Bt.g.* adult was accounted for by its blood; in the nymphs the proportion was a little higher.[39] In *P.a.* there was thought to be approximately 100 μl. of blood and different methods gave similar blood volume percentages. Using injection of a dye, the percentages found lay between 16 and 20, the nymphs averaging rather less[31] than the adults;[35] but using chlorine estimation on heat-fixed blood, the values were: nymphs 18% and adults 16%.[117] A more recent investigation found that the average and range of blood volumes as percentages of body weight in *P.a.* were:

(i) intermoult nymphs 17 (11–30);
(ii) moulting nymphs 14 (10–26);
(iii) individuals undergoing the final moult to the adult stage 21 (13–35);
(iv) 24 hr-old adults 15 (13–19);
(v) adults more than 24 hr old 19 (14–21).

The mean values correspond to 138, 109, 159, 114 and 165 μl of blood respectively,[105] but a centrifugal method produced in *P.a.* an average of 50 μl. of blood from females, and about 30 μl. from males.[91] In *Bt.g.* an average of $31 \pm 2·2$ μl. was found.[55]

Wharton *et al.* maintain that the reduction in blood volume, which they agree occurs after the final moult, continued for 4 days altogether, until it finally tapered off. Even then there were daily fluctuations in blood volume but not in the water content of the body under normal conditions.[104] In starvation of *Bt.g.* the amount of blood was reduced[39] but in starvation of *P.a.* both the water content and the volume of the blood increased, the latter reaching 36% for males 2–3 weeks old. It was thus clear that since the blood volume could change readily, but the total water content changed little there must be a considerable interchange of water between the tissues and the blood.[104] Just as remarkable was the observation that a cockroach could live, feed and move about actively for weeks with virtually no circulating blood.[63] On the other hand, roaches subject to extreme inanition lost both body weight and blood volume, but the ratio between them remained more or less constant.[117]

Salts present in the blood

Various estimates have been made of the concentrations of different salts in the blood of cockroaches, mainly the ions of potassium, sodium, calcium and magnesium (T). Although the sodium is more concentrated than the potassium, their ratio is much nearer to unity than is the case in vertebrates. In *P.a.* the concentration of sodium in the blood in mg/100 g was 246,[100] or 370[9] or 260 when fed on a diet of lettuce which has a sodium content of 30 mg/100 g.[75] For *Leucophaea maderae* the figure was 230.[102] The concentration of potassium in the blood of *P.a.* in the same units was 67,[100] or 31,[9] or 100 when fed on lettuce leaves with a content of 340 mg of potassium per 100 g.[75] In *L. maderae* the amount is 38 mg/100 g of blood.[102] For calcium the figures in *P.a.* are 17,[19] or 18,[8] or 16 for adults and 17 for nymphs.[9] For *L. maderae* it is 16·5.[102] *P.a.* has a concentration of magnesium in its blood of 7,[100] or 27·5[19] or 13·5 in the adult and 12·5 in the nymph,[8, 9] and in *L. maderae* 4·2 mg/100 g.[102] The method used by Tobias[100] and Clark and Craig[19] for the estimation of magnesium is considered to be less accurate than that used by Asperen and Esch,[8] but there are quite wide differences in any case (T). In part, these correlate with the diet[19, 67] and lettuce with its high potassium to sodium ratio was claimed to cause increase in the potassium of the blood and decrease in the sodium.[67]

Introduction of a solution of potassium chloride into the gut increased the potassium content of the blood three times[75] but even with large doses, the ratio of sodium to potassium did not become less than unity.[100]

Injection of sodium chloride caused water to be withdrawn from the tissues and the blood volume to increase, although some of the salt was taken up by the tissues if the concentration used was high.[58]

The ratio of calcium to magnesium is relatively stable but there is some evidence that changes in the concentration of magnesium are tolerated better than changes in the concentration of calcium. Much of the calcium is probably bound to proteins or other organic compounds and is not in an ionized form.[19] Surprisingly, *P.a.* is very tolerant of injections of very concentrated solutions of calcium chloride, magnesium sulphate and ethylenediaminetetracetate, and normal conditions are quickly restored.[9]

The blood of *P.a.* contains 0·73 mM of citrate.[47]

Lipoids of the blood

The neutral lipoid materials of the blood of *P.a.* is involved in blood clotting, and changes in lipid distribution can be correlated with moulting. Phospholipids, sterols and triglycerides are believed to be present also.[79] If *Bt.g.* is fed with a specially rich diet, fine fat droplets or lipomicrons can occur in the blood.[39]

Carbohydrates in blood

The total reducing substances present in the blood of *P.a.* has been stated to be 145,[9] 221,[101] 120 before a period of flight and 250 after,[68] and 74 at 4–5 weeks of adult age,[83] all expressed as mg glucose equivalent per 100 g blood. The figure for the blood of *Leucophaea maderae* is 228. The amounts of non-reducing sugars (in glucose equivalents and assumed to be trehalose) found were 677 mg/100 ml. in *L. maderae*,[102] and in *P.a.* 880 before flight and 380 after flight,[68] or 1,174 at 4–5 weeks of adult age and 1,400 at 3 months of adult age,[83] or 684 one day before moulting,[49] or 1,080[84] or about 737.[71]

Variations occur in all the carbohydrate constituents of the blood. Trehalose, for instance, is the main sugar used in flight[68] and it is probably the main precursor substance for chitin. Much of the carbohydrate is not free, but bound to plasma proteins in *P.a.* nymphs[50] and adults[48,107] and can be hydrolysed to give greater amounts of glucosamine, galactose and mannose with lesser amounts of galactosamine, glucose, arabinose and xylose. During a moult the amounts present vary,[48,80,107] and there is an increase in the proportions of mannose-rich and galactosamine-rich glycoproteins. By radioactive labelling, it has been found that, even in the intermoult period, the turnover is much greater for the amino sugars than for the neutral sugars.[48]

Proteins and amino acids

The total protein expressed in mg nitrogen per 100 ml. blood is 686·5 in *Leucophaea maderae*[102] and in *P.a.* 740[101] or 763.[9]

Electrophoresis has been used to analyse the blood proteins and, although there has been considerable disagreement about the number present, it is generally agreed that there are differences between the nymphs and adults,[28,80,81,86,87] between males and females[81,86,88,90] and at different ages of the adult. Three protein fractions have been found by Steinhauer and Stephen with migrations of 19, 43 and 61 mm in *P.a.*,[86,87] and in *Bt.g.*[90] Others claim 5 fractions are present,[80] or 6 if the number from one moult to the next is taken,[81] 4 being present in all instars.[79] The variations may be due to the changes which occur during the premoult stage after which there is a gradual return to intermoult conditions,[81] although even then the proteins are in a state of dynamic equilibrium.[79]

Steinhauer and Stephen reported that one fraction was present only at moulting time[86,87] and that another was more prominent during the intermoult period. A third fraction, comprising 80% of all the protein found, remained relatively constant in the nymphs but increased in the adults,[87] and more was present in the female than in the male.[86] This is probably the same fraction, containing a high proportion of neutral lipid and sterol, reported by Siakotos to be more concentrated in the female than the male.[79,80]

The blood cells may contribute to the changes in blood proteins,[79] but as their proteins are mainly in the form of lipoprotein or glycoproteins[80,81] it seems likely that they are more concerned with at least the transport of carbohydrates for storage or use in the moulting process.[81]

The non-protein nitrogen content expressed as mg/100 g blood is stated to be in *P.a.*, 260[101] or 227,[9] and in *L. maderae* 235.[102] The amino acid nitrogen found (in the same units) was 78 in *P.a.*,[101] 93 in *L. maderae*[102] and 56 in *Bt.g.*[70]

The free amino acids of the blood are subject to variations which depend in part on the diet in *Bt.g.*[10] and in *P.a.*, but are not correlated with either the stage of development or sex.[86] The blood of *Bt.g.* which had been fed on a diet containing α-amino-butyric acid, hydroxyproline, phenylalanine and taurine contained all of these amino acids, but DL-homocystine in the diet did not appear in the blood. DL-methionine produced α-amino-butyric acid and increased the amount of lysine and histidine.[10] A list of the amino acids found in *P.a.*, *Bt.g.* and *L. maderae* is given in Table 15.1.

TABLE 15.1

	P.a.	*Bt.g.*	*L.m.*		*P.a.*	*Bt.g.*	*L.m.*
Alanine	+	+	+	Hydroxyproline			+
β-alanine	−	+	+	Leucine	+	+	+
Arginine	−	+	+	Methionine	+	+	+
Asparagine	−	+		Ornithine			+
Aspartic acid	−	+	+	Phenylalanine	−	−	+
Citrulline		+		Proline	+	+	+
Cystine/cysteine	+	+	+	Serine	+	+	+
Glutamic acid	+	+		Taurine			+
Glutamine	+	+		Threonine	−	+	+
Glycine	+	+	+	Tyrosine	+	+	+
Histidine	−	?	+	Valine	+	+	+

Although the blood of *L. maderae* retains for at least three years the same protein fractions as fresh blood, this is not true of *P.a.*, which soon becomes useless for protein study.[89]

Other substances in blood

The uric acid content of the blood expressed as mg/100 g in *P.a.* was found to be 4·4,[2] or 14·3 [101] or 11 before flight and 22 after[46] and in *L. maderae* 12·4.[102] The amount found is very variable.[2]

Chitinase is present in strong concentration in *P.a.*, with an activity which liberates 4 mg of *N*-acetylglucosamine per ml.[103] There is also a β-glucosidase, which is not the same as the chitinase,[69] and several esterases have been found.[21] An agent may be present in the blood of nymphs of *P.a.* which is produced when they are artificially restrained and prevented from moving. It can be transmitted by transfusion, causes paralysis and death, and may be produced by hyperactivity of the nervous system.[11]

HAEMOCYTES

Various estimates have been made of the numbers of cells present in the blood, but the numbers vary so much in one individual[39, 65] that it is impossible to think of a 'normal' count and no conclusions about possible pathological conditions can be drawn from changes in the numbers present.[65] Only at the time of moulting is there a significant reduction in numbers of cells/μl.[64,65,98,105] In *B.o.* fixation of the blood with glacial acetic acid is said to double the numbers of cells counted,[31] but bacterial infection is reported to have either no effect on the numbers of cells[96] or alternatively to cause them to double.[98] Different sampling methods affect the results in *P.a.*,[105] and the number in a female producing an oötheca is stated to be above normal in both *P.a.* and *B.o.*[82] It has been shown by Wheeler that many of the variations occurring in cells per unit volume are due to changes in the volume of haemolymph circulating in the body and perhaps to selective adhesion of certain of the cells (cystocytes) to tissues and/or to the breakdown of these cells. The apparent increase in cells/μl. before a moult is due to these blood volume changes. The following figures show how the cells/unit volume and the total number of cells in the body vary during the later stages of the life cycle:

TABLE 15.2

	Cells/μl. (thousands)	Total number of cells in blood (millions)
Intermoult nymphs	96	13
Moulting nymphs	119	13
Last moult to adult	78	12·5
Adults during first 24 hr	80	9
Older adults	110	18

The older adults had a count range of 24 to 208 thousands/μl. and the other stages also had a fairly wide range of values; but the count at the adult moult had a significantly lower degree of variation.[105] The number of cells found in the blood of *P.a.* by Smith was 16·5 million[82] and no differences were found between the sexes.[82,98,105]

The haemocytes of *B.o.* are said to be greatly reduced by injections of arsenic, mercuric chloride or sodium fluorosilicate, but unaffected by carbon disulphide, hydrogen cyanide and ether.[32] But it is also reported that *B.o.* killed with carbon disulphide had little blood with few cells, while those killed with pyridine had little blood with normal cells.[78] In this roach, an average of 0·026% of the haemocytes were multinucleate: 1,313 had two nuclei, 31 had three, 6 had four, 1 had five and 2 had six, out of 5,190,000 cells examined.[96] Multinucleate haemocytes were reported from *P.a.* also, but only in pathological conditions.[30]

The percentage of cells undergoing division is very low: in *B.o.* 0·5[119] or 0·2[92] or 0·0–0·5.[93] Similar rates are found in nymphs, in male and female adults and amongst the supposedly different types of haemocytes. The average figures for nymphs are 0·203 (males), 0·194 (females) and for adults 0·186 (males) and 0·216 (females). Yet it is said that the animal can produce 2,000 haemocytes in 3 hr by mitosis of the circulating cells.[92] During a moult the numbers undergoing mitosis may increase to 1·0%, returning to normal within about 5 days.[93] One or two previous haemorrhages do not affect the number of dividing cells present,[119] but the cells themselves are nevertheless considered to be the only haemopoietic tissue,[92] or to come from an unknown origin[96] outside the blood system.[99] Division is apparently quick and infrequent in *Bt.g.* and the daughter cells are stated to have high nuclear to cytoplasm ratio.[39] The occurrence of mitotically dividing haemocytes may increase to 3·1% when *B.o.* is infected by *Staphylococcus albus*.[94, 95]

Types of haemocytes

Three main types of haemocytes have been described in *P.a.*[27, 30] The first, the prohaemocytes, have a diameter of 6–9 μ, much chromatin in the nucleus, which is large relative to the amount of cytoplasm present, and basophilic cytoplasm with a pH of 3·4–4·2. They are phagocytic and are believed to undergo mitosis to produce the other kinds of cells. Of the haemocytes of the adults 23% are of this kind, and of those of the nymph 18%.

The prohaemocytes become transitional haemocytes. They are the most numerous in the blood: 66% in the adult and 55% in nymphs. They are 9–18 μ in diameter, very active in phagocytosis but undergoing mitosis only in special conditions.

The transitional haemocytes in turn become large haemocytes with a diameter of 18–23 μ. The nuclei of these cells have a network of chromatin material and a nucleolus and the cytoplasm is weakly basophilic with a pH of 3·7–5·1. They are also strongly phagocytic, and more numerous in the nymph (28%) than in the adult (11%).[30]

These large haemocytes seem to correspond to the amoeboid cells of Taylor, which he describes as large cells, most active in migration, and in tissue culture. He rarely saw one in mitosis, but he found they increase at first in starvation or in thirst.[99] Such an increase is denied by Schlumberger.[74]

More recent work suggests there are two main kinds of haemocyte present, 60–95% being plasmatocytes[42] (Fig. 15.2). These are stated to be polymorphic,[105] often to contain spindle-shaped inclusions,[42] and to form many pseudopodia, or to round up when withdrawn from the body.[105] The other kind of haemocyte is the coagulocyte or cystocyte (Fig. 15.1), with a relatively large round nucleus in which the intranuclear material appears as a series of bars.[42, 105] The number of cystocytes in the circulation changes and for about two days during the period of the final moult the number is above normal.[105]

A third type of haemocyte is a granular cell only rarely found by Wheeler,[105] but noted by Smith who stated they had vacuoles, especially when they were breaking down. He was unable to identify mitochondria in these cells,[82] but Ermin stated that most of the granules were in fact rodlets or chains of mitochondria or sometimes phagocytosed particles.[30] Smith believed many of the supposedly different kinds of cells were due to different methods of obtaining and/or treating the blood. He found the haemocytes to be elongated, not more than 1 μ thick, uniform in outline and about 2·5 × 10 μ in size. The cytoplasm was hyaline, but lipoid globules were common and the nuclei were constant in form[82] contrary to the statement by Ermin that although the nuclei were usually rounded they could be spindle-shaped and in pathological conditions lobose polymorphs.[30]

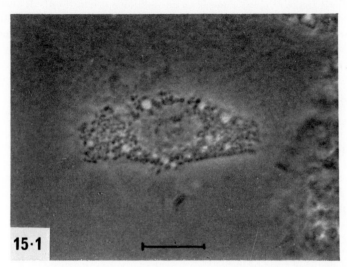

FIG. 15.1   *Periplaneta americana.* Cystocyte in coagulating haemolymph showing characteristic nucleus, hyaline cytoplasm, and many large mitochondria. Scale = 10 μ.
(Wheeler[105])

It was found by Jones that the plasmatocytes and cystocytes looked alike when the blood was fixed in ethanol, 1% acetic acid, 10% formalin or by heat[42] and even taking the blood out of the body of the roach made some of the cells form fine pointed pseudopodia which they never possess in the blood itself.[30] Jones, however, does not think all cells are variations on one basic type.[43]

No free oenocytes were observed in the blood.[30]

The only information relating to *B.o.* is that the commonest cells are ovoid, 22 μ × 18 μ, but some cells are 22 μ × 10 μ and some 28 μ × 11 μ.[96]

In *Bt.g.* Haber said there were three types of haemocytes which were the three stages of their life cycle. The cells of the first stage had nuclei and cytoplasm which stained heavily with few small vacuoles. These were the most common and active cells. The second stage had nuclei which were very large relative to the cytoplasm and both stained heavily. The third stage included those with many vacuoles in nucleus and cytoplasm, neither of which stained strongly, and the nucleus was relatively small. He also suggested that there may be platelets in which the nucleus and cytoplasm stain well but the nucleus may be irregular in outline and fragmentary.[39]

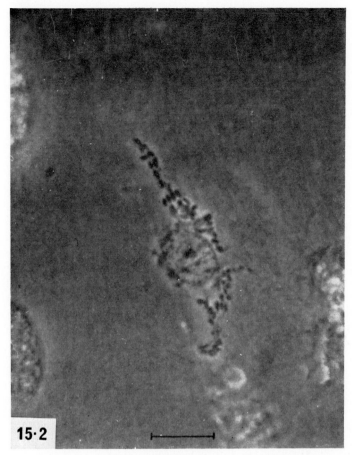

FIG. 15.2 *Periplaneta americana.* Plasmatocyte in coagulating haemolymph of moulting nymph showing characteristic nucleus and bacteriform mitochondria. Scale = 10 μ. (Wheeler[105])

The haemocytes of *Blaberus giganteus* have been studied by Arnold, principally in the wing veins. There were two main types noticed; (i) prohaemocytes of about 10 μ diameter, with a relatively large nucleus, and freely suspended in the blood. These became (ii) plasmatocytes which gradually changed to being more disc-shaped and polymorphic and less fusiform. In older animals the plasmatocytes tended to conform more readily to the shape of the place in which they found themselves, had filiform pseudopodia and readily clumped together. Both of these types of cells are said to divide by mitosis although this is uncommon.[3] Many of the cells observed with granular cytoplasm were very active and had an outer hyaline ectoplasm and an inner granular endoplasm. They had pseudopodia which were filiform or lamellar, possibly used to insinuate the cell into a small space. Some other cells were seen to possess filiform pseudopodia but they were

without movement and some smaller spherical hyaline cells had branched pseudopodia. These cells often had vacuoles and may be degenerating cells.[4] The movements found in the haemocytes include non-migratory movements of the
endoplasm, and probing movements of the pseudopodia.[6] Active migratory
movements, averaging 5 μ/min at 25°,[4] involved typical amoeboid movements,
but there occurred unusual movements in which hyaline pseudopodia were
produced. These resulted often in extreme, rapid elongation of the body,
enabling the cell to move quickly by means of almost leech-like extensions and
contractions, and to insinuate themselves into narrow interstices. At other times
when the cells entered an active blood stream they rounded up and passively
floated away in the blood.[6]

THE FUNCTIONING OF THE BLOOD AND ITS CELLS

The usually accepted functions of blood are the transport of dissolved substances, the transmission of hydrostatic pressure from one region of the body to
another, and as a reserve of water (T). The haemocytes are considered to have no
function in *B.o.*[96] and *P.a.*,[81] but they are said to be concerned in phagocytosis
in *P.a.*,[30,105] in coagulation of the blood in *P.a.* and *B.o.*[30,36,82,105,111,116,118]
and in wound healing in *P.a.*[27] Destruction of the cells of *P.a.* led to reduced
resistance to parathion,[64] and blocking the haemocytes with Chinese ink reduced
the resistance of the roaches to sodium arsenite, but had little effect on their
resistance to nicotine.[110] The haemocytes of *Bt.g.* are said to carry food
materials[39] and the plasma in *P.a.* to contain tyrosinase which melanizes foreign
bodies.[30]

Phagocytosis in *P.a.* begins with some of the haemocytes becoming laden with
the invading organism. These laden haemocytes congregate together and themselves become encapsulated masses due to the activity of more haemocytes,
which form a more or less unbroken pseudoepithelium round them. This
pseudoepithelium becomes fibrillar and ultimately the enscapulated masses break
down or remain inert.[30] Similar effects were found by Schlumberger when *P.a.*
was injected with talc. After 7 hours concentric layers of haemocytes were
surrounding the particles, the cells having pseudopodia and/or forming an
extensive syncitium. After 8–14 days, the central enscapulated mass began to
break down and become melanized.[74] The efficiency of the process is shown by
the fact that massive doses of *Bacillus subtilis* injected into the haemocoel were
all removed within 3 hours,[105] but in *B.o.* infection with *Staphylococcus albus* and
another unidentified bacterium caused vacuolation and disintegration of the
haemocytes. This disease may be transmitted by contact or cannibalism.[94,95]

Coagulation

Coagulation of the blood in *P.a.* may be brought about by the haemocytes[111,116] or by the plasma[81] or by both.[30,105] Yeager thought the plasma was
not involved in coagulation[116] but Ermin stated that the process begins with one
of the proteins of the plasma[30] and Siakotos considered that coagulation is
primarily concerned with lipoproteins in the blood which react to form further

lipoproteins one of which precipitates as an insoluble network.[81] Grégoire differentiates four patterns of coagulation in insects of which pattern 1, the most primitive, is that found in the Orthopteroid complex[35] (Figs. 15.3 and 15.4). In this process hyaline haemocytes or coagulocytes (but not granular haemocytes nor macronucleocytes[37]) become distorted in morphology and break down to release clouds of granules into the plasma around them.[36] This results in islands of coagulation which progressively link up by granular precipitation of the intervening plasma.[38] The granular clouds released by the disintegrating cells are perhaps the same as the masses of mitochondria which Wheeler believed were released by the cystocytes or coagulating cells in coagulation.[105]

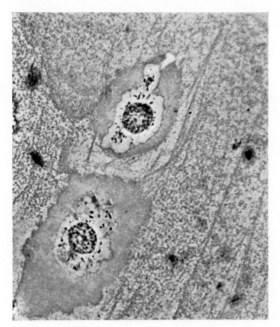

FIG. 15.3   *Periplaneta americana*. Undiluted haemolymph 12 min after withdrawal. Dense coagulation islands around several hyaline haemocytes. × 720. (Grégoire,[122])

The cells involved in coagulation in *P.a.* are said by some authors to round up and to form numerous filiform pseudopodia which become sticky and cause the cells to agglutinate.[30, 105] These masses of haemocytes now disintegrate and it is these cells which Smith thought were the ones with pseudopodia.[82] Plasma material may now be precipitated[105] and the whole mass becomes dried up and hardened and eventually blackened.[82] It is unlikely that the processes of cell agglutination and plasma protein precipitation are the same, since the amount of the anticoagulant versene required to stop the former is much less than to stop the latter.

The ability of the blood of *P.a.* to coagulate decreases during the four days prior to the last moult and after reaching the minimum at the time of ecdysis returns within an hour almost to the level before the decline began.[105]

In *B.o.* and *Bt.g.* the use of acetic acid vapour inhibited the coagulation of the blood, and the time required was inversely proportional to the temperature with variations due to age.[76, 77] This was true also of formic, propionic, butyric and valeric acid vapours with further variations due to the physical properties of the acids.[76] Acetic acid vapour did not affect the haemocytes.[78] Heat also inhibited blood coagulation, 60° for 10 min giving the best result, and it did not alter the cells[118] but blood treated at 40° produced abnormal cells.[77]

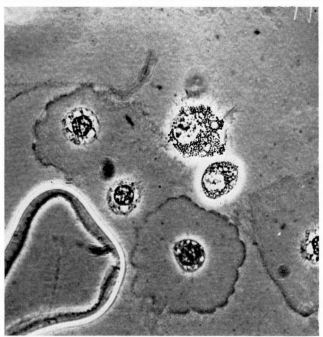

FIG. 15.4   **A**, *Blaberus (?)giganteus*. As in Fig. 15.3, but 60 min after withdrawal. (Grégoire, C. Unpublished, but reported in Grégoire[123])

Coagulation in *B.o.* is a result of the activity of the haemocytes. They round up and become more refractive, form filiform pseudopodia, and agglutinate into masses. These masses spread out and then disintegrate which causes a large increase in the viscosity of the plasma. There was no visible change in the plasma, and although some granules may be precipitated, no fibres are formed from the plasma.[116, 118]

WOUND HEALING

In *P.a.* the blood coagulated to form a scab by accumulation of masses of haemocytes, until the epidermis grew across beneath. In the adult the scar remained, but in the nymph it was lost at the next moult. The blood escaped from an abdominal cut for about 30 min but within 24 hr a network of haemo-cytes had formed an effective plug to the wound. Haemocytes migrated from all directions to add to the wound tissue of accumulating haemocytes, and after 2–5 days the closing of the wound to bacteria and fungi was complete. No cell divisions were seen in this haemocyte mass, but mitoses were much commoner in the rest

two passive granular haemocytes

three
coagulocytes
in areas of
coagulation

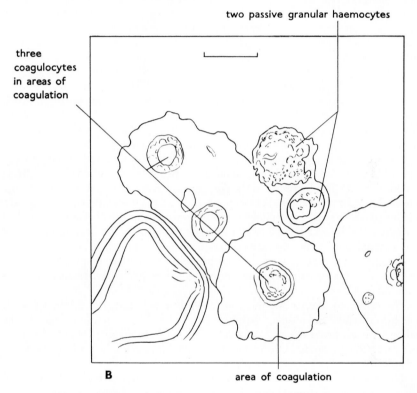

B   area of coagulation

15.4   **B**, diagram of the region shown in Fig. 15.4 **A**. Scale = 25 μ

of the haemocytes than in undamaged animals. About 8–10 days after the operation, the epidermal cells in the region of the wound began to enlarge, and soon they invaded the haemocyte mass, dividing it into an inner layer, which continued as a connective tissue layer, and an outer layer, which degenerated and was melanized. After a year, in the adult, the inner haemocyte layer had become fibrous, the outer layer heavily melanized, and the epidermal cells rounded and no longer elongated and spindle-shaped. Only epidermal cells formed new epi-dermis, no amitoses were observed and the oenocytes took no part in the pro-cesses.[30] A very similar account of wound healing is given by Schlumberger.[74]

THE HEART

The rate of heartbeat in *P.a.* is reported by several writers but little agreement exists amongst them (T). It is said to have a rate which settles down to 100/min 30 min after being dissected from the body,[45] or in vivo 110–120[59] or 120[12] or 100 (70–130) at 27°,[61] or 80–110 in vivo and 40–50 in vitro at 30°.[1] For last instar nymphs the figures range from 26 at 12° to 150 at 40°.[72] McIndoo reported a rate of 66 at the level of the bases of the first pair of segmental vessels and 72 at the base of the third pair, the rate decreasing towards the anterior,[53] but systole is also claimed to occur throughout the heart more or less simultaneously.[1,106] The beat may reverse in *P.a.*[53,85,113,115] and its speed is increased by feeding (13–21% for 2 to 4 hr),[25] by stimulation of the insect,[97] by the secretion of the corpora cardiaca,[15] or by irritation or constraint.[72] The effect of irritation must have occurred in many of the earlier experiments performed on the cockroach heart, and they are only reliable as exhaustion studies, especially as the amplitude of the contraction was often not included. (The amplitude is the percentage reduction in the diameter of the lumen from maximum dilatation.[62])

The secretion of the corpora cardiaca producing tachycardia was thought to be a peptide or protein,[24] but it may involve two peptides, one of which also affects the hind-gut.[14] The secretion of the corpora cardiaca is believed to stimulate the pericardial cells and causes them to produce, perhaps from a precursor,[24] an unidentified substance[26] previously thought to be indolealkylamine[24] or an *o*-diphenol.[15] Indolealkylamine was thought to occur in the opaque portion of the seminal fluid from the utriculi majores also,[22] though this is denied by Colhoun.[20] At the same time it must be pointed out that very large doses of corpora cardiaca extract were used to evoke the response and smaller amounts were ineffective.[23]

The optimum pH for the heart is 7·5 with a wide range of 3·5 to 10, acids having a diastolic and alkalis a systolic effect.[51] The best ionic composition of the saline for heart preparations was found to be NaCl 11·0 g, KCl 1·4 g, CaCl$_2$ 1·1 g per litre. They tolerate large variations in the Na/K ratio, but not in the K/Ca ratio.[52]

The effect of temperature on the heart of last instar nymphs of *P.a.* is to increase its rate in proportion to the rise in temperature between 12 and 40° but below 12° the relationship departs from linearity. In the intact animal, beating continues down to a temperature of 1·8° in cold-adapted, and to 4° in warm-adapted specimens, i.e. well below the temperature of cold stupor. There is no difference in rising and in falling temperatures, nor between the sexes. In hearts semi-isolated from the body the beating ceased at a minimal temperature of 8–9°. The activation energy or μ values varied from 7,000 with a Q_{10} of 1·3 above 25°, to 12–13,000 with a Q_{10} of 2 from 20 to 25°, and 18,000 with a Q_{10} of 2·5 below 20°.[72]

A similar change above and below 10° was found in the last nymphal instar of *B.o.* with μ values of 12,500 between 10 and 38°, but 18,000 below 10°.[33]

The heart rate of *B.o.* is stated to be 60–70/min at pH 7 and 20–30°,[44] or 75–100 (average 90)/min in saline for 4 hr.[114] When the heart was beating at

60/min systole took 0·1–0·2 sec and diastole 0·2–0·5 sec.[40] The amplitude at 20–30° was 0·3–0·5 mm, but above 40° this decreased irreversibly. Increase in temperature caused an increased rate of beating: at 20° the rate was three times that at 10°; at 30° it was twice that at 20°. Above 30° further increase occurred, up to an irreversible final systole at 40–45°, while at 6–8° the rate became intermittent and irregular. The blood was isotonic with 1% NaCl and when the preparation was suffused with hypotonic saline the heart slowed down, stopping in diastole in 0·6% saline. Hypertonic solutions caused an increased rate and decreased amplitude, with a 1·4% solution stopping the heart in systole. Changes in pH decreased both rate and amplitude.[44]

In *Bt.g.* the rate of beating in younger nymphs was less than 140/min, but was much faster than the hearts of older nymphs which were faster than adults. The sexes showed no differences in rate. Activity increased the rate, reaching a maximum in 5 min. After half an hour of forced activity, the rate was less than normal. Fasting decreased the rate and CO_2 stopped the heart in 20–40 sec, but this was reversible with the heart restarting after about 3 min. The heart stopped if it was injected with more than 1 μl. of water, but with less than this amount its rate increased temporarily. If saline was used 0·5 μl. was enough to stop the heart.[1]

It has been claimed that the heart in *P.a.* is neurogenic,[45,56,85] although others deny this, suggesting that the lateral cardiac nerves are the pacemaker to the heart, which is itself myogenic.[124] Since a 10^{-8} M solution of acetylcholine caused increased rate and amplitude of heartbeat, while anticholinesterase activated the heart, there is evidence that its innervation is cholinergic.[45,56] It is also stated that the automatic activity of the heart gets progressively less from posterior to anterior and it is not conducted from the abdomen into the thorax.[85] Thus the heart may have its own autonomic nervous system or it may be myogenic with additional nervous control.[54]

The action of the heart seems to involve no relaxation of the cardiac muscle fibres before systole, and contraction of one part of the heart is claimed to dilate another.[108] The contraction of the dorsal muscles does affect the heart action,[109] but the alary muscles probably only maintain a tonus on the heart. On the other hand, neither activity nor irritability of the alary muscles could be detected by Wilde even though they were seen to be innervated.[106] The heart in *P.a.* and *Bt.g.* contained many free haemocytes.[41]

The anatomy of the heart

In blattids the heart and aorta extend from the most posterior segment of the abdomen to the brain in the head. It is a cylinder whose wall is said to have in *P.a.* an adventitia of connective tissue, a media of muscle cells and an intima formed by the sarcolemma of the media.[106] In *Bt.g.* it is said to be only one cell thick.[29] In *P.a.* the heart has segmental excurrent arteries. McIndoo in one paper states that there is a pair in the mesothorax, the metathorax and between abdominal segments 2 and 3, 3 and 4, 4 and 5 and 5 and 6. Some adults appeared to be without excurrent vessels, but in the nymphs he noted that the

12 + B.O.C.

thoracic vessels are not present, and that there may be a pair between the sixth and seventh segments of the abdomen.[53] Nutting agrees with this account in respect of *Blaberus trapezoideus*.[60] However, in a later paper McIndoo shows vessels in the metathorax and abdominal segments 1, 3, 4, 5 and 6.[54]

There are 12 pairs of incurrent ostia[60] and in his figure 5A, McIndoo indicates that they occur on the ventral side of the heart.[53] He later shows them (figure 2C) as being lateral.[54] Nutting found the ostia to be lateral in blattids, where they are more or less vertical lateral slits whose borders are reflected to form valves. Dense groups of pericardial cells are present here.[60]

The segmental vessels in *P.a.* lie between the dorsal diaphragm and the cuticle, and may be covered by fatty tissue, especially at their distal ends. They are shorter (up to 1 mm) in the thorax than in the abdomen (up to 3 mm). They extend laterally to the edge of the dorsal diaphragm at right angles to the heart although not exactly opposite to one another on each side. They are depressed tubes and distally they widen considerably. They have peculiar cells forming a valve-like structure; these cells may be multinucleate.[53]

The pericardial septum may be considered for description to consist of alary muscles and a membranous dorsal diaphragm. Twelve pairs of alary muscles are found in blattids, those of the thorax arising on projections of the anterior tergal ridge and in the abdomen on the antero-lateral margins of the first 10 abdominal tergites. Many of the strands are, in fact, not muscle but connective tissue and some of these strands leave the muscle bundles medially to form a plexus which attaches the alary muscles and intervening dorsal diaphragm loosely to the heart wall. This dorsal diaphragm is fenestrated, and spreads amongst the alary muscles and between each pair of them. Laterally it extends rather indefinitely and may become a pleural fenestrated web investing the pleura and/or fat body, with free access for the blood between pericardial sinus and body wall.[60]

The circulation

The heart circulates the blood in the body; blood enters it via the ostia and leaves it by the segmental vessels[57] and by the aorta at the anterior end of the heart.[13] The circulation time in *P.a.* is said to be 30–60 min.[9] In *B.o.* the heart in the meso- and metathorax is muscular and no extra pulsatile organs are found.[13] This is in distinction to *Bt.g.*, which has pulsatile organs lying adjacent to the posterior basal region of the wing (jugal region).[16,18] The blood from the aorta passes mainly into the ventral sinus because the oesophagus largely occupies the head, neck and thorax, according to Brocher,[13] but in the later embryo of *Bt.g.*, Arnold states that the blood flows out from the head in a stream directed ventrally from behind the vertex through the neck towards the perineural sinus of the thorax. He also observed that the movement of blood across the openings of the head appendages was sufficient to aspirate blood from them, and so set up a slow circulation within them.[5]

In the thorax of *Bt.g.* the circulation was less vigorous than in the head and there were no pulsatile organs found to circulate the blood through the legs. They did possess a membrane running as far as the last tarsal podomere, so that at the base of the leg, one side of it was connected to the perineural sinus and the other to the perivisceral sinus. It may be that the slight differences in pressure in these two sinuses can partly account for the circulation in the legs, but since the ventral diaphragm is rudimentary it is not an adequate explanation. Possibly it is affected by an aspiratory mechanism, as in the head appendages.[5] In *B.o.* Bracher found that there was a median membrane only in the femora of the legs and he suggested that the activity of the muscles may be sufficient to maintain the circulation in the rest of the leg.[13] Each antenna has a basal pulsatile organ in *B.o.*[13, 66] equipped with a valve, which pumps the blood from the head sinus along a fine vessel into the antenna, probably by means of the muscle band connecting the two organs.[13] The antennae of *Blaberus giganteus* have an axial dividing membrane running to the penultimate article.[5]

The blood circulation in the wings normally is efferent in the anterior veins and afferent in the posterior veins in *B.o.*,[57] *P.a.*[115] and *Bt.g.*[16] In *P.a.* the blood passes outwards in both wings via the costal, sub-costal and proximal parts of the radial, medial and cubital veins, and returns by the distal parts of the radial, medial, cubital and vannal veins. In the nymphal wing pads the blood is efferent in all the main veins returning via the minor ones.[115]

Similarly in *Bt.g.* the flow in the fore-wing goes from the haemocoel into the anterior sinus, where the dorsal and ventral layers of the membrane are not fused, and then into the afferent veins, namely the costal, radial, proximal medial and proximal cubital. The blood returns via the distal medial, distal cubital and the vannal veins to the jugal region, where channels convey it to the axillary cord. This leads to the heart, passing through the valved pulsatile organ. There is in addition a basal sinus lying between the anterior sinus and the jugal region which receives some blood from the haemocoel via the anterior sinus. This passes out via the basal channel in the basal fold to the axillary cord.

In the hind-wing a similar circulation occurs, except that some of the remigial blood returns to the basal sinus from which it may become afferent again in certain vannal veins, usually 2 and 3.

The pterales are important in preventing the collapse of the anterior and basal sinuses, and the pulsatile organ is supposed to aspirate blood from the axillary cord and pass it into the heart.[16, 18]

Folding of the wing reduces the rate and extent of blood flow and conversely extension of the wings in flight increases them.[18] This was not the case in *Blaberus giganteus*, where a taenidial-like structure is present in the wall of the veins in the regions of folding and prevents their collapse.[7] The details of the wing circulation are completely flexible and it can adjust itself to constraints in *B.o.*[57] and to cuts in the wing in *Bt.g.* In the latter case, the circulation adjusts by using parallel channels or forming double circulations so that no part of the wing is without blood, although if the cuts are very large this eventually happens.[17] The circulation in the wing of *B. giganteus* is at a maximum in the early adults, but with age some of the smaller veins get blocked by clumps of haemocytes.[3] Now if the wing is deprived of its blood supply in *Bt.g.* it becomes dry and brittle, the tracheae, if present, coil and collapse and bubbles of gas are released.[17] This may account for the observation that in older specimens of *B. giganteus* some channels blocked by haemocytes contain bubbles of gas passed out from the tracheae.[3] There are always more channels available than are necessary, so that the flow of blood in any one of them can stop or reverse readily. This is independent of the reversal of overall flow which can occur in *P.a.* wings and wing pads with or without reversal of the heartbeat as well. Indeed, the blood can flow in opposite directions in left and right wings, the blood passing from the posterior basal region of the normal wing across the posterior tergal margin, and into the posterior part of the wing with the reversed circulation.[115]

Although the wings of *Bt.g.* have many tracheae, they are not present with the blood channels in the costal vein nor in the cross-veins.[16] The speed of blood flow was measured in the subcostal vein 1·7 mm long in *P.a.* The mean of the average times was 34·3 mm/min with a range of 14·5 to 65·2 mm/min. There was no correlation with changes in the heart rate.[97]

The differences in many of the figures reported for constituents of the blood are, in part, a reflection of the different diets on which the animals were fed and the techniques of investigation used. Many of the apparent contradictions in the accounts of the beating of the heart, the coagulation of the blood and the haemocytes also probably are due to different conditions at the time of study.

Further studies are needed of the anatomy of the heart, the segmental vessels, and the circulation in *P.a.* (T).

REFERENCES

1. ABOUL-NASR, A. (1960). Studies on the heart beat of the German cockroach *Blattella germanica. Bull. Soc. ent. Égypte*, **44**, 405–19.
2. ANDERSON, A. D. and PATTON, R. L. (1955). In vitro studies of uric acid synthesis in insects. *J. exp. Zool.*, **128**, 443–52.
3. ARNOLD, J. W. (1959). Observations on living hemocytes in wing veins of the cockroach *Blaberus giganteus. Ann. ent. Soc. Am.*, **52**, 229–36.
4. ARNOLD, J. W. (1959). Observation on amoeboid motion of living haemocytes in the wing veins of *Blaberus giganteus. Can. J. Zool.*, **37**, 371–5.
5. ARNOLD, J. W. (1960). The course of blood circulation in mature embryos of the cockroach *Blaberus giganteus. Can. J. Zool.*, **38**, 1027–35.
6. ARNOLD, J. W. (1961). Further observations on amoeboid haemocytes in *Blaberus giganteus. Can. J. Zool.*, **39**, 755–71.
7. ARNOLD, J. W. (1964). Blood circulation in insect wings. *Mem. ent. Soc. Can.*, **38**, 1–48.
8. ASPEREN, K. VAN and ESCH, I. VAN (1954). A simple microtitration method for determination of Ca and Mg in haemolymph of insects. *Nature*, **174**, 927.
9. ASPEREN, K. VAN and ESCH, I. VAN (1956). The chemical composition of haemolymph of *Periplaneta americana. Archs néerl. Zool.*, **11**, 342–60.
10. AUCLAIR, J. L. (1959). The influence of dietary amino acids on the blood amino acids of the German cockroach, *Blattella germanica. J. Insect Physiol.*, **3**, 127–31.
11. BEAMENT, J. W. L. (1958). A paralysing agent in the blood of cockroaches. *J. Insect Physiol.*, **2**, 199–214.
12. BETTINI, S., NATALIZI, G. and BOCCACCI, M. (1957). Osservazioni sul meccanismo di azione degli acidi iodo-, bromo- e chloro-acetico nella blatta, *Periplaneta americana. Rc. Ist. sup. Sanità*, **20**, 432–9.

13. BROCHER, F. (1922). Etude éxperimentale sur la fonctionnement du vaisseau dorsal et sur la circulation du sang chez les insectes. V. La *Periplaneta orientalis. Annls Soc. ent. Fr.*, **91**, 156–64.

14. BROWN, B. E. (1965). Pharmacologically active constituents of the cockroach corpora cardiaca: resolution and some characteristics. *Gen. Comp. Endocrinol.*, **5**, 387–401.

15. CAMERON, M. (1953). Secretion of an orthodiphenol in the corpora cardiacum of the insect. *Nature*, **172**, 349–50.

16. CLARE, S. and TAUBER, O. E. (1940). Circulation of hemolymph in the wings of the cockroach *Blattella germanica*. I. In normal wings. *Iowa St. Coll. J. Sci.*, **14**, 107–27.

17. CLARE, S. and TAUBER, O. E. (1942). Circulation of hemolymph in the wings of the cockroach *Blattella germanica*. II. Effects of cutting hemolymph channels in the normal tegmen and hind wing. *Ann. ent. Soc. Am.*, **35**, 57–67.

18. CLARE, S. and TAUBER, O. E. (1942). Circulation of hemolymph in the wings of the cockroach *Blattella germanica*. III. Circulation in articular membranes. *Iowa St. Coll. J. Sci.*, **16**, 349–56.

19. CLARE, E. W. and CRAIG, R. (1953). The calcium and magnesium content in the haemolymph of certain insects. *Physiol. Zööl.*, **26**, 101–7.

20. COLHOUN, E. H. (1963). Synthesis of 5-hydroxytryptamine in the American cockroach. *Experientia*, **19**, 9–10.

21. COOK, B. J. and FORGASH, A. J. (1965). The identification and distribution of the carboxylic esterases in the American cockroach, *Periplaneta americana. J. Insect Physiol.*, **11**, 237–50.

22. DAVEY, K. G. (1960). A pharmacologically active agent in the reproductive system of insects. *Can. J. Zool.*, **38**, 39–45.

23. DAVEY, K. G. (1961). The mode of action of the heart accelerating factor from the corpus cardiacum of insects. *Gen. comp. Endocrinol.*, **1**, 24–9.

24. DAVEY, K. G. (1961). Substances controlling the rate of beating of the heart of *Periplaneta. Nature*, **192**, 284.

25. DAVEY, K. G. (1962). The release by feeding of a pharmacologically active factor from the corpus cardiacum of *Periplaneta americana. J. Insect Physiol.*, **8**, 205–8.

26. DAVEY, K. G. (1964). The control of the visceral muscles in insects. *Advs. Insect Physiol.*, **2**, 219–45.

27. DAY, M. F. (1952). Wound healing in the gut of cockroach *Periplaneta americana. Aust. J. scient. Res.* (B), **5**, 282–9.

28. DÛCHATEAU, G. and FLORKIN, M. (1958). A survey of aminoacidemias with special reference to the high concentration of free aminoacids in insect haemolymph. *Archs int. Physiol. Biochim.*, **66**, 573–91.

29. EDWARDS, G. A. and CHALLICE, C. E. (1960). The ultrastructure of the heart of the cockroach, *Blattella germanica. Ann. ent. Soc. Am.*, **53**, 369–83.

30. ERMIN, R. (1939). Über Bau und Funktion der Lymphocyten bei Insekten. *Z. Zellforsch. mikrosk. Anat.* (A), **29**, 613–69.

31. FISHER, R. A. (1935). The effect of acetic acid vapor treatment on the blood cell count in the cockroach *Blatta orientalis. Ann. ent. Soc. Am.*, **28**, 146–53.

32. FISHER, R. A. (1936). The effect of a few toxic substances upon the total blood cell count in the cockroach *Blatta orientalis. Ann. ent. Soc. Am.*, **29**, 335–40.

33. FRIES, E. F. B. (1926). Temperature and the frequency of heart beat in the cockroach. *J. gen. Physiol.*, **10**, 227–37.

34. GLASER, R. W. (1925). Hydrogen ion concentrations in the blood of insects. *J. gen. Physiol.*, **7**, 599–602.

35. GRÉGOIRE, C. (1951). Blood coagulation in Arthropods. II. Phase contrast microscopic observations on hemolymph coagulation in 61 species of insects. *Blood*, **6**, 1173–98.

36. GRÉGOIRE, C. (1953). Coagulation de l'hémolymphe chez divers insectes Orthoptéroïdes. *Archs int. Physiol.*, **61**, 234–6.
37. GRÉGOIRE, C. (1957). Studies by phase-contrast microscopy on distribution of patterns of hemolymph coagulation in insects. *Smithson. misc. Collns.*, **134**, no. 6.
38. GRÉGOIRE, C. (1959). Further observations on distribution of patterns of coagulation of the hemolymph in neotropical insects. *Smithson. misc. Collns.*, **139**, no. 3.
39. HABER, V. R. (1926). The blood of insects, with special reference to that of the common household German, or croton, cockroach, *Blattella germanica*. *Bull. Brooklyn ent. Soc.*, **21**, 61–100.
40. HOSKIN, W. M. and CRAIG, R. (1935). Recent progress in insect physiology. *Physiol. Rev.*, **15**, 525–96.
41. JONES, J. C. (1953). On the heart in relation to circulation of hemocytes in insects. *Ann. ent. Soc. Am.*, **46**, 366–72.
42. JONES, J. C. (1957). A phase contrast study of the blood cells of the adult cockroach *Periplaneta americana*. *Anat. Rec.*, **128**, 571.
43. JONES, J. C. (1962). Current concepts concerning insect hemocytes. *Am. Zoologist*, **2**, 209–46.
44. KOZHANCHIKOV, I. V. (1932). Sketches on the heart activity of insects. I. Normal pulsation frequency of the dorsal vessel of *Blatta orientalis* and the effect of certain factors on it. *Bull. Leningrad Inst. Control Farm and Forest Pests*, **2**, 149–72.
45. KRIJGSMAN, B. J., DRESDEN, D. and BERGER, N. E. (1950). The action of rotenone and tetraethyl pyrophosphate on the isolated heart of the cockroach. *Bull. ent. Res.*, **41**, 141–51.
46. KUBIŠTA, V. (1959). Stoffwechsel der isolierten Insektenmuskulatur. *Sber. Ges. Beförd. ges. Naturw. Marburg*, **81**, 17–31.
47. LEVENBROOK, L. and HOLLIS, V. W. (1961). Organic acids in insects. I. Citric acid. *J. Insect Physiol.*, **6**, 52–61.
48. LIPKE, H. and GRAINGER, M. M. (1962). Mucopolysaccharides of the cockroach during molting. *Fedn Proc. Fedn Am. Socs exp. Biol.*, **21**, 170.
49. LIPKE, H., GRAINGER, M. M. and SIAKOTOS, A. N. (1965). Polysaccharide and glycoprotein formation in the cockroach. I. Identity and titer of bound monosaccharides. *J. biol. Chem.*, **240**, 594–600.
50. LIPKE, H., GRAVES, B. and LETO, S. (1965). Polysaccharide and glycoprotein formation in the cockroach. II. Incorporation of D-glucose-^{14}C into bound carbohydrate. *J. biol. Chem.*, **240**, 601–8.
51. LUDWIG, D., TEFFT, E. R. and SUCHYTA, M. D. (1957). Effects of pH on the heart of the American cockroach, *Periplaneta americana*. *J. cell. comp. Physiol.*, **49**, 503–8.
52. LUDWIG, D., TRACEY, K. M. and BURNS, M. L. (1957). Ratio of ions required to maintain the heart beat of the American cockroach *Periplaneta americana*. *Ann. ent. Soc. Am.*, **50**, 244–6.
53. MCINDOO, N. E. (1939). Segmental blood vessels of the American cockroach. *J. Morph.*, **65**, 323–53.
54. MCINDOO, N. E. (1945). Innervation of insect hearts. *J. comp. Neurol.*, **83**, 141–55.
55. MANSINGH, A. (1965). Water loss in malathion-intoxicated German cockroaches. *J. econ. Ent.*, **58**, 162–3.
56. METCALFE, R. I., WINTON, M. Y. and FUKUTO, T. R. (1964). The effects of cholinergic substances upon the isolated heart of *Periplaneta americana*. *J. Insect Physiol.*, **10**, 353–61.
57. MOSELEY, H. N. (1871). On the circulation in the wings of *Blatta orientalis* and other insects, and on a new method of injecting the vessels of insects. *Q. Jl microsc. Sci.*, **11**, 389–95.

58. MUNSON, S. C. and YEAGER, J. F. (1949). Blood volume and chloride normality in roaches (*Periplaneta americana*) injected with sodium chloride solutions. *Ann. ent. Soc. Am.*, **42**, 165–73.
59. NAIDU, M. B. (1955). Physiological action of drugs and insecticides. *Bull. ent. Res.*, **46**, 205–20.
60. NUTTING, W. L. (1951). A comparative anatomical study of the heart and accessory structures of the orthopteroid insects. *J. Morph.*, **89**, 501–97.
61. ORSER, W. B. and BROWN, A. A. (1951). The effect of insecticides on the heart-beat of *Periplaneta*. *Can. J. Zool.*, **29**, 54–64.
62. PALM, N. B. (1946). Studies on the peristalsis of the Malpighian tubes in insects. *Acta Univ. lund.*, **42**, no. 11.
63. PATTON, R. L. (1962). The specific gravity of insect blood and its application to physiological problems. *J. Insect Physiol.*, **8**, 537–44.
64. PATTON, R. L. (1961). Detoxication function of insect hemocytes. *Ann. ent. Soc. Am.*, **54**, 696–8.
65. PATTON, R. L. and FLINT, R. A. (1959). Variation in blood-cell count of *Periplaneta americana* during a molt. *Ann. ent. Soc. Am.*, **52**, 240–2.
66. PAULOWA, M. (1895). Über ampullenartige Blutcirculationsorgane im Kopfe verschiedener Orthopteren. *Zool. Anz.*, **18**, 7–13.
67. PICHON, Y. and BOISTEL, J. (1963). Modifications of the ionic content of the haemolymph and of the activity of *Periplaneta americana* in relation to diet. *J. Insect Physiol.*, **9**, 887–91.
68. POLACEK, I. and KUBIŠTA, V. (1960). Metabolism of the cockroach, *Periplaneta americana* during flight. *Physiologia bohemoslov.*, **9**, 228–34.
69. POWNING, R. F. and IRZYKIEWICZ, H. (1962). β-glucosidase in the cockroach (*Periplaneta americana*) and in the puffball (*Lycoperdon perlatum*). *Comp. Biochem. Physiol.*, **7**, 103–15.
70. PRATT, J. J. (1950). A qualitative analysis of the free amino acids in insect blood. *Ann. ent. Soc. Am.*, **43**, 573–80.
71. RALPH, C. L. and MCCARTHY, R. (1964). Effects of brain and corpora cardiaca extracts on haemolymph trehalose of the cockroach *Periplaneta americana*. *Nature*, **203**, 1195–6.
72. RICHARDS, A. G. (1963). The effect of temperature on heart-beat frequency in the cockroach *Periplaneta americana*. *J. Insect Physiol.*, **9**, 597–606.
73. ROUSCHAL, W. (1940). Osmotische Werte wirbelloser Landtiere und ihre ökologische Bedeutung. *Z. wiss. Zool.*, **153**, 196–218.
74. SCHLUMBERGER, H. G. (1952). A comparative study of the reaction to injury. I. The cellular response to methylcholanthrene and to talc in the body cavity of the cockroach *Periplaneta americana*. *Archs Path.*, **54**, 98–113.
75. SHAW, J. and STOBBART, R. H. (1963). Osmotic and ionic regulation in insects. *Advs. Insect Physiol.*, **1**, 315–99.
76. SHULL, W. E. (1936). Inhibition of coagulation in the blood on insects by the fatty acid vapor treatment. *Ann. ent. Soc. Am.*, **29**, 341–9.
77. SHULL, W. E. and RICE, P. L. (1933). A method for temporary inhibition of coagulation in the blood of insects. *J. econ. Ent.*, **26**, 1083–9.
78. SHULL, W. E., RILEY, M. K. and RICHARDSON, C. H. (1932). Some effects of certain toxic gases on the blood of the cockroach *Periplaneta orientalis*. *J. econ. Ent.*, **25**, 1070–2.
79. SIAKOTOS, A. N. (1959). An investigation of the conjugated plasma proteins of the American cockroach. *Diss. Abstr.*, **19**, 2377.
80. SIAKOTOS, A. N. (1960). The conjugated plasma proteins of the American cockroach. I. The normal state. *J. gen. Physiol.*, **43**, 999–1013.
81. SIAKOTOS, A. N. (1960). The conjugated plasma proteins of the American cockroach. II. Changes during molting and clotting processes. *J. gen. Physiol.*, **43**, 1015–30.

82. SMITH, H. W. (1938). The blood of the cockroach, *Periplaneta americana. Bull. New Hamps. agric. Exp. Stn.*, **71**, 1–23.

83. STEELE, J. E. (1961). Occurrence of hyperglycaemic factor in the corpus cardiacum in an insect. *Nature*, **192**, 680–1.

84. STEELE, J. E. (1963). The site of action of insect hyperglycaemic hormone. *Gen. comp. Endocrinol.*, **3**, 46–52.

85. STEINER, G. (1932). Die Automatie und die zentrale Beeinflussung des Herzens von *Periplaneta americana. Z. vergl. Physiol.*, **16**, 290–304.

86. STEINHAUER, A. L. (1958). Factors affecting the protein and free amino acid composition of blood of the American cockroach *Periplaneta americana. Diss. Abstr.*, **19**, 917–18.

87. STEINHAUER, A. L. and STEPHEN, W. P. (1959). Changes in blood protein during development of the American cockroach *Periplaneta americana. Ann. ent. Soc. Am.*, **52**, 733–8.

88. STEPHEN, W. P. (1958). Hemolymph proteins and their use in systematic studies. *Proc. 10th. Int. Congr. Entom.* (1956), **1**, 395–400.

89. STEPHEN, W. P. and JOHNSON, O. W. (1962). Qualitative changes in insect blood proteins after freezing. *J. Kans. ent. Soc.*, **35**, 189–96.

90. STEPHEN, W. P. and STEINHAUER, A. L. (1957). Sexual and developmental differences in insect blood proteins. *Physiol. Zööl.*, **30**, 114–20.

91. STERNBERG, J. and CORRIGAN, J. (1959). Rapid collection of insect blood. *J. econ. Ent.*, **52**, 538–9.

92. TAUBER, O. E. (1936). Mitosis of circulating cells in hemolymph of *Blatta orientalis. Iowa St. Coll. J. Sci.*, **10**, 431–9.

93. TAUBER, O. E. (1937). The effect of ecdysis on the number of mitotically dividing cells in the hemolymph of *Blatta orientalis. Ann. ent. Soc. Am.*, **30**, 35–9.

94. TAUBER, O. E. (1940). Mitotic response of roach hemocytes to certain pathogens in the hemolymph. *Ann. ent. Soc. Am.*, **33**, 113–19.

95. TAUBER, O. E. and GRIFFITHS, J. T. (1942). Isolation of *Staphylococcus alba* from the hemolymph of the roach *Blatta orientalis. Proc. Soc. exp. Biol. Med.*, **51**, 45–57.

96. TAUBER, O. E. and GRIFFITHS, J. T. (1943). Multinucleate hemocytes in the roach *Blatta orientalis. Trans. Am. microscop. Soc.*, **62**, 91–3.

97. TAUBER, O. E. and SNIPES, B. T. (1936). Velocity of hemocyte circulation in the elytron of the cockroach *Periplaneta americana. Proc. Soc. exp. Biol. Med.*, **35**, 249–51.

98. TAUBER, O. E. and YEAGER, J. F. (1935). On total hemolymph (blood) cell counts of insects. *Ann. ent. Soc. Am.*, **28**, 229–40.

99. TAYLOR, A. (1935). Experimentally induced changes in the cell complex of the blood of *Periplaneta americana. Ann. ent. Soc. Am.*, **28**, 135–45.

100. TOBIAS, J. M. (1948). Potassium, sodium and water exchange in irritable tissue and hemolymph of an omnivorous insect *Periplaneta americana. J. cell. comp. Physiol.*, **31**, 125–42.

101. TODD, M. E. (1957). The concentration of certain organic constituents in the haemolymph of the American cockroach, *Periplaneta americana. Jl N.Y. ent. Soc.*, **65**, 85–8.

102. TODD, M. E. (1958). Blood composition of the cockroach, *Leucophaea maderae. Jl N.Y. ent. Soc.*, **66**, 135–43.

103. WATERHOUSE, D. F. and MCKELLAR, J. W. (1961). The distribution of chitinase activity in the body of the American cockroach. *J. Insect Physiol.*, **6**, 185–95.

104. WHARTON, D. R. A., WHARTON, M. L. and LOLA, J. (1965). Blood volume and water content of the male American cockroach *Periplaneta americana*. Methods and the influence of age and starvation. *J. Insect Physiol.*, **11**, 391–404.

105. WHEELER, R. E. (1963). Studies on the total haemocyte count and haemolymph volume in *Periplaneta americana* with special reference to the last moulting cycle. *J. Insect Physiol.*, **9**, 223–35.
106. WILDE, J. DE (1948). Contribution to the physiology of the heart of insects, with special reference to the alary muscles. *Archs néerl. Physiol.*, **28**, 530–41.
107. WYATT, G. R. (1961). The biochemistry of insect haemolymph. *A. Rev. Ent.*, **6**, 75–102.
108. YEAGER, J. F. (1939). Significance of the presystolic notch in the mechano-cardiogram of *Periplaneta americana*. *Ann. ent. Soc. Am.*, **32**, 44–8.
109. YEAGER, J. F. (1939). Electrical stimulation of isolated heart preparations from *Periplaneta americana*. *J. agric. Res.*, **59**, 121–37.
110. YEAGER, J. F. (1942). The effect of blocking hemocytes with chinese ink and staining nephrocytes with trypan blue upon the resistance of the cockroach *Periplaneta americana* to sodium arsenite and nicotine. *Ann. ent. Soc. Am.*, **35**, 23–40.
111. YEAGER, J. F. and FAY, R. W. (1935). Reducing power of hemolymph from the roach *Periplaneta americana* with special reference to coagulation. *Proc. Soc. exp. Biol. Med.*, **32**, 1037–8.
112. YEAGER, J. F. and FAY, R. W. (1935). Micromethod for determining insect hemolymph specific gravity. *Proc. Soc. exp. Biol. Med.*, **32**, 1667–9.
113. YEAGER, J. F. and GRAHAM, J. B. (1937). Effects of the alkaloid nicotine on the rhythmicity of isolated heart preparations from *Periplaneta americana* and *Prodenia eridania*. *J. agric. Res.*, **55**, 1–19.
114. YEAGER, J. F., HAGER, A. and STRALEY, J. M. (1935). Some physiological effects of certain aliphatic thiocyanates on the isolated heart preparation from the roach *Blatta orientalis*. *Ann. ent. Soc. Am.*, **28**, 256–64.
115. YEAGER, J. F. and HENDRICKSON, G. O. (1934). Circulation of blood in wings and wingpads of the cockroach *Periplaneta americana*. *Ann. ent. Soc. Am.*, **27**, 257–72.
116. YEAGER, J. F. and KNIGHT, H. H. (1933). Microscopic observations on blood coagulation in several different species of insects. *Ann. ent. Soc. Am.*, **26**, 591–602.
117. YEAGER, J. F. and MUNSON, S. C. (1950). Blood volume of the roach *Periplaneta americana*, determined by several methods. *Arthropoda*, **1**, 255–65.
118. YEAGER, J. F., SHULL, W. E. and FARRAR, M. D. (1932). On the coagulation of the blood of *Periplaneta orientalis* with special reference to blood smears. *Iowa St. Coll. J. Sci.*, **6**, 325–45.
119. YEAGER, J. F. and TAUBER, O. E. (1933). On counting mitotically dividing cells in blood of cockroach *Blatta orientalis*. *Proc. Soc. exp. Biol. Med.*, **30**, 861–3.

ADDITIONAL REFERENCES

120. BETTINI, S., SARKARIA, D. A. and PATTON, R. L. (1951). Observations on the fate of vertebrate erythrocytes and hemoglobin injected into the blood of *Periplaneta americana*. *Science*, **113**, 9–10.
121. COON, B. F. (1944). Effects of paralytic insecticides on heart pulsations and blood circulation in the American cockroach as determined with a fluorescein indicator. *J. econ. Ent.*, **37**, 785–9.
122. DAS, P. C. and RAYCHAUDHURI, D. N. (1965). Electrocardiographic observations in the cockroach *Periplaneta americana* (Linnaeus). *Proc. zool. Soc. Calcutta*, **18**, 159–65.
123. GRÉGOIRE, C. (1953). Blood coagulation in arthropods. III. Reactions of insect hemolymph to coagulation inhibitors of vertebrate blood. *Biol. Bull. mar. biol. Lab. Woods Hole*, **104**, 372–93.
124. GRÉGOIRE, C. (1955). Blood coagulation in arthropods. V. Studies on hemolymph coagulation in 420 species of insects. *Archs Biol., Paris*, **66**, 103–68.

125. GUPTA, A. P. and SUTHERLAND, D. J. (1966). In vitro transformations of the insect plasmatocyte in some insects. *J. Insect Physiol.*, **12**, 1369–75.
126. KRIJGSMAN, B. J. and BERGER, N. E. (1951). Physiological investigations into the heart functions of arthropods. The heart of *Periplaneta americana. Bull. ent. Res.*, **42**, 143–55.
127. NELSON, D. R., TERRANOVA, A. C. and SUKKESTEAD, D. R. (1967). Fatty acid composition of the glyceride and free fatty acid fractions of the fat body and hemolymph of the cockroach *Periplaneta americana* (L.). *Comp. Biochem. Physiol.*, **20**, 907–17.
128. RALPH, C. L. (1961). Distribution of cardio-accelerator hormone in *Periplaneta americana. Am. Zoologist*, **1**, 381.
129. SARKARIA, D. S., BETTINI, S. and PATTON, R. L. (1951). A rapid staining method for clinical study of cockroach blood cells. *Can. Ent.*, **83**, 329–32.
130. YEAGER, J. F. (1938). Mechanographic method of recording insect cardiac activity, with reference to the effect of nicotine on isolated heart preparations of *Periplaneta americana. J. agric. Res.*, **56**, 267–76.
131. YEAGER, J. F. and HAGER, A. (1934). On the rates of contraction of the isolated heart and Malpighian tube of the insect *Periplaneta orientalis. Iowa St. Coll. J. Sci.*, **8**, 391–5.
132. YEAGER, J. F. and HENDRICKSON, G. O. (1933). A simple method for demonstrating blood circulation in the wings and wingpads of the cockroach *Periplaneta americana. Proc. Soc. exp. Biol. Med.*, **30**, 858–60.

16 Respiration

Abbreviations used for figures in Chapter 16			
a.	anastomosis	ldc.	latero-dorsal connective
bmp.	branches to mouth parts	llt.	lateral longitudinal trunk
d.	dilation	nct.	trachea of nerve cord
dbh.	dorsal branch to head	sp.	spiracle
dd.	dorsal dilation	vbh.	ventral branch to head
dtt.	dorsal thoracic trunk	vd.	ventral dilation
g.	gut	vtt.	ventral thoracic trunk
hrt.	heart		

The anatomy of the tracheal system

The anatomy of the tracheal system follows the typical insect pattern with ten pairs of spiracles, longitudinal trunks and small segmental air sacs,[13] but no illustrations of the respiratory system of *P.a.* is known to the writer (T).

The system in *Bt.g.* is shown in Figs 16.1 to 16.6.

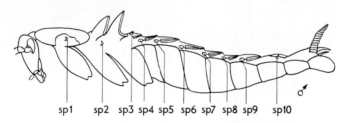

FIG. 16.1   Spiracle distribution on the body of *Blattella germanica*. (Haber[19])

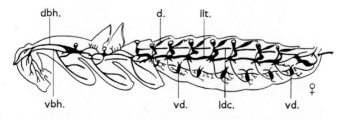

FIG. 16.2   Lateral view of tracheal system, *Blattella germanica*. (Haber[19])

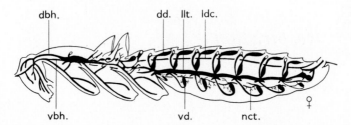

FIG. 16.3   Lateral view of tracheal system of a second specimen of *Blattella germanica*, to show the variability of this system. (Haber[19])

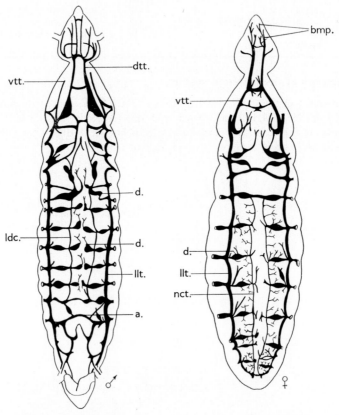

Fig. 16.4   Fig. 16.5

FIG. 16.4   Arrangement of mainly the dorsal tracheae in one individual. (Haber[19])
FIG. 16.5   Arrangement of mainly the ventral tracheae in one individual. (Haber[19])

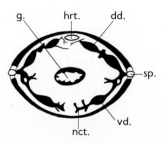

FIG. 16.6   Scheme of tracheal arrangement in a cross-section taken through the spiracular region of one of the abdominal segments. (Haber[19])

The larger tracheae of cockroaches are lined by a taenidial thread arranged in whole or broken annuli or in helices. The taenidium contains or is mainly composed of chitin micellae running longitudinally. Deep to the taenidium is a layer of chitin micellae running longitudinally, contributing to the proteinaceous endocuticle layer.[41, 44] Fibrils less than 100–300 Å diameter found in *P.a.* trachea are probably the chitin micellae.[43] The whole of the internal surface of the trachea is covered by a typical lipoprotein epicuticle.[43, 44] Irregularities are found in the intertaenidial luminal surface of the trachea whose origin is unknown.

In the smaller tracheae and the tracheoles of *P.a.* and *B.o.* chitin, as detected by the chitosan colour test, is not present.[44] Since the taenidia extend into the tracheoles,[41, 44] Richards and Korda have proposed that all the branches of the tracheal system less than 1 μ in diameter are called tracheoles.[44] The smallest branches have a diameter of 0·4 μ in *P.a.* and 0·3 μ in *B.o.* The tracheal end cells are absent from the crop, mid-gut caeca and wing muscles of *P.a.*, and the tracheae of the wing do not proliferate or migrate into an injured area.[11]

The trachea of *P.a.* may contain a sticky substance of unknown nature which often contains haemocytes,[48] while *Leucophaea maderae* and some other ovoviparous species secrete an odorous substance which is stated to be an alarm odour. It is secreted by whitish glands found in nymphs and adults on the wall of the tracheae close to the spiracles of the second abdominal segment.[45, 46] The substance in *L. maderae* is not a quinone as in many other cockroaches.[46]

An odd observation is that if a drop of water, 0·7–1·5% saline, acetic acid, benzene or ether, is placed on the surface of the intact or amputated leg of *P.a.* droplets appear within the trachea beneath. It seemed to Pal that this was not a condensation effect,[36] but Beament showed that a temperature difference of only 0·5° will cause the appearance of droplets; he pointed out that it indicates a high humidity within the tracheole.[3]

THE PHYSIOLOGY OF RESPIRATION

The R.Q. of *B.o.* when fasting is 0·75–0·85[9] or 0·78. Females kept at 15·3° for 20 hr on the average consumed 118 μl. of oxygen and produced the same volume of carbon dioxide to give an R.Q. of 1 when fed on sucrose. With protein as food, the oxygen uptake was 150 μl. and carbon dioxide output 119 μl., giving an R.Q. of 0·8 approximately.[16]

Young cockroaches had an R.Q. of 0·65–0·85 according to Gourévitch, and by feeding on fresh cream the R.Q. became about 0·8 and on starch it was about 1.[15]

The R.Q. of *P.a.* feeding on glucose was 1,[2] but the isolated metathorax of males of this species had a R.Q. of 0·88 when at rest.[25] During the first 4 min of flight the R.Q. was 0·97 and over the first 9 min, it was 0·90. As flight continued, the R.Q. declined, as did the frequency of the wingbeat. It can be calculated that the oxygen consumption of the red flight muscle during flight is 93 ml./g. fresh wt/hr, and at rest about 1 ml./g/hr. When these figures are corrected for the increased temperature occurring in flight it is found there is a 65-fold increase in the consumption of oxygen during flight from rest.[20]

The oxygen consumption of *P.a.* is said to be 0·38 ml./g body wt/hr (maximum) at 30°[17] or, in the isolated metathorax of *P.a.*, 0·64 ml./g/hr,[27] or 0·68 ml./g/hr,[26] or 0·368 ml./g/hr in males at 25°[37] and in males of *B.o.* it is about 0·325 ml./g/hr.[18] The consumption per gram body weight of the female is said to be 30% greater than that of the male,[40] but in *Leucophaea maderae* the opposite is true.[47]

In *P.a.* Q_{10} for oxygen uptake is 2·25 between 15° and 25°, with an activation value of 14,000–15,000 cal, between 3° and 35°.[40] The Q_{10} for *P.a.* in normal air at 11° is also given as 2·9 and in carbon dioxide-free air as 2·5.[51] In *B.o.* oxygen consumption is proportional to the temperature between 14° and 25°. Below 14° the oxygen uptake by *B.o.* is relatively more, and between 25° and 35° it is relatively less, than expected; but above 35° a disproportionate increase occurs up to 40°, when death intervened.[34] *P.a.*, however, shows adaptation to temperature, because if specimens are kept at 10° and then transferred to 20°, oxygen consumption is greater, compared with those which have been kept at 26° before being transferred to 20°. Smaller adults acclimated better than larger, and nymphs better than adults.[12]

Oxygen consumption is proportional to $W^{0.75-0.8}$ ($W=$ weight) in *P.a.*, *B.o.* and *Bt.g.*,[17] but in *B.o.* the metabolic rate was found to decrease as the animal grew from a weight of 0·08 g to 0·2 g, above which little further change occurred. Oxygen consumption also is increased by activity, in *B.o.*[9] and *P.a.*,[21] and is thus subject to the rhythmical cycles of activity exhibited by cockroaches. These are a main circadian cycle plus two less pronounced cycles of about 3½ hr and 48–54 min.[42] Oxygen consumption has been reported to increase during dehydration but this is a relative increase and is due to the loss in weight as the animal loses water.[18]

B.o. was found to be able to acquire enough oxygen from a 1% mixture with nitrogen, so that some earlier work is invalid unless special precautions were taken to exclude the last traces of oxygen. After a period of anaerobiosis the R.Q. was markedly decreased, the carbon dioxide being retained to restore the acid/base balance of the body,[10] but there is close agreement between the amount of oxygen debt and the amount of oxygen used in aerobiosis during an equal period of time.[9] In pure hydrogen, *Bt.g.* became inactive in 2 hr at 18° and in 1 hr at 25°,[10] although Nikitinsky says it takes 3 hr at 15°.[35]

The expired air of cockroaches contains about 4% of carbon dioxide and diffusion through the cuticle is negligible,[28] although in *Bt.g.* it has been suggested that carbon dioxide is lost from the wings.[8] The release of carbon dioxide from *P.a.* at 15° is fairly constant, though somewhat irregular according to Punt,[38] but it exhibits several rhythms according to Wilkins. He found that *P.a.* adults kept in alternately 12 hr light and 12 hr dark, in a stream of carbon dioxide-free air, of 80–90% R.H., showed a rhythm of carbon dioxide release every 14 min at 21°, but this was changed to 36 min, after an initial delay of 76 min when the temperature was reduced to 11°, and the amplitude of carbon dioxide output was halved. When the temperature was restored to 21°, the period became 13 min after a delay of 30 min. In normal air, the rate at 21° was every 16 min, but lowering the temperature to 11° made it 47 min, after a 45 min delay, again with the amplitude halved.[51]

Bt.g. becomes still in carbon dioxide in 10 to 15 sec, and in a mixture of equal parts of carbon dioxide and air, it takes 45 sec, at 15°.[35]

After anoxia by carbon dioxide or nitrogen, *P.a.* shows extra activity afterwards, and its usual daily peak of activity in the late evening may be displaced after even only one exposure.[39]

Bult studied the tracheae on the isolated mid-gut on *Bt.g.* in Ringer's solution. When the oxygen tension was low, the fluid was withdrawn from the ends of the tracholes in less than a minute, but if the oxygen tension was high the tracheoles quickly filled with water. He suggested that these effects were brought about not by changes in pH, but by changes in redox potential. This would have the effect of breaking the sulphur linkages of the proteins, so that they became hydrated, taking up the water from the tracheoles. He thought that the swelling of the cells indicated the swelling of the proteins as they inbibed the water. He also found that, when the permeability of all the cell walls was reduced by saponin or carbon dioxide in the saline, the cells absorbed water from the whole of the saline and not from that in the tracheoles. Thus he concluded that normally the permeability of the cell/tracheole interface is greater than that of the other walls of the cells, so that normally any absorbed water is taken from the tracheoles.

It was found that substances which stimulate oxidation or which interfered with reduction, checked the uptake of water from the tracheoles, and vice versa.[4]

Ventilation movements

In *P.a.* and other cockroaches the air is claimed to enter by the anterior four pairs of spiracles and to leave by the posterior six pairs, with the tenth playing the most important rôle. In quiet respiration all the expired air is said to leave this most posterior pair of the body.[28,29,30] The valves or lids of the spiracles alter to ensure the proper flow,[28,29] even reversing its flow if necessary.[30] In *P.a.*, however, it is also said that the air enters and leaves by all the spiracles, and that there is not through circulation of air in the longitudinal trunks of the animal.[22] In the Hawaiian cockroach *Nyctobora noctivaga* the air passes from anterior to posterior and the ventilation system is claimed to be able to create an internal pressure.[23] In *Bt.g.* the longitudinal tracheal trunks show peristalsis at almost the same rate as that of the heart.[1] They have swellings which have been called air sacs, but as they possess taenidia this name is inappropriate.[19]

During flight *P.a.* shows no obvious ventilation movements and after flying it shows them for only a few seconds if at all.[14]

The spiracles of *P.a.* open wider as the temperature is raised from $12°$ to $33°$, but at about $28°$ when they are one-quarter open they often show trembling movements. At $33°$ the spiracles are somewhat more than half open. If the roaches are put into a mixture of 10% oxygen and 90% nitrogen no changes are seen, but if the oxygen is dropped below 5%, ventilation movements begin after about half a minute.[22]

EFFECT OF CARBON DIOXIDE

With only a slight increase in carbon dioxide content, the spiracles open and ventilation movements begin. With slightly greater concentrations avoidance reactions are seen[24] and when the concentration reaches 10%, 8–10 ventilation movements/min occur. At 15% concentration the rate has risen to 150–180/min.[22] At 25% or more, no reactions are seen since the animal is anaesthetized or killed.[24]

Similar effects of carbon dioxide are commonly found in other cockroaches and injections of water with dissolved carbon dioxide, or 0.1% lactic acid cause dyspnoea.[28] Surprisingly, carbon dioxide is said not to affect the spiracles of the Hawaiian cockroach,[23] but the spiracles of *P.a.* possess sense organs sensitive to 2–3% of carbon dioxide, which is less than that usually present in the tissues.

The effect of carbon dioxide on these organs is to open the spiracles, but isolated spiracles require a concentration of 25–30% before they will open.[22]

In *P.a.* and *Blaberus craniifer* the actions of the spiracles are co-ordinated by the central nervous system,[5] but carbon dioxide also affects the respiratory system by a direct action on the ventral nerve cord in *P.a.*,[22,49] *B. craniifer*[6,7] and *Brysotria fumigata*,[31,32,33] and ventilation movements result.[6,33,49] The active phase of these movements in *P.a.* is in expiration. Thoracic ganglia in *P.a.* respond to a minimal concentration of 30% of carbon dioxide and they are the cause of ventilation movements of the abdomen. However, the abdominal ganglia can maintain a rhythm of movement set off by the thoracic ganglia and to start and maintain movements after anaesthesia, when the ventral nerve cord is cut between the thorax and abdomen.[49] In *Blaberus craniifer* the respiratory centre is in the metathorax and the first abdominal ganglion,[50] but Case states that the first abdominal ganglion and at least part of one of the adjacent ganglia are necessary for the rhythmic nerve impulses of ventilation to occur.[6]

In the females of *Brysotria fumigata* respiratory movements occur even at rest. In approximate figures, they happen in groups of 5[31,32] or 10[33]/min, with pauses of 7 min between each group.[31] If the insect is decapitated the breathing movements become continuous, but if the sixth abdominal ganglion is removed also, normal movements are restored. In such a preparation, ventilation movements result from bursts of impulses from the first abdominal ganglion which increase with increased concentration of carbon dioxide in the same way as they do in the intact insect. Thus the first abdominal ganglion contains the respiratory centre or ventilation pacemaker responsible for the rate and amplitude of the ventilation movements,[33] but the brain is in overall control. The threshold for carbon dioxide sensitivity is much lower in the abdominal ganglia than in the brain.[31]

In *Blaberus craniifer* the carbon dioxide works by the acidity it produces but pH is not the only factor affecting the sensitive ganglia. Weakly dissociated acids of the same pH as the carbon dioxide solution gave different effects, and it is suggested that the respiratory centre is protected by a barrier which is preferentially permeable to undissociated molecules and that it is also sensitive to pH.[7]

Oxygen does not affect the spiracles although lack of it does provoke ventilation movements in *P.a.*[22]

Much reliable work has been done on the physiology of respiration, and it is a pity that no study has been found of the anatomy of the tracheal system of *P.a.* The ventilation movements, and the supposed ventilation currents in the tracheal trunks, remain somewhat controversial points, but it seems unlikely that an animal as successful as the cockroach could not vary its ventilation activities in 'difficult' conditions. The presence of sensory structures in the spiracles, responsive to relatively low tensions of CO_2, suggests a useful local control mechanism, in addition to the central one in the nervous system, which could be used to select appropriate ventilation flow (T).

REFERENCES

1. ABOUL-NASR, A. (1960). Studies on the heartbeat of the German cockroach, *Blattella germanica. Bull. Soc. ent. Égypte*, **44**, 405–19.
2. BARRON, E. S. G. and TAHMISIAN, T. H. (1948). The metabolism of cockroach muscle. *J. cell. comp. Physiol.*, **32**, 57–76.
3. BEAMENT, J. W. L. (1964). The active transport and passive movement of water in insects. *Advs Insect Physiol.*, **2**, 67–129.
4. BULT, T. (1939). Over de bewegung der vloeistof in de tracheolen der insecten. Dissertation; Van Gorcum and Co., Assen.
5. CASE, J. F. (1957). The median nerves and cockroach spiracular function. *J. Insect Physiol.*, **1**, 85–94.
6. CASE, J. F. (1961). Organisation of the cockroach respiration center. *Biol. Bull. mar. biol. Lab. Woods Hole*, **121**, 385.
7. CASE, J. F. (1961). Effects of acids on an isolated insect respiration center. *Biol. Bull. mar. biol. Lab. Woods Hole*, **121**, 385.
8. CLARE, S. and TAUBER, O. E. (1940). Circulation of hemolymph in the wings of the cockroach, *Blattella germanica*. I. In normal wings. *Iowa St. Coll. J. Sci.*, **14**, 107–27.
9. DAVIS, J. G. and SLATER, W. K. (1926). The aerobic and anaerobic metabolism of the common cockroach, *Periplaneta orientalis*. I. *Biochem. J.*, **20**, 1167–72.
10. DAVIS, J. G. and SLATER, W. K. (1928). The aerobic and anaerobic metabolism of the common cockroach, *Periplaneta orientalis*. III. *Biochem. J.*, **22**, 331–7.
11. DAY, M. F. (1951). Studies on the digestion of wool by insects. III. A comparison of the tracheation of the midgut of *Tineola* larvae and other insects. *Aust. J. scient. Res.* (B), **4**, 64–74.
12. DEHNEL, P. A. and SEGAL, E. (1956). Acclimation of oxygen consumption to temperature in American cockroach. *Biol. Bull. mar. biol. Lab. Woods Hole*, **11**, 53–61.
13. EDWARDS, G. A. (1953). Respiratory mechanisms. In ROEDER, K. D. (ed.). *Insect Physiology*. Wiley, London and New York.

14. FRAENKEL, G. (1932). Untersuchungen über die Koordination von Reflexen und automatisch-nervösen Rythmen bei Insekten. II. Die nervöse Regulierung der Atmung während des Fluges. *Z. vergl. Physiol.*, **16**, 394–417.

15. GOURÉVITCH, A. (1928). Le quotient respiratoire des blattes en function de la nourriture. *C.r. Séanc. Soc. Biol.*, **98**, 26–7.

16. GOURÉVITCH, A. (1928). L'action dynamique spécifique chez les blattes. *C.r. hebd. Séanc. Acad. Sci.*, *Paris*, **187**, 65–7.

17. GUNN, D. L. (1935). The temperature and humidity relations of the cockroach. III. A comparison of temperature preference, and rates of desiccation and respiration of *Periplaneta americana, Blatta orientalis* and *Blattella germanica. J. exp. Biol.*, **12**, 185–90.

18. GUNN, D. L. and COSWAY, C. A. (1942). The temperature and humidity relations of the cockroach. VI. Oxygen consumption. *J. exp. Biol.*, **19**, 124–32.

19. HABER, V. R. (1926). The blood of insects, with special reference to that of the common household German or croton cockroach. *Bull. Brooklyn ent. Soc.*, **21**, 61–100.

20. HOFMANOVÁ, O., ČERKASAVOVÁ, A., FOUSTKA, M. and KUBISTA, V. (1966). Metabolism of the thoracic musculature of *Periplaneta americana* during flight. *Acta Univ. Carol.*, **1966**, 183–9.

21. JANDA, V. and MRCIAK, M. (1957). Čelková látkova premena hmyzu. VI. Pohybová aktivita svába amerického *Periplaneta americana* behem dne a její vztah ke spotrebe jyslíku. *Věst. čsl. Spol. zool.*, **21**, 244–55.

22. JORDAN, H. (1927). Die Regulierung der Atmung bei Insekten und Spinnen. *Z. vergl. Physiol.*, **5**, 179–90.

23. KITCHEL, R. L. and HOSKINS, W. M. (1935). Respiratory ventilation in the cockroach in air, carbon dioxide and nicotine atmospheres. *J. econ. Ent.*, **28**, 924–33.

24. KLOPFER, F. D. and QUIST, J. A. (1955). Reactions of the mealworm, honeybee and cockroach to some carbon dioxide concentrations. *J. comp. physiol. Psychol.*, **48**, 69–72.

25. KUBIŠTA, V. (1959). Stoffwechsel der isolierten Insektenmuskulatur. *Sber. Ges. Beförd. ges. Naturw. Marburg*, **81**, 17–31.

26. KUBIŠTA, V. (1966). Preparations of isolated insect musculature. *Acta Univ. Carol.*, **1966**, 197–208.

27. KUBIŠTA, V. and FOUSTKA, M. (1963). Anaerobic and postanaerobic changes of soluble phosphorus compounds in insect muscle. *Physiologia bohemoslov.*, **12**, 183–90.

28. LEE, M. O. (1924). Respiration in Orthoptera. *Am. J. Physiol.*, **68**, 135.

29. LEE, M. O. (1927). A note on the mechanism of respiration in Orthoptera. *J. exp. Zool.*, **49**, 319–20.

30. MCARTHUR, J. M. (1929). An experimental study of the functions of the different spiracles in certain Orthoptera. *J. exp. Zool.*, **53**, 117–28.

31. MYERS, T. B. (1962). Regulation of respiration in the Cuban burrowing cockroach. *Fedn Proc. Fedn Am. Socs exp. Biol.*, **21**, 358.

32. MYERS, T. and FISK, F. W. (1962). Breathing movements of the Cuban burrowing cockroach. *Ohio J. Sci.*, **62**, 253–7.

33. MYERS, T. and RETZLAFF, E. (1963). Localisation and action of the respiratory center in the Cuban burrowing cockroach. *J. Insect Physiol.*, **9**, 607–14.

34. NECHELES, N. (1924). Ueber Wärmeregulation bei wechselwarmen Tieren. *Pflügers Arch. ges. Physiol.*, **204**, 72–86.

35. NIKITINSKY, J. (1928). Über die Wirkung der Kohlensäure auf Wasserorganismen. *Zentbl. Bakt. ParasitKde*, **73**, 481–3.

36. PAL, R. (1947). Permeability of insect cuticle. *Nature*, **159**, 400.

37. POLACEK, I. and KUBIŠTA, V. (1960). Metabolism of the cockroach, *Periplaneta americana* during flight. *Physiologia bohemslov.*, **9**, 228–34.

38. PUNT, A. (1950). The respiration of insects. *Physiologia comp. Oecol.*, **2**, 59–63.

39. RALPH, C. L. (1959). Modifications of activity rhythm of *Periplaneta americana*, induced by carbon dioxide and nitrogen. *Physiol. Zöol.*, **32**, 57–62.

40. RICHARDS, A. G. (1963). The effect of temperature on the rate of oxygen consumption and on an oxidative enzyme in the cockroach *Periplaneta americana*. *Ann. ent. Soc. Am.*, **56**, 355–7.

41. RICHARDS, A. G. and ANDERSON, T. F. (1942). Electron micrographs of insect tracheae. *Jl N.Y. ent. Soc.*, **50**, 147–67.

42. RICHARDS, A. G. and HALBERG, F. (1964). Oxygen uptake rhythms in a cockroach gauged by variance spectra. *Experientia*, **20**, 40–2.

43. RICHARDS, A. G. and KORDA, F. H. (1948). Studies on Arthropod cuticle. II. Electron microscope studies of extracted cuticle. *Biol. Bull. mar. biol. Lab. Woods Hole*, **94**, 212–35.

44. RICHARDS, A. G. and KORDA, F. H. (1950). Studies on Arthropod cuticle. IV. An electron microscope survey of the intima of arthropod tracheae. *Ann. ent. Soc. Am.*, **43**, 49–71.

45. ROTH, L. M. and EISNER, T. (1962). Chemical defenses of arthropods. *A. Rev. Ent.*, **7**, 107–36.

46. ROTH, L. M. and STAY, B. (1957). The occurrence of para-quinones in some arthropods, with emphasis on the quinone-secreting tracheal glands of *Diploptera punctata*. *J. Insect Physiol.*, **1**, 305–18.

47. SAMUELS, A. (1956). Effect of sex and allatectomy on the oxygen consumption of the thoracic musculature of *Leucophaea maderae*. *Biol. Bull. mar. biol. Lab. Woods Hole*, **110**, 179–83.

48. SANFORD, E. W. (1918). Experiments on physiology of digestion in the Blattidae. *J. exp. Zool.*, **25**, 355–411.

49. SCHREUDER, J. E. and DE WILDE, J. (1952). Analysis of the dyspnoeic action of carbon dioxide in the cockroach, *Periplaneta americana*. *Physiologia comp. Oecol.*, **2**, 355–61.

50. SMALLEY, K. N. (1963). The neural regulation of respiration in the cockroach, *Blaberus craniifer*. *Diss. Abstr.*, **24**, 2629–30.

51. WILKINS, M. B. (1960). A temperature-dependent endogenous rhythm in the rate of carbon dioxide output of *Periplaneta americana*. *Nature*, **185**, 481–2.

52. BUCK, J. (1962). Some physical aspects of insect respiration. *A. Rev. Ent.*, **7**, 27–56.

53. SÄGESSER, H. (1960). Uber die Wirkung der Corpora allata auf der Sauerstoffverbrauch bei der Schabe, *Leucophaea maderae*. *J. Insect Physiol.*, **5**, 264–85.

54. WIGGLESWORTH, V. B. (1931). The respiration of insects. *Biol. Rev.*, **6**, 181–220.

17 Predators, parasites and symbionts

PREDATORS

As might be expected on the grounds of size, cockroach predators are to be looked for in the Arthropoda and Vertebrata. A large percentage of the predator species recorded came from isolated observations, and in some cases only environmental contiguity was shown; of greater interest are those observations suggesting a major prey–predator relationship. The many instances of the experimental feeding of cockroaches to other animals simply show that cockroaches form a generally acceptable form of food, without indicating any biotic relationship. In compiling lists of predators the monograph by Roth and Willis has proved a major source.[85]

A variety of Arachnids (20 species), ranging from Thelyphonids to Scorpions and Theraphosid spiders, have been seen to feed on cockroaches, but in many instances these were captive animals. It may be wondered whether some of the more sluggish Arachnids can capture such a quick-moving insect in a natural environment, and Cloudsley-Thompson reports having to disable specimens of *Periplaneta* before the scorpion *Euscorpius italicus italicus* would feed on them.[23] There is little doubt that many of the spiders that freely pursue other arthropods feed extensively on cockroaches when these are present. The Sparassid spider, *Heteropoda venatoria*, found in the West Indies, South America and Hawaii, has been observed by several authors to feed on a number of cockroach species found in these locations. In Hawaii it was specifically linked with *Periplaneta australasiae* present in large numbers beneath rock piles (Zimmerman). The cockroach is seized and then held on its back. It dies in about ten minutes, and then is gradually rolled up as the body contents are sucked out by the spider.[117]

Six species of Myriapod are reported as feeding on cockroaches and some will readily accept cockroaches as food in captivity. Lucas reports *Ectobius panzeri* as the natural prey of a species of *Scolopendra* in Great Britain, but in most cases the prey species was not identified.[66]

Of the insects associated with cockroaches a great many are parasites of the eggs, larval stages, or adults, and only a few species have been recorded as subsisting on cockroaches captured and eaten at each foray. Some Heteropterous bugs are found in proximity to cockroaches and there is good evidence that they feed on cockroaches. The Lygaeid *Clerada apicornis* was believed to feed on cockroaches, as was the Reduvid *Triatoma arthurneivai*. More direct observations by Pinto established *Spiniger domesticus* (Reduvid), as a predator of *P.a.* in dwellings in the Matto Grosso region of Brazil.[78]

The beetle *Dermestes ater* will feed on freely moving live *B.o.* and thus slowly kill them, in laboratory cultures of the latter insect. Roth and Willis also observed that the beetle larvae could enter oöthecae of *Bt.g.*, but not those of *P.a.* or *B.o.*[85] Other Dermestids may attack cockroach egg cases.

The killing of cockroaches by ants has been noted by various observers since the time of Bates (1863). A number of ants may combine their attack to overcome the larger, but sluggish and weakly-sclerotized cockroach. *E. pallidus* is preyed on by *Aphaenogaster picea* and *Lasius alienus* in the U.S.A. (Roth and Willis), and *Pheidole megacephala* followed and killed *Nauphoeta cinerea* and *Pycnoscelus surinamensis* as they burrowed in soil in Hawaii.[85]

It should be noted (see Chapter 1) that many cockroaches attack and eat members of their own species, but this may be a trait emphasized in captive populations.

Few records of fish eating cockroaches are available, although they are used as bait by anglers in various parts of the U.S.A.

The other vertebrate classes contribute a number of detailed observations. The lists given by Roth and Willis showing the numbers of predatory species in each class is as follows: 16 species of amphibians, 21 species of reptiles, 32 species of birds and 43 species of mammal. The more detailed nature of the observations on vertebrates as compared with predatory species of arthropods is undoubtedly contributed to by their ease of identification. In a number of instances the cockroach is an intermediate host for a parasite found in the vertebrate.

In the majority of amphibia in which counts of cockroaches were made from stomach contents, only small numbers of cockroaches and low incidence rates occurred (observed in less than 12% of food-containing stomachs). Nevertheless, *Bufo marinus*, the giant toad of the West Indies, Pacific Islands and Central America, has been shown to feed on *P.a.* and three other cockroach species, and is believed to eat considerable numbers of these insects. Several species of frog and one salamander are also cited as cockroach predators.[85]

A number of species of lizard, especially those frequenting houses, feed on cockroaches. In some instances the high incidence of cockroaches in their stomachs suggests that they form a major part of the food intake. The lizards most often containing cockroaches were as follows: in *Anolis leachi*, the total number of cockroaches/the total number of lizards—68%; these were *Periplaneta* sp. and other genera in Bermuda (Simmonds);[91] and in *Ameiva* sp.—45%, these were unnamed cockroaches in British Guiana (Beebe).[6] Many other species of lizard are recorded as having fed on cockroaches (3 species—8%), and in the gecko *Hemidactylus frenata* cockroaches comprised a large part of the stomach contents of 22 of these reptiles. In few cases is there any suggestion of host–prey specificity, although Darlington reports *Anolis sagrei* depending on *Pycnoscelus surinamensis* as a staple food.[27]

Many casual observations of birds eating cockroaches have been collected by Roth and Willis, but in the few cases where stomach contents were examined they revealed only small numbers of cockroaches. *P. surinamensis* was one of the few cockroach species to be coupled with a specific predator in different geographical areas, due to its rôle as the intermediate host of the nematode *Oxyspirura mansoni*.

The Peruvian bird *Troglodytes audax* is known as the Cucarachero and has been observed to feed on cockroaches, first removing the head and wings. There is little doubt that birds will readily accept cockroaches as food and as pointed out by Roth and Willis the more arboreal species of cockroaches might be expected to be taken by birds. One example is perhaps *Diploptera punctata* predated by a species of pheasant (*Phasianus* sp.), but in many instances the cockroaches were ground species.

A wide range of mammals (Marsupials, Insectivores, Chiroptera, Primates, Edentates, Rodents and Carnivores) has been observed to eat cockroaches. *Blattella germanica* appears to be especially favoured, although Carpenter recorded the rejection of an unidentified cockroach species by a Cercopithecid monkey, unless no other food was available,[20] and Roth and Willis cite Neill's description of a Callithricid monkey removing the head, viscera, wings and legs of a cockroach before eating it.

Periplaneta americana has been shown to provide a source of food for *Rattus norvegicus* and *Rattus rattus* in Denmark (Fibiger and Ditlevsen), and to harbour the parasitic worm of rats *Gongylonema neoplasticum*.[34]

Finally, cockroaches and their oöthecae have been used as food by man in Australia, Thailand, China, Japan and other parts of the Far East and they have also been consumed for medicinal reasons, according to Roth and Willis.

VIRUSES

Some types of insect virus, such as the polyhedral virus of Lepidoptera, have been extensively investigated, but there is not a great deal of information about viruses in cockroaches. This is a reflection of a low incidence of viral diseases compared with some other insects. Viruses are unlikely to be of great importance in limiting populations of cockroaches.

Periplaneta americana and *Bt.g.* have been used as experimental vectors for strains of poliomyelitis virus,[54, 37, 99] for encephalomyelitis virus,[98] yellow fever virus[36] and for Coxsackie viruses,[38] with varying degrees of success.

Natural vectors could only be found in the case of certain unspecified strains of poliomyelitis in *Bt.g.*, *Blattella vaga*, *P.a.*, *P. brunnea* and *Supella supellectilium* (see Dow for further details[31]).

The ability of cockroaches, which live associated with man, to pick up a virus and remain infective, is important. It seems likely that considerable variability exists. Fischer and Syverton found that after *P.a.* were given a single meal of Coxsackie virus they remained fatally infective to mice for 20 days, when the intestinal tracts were fed to the mice.[38] On the other hand, Gallardo, Forgash and Beaudette found that the Newcastle disease virus did not survive well in the gut of *P.a.*, and they concluded that some anti-viral factor was present in the gut of the cockroach.[42]

Rickettsiae

Very few species of rickettsiae have been recorded from insects, but recently Huger has published details of a new species from *B.o.* This author obtained excellent electronmicrographs of the organism which has been named *Rickett-siella blattae*. The rickettsial bodies appear as oval structures between 717 and 1,663 mμ in length, and 336 to 580 mμ broad (Fig. 17.1). The micro-organisms were found abundantly in the fat body, but other tissues were also infected.[55]

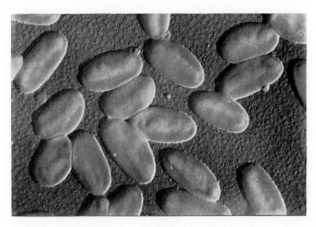

FIG. 17.1   An electronmicrograph of *Rickettsiella blattae* from *B.o.*, platinum shadowing. × 20,500 (From Huger[55])

BACTERIA

Over 150 species, types or varieties of bacteria have been isolated from cock-roaches, or passed into cockroaches in the course of experiments[83]. While only a small number of these bacteria appear to be endemic pathogens, a great number have been observed in the intestine or recovered from the faeces, and may be regarded as part of the normal gut flora. In no case was it clear to what extent the non-pathogenic bacteria of the gut contributed to the nutrition of the cockroach. A number of bacteria have been recorded as pathogenic to a cockroach when injected into the haemocoele but, as shown by Filatoff, a bacterium (*Bacillus flacheriae*) might be non-pathogenic when taken in via the gut (natural route), but pathogenic when injected.[35]

The bacteria which occur naturally in cockroach populations and produce death or marked debility in the infected insect are as follows:

(1) *Micrococcus pyogenes* var. *albus*. This has been recorded in *B.o.* (Tauber,[100] Tauber and Griffiths[101]), *Bt.g.* (Janssen and Wedberg[59]) and *Blaberus craniifer* (Wedberg *et al.*[109]). In *B.o.*, the organism occurred in the haemolymph. The symptoms were loss of appetite, sluggishness, irregular tracheal ventilation and paralysis. The body tended to become arched over, maintaining this position until death. The haemolymph was often whitish, and thick due to the large numbers of bacteria present.[101] Tauber believed that the infection might be spread by contact, or by other cockroaches eating the dead individuals. He was

able to show that infected individuals had a high haemocyte count, and many haemocytes were in the process of division.[100]

(2) *Serratia marcescens*. (Red strain.) Occurs naturally in *B.o.*, *Bt.g.*, *P.a.*, *Leucophaea maderae* and in a number of other cockroach species. A red colouration is typical of the dead or dying insects. The bacterium occurs in the haemolymph. There are few symptoms until the multiplication of the bacterium in the haemocoele has proceeded a long way and death is imminent, when the characteristic red colour appears. Death occurs when a critical level of infection is reached. Heimpel and West were able to show that in *Bt.g.* this critical level is near 84,000 bacteria, when these are injected into the cockroach. This or greater numbers of organisms causes the death of most insects within 24 hr. Injections containing 8,400 bacteria or less, were accompanied by little mortality before 7 days or after 11 days, and in some instances infected insects were observed to survive for 330 days. These authors concluded that the virulence of the bacterium for this cockroach is low.[50]

(3) *Bacillus cereus*. Occurs naturally in *Blaberus craniifer* (Wedberg et al.[109]) and *P.a.* (Hatcher[48]). This rod-shaped bacterium affects the host by enzymatic means. The internal organs are liquefied, the insect becoming discoloured and flaccid. The progress of the disease tends to be rapid.

(4) *Bacillus periplanetae*. Observed in *B.o.* by Tichomiroff (see Filatoff). Symptoms were diarrhoea; the liquid faeces were yellow-brown.[35]

(5) *Bacillus* sp. Jena M.E.T. Institute number 5896–8. Isolated and recorded by Heinecke from the haemolymph of *B.o.* It can be spread from the mouth, or from wounds. Course of the disease slow (85–90 days). Symptoms of paralysis were observed.[51]

FUNGI

A number of species of Thallophyte, about 60, have been observed in association with cockroaches. Perhaps the most striking are the representatives of the Laboulbeniales, most of them species of *Herpomyces*, which are usually found on the antennae and do not appear greatly to inconvenience their hosts.

Few species of fungi or yeasts have been definitely shown to cause the death of, or greatly affect the health of cockroaches infected by natural means.

Species of *Herpomyces*. Many of these are host-parasite specific; the following species have been recorded from the common domiciliary cockroaches.

Herpomyces periplanetae. Recorded from *B.o.*, U.S.A. and France (see Picard[77]), and from *P.a.* in the U.S.A., Africa and the Argentine (Spegazzini[94]). Has been found on other parts of the integument beside the antennae.
Herpomyces stylopygae. From *B.o.* in the U.S.A. and Argentina (Richards and Smith[84]). This species has been observed on various appendages.
Herpomyces chaetophilus. Recorded from *P.a.*, Brazil (Thaxter[102]).
Herpomyces ectobiae. On *Bt.g.*; distribution world-wide (Richards and Smith[84]). Usually found on the antennae but may occur elsewhere on the body.

Herpomyces tricuspidatus. From *Blaberus craniifer* in the U.S.A. (Richards and Smith[84]), and on *Leucophaea maderae* recorded from Fernando Po (Spegazzini[94]).

The haustorium of the fungus lies below the cuticle and communicates with the hair-like fruiting bodies on the surface of the integument through a fine perforation, or perforations, in the cuticle. Richards and Smith have published microphotographs illustrating many details of the relationship between host and parasite tissues. Three types of haustoria could be recognized: (a) Fine filaments up to about 1·0 μ in diameter. (b) Tubular haustoria 1·5–2 μ in diameter, thought to originate from the male plants; these expand into an haustorial bulb within the

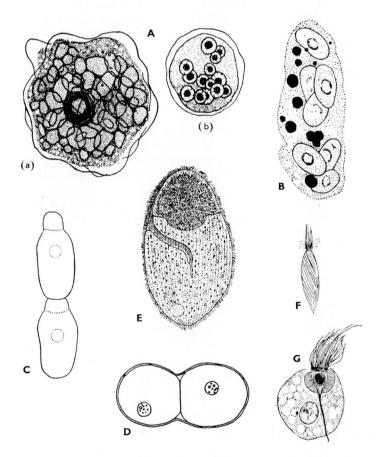

FIG. 17.2 Protozoa from cockroaches. **A**, *Endamoeba blattae* (a) trophozoite, (b) cyst. **B**, *Coelosporidium periplanetae*, trophozoite with spores and chromatoid bodies. **C**, *Gregarina blattarum*. **D**, *Diplocystis schneideri*. **E**, *Nyctotherus ovalis*. **F**, *Lophomonas striata*. **G**, *L. blattarum*. (Kudo[60])

host epidermis. (c) Large, less defined haustoria 2–5 μ in diameter, believed to be produced by the female plant. This type may also form an epidermal bulb.

Haustorial tubes passing through the cuticle are markedly argentophilic, but the haustorial bulb is not stained by silver. Nymphal cockroaches may get rid of the fungus by shedding infected cuticle at ecdysis, but adult insects retain the fungus throughout life.[84] Gunn and Cosway were of the opinion that infections of *Herpomyces* (= *Stigmatomyces*) *stylopygae* adversely affected the humidity receptors of the antennae.[47]

Among other Thallophyte species which may be regarded as parasitic are: *Metarrhizium anisopliae* from *P.a.* which, according to Bunting, grows on the female genitalia preventing oöthecal production;[17] *Aspergillus flavus* from the oöthecae of *P.a.* and *Bt.g.* (Roth and Willis),[87] *A. tamarii* from the oöthecae of *Bt.g.* (Roth and Willis).[86] A yeast-like micro-organism was isolated by Mercier from *B.o.* The parasite was found in the blood and fat body, and the abdomen became distended and soft.[72]

A number of species of different genera (*Aspergillus*, *Geotrichium*) are also associated with vertebrates.

PROTOZOA

All four major classes of protozoa are found in cockroaches, the great majority being found in the lumen of the gut or Malpighian tubules. While they are placed here under the title of parasites, there is little doubt that many of them live in a symbiotic association with their host and in a number of cases (as with flagellates in *Cryptocercus*) confer a benefit on the cockroach they occupy.

The following lists, largely prepared from Kudo[60], and Roth and Willis[85], set out the protozoan species naturally occurring in the five commonest domiciliary species of cockroach together with an author reference, and the site in the host where they were observed. (Some of the commonest species are illustrated in Fig. 17.2.)

TABLE 17.1

M = Mastigophora, Sa = Sarcodina, Sp = Sporozoa, C = Ciliata

Name	Tissue	Geographical location	Authority
Host: Blaberus craniifer			
Diplocystis sp. (Sp)	Haemocoele	U.S.A.	Nutting[74]
Host: Blatta orientalis			
Balantidium praenucleatum (C)	Anterior colon	U.S.A.	Meglitsch[71]

17.1—*continued*

Name	Tissue	Geographical location	Authority
Bodo blattae (M)	Hind-gut	England	Lankester[61]
Coelosporidium periplanetae (Sp) (*Nosema p.*)	Malpighian tubules	World-wide	Sprague[95]
Diplocystis schneideri (Sp)	Haemocoele	England	Jameson[58]
Endamoeba blattae (Sa) (= *Entamoeba blattae*)	Hind-intestine and rectum	World-wide	Meglitsch[71]
Entamoeba histolytica (Sa)		Peru	Schneider[88] and Shields
Entamoeba thomsoni (Sa) (= *Endamoeba thomsoni*)	Hind-intestine and rectum	World-wide	Chen[21]
Endolimax blattae (Sa)	Hind-gut	Germany, England and U.S.S.R.	Chen[21]
Endolimax blattae (Sa)	Hind-gut	U.S.S.R.	Zasukhin[115]
Gregarina blattarum (Sp) (= *G. blattae orientalis*)	Cells of intestine	World-wide	Sprague[96]
Haplosporidium periplanetae (Sp)	Malpighian tubules	Yugoslavia	Georgevitch[43]
Hartmanella blattae (Sa)	Hind-gut	Yugoslavia	Ivanic[57]
Herpetomonas periplanetae (M)		Italy, France	Lavern and Francini[62]
Hexamita periplanetae (M)	Hind-gut	U.S.S.R.	Zasukhin[115]
Lophomonas blattarum (M)	Colon	World-wide distribution	Zasukhin[115]
Lophomonas striata (M) (= *L. sulcata*)	Anterior colon	World-wide distribution	McAdow[68]
Monas sp. (M)	In the gut	U.S.S.R., Venezuela	Yakimov and Miller[113]
Monocercomonoides orthopterorum (+ *Trichomonas o.*) (M)	Hind-gut, common	Italy, U.S.S.R., England	Zasukhin[115]
Nyctotherus ovalis (C) (*Bursaria blattarum*)	Anterior colon	World-wide	Meglitsch[71]
Oikomonas sp. (M)	In the gut	U.S.S.R., Venezuela	Yakimov and Miller[113]

17.1—*continued*

Name	Tissue	Geographical location	Authority
Peltomyces periplanetae (Sa) (= *P. blattellae*)	Malpighian tubules	France	Debaisieux[28]
Plistophora kudoi (Sp)	Epithelium of caeca and mid-gut	U.S.A.	Sprague and Ramsey[97]
Plistophora periplanetae (Sp) (= *Nosema* sp.)	Malpighian tubules	Europe and U.S.S.R.	Debaisieux[28]
Plistophora periplanetae sp. (= *Nosema* sp.)	Fat body		Mercier[73]
Retortamonas blattae (M) (= *Embadomonas blattae*)	Hind-gut	England, U.S.A.	Bishop[9]
Stenophora sp. (Sp)	Mid-gut	India	Bal and Rai[2]
Trimitus blattae (M)	Hind-gut	France	Honigberg[52]
Tetratrichomastix blattidarum (M)	Rectum	U.S.A.	Young[114]

Host: Blattella germanica

(An asterisk indicates that the host may have been P.a.)

Bodo sp.* (M) Host uncertain		South Africa	Porter[81]
Coelosporidium periplanetae (Sp) (= *Nosema p.*)	Malpighian tubules	U.S.A., Germany	Wellmer[111]
Dobellina sp.* (Sa)		Egypt	DeCoursey and Otto[29]
Endamoeba blattae (Sa) Uncertain *(Entamoeba blattae)*	Hind-gut and rectum	Egypt	DeCoursey and Otto[29]
Endolimax sp.* (Sa) Host uncertain		Egypt	DeCoursey and Otto[29]
Entamoeba coli * (Sa) Host uncertain		Egypt	DeCoursey and Otto[29]
E. histolytica * (Sa)		Peru, Egypt	Schneider and Shields[88]
Entamoeba thomsoni (Sa) (= *Endamoeba thomsoni*)	Hind-intestine and rectum	U.S.A.	McAdow[68]
Eutrichomastix sp. (= *Trichomastix*) (M)		South Africa	Porter[80]

17.1—*continued*

Name	Tissue	Geographical location	Authority
Gregarina blattarum (Sp) (= *G. blattae orientalis*)	Cells of intestine	U.S.A., South Africa	Porter[80]
Iodamoeba sp.* (Sa) Host uncertain		Egypt	DeCoursey and Otto[29]
Lophomonas blattarum (M) (= *L. sulcata*)	Colon	U.S.A.	McAdow[68]
Lophomonas striata (M)	Anterior colon	U.S.A.	McAdow[68]
Nyctotherus ovalis (C) (= *Bursaria blattarum*)	Anterior colon	World-wide	McAdow[68]
Peltomyces periplanetae (Sa) (= *P. blattelae*)	Malpighian tubules	France	Debaisieux[28]
Plistophora periplanetae (Sp) (= *Nosema p.*)	Malpighian tubules	France, U.S.S.R.	Debaisieux[28]
Tetratrichomastix blattidarum (M)	Rectum	U.S.A.	Young[114]

Host: Periplaneta americana
(An asterisk indicates that the host may have been *Bt.g.*)

Balantidium blattarum (C)	Intestine	Indies, Gold Coast	Bhatia and Gulati[8]
B. ovatum (C)	Intestine	India, Indochina	Weill[110]
Balantidum sp. (C)	Intestine	Brazil	Magalhaes[70]
Bodo sp.* (M) Host uncertain		South Africa	Porter[80]
Coelosporidium periplanetae (Sp) (= *Nosema p.*)	Malpighian tubules		Lutz and Splendore[67]
Diplocystis schneideri (Sp)	Haemocoele	England	Jameson[58]
Diplocystis sp. (Sp)	Haemocoele	India, U.S.A.	Ray and Dasgupta[82]
Dobellina sp.* (Sa)			DeCoursey and Otto[29]
*Endamoeba blattae** (Sa) (*Entamoeba blattae*)	Hind-intestine and rectum	World-wide	Armer[1]
Endolimax blattae (Sa)	Hind-gut	World-wide	Armer[1]

17.1—*continued*

Name	Tissue	Geographical location	Authority
Endolimax sp.* (Sa) Host uncertain		Egypt	De Coursey and Otto[29]
*Entamoeba coli** (Sa) Host uncertain		Egypt	De Coursey and Otto[29]
*Entamoeba histolytica** (Sa)		Gold Coast, U.S.A.	Frye and Meleney[41]
Entamoeba sp. (Sa)		Gold Coast	MacFie[69]
E. thomsoni (Sa)	Hind-intestine and rectum	World-wide	McAdow[68]
Eutrichomastix sp.* (= *Trichomastix*) (M)		South Africa	Porter[80]
Gregarina blattarum (Sp) (= *G. blattae orientalis*)	Cells of intestine	World-wide	McAdow[68]
Gregarina legeri (Sp)	Intestine	Brazil	Pinto[78]
G. neo-brasiliensis (Sp)		Brazil	Cunha[25]
Hexamita periplanetae (M) (= *Octomitus p.*)	Hind-gut	U.S.S.R.	Zasukhin[115]
Iodamoeba sp.* (Sa) Host uncertain		Egypt	De Coursey and Otto[29]
Isotricha caulleryi (C)	Alimentary canal	Indo-China	Weill[110]
Lophomonas blattarum (M)	Colon	Egypt	De Coursey and Otto[29]
L. striata (M) (= *L. sulcata*)	Anterior colon	Indochina, Philippines, U.S.A.	McAdow[68]
Monocercomonoides orthopterorum (= *Trichomonas o.*) (M)	Hind-gut	Austria, Philippines	Hegner and Chu[49]
Nyctotherus ovalis (C) (= *Bursaria blattarum*)	Anterior colon	World-wide	Lom[65]
Plistophora periplanetae (Sp) (= *Nosemas p.*)	Malpighian tubules	Brazil	Lutz and Splendore[67]
Polymastix melolonthae (M)	Colon	England	Warhurst[107]
Protomagalhaesia serpentula (Sp) (= *Gregarina serpentula*)	Haemocoele and gut	Brazil	Magalhaes[70]
Tetratrichomastix blattidarum (M)		U.S.A.	Young[114]

17.1—*continued*

Name	Tissue	Geographical location	Authority
Host: Leucophaea maderae			
Gregarina rhyparobiae (Sp)	Cells of intestine	Uganda	Watson[108]
Hexamita (?) (M)		Philippines	Hegner and Chu[49]
Retortamonas (?) sp. (M)		Philippines	Hegner and Chu[49]

Not a great deal is known about the factors governing the growth and maintenance of protozoal populations in cockroaches. In this respect it is worth citing the recent work of Warhurst on the pH and oxidation–reduction potential of the hind-gut in *P.a.*, and the importance of these factors in determining the growth and survival of cultures of *Endolimax blattae*.

He found that the pH of the anterior colon was slightly alkaline (7·4–8·1), and that the oxidation–reduction potential was –84 to –241 mV. In vitro the optimum pH range for growth was 7·5–8·0, and reducing conditions. Oxygen partial pressures of 78 mm Hg suppressed growth, as did depletion of reducing agents in the medium.[106]

The reader should also refer to the work of Hoyte.[53]

HELMINTHS

A considerable number of helminth species have been identified from cockroaches. Although some of these have not been identified to species level, it appears likely that at least 80 species of Aschelminth, 5 species of Platyhelminth and 5 species of Acanthocephalan can be traced to cockroaches, or have been successfully introduced into cockroaches. While many of them occupy a good deal of space inside the body of the host, and must damage the gut, in those parasite species which pass through it, they seldom appear to cause death or grave debility in the host. In about half the species recorded, the cockroaches serve as primary hosts; in the remainder the cockroach is a vector of the helminth egg or is an intermediate host.

Cockroaches as primary hosts

A short list of the helminths naturally occurring in the common domiciliary cockroaches is given below in Table 17.2. One authority is given for further details.

TABLE 17.2

Helminth	Cockroach	Site	Place	Author
Binema mirzaia	*P.a.*	Gut	India	Basir[4]
Blatellicola blatellicola	*Bt.g.*	Gut	India	Basir[4]
Blatticola blattae	*Bt.g.*	Gut	World-wide	Bozeman[11]
Galebia aegyptiaca	*Bt.g.*	Gut	Brazil	Schwenck[90]
Hammerschmidtiella diesingi {	*B.o.*	Gut	World-wide	Lee[63]
	P.a.	Gut	World-wide	Lee[63]
	Leucophaea maderae	Gut	Brazil	Pessôa and Côrrea[76]
Hammerschmidtiella neyrai	*B.o.*	Gut	Spain	Serrano-Sanchez[89]
Leidynema appendiculata {	*B.o.*	Colon and rectum	World-wide	Lee[64]
	P.a.	Colon and rectum	World-wide	Lee[64]
Protrellus künckeli	*P.a.*	Gut	Brazil	Pessôa and Côrrea[76]
Schwenckiella icemi	*P.a.*	Gut	India, U.S.A.	Basir[4]
Thelastoma pachyjuli {	*B.o.*	Gut	Czecho-slovakia	Groschaft[46]
	P.a.	Gut	U.S.A., South America	Hatcher[48]
Thelastoma tireroi	*P.a.*	Gut	Cuba	Chitwood[22]

In many instances the primary hosts of helminths employing cockroaches as an intermediate host are not known. Table 17.3 gives a short list, largely compiled from Roth and Willis, of domiciliary cockroaches with identified vertebrate primary hosts. (N.B. *Leucophaea maderae* is abbreviated to *L.m.*)

TABLE 17.3

Helminth	Cockroach	Primary host	Author
Oxyspirura mansoni	*Pycnoscelus surinamensis*	*Gallus, Meleagris*	Roth and Willis[85]
Prosthenorchis spirula	*Bt.g.*	*Lemur coronatus*	Brumpt and Urbain[16]

17.3—*continued*

Helminth	Cockroach	Primary host	Author
P. spirula	*Bt.g.*	*Pan* sp.	Thiel and Wiegand-Bruss[103]
P. spirula	*Bt.g.*	*Nasua narica*	Brumpt and Urbain[16]
P. elegans	*Bt.g.*	*Callithrix chrysoleucos*	Brumpt and Urbain[16]
Protospirura bonnei	*L.m.*	*Rattus norvegicus*	Brumpt[15]
P. muricola	*L.m.*	*Aotes zonalis*	Foster and Johnson[40]
Gongylonema neoplasticum	*P.a.*	*Rattus norvegicus*	Fibiger and Ditlevsen[34]
G. neoplasticum	*P.a.*	*Rattus rattus*	Fibiger and Ditlevsen[34]

The eggs of a number of helminth species have been recorded from cockroaches, among them *Enterobius vermicularis*, *Necator americanus* and *Trichuris trichiura*.[85]

Apart from Manson's eye worm parasitizing chickens, there seem to be few instances of species of helminth, with cockroaches as natural vectors, which are either of economic importance or affect human health.

The helminth most likely to be met with in the course of laboratory work on

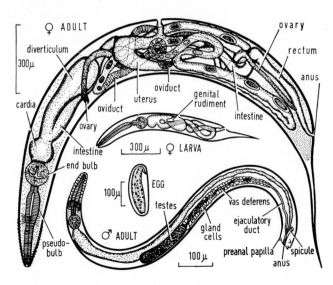

FIG. 17.3   Stages in the life history of *Leidynemia appendiculata*. (From Smith, after Dobrovolny and Ackert[30])

13—B.O.C.

cockroaches is *Leidynemia appendiculata*. The life history of this organism has been described by Dobrovolny and Ackert (Fig. 17.3). In collections made by these authors in Kansas, 85% of the insects contained numbers of the helminth. In some insects as many as 30 worms were present. When extruded from the parent worm the eggs are undeveloped or at an early cleavage stage. Development to the tadpole-like larva takes 36 hours. A few days later a quiescent stage occurs, and this is infective. The authors were not able to culture these developmental stages. After artificial infection the worms took 20–30 days to become mature.[30]

INSECT PARASITES

While the importance of the majority of parasites and predators as a permanent controlling factor of cockroach populations is not at all clear, there seems little doubt that Hymenopteran parasites and beetles belonging to the Rhipiphoridae may regularly destroy large numbers of cockroaches. Suggestions for the biological control of cockroaches have often been based on the destructiveness of these insects (Zimmerman).[117] The situation is complicated by the fact that some cockroach parasites have hyperparasites.[116]

A brief list of the insect parasites most likely to be met with is given in Table 17.4. For further details consult Roth and Willis.

TABLE 17.4

Name	Natural Host	Stage	Distribution	Authority
Ripidius pectinicornis (Coleoptera)	Bt.g.	Adults	On ships; Germany; South Pacific	Barbier[3]
The female is apterous. Eggs laid in a network of silk fibres. One to five larvae feed on host's fat body.				
Brachygaster minutus (Hymenoptera)	Bt.g.	Eggs	World-wide	Crosskey[24]
Evania appendigaster (Hymenoptera)	P.a., B.o.	Eggs	World-wide	Dumbleton[32]
Eggs laid within oötheca. Larvae may devour all the eggs in the oötheca and there pupate.				
Prosevania punctata (Hymenoptera)	P.a., B.o.	Eggs	Probably world-wide	Edmunds[33]
Development takes 40–57 days. Some eggs may develop pathenogenetically.				

17.4—*continued*

Name	Natural Host	Stage	Distribution	Authority
Anastatus tenuipes (Hymenoptera)	*P.a.*	Eggs	India, Hawaii	Burks[18]
(Development 32 days in *Supella*)				
Tetrastichus hagenowii (Hymenoptera)	*P.a.* (*B.o.*)	Eggs	World-wide	Roth and Willis[85]
As many as 261 parasites have been recorded from one oötheca, but usually less than 100.				
Tetrastichus periplanetae (Hymenoptera)	*P.a.*	Eggs	South Africa, West Indies	Roth and Willis[85]
Ampulex amoena (Hymenoptera)	*P.a.*	Kills and oviposits on nymph	Formosa	Sonan[93]
A. compressa (Hymenoptera)	*P.a.*	Kills and oviposits on nymph	India and E. Indies	Bordage[10]
Egg placed on host's mesothoracic coxa. Will enter houses in search of cockroaches.				
Dolichurus corniculus (Hymenoptera)	*Bt.g.*	Kills and oviposits on nymph	France	Benoist[7]

As with some of the other provisioning wasps part of the cockroach's antennae is removed. The whole cockroach, including the exoskeleton, is consumed by the larva.

The effectiveness of these parasites in destroying cockroaches may be gauged from the fact that in the case of the egg parasites, 30% or more of collected oöthecae may contain them. Cameron found that 29% of the oöthecae of *P.a.* collected in Saudi Arabia contained *Evania appendigaster*,[19] and Sonan found 30% of the oöthecae of *P.a.* and *P. australisiae* parasitized by *Tetrastichus hagenowii*.[92] Usman reported seasonal variations from 21–57% parasitization of *P.a.* by the latter wasp in India.[104]

Many field workers are of the opinion that wasp egg parasites make an important contribution to the control of cockroaches, at least in certain localities (Roth and Willis summarize conflicting views).

While no precise figures of cockroach mortality can be cited, the effect of provisioning wasps on cockroach populations may be considerable, and one successful example of biological control may be attributed to them. *Ampulex compressa* introduced into the Hawaiian islands in 1940 has considerably reduced the numbers of cockroaches there.[75]

MITES (Acarina)

Mites can be troublesome in cockroach cultures if allowed to multiply unchecked. Some species are able to pierce the integument of the cockroach easily, and if many of them become attached to a single individual, it may die.

There seems to be only one universally recognized species of mite associated with the commonest cockroach species. This is the Pterygosomid mite *Pimeliaphilus podapolipophagus* found on *P.a.* in the U.S.A. by Piquett and Fales (Fig. 17.4).[79] Cunliffe showed that it would also feed on *B.o.* and *Bt.g.* if introduced into the cultures of these insects. Adhesive eggs are laid on the host, and the life cycle occupies 28–32 days. They can destroy a cockroach culture, and an individual cockroach was observed to die after 5 hr when attacked by 25 mites.[26]

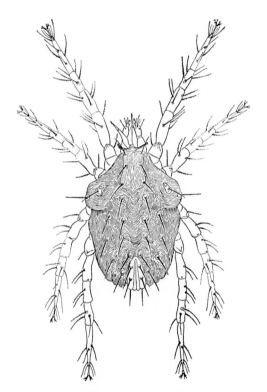

FIG. 17.4   *Pimeliaphilus podapolipophagus*, the cockroach mite. (From Roth and Willis,[85] after Baker)

Roth and Willis record a number of species associated with cockroaches, and quote Fisk as recommending a 5% spray or dust of p-chlorophenyl, p-chlorobenzene sulfonate against mites. The outside of containers were sprayed, and the inside dusted, including the cockroaches.[39]

See also Chapter 11, for other organisms reported to occur in the alimentary canal.

REFERENCES

1. ARMER, J. M. (1944). Influence of the diet of Blattidae on some of their intestinal protozoa. *J. Parasit.*, **30**, 131–42.
2. BAL, C. and RAI, B. P. (1955). On the occurrence of Stenophora sp. in the midgut of *B.o. Proc. Indian. Sci. Congr.*, **42**, 281–5.
3. BARBIER, J. (1947). Observations sur les mœurs de *Rhipidius pectinicornis*. Thunbg. et description de sa larve primaire. *Entomologiste*, **3**, 163–80.
4. BASIR, M. A. (1940). Nematodes parasitic in Indian cockroaches. *Proc. Indian Acad. Sci.*, **12**, 8–16.
5. BATES, H. W. (1863). *A Naturalist on the River Amazon*, 2 volumes. London.
6. BEEBE, W. (1925). Studies of a tropical jungle. One quarter of a square mile at Kartabo, British Guiana. *Zoologica, N.Y.*, **6**, 5–193.
7. BENOIST, R. (1927). Sur la biologie des *Dolichurus corniculus*. *Annls Soc. ent. Fr.*, **96**, 111–12.
8. BHATIA, B. L. and GULATI, A. N. (1927). On some parasitic ciliates from Indian frogs, toads, earthworms and cockroaches. *Arch. Protistenk.*, **57**, 85–120.
9. BISHOP, A. (1931). A description of *Embadomonas n.spp.* from *B.o., Rana temporaria, Bufo vulgaris, Salamandra maculosa*; with a note upon the cyst of *Trichomonas batrachorum*. *Parasitology*, **23**, 286–300.
10. BORDAGE, E. (1912). Notes biologique récueillies á l'Ile de la Réunion. *Bull. scient. Fr. Belg.*, **46**, 29–92.
11. BOZEMAN, W. B. (1942). An experimental investigation into the life history of *Blatticola blattae*, a nematode found in *Bt.g. Trans. Kans. Acad. Sci.*, **45**, 304–10.
13. BROOKS, M. A. and RICHARDS, A. G. (1956). Intracellular symbiosis in cockroaches. III. Reinfection of aposymbiotic cockroaches with symbiotes. *J. exp. Zool.*, **132**, 447–66.
15. BRUMPT, E. (1931). Némathelminthes parasites des rats sauvages (*Epimys norvegicus*) de Caracas I. *Protospirura bonnei*. Infections expérimentales et spontanées. Formes adultes et larvaires. *Ann. Parasit. hum. comp.*, **9**, 344–58.
16. BRUMPT, E. and URBAIN, A. (1938). Une curieuse épizootie vermineuse à acanthocéphale, devenue endemique à la singerie du Muséum. Mesures prophylactiques efficaces prises pour en arrêter les méfaits. *C.r. hebd. Séanc. Acad. Sci., Paris*, **206**, 1927–30.
17. BUNTING, W. (1956). Preliminary notes on some Orthoptera imported with bananas from Dominica. *Entomologist's mon. Mag.*, **92**, 284–6.
18. BURKS, B. D. in ROTH, L. M. and WILLIS, E. R. (1954). *Anastatus floridanus*, a new parasite on the eggs of the cockroach *Eurycotis floridana*. *Trans. Am. ent. Soc.*, **80**, 29–41.
19. CAMERON, E. (1957). On the parasites and predators of the cockroach. II. *Evania appendigaster* (L). *Bull. ent. Res.*, **48**, 199–209.
20. CARPENTER, G. D. H. (1925). *A naturalist in East Africa*. Oxford, England.
21. CHEN, L. (1933). Zuchtungversuche am parasitischen Protozoen von *P.a.* (*Endamoeba blattae, Nyctotherus ovalis, Lophomonas blattarum*). *Z. ParasitKde*, **6**, 207–19.
22. CHITWOOD, B. G. (1932). A synopsis of the nematodes parasitic in insects of the family Blattidae. *Z. ParasitKde*, **5**, 14–50.

23. CLOUDESLEY-THOMPSON, J. L. (1951). Notes on Arachnida: 16. The behaviour of a scorpion. *Entomologist's mon. Mag.*, **87**, 105.
24. CROSSKEY, R. W. (1951). The taxonomy and biology of the British Evanioidea *Trans R. ent. Soc., Lond.*, **102**, 282–301.
25. CUNHA, R. DE AL. (1919). Sobre a *Gregarina neobrasiliensis* Al. Cunha. 1919. Trabalho apresentado a Raculdade de Medicina de Bello Horizonte, Estado de Minas Gerais, Brazil.
26. CUNLIFFE, F. (1952). Biology of the cockroach parasite *Pimeliaphilus podapolipophagus* Tragardh, with a discussion of the genera *Pimeliaphilus* and *Hirstiella* (*Acarina, Pterygosomidae*). *Proc. ent. Soc. Wash.*, **54**, 153–69.
27. DARLINGTON, P. J. (1938). Experiments on mimicry in Cuba, with suggestions for future study. *Trans. R. ent. Soc. Lond.*, **87**, 681–95.
28. DEBAISIEUX, P. (1927). A propos des cnidosporidies des blattides. *C.r. Séanc. Soc. Biol., Paris*, **96**, 1404–6.
29. DE COURSEY, J. and OTTO, J. S. (1957). *Endamoeba histolytica* and certain other protozoan organisms found in cockroaches in Cairo, Egypt. *Jl. N.Y. ent. Soc.*, **64**, 157–63.
30. DOBROVOLNY, C. G. and ACKERT, J. E. (1934). The life history of *Leidynemia appendiculata* (Leidy), a nematode of cockroaches. *Parasitology*, **26**(4): 468–80.
31. DOW, R. P. (1955). A note on domestic cockroaches in South Texas. *J. econ. Ent.*, **48**, 106–7.
32. DUMBLETON, L. J. (1957). Parasites and predators introduced into the Pacific Islands for the biological control of insects and other pests. *S.P.C.q. Bull.*, **101**, 40 pp.
33. EDMUNDS, L. R. (1954). A study of the biology and life history of *Prosevania punctata* (Brullé) with notes on additional species. *Ann. ent. Soc. Am.*, **47**, 575–92.
34. FIBIGER, J. A. G. and DITLEVSEN, H. (1914). Contributions to the biology of *Spiroptera* (*Gongylonema*) *neoplastica* n.sp. *Mindeskr. Japetus Steenstrups Fds.*, **25**, 28 pp.
35. FILATOFF, E. D. (1904). Über das Verhalten einiger Bakterienarten zu dem Organismus der *Bombyx mori* (L) und der *Periplaneta orientalis* (L) bei artifizieller Infection derselben. *Zentbl. Bakt. ParasitKde. Abt 2*, **11**, pp. 658–86 and 748–62.
36. FINDLAY, G. M. and MACCALLUM, F. O. (1939). Epidemiology of yellow fever. *Nature, Lond.*, **143**, 289.
37. FINDLAY, G. M. and HOWARD, E. M. (1951). Observations on Columbia SK virus. *J. Path. Bact.*, **63**, 435–43.
38. FISCHER, R. G. and SYVERTON, J. T. (1957). Distribution of Coxsackie virus in experimentally infected cockroaches, *P.a. Proc. Soc. exp. Biol., Med.*, **95**, 284–7.
39. FISK, R. W. (1951). Use of a specific mite control in roach and mouse cultures. *J. econ. Ent.*, **44**, pp. 1016–17.
40. FOSTER, A. O. and JOHNSON, C. M. (1939). A preliminary note on the identity life cycle and pathogenicity of an important nematode parasitic of captive monkeys. *Am. J. trop. Med.*, **19**, 265–77.
41. FRYE, W. W. and MELENEY, H. E. The viability of *Endamoeba histolytica* cysts after passage through the cockroach. *J. Parasit.*, **22**, 221–2.
42. GALLARDO, E., FORGASH, A. J. and BEAUDETTE, F. R. (1957). An exploratory investigation of the effect in vivo and in vitro of cockroach tissues on the viability of Newcastle disease. *Ann. ent. Soc. Am.*, **50**, 192–8.
43. GEORGEVITCH, J. (1953). Étude de cycle évolutif de *Haplosporidium periplanetae* nov. spec. *Bull. Acad. serbe. Sci. Cl. Sci. math. nat.*, **12**, 98–102.
44. GHOSH, E. (1922). On a new ciliate Balantidium ovatum, sp. nov., an intestinal parasite in the common cockroach (*P.a.*). *Parasitology*, **14**, 371–4.

45. GLASER, R. W. (1946). The intracellular bacteria of the cockroach in relation to symbiosis. *J. Parasit.*, **32**, 483–9.
46. GROSCHAFT, J. (1956). Nalezý roupovitých (Oxyuroidea) in laboratorně chovaných švábů (Blattodea) (Oxyuroidea in laboratory rearings of Blattidae) (in Czech). *Cslka Parasit.*, **3**, 67–74.
47. GUNN, D. L. and COSWAY, C. A. (1938). The temperature and humidity relationships of the cockroach V. Humidity preference. *J. exp. Biol.*, **15**, 555–63.
48. HATCHER, E. (1939). The consortes of certain North Carolina blattids. *J. Elisha Mitchell scient. Soc.*, **55**, 329–34.
49. HEGNER, R. and CHU, H. J. (1930). A survey of protozoa parasitic in plants and animals of the Philippine Islands. *Philipp. J. Sci.*, **43**, 451–82.
50. HEIMPEL, A. M. and WEST, A. S. (1959). Notes on the pathogenicity of *Serratia marcescens Birzio* for the cockroach *Bt.g. Can. J. Zool.*, **37**, 169–72.
51. HEINECKE, H. (1956). Über einen pathogenen Sporenbildner in der Haemolymphe von *B.o. Zentbl. Bakt. ParasitKde*, **2**, 109, 324–535.
52. HONIGBERG, B. M. (1962). Evolutionary and systematic relationships in the flagellate order Trichomonadina Kirby. *J. Protozool.*, **10**, 20–62.
53. HOYTE, H. M. D. (1961). The Protozoa occurring in the hindgut of cockroaches I. responses to changes in the environment. *Parasitology*, **51** (3/4), 415–36.
54. HSIANG, C. M., POLLARD, M. and MICKS, D. W. (1952). The possible role of the cockroach in the dissemination of poliomyelitis virus. *Tex. Rep. Biol. Med.*, **10**, 329–35.
55. HUGER, A. (1964). Eine Rickettsiose der Orientalischen Schabe, *B.o.*, Neuursacht durch *Rickettsiella blattae* nov. spec. *Naturwissenschaften*, **51**, 1–3.
56. ILLINGWORTH, J. F. (1942). An outbreak of cockroaches, *Nauphoeta cinerea* (Olivier) in Honolulu. *Proc. Hawaii ent. Soc.*, **11**, 169–70.
57. IVANIC, M. (1937). Körper bau, Ernährung und Vermehrung einer im Enddarme der Küchenschabe (*B.o.*) lebenden Hartmanella-Art (*Hartmanella blattae* spec. nov). *Arch. Protistenk.*, **88**, 339–52.
58. JAMESON, A. P. (1920). The chromosome cycle of gregarines, with special reference to *Diplocystis schneideri* Kunstler. *Q. Jl microsc. Sci.*, **64**, 207–66.
59. JANSSEN, W. A. and WEDBERG, S. E. (1952). The common house roach *Bt.g.* as a potential vector of *Salmonella typhimurium* and *Salmonella typhosa. Amer. J. trop. Med. Hyg.*, **1**, 337–43.
60. KUDO, R. R. (1954). *Protozoology.* C. C. Thomas, U.S.A., 4th ed.
61. LANKESTER (1865). The parasites of the cockroach. The intellectual observer. *Rev. nat. Hist., Microsc. Res.*, **6**, 337–43.
62. LAVERAN, A. and FRANCINI, G. (1920). Herpetomonas et Spirochaeta de la blatte orientale. *Bull. Soc. Path. exot. Paris*, **13**, 331–3.
63. LEE, D. L. (1958). On the morphology of the male, female and fourth-stage larva (female) of *Hammerschmidtiella diesingi* (Hammerschmidt), a nematode parasitic in cockroaches. *Parasitology*, **48**, 433–6.
64. LEE, D. L. (1958). Digestion in *Leidynemia appendiculata* (Leidy, 1850) a nematode parasitic in cockroaches. *Parasitology*, **48**, 437–47.
65. LOM, J. (1956). Experiments with the cultivation of our three species of the genus *Nyctotherus*, and of *Balantidium entozoon* and *B. coli. Věst. čsl. zool. Spol.*, **20**, 16–61.
66. LUCAS, W. J. (1920). British Orthoptera. *Ray Soc. Publs*, 1–264.
67. LUTZ, A. and SPLENDORE, A. (1963). Über Pebrine und verwandten Microsporidian. Ein Beitrag zur Kenntnis der brasilianischen Sporozoen. *Zentbl. Bakt.*, **33**, 150–7.
68. MACADOW, C. M. (1931). Observations on some protozoan parasitic in cockroaches. M.A. thesis, Ohio State University.
69. MACFIE, J. W. S. (1922). Observations on the rôle of cockroaches in disease. *Ann. trop. Med. Parasit.*, **16**, 441–8.

70. MAGALHÃES, P. S. DE (1900). Notes d'helminthologie brésilienne. Matériaux pour servir á l'histoire de la flore et de la faune parasitaire de la *P.a.*—Une nouvelle espéce d'Oxyuris, O. Bulhoesi. *Archs. Parasit., Paris*, **3**, 34–69.
71. MEGLITSCH, P. A. (1940). Cytological observations on *Endamoeba blattae*. *Illinois biol. Monogr.*, **17**, 1–46.
72. MERCIER, L. (1906). Un organisme à forme parasite de la blatte (*B.o.*). Levure et Nosema. *C.r. Séanc. Soc. Biol.*, **60**, 1081–3.
73. MERCIER, L. (1908). Neoplasie du tissue adipeux chez des blattes (*B.o.*) parasitié par une microsporidie. *Arch. Protistenk.*, **11**, 372–81.
74. NUTTING, W. L. (1953). A gregarine Diplocystis in the haemocoele of the roach. *Blaberus craniifer. Psyche, Camb.*, **60**, 126–8.
75. PEMBERTON, C. E. (1949). The biological control of insects in Hawaii. *Proc. 7th Pacif. Sci. Congr.*, **4**, 220–3, Pacifi. Sci. Assoc., Auckland and Christchurch, New Zealand.
76. PESSÔA, S. B. AND CORRÊA, C. (1926). Notas sobre os Oxyurus parasitas das baratas domesticas, com a descripção de una nova specie: *Oxyurus australasiae* n.sp. *Mems Inst. Butantan*, **3**, 71–4.
77. PICARD, F. (1913). Contribution à l'étude des Laboulbéniacées d'Europe. *Bull. Soc. mycol. Fr.*, **29**, 503–71.
78. PINTO, C. F. (1919). *Contribuição ao estudo das gregarinas.* Tese, Rio de Janeiro, 113 pp.
79. PIQUETT, P. G. and FALES, J. H. (1952). Rearing cockroaches for experimental purposes. *U.S. Dept., Agr. Bur. Ent. and Plant Quar.*, ET-301, 12 pp.
80. PORTER, A. (1918). A survey of the intestinal entozoa, both protozoal and helminthic observed among natives in Johannesburg, from June to November, 1917. *South African Inst. Mem.*, **11**, 1–58.
81. PORTER, A. (1930). Cockroaches as vectors of hookworms on goldmines of the Witwatersrand. *J. med. Ass. S. Afr.*, **4**, 18–20.
82. RAY, H. N. and DASGUPTA, B. (1955). Occurrence of *Diplocystis* sp. as a parasite in the haemocoele of the cockroach. *Proc. Indian Sci. Congr.*, **42**, 281–2.
83. READ, H. C. (1933). The cockroach as a possible carrier of tuberculosis. *Amer. Rev. Tuberc.*, **28**, 267–272.
84. RICHARDS, A. G. and SMITH, M. N. (1956). Infection of cockroaches with *Herpomyces* (Laboulbeniales). II. Histology and histopathology. *Ann. ent. Soc. Am.*, **49**, 85–93.
85. ROTH, L. M. and WILLIS, E. R. (1960). The biotic associations of cockroaches. *Smithson. misc. Collns.*, **141**, 1–468.
86. ROTH, L. M. and WILLIS, E. R. (1960). Observations on *Aspergillus tarmarii* on oöthecae (unpublished), cited in ROTH and WILLIS.
87. ROTH, L. M. and WILLIS, E. R. (1960). Observations on *Aspergillus flavus* on oöthecae (unpublished), cited in ROTH and WILLIS.
88. SCHNEIDER, R. F. and SHIELDS, G. W. (1947). Investigation on the transmission of *E. histolytica* by cockroaches. *Med. Bull., Standard Oil Co.*, **7**, 119–21, New Jersey.
89. SERRANO-SANCHEZ, A. (1945). *Hammerschmidtiella neyrai* n.sp. en *B.o.* en Granada. *Revta. iber. Parasit.*, 213–15. Tomo Extraordinario, homenaje al C. R. Lopez Neyra.
90. SCHWENK, J. M. (1926). Fauna parasitologica dos blattideos do Brasil. *Sciencia méd.*, **4**, 491–504.
91. SIMMONDS, F. J. (1958). The effect of lizards on the biological control of scale insects in Bermuda. *Bull. ent. Res.*, **49**, 601–12.
92. SONAN, H. (1924). Observations upon *P.a.* and *P. australasiae* (in Japanese). *Trans. nat. Hist. Soc. Formosa*, **14**, 4–21.
93. SONAN, H. (1927). A taxonomic study together with observations of various families of egg laying wasps in Formosa. *Trans. nat. Hist. Soc. Formosa*, **17**, 121–38.

94. SPEGAZZINI, C. (1917). Revision de las Laboulbeniales argentinas. *An. mus. nac. hist. nat. Buenos Aires*, **29**, 445–688.
95. SPRAGUE, V. (1940). Observations on *Coelosporidium periplanetae* with special reference to the development of the spore. *Trans. Ann. microsc. Soc.*, **59**, 460–74.
96. SPRAGUE, V. (1941). Studies on *Gregarina blattarum* with special reference to the chromosome cycle. *Illinois biol. Monogr.*, **18**, 1–57.
97. SPRAGUE, V. and RAMSEY, J. (1942). Further observations on *Plistophora kudoi* a microsporidian of the cockroach. *J. Parasit.*, **28**, 399–406.
98. SYVERTON, J. T. and FISCHER, R. G. (1950). The cockroach as an experimental vector of the virus of spontaneous mouse encephalomyelitis. *Proc. Soc. exp. Biol. med.*, **74**, 296–8.
99. SYVERTON, J. T., FISCHER, R. G., SMITH, S. A., DOW, R. P. and SCHOOF, H. F. (1952). The cockroach as a natural extra human source of the poliomyelitis virus. *Fedn. Proc. Fedn. Am. Socs exp. Biol.*, **11**, 483.
100. TAUBER, O. E. (1940). Mitotic response of roach haemocytes to certain pathogenes in the haemolymph. *Ann. ent. Soc. Am.*, **33**, 113–19.
101. TAUBER, O. E. and GRIFFITHS, J. T. (1942). Isolation of Staphyloccus albus from haemolymph of the roach, *B.o. Proc. Soc. Exp. Biol. Med.*, **51**, 45–7.
102. THAXTER, R. (1931). Contribution towards a monograph of the Laboulbeniaceae. V. *Mem. Am. Acad. Arts Sci.*, **16**, 1–435.
103. THIEL, P. H. VAN and WIEGAND-BRUSS, C. J. E. (1946). Présence de Prosthenorchis spirula chez les chimpanzés. Son rôle pathogène et son developpement dans *Bt.g. Ann. Parasit. hum. comp.*, **20**, 304–20.
104. USMAN, S. (1949). Some observations on the biology of Tetrastichus hagenowii, Ratz—An egg parasite of the house-cockroach *P.a. Curr. Sci.*, **18**, 407–8.
105. VILLADOLID, D. V. (1934). Food habits of six common lizards found in Los Bãnos, Laguna, Philippine Islands. *Philip. J. Sci.*, **55**, 61–7.
106. WARHURST, D. C. (1964). Growth and survival, *in vitro* and *in vivo* of *Endolimax blattae*, an entozoic amoeba of cockroaches. Ph.D. Thesis Leicester University.
107. WARHURST, D. C. (1966). A note on Polymastix Bũtschli 1884 from the colon of *P.a. Parasitology*, **56**, 21–3.
108. WATSON, J. M. (1945). A new sporazoon *Gregarina rhyparobiae* in sp. from a tropical cockroach *Rhyparobia maderae*. *Parasitology*, **36**, 195–8.
109. WEDBERG, S. E. and BRANDT, C. D. and HELMBOLDT, C. F. (1949). The passage of microorganisms through the digestive tract of *Blaberus craniifer* mounted under controlled conditions. *J. Bact.*, **58**, 573–8.
110. WEILL, R. (1929). Notes protistologiques indochinoises (premier serie) la presence d'un infusoire du genre *Isotricha* (*I. caulleryi* n.sp.) chez un insecte *P.a. Archs. Zool. exp. gén.* (*Notes et Rev.*), **69**, 21–6.
111. WELLMER (1932). Sporozoen ostpreussicher Arthropoden. *Schr. phys.-ökon. Ges. Königsb.*, **52**, 103–64.
112. WIGGLESWORTH, V. B. (1953). *Principles of Insect Physiology*. Methuen, London.
113. YAKIMOV, V. L. and MILLER, G. A. (1922). Les protozoaires de l'intestin de l'homme en dehors de l'organisme de l'homme, L'examen de l'intestin du *B.o. Bull. Soc. Path. exot. Paris*, **15** (8–11).
114. YOUNG, M. D. (1935). Description, incidence and cultivation of *Tetratrichomastix blattidarum* n.sp. from the cockroach. *J. Parasitol.*, **21**, 309–10.
115. ZASUKHIN, D. N. (1930). Lebensbedingungen, Cytologie und Entwicklung von *Endamoeba blattae*. *Arch. Protistenk.*, **70**, 681–6.
116. ZASUKHIN, D. N. (1934). Hyperparasitism in protozoa. *Q. Rev. Biol.*, **9**, 215–24.
117. ZIMMERMAN, E. C. (1948). *Insects of Hawaii*, vol. 2, Apterygota to Thysanoptera, pp. 1–475, Honolulu.

18 Control and insecticides

Eradication techniques

All parts of the room affected should be kept clean and free from food particles. Spaces left between hot water or gas pipes and the wall should be sealed with putty, and holes in walls or below skirting boards filled in. If cockroaches are denied food and living space their eradication by means of insecticides will be facilitated.

Lacquers containing pyrethrum, if painted in strips near places known to be frequented by cockroaches, continue to be lethal for over a year. Dusts and sprays containing 0·5% Dieldrin may also be effective, although their effect does not persist as long as insecticidal lacquers. Dieldrin dusts do not last well above 25°. Diazinon (0·5%), Malathion (1·5%) or Pyrethrum (1·3%) may be employed as alternatives to Dieldrin, in the form of sprays.

Resistant strains of *Bt.g.* to Dieldrin and Diazinon have been reported in Britain and elsewhere. Van den Heuvel and Shenker[67] investigated the fate of the oöthecae of Dieldrin-resistant *Bt.g.* following the work of Parker and Campbell,[51] and Woodbury,[73] who had shown that pyrethrins had the effect of making the cockroaches deposit oöthecae prematurely. Van den Heuvel and Shenker found that if such oöthecae fell on a non-insecticidal surface, they hatched with a high degree of success, although some oöthecae were affected by desiccation, presumably due to the incomplete formation of the oöthecal cuticle. Fungal infections might also occur. When non-persistent chemicals are used, a second treatment at 3 to 7 weeks is required to kill emerging nymphs.

Bills[3] and Tyler[66] have shown that Kepone supplied in the form of a bait may be useful in killing cockroaches (especially *Bt.g.*) that have been reduced to small crevice-haunting populations by the use of sprays. The bait was eaten, even when alternative non-poisonous food was available.

Bills[3] and Ebeling[22] also found that dichlorvos ('Vapona') used in the form of strips from which the insecticide was slowly emitted, would successfully control cockroach populations. The method relies on small air volumes in which the vapour can be concentrated, and Ebeling applied it successfully to water meter boxes and dustbins. The inaccessibility of many of the preferred sites of cockroach populations often makes eradication difficult, and this situation may sometimes be exacerbated by continuous illumination, which makes foraging behaviour erratic. The success of bait and lacquer strip methods depends on mass sorties. Bills found that introducing pyrethrin aerosol into small cavities under the pressure provided by an electrically operated hydraulic paint spray successfully eradicated such persistent populations.

Döhring compared the lethal properties of diazinon, malathion, fenthion, fenitrothion (organic phosphoric esters) and propoxur (carbamate), on both sexes, and larvae of *Bt.g.*, and larvae of *P.a.* Propoxur had the strongest initial effect, achieving a 90% knock-down of *Bt.g.* within $1\frac{3}{4}$ hours on a 1-day-old deposit. It had an equally strong effect on *P.a.* larvae, which tended to be more resistant than the other subjects.[18]

Volatile agents, anaesthetics

Substances such as chloroform, diethyl ether, carbon tetrachloride, carbon disulphide and ethylene dichloride when injected into the spiracles of *P.a.* destroy the normal birefringence of lipid nerve membranes, but this does not occur if these substances are applied as vapours even at lethal concentrations.[53] Other effects may be produced. Shull *et al.* showed that carbon disulphide vapour causes a reduction in blood volume in *P.a.*[59] It did not reduce the haemocyte count in *B.o.*, although the ability of the haemolymph to coagulate was slightly inhibited by diethyl ether while leaving the haemocyte count unaffected according to Fisher.[24]

INSECTICIDES

Axonic poisons

Hyperactivity, tremors and paralysis are produced in *P.a.* by benzene derivatives such as phenol, aniline, hydroquinone, *p*-dichlorbenzene[43] and by DDT.[64]

DDT and its effects have perhaps been more investigated than any other insecticide. No doubt this is due to its proven effectiveness against a large number of insect species.

Tobias and Kollros describe the symptoms as continuous tremors of the body and appendages accompanied by unusual irritability and activity. Movements become uncoordinated, and eventually the insects fall on their backs, and are unable to rise. The legs continue to move, and slow and fast components attributed to the dual nature of motor innervation can be distinguished. Paralysis begins to set in. Twitch responses disappear, followed by slow contractions, and finally heartbeats fail. Electrical stimulation of the insect is without effect. One of the striking features of DDT poisoning in its later stages is the rapid desiccation that takes place, so that soft-bodied insects shrivel up.[64] Desiccation is evident in the cockroach according to Heslop and Ray, who also describe the body muscles as contracted, although it seems more probable that the muscle proteins are denatured at this stage.[33]

Investigation of the sites of action within the body confirms external observations in demonstrating striking effects on nerve and muscle. Roeder and Weiant showed that afferent neurones were caused to discharge repetitively by DDT contact with the peripheral cell bodies. Recordings from the crural nerve (n.5) exhibited high levels of activity much of which could be traced to the campaniform sense organs on the legs. It seems, however, that direct effects on the axon membrane of efferent and inter-neurones follow initial stages of poisoning and the direct effect of DDT on the axon membrane can be demonstrated in dissected specimens.[56]

Various authors[56,63,70] have described trains of impulses with frequencies between 250–500/sec (i.e. up to limits of frequency response imposed by utilization time), each train lasting 0·1–1·0 sec, from the central nervous system. DFDT and methoxychlor produce somewhat similar effects.[70] Yamasaki and Narahashi showed that the form of the action potential in large central axons when exposed to DDT was characteristic, the return to the normal resting potential level being delayed (prolonged negative after-potential).[75] In this unstable state, the membrane tends to produce a multiple response instead of a single response. It is suggested that the high potassium conductance of the membrane, normally accompanying repolarization, is inhibited.[77]

That DDT may have a synaptic effect has been put forward by Yeager and Munson,[81] Tobias and Kollros,[64] and Dresden.[19] Blocking ganglionic conduction reduces the effect of low concentrations of DDT as reflected in axonic transmission. Smyth showed that trans-synaptic conduction was directly affected in *P.a.* following partially desheathing the ganglion.[60] Since synaptic transmission involves the electrical properties of adjacent membranes as well as synapse-limited chemical properties, and direct effects on peripheral fibres are so readily demonstrated, it seems likely that synaptic susceptibility to DDT poisoning is secondary to membrane poisoning.

Evidence for synaptic effects produced by DDT can be sought amongst studies on ACh and AChase. In *P.a.*, Richards and Cutkomp,[53] and Hartley and Brown[31] showed that DDT did not markedly inhibit cholinesterase in vitro. The latter authors showed that there was very little effect, especially as compared with organophosphorus compounds. In one series of experiments, the substrate was added to the enzyme prior to the insecticide; in the other series, the insecticide was added initially. The results from both series were generally similar. In terms of the mm^3 of CO_2 evolved, for series 1 the results were: 139 (control) compared, with 138 (experimental); and for series 2: 104 (control) compared with 100 (experimental).[31] Tobias *et al.* showed that free ACh increased in the nerves of DDT-poisoned *P.a.* in the first stage,[65] but Colhoun demonstrated that this initial rise was followed by a return to normal levels, followed by a more substantial increase during prostration.[15]

Although no changes were found by Richards and Cutkomp in the structure of DDT-poisoned nerve cells,[53] Chang demonstrated striking changes in the dictyosomes of neurone cell bodies in *P.a.* When stained with silver nitrate, the dictyosomes become less and less dense as the stage of poisoning advances, until at the time of death they are no longer stainable (Fig. 18.1).[13]

Eaton and Sternburg showed that while the general toxic effects of DDT on *P.a.* have a negative temperature coefficient, for part of the nervous system, the effects become more marked with rise in temperature. A number of authors have demonstrated the reversibility of general DDT poisoning. Symptoms visible at a certain temperature disappear at a slightly higher temperature, to return when the temperature is lowered.[68] Eaton and Sternburg were able to show that afferent fibres in the crural nerve responded positively to a rise in temperature; the reverse was true of the central nervous system where a sufficiently high temperature completely eliminates abnormal trains of impulses. Saline perfusion and deafferentation also eliminated abnormal discharge in the central nervous system when applied together, but saline perfusion did not abolish abnormal discharge in afferent fibres.[21] The positive coefficient of DDT effects on sensory axons was confirmed by Yamasaki and Ishii.[74]

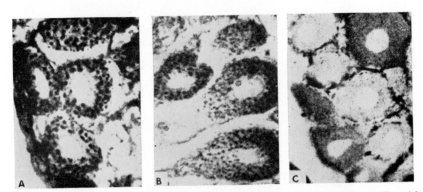

FIG. 18.1   Changes in the stainability of the dictyosomes of ganglion cells with DDT poisoning. **A**, normal insect; **B**, at knock-down stage; **C**, at time of death. (From Chang[13])

That the elevated frequency of response may persist in afferent fibres after recovery from low concentrations of DDT was noted by Yamasaki and Ishii and may be compared with the finding of Yamasaki and Narahashi that intracellularly recorded action potentials of *P.a.* giant axons go on showing prolonged negative after-potentials following recovery. These findings suggest that the striking response of the nervous system to DDT may not represent the primary effect of the insecticide.[77]

A number of workers have shown that DDT poisoning is accompanied by the appearance of a toxin in the haemolymph distinct from DDT. Treatment with TEPP or strong electric shocks has a similar effect. Sternburg and his co-workers[62, 63] have made detailed studies of the origin and properties of this toxin. Bot found that blood from DDT poisoned *P.a.* could produce typical DDT symptoms in flies,[5] but Sternburg and Kearns were able to show that the blood toxin was not DDT.[63] Roeder and Weiant had demonstrated that DDT did not produce abnormal discharge in the nerve cord when topically applied.[56] Sternburg and Kearns found that the blood toxin did have this effect. Discharge rates increased immediately but high frequency impulse trains took a few minutes to develop and eventually these became more or less continuous. This phase is succeeded by a complete block of activity lasting 1 to 15 minutes, and this is followed by a gradual return to normal levels (Fig. 18.2). The toxin was not extracted by benzene or ether, a method which would remove DDT.[63] In a later paper Sternburg, Chang and Kearns showed that the toxin was chromato-

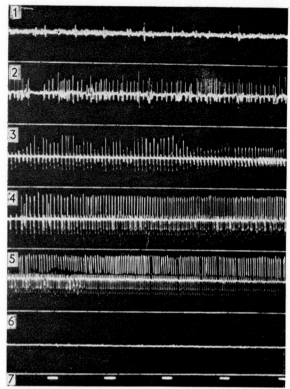

FIG. 18.2   Electrical response of the isolated nerve cord to the blood of DDT-prostrate cockroaches. Minutes after exposure: **1**, 0; **2**, 2; **3**, 5; **4**, 7; **5**, 7·5; **6**, 8. Gain reduced at **3** and **5**; calibration 10 c/s. (From Sternburg and Kearns[63])

graphically different to a number of transmitter substances (acetylcholine, epinephrine, norepinephrine, histamine, γ-aminobutyric acid and 5-hydroxy-tryptamine). They also came to the conclusion that the substance was produced by the central nervous system as a result of afferent activity.[62] This would fit in well with its time of appearance. Further analytical investigations by Hawkins and Sternburg using cockroaches (*P.a.*) and crayfish (*Oronectes*) showed that the active substance was probably an aromatic amine and an ester. The toxin appears similar to the substance released by nerve cords treated with TEPP or TMPP.[32]

Beament showed that cockroaches that have been forcibly immobilized for several days exhibit similar symptoms to those produced by DDT poisoning, and a similar neurotoxin accumulates in the blood;[1] and Colhoun provided evidence for the release of a catecholamine into the blood from the corpus cardiacum as a result of DDT treatment.[15]

A slight increase in the variability of rate of heartbeat as a result of injected DDT was observed in *P.a.* by Orser and Brown,[49] but Naidu found that the isolated heart responded by irregular, slower rhythms and this effect was not prevented by atropine.[44] Orser and Brown compared the heartbeat in intact and decapitated insects, and both showed a slight increase in maximum and minimum rates.

Merrill *et al.* showed that the neuromuscular symptoms of DDT poisoning could be prevented in *P.a.* by anaesthesia with cyclopropane, but they appeared again subsequently.[41]

Various authors have reported changes in the amino acid content of the haemolymph in different insect species, but results are contradictory. Corrigan and Kearns found that major amino acids were unaffected in DDT-poisoned *P.a.*, but proline decreased progressively.[17] There seems little doubt, however, that DDT can affect oxidative enzymes. Inhibition of cytochrome oxidase has been demonstrated by Morrison and Brown using homogenates,[42] and Ludwig *et al.* working with isolated leg muscles of *P.a.*;[39] although Brown and Brown found little decrease in the activity of this enzyme during DDT poisoning in the whole insect,[8] and results obtained by Fukami supported this contention.[26] The results obtained by Morrison and Brown were rather complex in that there was often an initial rise in cytochrome oxidase activity as measured by oxygen uptake, and this was prolonged for 100 min at 10–5 M concentrations before inhibition set in.[42] A point that is noteworthy in connection with Brown and Brown's in vivo analyses is that the variability of the controls in 2–8 hr experiments was about 20% and this may have masked changes due to poisoning. In this and in longer experiments (48 hr), however, the lowest values were obtained in the advanced stages of poisoning.[8] It is interesting to note that McAllan and Brown also found divergent results of a similar kind from in vivo and in vitro experiments on the effect of insecticides on transamination.[40]

The effects of the chlorinated hydrocarbon Lindane on nerve and enzyme systems differ considerably from those of DDT. Becht showed that it has virtually no effect on the electrical discharge from campaniform organs,[2] while Orser and Brown demonstrated striking effects on the heartbeat as a result of applying this substance to *P.a.*[49] In the intact insect, the heartbeat is very irregular in frequency and may ascend to 150 or more beats per minute (normal—130). The heart of the decapitated animal on the other hand, which is usually 20 beats/min slower than in the intact insect, is accelerated to a rate varying around 130/min. The general effect is one of acceleration, and can be contrasted with the result of applying chlordane in which the rates for both intact and decapitated insects are lowered (100 and 80 respectively). Morrison and Brown found that Lindane at a concentration of 10^{-3} M produced clear-cut inhibition of cytochrome oxidase in vitro after 60 min, as measured by oxygen consumption.[42] Forgash has shown that Lindane has an adverse effect on growth of the larval stages,[25] but Harshbarger and Forgash found that this was not due to a reduction in the intestinal micro-organisms, although Lindane-sensitive forms were observed.[29]

Pyrethrins

Many of the symptoms of poisoning with pyrethrin parallel those following DDT treatment. Hutzel showed that afferent nerve fibres were stimulated in

Bt.g., an effect that was independent of nerve cord transection.[35] Coon found that the effect on the heart, like that of certain drugs, varied with concentration. Acceleration was produced by sub-lethal doses, lethal doses depressed and finally stopped the heartbeat (*P.a.*),[16] arresting it in systole in *Bt.g.*,[80] and similar effects were observed in the isolated heart by Naidu.[44] The latter author obtained a reduction in the effect of pyrethrin in the presence of atropine. While the observations of Hutzel suggest that the primary effect on the nervous system is on sense organs, the electrical behaviour of the nerve cord alters considerably evoking repetitive trains of impulses.[23,36,38,70] Roeder suggests that pyrethrins unstabilize the membrane, a view supported by the observations of Narahashi who detected accentuated negative after-potentials in giant axon impulses following treatment with allethrin. High concentrations blocked conduction.[45]

A neuroactive substance is found in the blood of pyrethrin-poisoned cockroaches (*P.a.*) at low temperatures but not at high ones, according to Blum and Kearns.[4]

Well-defined inhibition of cytochrome oxidase by pyrethrin and allethrin at 10^{-3} M, but not at 10^{-5} M, was demonstrated by Morrison and Brown. Inhibition occurred more smoothly in allethrin than with pyrethrins.[42] However, Fukami found no reduction in the oxygen consumption of muscle, in vitro or in vivo, after treatment with pyrethrins.[26]

Pyrethrins penetrate the cuticle readily,[50] then diffuse to deeper lying regions of the body via the nerves[35] and the haemolymph;[57] they may accumulate locally in the fore-gut according to Zeid.[82] The structural changes produced in the nervous system by pyrethrins were investigated by Richards and Cutkomp. They observed a loss of birefringence in axons and sheaths which coincided with lowered sensitivity, and nuclear pycnosis in the nerve cord. Vacuolization and chromatolysis of neurone cell bodies occurred at a later stage (Fig. 7.1).[53]

Compounds which synergize pyrethrin action have been demonstrated in a variety of insects. Chamberlain showed that piperonyl butoxide inhibited the lipase activity of tissue homogenates of *P.a.*, and in other instances, the synergist acts by oxidative inhibition of detoxification processes.[11] Nevertheless Zeid and his colleagues believe the detoxification of pyrethrins to be mainly hydrolytic rather than oxidative.[82]

Veratrine alkaloids such as cevadine and veratridine produce effects and symptoms very similar to those resulting from pyrethrin treatment. Harvey and Brown demonstrated slight increases in O_2 consumption in *Bt.g.* following treatment with veratrine alkaloids,[30] but Morrison and Brown found that 10^{-3} concentration of the alkaloid (Sabadilla seed extract) produced quite a marked inhibition of cytochrome oxidase from *P.a.* leg muscles.[42]

Synaptic poisons (Non-anticholinesterases)

γ-Benzene hexachloride (Gammexane) is a fast-acting insecticide which produces tremors, ataxia and convulsions, followed by prostration when applied to *P.a.*[58] According to Harvey and Brown, initial tremors and convulsions are accompanied by a large increase in O_2 consumption ($\times 5$).[30]

BHC has little effect on the characteristic activity of the campaniform sensillae,[2] and Bot found that the sensori-motor arc must be intact for the leg muscle tremors to develop.[5] That the effects of BHC are localized at the synaptic level was shown by Yamasaki and Narahashi, who detected a prolonged response in post-synaptic fibres to single shocks applied to the presynaptic fibres, in the cercal sensory-giant fibre preparation of *P.a.*[76] Although Tobias showed an increase in free ACh in the nervous system of BHC-treated insects,[7] Hartley and Brown produced evidence against the suppression of AChase activity by BHC.[31]

Certain substances may antagonize the insecticidal function of BHC, and Srivastava found that the dietary factor meso-inositol reduced BHC poisoning in *Bt.g.*,[61] but Dresden and Krijgsman detected no protectant effect of this substance in *P.a.*[20]

Disturbed lipid metabolism may be involved in the action of BHC. Srivastava demonstrated an increase in fat droplet deposition both in the fat body and in the neuropile.[61]

The action of the cyclodiene derivatives aldrin, dieldrin, endrin, chlordan, heptachlor and toxaphene has been the subject of numerous investigations, and detailed effects can be traced. The symptoms of poisoning by these substances develop slowly; in an extreme example, *Blaberus fusca*, contact poisoned by heptachlor, may take a week to die.[37]

In *P.a.*, the symptoms of Dieldrin action resemble those produced by other nerve poisons, that is ataxia, convulsions and eventual paralysis. Yamasaki and Narahashi traced the action of Dieldrin to an increase in postsynaptic responses in the sixth ganglion, a very similar result to that produced by BHC.[76] These heightened discharges are antagonized by nicotine according to Gianotti, Metcalf and March, who found that isolated legs were unaffected by dieldrin,[27] and Bot showed that chlordane had no action on the motor nerves.[5] Multiple discharges do not develop for some time in the central nervous system according to Lalonde and Brown as a result of treating *Bt.g.* with endrin, aldrin, heptachlor or chlordane.[36] Lhoste and Roche were able to show the loss of some stainable material, possibly ribosomal, from the cytoplasm of motor neurone cell bodies (Fig. 18.3). These authors also described a more localized effect in globuli cell bodies of the corpora pedunculata in *Blaberus* subjected to slow heptachlor poisoning. By the third day, the globular nuclei were markedly pycnotic, and it seems quite probable that symptoms of ataxia visible at this time are due to malfunction of higher centres such as the corpora pedunculata.[37] Brown noted that chlordane decreased muscle tonus in *P.a.* movements weakening before they became coordinated, and might show an exaggerated response to stimuli. This latter symptom may depend on the function of the corpora pedunculata as a sensory mixing area, suggested by Vowles.[69]

Harvey and Brown showed that cyclodiene derivatives produced a large rise in O_2 consumption in *Bt.g.*[30] At low concentrations, Morrison and Brown found that $(10^{-5}$ M) aldrin, and chlordane, β-chlordane, toxaphene and heptachlor produce small increases in the O_2 consumption of cytochrome oxidase from *P.a.* muscle, but at concentrations of 10^{-3} M inhibition occurs more or less sharply after 30 min.[42]

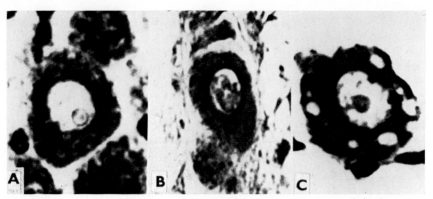

FIG. 18.3   Changes in thoracic ganglion cells following exposure of the insect to, B, aldrin and, C, parathion. A shows a normal cell. (From Roche and Lhoste, in Brown[7])

Heart muscle is little affected by chlordane over a 100 min period, according to Orser and Brown, but their graph shows rather high rates for heartbeat of decapitated insects treated with toxaphene. Effects were generally slight.[49]

Heptachlor, endrin and dieldrin inhibit the excretion of carmine by Malpighian tubules,[52] but toxaphene and endrin could not be clearly seen to affect trans-amination according to McAllan and Brown.[40]

Gianotti *et al.* showed that injected aldrin is partially converted to dieldrin, probably in the fat body, and that absorption and transport is rapid. Dieldrin produces a large loss of water in *Bt.g.*[27] according to Clark and Butz, and this may contribute considerably to the lethal effect of these insecticides.[14]

Nicotine has long been employed as an accelerator of nerve and heart muscle activity in physiological experiments, but its usefulness as an insecticide has been somewhat overshadowed by that of other substances. Its application results in prolonged bursts of activity in the nerve cord terminated by complete block,[54] and in low concentrations it accelerated heartbeat, an effect antagonized by atropine.[44, 79] Hartley and Brown showed that cholinesterase was not involved.[31] Nicotine-poisoned cockroaches develop convulsions very rapidly: *Bt.g.*—2 min; *B.o.*—3 min; and *P.a.*—6 min, according to O'Kane *et al.*[48]

Organic thiocyanates have been employed with success as insecticides, especially Thiocyanoethyl laurate (Lethane 60), and Butoxy-thiocyanodiethyl ether (Lethane 384). Their action is swift. Lethane 60 injected into *Bt.g.* causes a brief initial phase of hyperactivity, followed by extension of the legs and paralysis according to Brown.[6] Lethane 60[49] and Lethane 384[16] depress the heartbeat of *P.a.*, and thiocyanates eventually arrest the heart of *B.o.* in diastole.[80] Experiments with other insects suggest a disruption of central nervous structure and function to be a major aspect of thiocyanate poisoning,[7] although Morrison and Brown demonstrated a clear-cut inhibition of muscular cytochrome oxidase resulting from Lethane treatment.[42]

ANTICHOLINESTERASES

Some of the most powerful anti-Chase insecticides are organo-phosphorus compounds. Those in which the systemic effects have been closely investigated are: Tetraethyl pyrophosphate (TEPP), diethyl *p*-nitrophenyl thiophosphate (Parathion), and *O,O*-dimethyl-dithiophosphate of diethyl mercaptosuccinate (Malathion).

TEPP produces a phase of hyperactivity, followed by exaggerated tonus, ataxia and eventually paralysis and death, according to Chadwick and Hill.[10] In both TEPP and parathion the action of the insecticide may be rather slow; death may not occur for 36 hr and with Parathion the onset of symptoms may be delayed for 7 hr.[12] Malathion poisoning may be even more gradual, and O'Brien noted that death might not occur for 3 days.[47]

The action of carbamates has been reviewed by Casida. Carbamates are esters of methyl and dimethylcarbamic acid and have been employed for some time as parasympathomimetic agents. Physostigmine or eserine is the only known naturally occurring carbamate ester, and is obtained from Calabar seeds. Synthetic analogues are numerous and many have been embodied in insecticides. They act by the inhibition of AChase.[9] This effect has been demonstrated in *P.a.* by Tobias, Kollros and Savit,[65] and also by Chadwick and Hill.[10] Roeder demonstrated that the main effect is on the synapses where AChase is localized.[55]

Wiesman and Kocher studied the effects of the related substance Pyrolan (1-phenyl-3-methyl-5-pyrazolyl-dimethylcarbamate) on the heart, spiracles and nervous system of *P.a.* Nerve section demonstrates that there is a necessity for the reflex arc to be intact for carbamate action to be effective. It is centred in the motor part of the thoracic ganglion. Blood and muscle pH drop considerably, probably due to lactic acid production. Death is probably due to exhaustion and auto-intoxication.[71]

According to O'Brien the ionized carbamate does not readily penetrate into the nerve cord.[46] Cholinesterase inhibition is easily reversed, and cockroaches recover from slight poisoning after developing marked symptoms in Chadwick and Hill's experiments.[10] Winton, Metcalf and Fukuto showed that topical application of *m*-tert-butyl phenyl carbamate produced partial inhibition of neurons and ganglia followed by recovery after 2 hr, probably due to inhibitor destruction.[72]

The metabolism of carbamates is little understood. Hodgson and Casida observed that the application of naphthyl-1-^{14}C methyl carbamate yielded 6 metabolites in *Bt.g.* One metabolite was believed to control the overall rate of conversion. Some information on the nature of these metabolites is provided by these authors.[34]

Entry of these insecticides may not be effective through the gut. Wiesman and Kocher found that if pyrolan is ingested by *P.a.* it remains relatively inert. If injected into the heart, no toxicant was left in the blood after 1 hr, but after 2 to 4 hr toxic products remained in the gut, fat body, muscle and thoracic ganglia.[71]

Some substances block detoxification and synergize carbamate activity.

Gordon and Eldefrawi found that Dimetilan, but not Isolan, synergizes Pyrolan and Sevin in the German cockroach *Bt.g.*[28]

Phenothiazine

Phenothiazine has been shown to have a clear-cut inhibitory effect on neuro-muscular transmission in crustacea, and it is probable that a similar local poisoning occurs in insects. Contact poisoned *P.a.* exhibit locomotory ataxia followed by paralysis according to Zukel,[83] but oxygen consumption was only slightly affected in *Bt.g.* in Harvey and Brown's experiments. Phenothiazine does not appear to block neuromuscular transmission by altering cholinesterase levels.[30] Hartley and Brown found that cholinesterase activity in tissue homogenates of *P.a.* was little affected by phenothiazine treatment;[31] on the other hand, Morrison and Brown found that cytochrome oxidase was strongly inhibited.[42]

In some cases recovery from phenothiazine poisoning has been noted in cockroaches and Zukel traced this to the rapid excretion of leucothionol by the Malpighian tubes. Phenothiazine is oxidized to leucothionol when it enters the body.[83]

REFERENCES

1. BEAMENT, J. W. L. (1958). A paralysing agent in the blood of cockroaches. *J. Insect Physiol.*, **2**, 199–224.
2. BECHT, G. (1958). Influence of DDT and lindane on chordotonal organs in the cockroach. *Nature, Lond.*, **181**, 777–9.
3. BILLS, G. T. (1965). Kepone and dichlorvos for controlling cockroaches and vinegar fly. *International Pest Control*, **7** (5), 8–11.
4. BLUM, M. S. and KEARNS, C. W. (1956). Temperature and the action of pyrethrum in the American cockroach. *J. econ. Entomol.*, **49**, 862–5.
5. BOT, J. (1952). The action of DDT, hexachlorocyclahexane, chlordane and toxaphene. *Documenta Med. georg trop.*, **4**, 57–70.
6. BROWN, A. W. A. (1951). *Insect control by chemicals*, pp. 1–817. Wiley, New York.
7. BROWN, A. W. A. (1963). Chemical Injuries. *Insect Pathology*, ed. STEINHAUS, pp. 65–131. Academic Press, New York and London.
8. BROWN, B. E. and BROWN, A. W. A. (1956). The effects of insecticidal poisoning on the level of cytochrome oxidase in the American cockroach. *J. econ. Ent.*, **49**, 675–9.
9. CASIDA, J. E. (1963). The mode of action of carbamates. *A. Rev. Ent.*, **8**, 39–58.
10. CHADWICK, L. E. and HILL, D. L. (1947). Inhibition of cholinesterase by diisopropyl fluorophosphate, physostigmine and hexaethyl tetraphosphate in the roach. *J. Neurophysiol.*, **10**, 235–46.
11. CHAMBERLAIN, R. W. (1950). An investigation on the action of piperonyl butoxide with pyrethrum. *Am. J. Hyg.*, **52**, 153–83.
12. CHAMBERLAIN, W. F. and HOSKINS, W. M. (1951). The inhibition of cholinesterase in the American roach by organic insecticides and related phosphorus-containing compounds. *J. econ. Ent.*, **44**, 177–91.
13. CHANG, P. I. (1951). The action of DDT on the Golgi bodies in insects' nervous tissue. *Ann. ent. Soc. Am.*, **44**, 311–26.
14. CLARK, H. B. and BUTZ, A. (1961). The effects of some insecticides on the metabolites of *Bt.g. J. econ. Ent.*, **54**, 1022–4.

15. COLHOUN, E. H. (1959). Acetylcholine in *P.a.* III. Acetylcholine in roaches treated with tetraethyl pyrophosphate and DDT. *Can. J. Biochem. Physiol.*, **37**, 259–72.
16. COON, B. F. (1944). Effects of paralytic insecticides on heart pulsations and blood circulation in the American cockroach as determined with a fluorescein indicator. *J. econ. Ent.*, **37**, 785–9.
17. CORRIGAN, J. J. and KEARNS, C. W. (1958). The effect of DDT poisoning on free aminoacids in the hemolymph of the American cockroach. *Bull. ent. Soc. Am.*, **4**, 95.
18. DÖHRING, E. (1965). Zur schabentotenden Wirksamkeit von Phosphorsaureestern und Carbamaten in Sprühmitteln. *Z. angew. Zool.*, **52**, 145–72.
19. DRESDEN, D. (1948). Site of action of DDT and cause of death after acute DDT poisoning. *Nature, Lond.*, **162**, 1000–1.
20. DRESDEN, D. and KRIJGSMAN, B. J. (1948). Experiments on the physiological action of insecticides. *Bull. ent. Res.*, **38**, 575–8.
21. EATON, J. L. and STERNBURG, J. (1964). Temperature and the action of DDT on the nervous system of *P. americana. J. Insect Physiol.*, **10**, 471–85.
22. EBELING, W. Tests with vapona insecticide resin strips, *P.C.O. News*, **24** (4), 23.
23. ELLIS, C. H., THIENES, C. H. and WEIRSMA, C. A. G. (1942). The influence of certain drugs on the crustacean nerve muscle system. *Biol. Bull. mar. biol. Lab.*, Woods Hole, **83**, 334–52.
24. FISHER, R. A. (1936). The effects of a few toxic substances upon the total blood cell count in the cockroach *B.o. Ann. ent. Soc. Am.*, **29**, 335–40.
25. FORGASH, A. J. (1962). Failure of myo-inositol to prevent the growth inhibiting effects of lindane in *P.a. J. econ. Ent.*, **55**, 308–12.
26. FUKAMI, J. (1956). Effect of some insecticides on the respiration of insect organs, with special reference to the effects of rotenone. *Botyu-Kagaku*, **21**, 122–8.
27. GIANOTTI, O., METCALF, R. L. and MARCH, R. B. (1956). The mode of action of aldrin and dieldrin in *P.a. Ann. ent. Soc. Am.*, **49**, 588–92.
28. GORDON, H. T. and ELDEFRAWI, M. E. (1960). Analog synergism of several carbamate insecticides. *J. econ. Ent.*, **53**, 1004–9.
29. HARSHBARGER, J. C. and FORGASH, A. J. (1964). Effect of Lindane on Intestinal microorganisms of the American cockroach *P.a. J. econ. Ent.*, **57**, 779–80.
30. HARVEY, G. T. and BROWN, A. W. A. (1951). The effect of insecticides on the rate of oxygen consumption in *Bt.g. Can. J. Zool.*, **29**, 42–53.
31. HARTLEY, J. B. and BROWN, A. W. A. (1955). The effects of certain insecticides on the cholinesterase of the American cockroach. *J. econ. ent.*, **48**, 265–9.
32. HAWKINS, W. B. and STERNBURG, J. (1960). Effect of Insecticides on Neurophysiological Activity in Insects. *Agriculture and Food Chemistry*, **8** (4), 257–61.
33. HESLOP, J. P. and RAY, J. W. (1959). The reaction of the cockroach, *P.a.* to bodily stress and DDT. *J. Insect Physiol.*, **3**, 395–401.
34. HODGSON, E. and CASIDA, J. E. (1960). Biological oxidation of N-N-dialkyl carbamates. *Biochim biophys. Acta*, **4з**, 184–6.
35. HUTZEL, J. M. (1942). Action of pyrethrum upon the German cockroach. *J. econ. Ent.*, **35**, 933–7.
36. LALONDE, D. I. V. and BROWN, A. W. A. (1954). The effect of insecticides on the action potentials of insect nerve. *Can. J. Zool.*, **32**, 74–81.
37. LHOSTE, J. and ROCHE, A. (1956). Action de l'heptachlor sur les ganglions cérébroïdes de la Blatte *Blabera fusca. Archs. Anat. microsc. Morph. exp.*, **45**, 302–10.
38. LOWENSTEIN, O. (1942). A method of physiological assay of pyrethrum extracts. Effect of pyrethrius on cockroach nerve cord. *Nature, Lond.*, **150**, 760–2.
39. LUDWIG, D., BARSA, M. C. and CALI, T. C. (1955). The effect of DDT on the activity of cytochrome oxidase. *Ann. ent. Soc. Am.*, **48**, 165–70.

40. MACALLAN, J. W. and BROWN, A. W. A. (1960). The effect of insecticides on transamination in the American cockroach. *J. econ. Ent.*, **53**, 166–7.
41. MERRILL, R. S., SAVIT, J. and TOBIAS, J. M. (1946). Certain biochemical changes in the DDT poisoned roach and their prevention by prolonged anaesthesia. *J. cell. comp. Physiol.*, **28**, 465–76.
42. MORRISON, P. E. and BROWN, A. W. A. (1954). The effects of insecticides on cytochrome oxidase obtained from the American cockroach. *J. econ. Ent.*, **47**, 723–30.
43. MUNSON, S. C. and YEAGER, J. F. (1945). DDT-like effect from injection of other compounds into roaches. *J. econ. Ent.*, **38**, 618.
44. NAIDU, M. B. (1955). Physiological action of drugs and insecticides on insects. *Bull. ent. Res.*, **46**, 205–20.
45. NARAHASHI, T. (1962). Effect of the insecticide allethrin on membrane potentials of cockroach giant axons. *J. cell. comp. Physiol.*, **59**, 67–76.
46. O'BRIEN, R. D. (1957). The effect of ionization upon the penetration of carbamates into the nerve cord of the cockroach. *Ann. ent. Soc. Am.*, **50**, 223–9.
47. O'BRIEN, R. D. (1957). Properties and metabolism in the cockroach and the mouse of malathion and malaoxon. *J. econ. Ent.*, **50**, 159–64.
48. O'KANE, W. C., WALKER, G. L., GUY, H. G. and SMITH, O. J. (1933). Reactions of certain insects to controlled applications of various concentrated chemicals. *Bull. agric. exp. Stn, New Hampshire*, **63**, 1–8.
49. ORSER, W. B. and BROWN, A. W. A. (1951). The effect of insecticides on the heartbeat of *P.a. Can. J. Zool.*, **29**, 54–64.
50. PAGE, A. B. P., STRINGER, A. and BLACKITH, R. E. (1949). Bio-assay systems for the pyrethrius. I. water base sprays against *Aedes aegypti* and other flying insects. *Ann. appl. Biol.*, **36**, 225–49.
51. PARKER, B. A. and CAMPBELL, F. L. (1940). Relative susceptibility of the oötheca and adult female of the German cockroach to liquid household insecticides. *J. econ. Ent.*, **33** (4), 610–14.
52. PATTON, R. L., GARDNER, E. J. and ANDERSON, A. D. (1959). The excretory efficiency of the American cockroach, *P.a. J. Insect Physiol.*, **3**, 256–61.
53. RICHARDS, A. G. and CUTKOMP, L. K. (1945). Neuropathology in insects. *Jl N. Y. ent. Soc.*, **53**, 313–55.
54. ROEDER, K. D. and ROEDER, S. (1939). Electrical activity in the isolated ventral nerve cord of the cockroach. I. The action of pilocarpine, nicotine and eserine. *J. cell. comp. Physiol.*, **14**, 1–12.
55. ROEDER, K. D. (1953). *Insect Physiology*, pp. 423–62. John Wiley, New York.
56. ROEDER, K. D. and WEIANT, E. A. (1948). The effect of DDT on sensory and motor structures in the cockroach leg. *J. cell. comp. Physiol.*, **32**, 175–86.
57. ROY, D. N., GHOSH, S. M. and CHOPRA, R. N. (1943). The mode of action of pyrethrum on the cockroach *P.a. Ann. appl. Biol.*, **30**, 42–7.
58. SAVIT, J., KOLLROS, J. J. and TOBIAS, J. M. (1946). The measured dose of gamma hexadichlorocyclohexane required to kill flies and cockroaches and a comparison with DDT. *Proc. Soc. exp. Biol. Med.*, **62**, 44–8.
59. SHULL, W. E., RILEY, M. K. and RICHARDSON, C. H. (1932). Some effects of certain gases on the blood of the cockroach *B.o. J. econ. Ent.*, **25**, 1070–2.
60. SMYTH, T. (1960). Action of DDT at an insect synapse. *J. econ. Ent.*, **53**, 170–1.
61. SRIVASTAVA, A. S. (1951). Studies on the modern insecticides, mechanism of the physiological action of gamina benzene hexachloride. *Indian med. Rec.*, **71**, 43–50.
62. STERNBURG, J., CHANG, S. C. and KEARNS, C. W. (1959). The release of a neuroactive agent by the American cockroach after exposure to DDT or electrical stimulation. *J. econ. Ent.*, **52**, 1070–6.
63. STERNBERG, J. and KEARNS, C. W. (1952). The presence of toxins other than DDT in the blood of DDT poisoned roaches. *Science, N. Y.*, **116**, 144–7.

64. TOBIAS, J. M. and KOLLROS, J. J. (1946). Loci of action of DDT in the cockroach *P.a. Biol. Bull. mar. biol. Lab., Woods Hole*, **91**, 247–55.
65. TOBIAS, J. M., KOLLROS, J. J. and SAVIT, J. (1946). Acetylcholine and related substances in the cockroach, fly crayfish and the effect of DDT. *J. cell. comp. Physiol.*, **28**, 159–82.
66. TYLER, P. S. (1964). Kepone bait for the control of resistant German cockroaches. *Pest Technol.*, **6** (5), 10–11.
67. VAN DEN HEUVEL, M. J. and SHENKER, A. M. (1965). Cockroach control using nonpersistent insecticides. *Pest Technol.*, **7** (6), 10–11.
68. VINSON, E. B. and KEARNS, C. W. (1952). Temperature and the action of DDT on the American roach. *J. econ. Ent.*, **45**, 484–96.
69. VOWDES, D. M. (1955). The corpora pedunculata of Hymenoptera. *Q. Jl microsc. Sci.*, **96**, 239–55.
70. WELSH, J. H. and GORDON, H. T. (1947). The mode of action of certain insecticides on the arthropod nerve axon. *J. cell. comp. Physiol.*, **30**, 147–71.
71. WIESMAN, R. and KOCHER, W. (1951). Uber ein neues, gegen resistante *Musca domestica* wirksames, Insektizid. *Z. angew. Ent.*, **33**, 297–21.
72. WINTON, M. Y., METCALF, R. L. and FUKOTO, T. R. (1958). The use of acetylthiocholine in the histochemical study of the action of organophosphorous insecticides. *Ann. ent. Soc. Am.*, **51**, 436–40.
73. WOODBURY, E. N. (1938). Test methods on roaches. *Soap sanit. Chem.*, **14** (8), 86–90.
74. YAMASAKI, T. and ISHII, T. (1954). Studies on the mechanism of action of insecticides. VIII. Effects of temperature on the nerve susceptibility to DDT in the cockroach. *Botyu-Kagaku*, **19**, 39–46.
75. YAMASAKI, T. and NARAHASHI, T. (1957). Increase in the negative after-potential of insect nerve by DDT. Studies on the mechanism of action of insecticides. XIII. *Botyu-Kagaku*, **22**, 296–304.
76. YAMASAKI, T. and NARAHASHI, T. (1958). Nervous activity as a factor of development of dieldrin symptoms in the cockroach. *Botyu-Kagaku*, **23**, 47–54.
77. YAMASAKI, T. and NARAHASHI, T. (1957). Intracellular microelectrode recordings of resting and action potentials from the insect axon and the effects of DDT on the action potential. XIV. Studies on the mechanism of action of insecticides. *Botyu-Kagaku*, **22**, 305–13.
78. YAMASAKI, T. and NARAHASHI, T. (1957). Effects on the metabolic inhibitors, potassium ions and DDT on some electrical properties of insect nerve. *Botyu-Kagaku*, **22**, 354–67.
79. YEAGER, J. F. and GAHAN, J. B. (1937). Effects of the alkaloid nicotine on the rhythmicity of isolated heart preparations of *P.a.* and *Prodenia eridania*. *J. agric. Res.*, **55**, 1–19.
80. YEAGER, J. F., HAGER, A. and STANLEY, J. M. (1935). Some physiological effects of certain aliphatic thiocyanates on the isolated heart preparation of the cockroach. *Ann. ent. Soc. Am.*, **28**, 256–64.
81. YEAGER, J. F. and MUNSON, S. C. (1945). Physiological evidence of a site of action of DDT in an Insect. *Science, N.Y.*, **102**, 305–7.
82. ZEID, M. M. I., DAHM, P. A., HEIN, R. E. and MACFARLAND, R. H. (1953). Tissue distribution excretion of CO_2 and degradation of radioactive pyrethrins administered to the American cockroach. *J. econ. Ent.*, **46**, 325–36.
83. ZUKEL, J. W. (1944). Some effects of phenothiazine, phenothiazone and thionol on *P.a. J. econ. Ent.*, **37**, 796–808.

Index

NOTE: *Figures in bold type denote illustrations*